I0188347

The doG House of Cards

Darrel F. Loyd

The doG House of Cards

ISBN 13: 978-0-692-98961-6

SYNOPSIS

The doG House of Cards is a creative memoir of self-discovery with a spiritual edge—a story about overcoming adversity and having the grit to persevere in the midst of hopelessness. Once it became clear to me that I was not born to be just another person in the world, I began to take a closer look at my life…and I've come to believe that I was created with a purpose and a destiny.

This story is about the coincidental occurrences in my life that have enlightened me to my purpose—and ultimately brought me to a place where I didn't even know I belonged. It unfolds over decades and through a twisted chain of events I'm led to discover my place of belonging.

When I reach a point in my life – and find myself isolated in a desert – I become terrified and begin to believe I may never survive the perils that I encounter in that desert valley. Due to a constant stream of wrong choices that I kept making throughout my life, I'm brought to my knees. In my darkest hour, I unexpectedly come face-to-face with what I believe to be my guarding angel. She delivers a message of *hope*, which gives me courage to overcome a hopeless situation. My faith is founded, and I begin to believe that there's more to life than what I could see before I found myself in my hour of despair. Within the cracks and crevices of my life, I start to look for and find a spiritual presence. I begin to build a relationship with this spirit that would eventually change my life forever.

When I finally began to look closer at my circumstances in a way that I had not considered before encountering the presence of this spirit, the more I could see, the happier I became, the more I felt like I belonged—and the less afraid I was—until I finally ended up here…sharing my love story with all of you.

DEDICATION

This book is dedicated to those who have gone before me, but especially to three individuals that impacted my life in their own way: Tim Tingley, Ryan White, and Lance vanGils.

Tim was a former boyfriend. In loving memory of him, a portion of the proceeds from this book will be donated to an organization that helps improve the conditions of those who are living with AIDS.

I did not have the pleasure of knowing Ryan when he was alive, or have the opportunity to meet his parents. I remember hearing about Ryan's story, as it was major headline news. Several decades later, I became familiar with the specifics of his legacy, the Ryan White Foundation, which allowed me to have medical coverage when I lost a job and was unable to find an employer that offered group health care insurance. As horrifying as it must have been for his parents to lose their son, I hope with all my being that it gives them some comfort to know that, if not for their son and his life's path, many people would have lost their lives, many would have suffered greatly from lack of medical care prior to their death, and many more would have lost their loved ones before their time. I thank God that I have the opportunity to express my gratitude to Ryan's family for the good they have done in his memory, and believe it is God's wish that I do so. Ryan is a hero of mine and I'm sure he is one of God's special Angels in heaven.

I met Lance when he was twenty-one. I introduced myself to him eleven days before his twenty-second birthday—at Gold's Gym in downtown Los Angeles. Sadly, he wouldn't live to celebrate his twenty-third birthday. I had the great pleasure to know him between November 13, 2012 and July 11, 2013. Although our time as friends only lasted eight months, Lance and I developed a close friendship. I believe God had a hand in bringing us together for a reason that neither of us could comprehend at the time. By building a friendship with him, I became a better human being. He had an enormous impact on my life while he was alive and he has equally influenced my life now that he is gone. Even though there was a thirty-year difference between us, I learned much from him. Christina Borraez and Gerard vanGils, his parents, raised an amazing young man. His passing gave purpose to a passion of mine that I believe God placed in my heart. It is my hope that I will be able to establish and fund a non-profit organization, through the efforts of this book, which will assist the less fortunate of the world with housing and education—in memory of my friend Lance.

CONTENTS

I believe heaven's daily task is to look after us and help us achieve our destiny.
I sincerely believe that God works in ways that sometimes we cannot understand –
and for some of us, we may never really understand.
I also believe, given the opportunity, that God will use all 'things' for good,
for if God is for us, who can be against us?

Darrel F. Loyd

INTRODUCTION

This is a story of how my imaginary childhood friend, BoBo, became real and awakened me to his spiritual presence, resulting in Him becoming my best friend much later in my adult life. Through this relationship founded in the early years of my childhood, my imaginary friend manifested from make-believe into the essence of the word love. A magical sequence of events that take place over half a century, ultimately lead me to explore the greater meaning of my existence. This story is intended to engage you much like a Hollywood blockbuster film that you might enjoy—whether it's based on fact or fiction. My story is based on fact and represent a series of incidents that enlightened me to a spiritual awakening. It's not about religion; it's about hope and understanding that manifested into a love story. I hope you find it interesting, insightful, entertaining, and – of course – a wonderful heartfelt testimony of a life-long affair.

Some of the common synonyms for the word imaginary are *fictional*, *pretend*, *make-believe*, *mythical*, *mythological*, *fanciful*, or *fairytale*. The existence of a deity is certainly not something that is normally referenced as imaginary, although to a small child the existence of a higher power may seem very much like the existence of a made-up character, as it did for me when I was a little boy. I call my friend BoBo in the hope that it will allow those who do not believe in a spiritual being, that any of us can confirm without debate, the opportunity to view this story much like a fairytale. Possibly you too may begin to believe.

As a young boy, I attended church services with my family, comprised of my mother, my father and two brothers. After church ended, my brothers and I would sometimes attend Sunday school. On several occasions, over various summers that I stayed with my grandparents in Joliet, Illinois, I would attend services with my grandmother Loretta. She enjoyed going to church very much and I specifically remember spending Easter Sunday and Christmas time with her in BoBo's house. I have vague, but fond memories of attending services with her, as she seemed genuinely happy to be in church with her grandson. I was very young and do not remember anything about the sermons being preached. Although I can recall attending church and

Sunday school, and being told by my parents that I was baptized when I was a baby, for some reason – when I was around eight years of age – my parents drifted away from our church. Shortly after my family ceased taking us boys to services, I stopped giving much thought or consideration to the church or to BoBo. However, my spiritual foundation had been laid in the early years of my childhood for a much greater awakening.

From the early days of attending church with my parents and grandmother and until my late forties, I emphatically believe BoBo had been pursuing me and I eventually came to realize he had left a trail of his presence throughout my life. Once I acknowledged that presence, the trail led me to a place where I did not know I belonged. I started to make the turn from living a self-absorbed existence to embracing a more compassionate life. I began to explore how the concept of a divine presence could be a reality in my daily life, rather than something that was sought one day of the week, on a Sunday morning, in a place called church.

Whether you believe in the God of Abraham, Isaac and Jacob, Jesus of the Holy Bible, or Allah of the Holy Quran, all roads seem to lead to the same place. I believe a very similar path is true for those who simply may not believe in anything greater than mankind. Whatever your beliefs, I hope my story provokes you to become aware of all things around you, while at the same time, allowing you to embrace the similarities in each of us and, more importantly, the differences in one another. I believe the real power here on earth lies within us, in a world that's so complex that it defies all logic, although it can be explained in one simple word…love.

Before I developed my adult relationship with BoBo, I initially greeted all the coincidences that took place in my life as isolated and unrelated events. They usually caused more confusion than clarity, and in some cases, they generated fear. I believe whenever we encounter something that we do not understand, or that we can't comprehend, there is always a good chance we will ignore it or fear it. I now feel that most of the various circumstances I was faced with, over many years, were revelations from a spiritual place. Some of these so-called coincidences made sense to me at the time and others did not. I later came to recognize that some of the events that took place at a certain point were signs that were meant for a future purpose. As I developed my awareness, the coincidences began to have new meaning—until I was finally able to identify most of the events that had taken place over a lifetime as confirmation of a divine presence.

As a child, and for at least half of my adulthood, I experienced constant feelings of unrest. During that time, I felt alone in the world. I was unhappy and lonely and struggled with feelings of not being loved. Many years came and went where I didn't care if I lived to see another day. I had most of the material things in life that people work their entire lives to achieve, although I felt as if my life did not matter. There was an emptiness to my existence.

Living without BoBo in my life seemed like a very natural way of living, until one day when I had an epiphany. I came to realize that my life without Him to give me hope, understanding, and love, was a life that made very little sense. Once I entered into a relationship with Bobo, I came to view my life and my fellow man differently. Not until that time, did I appreciate how a relationship with Him could provide clarity and play an important role in my day-to-day existence.

When I began to add BoBo to the storyline of my journey, I finally embraced my life and became more content and humble. In the Bible, there is a reference that we must humble ourselves like children. "Truly I say to you, unless you are converted and become like children, you will not enter the kingdom of heaven. Whoever then humbles himself as this child, he is the greatest in the kingdom of heaven." Knowing BoBo as a little boy was how I was able to relate to a higher power in a way that I could comprehend when I was but a humble child.

I was born on the fourth of May in 1960, in the county of Los Angeles, California. When I was still a baby, my parents moved me and my older brother to Chicago, Illinois. The Midwest region of the U.S. is where I grew up to become a shy gay man and where I would spend the next four decades. I graduated from high school at the age of seventeen, six months earlier than most of my classmates. I worked as a part-time stock boy on a retailer's loading dock for several years while attending high school. Four months before my eighteenth birthday, on the day of graduation, I was promoted to Shipping and Receiving Manager of the loading dock. The retailer, with whom I was employed, was a family-owned, full service department store that had been in business for over one hundred years and had thirteen department stores in the Chicago-land area. At the time of my promotion, I certainly thought I was mature enough for the position. Looking back, I can now clearly see that I was very fortunate to have been offered a position of such responsibility at a young age. In my new managerial role, my life soon became all about the working world and the things I could afford to buy. Every eighteen-year-old young man dreams of owning a brand new car and, shortly after I was promoted and received my corresponding salary increase, I bought a brand spanking new car with bucket seats. Over the next thirty years, I would devote my time and energies to advance my professional career, go to fine restaurants for dinner, shop for new clothes, travel whenever possible, go to clubs, party, get my own apartment and eventually purchase a home, and upgrade to more expensive new automobiles. During these years, I did not give BoBo or the church any real thought in my day-to-day life. It was all about me and the material things that life had to offer. I was a generous person and a good friend to those who were close to me, but unfortunately, my generosity and general concern for my fellow man never went any further than my immediate circle of family and friends. I was self-absorbed and totally focused on superficial desires.

At twenty-seven years of age and during the time in America when the AIDS epidemic ravaged the country and its gay community, I became a statistic of the epidemic and contracted the HIV virus. In the early years of the disease that we know today as AIDS, almost everyone who contracted the virus eventually died. After I was diagnosed as being positive, I would endure years of fear that any day I would get sick and die a horrible painful death. Due to the hysteria that surrounded those who were sick from the disease, I quickly developed a fearful existence and this fear rapidly manifested itself into denying that I had HIV. At the age of thirty-two, I started experimenting with illegal recreational drugs on the weekends when I frequented clubs to party. My mindset was that I had to cram as many decades of living into the next several years. Due to the information that was being presented at the time by the medical community, I naturally assumed I only had a few additional good years to enjoy—before the illness would consume my entire body and I would die.

During the initial years of facing my fatal diagnosis, I earned a salary in the six figures. I enjoyed most of the luxuries that life had to offer, without the reassurance that I had another healthy year ahead of me. In the early years of testing positive, I was enrolled in a group healthcare plan with my then employer. Assuming I might be changing employers at some point, I paid for all my HIV-related medical expenses out of my pocket. Once diagnosed with having AIDS or identified by the insurance companies as being positive – if you opted out of your current group healthcare plan for any reason – you would not be able to secure health care due to the pre-existing condition clause that all insurance companies had and exercised under the law at that time. It was a very scary environment and a medically complex time for a gay man in America to be positive or to be diagnosed with having AIDS.

In the late eighties and early nineties, the intolerance within the gay community for those who were affected by HIV or AIDS resulted in a high level of discrimination. In many circumstances, the straight community, as well as some of those in the gay community, treated people who had AIDS or who were positive, like lepers. I began to isolate myself from those who would have judged and rejected me for my status and, in doing so, my feelings of loneliness became an overwhelming issue for me. In my attempt to mask my feelings of being segregated from within my own community, my recreational drug use began moving toward harder drugs.

Many gay men were faced with the belief by the religious community that AIDS was the wrath of God placed on them for their sexual preference. I never felt this way, although the reality of the allegations is a very emotional set of circumstances to sort through when you're staring the epidemic in the face. To this day, a majority of the so-called leaders of today's organized religious establishments still do not openly accept those who are gay. The

Holy Bible states, "God is no respecter of persons." I'm so very thankful that God accepts all of creation in the same manner and does not divide the world by continent, country, culture, religion, race, gender, or sexual preference.

To this day, I've never been diagnosed with having AIDS, or any HIV or AIDS-related illnesses in the twenty-seven years of being positive. At the time of writing this portion of my testimony, my viral load is undetectable and my CD4 count is over fourteen hundred at forty-three percent. For a non-positive individual, these numbers would be considered extremely good and in very good health. In my specific case, considering the fact that I've been positive for nearly 30 years, these numbers are extraordinary. I believe my health status is a perfect representation of God's grace in my life and the reality of miracles.

I've come to believe, as an adult, that God has a story he would like for each of us to proclaim to the world, and this story that we're to declare, comes through our testimony. While I make references to "my story", I believe this book represents one of the many stories of God. *I will reveal myself to the world through my people.* As I begin telling mine, I recall a revelation that I believe came to me from a heavenly place. When I was forty-seven, I moved from Chicago, Illinois and relocated to Palm Springs in the desert region of California. In hindsight, I believe, without a doubt, God had a hand in moving me to the desert and isolating me from my family and friends—in a place where he knew he would be able to get my attention. The time had come for me to change my life of partying, drinking alcohol in excess, having anonymous sex, and doing recreational drugs.

After relocating to the desert, I saw three moons one night in the desert sky over the house. It seemed as if one of the moons was fading or dying off. It certainly seemed like a vision. I'm not sure how else to label what I saw. After much contemplation, I came to see the vision of the three moons very much like a riddle, where the three moons represented three worlds. I found this potential revelation to be confusing and overwhelming. I had to ask myself whether I was really experiencing a revelation or was I simply losing a grip on reality and making it up in my mind. In either case, I felt compelled to give more thought to the theory of the three worlds, even though the notion of three worlds made no sense to me. Over the following weeks and months, I came to realize the revelation that I felt originated from a spiritual place, did in fact have some merit. Thus, it was in the desert region of Coachella Valley when my spiritual awakening came to fruition and where I believe God began to reveal himself to me.

The first world, Earth, was the only one of the three with which I was able to make a viable connection. As a child, I was introduced to the biblical creation of the Earth when I went to church and Sunday school. I also learned about the scientific approach to the creation of the Earth when I was enrolled in a public school. Earth was obviously a very easy concept for me to accept, whether I believed it was the creation of a higher power or a scientific phenomenon.

The second world that I came to know consisted of man-made islands in Dubai, which were formed to emulate the shape of the world that God created and are known as *The World* or *World Islands* in Dubai.

Three years earlier, I had secured a sales appointment in Seattle, Washington with a large architectural firm. During my sales presentation to the design group, one of the architects on the team began talking about an unrelated topic that he saw as an interesting creative project that he wanted to share with the group. The project was one of many that the Crown Prince of Dubai had under construction at the time. The Prince decided to construct a group of islands off the shore of Dubai that replicated the shape of United States and he was going to sell these various islands to private investors. As I heard the story, I quietly thought to myself that the design concept of this project, led by the Prince, was an amazing creative vision by all accounts. After that day in Seattle, and upon the completion of my sales appointment, I didn't give the man-made islands in Dubai much more thought. After several months, I completely forgot about the fantastic design concept of these islands under construction in the Emirate of Dubai.

Several years passed and one day in Palm Springs, after receiving what I believe to be the revelation from God regarding the three worlds, I recalled the conversation about the project in Dubai. I immediately went to my computer and googled *The United States of America islands built in Dubai*. To my amazement, the World Islands showed up in my search. The project was not about replicating the United States as islands, as I originally thought. The design concept must have changed direction at some point or I had misunderstood what the architect was explaining when he was sharing the scope of the project. In either case, the actual design consisted of various small man-made islands that were to replicate the rough shape of the world map.

If you've seen the movie *Slum Dog Millionaire*, you probably know how I felt at that exact moment. The movie revolves around a young boy that has grown up in the slums of India. As a young adult, he gets the opportunity to become a contestant on a game show. Toward the end of the movie, he becomes one of the finalists because he knows all the answers to all the questions that are being posed to him. The organizers of the show concluded that he must be cheating somehow, as they could not understand how a poor uneducated man from the slums of India could possibly have the correct answers to all the questions. It turns out that his entire life's experiences have led him up to this moment. The reason he knows all the answers is because his life experiences mirror the questions being asked and the situations that he experienced, first as a boy and later as a young man, allow him to possess the knowledge to know the answers to the questions. He eventually becomes the grand prize winner of the game show, hence the title of the movie. Did the coincidences in his life lead him to know the answers to all the questions? Or did the movie portray an example of how God used the young man's experiences for a greater purpose?

The third world was a floating cruise ship where you could buy a residence and cruise the open waters of the world. Similar to the islands in Dubai, I had no idea that this third world – a floating cruise ship named *The World* – was being built. Coincidentally, several days after discovering the existence of the *World Islands*, a friend sent me an email introducing *The World*—a cruise ship that was under construction where you could buy a residence on board, if you had the funds. I never told anyone my story regarding the three worlds or my belief that I received this message from a spiritual place. The email was sent to me randomly and it was unsolicited. My friend simply thought I would find the project interesting from a design perspective. Was God intervening and motivating my friend to press the send button on his computer when I had the subject on my mind?

Before seeking a relationship with God, my life was full with what I believed to be random coincidences. After an encounter with God, I came to understand that He was utilizing my life experiences for a much greater cause and came to see that many of the coincidences had deeper meaning. These coincidental events seemed to represent pieces of a puzzle. Much like Slum Dog Millionaire, my life represents the importance of taking note of the little occurrences that take place in our daily lives. Prior to God placing the thought of the three worlds on my mind, I was clueless to the existence of the two additional man-made worlds in the world that He created. Once I was able to connect the dots and make a connection to the three worlds, I asked myself why He wanted me to know it.

I do not believe you'll find God in a book, or in a church for that matter, for I believe God is a lifestyle. In my search for a relationship with Him, I believe I must begin to understand the powerful importance to the ramifications of who and to what I listen. In understanding how these two scenarios mirror my vision and my speech is to grasp the wisdom of how I see myself viewing the world. I emphatically believe my viewpoints and opinions will have a direct effect on the connection I have with my inner self. I believe it's this connection that will dictate the type of relationship I develop with God. This link between my inner self and Him will ultimately determine my destiny.

THE END | DEAD MAN'S HAND

At the age of forty-eight, when I received the revelation of the three moons, my lifestyle as I knew it, came to an end. Many months later, after much contemplation and heartache, I believe I received a promise from God. Due to this promise, I began the long journey to change my lifestyle and my life is no longer without purpose. I can't begin to make the claim that I'm able to predict the future and say how this story will end. But on the other hand, I can say I'm optimistic that by the time I complete telling this story I will be able to paint you a picture that allows you to see a life filled with hope, understanding, and love from "the beginning."

Several years earlier, an event took place that I found to have a considerable deeper meaning, many years after the episode occurred. I was in Atlanta, Georgia surrounded by my boyfriend and two of my best friends who almost always traveled with me when I attended one of the parties on the gay circuit. The circuit consisted of thematic dance parties in large venues that were held in various cities in the United States, orchestrated by different party promoters. On a particular evening, Rick and Tony, my best buddies, were standing next to me on the dance floor. We were inseparable, just like the Three Musketeers. We lived in Chicago and had been friends for many years. When traveling to the various gay circuit events, the three of us, who were single, usually traveled together. After I met a man named Alex, and we became boyfriends, I added him to the Three Musketeers clique as my plus one.

It was in Atlanta where my relationship with Alex would result in *Dead Man's Hand* becoming a more apt description for the party boys than the Three Musketeers. The phrase Dead Man's Hand came about in the Old West in the U.S., when Wild Bill Hickok was holding a two-pair poker hand consisting of black aces and black eights along with a kicker card when he was murdered at a poker table. A kicker card is defined in Wikipedia as *"a card in a poker hand that does not itself take part in determining the rank of the hand, but that may be used to break ties between hands of the same rank."* Rick, Tony, Alex and I theoretically represented the pair of eights and the pair of aces when the defining kicker card was dealt.

The four of us were at Hotlanta, one of the larger parties in the gay circuit. We saw and greeted the occasional individuals that we met over the years during our travels and who we would see at these events. We only hung out with our circuit friends a few times a year and we acted like we were all close friends, even though we only met and associated with one another during these parties. In Atlanta, the kicker card in our game was revealed, a play that set in motion a hopeless competition for the Latin Queen of Hearts.

It was the typical gay circuit crowd. There were the usual party muscle boys that always attended these events and the vast room was filled wall-to-wall with beautiful shirt-less gay Adonises dancing until all hours of the morning. On the dance floor, people we had just met that weekend danced around us. Like most events that attract a lot of handsome and pretty people dancing like a bunch of peacocks that are strutting their stuff, there's bound to be at least one, if not several, of the prancing peacocks that have their eyes set on one that has already been courted. My boyfriend Alex was a Puerto Rican with a well-defined body and he was an incredible dancer. One might easily have gotten the impression that he was a peacock from the way he was always strutting his stuff on the dance floor. Through the crowd an invading boyfriend snatcher approached. He was someone that Alex and I met on one of our many gay party junkets that we attended that year. We traveled from Chicago to Atlanta for Hotlanta...to Columbus, Ohio for the Red Party...New York for the Black Party and Gay Pride...Palm Springs for the White Party at Easter...San Francisco for Magnitude during Folsom Street Fair...Los Angeles for Labor Day LA and to South Beach in Miami for the White Party at Thanksgiving. We also attended Chicago's very own Hearts Party held around Valentine's Day. Alex and I spent forty thousand dollars on traveling the gay circuit that year, which included our party favors.

I was minding my own business, trying to protect my small portion of real estate on the dance floor while enjoying my party favors. The invading boyfriend snatcher offered a bump of K, then the drug of choice. K, or Ketamine as it's clinically called, is a dog and cat tranquilizer and it was very popular in the gay community in the nineties. The drug came in liquid form, but if you baked the liquid in the oven or microwave it was transformed into a powder-like substance. Once in powder form, you snorted it like you would snort cocaine, although in much smaller amounts— in bumps, not lines. It was fashionable to flavor your K and add vanilla or strawberry extract to make it smell and taste better. The snatcher's offering, like so many people who come offering you something for nothing, came with a catch or in this case, a kicker. He had hoped to catch a few minutes alone with Alex, while placing or kicking me in some other dimension, better known as a k-hole— a catatonic state where you would end up if you ingested too much Ketamine in a single dosage.

When ingesting most drugs, there is an art to the recommended dosage that one can consume at a specific moment, and the dosage can also vary depending on what drug you're consuming. Like so many drugs, the dosage that one person can tolerate may also vary from one person to another. There I was, on the dance floor at a mega gay event and for no logical reason that I can recall other than I was duped, I had what seemed to be an out of body experience. After accepting the boyfriend's snatcher's gift of a gratis bump of his K, I suddenly found myself standing in front of Jesus and his Disciples. Several years after this incident took place, I found myself standing before Jesus and his Disciples again, though the second time was in Milan, Italy during a trip to Europe when I viewed the actual fresco of Leonardo daVinci's Last Supper.

In Atlanta, immediately after I ingested the bump of K, I was transformed to a place where it seemed as if I was actually at the Last Supper with Jesus and the Apostles. A very similar scenario was playing out in my mind as it did in the actual Last Supper. I too had been betrayed—in my case, by a party friend that we had met on the circuit. The bump of K that kicked me into another dimension had been laced with acid, the old fashioned 1960's San Francisco peace, love, sex and rock-n-roll type of acid. The snatcher failed to mention, or he deliberately failed to disclose, that he had laced his K with acid to add a kicker to its overall effect. I would've proceeded with more caution or possibly passed altogether on the free bump had I been forewarned about the acid in his offering. My altered state of mind may not have been so dramatic if I had been made aware that he had laced his K prior to me snorting the bump. "This is it?" These were the only words I could utter immediately after ingesting the drug, and in my mind I was asking Rick, "this is where I die?" It made sense that it was truly the end. My hand had been played just like Wild Bill Hickok's hand a century earlier. Why else would I be standing in front of Jesus at the Last Supper if I was not going to die at that exact moment? I recalled that Jesus was sold out for thirty pieces of silver and I had sold myself out for a single bump of K laced with acid. My mind was reeling. I felt the vision that I was experiencing must have some relevance to how Jesus was also betrayed by someone he knew. The laced K offering resulted in me becoming a pawn in the game of love. This kicker did not take part in determining the rank of the game, but it could be used to break the tie between two fags that were attracted to the same man. I felt betrayed by the boyfriend snatcher for his attempt to woo Alex away from me while I was unable to speak or move except for uttering those three words, "this is it?"

Did this unforgettable situation have meaning for a greater message and was this why, at the precise time of my assumed demise, I experienced that vision? Was my drug-induced revelation, a premonition of what was yet to come? Or was I simply experiencing a tragic drug-induced moment that had no greater relevance? I believe that God will use all things for good. He will intervene on our behalf and use a bad experience in our life for the greater good, if we allow him to do so. Even during my messed-up behavior of partying and using illegal substances, I believe God was present and eventually he would utilize this experience to develop me spiritually.

Over a decade later the phrase "this is it" would have a larger significance to the world than what took place on the dance floor that night in Atlanta. In Los Angeles, California, the King of Pop would utter those exact three words, the name of his last concert tour, shortly before being administered a drug overdose, by someone he trusted, which would result in his tragic demise and **The End** to an era.

1 | THE QUEEN OF HEARTS

I met Alex in a gay dance club one evening when I was living in Chicago. I happened to be out partying alone, which was somewhat unusual for me since I very seldom ever traveled the gay scene solo. As I entered the club, I headed to the coat check. It was another very cold night in Chicago, as most evenings are during the winter. Once in line to check my coat, I casually glanced around the front bar area as if looking for someone, although very careful not to make eye contact to not give anyone any pre-conceived notions. As I finally made it through the line, I checked my coat and immediately headed to one of the many bars inside the club. Since the winters are freezing cold in Chicago, you need to drink to keep warm, or so I told myself. I happened to glance toward the dance floor in the center of the club. I spotted a lovely Latin man dancing with another man. The Latin dancer had not only caught my eye, he had my undivided attention.

At this point in my life, I was fortunate to be financially successful in my professional career. I held the position of vice president of store development and visual merchandising for a high-end men and women's retail clothing chain in Chicago. I was very seldom shy when it came to conducting business matters on a professional level, although approaching men and engaging them in conversation for a potential sexual encounter at a club or another type of social setting, came with a different set of circumstances altogether. I often felt like a shy mouse when it came to playing the cat and mouse game. Up until that night, I rarely approached guys with whom I had a physical attraction. Usually, I interacted with men that approached and engaged *me* in conversation.

I positioned myself at the main bar, in the front of the club. I strategically stood at the slightly-elevated edge of the bar area, closest to the dance floor. This location gave me the vantage point of being able to observe the lovely Latin man, who was prancing like a peacock, from close proximity. He truly was an amazing dancer and had a fantastic six-pack. After standing in the same spot and watching his every move for what seemed like hours, I couldn't help but think that the man he was dancing with must be his boyfriend. If this was the case, and they were boyfriends, it certainly would have prevented me from making any advances. Earlier in my life I had learned the hard lesson of getting involved with someone who had a partner. That evening, destiny was on my side. The peacock's dancing partner stopped dancing and walked off the dance floor and – as he pushed himself through the crowd – he walked right pass me, brushing his arm across mine. I did what any respectable gay man on the prowl would do in this type of situation. I followed the guy. He ended up at one of the four bars in the club and I managed to position myself next to him. As always, the club was packed. It was Saturday night and with this being the only real gay dance club in the city, it was standing room only. Then destiny smiled upon me twice in the same evening. The bartender at the station where the guy went to get drinks was Jeff, a good friend of mine. Jeff was seven years younger than me and was an extremely handsome man with an amazing body—very masculine and wonderfully buff. He traveled with his own fan club. Most people wanted to have a physique like Jeff's and, if that was not the case, then they certainly were interested in getting into his pants. I was able to get Jeff's attention when he came over to the area where I was now standing shoulder to shoulder with the guy. Jeff yelled out *Mary* in my direction. He called every gay male that he liked Mary, and I soon picked up this habit from him. Jeff nodded his head, as to give me the go ahead to tell him my drink order. This gave me the opportunity to turn to the guy and say, "you were here first, what are you having?" As he muttered his drink order to Jeff, all I could think of at that exact moment was how I was going to find out the story about the guy with whom he was dancing. Were they boyfriends? Or were they only friends out dancing together for the evening? Just as he was about to walk away with drinks in hand – and all hope of ever finding out the story regarding his dancing partner was fading – the mouse spoke. "Are you and the guy you're dancing with boyfriends?" I asked. Having his back positioned to me, he turned his head slightly as not to give me his full attention and replied, "no, although we were boyfriends at one time, we're just friends now." My biggest mistake at that moment was not asking one additional very critical question: does the guy that you're dancing with have a boyfriend? As the saying goes, I heard what I wanted to hear and I failed, possibly deliberately, to ask any additional questions. With this information in hand, I grabbed a pen from Jeff, wrote my home number on the back of my business card and headed back to the observation deck where I had been previously standing. After so many years of giving out my number to strange men in clubs, I should have had my home phone number printed on the back of my business cards, although, I'm not sure how that would have gone over with my boss.

As the evening went on and the drinks became many, I finally mustered up the balls to walk up to the guy and present him with my card. I said something to the effect of "if you're interested in getting together sometime, feel free to call me." I don't think I had fully gotten the last two words out of my mouth when I turned and began to walk toward the coat check to retrieve my coat and get the hell out of the club.

The next morning, I was awakened early by the ringing of my home phone. I was hung-over and not sure to this day why I answered the phone, although I did. The voice on the other end of the line said, "Hey, this is Alex." I could barely utter the words, "Alex, Alex who?" When he replied, "It's Alex from the club", I asked myself whether this man, who I admired from afar earlier that morning, could be as interested in meeting me as I was in meeting him. Although the larger question that was running through my mind was…what type of potential trick calls before nine o'clock on a Saturday morning, especially if they know you've been out drinking until three o'clock that morning? So much for my infatuation with the man with the incredible abs from the night before. My hangover had a mind of its own that morning and it did not include dick that went by the name of Alex. Once I understood it was *the Alex* from the club, I quickly excused myself from speaking any further with him and inquired if we could continue our conversation later that day once my hangover subsided.

At this point in my evolution as a gay man, I never found myself sexually attracted to Latin men, so this was an unusual circumstance. Alex was born in Puerto Rico and although he was so outside of my normal dating pool, there was something about him that was so sexy. He definitely had my interest. I never gave much thought to whom I was attracted until this point. Typically, all the men that I dated or hooked up with for sex were white guys much like me. While my best friend at the time also happened to be Puerto Rican and I had a good friend that I worked out with at the gym who was black, I personally never found myself encountering any of the Baskin Robbin's flavors of gay men – other than vanilla – when having sex. I was thirty-six when I met Alex and was not very savvy to the ways of the world. I had unintentionally limited my exposure to the many varieties of men in gay culture. My first real gay relationship that involved the two of us living together was with a man named Tony who was twelve years my senior. He was Italian and was a hairdresser by trade. We lived together in the suburbs of Chicago for seven-and-a-half years until we split from one another when I was twenty-seven.

Shortly before the end of my relationship with Tony, I met a man named Tim where I worked, who was a few years my junior. I was employed as a visual merchandising manager at Madigan's, a family-owned retail company that had six stores on the west side of Chicago. At the initial stage of Tim's hire, he was assigned to my display crew, as one of the visual team members that made up my creative staff. I was instructed to be his mentor throughout his introduction to the department. He had expressed his attraction toward me several months prior to me finding myself accepting his advances. Tim was a lovely, young, light-skinned white man. He was five feet six inches tall, with dishwater blonde hair and was an amateur body builder. Up until now,

I'm not sure why it took so long for me to accept Tim's affection.

I was very slim with little muscular definition. Most people would have probably described me as a skinny little queen. At that point in my life, I did not give much thought to my body or working out; I had been concentrating on building my creative career. Going to the gym would not become one of my life's passions until several years after meeting Tim. At the time, I remember wondering how this hot muscular man – who looked like a handsome rock-hard Adonis – be interested in a slender man like me. To this very day, my life encounter with Tim has left an everlasting and profound mark on my existence.

The corporate director of the creative team at Madigan's was a middle aged gay man that I later came to realize, had a crush on Tim. In reality, I think it was Tim's body that got him the job. Tim and I were the only gay men on a crew of four. The other creative members were Katie and Gina, two straight women in their early twenties. Each store in the chain had its own display crew, although all the field visual merchandising personnel that worked in the retail stores were considered to be corporate employees. My four-person visual crew, where I was the managing creative lead, worked very well together. We always finished our scheduled daily tasks and kept our creative commitments to the store and to corporate, although we always found time in the day to gossip and laugh hysterically. On occasion when Tim and I were alone in a window working on a new display and near one another, he would position himself in some manner as to casually brush that incredible tight and hard body of his against mine. I usually ended up having a major hard-on for hours during the day, due to Tim teasing me.

One day, after installing two display windows, I stopped to use the restroom in the store prior to going home for the evening, on the south side of Chicago, were I lived with Tony. Tim followed me to the bathroom and approached me with a sexual proposition. Needless to say, after many months of fighting off his sexual advances, I finally gave in to Tim and his rock-hard body. Very soon, something else was hard in the bathroom besides his muscles. We left work immediately, after his proposition was greeted with overwhelming acceptance.

One of the Madigan's where we worked was in a shopping mall and, as fate would have it, there was a hotel conveniently across from the shopping center. Since the sexual energy had been building for months prior to our hookup that evening, we ended up having amazing hot indulgent sex for hours. This hotel, where we initially explored our interest in one another's bodies, would soon become our home away from home for any months to come. Whenever possible, we continued to hook up after work at the same hotel and screwed for hours. Katie and Gina had no idea that their co-workers where fooling around right under their noses. Every Saturday, Tim and I would make a point of getting together and sexually exploring every inch of one another for an entire eight hours in a single day. I've always been a sucker for a man that will bring me flowers – I always have and always will – and Tim would sometimes surprise me and show up to the hotel with flowers. On occasion, we ordered room service and lay in bed naked enjoying every minute we had together. This was the first time I had sex with a man that went to the gym and who took such great physical care of his body. The entire experience on all levels was very hot. Tim was also an amazing lover; I could not get enough of him. He referred to me as his "little guy." I think he gave me that nickname because I was so skinny. I found Tim to be so endearing. He made me laugh and he was so incredibly attractive and fucked like a rock star. There was great chemistry between us and I found myself falling in love with him.

One day, which I can still recall like it was yesterday, Tim decided he wanted to top me. Prior to that day, I was always the top when we had sex. It was in the eighties and I was in the midst of ending my relationship with Tony. It was also the beginning of the AIDS epidemic. During the years that Tony and I were together we had a monogamous agreement and, in that time, I was tested for the HIV virus to secure a life insurance policy. I had been approved by the insurance company and received the life insurance—so I knew without a doubt that I did not have the virus prior to meeting Tim. I was naïve enough to believe that all couples in a committed relationship were monogamous. I unfortunately had a lot of life lessons to learn in the coming years. Coincidentally, Tim had the same situation at home that I did. Like me, Tim was involved in a long-term relationship with Steve, an older man who had been his partner for seven years. The affair between Tim and me was a perfect example of the so-called "seven-year itch."

I certainly was not a virgin to the concept of being a bottom, although I only bottomed on a rare occasion and it would become a new role for me in my sexual relationship with Tim. At that stage, I was somewhat shy and not very comfortable with my sexuality and was reluctant to have my legs up in the air. For some sexually-insecure reason, I felt feminine when giving my ass to a man. I eventually came to enjoy the bottom position when connecting with the right sexual partner—so perhaps Tim knew me better than I knew myself and this is one of the main reasons I was so attracted to him.

As Tim was aggressively seeking my ass, I quietly thought that we probably should be practicing safe sex. I know I was being a hypocrite by thinking I should ask Tim to wear a condom when I certainly had not bagged my pecker when I fucked him. I had also convinced myself that since I knew I was negative, then he too must be negative, as he was in a long-term relationship prior to the onset of the AIDS epidemic.

After Tim and I decided to leave our boyfriends and cohabitate as lovers, our relationship was inadvertently exposed to our associates at our workplace. Our outing was not a pleasant time for us in any way, shape, or form, and I was finally forced to take responsibility for my actions. I had become the talk of the corporate visual department. I was the Manager that slept with one of their employees. It seemed that Tim had become the forbidden fruit. It was not long before I was summoned to the corporate office by the executive assistant to the president of Madigan's, who wanted to speak with me regarding my extracurricular activities with Tim. Mr. Joe Madigan was an older straight man who was part of the second generation of the Madigan family that founded the company many decades earlier. He was known for his outlandish and often unannounced conduct, which oftentimes resulted in angry rants for no apparent reason. My single and most important asset that I had going for me at that moment was that Mr. Madigan happened to be a big fan of my creative ability. As I arrived at the corporate office, I became sick to my stomach. Tim and I had just moved in together and our rent was fairly expensive. Both of us had been living with our older and somewhat successful boyfriends, so we were slightly spoiled in our lifestyles, hence the expensive apartment. When I arrived at Mr. Madigan's office, I informed his secretary that his executive assistant called me to the office. She politely ushered me to the conference room, where I waited alone and with anticipation of what was to come. I sat by myself in the conference room with nothing but my thoughts, and I quietly asked God to let me get out of this room without getting fired. When I found myself facing a difficult circumstance, I certainly did not hesitate to pull out the God card and ask for help. I was like so many people who do not have a relationship with God, although when they get into a troubling situation they tend to seek immediate relief from the heavens. I thought that it certainly couldn't hurt to ask for His divine assistance. Shortly after my repeated attempts to ask for His intervention, the door to the conference room opened and the owner of the company entered. I could immediately sense, as he closed the door behind him, that God may not have been available when I was asking for help. Or possibly He was available and listening, although He was keeping His presence quiet in the conference room while He was observing how I was going to handle the situation. Mr. Madigan inquired if I knew why I was called to his office and I nervously nodded my head several times in response to his request. He continued his questioning by asking me to explain myself in detail as to why I believed he called me to his office. As I struggled to form the words to recall the correct chain of events that led up to my involvement with Tim, I said something that triggered Mr. Madigan, known for his outbursts.

Somewhere around the point where I was explaining that Tim and I were attracted to one another, he jumped up from his chair and yelled for me to get out of his sight. I gladly headed toward the door of the conference room, but Mr. Madigan repositioned himself by the exit—pinning me between him and the door. With my back to the door and his shaking clenched fist in my face, I thought nervously, this is the type of bullish behavior that I heard about. If the stories about his temper were true, then I was not sure if I was going to get out of the room without receiving a black eye or with my job intact. Not only was I fearful of him snapping at any moment – and delivering those words that I was so fearful of hearing, "you're fired" – but I could possibly also be sporting a black eye and be unemployed. As he yelled at me to leave the room and not return to my store, he calmly changed the tone of his voice. In a less angry manner, he said not to worry about losing a half day's pay for he would ensure that I was compensated for a full day's work. I quickly turned the doorknob and opened the door with my back still pressed tightly against it. I moved as far away from the shaking fist as I could get while attempting to leave enough room to open the door slightly to orchestrate my escape. As soon as there was enough space for me to slide through a small opening, I made a mad dash out of the conference room and headed for the company parking lot where my car was parked. As I walked nervously and a little shaken to my car, I was not exactly one hundred percent sure what had just transpired. On the other hand, I knew Mr. Madigan was not happy with Tim and me, which I could certainly understand. The next day I was informed by my peers, who were near the scene, that shortly after I left the conference room, Mr. Madigan went around the office asking if I was still at the corporate headquarters. From what I was told by my associates, he seemed very calm when inquiring about my whereabouts. I wonder if he was looking to locate me so he could finish what he started in the conference room.

On my drive home that afternoon, I kept thinking how thankful I was that I had made it out of the corporate office with my job still intact. I hoped that keeping my job was not going to end up becoming a temporary situation since Mr. Madigan had been looking for me after he sent me home. I laughed out loud in the car as I recalled my desperate plea to God that day. He not only granted my request for me to keep my job, He also made sure I knew I was getting paid for the entire day, even though I was being sent home early. Whoever said God doesn't have a sense of humor, obviously never experienced a similar situation as I did that afternoon in the conference room at Madigan's corporate office.

After my encounter with Mr. Madigan, I went directly to the apartment that I was renting with Tim and immediately located the newspaper. I began looking through the employment section of the Chicago Tribune for other potential career opportunities. For those who have no idea what I'm talking about…before the internet you looked for current job openings in the career section of your local newspaper, which now seems so archaic, even to me. I found that Bloomingdale's was opening their first store in Chicago and they were seeking candidates for the visual merchandising department. God does work in mysterious ways and I think He was present that day in the corporate conference room, although He was being very mysterious. After I read the ad posted for the visual merchandising positions, I immediately typed my résumé and sent if off that afternoon to Bloomingdale's in New York City. Several weeks after submitting it, I was contacted for an interview. Shortly after the interview process was completed, I received an employment offer as visual merchandising coordinator of the men's floor. Soon after receiving the new job offer, I submitted my resignation at Madigan's and was able to retain some of my dignity for my actions resulting from my relationship with Tim. He also left Madigan's shortly after our relationship became public information. He was still working in the visual merchandising industry, although he was now employed with I. Magnin, a high-end retailer at a suburban mall in Oakbrook, Illinois.

Reflecting on my choice to pursue a romantic love affair with Tim, I would not have changed my decision to explore the affection that Tim and I had for one another. But on the other hand, I would certainly caution anyone that might be in the midst of entertaining a heated sexual encounter with a co-worker or an employee. A love affair at one's place of employment is as complicated as you could imagine. The individual that came up with the saying *'tis better to have loved and lost than never to have loved at all* obviously didn't have their job on the line.

Tim and I continued our relationship for three more years after being outed and, during a point in this three-year period, Tim lost his job with I. Magnin. I was the person in the relationship that did all the worrying for the two of us. Due to my concern for Tim's health, I pressured him into applying for a private health care policy, since he was not covered by a group plan during his unemployment. Anyone who attempted to secure a private health care policy was required to submit to a physical and a blood test. It was the late eighties and the AIDS epidemic was on everyone's mind, especially those in the health care insurance. After Tim's health screening, he received a call from the doctor's office that conducted the physical. The doctor wanted to see him. Tim and I expected and prepared for the obvious, which was our worst-case scenario. Tim went to the appointment and received the news that he had tested positive for HIV. I was heartbroken for Tim and tried to comfort him as much as I could. I was very much in love with him and the news of him being HIV positive was a death sentence at that juncture of the epidemic.

It's impossible for me to put into words how horrifying and impactful those three letters are to hear when they're followed by the word positive and especially when they're applied to someone you love. I was also very worried about my own health status. I tried extremely hard not to show any signs of being concerned about my potential and most probable diagnosis that I too was positive. I tried to be there for Tim one hundred percent and besides, what was done was done. Unlike Cher's song, *If I could turn back time*, there was no turning back, especially where those three letters were concerned.

I was confused as to how Tim ended up testing positive if he was in a committed relationship prior to us becoming boyfriends. In my previous relationship with Tony, we had been together for over seven years and during that time, except for one incident where Tony and I broke up for a few months and I was with another man, I had been monogamous. After Tony and I rekindled our relationship, and a few years into reuniting with one another, I was tested to obtain the life insurance policy, which I received, so I knew that I did not have HIV prior to meeting Tim.

Boys and girls, ladies and gentleman, moms and dads…this would be a huge learning experience for me in realizing the sexual mores of the world. My experience with Tim taught me a very important lesson in life. I now knew that just because I conducted myself within a certain set of ethical and moral standards, it did not mean that everyone operates on the same level. I was naïve and had been enlightened by Tim's diagnosis and to other interpretations of what is deemed appropriate when it comes to an individual's ethical and moral conduct. I believe it's certainly everyone's prerogative to conduct themselves as they see fit for their life. With this said, I absolutely also believe that we all need to be held accountable for our behavior and the choices that we make in life. Very shortly after receiving the news about Tim's health issue, I would be forced to face the ramifications of my choice to have unprotected sex with him. I had not gone to the doctor to get tested and felt denial was probably my best option at that juncture, although deep within my subconscious I naturally assumed that I was more than likely to test positive since Tim and I had been having unprotected sex.

I needed to face the consequences of not having a conversation that required full disclosure of someone's previous sexual conduct prior to having sex with them. After a lengthy conversation with Tim that evening, I was informed that Steve, Tim's previous lover, was very sexually active. During their seven-plus year relationship, Steve and Tim had three-ways with numerous guys at various times and cities across the U.S. One of their threesomes was with a gay man that resided in San Francisco, California—one of the places where the disease took an initial foothold and where it had a devastating effect on the gay community. This man in San Francisco that Tim and Steve visited on occasion was later diagnosed with AIDS after the epidemic broke out in the city.

I've certainly learned a lot about the gay lifestyle, as well as people's sexual behavior, since the time I was in my late twenties and became positive. Up until that point, I thought and very much believed that if you were in a committed relationship you were monogamous. Monogamy is a choice that I believe works best for me when I'm in a relationship with another man. More importantly, I made my position on monogamy perfectly clear to Tim – and later in life with Alex – when we initially met. I verbally received a confirmation to be monogamous from Tim, and from Alex, before entering into a relationship with either of them. I grew up in a conservative family with two brothers who were straight and was raised to believe in fidelity. I know today that my assumption about monogamous relationships may seem a little ridiculous to many, although I still have hope that somewhere over the rainbow the fairy tale of monogamy is still alive. Later in life I came to realize that the concept of fidelity would be a difficult attribute to find in a gay male partner. I hope that gay male couples still engage in fully monogamous and loving relationships. I believe when a loving commitment exists between two individuals, who care for one another, that they should protect that love with all their heart. For I believe there's no greater gift in life than finding someone that you love with all your being and knowing without a doubt that they love you even more than they love themselves.

I take responsibility for my choices and, in doing so, I do not blame Tim as the reason I contracted HIV. To know Tim was to love him. He was passionate about fashion and attended and graduated from the Fashion Design School at the Art Institute of Chicago. He always hoped to work in the fashion industry and his true passion and dream was to become a woman's fashion designer. As in so many cases and for so many individuals that were diagnosed with the disease in the early stages of the epidemic, the disease had a plan of its own—and for Tim that plan would not allow him to develop a career in fashion that he would have loved so much.

Tim was instrumental in mentoring and nurturing a positive attitude within me where I began to understand the importance of taking physical care of my body. Going to the gym on a regular basis and eating a proper diet became my foundation to begin a life of healthy living. Until I met Tim, the concept of working out and eating a proper diet was a foreign concept in my world with its fast food eating. His dedication to the gym was the reason I began working out. It was no easy task getting accustomed to going to the gym three or four times a week. In the first year, as I began my workout regimen, I absolutely detested it! I would've never kept my commitment to work out had it not been for Tim and his influence. As a body builder, Tim was married to the gym. I could see and physically enjoy the benefits of his workouts. It took me a full year of lifting weights – and hating every minute of it – before I began to see a small physical difference in my own body. After I began to notice a change for the better in my physique, my drive to frequent the gym became part of my everyday lifestyle. Tim's perseverance in getting me into a regular workout schedule played an enormous part in keeping me healthy all these years and ultimately has increased the quality of my life. Tim may have been one of the key elements that resulted in placing my life in jeopardy, by exposing me to HIV, but on the other hand he was equally instrumental in saving my life on many levels.

Tim was a character. He was always making me laugh and I could never help but fall in love with a man that made me laugh. On occasion, he strutted like a runway model when exiting the elevator and walking up the hallway to our apartment and he always had me laughing in hysterics when he did his runway model impersonation. I also found him to be very sensual. He was the first man that I was truly attracted to on a physical level. Despite the many obstacles that tried to keep us apart, we still managed to overcome those difficulties and develop a loving relationship. I know without a doubt that Tim truly loved me for who I was and more importantly, I wanted to be loved by him.

We lived together in a newly constructed high-rise apartment building in Chicago. After a few years of being monogamous, he wanted to explore what he called the great outdoors...men outside of our relationship. Tim approached me with the idea to open our relationship to include a third. At this point in my sexual evolution this was not a concept that I was comfortable in entertaining and especially in my commitment with the man that I loved. Due to my everlasting devotion for Tim – and after much debate and reservations on my part – I considered the idea of a three-way. I recall the chain of events that led me to agree to have sex with Tim and another man at the same time as if it took place yesterday. I'll spare you the details of this encounter and I'll spare myself the visual image of having to relive the event. I will say that, yes, we practiced safe sex. Bringing a third person into our sexual activities was the beginning of the end of our relationship.

As in any relationship, there are high and low points that we all experience at various times during our personal or professional encounters with certain individuals. I believe it's the maturity of the two individuals in the relationship that dictate the outcome of the low points. In many situations, couples do not survive the low points in the roller coaster ride of life due to their level of immaturity and their unwillingness to compromise. I believe the lack of maturity that Tim and I had – when we were in our middle to late twenties – was a contributing factor in determining the outcome of our relationship.

Tim became preoccupied with his medical condition and eventually became restless. He was looking for more than the complacent relationship that I could offer him. Possibly Tim wanted answers for why he ended up positive, which was something that I could not provide. Tim believed, as so many people did at that time of the onset of the AIDS epidemic, that in a few years he would probably become ill and eventually die from his condition. I've come to understand that when an individual is staring death in the face, it's natural for them to let their mind wander toward visualizing their future or lack thereof. In so many cases, the future for terminally-ill individuals leaves them feeling nothing but hopelessness, which turns to despair. The only drug that was available to treat HIV and AIDS in the early nineties was the drug known as AZT. In a short time, the gay community learned that if the disease didn't kill you the AZT drug that treated the disease certainly would. In my opinion, that's about as much hopelessness that anyone can endure, not to mention having to accept and live one's ultimate destiny of doom and gloom.

During the three plus years that Tim and I were together, we were inseparable. After we engaged in the three-way encounter, I realized that this was not the type of relationship I wanted with him. It was difficult for me to consider the possibilities of letting him go, although the alternative of sharing him sexually with another man was even more difficult for me to accept. Shortly after our three-way, Tim moved out of our apartment and accepted a new visual merchandising position on the East Coast. Tim wanted to spread his wings and soar with the eagles and experience what life had to offer—for what he believed was left of his life. Since Tim had a passion for fashion and he was seeking some type of immediate fulfillment, he landed in New York City, where so many soaring gay eagles nest, and the Big Apple became his new nesting place.

I was now nursing what I believed to be a broken heart over the fact that Tim and I were no longer together. I also found myself a little envious of his new living environment as he was going to be residing in New York. Ever since I was a teenager, I had a fascination to live and work in Manhattan. To add insult to my injury, Tim met an incredibly handsome man with an equally incredible body shortly after he moved to the Big Apple, at a popular gay bar called *The Eagle.* I was no longer envious of Tim living in New York, I was downright jealous of him and his new beautiful boyfriend. Tim and I didn't speak for years after the new boyfriend entered the scene. I needed time for my wounds to heal and time to adjust to the idea of the incredibly handsome body builder boyfriend that Tim was living with, while I was living alone. I also needed to come to grips with the idea that Tim, the man that I wanted in my bed, was never coming back to it or to me.

Where do broken hearts go? In my case, I decided to stay in my apartment alone after work for the next six months—crying myself to sleep every night. I had moved out of my parent's house at the age of twenty and moved in with Tony. After my relationship with Tony came to an end, I immediately moved in with Tim. During those ten-plus years of being in two different committed relationships, I concentrated on my career and boyfriend with whom I was involved, which left me with little time for developing new friendships. I was now thirty years old and living alone for the first time in my life, in the apartment that Tim and I had shared.

I was still employed with Bloomingdale's and I decided to pour my efforts into my job and getting into the best physical shape possible. I needed to keep my mind engaged and stay busy so I would not think about Tim and his new life. I took the opportunity to make new friends and began to construct a new life for myself, while simultaneously trying to outrun the dark cloud of my HIV status. It was a dark time. It was three and a half years since the afternoon that Tim initially topped me for the first time, the day, or very soon after, when I contracted the HIV virus. Shortly after splitting with Tim, I realized a guardian angel was hiding in that black cloud that was now hovering overhead. I expect most people have heard the expression that every cloud has a silver lining. I soon came to realize the true meaning of this saying and how it applied to me.

They say you never forget your first love and I certainly have not forgotten Tim. The love that this man expressed toward me was something I will remember for the rest of my life. I will fondly and forever hold the memory of Tim near to me. Up to this day, I still wear the simple gold band ring that Tim gave me when we moved in together all those decades ago; it represents Tim's loving commitment to me and mine for him. As the saying goes "something good always comes out of something bad." Even though Tim is the person from whom I contracted HIV, it was the love that we shared for one another that eventually overshadowed the disease. I realized many years later that the disease came with something good other than Tim's love. I managed to use this unfortunate circumstance of becoming positive to become a better human being. I've learned over the years not to be so judgmental of people and I've also developed a greater depth of compassion for people and the "things" they have to endure in their lifetime. I believe this is another example of how God will use all things for good, even the not so good, if we allow Him to do so—a very hard concept for one to grasp and even harder for one to live by, although this concept has allowed me to have an amazing transformation in how I view the world. Once I was able to fully understand the magnitude of this hypothesis, I was able to have more joy in my daily life and was able to have more compassion for my fellow man.

A PARABLE | POKER FACE

I began to write my story in February of 2011, while still living in Palm Springs, California. In April of that same year, I moved to Los Angeles after residing in the desert for almost four years. That August, I struggled with the concept of whether I was creatively capable of writing a story about my life's journey. For several weeks, I had been contemplating whether I was gifted enough to tell my testimony in a style that could move people's spirit so they would have a genuine interest in taking the time to read it. I wondered if I was afraid of failing in my attempts to be a creative storyteller, which may have been why I was looking for an excuse not to try. If this was true, was I potentially going to cheat myself out of an amazing experience and a great success? At that point, one of those so-called coincidences popped-up in my life once again. Could there be more to these coincidences that have been taking place during my lifetime and, if so, had I failed to give the proper credence to these mysterious events?

I owned my own business and worked from my home office, in a loft apartment in downtown Los Angeles. Working from home allowed me the luxury to enjoy a little television break while having lunch during my workday. One afternoon, there was an episode of *Sex in the City* on the television and the storyline involved a celebration party that Carrie Bradshaw was attending. Carrie had recently finished writing a book and her publisher was having a party to celebrate the launch of the manuscript. At some point during the evening's festivities, Carrie decided she was no longer enjoying her party. At that moment, I began to give closer consideration to the storyline and upon doing so, I decided this was a good reminder for me to get up off my ass and begin writing once again. Upon Carrie's exit from her event, she stepped off the curb of the sidewalk and into the backseat of the town car she had ordered. Once seated, and prior to shutting the door to the car, she casually glanced down at the ground. She spotted a single card from a deck of playing cards between the open door of the car and the gutter of the street. The timing of seeing this card by Carrie must have had some relevance to the show's storyline. Although, all I could think about was how I had placed my writing on the back burner for several months. Just as I was questioning whether I was capable of writing a compelling story, *Sex in the City* played on the television, with a plot about a person who wrote a story about their perspectives and who was celebrating the success of that effort in the form of a published book.

As Fate knows, I'm a little slow when it comes to receiving and deciphering my messages from the beyond. She – for I believe if Fate had a gender, *she* would be a woman – had placed a single playing card in the storyline—at the exact moment that I was watching television and contemplating my creative ability. Possibly Fate wanted me to make the connection to the potential success of my book with the success of Carrie's book and this is why the specific episode had a playing card placed so strategically in the plot. Coincidently, in writing *The doG House of Cards*, I had begun to label each chapter by referencing a single playing card or a gaming expression that is used when playing a card game and I believe the timing of me viewing this specific episode of *Sex in the City* was more than a coincidence. Although, for me to make the connection between what was being portrayed on the television screen and how it could be relevant to my life and my potential writing capability, I would need to put forth the effort and begin writing once again. I was left with the task of having to decipher if this was a sign to inspire me to restart my writing or just a simple random coincidence that had no meaning whatsoever.

I now had renewed motivation to begin writing and attempt to construct this story. After work, I began to get myself ready to head over to the local coffee shop, a few blocks from my apartment, when I began to contemplate how I was going to format my thoughts into words and then into sentences that would begin to convey my feelings on the subject of living the majority of my life in fear. I was fearful that I could become seriously ill from a disease that was directly related to my HIV status, resulting in me not being able to work. I would lose my job and not able to pay for my living expenses, ending in my becoming indigent. I was fearful for many years that I was going to get ill any day and die of AIDS. I was fearful that my boyfriend was going to cheat on me—which they always did. I was fearful that my friends were talking poorly about me behind my back. I was fearful that the people closest to me were lying to me and mistreating me. I became fearful of the possibility of failing in writing my story in a manner that would appeal to a general audience. Ultimately, I was afraid of yet another failure in my life. How was I to convey my feelings of living my entire adult existence in fear, of having one scared thought after another? My fears were affecting the decisions that I was making and the life that I was able to lead.

Suddenly, while in the shower, and as I was getting ready to head to the local coffee shop to begin writing, I called out loud for divine assistance to rid my mind of this fear. When I stepped out of the shower and began to dry off, I had renewed enthusiasm to be more optimistic about life and my writing capabilities. At that exact moment, as I was exiting the bathroom and entering the living room, I heard a voice say… "as I walk through the valley of the shadow of death, I shall fear no evil." On the television, there was now an episode of the *X-Men.* Was this yet another crazy, but calculated coincidence that had a message for me at the precise moment I had the same subject on my mind? Or possibly was this just another random incident that had no real relevance to my situation? The timing of these two scenarios from *Sex in the City* and *The X-Men* took place on the same day, a few hours apart. It seemed that someone or something was attempting to give me a sign to reassure me that I could write this story. The situation reminded me of the movie *The Poltergeist,* when the spirits speak to Carrie Anne through the television and Carrie utters the words, "they're here." I believe a spirit was present and it was using the television to get their voice heard and reassure me that I could write my testimony. Where else than in Hollywood, California would Fate utilize multi-media as her preferred messenger?

I never made it to the coffee shop. I was a little overwhelmed and needed some time to process the meaning of the occurrences that had taken place that afternoon. A few days passed before I sat at my computer and began to attempt to write once again. I had gone to the gym to work out and upon returning to my apartment, I turned on the television for some background noise. Then a phenomenon confirmed what I've previously expressed.

I was sitting at my desk and working on finessing the above paragraphs, when I found myself struggling to assemble words in a manner that expressed my feelings and that would make sense to others. I was having difficulty in making a cohesive thought when I heard a knock at the door. My two miniature schnauzers, Aston and Bentley, both got up and started barking and went to the front door of the apartment. I got up from my chair and walked over to the front door and as I began to open the door I heard a voice coming from the television, "who's there?" The next few words got my attention. "It's the Vatican." There was no one at my apartment entrance. The knocking that the dogs and I heard had come from the television, as had the voice that I heard proclaiming "who's there?" It was Brian, the talking dog from the television show *Family Guy.* The episode involved a person knocking at the door of Brian's house and when Brian opened the door there was a priest at the entrance of the house who said, "it's the Vatican."

Was this another random coincidence, or was this verification from Fate that I received these three communications from a spiritual place? Like God, I believe Fate has an amazing sense of humor and an outstanding sense of timing. I believe these messages were intended to give me encouragement or comfort that I was on the right track in compiling my thoughts for this story. The amusing part of this coincidence was Brian and the priest knocking at the door. Both characters can be construed as having relevance to this book's title, *The doG House of Cards.* God spelled backwards is dog and this story is my testimony, which can be tied to the priest at the door. I was fascinated and entertained by the various coincidences that seemed to give me encouragement to at least try to write my story. Adding the perfect timing of these events to the equation of my skepticism in my writing capabilities, I felt reassured and comforted. I was convinced that there was more than what meets the eye to these random situations. I felt empowered to at least try to write while putting forth my best efforts to express my thoughts in a creative and interesting way.

I understand that these three scenarios can certainly be argued as simply random occurrences that didn't have any meaning, spiritual or otherwise. One can argue that I was looking to make a connection and I did. I also understand that believing Fate was using the television as a means of communication can also be construed as a very unconventional means of hearing from the beyond.

Let's entertain another assessment of the facts. I believe messages from a spiritual realm can come to us in what we refer to as a "gut feeling." We're not sure why we feel a certain way about a certain situation, although something, possibly Fate, is telling us that a situation just does not feel right. Therefore, we proceed with much reservation toward a person, situation, or circumstance. For example, we may have an overwhelming desire to take on a project in an area where we don't have any formal training, although our gut is telling us that we should feel confident in our attempt to achieve success. Are these feelings a result of a random set of situations that are occurring around us? Or are these positive or negative feelings, regarding a specific event or person, a result of Fate showing up in our life to offer her assistance? I don't believe that you have to be in a church or in a holy place to hear, see, or receive a spiritual message or to have Fate offer her promise of wisdom and protection.

I realize that I can debate these situations until the end of time or I can – and I have – begun to see that my life coincidences have two options that they offer me. I can choose to ignore these coincidences as unrelated events that have no relevance in my life and with no real bearing on my life's journey. Or I can embrace these incidences as road signs in my life's path that will require some interpretation on my part to understand how they have tidbits of important information that will allow me to make more informed choices. How I acknowledge and react to these signs will dictate the path that I will travel. Potentially, these signs will lead me closer to my intended destiny or simply closer to something I want or that I'm trying to achieve in my professional, personal, or spiritual journey. Some of these signs are just simple reminders to let me know that there's more to life than I understand. I chose to pay attention to these so-called coincidences, signs, or gut feelings so I may identify the wonders in life. I believe God allows heaven to speak to us on his behalf and even though He doesn't speak with us directly in every circumstance, I believe he is aware of all communications that take place with us from a spiritual realm. Fate speaks to us in many ways and sometimes she may do so through unconventional means—and what makes sense to one individual may not make sense to another. I've begun to pay very close attention to the little things that take place in my life as I've learned the largest messages are usually disguised in the smallest events.

Wikipedia defines faith as confidence or trust in a person, thing, deity, view, or in the doctrines or teachings of a religion. It can also be defined as belief that is not based on proof and it is often used as a synonym for hope or trust. What if coincidences are Fate's or the universe's way of lining up a chain of events for us on a specific day that have a personal message—and to receive that message we need to have faith in Fate? Perhaps the circumstance that is to take place is time sensitive and, therefore, the encounter with the intended recipient takes place at a specific time and on a specific day. Maybe the onset of the coincidence is a unique message that only has meaning for that particular person of faith. To the average person this event may seem like a normal set of circumstances that may happen on any given day and the event may certainly not be an earth-altering circumstance for anyone else other than the intended recipient.

Being in the right place at the right time or good or great timing is certainly a key element in becoming the recipient of good fortune in life. The timing of the events relayed through the television programs only had a positive effect on me because my mind was synchronized with the events as they were taking place and I had faith that I could write a compelling story. Had my thoughts been focused on different subjects other than this book, the messages that I believe were sent from an unconventional source would've had little if any relevance to me at the time they took place. My mind was focused on the right subject, at the right place, and at the right time…and I was able to receive what I believe to be my messages of encouragement that day. Whether it's a gut feeling or just a simple reading between the lines when it comes to encountering a coincidental event, I believe we've all had one or more of these experiences take place in our lives. If we develop a mental presence in our daily routines to acknowledge the signs and wonders at the time they're taking place, then possibly we can have more control over our random life occurrences than we previously believed possible. In doing so, we may be able to execute the philosophy of a positive cause and effect on our specific circumstances—resulting in us being able to achieve a more satisfying existence.

Apophenia /æpə'fiːniə/ is the experience of seeing patterns or connections in random or meaningless data.

2 | A FULL HOUSE

For fifteen years, starting in 1990, I traveled to New York City three to four times a year for business meetings and tradeshows. Whenever I was in New York, I always found time to go to the clubs to enjoy all that Manhattan nightlife had to offer. One night, in the early nineties, I decided to go out to a disco. The hot spot for gay men to party then, on that evening, was a warehouse that had been converted into a club called the Men's Room. The nightclub was in midtown Manhattan and had only recently opened. It was fashionable then for gay men to wear sweatpants to a club. Once you arrived, you removed your sweatpants and checked them at the coat check. Summer or winter—it did not matter, it was all about dancing in your underwear…and Calvin Klein underwear was the popular choice in the gay community at the time.

It was the middle of winter in New York and there I was, dancing in my white Calvin Klein tight fitting boxer shorts, looking buff and feeling pretty good from the prior months I spent at the gym. I was enjoying the music and breaking a disco move when I spotted Tim with Ron, his incredibly handsome body builder boyfriend, dancing a few feet away. Tim and I noticed one another at the exact same moment. They were not dancing in their underwear, although they both looked amazingly healthy and very happy together. This was the first time I had seen Tim in a year and I felt a little uncomfortable about our impromptu encounter. I quickly exchanged pleasantries with them and then I excused myself and went up into the bleachers to lick my wounds. After that evening, Tim and I began speaking to one another once again. We renewed our commitment, although this time it was all about developing a close friendship.

Two years later, Steve, who had been Tim's lover when he and I met in Chicago, became ill and died of AIDS. Steve had remained in the Chicago area after he and Tim broke-up and was still residing in a suburb of the city when he passed away. Tim was not in the best of health then and was unable to travel back to Illinois when Steve died. A friend of Steve's had moved all his furnishing and personal articles into a storage facility when Steve was in the hospital prior to his death. Since I was living in Chicago, Tim asked if I would go through Steve's personal items for him. He wanted me to sort through Steve's possessions, keeping items that could be of personal use. Otherwise, I was instructed to give away the remaining items or throw unwanted things in the trash. Steve parents were in their eighties and did not know that he was gay until just before his death. Steve's mother and father didn't approve of his lifestyle and had no desire to go through their son's personal things. I was now asked to sort through this man's life that I barely knew and make the decision as to the fate of his life's treasures and possessions.

Shortly before Steve died, Tim became ill and I was forced to look in the mirror and ask myself if I was next on the grim reaper list. Were Steve's death and the onset of Tim's illness a glimpse into my own pre-destined demise? Did my future include a person that I barely knew deciding the disposition of my life's treasures, as I was asked to determine the fate of Steve's? Several years after Steve's passing, Tim too died of AIDS. I was devastated. The fear associated with his death kept me from dealing with my emotions. I was terrified that I would become ill at any moment, which kept me in a state of denial, but it forced me to have a new perspective on the meaning of life and what little time there may be left of it.

At this point in my career, I worked at Bigsby&Kruthers, a high-end retailer, as vice president of store development and visual merchandising. During my six plus years of working there, the company acquired a new division formed in partnership with Michael Jordan, the amazing basketball star that played for the Chicago Bulls. As part of the partnership, Bigsby had a very large financial interest in a small five hundred square foot retail store that sold Michael Jordan memorabilia within the Michael Jordan restaurant. The retail shop fell under my department's responsibility and due to the enormous success of the retail store I needed to hire an employee to maintain the windows and merchandising standards. Over the course of my career, I had a very close professional relationship with the personnel in the various departments that I managed and long considered my staff to be a very intricate part of my success at Bigsby. Not surprisingly, over the years, I developed a close friendship with each of my staff members, who were like family to me.

Rick, the new hire for the Jordan retail shop was a friend of Tony, my workout partner and my best friend at the time. They had been best friends for many years and Tony introduced us. Tony and I met when he was employed at Bloomingdale's as a salesperson in the men's fragrance department, on the same floor as the men's area where I was responsible for the visuals. I was in the final stages of getting over my breakup and emotional attachment to Tim, when Tony and I began a friendship and started to work out together at Gold's Gym. After a few years, I began to refer to Tony as my best buddy. After Tony introduced me to Rick, we three developed a very close friendship that would last for close to a decade. Tony is of Puerto Rican decent and Rick is from Mexico. Prior to living in Chicago, I had been raised in one of its' small suburbs – on the southwest side – where there were not many opportunities that allowed friendships to be developed with other races and cultures, other than the average white suburbanite like myself.

Tim had introduced me to the gym a few years before Gianni Versace introduced muscle men into his fashion campaigns. The photo spreads in these ads involved numerous and outstanding muscle boys wearing Gianni Versace's latest and greatest creations, shot in South Miami Beach. Versace published a book of his photography and encased these beauties in a hardbound book that you could find on almost any gay man's coffee table at that time. His photography became the standard for every gay man who wanted muscles and, to this day, I still have Gianni's amazing book. In my opinion, it was Versace's influence that was instrumental in promoting what became the gay community's obsession with the muscle scene. Many gay men, including myself, wanted to look exactly like those Versace models and this esthetic became the ideal in the gay community.

Tony's desire to become my workout partner was fueled by his passion to have his share of the popularity that surrounded the boys sporting those beautiful muscles. Tony was five feet, eight inches tall and passably good looking, although he was a little on the skinny side. After several years of working out at the gym, his dedication began to produce results and while he worked diligently to develop his body, he failed to continue to evolve as a person. I believe Tony became jealous of the friendship that Rick and I established and this jealousy clouded his judgment and eventually this envy became his major shortcoming, as a person and, more importantly, as a friend.

After Rick began to work at Bigsby, we had the opportunity to have daily interaction with one another and soon developed our very close working relationship and a friendship outside the office. When he was younger, Rick had fallen deeply in love, but it had not been reciprocated. This had a profound effect on him—but it never dimmed his positive outlook on life. He had two mottos that he was known for quoting on a regular basis. His expressions would eventually make their way into my thoughts and I would ultimately find myself utilizing them throughout my lifetime. Rick's first motto was "how hard can it be?" Whenever I gave him a project at work that was somewhat challenging, I can always recall him saying those five words. I believe this was to encourage himself, as well as reassure me that the project that had been assigned to him would be completed as requested and more importantly, that the project would be completed as expected. Over the decades to come, whenever I came across a difficult task in my life, I could hear a little voice in my head uttering those five words, "how hard can it be?" Somehow these words allowed me to keep things in the correct perspective and not to become overwhelmed with the task at hand. Rick's second motto was "better alone than badly accompanied," one I believe he learned from his father and which he followed. This motto was a very wise set of words to live one's life by, although it would be many years before I eventually realized the importance and the magnitude of executing these words in my daily life. I'm a very slow learner and usually repeat my mistakes over and over before I learn my life lessons—and this was especially true when it involves friendships and romantic relationships.

On the Sunday afternoon that I promised Tim I would sort through Steve's personal things, I asked Rick to accompany me to go through Steve's storage locker in a storage facility in a suburb of Chicago. Rick and I had been out partying the night before and were both somewhat hung-over and not looking forward to the task awaiting us. Hangover or no hangover, I had to do what I promised.

When we arrived at the storage facility, we stumbled from locker to locker until we eventually located the one that belonged to Steve. As I lifted the rollup door to the storage space, some of Steve's stuff tumbled out and landed at our feet. It seemed as if someone had packed Steve's things in the middle of the night and just tossed whatever he or she could get into any random boxes they could find. I remember thinking how Steve had achieved such a level of success as an executive at a major car manufacturing plant in DeKalb, Illinois…and how sad it was that this man's personal possessions had been reduced to what resembled a quick move out in the middle of the night. It was chaotic; Steve's things were not correctly packed and there was no rhyme or reason on how his stuff had been stored. The entire scenario was very unsettling and a very depressing situation with which to be dealing. I remember thinking that Steve was watching Rick and me as we were going through his things. Needless to say, it was not about being selective and detailed as we rummaged through the numerous boxes; it was all about getting out of there quickly. While we selected some items to take with us, Rick and I ended up tossing ninety percent of Steve's things into a dumpster. I'm not sure why I didn't call Goodwill to come and retrieve his discarded items. I think my fear had gotten the best of me. I was afraid…scared that I was looking at my own future with someone that I barely knew rummaging through my personal treasures in some suburban storage facility and not really taking time to evaluate the importance of these items that took my entire life to collect. I wanted nothing to do with the situation and it took all the mental energy that I could muster to complete the task at hand, as fast as possible. In dumping Steve's items quickly, I was able to maintain the denial of my HIV status while simultaneously upholding my commitment to Tim.

Several years after Tim and I broke up, I was forced to deal with my possible and most probable diagnoses of being positive, which was a rude awakening. At the time, the ignorance, fear and downright hatred that was being projected onto those who were positive or who had AIDS was absolutely shocking. The haters were prevalent in the straight and the gay community. Being shunned by some of those in my own community was the most shocking situation for me to accept. The majority, if not all of these haters, were not positive or were not personally affected by knowing someone that had contracted the HIV virus or who had full-blown AIDS. In hindsight, I understand most of these haters were people that were experiencing fear because they themselves were afraid of what they did not understand, as I believe its human nature to be afraid of what we do not understand and, more importantly, what we cannot control. One might even expect or be able to explain away this type of behavior from the straight community, although this was a hard concept to grasp in my mind coming from the gays. Where was the compassion for these terminally ill people? The mental anguish and isolation that the positive and AIDS-stricken individuals were left to deal with is beyond most people's comprehension. I'm not sure I can put into words how I was left to feel about my self-esteem and my self-worth during this time. I believe it takes a very special person to be able to walk among those who would reject them should the truth be known of their specific circumstance. In my case – during the early years of my diagnosis of being positive – there would have been an enormous negative effect on my life had my HIV status been openly revealed to my family, friends, and professional associates.

While I was aware of the concept of God learned in my early years with my grandmother and parents, I had no interest at this time in pursuing the reality of how God could have an effect on my life any more than what I was exposed to as a child. Ironically, I did find some comfort in the portion of the Bible that speaks of Jesus and the time that he spent with the lepers. I can actually imagine the great comfort that these lepers must have felt by knowing that this man, admired by so many, was not afraid of their disease and spent time expressing genuine love towards them. I believe if there's just one item that encompasses the legacy of the Bible, it's the never-ending love story for all of mankind exemplified by Jesus. As the Bible proclaims, God came for the lost and discarded or, should I say, he especially came to seek the lost and discarded, the meek that shall inherit the earth.

In my early years of being positive, I became very introverted and protective when it came to divulging my health status to anyone. It goes without saying, although I'll say it anyway, it was very difficult to find anyone that was remotely interested in getting romantically involved with someone that was positive like myself. Most positive people concealed their status and I avoided the dating process altogether, as it always inevitably led to the question of when was the right time to disclose "the issue". Was it proper to discuss your status with a date on the first date or on the second date? If not by the first or second encounter, then definitely l would be obligated to have the discussion no later than on the third date, right? How many gay men do you know that have three dates before they have sex? Since gay men, including myself, were so eager to have sex so early when getting to know one another, I basically stopped looking for anyone to get involved with romantically. Besides, I thought, I only had a short number of years to live and why would I drag another individual into my nightmare. I began to believe I didn't deserve the happiness that comes with a healthy and blissful relationship and my self-esteem declined dramatically. Each morning upon starting my day, I lay in bed contemplating if this was going to be the day that I became ill—a very emotional and somewhat overwhelming way to begin my day every morning for the next five years.

After a brief period of working with Rick at Bigsby, we developed an extensive social calendar. On most weekends, we frequented the gay clubs. Several times during the week we went to dinner with friends and we always celebrated the major holidays together. A few years into our friendship, we began traveling together. When we took our first trip, we were living in Chicago and still working for Bigsby. We had planned a personal trip to Los Angeles, where we attended a gay circuit event called Labor Day LA. This was an annual circuit party weekend that donated a portion of its proceeds to AIDS research. We had a great time, although our friend Tony was not pleased that we traveled to Los Angeles without him and he didn't speak to us for weeks after we returned. To this day, I'm not sure what Tony's real issue was regarding the trip since I had invited him to join us. Many years later, looking back, I now see that Tony was envious of my friendship with Rick and the mutual interests that we shared together. While we had different personalities and interests, we complemented each other well. We both liked to travel and explore different cultures around the world. We both liked to experience new things and were interested in architecture, fashion, and the culinary arts. Rick introduced me to art and history. I introduced him to visual merchandising and graphic design. We made each other laugh. Most importantly, we had a genuine appreciation and respect for each other.

The three of us had gone out the night before Rick and I traveled to Los Angeles. We got very drunk, which was nothing new, as we were young and drank a lot in those early years of our friendship. In my drunken state, I met a cute guy at the bar where we ended the evening. I left Rick and Tony at the bar in boystown and, with trick in tow, I went home to my high-rise apartment in downtown Chicago. All I remember was taking this guy that I picked up at a gay bar back to my place—and the next thing I remembered, after getting home and into bed, was waking up alone at five in the morning. I was sure I brought someone home with me from the bar, or was I so drunk that I was mistaken? I went back to sleep and awoke several hours later, although this time I had an enormous hangover, probably I was still drunk from the night before. We had a morning flight and, in those days, I was always on time or, in more cases than not, I was early for my commitments. With a killer hangover, I managed to get ready for our trip and eventually made it out the door of my apartment, down the elevator and to the garage across the street, where I had parked my car. Rick was also a high-rise living fag and I had arranged to pick him up at his apartment building in boystown, which was on the way to the airport.

I had recently received a promotion at Bigsby as vice president of development and visual merchandising and was looking to hire a visual director to fill my former position. Coincidently, the recruiting company that Bigsby hired to fill this position had a potential and promising candidate for me to interview in Los Angeles, employed with Ralph Lauren and living there. I thought I would mix a little business with pleasure that weekend and travel out a day early and interview this candidate while attending the Labor Day LA event.

I'm very conscientious when I travel and I usually like arriving at the airport with enough time to spare to comfortably make it to my gate without being anxious about the process. I wish I could say the same about Rick. He was notorious for being late at this point in his life. When I arrived to pick him up, I woke him up from a sound sleep and he had not showered or even packed his clothes. The race was now on for him to pull it together and do it quickly.

Rick was cursed when it came to over sleeping and being late. This irritating pattern would follow us from city to city as we traveled and he would usually oversleep on the days of our departure during our travels to Europe. He was the designated individual responsible for our international plans and the ground transportation fell within his responsibilities. On more occasions than not, we found ourselves scrambling in the morning of our departures. In this instance, his tardiness, was related to us being out until the wee hours of the morning the night before.

As I waited in my car for Rick, I could not stop thinking of the numerous times that Rick had overslept on similar occasions. He must have been in his apartment running about like a Tasmanian devil as he attempted to get himself ready. I'm sure he knew the longer he kept me waiting the more impatient I became. I do get very irritated when someone keeps me waiting, especially when I had previously confirmed a time to meet, and I kept calling him every five minutes just to rattle him a little more than he already was for not being ready at the appointed time. Rick eventually emerged from his apartment building with packed suitcase in hand. He jumped into my car and we were finally on our way.

As we drove to the airport, Rick and I discussed the events from our previous evening. I mentioned that I went home with the cute guy that I met at the bar. Rick then assured me that I had not. I was a little confused as to why he believed that I had not gone home with the cutie. I knew I was definitely over-served the night before, but I was sure I had trick in tow when I arrived at my apartment the previous evening—even if he was not there when I awoke. That morning, in fact, I happened to find a man's watch on the nightstand in my bedroom, which I knew was not mine. With watch in hand, I knew for sure that someone had to have been in my apartment and it must have been the cute guy from the bar. After several repeated attempts to recall the foggy events from the night before, I reiterated to Rick that I indeed went home with the cute guy. Clearly, I have no idea what his name was. Rick still insisted that I could not have done so. I was a little irritated that he was so persistent that I was incorrect. I asked him why he believed that I was mistaken and he replied, "Because I went home with him."

How could he have gone home with the same guy on the same evening that I did? This made absolutely no sense to me whatsoever. I was very confused and somewhat annoyed, to say the least. Rick and I eventually realized that I took the cute guy back to my place and passed out. The trick inadvertently left his watch on the nightstand, as he dressed to catch a cab back to the bar where I originally met him. Once back at the watering hole, he ran into Rick, who didn't realize that the guy had left with me earlier in the evening and so…he took the guy back to his place to complete what I had not. Rick and I were both suffering from serious hangovers on our way to the airport, but we were still able to determine that the chain of events that took place the prior evening was somewhat disturbing. Within a few minutes though, we both managed to see the humor in the situation and were able to have a good laugh at our own expense as we arrived at the airport. Our laughter allowed us to forget about the tension that had been created earlier that morning when I arrived at his apartment building to pick him up and he was not showered or packed for our trip to the *City of Angels*, or as I like to refer to it: *The land of Oz*, where wishes are free and dreams come true.

By the time we got to the airport and found our gate to board our flight, I was absolutely exhausted. The alcohol I consumed the night before had finally left my system and I was to pay the piper. Once we boarded the plane – with Rick going in first – and found our separate seats, I decided to take a trip to the bathroom. On my way back to my assigned seat, I noticed an entire row of seats that were empty in the back of the plane and decided to re-ticket myself for that empty row that I turned into my in-flight bed. I was now able to lie down and sleep for the duration of the flight. I know most people would argue this point with me, but I believe Fate was flying coach with me on that flight. Even though I now believe it's wrong to drink until we can't remember who slept in our bed the night before, I also believe God loves to show up when we least expect it and, most of all, when we least deserve it. I believe the entire row of empty seats on the plane was a gift from heaven as I was in desperate need of sleeping off my tremendous hangover before landing in California. Four and a half hours after leaving Chicago, our plane landed and my in-flight nap came to an end.

Los Angeles always gives me a feeling of home.... a feeling of familiarity and endearment derived from my love for palm trees and the fact that I was born in Long Beach. Since I re-seated myself in the back of the plane, Rick had to wait for the entire plane to disembark before I could make my way down the jet-way ramp and into the terminal where he was waiting. He became very nervous when he noticed most of the people had gotten off the plane and I still had not shown up. He thought that I may not have gotten on the flight and was still sitting in Chicago at the airport. Later that day, I would laugh about Rick sweating my whereabouts when we landed. His anxiety should have served as a fantastic reminder not to sleep with my tricks, at least not on the same night as me. We made our way to the baggage claim area and with luggage in hand we jumped on the shuttle to the car rental office to pick up the convertible that we rented for the weekend. I booked a room for us at the J.W. Marriott on the Avenue of the Stars in Century City, conveniently located near Beverly Hills. I often stayed at this hotel when I was in LA, as I enjoyed its' spacious rooms and the great amenities. The hotel was also close to West Hollywood or should I say WeHo, a place with not a wee number of hos.

Once we arrived at the hotel, we valeted the convertible and were able to get checked into our room earlier than expected. Upon entering our room, I mentioned to Rick how exhausted I still was from our drunken adventure the night before. My in-flight nap was beneficial although it did not cure my hangover—and we had so many activities planned in LA for this weekend and no spare time to catch up on our rest. At that exact moment, an acquaintance of mine from Oz, knocked on our door. As I opened it, Kevin – who I called "the wizard" – sauntered into the space and welcomed us "bitches" to the "land where the fruits are many and the nuts have wings." The next words out of his mouth had an enormous impact on my life for many decades to come. Kevin told us, "I've been carrying a bag of crystal meth in my wallet for a year and you're welcome to it, if you need a pick me up." A drug dealer had given him the baggie of meth a year earlier when he had stayed at his apartment for the weekend and Kevin had carried the substance in his wallet ever since that day...and maybe it was for such a day and time. It was the middle of the nineties and the crystal phenomenon in the gay community had just begun its' debut in the party scene. The drug gained in popularity over the next several years and eventually became part of the mainstream gay culture almost a decade after its initial introduction. The gays eventually christened the drug "Tina" and she was certainly calling my name from Kevin's wallet that day at the J.W Marriott. She wanted to come out to play and she was definitely interested in becoming the life of the party. Up until that point, my group of friends and I were weekend partygoers who partied on alcohol, ecstasy, cocaine, and ketamine. These four were our typical choices when we went out to the clubs to party, maybe not all of them at the same time, but certainly a combination of two or three on the same evening. I kept hearing Tina calling my name and I had to let her out to play. I was not only introduced to Tina that afternoon, I found myself entertaining the bitch for too many years.

From that point forward, she became a frequent guest who I invited to accompany me to parties and who in a very short time overstayed her welcome. When given the opportunity, she would be my number one choice, over coffee, to begin my day. Though at times I make light of the use of crystal meth for entertainment and for humor's sake, make no mistake, Tina is not something that should be taken lightly under any circumstances. Tina had an impact on my life and created many hardships. I eventually came to the hard realization that the use of methamphetamine plays a specific and dramatic role in ruining many people's lives. However, I hope this story sheds some light on how I was seduced by Tina and assists you in understanding the demons that were created from my weekly party agenda. I allowed Tina to lead me down a dark one-way path—one that I would not have chosen for myself had I said no to her that day in Los Angeles at the J.W. Marriott. God eventually used Tina, and the darkness that surrounded the drug and her followers, to expose the ugliness and sadness that encompassed the world that she ruled. Without God in my heart and mind, Tina and her users would have destroyed everything that I believed to be good in life. I've learned through my love for God that evil has no power—other than the power that we allow it to have over us. In Tina's case, she was just another annoying guest that I should have removed from my life on the same weekend that I invited her to accompany me to the Labor Day festivities.

At the exact moment when I snorted Tina up my nose for the first time, I instantly no longer felt the presence of a hangover that had been lingering. Tina was now my BFF, my best friend forever, and we hung out together for the entire weekend while in LA. She comforted me and made everything feel better or so it seemed. Little did I know, this was the calm before the perfect storm. I believe Tina is the drug of the devil, for no God-loving or God-fearing person would ever manufacture such a chemical for human consumption. Only God himself could have known what Tina had in store for my future and the tricks she had up her sleeve or, more appropriately, the tricks she had going up my nose. As the Bible states, "if God be for us, who can be against us?" …nobody—certainly not Tina or any drug lord for that matter!

I eventually made it to my appointment with the candidate that I was interviewing for the Bigsby position. The individual I was interviewing was presently working at the Ralph Lauren store on Rodeo Drive in Beverly Hills, as their visual merchandising manager. After meeting with him and spending a few hours chatting over lunch, and upon my return to Chicago, I gave my stamp of approval for this tan, tall, slim LA queen named Don to be interviewed by the CEO of Bigsby. A few weeks after our initial meeting, Don flew to Chicago for further interviews with Gene, the CEO, and a few of the merchandise buyers. His interview went well and he was offered the job shortly after. He became one of my department heads reporting to me. He was to oversee the visual merchandising of the men and women's clothing division at seven Bigsby locations in the Chicago area, as well as the supervision of a field staff of three. My decision to hire Don to manage the visual team in Chicago was like taking a flamingo out of its habitat in Florida and moving it to Alaska. Don was never able to fully adjust to the huge culture difference and climate change between Beverly Hills in the sunny west coast and the mid-west winters of the Windy City.

I was employed at Bigsby for just over six years with great success. Within this time, my department designed and oversaw the construction of forty-three accessory stores across the U.S. known as the Knot Shops. In the Chicago area, I also remodeled two existing Bigsby men's stores, designed and opened two new Bigsby women's concept stores, and assisted on the design of the Michael Jordan retail store within his eponymous restaurant.

At Bigsby, I was the only creative director that was able to stay on the job for more than a single year, in the entire history that it was in business. My predecessors either quit or were fired within the first year. Gene, the owner and CEO, was impossible to work with and no individual maintained employment in my role for longer than a year under his supervision. He was an egotistical, narcissistic, self-centered, self-absorbed, womanizing male boss who always had to be right with all his opinions and creative guidance. He was the head of all three divisions and there was no escaping his micromanagement tactics, especially when it came to the creative direction for the three companies. Gene always thought he knew best, no matter what subject you were discussing, when it came to the Bigsby business model. His ego was so large that when the business relationship between Michael Jordan and Bigsby soured, Gene sued Jordan, and the ego lost; Jordan won.

I often referred to our relationship as a very dysfunctional and abusive marriage. Guess who was the one getting abused? Being a gay man and still quite young in my professional life experiences, I had not developed skills in exercising self-control when it came to editing what I was thinking and what came out of my mouth at any given moment. I often got myself in trouble with Gene by challenging his directive, although I believe he respected me for standing my ground when I believed I was right. Most of my managerial co-workers under his supervision crumbled in fear of the consequences that they may or may not endure by taking the risk in challenging one of his directives. Gene's style was to manage by fear and this behavior only worsened as the company grew larger. He was the only boss that I reported to in my adult career that actually reduced me to tears. On three separate occasions during my tenure at the company, he reprimanded me to the point that I broke down and cried at the office. Though I never let myself cry in front of him because I would not give him the satisfaction of seeing me in that state and letting him know that he emotionally broke me down.

He was notorious for calling his direct reports after office hours, on a constant basis for many years and at all hours of the night. He often called me late at night to discuss the creative ideas that happened to come to his mind at any given moment and on any particular evening. The after-hours phone calls often took place as late as midnight and it didn't matter to him if it was a weeknight or on the weekend. He didn't respect professional boundaries when it came to nonbusiness office hours, but, as this was the time before everyone carried a cellular phone, I could hide behind my home answering machine on most occasions.

Gene was the type of supervisor that not only managed by intimidation, he also managed by sight. The closer you were to interacting with him daily, the more things with which he found to interact with you. My fellow executives at the office had a standing joke to not pass Gene's office when his door was open…otherwise you were sure to get pulled into some type of *thought* that he had or an impromptu meeting that would last for hours. He was always changing his mind; just as he gave you a specific direction, he changed it. On more occasions than not, I executed what I felt was in the best interest of the company, based on my professional experience, and not necessarily the directive that was imposed on me by Gene. These decisions to follow my instincts, and not Gene's commands, were a risky endeavor, to say the least. My creative background and talent usually helped in making the correct decision and my decisions to take risks generally worked out in my favor. On occasions, Gene would challenge my creative choices and the confrontation was usually painful, with hell to pay for going against his directive. On the rare occasion when I did get busted for going against one of his crazy creative tangents, I told tell him that it was what he instructed me to execute. Nine out of ten times he could not recall his final directive to me on a specific project because he changed his mind so many times during the process, so I was able to skate through. The creative staff in my department came up with a nickname for him and hence referred to him as *The Mad Scientist.*

While he was absolutely and positively nuts, Gene was also a very creatively-driven man. However, within several years of working for him, I would use up all my professional and personal favors from the vendors that supported my department and its' endeavors. Gene would frequently change his mind in the midst of a construction project and still expect the cost and time frame of that project to remain as originally negotiated. I never moved so many mountains or pulled so many rabbits out of my ass as I did when I worked for this man. I was a frickin' magician that had used up all his tricks entertaining The Mad Scientist and his ideas of grandeur.

Despite the negative attributes that surrounded Gene as a leader, he was very charismatic and had many great talents. He was a phenomenal salesperson when it came to selling the company's vision and was able to attract incredible leaders in their field of expertise to the organization. He had the bullshit sales tactic down and could sell a blind man a pair of reading glasses. He could make you feel like the most important person in the world if he wanted something from you and he often left you with the impression that the company could not survive without you.

When confronted with his micromanagement style, Gene swore to me that he would change his ways and not be so overbearing when it came to controlling my creative efforts. For those who have not had a boss like Gene, take my word for it—they will never change, no matter how convincing they may make the argument that they will. I received the declaration and heard the words of redemption in person and directly from the mouth of the Mad Scientist himself…he convincingly said he would become less of a dictator and more of a mentor, although he never followed through with his promise. I suppose the dictator loves his power more than he loves his people.

At Bigsby, my biggest claim to fame, my fifteen minutes, was the creative design, development and implementation of a new, twenty thousand square foot flagship store. It consisted of two retail floors in a historic building on the famous Magnificent Mile in Chicago. The design and construction for this new flagship location took eighteen months of my career, during which I submitted my resignation to Gene on two separate occasions. My first attempt was submitted as construction was underway. Upon tendering my first resignation, Gene offered me a bonus of twenty five thousand dollars to stay on. I then rescinded my resignation…and deposited my self-respect, along with the check for twenty five thousand dollars, into my checking account.

During my years of working for Gene, I observed that he was a great and loving father. He invited me to numerous social events that he hosted for his family. The first invitation was to his son's Bar Mitzvah and I had the pleasure of becoming acquainted with his wife and children. I was a big fan of his wife; she was a lovely lady and I'm not sure to this day what attributes of Gene she found to be so attractive. I was unable to see what she saw in him and perhaps this speaks to her character or to the old adage that love is blind. During the years that followed, I learned a good life lesson. A Bible verse states, "judge not, and thou shall not be judged", a difficult concept to live by, but a liberating one once it's learned. This is especially true when it comes to evaluating a couple's romantic relationship—as I was doing with Gene—by judging how his wife could be in love with a man that I was not able to embrace as a person.

My second and final resignation to divorce myself from Gene was handed to him upon the completion of the new store. I just could not ride the bipolar roller coaster any longer. I was ready to throw-up all over myself and all over Gene if I stayed employed at Bigsby anymore, under his authority.

As the new flagship store opened, the company was starting to experience financial difficulties due, in no small part, to Gene's outrageous spending habits. The financial stress on the company was compounded by softening retail sales in the suit business, Bigsby's bread and butter, due to the arrival of casual Friday. Gene refused to acknowledge that fashion in the business world was changing from formal business attire to a more casual way of dressing. By the time he finally embraced the concept, it was too late for Bigsby to alter its' merchandise selection and for the company to attempt to rebound. His arrogance had finally caught up with him and his companies, and casual Friday was the beginning of the end for the Bigsby empire. As with the end of all great empires, its demise came with mixed emotions. While I had given my last breath of energy to this man and his companies, I was grateful for the creative opportunities that I had been given and for what I had been able to learn during my tenure there. I'll never forget the great experiences and the fantastic projects that I had the pleasure to work on while working under the leadership of this Mad Scientist.

Up to that point, working at Bigsby was the crown jewel of my career, despite my dysfunctional relationship with Gene. It was the place where I was able to flourish as an interior designer and visual merchandising manager. I developed my talents and became the designer that I had always dreamed of being. I was recognized and received many national awards within the retail design industry, including an industry award as one of the *Top 40 designers in America, under 40* in 1997.

The challenging conditions that I had to endure at Bigsby are a perfect example of how I was able to find self-satisfying achievements amidst overwhelming frustrations that came with the job. At thirty-two, I was earning a six-figure salary, which is not bad considering that I didn't have a formal design education or a college degree. Like most things in life, my achievements came with a price of working under very challenging conditions. I had become aware of my HIV status while working at Bigsby, though I only revealed it to a few select individuals in my immediate department and I believe Gene had no idea of my health situation—a perfect example of how two people can work so closely together daily, for so many years, and never truly know one another on a personal level.

I met Alex when I was thirty-six, still employed at Bigsby, and still looking for love in all the wrong places. Until meeting him, I had failed in the love department, except for my amazing, but brief three-and-a-half-year relationship with Tim. After my relationship with Tim ended, I had not truly experienced another deep and long-lasting love affair with another man.

Then the ringing of my home phone awoke me that cold winter weekend morning in 1996. The caller was Alex and I was very interested in speaking with him, as you can imagine—after I had slept off my hangover. Alex was calling to express his interest in furthering our brief encounter, and I wanted to know more about this man that I had so admired the night before on the dance floor, as he strutted his stuff in the club. While I was certainly curious, I was also leery as to why Alex was interested in reciprocating my interest so quickly; it had been less than six hours since I approached him in the club.

3 | DEALER'S CHOICE

As a young boy, I recall being attracted to men and thinking that I was not supposed to feel that way about the same sex. I thought my attraction to men was a pre-adolescent fad that I was going through. Around the same time, I heard on the television that it was natural for young boys to be attracted to older boys or other young men like themselves. It was also mentioned that when boys matured into young adults, the male-to-male attraction would fade and then the boys would naturally be drawn to girls. But as I grew into a young man, my attraction to men increased and my physical attraction to girls never seemed to blossom as the narrator on the television had said. During my pre-adolescent years, I messed around sexually with other boys who were usually older than me. These teenage boys seemed to identify that I was interested in interacting with the same sex. I'm not exactly sure how they knew I was gay when, in fact, I had not realized it myself. Did I give off a gay vibe? Was I showing up on their gay radar? Or, was it because as a young boy, and later in life as a young adult, I was very shy and introverted? Did these characteristics contribute to making me a vulnerable target? I often thought being a young introverted gay boy in America was comparable to being the vulnerable pray in the animal kingdom—where the strong conquer the weak. Much later in life, I realized that, as a rule, many people will pray on the shy, timid, and weak for their own pleasure and personal gain.

Around the same time that I was experiencing these new feelings of unexplained attraction to other boys, my parents befriended a married couple and developed a close friendship with them. They were an older couple that had been married longer than my parents and had produced three boys in the early years of their marriage who were teenagers when my parents befriended them. Much later in their marriage, they had a second set of children and they were closer to my age. When my parents and the older couple would get together – usually going out to dinner and dancing – their teenage boys would babysit their younger siblings, as well as me and my brothers. The three teenage brothers were close in age and one of these brothers would always have me sleep with him in his room. Looking back, I now realize he had an agenda and he isolated me from his siblings and from my own brothers. I don't remember the specifics of how he persuaded me to perform sexual acts on him, but I recall the acts that he had me perform. I was too young to comprehend what he wanted me to do meant. I didn't understand the specifics around the birds and bees, although I knew that I needed to be quiet about our nighttime activities. I was so naïve that I was not yet aware that guys ejaculated seamen when they sexually climaxed. I had not hit puberty and I was confused when he ejaculated for the first time. I do not claim that what happened between this teenage boy and me to be child molestation, although some experts in the field may disagree with me. I know for a fact, without any doubt, that the sexual acts with this older boy were not the cause of me becoming gay nor did it turn me into a child molester later in life. As I became a little older and entered my teens, I found myself sexually attracted to older men. To this day, I'm not sure if my initial physical attraction to more mature men, as I became a teenager and into my twenties, had anything to do with the sexual encounters that took place between me and the older boy.

Like most young teenagers who go through puberty, I struggled with being comfortable with my sexuality. Whether you're born straight or gay, I believe that most teenagers find the process of moving from a boy to a young man an awkward time. The addition of my homosexual feelings, as I transformed to a young teenager, caused much more confusion. I was confused about why I was physically attracted toward men and not women. As most individuals that find themselves isolated, I wondered if I was the only one in my high school, or in my small town where I grew up, who was having these types of feelings. I couldn't help but think there was something wrong with me. When I finished my senior year of high school, I found myself without having had a romantic relationship with a girl. I had a few female friends where the relationships could have been construed as potentially being romantic, but these relationships were nothing more than close friendships, and in some cases were deliberately staged on my part to give the perception that I was romantically involved with a female. Concealing my true intentions from girls was something that I did because I was expected by society to be physically attracted to the opposite sex. If I felt I had a choice at the time, I certainly would not have chosen this type of behavior. Deceiving people, or at the very least giving them the wrong impression of my true intentions, was not something with which I was comfortable. However, the alternative of having my classmates find out about my potential homosexual tendencies was not an option that I was willing to entertain. I was confused and afraid of openly exploring the alternate option to dating girls.

At sixteen, I worked as a stock boy on the loading dock of Wieboldt's. It was one of the major department stores that anchored the Lincoln Mall Shopping Center in Matteson, Illinois. Upon completing my classes for the day, I would leave high school after having lunch in the school cafeteria and headed over to the mall to work. I was enrolled in a work release program that allowed me to attend a half-day of school and spend the rest of my day getting practical work experience in a place of business, which counted toward my education. My main responsibilities were to go from department to department on the first and second floor of the store and collect the trash, pick up merchandise that customers had bought and wanted to have shipped to their homes, and gather goods that were being transferred to another location. In a short time, I developed a friendly relationship with the various department managers. They quickly became familiar with my daily schedule and knew when I would stop by their department for my rounds. These managers would have their customer sends or inter-store transfers ready for pickup when I arrived and I always made time for a few minutes of pleasant conversation with the salespeople and, more importantly, with the managers as I went from department to department.

During my second year of working at Wieboldt's, I met Larry, a twenty-seven-year-old man who I found to be extremely attractive…and I soon found myself pining for his attention. Larry worked in the furniture department and he always chatted me up when I passed his area. There were numerous saleswomen throughout the store that were also obsessed with Larry. I was seventeen and up to that point I had not openly pursued another man. He was the first guy I flirted with in public, without divulging the exact nature of that interest. It was a very exciting time, although a scary endeavor for me to act upon should my advances not be reciprocated. What would happen to my job if my casual advances toward this handsome man of Czech decent were not appreciated or welcomed? What if Larry was not sexually interested in men and he realized that I was after him for more than a friendship? Would he out me at work? I was extremely shy and somewhat of an introvert but – while suppressing my homosexual interest – I was trying to drop hints of my curiosity to explore a closer interaction with him.

After a year of taking every opportunity to walk by Larry's department, in hopes of seeing him and possibly having the chance to speak with him, he eventually realized that I apparently had more interest in him then just a casual work friendship. One evening at work, he suggested that we get together for a drink after our shifts ended. The legal drinking age was twenty-one and, as I was under the legal age for consuming alcohol, our options where we could have a cocktail were limited. After we had a few drinks at a local restaurant close to mall where we worked, he finally made a move to let me know that he was definitely interested in men and, at that moment, his interest was focused on me. This sexy lady's man that all the women at work adored placed his cards on the table and under that table he placed his hand on my leg. I was excited to finally have my interest reciprocated and I was very interested in seeing where the hand on my knee would lead, although these feelings came with mixed emotions. Larry was also closeted at work and he understood my reluctance to act on my sexual interest with a male coworker. This was the first time I openly admitted to myself that I preferred men over women. I was thrilled about a potential sexual encounter with Larry, but I was also scared out of my mind when it came to acting on those feelings. Almost all my coworkers on the loading dock were young men slightly older than me—and very straight. The year was 1977 and being openly gay was not something that was as widely accepted as it is today. My working environment would have become somewhat hostile if anyone discovered that I was more interested in my fellow male colleagues on the loading dock than I was in dating a young woman on the sales floor.

During my employment at Wieboldt's, I had the pleasure of befriending Toni – a twenty-six-year-old, single Italian lady, five feet one inch in height – who always wore at least four-inch high heels. She managed the linen department. My first impression of her was that she seemed a little naïve. This innocence was her single most appealing trait and she had a very refreshing attitude about life. She lived at home with her parents and her older sister and she was the baby of the family—and certainly daddy's little girl. During the nine years I worked at Wieboldt's, we became very close friends and I became acquainted with her family. Most of the people with whom we worked had the impression that Toni and I were more than coworkers. You could say that Toni became my beard at work and she was instrumental in helping me keep my homosexuality a secret. Whenever possible, Toni and I hung out at work and usually spent our breaks and lunch hours together. She had an Italian boyfriend named Brian, a very nice guy, or so I thought at the time of our introduction.

Toni and Brian got married and I attended their wedding. They seemed so happy together. I was just seventeen when she and I initially met and, during the near decade of our friendship, I learned that when it came to judging Brian's character, I had not done a very good job. Toni eventually caught Brian cheating and she was devastated. To add insult to injury, Brian's new lover was someone with whom Toni and I worked. Before she discovered she had a lying, cheating, and no good husband, I had divulged my big secret to her and she was instrumental in bringing Larry and me together. What are good friends for, if not for hooking you up?

After two years of working on the loading dock, I was promoted to shipping and receiving manager. At eighteen, I was the youngest person in the history of the company to be promoted to that position, a big step up from my early years at the company. The relationships I was able to build with the department managers – while picking up the trash – proved to be very beneficial to my success at the store. These managers were influential in convincing the general manager to offer me the position, even though I was only eighteen. The specifics that led up to me receiving the offer to become part of the management staff are memorable. The general manager presented and offered me the promotion on the same day that I graduated from high school—and I felt like I had arrived in the business world. I had always planned on attending college directly after high school, although it was never an absolute that I had for my life. After being offered the managerial position, I revised my plan to attend college immediately and now planned to work for two years before I enrolled in an institution of higher learning. I thought I would work for a couple of years and earn enough money to pay for my college education.

Shortly after starting my new position, I purchased a brand-new car…and my first two years of working as a manager at Wieboldt's came and went—and so did my interest in going to college. I have no regrets in not pursuing a degree. I feel that I made the right decision at the time by accepting the management position and the seven years of practical experience in management that I was able to attain, together with the opportunity to manage thirty plus people, was equivalent to what I would have learned in a four-year institution of higher learning. I learned many things in the working world, at a young age, which I would not have experienced from attending college. I also developed some of the most amazing professional relationships of my career while working there as a young adult. Even though I never attended university, I felt that Wieboldt's was my fraternity.

I learned many life lessons in my first years at Wieboldt's. I had met Toni, my first best friend outside of high school, who was also the first person to whom I came out. I met Larry, who became my first boyfriend. In turn, Larry introduced me to gay culture—going to gay bars and clubs in Chicago, which was incredibly exciting. At eighteen, and at the rate I was advancing in life, I thought I would conquer the world by the age of twenty-five.

Working at Wieboldt's was a fantastic experience for me as a teenager. On many occasions, I frequented the local bars and clubs with the single or divorced managers who were in their middle to late twenties. My older colleagues were always very committed to having me party with them. Since I was under the legal drinking age, the ladies usually went out of their way to convince the doormen at the bars and clubs that we frequented to let me enter. These ladies partied like rock stars. Though they didn't partake in drugs, they loved their cocktails, and especially loved to drink their shots of tequila. On more occasions than not, I usually ended the evening by throwing up the tequila shots that were bought for me on any given night. I was young and inexperienced and, as I couldn't hold my liquor, was considered a lightweight amongst the group. To this day, I am grateful to the lovely and wildly fun ladies at the Wieboldt's in Lincoln Mall for the many evenings of entertainment we had during the many years we spent together, as coworkers and, more importantly, as loving friends. These special friendships would leave an everlasting impression upon me.

Larry and I dated for a short time before we eventually became boyfriends. He took me to my very first gay club, the Bistro, on Hubbard Street in Chicago. At the time, the police were randomly raiding gay clubs and it seemed strange to me that the Bistro was directly across the street from a police station. Eddie Dugan, one of the owners, was to the Bistro in Chicago as Ian Schrager was to Studio 54 in New York. There was a rumor circulating that Eddie was paying off the police to stay out of the club. Whatever the case, the disco was never raided and the patrons were never harassed by the police.

As you entered the club, you walked down a small hallway that opened up to a huge room that held the main bar. The bar was in the shape of a huge oval that took up about two thirds of the space on the main floor. This fantastic oval-shaped monstrosity served as a meeting place for the gays to cruise one another, and sat nearly a hundred people, plus countless others that would stand in between the seats trying to be noticed. It was the perfect layout for cruising potential tricks. When sitting at the bar, the opposite side was about twelve to fourteen feet away…close enough to make eye contact with the people directly on the other side, yet far enough to have a conversation with someone next to you without the person on the opposite side being able to hear your conversation over the din of the music. When spotting an interesting prospect, you might have the bartender deliver a drink to the person, always a great way to break the ice with someone that you found attractive and wanted to meet.

This was decades before the internet and most, if not all, gay men went to bars or clubs to hook up with other guys for sex. I preferred this period in gay history to the current gay culture where most gay men go online to interact or meet other gay men for sex or dating. Then, people would get dressed up for the night and go out to interact with one another for social and sexual encounters.

The Bistro was famous for their dance floor, which was lit from underneath. You had to walk up a dozen steps to reach the cavernous room that contained the disco, as well as another large bar with wait and bottle service, a very upscale venue for a gay bar in the late seventies. On many occasions, I fell down those same twelve steps leading to and from the dance floor, as did probably half of the other patrons that frequented the club.

There was an amazing DJ, Lou DiVito, who spun at the club for the pleasure of the crowd and, as you arrived, you were greeted by the Bearded Lady, the club's infamous hostess, who was an enormous hit, an icon really. One might have gotten the impression upon entering the club that they were at the circus. Upon seeing the Bearded Lady, a large drag queen with a full men's beard, you would certainly get the impression that you were partying under the big tent. It was joyous, it was wild, it was hedonistic, and it was an insane place for its time—just like a circus.

On occasion, after the club closed for the evening, Eddie would host a private party in the basement and I had the thrill of being invited. There were always pretty people at the after party – all the connected people and the beautiful men that happened to visit the club that evening – along with cocaine and Quaaludes, which were prevalent and freely used in the venue.

Once a year, Eddie closed the club for a week to refurbish it and some years the refurbishing turned into a major remodel. He kept recreating new experiences in the same space, which kept his clientele from becoming bored with the club. He hosted a private party for all the regulars each evening before he closed the place for refurbishment. It was invite only and you had to get a personal printed invitation from someone that was on the staff. Year after year, the White Party, as this annual event came to be called, was the event of the season. The guest list included all the beautiful people you ever hoped to see in one location and at the same time and, every year, I looked forward to being part of the experience. I'll forever have fond memories of this amazing place that closed its doors in the early eighties.

The club became my home away from home for several years and I went there every Thursday and Saturday night for one hundred and ten consecutive weeks. On Thursday nights, they had quarter night when all drinks were just a quarter. Quarter drink night made the hour drive back to the suburbs, at three in the morning, a challenge. I got shit-faced drunk and made the drive from the club to the suburbs twice a week. One Saturday night, after a long night of drinking, I drove home where I still lived with my parents, and fell asleep behind the wheel. When I woke up, I found myself in the middle of the medium between two highways. I did some crazy shit when I was young and, looking back, I realize I was lucky that I didn't flip my car over or hit another oncoming vehicle. I often wondered how I made it out of those crazy party years of excess drinking without killing myself or, even worse, killing some innocent individual.

At that point in my life, I didn't think about God or how my life played into the world. Many decades later, I now realize God was without a doubt watching over me. He must have been the one who kept me safe from myself and, more importantly, made sure that I didn't hurt anyone else on those nights that I drove home drunk from the Bistro. I believe there's no other explanation for my making it out alive from those years of driving under the influence. It's an example of another miracle that has taken place in my life, without my noticing it, and I'm thankful to my guardian angels that kept everyone, including me, safe from my irresponsible and reckless behavior.

Larry introduced me to many aspects of gay life that I didn't know existed. I finally realized, for the first time, that there were numerous people in close proximity that had the same sexual preference as me. I felt liberated. Larry also exposed me to various gay subcultures, like the leather and biker communities, and introduced me to a subculture that existed in the gay community – or should I say in the straight community – that I had no idea existed.

One sunny afternoon in a summer month, Larry wanted to take me to one of the many forest preserves in the Chicago area to sit outside and have lunch while we enjoyed a beautiful summer day. The preserve was off the Stevenson expressway at the La Grange Road exit. Upon arrival, we drove into the entrance down a winding road. Once far enough into the forest preserve, and away from the viewing area of any passing cars from the La Grange road traffic, Larry parked the car. When we exited, I noticed there were many picnic tables in the immediate area and we decided to sit at one of the unoccupied tables to enjoy the day and eat our lunch. I could not help but notice the number of cars that were driving into the preserve. Some drivers would park their cars and some would just slow down as they leered at us, and then continue to drive on. The parked cars always had a single male driver who got out of their car and then walked into the woods. I observed this rather strange phenomenon, which went on for thirty minutes, before I finally realized something was taking place. What were these guys who were walking in the woods up to? I finally turned to Larry and inquired what they were doing and he laughed, "I was wondering how long it was going to take you to notice what was going on right in front of your nose", he answered. What was going on right in front of my nose? As any inquisitive gay male in the forest preserve, with his picnic basket and lunch in hand would do, I repeated my question. "This is a gay cruising place and these men are hooking up for sex", Larry answered. I was absolutely shocked and a little horrified at what Larry had just told me. I was a newlywed and very new to the gay scene and only being eighteen, I was very naïve to say the least. After many questions from me and answers from Larry, I discovered that many of the guys who were stopping and entering the woods – for a little picnic lunch where they reached for someone else's basket other than their own – were so-called straight men. Many of these guys who were cruising the woods, were not only so-called straight men, they were also married to women. For the second time in one afternoon, I was shocked, and horrified that the woods were filled with straight, gay, and bisexual men that were seeking a little afternoon delight, in plain sight. That day, I was introduced to the big bad wolves looking for their male version of little red riding hood.

Now a year into our relationship, Larry and I dated for another year before we finally broke-up. When we split, we still worked at Wieboldt's, in the same building, which was awkward. In the end, my first boyfriend turned out to be a jealous, possessive, and crazed individual who was very mean when he drank and became intoxicated. After we split and went our separate ways, he stalked me for several years. They say you never forget your first love, and although Larry was not my true first love, I believe I was his and perhaps that's why he had such a difficult time forgetting me. Maybe I am flattering myself, or giving Larry the benefit of the doubt, but possibly he wasn't crazy and possessive after all and may have simply been heartbroken—and the reason he was so irritable when we split.

Shortly after we broke up, I met Tony, the aforementioned hairdresser. He was twelve years my senior and became my second boyfriend. Toni, my best friend with whom I worked, introduced me to him at one of the White Parties at the Bistro. After Toni divorced Brian, she would accompany me on many occasions when I went to the gay clubs in Chicago and, with her in tow, I met more gay men on any given evening than I ever did when I went out alone.

Tony and I become lovers and were together for seven and a half years. During this time, I moved out from my parent's house and into an apartment with him. After many years of renting places in different suburban cities, we finally became homeowners for the first time. We bought a townhouse on the Southside of Chicago and set up house as an openly gay couple. I finally began to feel like an adult for the first time. After nine years at Wieboldt's, at twenty-five, I resigned. I realized my dream of conquering the world by the age of twenty-five could not have been further from reality. While I had finally admitted to myself that I was gay during my early years there, I remained in the closet for almost my entire career at the company.

After leaving Wieboldt's, I became employed at Madigan's. Working in the visual merchandising field allowed me to showcase my creative talents. I had the great fortune to be initially hired as a senior trimmer with management opportunities in my future. For the first time in my life, as an adult in the working world, I could openly embrace my homosexuality. In fact, if you were a male and working in the visual department at Madigan's, it was naturally assumed that you were gay, unless proven otherwise. Jim, the creative director, was also openly gay and he was a very creative person and a very nice man too; not pretentious like so many other people in the design industry.

Shortly after my interview with Jim, I contemplated whether I had the creative ability to hold my own against their talented visual merchandising artists. Madigan's was well known in the creative arts field for their imaginative window displays and merchandise presentations. Madigan's was fashion-forward department store, known for its stylish clothing lines in the medium price category. It was a well-respected company by its customers and by its competitors. The owner held the visual merchandising team in high regard and funded the department as if it was his ad agency. Each visual manager and their staff were assigned to a specific retail location, although we were considered to be corporate employees. The visual department was the pulse of the stores. We oversaw the purchase and allocation of the store fixtures, visual props, the design and implementation of the window displays, and maintained proper lighting for the merchandise on the selling floor. We assisted the store personnel with all aspects of presenting the merchandise, while upholding the brand. Most associates in the store loved the visual teams, but there were an isolated few that were not as accepting of – what seemed to them – our alternative lifestyles. But we were loved by many for everything that we did to help the department managers hit or exceed their sales goals, although, like most relationships, there were those days of wanting to strangle the ones you love.

For creative people who did not have prior visual merchandising experience, and who were seeking an opportunity to break into the industry, Madigan's was the place to learn—and it was to the visual industry as boot camp is to the military. You would earn little money at first, although if you made it through the rigorous training process, you would not only be compensated for your efforts, you usually ended up with a fantastic creative portfolio that was critical to secure an artistic position with one of the larger and more exclusive department stores on Michigan Avenue in Chicago.

I was sent to the oldest store in the chain to be part of a three-person creative team. I worked for Amy, a female display manager whom I believe was bipolar. At times, she was very sweet and a pleasure to be around and other times, and for no apparent reason, she was just a hateful bitch. She was married, although I don't think she liked men very much. The best part about being assigned to this location was Claudia, the other woman that worked on the creative team and a real delight. She was Argentinian and very pretty, thin, five feet eight inches tall, with jet black hair. We quickly became good friends. When you're working for a boss that may go off on a rant, at any time for whatever reason, you quickly learn to join forces. Amy soon became jealous of our friendship and she would try to separate us whenever possible. I worked for Amy for six months when, one day, the three of us were working in a children's display window. Amy was having difficulty in getting a prop wired in place. Upon my offer to help wire the mannequin to the platform for her, she lost it and started yelling at me and threw a screwdriver in my direction. Just like anyone else, I can be an asshole when I want to be, although in that particular situation I was sincerely trying to be of assistance and keep her from losing a grip on reality and hurting someone in close proximity. My suggestion to help was also offered for selfish reasons, because if she lost it and started hurting people in the display window, Claudia and I were the closet ones to her. Shortly after this incident, I called the corporate office and requested a transfer to another Madigan's store. I felt guilty about going behind her back and asking for a transfer, but shortly after my request, I got moved to another location, even as Claudia was stuck with her. Amy genuinely liked Claudia and other women in general and she was nicer to Claudia than she was to me.

Be careful of what you wish for, goes the common expression. Due to my request for a transfer away from the crazy bipolar bitch, I had been transferred to the largest store in the Madigan's chain. This store was also the most challenging due to the amount of work that the location required visually. The store had a visual crew of four, including me. I was the only gay male on the team, comprised of three other trimmers who were young, straight, creative women. The visual merchandising manager was a very talented woman with a great taste level, although like most creative people, she was a little disorganized, which made it more difficult for the rest of the crew. I was at that location for six months when I was promoted to visual manager and was transferred back to my previous store that had a new crew by then. I was very proud of my creative accomplishments and had earned the respect of my creative peers as well as notice from the director of the department. I had now been at Madigan's for three years, since I began as a senior trimmer, and during this time I moved from store to store and eventually ended my career at Madigan's as the visual merchandising manager of the largest store in the chain. I managed to create a name for myself in the industry due to my creative accomplishments and even earned the respect and appreciation for my efforts from the owner and president of the chain. Mr. Madigan loved my work and I became one of the managers that were favored by the creative director. I was chosen by him to travel to New York on several occasions for the visual merchandising shows that took place twice a year and I also traveled to California to attend the West Coast visual market once a year. This perk of attending the visual merchandising markets did not go over well with the other visual managers, although I never let it bother me. I was equally as creative as my coworkers, although I had one big advantage over all the other managers—I was more organized in the planning of my windows and seasonal change-outs. My crew and I consistently planned and scheduled our creations months in advance, immensely pissing off the other visual managers and creative teams. I learned during those years that being organized came with many advantages and the most coveted advantage for me during this time, was being chosen on a consistent basis over my coworkers to attend the creative markets in New York and California…boom!

After I met Tim, my love affair with him would be the beginning of the end of my career with Madigan's. My sexual involvement with him had required me to abruptly exit my job. You've heard the phrase don't shit where you eat? In my specific case, it was more like don't fuck where you get your paycheck. After I left Madigan's, I became close friends with Jim and later in life, he was diagnosed with AIDS and, after years of battling the disease, he would lose the fight and become another amazingly talented person that would be lost to the epidemic.

Madigan's was a great place for me to start my visual merchandising training. The company was very well respected in that field by the industry and by the other high-end retailers in the Chicago area. My time spent there helped me secure employment at the new Bloomingdale's store that opened on the world-renowned Michigan Avenue. I began working there as the visual coordinator of the men's floor. This Bloomingdale's was the first store in the retailer's chain to be opened in the Chicago area when I received an offer to work for them—a great moment in my career. It was considered a world-class retailer and a monumental addition to the high-end stores that lined the avenue. I can recall the very first time I visited their New York flagship location on 59th Street in Manhattan—an opportunity that I experienced during my travels to New York for the visual merchandising shows when I was Madigan's golden boy. I also became familiar with the Bloomingdale's brand through magazines and, when the upscale store decided to join the retailers on Michigan Avenue, I was honored to become part of their Chicago history. Bloomingdale's then became the first of my two Chicago retail experiences where I was part of their grand opening ceremonies. The opening, and the store itself, were a tremendous success and, at the time, their Chicago location was the largest producer outside their flagship store in Manhattan. The visual crew worked crazy long hours during the months that led up to the day the store opened its door for business and, for almost a full year afterward, our work schedules became so hectic that it wasn't unusual to work ninety hours in one week. It took a year after the store opened before things started to slow down to the original sales projections and we could begin to experience some normalcy in our daily work schedules.

Working at Bloomingdale's provided my first chance to work with high-end designer merchandise. I purchased my first two real designer sport jackets there, designed by Gianfranco Ferre that I still have to this day. The jackets originally sold for almost two thousand dollars each. After several markdowns, including a third or fourth markdown in price, plus my twenty percent employee discount, I ended up buying the jackets for less than four hundred dollars for both. Since I was responsible for the visuals on the men's floor, I interacted with the department managers daily and developed a great working relationship with them. They would let me know when they were going to take their markdowns and I was always part of the select group that had the first chance to purchase designer goods at great reductions. Ferre, to this day, is still one of my all-time favorite designers and this was the beginning of what would become a life-long love affair with fine clothing. In my opinion, the difference between non-designer clothing and fine designer clothing is comparable to the difference between an average lover and a high-quality lover. The average lover seems sufficient to you when that is the only point of reference you know. Once you've had the good fortune to encounter a great person that also happens to be a great lover, there's no going back to what once seemed sufficient.

I learned a great deal from Steve, the creative director at the store, who had a natural creative talent for the theatrics of visual merchandising. The team under Steve's supervision got their overall direction for the seasonal promotions from corporate headquarters in New York, but Steve's great claim to fame was that he always layered on top of the corporate design packages that were distributed to the Chicago store. His additional layer of creativity, added to the corporate directives, resulted in our programs having greater visual impact. His creative eye not only took the corporate concept to the next level, it also branded the look of the executed designs as Chicago's very own. Since this was still a relatively new store that was exceeding corporate sales projections, we were under a tremendous amount of scrutiny from the New York executive staff to maintain the sales momentum that had been created during the first few months after the store opened its doors. It was a wild and crazy time to be part of the Bloomingdale's culture and this period would not be repeated.

I worked at Bloomingdale's for several years and during my initial time there I took over the visual merchandising responsibility for the main floor cosmetics area, while maintaining my current responsibilities for the men's floor...and was eventually promoted to assistant visual director for the entire store. I was now thirty years old and becoming very ambitious and driven in my career. After becoming assistant visual director, I leveraged this experience to land the position of corporate visual merchandising director for Bigsby&Kruthers, the much more exclusive high-end men's clothing retailer in Chicago. My second store opening on Michigan Avenue would follow almost a decade later, when I designed and debuted the new Bigsby&Kruthers flagship store.

4 | GO FISH

The phone ringing that fateful Saturday morning suddenly awakened me and I was surprised at who was calling for the second time that day. It was Alex who I supposed was showing his interest in getting to know me a little better. The specifics of that conversation escape me, other than the basic formalities of introducing each other and the general questions one may inquire when speaking with someone for the first time—I asked what part of the city he lived in and what he did for a living. Alex quickly got to the reason he was calling. He was interested in securing a date and meeting up with me at my place later that week. Many years later, when I reflected on our initial conversation, I realize that I failed to ask the single most important question on that initial call. I should have inquired if Alex was dating anyone or if he was currently involved with someone. In my defense, why would I ask such a question? Why would this man be calling me if he had a boyfriend?

Several evenings later, with flowers in hand, which I love getting, and as promised, Alex showed up at my place. As I opened the door to greet him, I wondered if Fate had brought Alex to my door or was I mistaken and it was Fate's evil sister, Lust.

Early in our conversation with one another that evening, I discovered that Alex indeed had a boyfriend and, to add insult to injury, they were living together. He justified his actions by proclaiming that he was in the early stages of dissolving the relationship and ending his commitment. I convinced myself that Alex was operating in good faith so I allowed our date to continue, exploring the rest of what our evening had to offer. The major reason I continued seeing Alex, after he disclosed that he had boyfriend, was because I had experienced a similar situation when I met Tim. Like Alex, I had been in a relationship where the romance had come to an end and I also made the decision to end the relationship around the same time that I met someone else, although, unlike Alex, I had not started to finalize the breakup. In my case, Tim was the catalyst that motivated me to end my relationship with Tony, the hairdresser, so I could pursue a different romance.

In retrospect, I now know I was making excuses for my behavior. Upon hearing that he was in a relationship, I should have ended our time together.

I was totally in the wrong when I made the decision to continue seeing Alex. I should have required him to end his relationship with his current boyfriend and, when he had done so, we could discuss the possibility of dating. Reflecting on that specific moment later in my life, I must say that I now believe that my involvement with him was preordained. I believe the path that I eventually traveled with him was a journey that I was meant to experience. Many years would come and go before I knew without a doubt that it was Fate that was knocking at the door on the evening when Alex arrived. Only Fate and God were aware the road yet to be traveled and a full decade would come and go before I could truly understand why Fate allowed us to meet.

After a very brief dating period, Alex and I made the decision to live together. When he moved in with me, I was living at the edge of downtown Chicago, in a two-story townhouse. Unlike Alex, I was living alone so he moved his personal belongings into my place so we could begin our life together. I was working for Bigsby at the time, and during my employment, I certainly adapted the philosophy of *dress for success and become a success*. As Alex moved into my townhouse, he came with very little furniture or personal items. As he was moving his things in the middle of the night, I remember thinking that he reminded me of a gypsy. This feeling should have been another red flag for me to notice and heed. He made several trips that same evening to bring his belongings to my place and, for several hours, he would drop a load of clothes off and would go back to his former apartment and load up his car once again. He moved into what soon became our place using only his car, which should give you a good indication that he didn't have many large items to move. As he dropped off his clothes, I sorted through his belongings and, being the clothes snob that I had become, a large portion of his shirts and suits ended up in the dumpster before he made it back to my place with his last load of the evening. There was no way that I could allow a boyfriend of mine to wear cheap suits to his place of employment. Right from the start, I was very much in love with Alex and wanted the best for him. I wanted him to look his best at all times and it made me feel good to see that my man was well dressed. He and I were about the same weight and height and he could wear most of my suits and so, essentially, he doubled his wardrobe. Shortly after we settled in as live-in boyfriends, I regularly purchased new suits, ties and dress shirts for him to update and upgrade his wardrobe. I was certainly a clotheshorse and, in a very short amount of time, I also turned Alex into one. As an executive at Bigsby, I received a substantial discount on all my purchases, which made it easier on the wallet when purchasing new designer suits and sportswear for him. Alex soon became known as the best-dressed man in his office and after he moved in with me and we upgraded his personal appearance, coincidently, he became very successful at work. Was his new position as the best-dressed man at the office just a coincidence or did he finally look the part? Did the man make the clothes or did the clothes make the man? I would eventually realize that, in Alex's case, it was neither.

The love that I immediately felt for this man was like nothing I had ever experienced before. Jeff told me he was shocked at the level of change in my personality. He said, "You seem so much happier since you've met Alex and it shows in the way that you conduct yourself." Since the time I heard this observation, I've come to believe that a pure love will have that effect on a person and that this type of love is what God has intended for us all—a love that will ultimately enhance our existence, as we unite with our mate.

When I met Alex, he seemed to be everything that I always wanted in a loving partner. One of the most amazing characteristics of his love for me is that he had no issues with me being positive. I had been single for more years than I care to remember prior to meeting him and I had become very lonely and somewhat sad and isolated due to my HIV status. Before meeting him, I had started frequenting sex clubs and male erotic bookstores – often late at night – when I was drunk and feeling lonely. I do not judge others for going to these places, as I myself frequented them and believe they serve a purpose, but I would've preferred a monogamous loving relationship over the anonymous sexual encounters that I engaged in at these places. Deep down, I felt I didn't deserve a quality relationship due to my HIV status so I frequented all the wrong places looking to mask my feelings of sadness, loneliness, and unhappiness.

Before meeting Alex, I had a relationship with Matt, who was younger than me and HIV negative. Unlike Alex, he was absolutely against dating or getting involved with anyone that was positive. While its own long story, Matt and I dated for a few months and, after a brief dating period, we moved in together, which was big mistake on both of our parts. We genuinely cared for one another in the beginning, but I do not think we were in love to the level that we needed to be to deal with the difference in our HIV statuses. Matt was the only boy in his family and had been very spoiled by his parents. He was four years my junior and not very mature when we met. Although very handsome by all accounts, he was a tad selfish and on the lazy side. I myself had numerous character flaws during the time that he and I dated—and was the angry one in our relationship. I was angry that I was positive and feeling like I was damaged goods and the lessor of the two. At twenty-eight, Matt was still mostly in the closet and not out to his parents and work associates. I found this to be a difficult situation to cope with, as I was thirty-two and very much out of the closest. Our relationship only lasted a year and during this time I became very insecure due to Matt having issues with me being positive and, in many ways, Matt made me feel dirty and unworthy in the bedroom. He was afraid of me sexually and looking back on our relationship, we had absolutely no businesses being together. I felt, and still do, that he was more attracted to the amount of money I was earning at the time we were together than he was with me as a person and as his boyfriend. I was so desperately seeking intimacy and love from a man that I settled for someone that was afraid to be with me and know now that the relationship between us was doomed from the beginning.

After Matt and I ended our relationship, I began having drunken weekends at bars or clubs and usually ended those weekend evenings by frequenting a gay adult bookstore or a gay bathhouse, seeking a warm body that would love me, even if it was only for a few brief moments. This reckless behavior, after I split up with Matt, went on for years, as it was all I felt I deserved, or possibly could really expect, due to my HIV status. In some way, looking back on my circumstances at that time, I find my thought process of not being worthy of a healthy relationship somewhat amusing, considering I was found to be attractive, or so I was frequently told. I went to the gym four days a week and took very good care of myself physically and I also made a concerted effort to be well groomed and well-dressed at all times. I was fortunate enough to reside in a beautiful apartment and to have a good job making decent money. But the fear that was associated with those three letters overrode any physical and monetarily attributes that anyone had to offer, especially with the majority of the gay community at that time. In everyone's defense, it was still relatively early in the onset of the AIDS epidemic and the majority of the gay communities around the country still feared those who had AIDS or were diagnosed as being positive.

Several years after Matt and I broke up, before meeting Alex, I meet a handsome guy online. We talked on the phone several times during the week before we met for a date and at no time during our conversations did he inquire about my HIV status. As far as I was concerned at the time, I assumed all guys were potentially positive and I attempted to conduct myself accordingly. By doing so, I put myself in control of my health rather than allowing someone else to make that decision for me. I had failed to protect myself during sex with Tim many years earlier and I did not want to repeat the same mistake.

My online date met me at my apartment in downtown Chicago and he and I walked to the place where we had dinner. We had great conversation during our time together, probably drank a little too much, but managed to flirt a lot with one another during the course of our meal. After dinner, on the way back to my apartment, the online guy had his hands all over me. He made it clear that he was interested in having sex with me, as I was with him. At no time during dinner, or on the walk back to my apartment, not even when he had his tongue down my throat, did he inquire about my status. I understand some people will question why I didn't tell him about my situation when we spoke on the phone or when we had dinner together. My thought process at the time was that if it was important for an individual to hear the words of my status prior to having sex, then I assumed they would inquire.

In the earlier days of the epidemic, years before President Clinton passed the law that required insurance companies to insure an individual with a pre-existing condition – which included HIV and AIDS – I was very selective with whom I disclosed my status. During this time, there was still much HIV discrimination in the healthcare industry and certain employers were biased against individuals that were positive. I knew I was not going to be employed at Bigsby for my entire career and so I was very choosy when sharing my status, attempting to minimize the risk of my personal health information becoming public knowledge. I've certainly come to realize that you never really know for sure if you'll get the truth from someone as to their status and there's certainly the possibility that the person does not know himself unless they have recently been tested and, in some cases, they still may not have the most accurate information. There are many different opinions on how to handle the specifics of this situation, although, all I can say is that I've learned the hard way that I'm the person responsible for keeping myself safe.

Upon entering my apartment, my online date was all over me as we undressed each other, wanting to get naked and between my sheets as fast as possible. Once we were mashing between the sheets and I began sucking his dick, he finally decided it was important to ask about my status. His timing was as off the mark as it could have been and, as I stopped what I was doing, and looked up at him and stated those eight letters, he replied with an incredulous "what?" I again replied that I was positive and could tell he was freaked out by my answer, although he allowed me to continue to blow him until he ejaculated. Once he had gotten his rocks off, he got dressed and wanted to exit my apartment as fast as he entered. I couldn't help but feel used by this guy and once again I was left feeling a little dirty for being positive. I was also experiencing feelings of rejection and isolation from the online guy, which made me feel, again, like a leper—a familiar type of rejection and isolation that I experienced with Matt when we also had sex together. Fortunately, I was able to muster the self-worth to walk the online guy to the door of my apartment and – like a gentleman – I wished him a good evening. I went from being the center of someone's attention that I found attractive, to the opposite of that spectrum, by uttering one single eight-letter word. The most tragic portion of this situation was that this person – who'd been so mutually attracted to me before I revealed my status – experienced his repulsion for me in my own home and in my own bed…and I'll never forget the overwhelming level of discrimination that I felt from my own community.

This experience was a rude awaking. As I closed my apartment door behind the online guy, I chuckled to myself to mentally survive the incident, although I knew in my heart that if I allowed myself the opportunity to react to this experience, it would've had a major negative effect on my self-esteem and my self-worth. I had to choke down the feelings of rejection and the feeling of being dirty and unworthy, so I had to chuckle and move on. What other choice was there for me in dealing with this situation?

I relate this experience with the online guy and my relationship with Matt as the closest comparison in my life for how Jesus must have felt when he was rejected by his people and the religious leaders of his time. Most certainly, Jesus's life was a different set of circumstances than mine altogether, although rejection by your own community and peers is rejection on an epic scale no matter what the circumstances. As the years passed and drugs became available to treat HIV, some of the stigma dissipated—paving the way for gay dating sites for people who were positive. On some of these hookup sites an individual could openly reveal their status in the hopes of connecting with a similar or an accepting individual. Now, almost three decades later of living with HIV, I now comfortably have the conversation on the first date or have openly posted my status on my online dating profile.

The first six months of my relationship with Alex were incredible. I wish everyone could feel the level of love for another human being that I felt for him. I had an amazing love connection with this man—and for me it was all so real and just so wonderful. From the time I received the news that I was positive to many years later when I met Alex, he was the first man since receiving that information that actually made me feel comfortable in a relationship and genuinely happy in my daily life. Alex allowed me to forget the fact that I was positive and for the first time in five years it was not the first thought when I woke up in the morning. After six blissful months of loving Alex and living together, we decided to purchase a condo in a building that was being converted from a factory into loft apartments near the famous Merchandise Mart in Chicago.

Our new loft was an amazing seventeen hundred square foot, two-story unit, with sixteen-foot ceilings. One exterior wall had floor-to-ceiling glass windows, which gave the space a sunny backdrop to set up our new home. The unit cost us two hundred seventy nine thousand dollars, which seemed like so much money. At the time, it was a lot of money, although today it certainly seems like a deal for that type of space in downtown Chicago. Being a designer, I found purchasing new furniture and managing the construction schedule for our new home to be very exciting. I had the general contractor wire the entire apartment for a central sound system and I ordered custom light fixtures from Italy for every room. Since Alex worked in the technology sector and had no interior design experience, he left the design of the loft and its furnishings to my expertise.

Being so much in love with Alex, I was thrilled that we were purchasing our first home together. Our new furniture and custom light fixtures were starting to be delivered and these had to be stored in our current apartment while the loft was being readied. We were a good couple and we seemed perfect for one another. We seldom argued or got into a confrontation—which was a first for me in a relationship with another man, as I argued with all my previous boyfriends and, for some reason, was not able to nurture a harmonious partnership with any of them. The feelings that I was now experiencing were very different from my previous relationships and life was good—and it seemed like most aspects of my life were now moving along as well as I could have expected and hoped.

One morning, for no apparent reason than I can recall, when I woke up and started my day, something felt different. I began to have an uncomfortable feeling that there was something not quite right in our relationship. I was not sure why I was feeling this way, but I began to look at Alex in a different manner. After much doubt and confusion, I began to watch him much more closely than I had before. I began to question his whereabouts when he had unaccountable free time in his schedule. I began checking his pockets for any clue that would confirm my suspicions regarding his conduct. This cat and mouse game of me checking up on his whereabouts went on for six months. We had now been together for a year and the loft was almost ready for us to close on the property and take occupancy. By this time, I had become very suspicious of his intentions and was struggling with my emotions. Why did I have these feelings of doubt, when the first six months of our relationship seemed so perfect?

Looking back, the first six months were truly a wonderful time for me, and I like to think it was as equally as wonderful for Alex. Even though he and I were never officially married, I expect that the initial marital bliss that I was experiencing was partially due to the fact that we were still in our honeymoon period. In the initial six-month phase of our affection for one another, he concentrated his efforts on seducing me and getting me comfortable in the relationship. After the honeymoon had passed, I began to wonder if he had altered the monogamous commitment that we had made to one another without consulting me, which prompted my noticing changes in his behavior. While we all have a past, what I didn't realize at the time was that Alex too had a past that was dictated by a behavioral pattern – an addiction really – that would come to light later rather than sooner.

Without a doubt, I absolutely knew that Alex was my soul mate. What I didn't know was how dangerous a love like this could be, should the love not be based on truth. I've since come to understand that you cannot have true love without truth being the foundation of the relationship, for the truth will allow you to love freely, or at least the truth will allow you the option to be free. Free of all the hateful feelings of self-doubt that one will experience when someone lies to their face, especially when those lies are being delivered by their mate whom they love. I've found, as a result of my personal experiences, that whenever I've posed a question to someone with whom I share my most intimate moments – as well as my home and my money – and their answer is something that does not engender a comfortable feeling within me to be a difficult set of emotions to manage.

I've discovered that when something just doesn't feel right in my gut, it's usually for a valid reason. When faced with what I perceive to be a lie, I may ask the same question in a different manner. In most cases, I've found that when my partner is responding with an untruth to a question, it does not matter how I pose the question or how he may formulate his answer; it almost always leaves me with that uncomfortable feeling of doubting my partner or, possibly the worse version of all doubts—doubting myself. What does one do with these feelings of doubt?

I've also discovered that paranoia develops from a bad experience that you've endured at some point in your life and wanting to be very cautious to not repeat the same circumstances that led you to become involved in the bad situation in the first place. I've also found that the liars of the world will say that you're being paranoid when you challenge them on their dubious response to a question that you have proposed to them. In my particular case, the feeling of paranoia usually surfaces when I've been lied to by a close loved one and begin to question the truth of the information that's been presented to me. I once heard Oprah say that if you have suspicions of your spouse cheating on you, there's a ninety plus percent chance you're right. If she is correct – and I believe she is – then I also believe those feelings of paranoia is your subconscious telling you something is not right and your suspicions are present as a warning system. Was this amazing love affair between Alex and me real or was it Memorex? Was I blinded by the love he showed me and that I developed for him and, if so, was the forest burning in the distance? Because if there's smoke on the horizon…usually the flames of the fire are not far behind. If I needed to escape from this relationship would my route to safety be engulfed in self-doubt and paranoia?

Alex's behavior left me doubting myself and questioning how I could so overwhelmingly love this man that I mistrusted. I started to experience immense uncertainty and had questions on top of questions regarding our commitment. Alex quickly took control of the relationship and had me entertaining the notion that I was crazy for feeling this way—and he had me questioning myself that there was something wrong with me. This self-doubt that I was feeling was the worst experience during this time of confusion. Why *was* I feeling this way and *was* there something wrong with me physically that was causing these emotional feelings of mistrust for Alex and causing me to doubt those feelings at the same time?

In my experience, the goal of a liar is to get you to question yourself and, once the self-doubt begins to take place, the liar takes control of the situation and you. Often, this scenario will lead you down a road of no return and usually the road to recover one's confidence after experiencing a compulsive liar for a partner can be a long and difficult journey. For six months, it became an all-consuming effort on my part to become the best detective to get to the bottom of Alex's true intentions…and the pressure of looking in the cracks and crevices of his whereabouts began to take its toll on my emotional stability. Keeping my feelings bottled up from my friends, and being silent about my suspensions regarding his behavior, was creating a tremendous amount of emotional pressure on me.

Alex and I had a mutual friend, Chuck, who lived in Los Angeles and who was having a birthday in February. My good friend Rick in Chicago was also having his birthday very close to the same date so I decided to get a group of seven friends – including Alex and I – that all knew the birthday boys and surprise them with paid airfare to New York to celebrate their birthdays. I also reserved two adjoining rooms in a hotel in midtown Manhattan. The adjacent rooms allowed the seven of us to party the entire time together while celebrating—seven gay men having a slumber party for a three-day extravaganza and all the gayness that New York had to offer. There was one additional guest that weekend, Tina. She was supposed to be the life of the party and anyone who is familiar with her knows firsthand, or from afar, that once she arrives on the scene, she never sleeps—and neither did we.

We arrived in New York City on a cold Friday night. We all traveled in a limousine that I had ordered to take us from LaGuardia airport to our hotel in Times Square. As we had planned, we went to Twilo, a gay dance party at a club in Chelsea on the evening of our arrival. That night became known as the straw that broke this camel's back. There were many things in play that evening in New York besides seven gay friends celebrating two birthdays. Everyone seemed to have their own thoughts on the celebration agenda for that weekend and it seemed to be adding to the tension that I was experiencing from my suspicions about Alex. One of my mottos was *the more the merrier* and I enjoyed getting my friends together when going out for a night of partying. On this trip, I was the main mutual friend that was the common denominator to most of the other five guys that joined us that weekend. Most of them knew one another based on their association with me and had become friends as a result. I was the glue that bound the five of them. Alex did not know my other five close friends prior to me introducing him into the group as my boyfriend. Tony from Bloomingdale's was part of the party that weekend, who by then had been replaced by Rick as my best friend. Chuck, the other birthday boy, was the only person that was not living in Chicago at the time we got together in Manhattan for that infamous birthdays celebration.

The seven of us were partying and getting high at Twilo on that first evening of what became many outings that we had planned. We were all behaving with such confidence, as if we owned the club. As we danced, my friends were strutting whatever they thought they had to offer on the dance floor in the hopes of attracting a suitable mate for the evening. To my dismay, Alex was also doing his peacock dance as I believe he too was hoping to have a sexual encounter of his own that did not include me. Chuck left for the night and headed back to the hotel, as the club had closed the bar for the night, and converted the venue into an after-hours party. Chuck went back to the hotel with Jeff, the bartender from Chicago, and John, who was not only a friend of mine, but also worked on my team with Rick and me at Bigsby.

Rick, Tony, Alex and I decided to stay at the club and continue the celebration. What took place later in the evening, as the party went on into the early morning hours, is unforgettable…and the image of this event is embedded in my mind forever and burned into my memory. I had suspected Alex of cheating on me prior to arriving in New York and my gut feeling was telling me that something was not as it seemed. I was high and had been partying for at least eight hours, when the incident took place. Now I understand I was extremely sensitive due to the heightened emotional roller coaster that I had been riding for six months—and being under the influence of an illegal substance certainly did not help me in being able to properly judge the oncoming event, on the dance floor, right in front of my eyes.

The four of us were dancing together when I began to notice a change in Alex's behavior. Alex was not showing any affection toward me whatsoever and he was acting very distant, as if I was not present. Was I possibly over-reacting and reading too much into the situation because I had been partying for many hours? Or was Alex possibly too high himself to understand the ramifications of his actions? High or not, I was convinced I was correct in my assumptions, but, as the saying goes, Alex was innocent of all charges until I proved him to be guilty. Certainly, if you were to use my five close friends on that weekend as a jury of his peers, their verdict would've been that he was innocent of all charges. It was like watching the O.J. Simpson trial. It sure looked like this man was guilty, although O.J. was famously found innocent of all charges by a jury of his own peers.

The one defining moment from this weekend would be that my perception of the situation between Alex and me was the key to dissecting the problem at hand. I was the closest to him and naturally noticed changes in his behavioral pattern before my friends. Alex was the center of my life and because of my romantic involvement with him I became obsessed with watching his behavior to confirm my suspicions of his possible infidelity. While properly navigating my course of action that evening, I lost sight of the fact that my relationship with Alex was not the same center of observation for my five friends, as it was for me. I had not yet confided my suspicions of Alex's infidelity to them and they had not been alerted to observe his behavior more closely.

Each time I positioned myself in front of Alex on the dance floor, he would causally look to Tony and begin to reposition himself so he was facing Tony and not me. Again, I thought to myself…am I going crazy? Were the drugs distorting my perception? After much internal debate, I concluded that Alex was doing exactly what I thought he was doing and it was making me very uncomfortable and pissing me off big time. Could his screwed-up behavior be more inappropriate than I had originally imagined? Could Alex be messing around with one of my closet friends and acting improperly right in front of my face? How messed up was my relationship? Was it possible that one of my closest friends was disrespecting me by flirting with my boyfriend while we were all dancing together? The evening's events made me question everything about my existence and the people with whom I surrounded myself. After going around and around with Alex on the dance floor and trying to get his attention to be directed back to me, I finally hit my limit with the debate I was having with myself about my assumptions. I simply could not be silent about my suspicions regarding Alex and his shenanigans any longer. I turned to Rick and said that I had to go to the bathroom and asked him if he had to go. He replied no, and upon receiving his answer, I turned to him and said, "Yes you do, come with me, now!"

Rick was gracious enough, or high enough, to agree to accompany me. As he followed me off the dance floor, I stopped halfway to the bathroom to gather myself and mustered up enough balls to approach Rick about my feelings regarding Alex and the situation at hand. I had been living with Alex for a year and for six months of that year I had been dealing with my suspicions of his infidelity without sharing them with anyone. I was feeling isolated for not being able to talk about my feelings, that I had been experiencing daily, with anyone. Finally, on this Friday night in February in New York, I was going to make contact with another human being about how I was feeling. I felt like I had been on the moon for the past six months, looking for answers to many questions. After many exhausting months of searching for the truth, I was finally going to have a conversation with a close friend about my findings. "Houston, we have contact."

I was consumed with overwhelming emotions about Alex's behavior that night; it was all I could think about. My detective work had become all too consuming. Looking for clues to my suspicions was on my mind from the time I woke in the morning until the moment I closed my eyes and went to sleep at night. At last, now was the time for me to share my burden that I had carried for so many months and divulge my findings to someone that I trusted. However, timing is everything in life and, in this circumstance, I could not have chosen a worse time or place to plea my case to someone else regarding my suspicions and conclusions.

Upon leaving the dance floor with Rick, I positioned us far enough off the dance floor so Alex and Tony could not see us, but close enough so that Rick and I could observe their every move. I was trying to muster up the correct sequence of words to approach the subject with Rick, when I suddenly found it difficult to get the words out of my mouth. I realized at that moment, that once I voiced my suspensions to another person about Alex, it would open Pandora's Box and there would be no turning back. I suddenly thought…if I expressed my concerns openly to Rick, would my words change the dynamics of the relationship between my friends, Alex, and myself forever? I was distraught over the possibility of diluting the groups' dynamic and this was something that I did not take lightly, especially on this weekend when we were all together celebrating the birthday boys' special day. Little did I know…it not only changed the dynamics of that weekend, but my life was about to change too.

I finally decided to broach the sensitive subject with Rick. I struggled with forming my words on how to approach the topic. I decided to confront the situation in a way that I felt would make sense to Rick as an outsider in my relationship. I began to explain my suspicions and highlighted that Alex was wearing a belt that evening that I believed was not his. I was very familiar with all the clothing and items that Alex moved into my apartment and was certain that he didn't have that belt when he moved in. Since I purchased all of Alex's clothes at Bigsby using my employee discount, I knew I had not purchased this belt. I asked Rick, "Where would Alex have gotten this belt, if I didn't purchase it for him?" Here I was, in a situation where I was so overwhelmed by the circumstances that I referenced something to attempt to get my point across and instead of making my point, I confused the situation even more. This was now the case. Rick replied, somewhat indignantly, "*I* gave that belt to *you* last year for *your* birthday."

Oh my God! I don't think I could have used a worse example in my attempt to get Rick to see my point of view and look a little closer at Alex's behavior. At this point, Rick was questioning my thought process and was wondering what this crazy bitch was talking about. Rick was not privy to any of my other suspicions regarding Alex and his behavior that led up to this moment and I'm sure he must have also thought to himself, "This bitch is off her rocker and he is definitely over-served." Many years later, when I recalled that moment, it brought a smile to my face. There I was in New York, celebrating Rick's and Chuck's birthdays, partying, and dancing in a club full of hot shirtless muscle men and all I was concerned about was last year's leather accessories…hysterical.

I thought Alex was such a catch; he was the big fish that I had been waiting for my entire life, my soul mate. In my search for love, I had fallen overboard and found myself drowning in the love that I had for this man. My affection for him had developed so quickly and my love for him grew each day that I spent with him. My initial attraction to him was like the fisherman that tells the story about his big catch of the day and by the time the same story has been told for the sixth or seventh time, the original fish that was caught in the beginning of the story has now become twelve times its original size. My love for Alex seemed very similar to that fisherman's story—Alex seemed like a regular average guy when I met him, although very quickly the love that I had for this man became bigger than life and all consuming. At the height of my love for him, I certainly thought he was the one that I was meant to be with and while I could have been mistaken, it's possible that God chose Alex as the person he would use to reveal what I believed to be true love.

Soon after that evening in New York, Alex secured a new career opportunity. As with most corporate positions, Alex had scheduled an exit interview with the personnel department from his previous employer due to take place sometime within the two weeks following his resignation. Over the following weeks, Alex took a few days off after ending his employment and before starting his new job. One morning, as I was getting ready to go to my office, Alex informed me that he was going to have his exit interview with the personnel manager that afternoon. I didn't give much more thought to his exit interview, as it was a common practice with most companies. Alex was still enjoying his few days of relaxation prior to starting his new job on the day his exit interview was scheduled.

By this time, I had already left Bigsby, and had recently accepted a new position as director of national accounts for a family-owned lighting design firm. Jim, who owned the company, was also my new boss. He was Jewish and the business was family-owned and operated, much like the former company where I worked. Jim's brother and father helped to run the business, so it was very much like Bigsby—another Jewish family operated company owned by Gene and his brother, Joe.

My office was close to the townhouse that we were renting, while we were waiting for our loft to be completed, and from time to time, I would come home for lunch. On the afternoon that Alex told me he was going to have his exit interview, I randomly decided to go home for lunch. When I arrived at the house, Alex was not home, as he was having his exit interview. While having my lunch, leftovers from the previous night's dinner, the phone rang. Upon answering the phone, I was greeted by the personnel lady from Alex's previous employer. She wanted to know if Alex was at home. When I informed her that he was not present at the moment, I asked her if I could give Alex a message. "Absolutely", she replied, "I'm following up with Alex as he had his exit interview scheduled for this afternoon and he never showed up for our appointment, and I wanted to know if he was going to reschedule." I informed her that I would relay her message to Alex when I saw him that evening. As you can imagine, I was wondering what he was up to and why he never made it to his appointment that he had said he was going to attend. While this now seems strange and funny at the same time, this incident took place before everyone carried a cellular phone so my inquiry to Alex on his whereabouts would need to wait until that night when we were both at home and I could have a face-to-face conversation with him. On my way back to my office I found myself becoming overwhelmed with the anticipation of confronting Alex.

Upon arriving back at my office, I found that I was not able to fully concentrate on my work. For the rest of the day, I was preoccupied with pondering Alex's whereabouts. I was bursting from the anticipation of presenting the news that I received that afternoon when I unexpectedly came home. I believe Fate wanted to have lunch with me that afternoon, as she was expecting a call and wanted me to be at home to answer the phone. While I can't specifically recall if Alex was already home once I arrived at the house that evening, or if he arrived home later, I can clearly recall the events that followed, as if they happened today. Alex and I were in the kitchen getting dinner ready, when I asked about his exit interview. He replied, "It went well, just the usual corporate exit interview questions." Well, well, I thought to myself, little lying Miss Mary just got caught in her fib. I told Alex that I had answered the call from his former employer and confronted him as to why he lied about his whereabouts and, more importantly, I wanted to know where he was that afternoon. The next few sentences out of his mouth were the most insensitive lies that I ever heard based on an impromptu set of circumstances. "I decided to go to a free clinic to get an anonymous HIV test and it just so happened that the test came back positive", Alex replied. He continued to say that he was so genuinely distraught by the information that he began to walk aimlessly around the city, thinking about the ramifications of what he was just told.

I recalled Oprah's statement that ninety plus percent of women that think their husbands are cheating usually have these feelings for a legitimate reason. I'm certainly not a woman and Alex and I were not legally married, although I was ninety plus percent sure that this man that I loved was lying to me regarding his whereabouts and his newly discovered HIV status. Since Tim had died of AIDS, and I had been positive for many years prior to meeting Alex, I took his words very seriously and very much to heart. By this time, Alex was in full drama mode. He was shedding tears and stated that he didn't think he got the virus from me, as we were as safe as we could be, and he thought he may have gotten the virus from his ex-lover, as he too was positive.

There they were, those little hairs on the back of my neck just standing on end waiting for me to tell this man that I loved more than life itself, that he was an absolute out right bullshit artist and he should be ashamed of himself for telling such an outlandish story, but instead I cried too and I reached out to him and we held each other and cried together before sitting down to dinner. I chose not to be as insensitive as Alex had been with me by telling his bullshit cover story to justify his whereabouts that afternoon. I believe Alex knew that I would not challenge his story since I had endured Tim's death and because I was positive myself—so he used the HIV trump card to avoid going to the doghouse that evening. I thought to myself, is there a possibility that I could be incorrect in my assumptions? This incident exemplified the self-doubt with which I struggled. I decided not to call his hand. With many reservations on my part, I reluctantly decided to fold my position and went to bed to address this conundrum another day.

After Alex delivered what I believe to be a fairytale about his whereabouts on the afternoon he missed his appointment for his exit interview, I was experiencing much guilt for not believing the story of this man with whom I was so in love, and began to have feelings of remorse and was very concerned and worried about his health and his overall well-being. At the time I met him, I had been positive for many years and had experienced the initial feelings of fear, hysteria, and isolation that were associated with HIV. By the time Alex delivered the news about his newly founded HIV diagnoses to me, I had finally adjusted to accepting my health status. I owe much of my success in conquering my fears about being positive – and my eventual acceptance of my health situation – directly to Alex…and the love that he initially expressed toward me daily. I was no longer afraid or worried about becoming ill. I was confident that I was going to be able to manage my status and live a healthy and full life. Now, my own concerns about living a healthily existence had been redirected and I was now consumed with concerns about Alex's future health. I would rather die myself, than have to experience and endure yet another person that I loved suffer and pass away from AIDS.

One other evening after work, I was at the townhouse making dinner and doing laundry before Alex arrived home. He was on his way to our place from his new job that he had recently started a few months earlier. Once again, I believe Fate just so happened to be at the house waiting for a phone call. While preparing dinner, the phone rang. The person on the line was Alex's regular medical doctor wanting to know if Alex was available. I explained to the doctor that he was not yet home. The doctor then inquired to whom was he speaking with. "I'm Darrel, Alex's boyfriend", I informed him. The doctor was aware of Alex's relationship with me and so he provided me with information to give to Alex. He wanted me to relay the good news about Alex's recent HIV test. The doctor continued to explain that the test had come back negative and all was well with Alex's health. My heart skipped a beat, or possibly two, upon receiving this confirmation of what I already knew in my gut to be the truth. I tried to keep my composure while I was experiencing heart palpitations and, fortunately, I was able to muster the energy to pleasantly reply, "I'd be thrilled to relay your information to Alex when he arrives home."

Once again, Fate was relentless in her quest to ensure that the truth was told and received by me. I believe she wanted to ensure that the good news relayed by the doctor was given to the person who needed to hear it the most. The other interesting portion of this scenario was that Alex never informed me that he was going to his regular medical doctor to be re-tested prior to me answering the phone call. Fate revealed the cards that Alex was holding, Go Fish.

I have my own thoughts and beliefs on the types of relationship agreements that I believe can be effective for couples. Some couples in a gay or straight relationship may have agreements in place where each person in the relationship can have sex outside the relationship and they may have a don't ask, don't tell policy. Other couples may explore the option of bringing another person into their relationship for a three-way, or more, encounter. In this type of agreement, a couple may only include another person or another couple in their sexual activities when they're together and this extra-curricular behavior never takes place without both parties in the relationship being present. Whatever mutual arrangement exists between two people for their sexual escapades, the key words needed to achieve success in the agreement, and therefore in the relationship, would be that it be *mutually-agreed-upon*. Both partners must honor each other and the agreement must be upheld by both parties and at all times. I also have lived long enough to understand that the sex in long-term monogamous relationship does change over time and may become a little monotonous for one or both partners. Therefore, if an individual feels the need to step outside the monogamous arrangement that was previously agreed upon by both parties, then I believe both individuals should renegotiate their agreement with one another. If either individual cannot achieve a mutual compromise with his or her partner, then I believe the relationship should be dissolved. I try very hard not to be judgmental of others and whatever relationship agreement they have. In my situation with Alex, I didn't want to, nor did I expect to, be sharing the man that I loved with another. When consummating our relationship, Alex and I had mutually agreed on a good old fashion monogamy arrangement. I had been honoring the monogamous agreement between us and I absolutely expected and demanded Alex do the same, or he should have come back to the table to renegotiate the terms. Alex knew that I would never agree to an open relationship so he opted not to seek my permission to alter our agreement and quietly decided to conduct himself under his own set of rules. I'm sure Alex was thinking that he would never get caught cheating and should something go wrong to expose his behavior, he would ask for my forgiveness.

When Alex arrived home in the evening, I was in the laundry room near the kitchen, folding clothes from the wash that I had started while awaiting his arrival. He entered the house with his usual cheerful disposition and came up to me immediately with hugs and kisses with which he usually greeted me. This is one of the main reasons why I was so in love with this man, he always made me feel so loved and important. Looking back, I often wonder if he did truly love me, or if the constant hugs and kisses were nothing more than him feeling guilty for cheating on me. I was now bursting with anger and wanted to deliver the so-called good news from his doctor. When I confronted him about his doctors' message, he acted as if the reversal of the original diagnoses would bring me much happiness and assist in defusing the issue of his whereabouts on the day in question. Alex seemed to expect that with the deliverance of the diagnoses, he would no longer be sitting in the doghouse and, to the contrary, now expected to be sitting on a throne of redemption. Instead, I found his behavior to be extremely insensitive and overwhelmingly selfish on his part. Looking at the situation from Alex's point of view, I'm sure his strategy must have seemed very effective in his attempt to cover his tracks. I would be lying if I said I was not happy to receive the confirmation of what I already suspected—that Alex was negative and in good health. Which still begged the question, where the hell was Alex on the afternoon that he failed to arrive for his exit interview?

In retrospect, I believe Alex was feeling guilty for the burden that he had placed on me for delivering the news regarding his fake HIV status report. I'm sure he realized that I was genuinely concerned and becoming increasingly worried about his health and I believe this is why after several months of noticing my growing concern, he decided to let me off the hook. The charade of being re-tested to make it look like he was following up on the first diagnosis, to confirm or deny the positive report that he previously received, was just that, a calculated charade. Alex already knew what the results of the re-testing would be. While I believe Alex was a good guy at heart, he was also a compulsive liar—a major flaw in his character.

5 | TIPPING YOUR HAND

During the time that Alex and I spent as a couple we attended many social functions together. One of the most monumental of these was the Hearts Party, a lavish weekend event held each year in Chicago on or near Valentine's Day. The party was held over two or three days, with each evening's venue varying from location to location. Some of its proceeds were donated to HIV and AIDS causes and research.

In the year that Alex and I attended, the first evenings' event was a formal black-tie party held at the Merchandise Mart. The building, considered to be an icon of Chicago's architecture, had recently completed the renovation of its entire first floor lobby – prior to the black-tie fundraiser – and it was a fantastic venue to host the event due to its enormous size. Hosting the Hearts Party there allowed the building owners to showcase their newly renovated space. Before the renovation, the Mart was only accessible to those in the design trade and so the party helped the owners debut the newly renovated first floor of the design center – and its newly available design solutions – to the public.

On the evening of the black-tie event, a silent auction took place during the cocktail portion of the party. As the evening festivities commenced, we strolled around and looked at the items up for auction and, as the cocktails became many, I became preoccupied with a miniature schnauzer puppy that was being offered as part of the auction. The adorable puppy had been donated from a canine farm somewhere in one of the southern states of the United States. I was a little drunk so I thought the little guy would be a good addition to our newly formed family and to our new loft apartment that we were getting ready to close on and occupy. I placed a bid on the puppy and walked away to have a few more cocktails while chatting with people that I knew. I made a point to keep a close eye on my last bid and, more importantly, to ensure that I placed a higher bid than anyone else had done. By this time, I was well over served and was obsessing with the possibility of taking the little guy home with me that evening—although I had enough sense to not bid outrageously over the other bidders. After I placed my last bid, I decided to head to the bathroom. Rick attended the party with Alex and me and on my way to the restroom I told them that I would catch up with them after I returned. On my way back, I noticed that the puppy was gone from the area where he had been placed for the silent bidding. Once I located Rick, I inquired what happened to the little guy. Rick told me that the event organizers had taken the puppy to the main stage and had a live auction to generate as much money for him as possible. Certainly this made sense to me, even intoxicated. Like most things in life that we want and know that we can't have, I now had an overwhelming desire to have the little puppy more than ever. Since he had been auctioned off and was now unavailable to me, I was overwhelmingly disappointed. I started to pout like a little boy who just lost his puppy and I asked Rick if he knew of Alex's whereabouts, as I wanted to leave.

Rick and I began making our way toward the main entrance of the Mart, which was now our exit. As I was looking for Alex to head out, I saw him in the distance. Alex was walking toward us and he seemed like he was in a hurry and very excited about something. Once Rick and I met up with him, he requested that we go with him as he had someone for me to meet. I wasn't really in the mood to do any more socializing since I was still pouting about the puppy that I didn't win in the silent auction, but I reluctantly followed him through the crowd. As Alex reached a certain point past the crowd, I saw the miniature schnauzer in a cage and a huge smile on Alex's face. In the time that it took me to visit the restroom, combined with the time it took the organizers to auction off the puppy, Alex had placed the winning bid on the schnauzer during the live auction, paying a lot of money for this little dog that became the new addition to our family.

I'll never forget this lovely gift that Alex gave me that evening; it was a huge surprise, an exceedingly kind gesture, and an outstanding act of love. Despite his faults, Alex could be very thoughtful and I'll forever remember and adore him for his thoughtfulness when it came to giving me this little schnauzer that became known as *Papi.* It's certainly a wonderful experience to receive a gift from anyone—and when that gift is given in a loving manner, as the gift that Alex had just given me, the act of love behind the gift is so much greater than the gift itself. Papi would become my four-legged best friend and I also believe he was a gift from God. Rick was as excited for me as I was in receiving the adorable little puppy. You know you have a good friend when he is as equally as excited – or even more excited then you are – when someone does something to make you happy. Rick's true friendship was on display that evening that Papi came home with me and Alex.

I had now been positive for many years and had experienced a great amount of heartache – feeling that I was less deserving of a loving relationship than someone who was negative – so the Hearts Party had great personal meaning to me. This fundraising event happened to take place on Valentine's Day weekend and Papi was a gift of love—and love him I would for the next eleven years of his life and for many years after. Papi was also a threefold gift. First, he was given as a gift by the puppy farm to the event to raise money. Second, Alex purchased the little guy for eight hundred dollars, raising a substantial amount of money for the beneficiaries. Third, he was a loving Valentine's Day gift from Alex to me. Redemption does come in the morning – or at least in Alex's case it came at an opportune time – because whether Alex realized it or not, he had redeemed himself in my eyes for his genuine act of kindness. His loving gesture and his kindheartedness now overshadowed his earlier alleged lie regarding his HIV status.

Papi received his name because Alex was Puerto Rican and I thought it would be fitting if the puppy had a Spanish name. He was a typical miniature schnauzer and, like most schnauzers, he was a little barking monster. His ears were clipped and they were as sharp as radar; he heard everything and barked at everything. As a young boy, we had several family pets that were dogs and these canines always seemed to gravitate toward me. Papi was the first dog that I had as an adult outside of my parent's house and I never realized what I was missing until Papi came to live with us. The love that Papi brought into our house that day would change me forever. The affection that I developed for him became an essential part of my relationship with Alex; he was like our first child that we had together. Many gay and straight couples do not have children and so their pets become their family—and Alex and I were no different. After several years of being together, Alex and I discussed the possibility of expanding our family. We had planned on adopting a child at some point in our relationship, but unfortunately our desire to adopt a little boy or girl did not have an opportunity to become a reality. Not having the chance to become a father to a child is probably the biggest disappointment that I have in my life today. I always dreamed of having a loving family, a handsome husband and a child, or possibly two, as well as a family dog—and my vision also included having a house in or near a major city. My visualization of my family was very much my gay American dream and, in the absence of children in our relationship, Papi and the new loft apartment was the beginning of establishing and living *my* gay American dream.

As anyone who has had a puppy at one time in their life, you know they take a lot of your time and attention to teach them to become well-adjusted and responsible members of the family. When Papi was not being supervised, he liked to chew on the electrical cords in the house that were attached to the major appliances. For his safety, and for the sake of preserving the integrity of our appliances, we crate-trained Papi when he was a puppy. The crate-training also helped in getting him to understand the concept of doing his business outside of his crate and, more importantly, outside of the apartment. As Papi became adjusted to his new living environment, and learned the importance of doing his business outside, he began to receive more privileges and received extended access to our living space. During one of his extended privileges, an incident occurred between Alex and Papi in our bedroom. Papi was getting ready to tell me something about Alex without ever speaking a word.

When we were still residing in the townhouse, before moving into the loft, Alex and I had bought a new mattress set for our bedroom, in the midst of purchasing other furniture. In the master suite of the townhouse, the bathroom and bedroom connected to one another. The entrance from the bedroom into the bathroom was positioned directly opposite the middle of the vanity of the bathroom, and above the vanity there was a mirror that covered the entire wall. The bed with the new mattress set was positioned in the bedroom on the opposite wall from the bathroom and if you stood at the vanity facing the mirror with the bathroom door open, you could see the entire bed in the mirror's reflection.

One day, Alex was on the bed playing with Papi while I was in the bathroom brushing my teeth and I could see them in the reflection of the mirror even though my back was positioned to them. Papi then did something that shocked me beyond my understanding. In the mirror, I saw Papi position himself behind Alex on the bed and, in a split second, Papi lifted his leg and pissed on Alex's back. Papi did not only just urinate on Alex, there was dog piss running onto the mattress that we had just purchased. I was absolutely horrified by Papi's behavior and could not understand why he would do such a thing. I ran from the bathroom with a towel in hand to catch as much of the dog piss that I could from soaking into the mattress. I was very unhappy with Papi and asked Alex, "what is wrong with this little dog and why would he do such a thing?" At that moment, I quietly thought to myself that I had a problem child on my hands. Needless to say, Alex was livid and Papi was in big trouble for urinating on him and on the bed and was to receive his punishment—he got a whopping and once again had to sleep in his crate, losing his privileges to access the bedroom for several weeks.

After I left Bigsby, my former creative assistant entered the design of the new Bigsby&Kruthers flagship store on Michigan Avenue, which we had recently completed in a design contest and – shortly after the incident with Papi – I received an award for its design from the retail design industry. I had been the design lead and overall manager for the project and the acknowledgement by my peers for my team's creative accomplishments was a huge honor for my department and me. The award, *Store of the Year for Large Retailer over 10,000 square feet,* was one of the categories being honored to retail designers by Chain Store Age magazine and which my department won first place. The awards ceremony was being held in Nashville, Tennessee at the Opryland Hotel. The coolest part of the awards ceremony was the seating arrangement. I was to be seated at the table with the design firm that created the vision for the Virgin mega store in Times Square in New York. At the time of the awards dinner, the Virgin store in Manhattan was the first location to have been built in the chain with a multitude of locations to follow. The interior design of the store and the overall building architecture were outstanding and an inspiration to all who visited. The honor and having the pleasure to be seated with this amazingly talented group of designers and architects meant more to me than the actual award that I was to receive.

On the day that I was to travel to Nashville to accept my award, I was experiencing a level of anxiety that I had not experienced prior to that day. Earlier in the week, Alex said he would drop me off at O'Hare airport on the Saturday that I needed to travel to Nashville. He wanted to take me to the airport since he was not joining me for the awards dinner. When Saturday arrived, Alex was acting a little jumpy and was overly anxious about something. His behavior put me on heightened alert that he had more on his mind than dropping me off at the airport. In the late morning on the day of my flight, Alex asked if I could take a cab to catch my flight. We had confirmed on several occasions that he was going to take me to the airport that afternoon so I was a little pissed off that he wanted to change our plan at the last minute for no apparent reason. My suspicions regarding his anxious behavior combined with the last-minute change in plans made me very leery. Alex came up with some bullshit excuse as to why he could not drive me to the airport. More than likely he used the excuse that he had to go to the office, as this was his standard reason to get out of the house. Due to the apparent change in my attitude over his request for me to take a cab, he quickly folded and stood by his original agreement to drop me off at the airport. Based on the abrupt change in his demeanor, combined with his lame excuse of wanting to get out of the house, I became very anxious about traveling to Nashville and leaving Alex unsupervised. I became unsettled with the idea of going away, as I knew in my gut he was up to something, although I had no actual proof as to what that might be. Soon I would be on a plane to Nashville without any way of checking on his whereabouts. Little did I know that Papi was taking on the responsibility to become my personal spy and detective while I was out of town.

Alex and I finally headed to the airport. Once we arrived, Alex dropped me off at the curb of my airline terminal. As he pulled away and drove off into the distance, I hoped that he was heading back to our townhouse or the office, like he said. I was in turmoil; my stomach was doing flip-flops. I knew that the man I loved was up to no good and violating the terms and conditions of our monogamous relationship. I had suspected Alex of cheating on me for the past six months though I had not found any proof to substantiate my suspicions and, truth be told, I was conflicted that I could possibly be overreacting and reading more into the situation than what may have actually existed. Was I being a nervous nelly and could Alex be innocent of the alleged charges that I was secretly accusing him of? From the moment I boarded my flight, and exactly when the door closed to the plane, I began to become increasingly upset about Alex's behavior at the house earlier that day. All I could do at that moment, about my increasing suspicions about Alex and his possible infidelity, was to stew about it alone in my seat. Once my flight was in the air, I grabbed the phone in the back of the seat in front of mine. At several thousand feet in the air, I realized the flight was going to be an expensive endeavor as I swiped my credit card and placed a call to Tony. As I began to explain my discomfort and unrest to him, the plane climbed to thirty thousand feet…and all I could think of was that I wanted to jump out of the airplane and land right on top of Alex, squelching him and whatever he was up to. Tony and I discussed the situation at great length from my seat in the air and he was eventually able to calm me down to a point that I no longer wanted to jump out of the plane—and we both had a good laugh or two at my expense before finally concluding the call. The fact that I could find humor in a humorless situation was something that brought a smile to my face for at least my sense of humor was still intact.

Upon the airplane landing in Nashville, I exited the plane and took a cab to the Opryland hotel. Once I checked in and arrived at my room, I promptly called Alex and we spoke briefly before I went to bed for the night. As planned, I arrived at the awards dinner the following Sunday. I received my award and was honored by my peers for my creative accomplishments—an event now being overshadowed by the concerns I was having about Alex's actions while I was out to town. I ended up cutting my trip short and traveled back to Chicago earlier then I initially planned because I was feeling anxious again and felt like I needed to checkup on Alex and his whereabouts.

After landing at the airport, I took a cab to the townhouse, as I arrived back home earlier than planned. Upon reaching the house, I found Papi home alone and locked in his crate. I immediately let him out and I was a little surprised when he ran directly upstairs without greeting me; something he had never done before. I followed him up the stairs, curious to know why he was in such a hurry to go to the second level of the house. He ran into the master bedroom and jumped on the bed and began sniffing the comforter as if there was an unfamiliar scent on the bed. His behavior made me very uncomfortable and I began to look around the room for anything that seemed out of place. I looked in the laundry hamper in the walk-in closet to see if there were any suspicious items that might offer a clue to Alex's potential shenanigans while I was away. To my amazement, all the clothes that were in the hamper prior to me leaving for my trip were now gone; Alex had done the laundry while I was away. This was strange behavior on Alex's part since he never tended to the laundry; this was usually a chore that I handled.

Little Papi then came over to where I was standing in the closet and he placed his head in the hamper. Curious once again, I looked into the hamper, reached down, and pulled a single pair of Alex's jeans left in the basket that he was wearing when he took me to the airport. As any good snooping husband with his little nose-sniffing assistant would do, I began checking the pockets for any clues that Alex may have left behind. I ended up pulling out a piece of paper…a single ticket stub from a pant pocket. Did I just find the winning ticket that would lead me to the answers of the all the questions that I longed to have resolved? Would this ticket provide the answer that would change the dynamics of the relationship between us? If I had in fact found a clue that would solve the mystery of Alex's whereabouts and confirm his infidelity while I was away, would I end our relationship and leave this man that I adored? In a very short time, I soon came to realize that Alex and I were both on the losing end of the discovery that Papi helped me make—and the only one winning that evening would be Papi, who received a treat for a job well done! Had Papi, a miniature schnauzer bred to catch rats, exposed the biggest rat of all?

I believe God works in mysterious ways and the evening's events soon proved that this notion is certainly a fact. Had Fate been standing by my side the entire time I was away? Did Fate utilize Papi to lead me to the ticket that I found in Alex's pocket and to alert me that Alex had someone in our bed? Or was this all another simple and random coincidence that had no relevance to my suspicions about Alex's behavior?

Prior to meeting Alex and us becoming boyfriends, when I had been out drinking heavy for the evening, I often frequented various gay bookstores, adult movie theaters, and bathhouses where I randomly hooked up with guys for sex. When I began to examine the ticket that I pulled from Alex's jeans, it had a very familiar look. It was the same type of ticket that I received at the door of an adult movie theater where I had paid an entrance fee to enter the backroom area…and the gay movie theater – where I believe the ticket was from – was located near our townhouse. I needed to be patient and wait out the hours between the time I found the ticket and the time Alex arrived home, before I could confront him face-to-face. The future of our relationship was now tied up in a single ticket that Alex had overlooked and left in his pant pocket. Did Alex seal his own demise when he purchased Papi for me at the Hearts event? If it had not been for Papi, my little spy and detective, I may not have been tipped off to reach into the hamper and have proof of Alex's shenanigans at last.

On a professional level, my new job at Superior Lighting was a difficult transition for me. I was thirty-six years old when I decided to make a life changing career move from visual merchandising and store development to lighting design and distribution. One of my new responsibilities was to develop a national sales account business and this would be the first time in my professional career that I had to develop a sales territory. At Bigsby, I had a staff of nine—comprised of a creative assistant, an administrative assistant, two visual merchandising directors, two graphic designers, and a visual merchandising field staff of three. At Superior Lighting, I had no staff and I quickly needed to learn to become 'a jack of all trades' and, for several months, I found myself being the master of none. I was placed in an open bullpen sales and design area, in a cubicle with a desktop computer. I previously enjoyed the comforts of a lavish office at Bigsby and, while I didn't have a computer there, my secretary had her own company computer. My new working environment was certainly a far cry from what I was accustomed to and I had to become comfortable with operating without a staff and working in a cubicle. This was also the first time I used a computer and I had a lot to learn in a very short amount of time if I was going to be successful in my new career. Between getting settled in my new job and attempting to build a sales clientele, combined with managing the construction of the loft, I was overwhelmed and under much stress at work and at home.

My professional confidence was at its lowest point in almost a decade and the suspicions that I was feeling in my relationship with Alex, added to my anxiety. I was forced to deal with my angst daily and I soon turned to Tina to muster the energy to get out of bed in the morning and confront my issues. The biggest factor that I believe contributed to my going from a recreational drug user on the weekends, to someone that used daily to get out of bed in the morning, was because I was conflicted about my suspicions about Alex's potential infidelity…and it was starting to gnaw at me and eat me alive from the inside out. I was left to discern between what I believed to be lies being fed to me by Alex, and the truth that I believe my gut was trying to get me to embrace. I found myself overwhelmed and preoccupied with dealing with my relationship concerns, which became exhausting to deal with each and every day—hence my friend Tina coming to my rescue. While many factors drove me to turn to her to help me deal with my issues, I believed, first and foremost, that Tina would be a temporary solution to my problems and thought she would give me the additional energy I needed to deal with them. I had become consumed with looking for clues regarding Alex's shenanigans, which was exhausting, and I needed the additional boost that Tina provided to perform my newly assigned duties as a full-time director of national accounts at Superior Lighting.

I have serious issues with someone lying to my face, I believe it's the disrespect for me as a person that bothers me more than the actual lie. I felt like Alex was playing me for a fool and he thought I was too dumb to catch him in his lies. I was also becoming very concerned about laying out tens of thousands of dollars – that took my entire adult life so far to save – for the down payment on the loft apartment, if Alex was lying to me. If I was correct about him, then certainly that was an unacceptable condition based on our relationship agreement.

As the days became weeks and the weeks became months, I began to unravel from the inside. I managed to maintain a good outward appearance although, on the inside, I was about to explode from the pressures of trying to juggle all the secret detective work that I was performing, while simultaneously trying to be a full-time employee at my new job. The sheer volume of scenarios that I had swirling around in my head, to make sense of Alex's unsubstantiated claims for his whereabouts, were exhausting me.

During that crazy time, I learned as a person, and more importantly as God's creation, that we as his people have been individually and uniquely designed for a purpose. I began to realize that I had one amazing characteristic that would not only allow me to endure, but it would also allow me to be the victor in the catch me if you can game that Alex and I were playing with one another. During this period – and for whatever reason – but maybe from the presence of Tina, I was not able to retain or recall the names of new acquaintances to whom I had been introduced five minutes earlier. My short-term memory for recalling names and numbers was almost zero. On the other hand, I had the capacity to store and retain hundreds of details from various situations…and I could remember these countless details for years on end. This God given talent to retain specific information became extremely beneficial when having to store Alex's tales. I could reference his previous stories and compare them with his currents ones to verify the truth and note conflicting information that could potentially lead me to catching him in a lie.

In our relationship, I maintained our finances and was the one that paid all our combined and individual bills. We put our money into one shared account and I handled the finances and balanced our checkbook. Since we both had numerous business expenses that were reimbursed to us through our employers, we needed to keep these funds separate from our personal income. I reconciled our credit card statements against our expense reports to ensure that we didn't spend the money that we received for our reimbursable expenses prior to receiving the bill from the credit card companies. To accurately account for all charges, I was constantly reviewing Alex's expenditures. Each month, Alex had several consistent charges for fuel that were showing up on his monthly statement from a specific gasoline station in Countryside, the same town that Larry and I had visited those many years ago, when he took me to the forest preserve off La Grange Road. Was this yet another simple random coincidence or was this not a coincidence at all? Alex had clients in Chicago and in the surrounding suburbs and was required to make regular visits to new or existing customers to present sales proposals or to follow up on existing business…and he certainly could have had a client in the Countryside area, which would explain the consistent visit to this particular gas station.

Was I reading too much into an innocent situation or was Fate lining up the stars that would lead me from what seemed like a harmless adventure with Larry twenty years earlier to a preordained destiny with Alex two decades later at the same exact location? It was these types of questionable coincidences that continually led me to believe that my gut was correct in supposing Alex's infidelity and it was these same coincidences that were now beginning to extract their toll on me. The circumstantial evidence against Alex was mounting, which had me in an ever-growing tailspin. Tina was now controlling the situation and there was no parachute in sight. Alex now had me questioning everything in my life. I was not only questioning the integrity of my relationship, I had begun to question the stability of my own sanity. I began to doubt everything about my life and every decision that I had made. I questioned the commitment I made to my new employer and whether I was capable of breaking into a new industry and building a national sales business. I doubted my financial decision to lay out tens of thousands of dollars of my own money to purchase a new loft apartment with Alex. The most tragic doubt was that I started to second guess my gut feelings—and began to think I was being paranoid about Alex and his possible infidelity. This was the most unsettling aftermath from the chain events with Alex and his lies that contributed to my drug use…I had begun to doubt myself in every aspect of my life. Alex now had the upper hand, as I became increasingly unstable. At that time, to mentally survive the present day and to live to fight another day, Tina helped me make the choice to emotionally check out. With the mounting stress, I felt very much like the tension in a rubber band that was being stretched to its limit. By taking a pair of scissors and cutting an extremely stretched rubber band, it releases the pressure on the band. You still have the left and right side of the rubber band, although the tension that was being created by pulling on each end, no longer exists. I felt like that rubber band that was being stretched to its limit and Tina was the scissors that relieved the pressure. Much like the rubber band, I was still present, although I no longer felt like my emotions were pulling me in two directions. I became emotionally detached, or at least that's what I convinced myself to believe and feel.

My suspicions continued to mount. I could no longer ignore my gut as it was gnawing at me day and night. I was concerned that I was building my life with Alex on a foundation of lies and my demeanor began to show signs that I was becoming unhinged. My instability was most evident in my personal life, although it had not spilled over into my professional career, at least for the moment. My circle of close friends expressed their concerns, as they doubted how I was feeling because they saw no real basis for my suspicions regarding Alex and his alleged infidelity. With much skepticism coming from my immediate surroundings, I became increasingly confused about my feelings, as I had not been able to secure any tangible proof that Alex was being unfaithful.

Finally, I went to see Gary, my doctor, to seek medical help. I thought, and Alex also encouraged me to believe, that the HIV drugs that I was taking to treat the virus were having an effect on my metal stability. After visiting Gary, who was not only my doctor, but also a good friend, he shared that my stress and doubts were part of a natural process that many people who enter into a committed relationship and purchase a home together experience. He also indicated that there was no medical issue with me that was causing my emotional duress and diagnosed my condition as a case of pre-wedding jitters. He felt that the emotional and financial commitment that I was making to Alex came with doubts, which was natural. I left his office feeling a little better than when I entered and was thrilled to hear that my condition was not a result of my medical treatment. I was also happy to have a medical professional diagnose me as going through a natural process of having second thoughts as I was entering into a major commitment. Although it was great to get Gary's opinion on the situation, I was not totally convinced that it was as simple as me having commitment anxiety or a case of pre-wedding jitters. In a short time after leaving the doctor's office, my gut would again tell me that I was correct in my original assumptions. Alex was as cunning as a fox and as dirty a pig in shit.

Back at the townhouse, my little detective Papi and I waited for Alex to arrive home after I found the ticket in his jean pant pocket. As Papi and I sat alone in the house awaiting Alex's arrival, with nothing but our thoughts and each other to keep our time occupied, I was thrilled to have finally cornered the fox. In the midst of experiencing the joy of knowing that I was not crazy in thinking he was cheating on me, I suddenly became very sad that my suspicions had been correct.

When he finally arrived, I verbally and aggressively confronted him, as I was bursting at the seams to deal with his lying behavior. He took no responsibility and denied any wrongdoing or having been to the gay adult movie theater while I was out of town. He tried to pawn off the ticket that I found in his pant pocket as belonging to someone else. He claimed that he had been cleaning his car when I was away in Tennessee and found the ticket in the backseat. I had used Alex's BMW a week earlier and had gone out with Tony and Rick to Vortex, the same gay dance club where Alex and I met. Alex did not go out with us that night and he claimed that the ticket must have belonged to Rick or Tony. He was a master at lying and when he was confronted with a situation he could hit the ground running with a completely fabricated story to cover his tracks, while never missing a beat in his made-up fairytale. I often wondered if his ability to lie on command played a factor in his success as a salesperson. Later in our relationship, I came to realize that Alex's lying behavior was a way of life for him and he had made a life-long commitment to the profession. I loved a man that attended the college of cheaters and received his master's degree in the art of lying.

The confrontation between Alex and me became heated. The more he claimed he was innocent, the more angry and volatile I became. I was so pissed off that he was trying to tell me another fairytale that I became very aggressive in dealing with him in a physical manner. I cornered him and pushed him up against the wall in our living room. With his back against the wall – and no room for him to move back any further – I positioned myself so I was standing directly in front of him with absolutely no space between the two of us. I got in his face and demanded that he get his ass in the car as we were going to drive to the theater where I believed the ticket was purchased. I told him that once we arrived at the adult movie theater I was going to enter the venue and pay to get in. I had been to this theater on several occasions prior to meeting Alex, so I knew patrons entered an area in the back and above the theater where they would go to cruise and have sex with each other. Upon paying your entrance fee, they would issue you a ticket. If the numbered ticket that I received that evening was close in numerical order to the one found in his pocket, it would prove that it could not have belonged to Tony or Rick or been from a week ago, as he claimed. With this prospect and dilemma now facing him, and my anger over the situation becoming evident, he began to cry and admitted and confessed to going to the adult theater the day he dropped me at the airport on my way to receive my design award in Nashville, Tennessee.

At long last, the fox had not only been cornered, it had been captured—eighteen months into our relationship. For the first six months, our time together was blissful. In the second six months, I began to doubt his sincerity. The last six months of that year and a half would bring chaos to my life. After investing eighteen months, the truth had finally come to light. Alex was the lying cheating bastard that I reluctantly believed he was after living with him for six months. The question yet to be answered in the coming days would be whether the truth would set me free from him. At the exact moment that Alex professed his guilt, I certainly became freed from all the paranoid feelings that I had been harboring for the last year. What was I now to do with him? Should I slap him silly where he stood or simply set him free and let him go back into the forest preserve from whence I thought he came?

My mind was racing. I could not help but reflect on the situations that brought us to that exact moment. First, when Papi had peed on Alex's back that evening in our bedroom…it was because Alex was bringing men to our house and was having sex in our bedroom when I was not there. Alex and these other men had been fucking around in our bed and little Papi was telling a story – without ever speaking a word – when he lifted his leg and pissed on Alex's back. Papi was doing what dogs naturally do; he was simply marking his territory, like most dogs. Then, after letting Papi out of his crate on the afternoon that I arrived home from Nashville, Papi ran upstairs and began sniffing the comforter on the bed. Alex had once again brought someone home and once again Papi was telling me what had taken place on the bed when I was away. Thirdly, I believe Fate had led me to the forest preserve in Countryside almost twenty years earlier when Larry introduced me to that gay cruising area. I soon had confirmation from Alex that he had been going to this exact forest preserve seeking the big bad dick-seeking wolf for several months. He would use his credit card to purchase gas and a newspaper at the service station in Countryside before going to gather nuts on his knees in the woods. He would read the newspaper as a cover while sitting in his car as he waited for men to arrive with whom he would cheat. Fate had left a trail of clues…namely a random forest preserve outing that I would recall taking two decades earlier, many miles from where Alex and I lived. This clue would lead me from his credit card statements to his escapades in that exact same forest preserve.

Once Alex confessed to cheating on me while I was in Nashville for the awards dinner, he attempted to control the situation between us by using his standard modus operandi. Prior to his confessions of infidelity, he always threatened to leave me when I confronted him about his potential extracurricular sexual activities. As I had no proof that he was cheating on me, I always ended up backing away from pursuing my accusations, afraid that I might be falsely accusing him. I certainly did not want to end our relationship on an unsubstantiated hunch. Now, just like all the other times when I had confronted him, he decided to use his usual means of controlling the situation—by threatening to leave our relationship. Now that I finally had proof and admission of his infidelity, I welcomed the opportunity to call his bluff. He threatened to leave the house if I didn't calm down…playing the same old game he had been playing for many months, although I was now in possession of the truth. With truth in my hand, along with a ticket and his confession, he was no longer able to control me with his toothless threats.

While he threatened to leave the house if I did not calm down, I was not able nor did I want to get myself under control. For the first time in eighteen months, I had a legitimate reason and substantiated proof to be out of control. As threatened, Alex did leave the house to go lick his wounds. I was relieved that he was out of my immediate sightline, as I needed time to reflect on what I was going to do now that I had confirmation that Alex was not only cheating on me, but had also been lying to me for almost a year. I found myself having mixed emotions about what actions, if any, should be taken on our immediate living arrangement and whether I should end the relationship altogether. As I paced around the house and thought what the hell I was to do about our relationship and our immediate living arrangement, the phone rang. Thirty minutes had now passed since Alex walked out of the house on Papi and me and the caller was Alex—phoning to see if he could return home. I laughed out loud and replied, "I never told you to leave the house in the first place; that was your idle threat—not mine."

Several months later, I applied much pressure on him to tell the truth about his initial faked HIV status. He then confirmed what I already suspected. He had lied when he said he tested positive. He had been preoccupied with getting dick on the day of his exit interview so he missed his appointment, which prompted the phone call that I intercepted from his personnel department requesting to reschedule his exit interview. Alex confessed that he didn't know what to tell me when I confronted him about missing his appointment and so the story of testing positive at the free clinic was the first cover story that came to his mind to account for his day of dick in the park.

6 | DON'T GET LOST IN THE SHUFFLE

The following day, Alex and I came to the agreement that it was best for the situation if he moved out of the townhouse. He then went to live with David, his best friend, as it were, while I tried to sort through my emotions. I was still very much in love with Alex, even after all the crazy shit he had put me through. Was the love that I had for him strong enough to mend the web of lies that spewed out of his mouth time after time? As if the cheating was not enough to endure, I also had the financial commitment for the new loft that we had bought hanging over my head. We were under contract for the unit and the construction was nearly completed—and to back out of the contract at this point would have resulted in the loss of a large sum of money. We had also customized the unit with numerous upgrades and ordered custom furniture and European lighting fixtures, which added to the overall cost, and it was not an option to cancel those orders at that point. It was difficult enough to deal with the emotional turmoil that this man caused and, when you added a potential financial calamity to the equation, it was almost more than I could bear. It felt like the walls were closing in and the roof was about to fall on my head. What was I supposed to do? Did Alex, the most important person in my life, not understand the ramifications of his lies and his actions or did he simply not give a damn?

As so many people who use a crutch in life to get through the day, I once again turned to Tina, my own crutch, for emotional support during that time of unrest. For those who don't know, there are three ways to ingest meth. You can snort it up your nose in powder form. You can also smoke it…lighting the rock crystals in a glass pipe to inhale the resulting fumes into your lungs. You can also inject it directly into your bloodstream using a syringe—clearly the most dangerous option of all. Each option offers a different type of high. Typically, the recreational user will begin using Tina by snorting it…and over time they may gradually become more addicted and seek a more intense high through smoking it or possibly injecting it. Users may begin to use the drug for whatever reason, but by the time they become sick and tired of being sick and tired of doing the drug, they have usually gone down a path that they wished they had never traveled. This was certainly the case with Tina and me.

After Alex moved out, I felt like a newborn puppy that had just been torn away from its family before it was ready to separate from its mother. I cried myself to sleep many nights. Papi consoled me and brought me comfort, as I laid in bed feeling very sad and sorry for myself. Much like that puppy that leaves his family, I too needed to begin to re-establish a support foundation for myself to help me in getting through the days and weeks ahead and so I turned to my friends for emotional support. My four very close friends – Rick, Tony, Jeff and Chuck – were very supportive as they listened to my tales and took me out to the bars to forget and drown my sorrows. Internally, I was being pulled in two different directions…my head was telling me to leave Alex, but my heart was telling me to reconcile with him. Since we had separated, I scheduled a meeting with him to discuss what direction our relationship was going to take…should we reconcile or should we dissolve our involvement altogether?

As much as I would've preferred our relationship to survive for the long run, looking back on the conditions in which we met…Fate was reminding me that I had entered the relationship on a lie, so why would I expect something more than what had come to pass? I was not aware at the time we met that he had a pattern of jumping from one relationship to the next. I believe somehow in his mind he thought he was upgrading his boyfriends. This behavior is common in the gay community; men are always looking for the next best thing in a man. Possibly they're seeking a man with a bigger dick, more money, a better body, or other endless options—behavior that is tiresome for all involved.

I met with Alex on a Sunday evening at the townhouse to discuss not just our relationship, but also the loft that we had under contract. I had been out with Jeff that afternoon and when I arrived at the townhouse, Alex was already there. I had been drinking and started acting more aggressively than I normally would have. I was hurt and still very angry over the situation and the alcohol fueled the angry fire that was raging within me, so I acted somewhat like a dictator as I delivered my conditions and demands for a possible reconciliation. I had had enough of his manipulations to last me a lifetime so my demands were non-negotiable. Alex acted like a sad puppy that had been disciplined for bad behavior and placed outside and like that disciplined puppy that is sorry for what he had done, Alex just wanted to be loved once again and let back in the house.

I would've preferred to forget Alex's lying, manipulative, disrespectful, and cheating ways…and accept him back in the relationship as if nothing had ever happened. Realistically though, I knew this was not an option for me. I found myself asking why I wanted him back after all the days, nights, weeks and months that his nasty behavior poisoned our relationship. I also asked myself why I wanted to reconcile with a man that did what Alex had done.

What I didn't know was that the lies were only just the tip of an iceberg. The glacier of deceit and manipulation that encompassed Alex's cheating behavior was yet to be revealed.

I got Alex to admit that he had many sexual encounters with many other men in the year that I suspected him of cheating, though I knew there were many more. What was wrong with me that I would consider reconciling with him? It was simple really…I loved Alex with all my heart. My love for him was large and the sacrifices that I was willing to make for this man were equally as enormous. The depth of my love for him was such that if we happened to be walking down an alley together and a stranger pulled a gun, and stated that he was going to shoot one of us, I would've told the stranger with the gun to shoot me. I loved him more than I can express in words and would've laid my life down to protect him. The sad part about this is that by sacrificing my life for Alex's safety, I would've given up my life in vain. Alex was selfish when it came to how he loved and I believe he loved himself and his anonymous sexual escapades more than he ever loved me.

During our conversation that night, Alex continued to act timidly and overly cautious. At one point, he abruptly ended our conversation and stated he was going to leave, which I found to be disheartening and frustrating. Was he not sorry for what he had done and was he not willing to try to make amends for his actions? Later, I discovered that David, his best friend, had advised him to leave the house if I seemed agitated as I might end up physically hurting him. I was angry and pissed off and my anger was being projected in my aggressive behavior. I wanted to bully Alex a little for what he had put me through—not very adult behavior on my part…although I saw it as very much a natural reaction.

After much discussion, Alex and I agreed to reconcile and attempt to fix the relationship, although this would be easier said than done. I would soon learn that reconciliation would prove to be very difficult. Alex had played with my mind and had released the demons of self-doubt and mistrust within me and I doubted every thought that I had, and every decision that I made. I now had a very difficult time trusting anyone that was remotely close to me.

We also decided to move forward with our plans to purchase the loft, but we agreed to remain separated while we began to date each other once again to try to rekindle our relationship. We were going to attempt to repair the trust that had been destroyed and was now non-existent. In my heart, I wanted Alex to immediately move back in to our home and attempt to put all the lying and cheating behavior in the past, although I knew it wasn't as simple as that. On the other hand, if Alex's behavior was just simple acts of infidelity, if there is such a thing, and he was truly remorseful for what he had done, then a fast and successful reconciliation might have been a possibility while he attempted to clean up his act. As we talked, my subconscious was telling me that there was much more to this situation than meets the eye, so

I proceeded with much caution and reservation when it came to forgiving him. Even though Alex and I were to be co-owners, we agreed that I was to occupy the loft alone once the unit was ready. He was to stay with David, as I attempted to mend my broken heart and, more importantly, tried to extradite the demons of self-doubt and mistrust from my mind that he had placed there.

As far back as I can recall, I always wanted the same things out of life that I believe most straight couples want in a relationship. My own American gay dream included a loving partner, a monogamous relationship, children – in my case, through adoption – a family dog, a great house to raise my family and, of course, like most men, I also wanted a beautiful car. Alex was the first man that I fell head over heels in love with, while at the same time, believing he was my soul mate. I had hoped we were on a path to establish a foundation for our dreams to come to fruition. In the middle of our storm, I thought it would have been easier to walk away from my commitment with Alex than it would have been to heal my bruised ego and attempt to put our relationship back together. However, I ended up compromising my morals and my standards of what I was willing to accept in a mate, as I tried to reconcile and re-establish a new foundation with him. Forgiveness is something that God requires from each of us and although I would learn to forgive Alex in time, forgiving myself was going to be much harder than I could have ever imagined. I learned a great deal about myself in the coming months…and going against the core of my existence to begin to trust him once again was going to be the largest mountain I had yet to climb.

It took six months before I could entertain the thought of trusting Alex again. During this time, we closed escrow on the loft and I moved into the new home. Shortly after, I allowed him to move in with me and Papi so we could begin to re-establish a home together. Christmas was just around the corner and on this holiday season we would soon have a new addition to the family. Alex gave me a wonderful gift that Christmas…a fawn colored pug who I named Puck or, as I liked to call him, Puckles.

At some point in our relationship after that Christmas, I was finally able to rid my mind of those demons of mistrust and self-doubt and was able to begin trusting Alex once more, but after a few months of feeing like our relationship was on the right track, I began to experience those same feelings again that something was not right. Was I just being paranoid? Were these recurring feelings of doubt understandable based on what had taken place in our past? Or were these feelings harbingers of my worst-case scenario and was Alex back to his old tricks? These feelings lingered and remained foremost on my mind.

About eight months after we reconciled, Alex was offered a promotion at work, one that required him to relocate to San Francisco, California. I received this news with mixed emotions. I had begun to question Alex's fidelity again and was concerned with the risks of relocating our home to an unfamiliar city with a man that had proven to be a cheating and compulsive liar. I was doing well at work, having recently been promoted to vice president of operations and national accounts. If Alex was to accept the promotion in San Francisco, I needed to decide if I was going to follow him and give up my new vice-presidential role. During this time, I still believed in my heart, mind, body and soul that Alex and I belonged together and, at that point, I probably would've followed Alex all the way to the gates of hell.

I was now thirty-seven years old and had held two vice presidential positions in my professional career at two different companies. Since I had managed to professionally achieve more than I had ever expected, I decided that I wanted more than just a professional career; I wanted a loving partner and my own American gay dream.

My older brother and I were born in Los Angeles County. When I was still a baby, my parents moved the family to Illinois where I was raised and spent most my adult life although I had always hoped to someday move back to California. Alex decided to accept the position in San Francisco, providing we relocated as a couple. I thought Alex's acceptance of the position could eventually lead us to reside in Los Angeles as a family, which I had always dreamed about doing. I certainly had a vision and a long-term plan for our life together. This choice to leave my position and sell the loft to begin a new life with Alex in an unfamiliar city was not a decision that I came to without much debate and concern. Was I doing the right thing in following a man that had a difficult time keeping his pecker in his pants?

Nineteen years earlier, when I was eighteen years old, I had visited San Francisco when I went on vacation with my good friend Toni, who was then the manager of the linen department at Wieboldt's. I was still living with my parents and this was my first trip to Northern California. It was a time of many firsts for me. It was the first time I went to a Macy's store on the West Coast (once a retail queen, always a retail queen), it was my first time visiting the Castro, and it was my first introduction to the gay life in California. We stayed at the Grand Hyatt hotel in Union Square—the same hotel that Alex and I would stay at almost two decades later during our first trip to San Francisco to seek housing.

Prior to arriving in San Francisco with Alex, I investigated the real estate market...and we were immediately overwhelmed with the difference in price between the Midwest and the West Coast. The dot com boom had started to take hold in the Bay Area and it had dramatically driven up the cost of residential real estate. There was very little new construction-taking place in the city and the inventory was low, but the demand for housing was high. We soon realized that if we wanted a single-family home we needed to look in a more affordable area, possibly east over the Bay Bridge to the East Bay or north over the Golden Gate Bridge to Marin County.

We decided to explore homes in Marin. On our first day of looking for housing, we again experienced sticker shock as we tried to find a house in the area that would fit our budget. Our loft in Chicago had cost us two hundred-seventy nine thousand dollars and that was more money than I could've ever dreamed of spending on housing at the time. Now, it was less than a year after closing on the loft, Alex and I were in Marin County looking at homes in the half million dollar price range. In his new position, Alex had received a substantial salary increase that allowed us to consider houses in that price range, which was exciting, no doubt. It's a common occurrence that when a couple is experiencing troubling times, often they'll have their first child, or more children, to mask their marital issues. This was certainly our case, although instead of adding children to the mix, Alex had given me Puckles and – here we were – buying a larger and much more expensive house in an unfamiliar city. I welcomed the distraction of the new puppy, the new house, and the new city from my renewed suspicions about Alex's bad behavior.

On that first day of looking for a new home in the Bay Area, we looked at thirty different houses. We eventually ended up in San Rafael, a small town in Marin County that was a thirty-minute drive north from San Francisco. A new housing development was under construction a few minutes off the main local freeway, close to San Francisco Bay. The development had vast array of designs and styles to choose from and the floor plans differed from model to model, with various façades available for each style of house, certainly a designer's dream come true. The prices started at four hundred thousand dollars without a finished backyard or without any upgrades…and phase one of construction was already sold out. The developers were now selling phase two of the development, which did not fall within our time frame. We needed a house that would be available for occupancy in three or four months and phase two would not be completed for six or more months. As Fate would have it, a house in phase one of the construction – and in a style that we were interested in purchasing – fell out of escrow after the shell of the house had been completed and it could be finished in roughly three months, with the customized interior finishes that we preferred. So, on our first day of scouting out homes, we had found the house we wanted. Our dream home in the Bay Area, our piece of paradise, could come to fruition with a price tag of five hundred and fifty thousand dollars.

The following day, a Sunday, we returned to San Rafael to look at the house one more time. Since the house was at the high-end of our price range, we decided to check out the surrounding neighborhoods and towns prior to making our final decision. While I would've preferred to live in San Francisco, the houses in the city were out of our price range, being closer to a million dollars or more for what we wanted in a single-family home. The new housing development in San Rafael offered us more value for our money, at half the cost of the same type of a house in San Francisco. The upside to purchasing a new house under construction was that it allowed us to customize it to our taste level. We chose the exterior paint color for the house and designed the backyard to our liking. Overall, Alex and I felt like we had found the perfect home in a good location, and it felt like a great day. That same Sunday afternoon we decided to buy the house and placed it under contract.

We spent more money than I could've ever dreamed of spending on a home, but I was genuinely excited about purchasing this new house and the possibilities of exploring a new life in a new city with Alex, Papi, and Puckles. We had found a beautiful home close to the city that allowed us to enjoy all that San Francisco had to offer with the beauty of living in Marin County. I felt truly blessed and so fortunate. My American gay dream was becoming a reality. Once we closed escrow on the house in San Rafael, the only thing missing from my dream was the adoption of a child or two.

That same Sunday evening, I traveled back to Chicago, as I had to work on Monday morning. Superior Lighting was not aware of my plans to relocate to the West Coast…and due to the extraordinary cost of the new house in Marin that we had just placed under contract – plus the mortgage for our loft that we owned in Chicago – I needed to retain my employment with them until I resigned. I was terrified that I would find myself without a paycheck before we were financially ready for that to take place.

When I left San Francisco, Alex stayed behind at the Grand Hyatt as he was going to work at his new office in the Financial District for a few weeks before returning to Chicago—getting acquainted with his new business associates. Upon my return to Chicago, I had a renewed sense of hope for our relationship. I believed Alex was truly sincere about starting a new life together and that he was finally serious about honoring our monogamous commitment to one another. If this were not the case, why would he insist on my moving with him to the West Coast and buy such an expensive new home? He certainly could have moved to San Francisco, the gay capital of Northern California, on his own and cruise Muir Woods to his heart's content, while looking for Woody Woodpecker. I really wanted and hoped with all my heart that our relationship would finally get on track and Alex and I could eventually adopt children in the coming years. Alex continued to be everything that I had wanted in a man. He was kind, funny, charming, loving, caring, non-confrontational, a good lover and…most of all, I considered him to be a best friend. I was crazy about him on so many levels and saw him like a precious diamond, definitely my rock. Unfortunately, like many diamonds, Alex also had a flaw. It seemed that he was unable to keep his dick in his pants when he was out of my sight and – at that point in our relationship – it was unfathomable for me to understand the enormous depth of this man's irrefutable flaw that he had been so careful to conceal from me.

We had been a couple for two years and during this time we traveled the gay circuit within the United States. We usually traveled with our close friends and joined thousands of other gay men from around the country for a weekend of dancing and partying. While there were many other gay circuit parties in various parts of the world, our group only traveled the domestic circuit. Being a well-traveled gay man, I certainly realized that dick could be found anywhere in the country and at any given moment. I did have reservations of moving to the lion's den, with its readily available amount of gay dick that could be found in the San Francisco area, but even though the city was known for its large gay population, I realized that if Alex was going to cheat in our relationship, he could make that happen no matter where we lived.

I felt blessed to have met Alex and to have had the opportunity to build a relationship with him—and felt equally as blessed to have had the chance to build several close friendships after Tim and I split up and before meeting Alex. I was very careful not to forget my friends when Alex and I began dating and made it a point to continue spending time with my buddies even though I was involved in a relationship. I integrated my close friends into my new life and they were supportive of my relationship in the beginning stages. After Alex's infidelities came to light, several of them, especially Jeff and Tony, were not as supportive of the relationship as they had been. Alex, to his credit, was humble and determined to mend the broken relationships that developed with them because of the lies that he told to conceal his behavior.

My friendship with Rick had grown immensely from the time we met and we began to work together at Bigsby. When Rick was still working at Bigsby and after I went to work for Superior Lighting, I recommended to Alex that he offer Rick a position on his staff. Alex was a department head at the company where he was employed and he sold technology consulting services and had a team that delivered those services. Since Alex was looking to grow his team, he offered Rick one of the open positions in his department, which he accepted. In a very short time, he proved his worth and became a very valuable employee to Alex and the efforts of his department. He thrived as a technology communications consultant, quickly learning new technologies and picking up new skills. When Alex and I decided to relocate to San Francisco, I requested that Alex consider transferring Rick to his San Francisco office, which was booming at the time. With Rick's potential transfer, my best friend would be living in San Francisco, which would make the move to this unfamiliar city seem a little less challenging. As Rick was a valuable employee to the organization, Alex could justify the transfer…so he graciously honored my request—and approached Rick about his interest in relocating to the West Coast office. Being one for adventure and trying new things, Rick was excited about the relocation offer and the possibilities of exploring a new city and he accepted the transfer offer almost immediately. He too would move to San Francisco six months after us.

Life was good. I had a new single-family home being built in California and my best friend was also relocating to join us in our new endeavors and I was happy and extremely excited about starting a new life on the West Coast. On the immediate horizon, it seemed that Alex was honoring our commitment and it very much looked to me that achieving my American gay dream was closer than ever.

The house in San Rafael wouldn't be ready for three to four months after Alex was required to be in San Francisco to begin his new responsibilities—so Alex's company placed him in a temporary corporate apartment in the city while the construction on the house in Marin was being completed. We agreed that I would stay in Chicago for a few months longer to sell our loft and get us organized for the physical move of our possessions. I also needed to give my resignation at work and begin transitioning my work responsibilities. Every other weekend, Alex traveled back to Chicago, so we could spend some time together while we waited for the house in Marin to be finished. While very excited about relocating to California, I was equally as sad to be leaving my family and friends and so it became bittersweet. I was not only down about moving away from the city that I considered home for my adult life, I had become very apprehensive about leaving what was familiar to me. Chicago was my home and had been my support center for over three decades. I was leaving my life-long friends, my family, and the home that Alex and I put so much effort into completing to our specifications.

On the other hand, I was thrilled to be managing the upgrades that we purchased for the house that we were building in Marin. I designed a custom metal staircase that was being manufactured and I purchased numerous European light fixtures that were being installed throughout the house. Our home was on two stories with over twenty-three hundred square feet of living space, a designer's showcase, at least in my eyes. We chose the interior finishes for all areas of the house to our liking...the floors, the kitchen counter tops, the paint, the bathroom fixtures, the kitchen appliances, and so much more. The residence was certainly a home that Alex and I could be proud to own and we mutually felt like it was representative of what we could achieve as a couple in a short time. I failed to understand what might be waiting for me in San Francisco upon my arrival—when I was engrossed in managing the construction of the house and getting the loft in Chicago ready to go on the market. Soon I would be isolated on the West Coast from my family and friends back in Chicago and I would find myself without the support system that I had taken for granted all those decades. The situation in California would leave me with many lonely days, weeks, and months.

A month later, we received Alex's credit card statement in the mail that had the hotel expenses from our weekend of house hunting. Upon receiving the statement, I opened it, as I reconciled all our bills, and reviewed the charges from the Grand Hyatt hotel, where we had stayed on our initial visit to look for housing. The charges on the credit card statement for our stay were four hundred dollars more than what Alex had claimed on his business expense report. When I asked Alex why there was such a significant difference in the expensed amount compared to the amount that was reimbursed, he told me that the hotel must have made a mistake and overcharged his credit card. I was suspicious about his answer, but if he was telling me the truth there should be a credit to follow on an upcoming statement.

There were a few other questionable items that were taking place at the same time in our relationship and Alex felt like he needed to justify the correct hotel charges with me as quickly as possible. Alex had been in Chicago for the weekend and decided to stay longer, so we could spend more time together. During that time, he worked from his company's office in the city. A few days passed and he presented me with an invoice from the Grand Hyatt for the weekend stay. He claimed that he retrieved the invoice from his accounting department at work to prove that the hotel charges were as he expensed and that the hotel did in fact make an error when billing his credit card. That morning, as we were both getting ready to walk out the door on our way to work, he showed me several pieces of paper that resembled a hotel invoice. At a quick glance, the invoice looked legitimate and depicted the same charges that he expensed and that his company reimbursed, although the credit card bill reflected a higher amount. I glanced at the hotel bill quickly and told him that it was not necessary for him to have gone to the trouble of getting the original invoice from his accounting department. He insisted that it was important for him to prove to me that he was telling the truth based on what had taken place in the past. He then took back the invoice that he showed me, stating that it was the original and he needed to return it to his companies' accounting department that same morning. His statement certainly made sense to me or at least it did at that specific moment.

A few days later, Alex traveled back to San Francisco and began working out of the West Coast office full-time while I was getting our personal belongings organized and ready for the movers to pack and load for transportation to California. My subconscious suddenly flashed a vision of that hotel bill that Alex presented to me on the morning when we were getting ready to walk out the door on our way to our offices. The scenario kept playing over and over in my head. For no apparent reason, I made the visual connection that the hotel invoice that Alex showed me was printed on regular-sized, eight-and-a-half by eleven-inch paper. Back in those days, hotel bills were not printed on regular paper, but on a type of paper that had perforations on both sides. When you checked out of a hotel, the invoice was printed in triplicate on carbon paper; it was an industry standard at the time. The 'original' that Alex had shown me was a copy printed on a desktop printer without the perforations on each side. Was I correct in my assumptions and, if so, what difference did it make? I needed to take charge of the situation to confirm if my suspicions had any merit. I decided to call the Grand Hyatt and asked for the accounting department to request a copy of the original invoice for our stay. As I called the hotel, I pretended that I was Alex and explained to the woman on the phone that I had lost my copy of the hotel invoice and needed a replacement receipt for my stay to expense the charges on my business expense report. "Alex", she replied, "would you like me to fax you the original copy of the hotel charges for that weekend or the one that you requested us to revise and that we've already sent to you?" I almost fell out of my chair when I heard her response…my suspicions regarding the hotel invoice did have merit and Fate was again being merciless toward Alex. "Please fax me a copy of the original hotel charges", I muttered back. I gave her the fax number at my office and Fate and I then waited for the fax to come through.

I was pissed off and sick to my stomach. What the hell was so incriminating on the hotel invoice that he needed to conceal the original invoice from me? I walked over to the fax machine in the public area of my workplace to retrieve the incriminating document. My heart was pounding out of my chest. As I reached for the incoming fax that had come through from the hotel, I thought how I had already given my resignation and was transitioning out of my position. We had also placed the loft on the market and had a home worth over a half million dollars under contract. I grabbed the fax and slowly walked back to my office to review the information. I was a nervous mess. I closed the door behind me and sat down at my desk to review the fax. The room charges, room service, and parking for our stay for that weekend were all in order. However, there were numerous phone charges that added up to four hundred dollars. During this time, hard-wired car cellular phones existed, but personal cellular phones were not yet available—so we still used hotel phones to make calls when traveling on business trips or on vacation. In practicality, hotel phones were the only real option for calling someone when you were out of town and staying at a hotel, unless you had a calling card. If you had a calling card, the phone charges could be charged to your card and these would not be placed on your hotel bill.

I finally had the truth in hand. I found the additional four hundred dollars in expenses that Alex had attempted to conceal from me, although I didn't know who was on the receiving end of these calls. All the questionable charges on the hotel invoice were made to the same number and on the same Sunday evening that I traveled back to Chicago after I left him alone in San Francisco. As any good investigative gay husband would do, I picked up my office phone and dialed the phone number that he had called, listed on the hotel bill.

Like so many children, I certainly told my share of lies when I was a young boy. Most of those lies were told to my parents so I didn't get in trouble for doing something that they told me I couldn't do. As I grew up and became an adult, I tried very hard not to tell lies. I also deliberately surrounded myself with people that behaved in a manner where I didn't have to sort through their stories to determine whether they were lying—so Alex's ongoing web of deceit was conduct that was completely new to me. At thirty-seven, I was naïve to his lying behavior, although I was learning fast.

Imagine my surprise when I called the number on the hotel bill and discovered that Alex had spent four hundred dollars calling a sex line. In retrospect, it wasn't a big deal to me that he called a sex line. What was a big deal was the great lengths that he had gone through to conceal these calls from me. Certainly, the reintroduction of lies back into our relationship was a major problem for me, although there was another underlining concern that I had and it was a financial one. Since I would soon be unemployed until I secured a new job in California, we needed to be very carefully with our money due to all our upcoming expenses. Shortly we would be responsible for paying two mortgages, the mortgage on the loft – until it sold – and the upcoming mortgage on the new house in San Rafael. Alex's blatant disregard for our financial commitments, on top of the lies, was something that I found to be very disturbing and disrespectful. My next call was to Alex in San Francisco. I was anxious to confront him and the web of lies that he was spinning once again. Charlotte had some explaining to do.

As I dialed the phone, I became deeply concerned about my decision to quit my job, as I would no longer have medical coverage through my employer. Alex's company was progressive in its insurance coverage to its employees and they offered domestic partner medical coverage. Alex and I agreed to add me to his medical plan and so we were extremely intertwined on a personal, financial, and medical level.

With the added stress of being positive, and needing medical coverage to maintain my monthly medication, I was freaking out over Alex's behavior. I was becoming emotionally fragile from trying to figure out what was going on in Alex's mind and why he was behaving in this manner. I felt like Humpty Dumpty, although, instead of sitting on a wall, I was sitting on two mortgages and, at any moment, I could have a great financial fall. I was in my office holding the phone and visualizing the cracks that were forming in our relationship. I was not sure how long the relationship would hold together before everything that we were trying to build with one another came crumbling down around us. While little Miss Charlotte was running around spinning more lies to attempt to hold our relationship from falling apart, I had turned to my old friend Tina to attempt to help me in pulling myself together. How long would it be before Tina and Charlotte would cause Humpty Dumpty to fall to his demise?

I was very angry with him and genuinely concerned about our financial stability. Even though I was upset, I was going to attempt to be non-confrontational and allow him the opportunity to tell me the truth. When Alex answered the phone, he seemed to be in a very good mood. Soon, his demeanor would change based on the subject of the conversation that was about to take place. I inquired if he was alone in his office and he replied that he was. I requested whether he could close his office door for a private conversation. "Of course," he replied. As I waited for him to close his door, I began to feel sick to my stomach. This confrontation was going to be more uncomfortable for me than I had imagined. When Alex picked up the phone again, he asked "what's up?"

I said to him, "the following question that I have for you is very important and your response is equally as important to our relationship, so you need to answer my question with the truth." I asked him if he understood what I was requesting of him and he replied that yes, he did. I once again asked him what the four hundred dollars charges on the hotel bill were about. He maintained his original story that it was an overcharge by the hotel and he was working on reaching the hotel's accounting department to get the amount credited to his account. I stopped the conversation there and reiterated the importance of him telling me the truth. I asked the same question once again. Now, you would think that at this point he would've suspected that I knew or had in my possession something that made me think he was lying, although he held firm to his original story. I had come to understand the pattern of a true liar. A compulsive liar will never change their story, as they know inconsistencies to their original version of the story will lead to speculation of the truth. They'll maintain the integrity – now there's an oxymoron if I have ever heard one – of their untruthful version of the story, at all costs. Alex did not realize that I had the evidence in hand that would require him to very shortly recant his version of the story. I was extremely angry and proceeded to call Alex a liar! I had given him two opportunities to tell the truth and, on both occasions, he chose to lie. Adding insult to injury, I expressed the magnitude of him telling the truth and the negative affect it would have on our relationship if he did not. I threw every profanity that I could think of at that moment at him and reiterated once again that he was an outright liar and he should be ashamed of himself. I then explained how I knew for a fact that he was a perpetual liar, telling him that I had a copy of the original hotel invoice that was faxed directly to my office from the hotel. Upon hearing my explanation, he immediately began to cry. Charlotte had spun one to many lies and got herself caught up in her own web of deceit.

I was lost somewhere between the reality of what Alex and I had together in Chicago when we first met versus the dream of what we potentially could achieve in San Francisco. Was I caught up in the material things of our relationship or was it the American gay dream that I was chasing? It no longer seemed to matter what I wanted, I was now disoriented and perplexed on what my next move should be. The movers were scheduled, the loft was on the market, we were under contract for the purchase of the house in San Rafael, and I had resigned from my job. There appeared to be no end in sight to the trials and tribulations in our relationship. A mammoth dark cloud had been cast over the love that I had for Alex and it would begin to engulf me in its darkness, sadness, and despair.

7 | PLACE YOUR BETS

Shortly after our phone conversation ended with Alex crying in his office, he boarded a plane in San Francisco and headed back to Chicago. We needed to discuss the future of our relationship and the magnitude of the ramifications to our financial stability if our commitment to one another failed. In a situation in which we now found ourselves, there's a negotiation factor that required each party to bring something to the table to strengthen the deal. At that point in the game, I was not convinced that our love for one another was enough to get us through yet another storm in our already tumultuous relationship. I had hoped and believed that our West Coast adventure would allow the sun to shine on our commitment to one another again.

My friends, I felt, were betting that our relationship would not pass the test of time. Jeff had begun to notice that the wear and tear from Charlotte's web of lies had begun to take its toll on me and he was starting to doubt whether Alex was a good choice and a suitable partner for me—and was applying pressure for me to reconsider my decision to move to San Francisco.

At some point in my relationship with Alex, I noticed that he had a motive in how he dealt with me. In the first six months, he concentrated his efforts on seducing me on a physical and emotional level, ensuring that I would be drawn to him. He was exceedingly good at assessing a situation. On our first date, he brought me flowers when he arrived. It was a simple gesture and certainly thoughtful and gentlemanly. On our second date, having had the chance to see my apartment, he brought me a blue, frosted, hand-blown glass vase, which on its own was thoughtful and generous. I found his gift to be fascinating because I was a big fan of collecting colored glass items to accessorize my home. Modern, colored glass accessories was something of a novelty and I was keen on collecting quality designer pieces. This fascination with colored glass accessories would be one of my passions for many years. The vase that Alex gave me was the exact one in the same color that I had been eyeing from Marshall Field's, then one of Chicago's finer department stores. It was expensive and I had been mulling the idea of purchasing the piece for myself before making a final decision to buy it. At no time did I mention the vase to him, or my interest in collecting these types of pieces, and I'm still impressed that Alex had the foresight to assess my home in one single visit and then be able to choose the exact personal item – out of hundreds of stores in Chicago and probably thousands of colored glass accessories – that I would've chosen for myself. I was impressed by his gift, and by his perception, and was captivated by the fact that he paid such close attention to something that was of so much interest to me. After we started dating, he sent me flowers at my office once a week. I loved getting flowers from him on a regular basis and it made me feel special. The women with whom I worked always made a big deal out of the flower deliveries and I think they were as excited to see the arrangements being delivered as I was to receive them.

After six months of investing much of his time and attention to secure my affection, my devotion to him was guaranteed. Once he was certain that I was committed to the relationship, he began to alter our commitment, without once having a conversation with me.

The material items that we acquire or seek to acquire in life are just 'things' and I've come to understand that these things can't make you happy on their own, although they do offer much comfort depending on the situation in which we've acquired them. It took me decades to learn that no matter your passion – whether it's collecting quality colored glass, designer clothing, fine cars, jewelry, dining at great restaurants, vacationing in foreign lands, collecting rare art, having an expensive home, or simply sitting in your house and wallowing in the large number of dollars that you've managed to acquire – they on their own merit cannot bring you happiness. A person can have all the best of the material things that life has to offer, but without their health being in good standing, these items are of no importance if the individual is too sick to enjoy them. By the time I met Alex, I had been infected with HIV for nearly eleven years and by all accounts I should've been showing signs of some type of health issues, although by the grace of God, all was well. I certainly could have and possibly should've ended the relationship with Alex by that point, but my love was blind. In my case, the love that I had for Alex made me deaf, dumb and stupid when dealing with my emotions, which was compounded by the material things that Alex and I had acquired while we were together. By the time I realized what was driving Alex's lying and cheating behavior, we were so intertwined that I felt like I had no choice but to explore and exhaust every possible option before I could consider ending our relationship.

In telling this story, you'll come to realize that I seldom learn my lesson the first time around, although I seem to eventually end up learning—by repeating my mistakes again and again. A common definition of crazy is repeating the same behavior over and over while expecting a different outcome. In my case, the good news is that I eventually began to realize I was not crazy for repeating my mistakes continuously while expecting a different result. I am just an extremely stubborn person and need to be sure of my choices. I needed to ensure that I was making the correct decisions about my relationship with Alex no matter what the emotional cost. I was also trying to manage my feelings while attempting to be financially responsible. I didn't want to jeopardize the assets that we had acquired without knowing for certain that Alex was not the loving and caring person that I believed he was, even though his behavior was telling me otherwise. Sometimes, to ensure that we're making the correct choices in life, we may be required to put ourselves in a circumstance that will require us to repeat the mistakes of our past. This may need to take place for us to ensure that our decisions about a specific circumstance is the best decision for us, otherwise we risk losing something of value. In my case, my 'something of value' that I was worried about losing without putting forth the effort to salvage it – if it was worth salvaging – was my relationship with Alex. I understand many people would disagree with me and they would rather risk losing a person of value in their life than having to go through a difficult and painful experience. I soon began to question if my pursuit to salvage my relationship was being done in vain. Did Alex want to change his behavior and was he truly in love with me? Possibly, I underestimated the situation altogether and Alex was not capable of change. The inevitable truth to these questions would soon be unveiled, but not before there was a painful pursuit of that truth.

There certainly have also been times in my life when I've taken the longest route possible to get to a specific designation in my life's journey. I often wonder if I wasn't paying enough attention to the road signs of life, or whether my unfortunate circumstances were possibly all meant to be. Was I destined to wonder aimlessly and repeat my mistakes over and over until the end of my days? Throughout my life, so-called friends and acquaintances deliberately created 'situations' that were nothing more than mind games in their attempt to get me to react or change my direction, better known as manipulation. These individuals should've been bearing an 'approach at your own risk' life sign. I was stupid to the ways of a manipulator so I was easy prey for these types of individuals. My poor choices in friends, acquaintances, and Alex ended up creating a behavior within me that was a by-product of their dishonest ways. Because I had been manipulated on many occasions – even when the signs were quite clear to abort a particular situation or circumstance due the red flags that were present – I doubted my intuition and chose to ignore the obvious. This type of behavior resulted in many hardships in my life that I could've avoided. The battle wounds from my relationship with Alex, compounded with my poor choice in friends, and the added mix of bad acquaintances, had begun to affect my ability to properly assess a situation. For the first time in my adult life I became unsure of myself, doubting my capabilities and my existence. The dark cloud cast over the love that I had for Alex changed the landscape of our relationship. I was no longer confident that Alex and I would be able to sustain our relationship due to the aftermath that came about from the chain reaction that he had put into play by his web of deceit.

Since Alex and I had financially committed to the house in Marin, and since I was still in love with him, I made the decision to throw all caution to the wind and move forward with my plans to move to San Francisco. Before I told Alex that I had made my final decision and was moving forward with my plan to relocate to the West Coast with him, he pulled a sympathy card to the hand that was in play between us. He knew that my decision to relocate could've gone either way and he was taking no chances. He informed me that an uncle had sexually abused him when he was a young boy. He claimed he was traumatized as a child from the sexual abuse that he experienced, which resulted in his having physiological issues, causing a behavioral pattern that an expert diagnosed as a sex addiction. I had not heard of this expression, nor did I know that this type of addiction existed. I am uncertain if Alex was telling the truth when he told me the story about his uncle sexually abusing him, although it could have been true. I did know that he certainly had an issue with keeping his pecker in his pants and had thought this issue was a simple case of him being a whore and not wanting to contain his activities. Little did I know that the real problem was with his pecker—it was addicted and it could not be contained. While I can laugh for a moment because this shit sounds funny now, it was devastating at the time. Alex had become the adult version of the children's story that I would come to refer to as *Charlotte's Web of Lies and Deceit.* I would also come to see him as the protagonist of an adult animated short story, the *Addicted Pecker that Couldn't get Enough Wood.* Almost two decades later, due to my relationship with God, I can now see humor in the darkest times of my life. God is amazing.

When Alex delivered the news about his sex addiction, he pleaded that we continue to move forward with our plans to relocate to California. He proclaimed that he would seek professional help to get his addiction under control if we stayed together. He continued by stating that he could not be successful nor could he be happy in San Francisco without me and the puppies joining him. In his defense, he seemed sincere and genuine in his pleas, but in my defense…that's what a professional liar does—they always make you feel as though they're being sincere. He again assured me that if I continued with our plans, he would seek the professional help to deal with his addiction. Was this his first step toward true redemption and the beginning of his recovery process? They say that the first step in recovery is to admit that you have a problem and now I understood the underlining issue that was potentially driving his extra-curricular activities. However, I had serious concerns that I was the proverbial lamb being led into the slaughter. How was I to police Alex in the sexually-free environment of San Francisco?

Would my efforts to ensure that he honored his word to change his ways be in vain? Was I being played for a fool once more? Was Charlotte spinning me further into her web?

On top of all this, Alex came bearing gifts in the form of a brand-new Mercedes E320 just off the showroom floor. The automobile was the make and model that I had been eyeing for many months and was an outstanding driving machine. Was this a gift of love and reconciliation or was it a bribe? Either way, it was a lovely gift by any means and, if the car was a bribe, it was going to cost Alex a whole lot more than the price of a new E320 Mercedes, thank you very much.

Despite Alex's behavior in our relationship, he managed to become very successful while we were together and his professional achievements were something to be respected and admired. When we first met, my annual income of a hundred thousand dollars was twenty five thousand dollars more than his. About eighteen months after we began living together and shortly after he took on his new job, he surpassed my annual income. After receiving a salary increase for the promotion to the West Coast, plus a salary adjustment that he received to make up for the cost of living in San Francisco, he was grossing nearly double the annual income that I was making when we initially met.

During the first few weeks of dealing with the news of Alex's newly claimed addiction, I traveled to New York to interview for a national sales position with a newly-formed company based in Manhattan, although the position that I was interviewing for would be based in California. As Fate played out my day in the Big Apple, I was offered the position on the same day of my interview and I flew back to Chicago that evening with confirmed employment. Now that I had a job offer and the opportunity to earn a salary in San Francisco, it made my decision to follow my heart and my pursuit of my American gay dream that much easier. I gave Alex my final decision to move to San Francisco with him, if he honored his commitment to seek professional help for to his addiction.

It seemed as if our train had finally left the station. Was it possible that our relationship was moving in the right direction and on the right track for the first time since we met? Life offers several paths to get us from point A to point B. Sometimes, the end of our journey is the same no matter what path we may have chosen. It's the experiences we encounter along the way that vary depending on the paths we take. Some individuals get detoured in life by unforeseen circumstances and don't end up traveling on the path intended for their life, a phenomenon that I attribute to the homeless. For whatever reason one becomes homeless, this is certainly not a path that would be chosen by anyone, given a choice.

How is anyone to embrace life, people and their surroundings if we are always deciphering the poor behavior of the people around us? It seems that we've all become tolerant or acceptant of behaviors that distract our time and energy from our goals in life. Like the friend or co-worker that lies to us or the spouse that creates an untruthful and elaborate story to cover his or her tracks when they're confronted on their unfaithfulness. Many of us have encountered these two scenarios to some degree, but unfortunately, if the truth were to be told about us, we've all probably engaged in some type of behavior that has been counter-productive to someone we know and love.

On the flip side, I've come to realize that on occasion Fate will place people and circumstances in our path to purposely distract us. This could be for our own good and for our own safety without us ever realizing it. Possibly, it's to lead us down a path that we would not have chosen for ourselves, although for whatever reason, this is a road that we must travel. But I believe that God will use all things for good, even the not so good things that take place in our life—if we allow him. Did Alex and I get detoured from our intended path? If so, were we finally on board with one another and traveling in the right direction? Could we, and would we, achieve what God had intended for our lives when He brought us together?

Before meeting Alex, when I awoke in the morning, I would – for no apparent reason – be in a troublesome mood. Sometimes, on some mornings, I was afraid to open my eyes because I was terrified that I was going to have one of those bad days. On those days, my world seemed so heavy and pointless. During this time in my life there seemed to be no answer for controlling my mood swings, which were really bouts of depression. As far back as I can remember, I suffered from depression and my situation got progressively worse as I got older. I feel that creative people march to a different drummer than other people and believe that many creative individuals tend to suffer from some type or level of depression. As I saw myself as a creative individual, I believe I stumbled through life for many years with this condition

I was emotionally invested in my relationship with Alex and this was enhanced by my belief that we were meant to be together. Alex was very thoughtful and kind when it came to expressing his love for me and for Puckles and Papi, our little babies. During the first six months with Alex, the bad days seemed to be far and few, but my new sunny disposition didn't last long. The heavy days returned with my suspicions that something was not as it seemed with Alex and our relationship.

Since I was able to secure a job prior to relocating to the Bay area, I thought Fate was giving me the heads-up to follow my heart and Alex to the West Coast. So, it was an exciting day when the moving truck arrived at our new home that had been completed to our liking in San Rafael. Puckles and Papi were running around in their new backyard and when our personal belongings and the Mercedes were off-loaded from the moving truck, California was once again home sweet home. I once heard Cher say that "home is where the heart is" and my heart was now with Alex and the bay area was our new home. As we began to set up our new house and start our new lives together, it seemed as if the dark clouds that had been hovering over the relationship in Chicago had not made their way to California.

Alex began to see a therapist for his sex addiction twice a week in San Francisco. He seemed earnest about keeping his commitment to me and to himself and was conscientious about going to his therapy appointments regularly. We never discussed what he and his therapist talked about during his visits. I felt like this was something Alex needed to do for himself and if he wanted to share information, he would do so when he was ready. I was just thrilled that he seemed to be taking positive steps to get his situation under control.

I was not so naïve to believe that Alex was going to be cured from his addiction simply by going to therapy. Most people who are trying to overcome an addiction usually go through a trial and error process. In many cases, an individual will have a relapse while they're trying to get their addiction under control. Alex's commitment to begin the healing process via professional help was a viable approach to the situation and one that I could understand. This approach certainly made more sense to me then if he had told me that he was going to go cold turkey and try to deal with his addiction on his own. I was hoping for the best, while keeping a close eye on his behavior and his whereabouts, but realizing that he was working in San Francisco, where there was much gay wood for the pecking, I certainly could not watch his every move if his pecker wanted to come out and play.

While he was working in San Francisco, I worked from our house in San Rafael where I converted the third bedroom into a home office. The New York-based company that I now worked for designed and manufactured store fixtures for the retail and architecture industries. They didn't have an office in California so I had become their account sales executive to introduce and establish their presence on the West Coast. The president and co-owner of the company was someone with whom I had been involved on a business level for many years prior to him starting the company. I was genuinely excited about being an intricate part of an organization from the ground up, but it was going to be challenging. With anything that you build from the foundation, especially in sales, it takes much dedication and discipline to be successful, and it takes time. Rome was not built in a day and neither is a successful client base.

In a year of living in the Bay area, Alex and I accomplished much. After we got settled into our new home, we hired a landscape architect to design the backyard patio. Once the designer installed the patio and walkways around the house he landscaped those areas and we purchased a stainless-steel barbecue and a six-person Jacuzzi. Our circle of friends in the Bay area grew quickly. Alex was a fairly good cook and we enjoyed entertaining in our newly finished home on the weekends and met and befriended several gay couples. One couple resided in San Francisco and the other couple happened to be our neighbors. Rick had also relocated from Chicago and was living in the city. I became friendly with Laura, Alex's personal assistant who we both considered a friend. Gary, my doctor in Chicago, also followed us to San Francisco shortly after Alex and I moved into the house. We often had friends come on the weekends for cocktails, dinner, conversation, and a dip in the Jacuzzi for those who wanted to relax after dinner. We enjoyed our new home greatly and it was wonderful to be able to share our hospitality and good fortune with our close circle of friends. I feel having financial success in life is without value if you don't have people to share it with and I also felt blessed to be able to share our new home with our new friends that were good-hearted people who genuinely cared for us both.

But alas, it was not long before Charlotte began spinning a more intricate and twisted web of lies and our happy days in paradise would soon come to an end. The dark cloud that had been hovering over our relationship in Chicago would soon bring a downpour of deception to San Rafael, like El Niño, the weather pattern that was now raging in the Pacific and would settle over the Bay Area for months that winter.

Around that time, Bill Clinton's sex scandal with Monica Lewinsky hit the national news. I was frustrated with President Clinton's proclamation that he didn't have sexual relations with Ms. Lewinsky, a statement that he would later need to recant—or at least define what he meant by sexual relations. At the time, I was trying to get Alex to understand the importance of honoring his monogamy agreement, not just verbally, but also in practice. If the President of the United States of America, the highest office in the land, was partaking in the same type of behavior that I was telling Alex was inappropriate, then why would Alex think he was doing anything wrong? I must have seemed like a nut to him. If the President of the United States was having extra-curricular activities in the Oval office, I'm certain Alex wondered what the big deal was with his gathering nuts on his knees in the woods.

Like most people, the main issue that I had with President Clinton is that he lied about his level of involvement with Monica until her dress with his DNA surfaced—the same behavior Alex was exhibiting. He would lie at great lengths to cover his infidelity but, when confronted, he maintained his story until evidence was presented that would force him to recant his web of lies. His actions exhausted me in attempting to bring the truth to light and I'm sure Alex was equally as exhausted from trying to cover his tracks and keeping me from discovering the truth about his adulterous behavior.

Sorting through the lies and the underling layers of deceit became a main component in our relationship and my mood worsened. My Tina use compounded my mood swings, resulting in my becoming very aggressive toward Alex. My disposition was all over the spectrum and changed on any given day and at any given moment. I had a very difficult time concentrating on anything other than the scenarios that kept playing over and over in my head. I kept thinking of the lies that Alex was feeding me to cover his cheating ways and I became preoccupied with trying to discern the truth. I felt like an investigative reporter looking for the true story behind the bullshit cover story that I was being told. The similarities to the ongoing Lewinsky story were striking. I was working overtime to sort through the various scenarios in my head to come up with answers that could provide me with the truth. I was truly naïve to the depths to which a professional liar would plummet—to conceal whatever it is that they want to hide. Since the master of all liars was training me, I would soon have my master's degree in dissecting the liar's ways. It was a totally messed up situation, but what choice did I have if I wanted the truth? I didn't have the national news networks to assist me in my investigations; I had to do the work on my own.

Many years after I built a relationship with God, I was able to separate my feelings about President Clinton's sex scandal from his accomplishments that he achieved while in office. I'm not exactly sure why God unveiled his scandal at the same time I was experiencing my issues with Alex, although I've come to understand that this was another example of how God will use all things for the greater good, if we allow him. That President Clinton was able to take the country from a budgetary deficit during his terms in office and transform that deficit into a monetary surplus is an indisputable achievement. One of his most memorable accomplishments during his presidency was that he signed a bill – making it a law – that healthcare insurance companies could no longer discriminate for a pre-existing medical condition if an individual was switching from one group medical provider to another. This was a major milestone for those people that were HIV positive, but otherwise healthy, who could now change employers. Prior to this change in the healthcare law, people who were HIV positive were not able to get re-insured if they changed jobs and so this was a major act of compassion by President Clinton for many people. In my view, possibly God wanted me to understand that there's good to be found in every aspect of life—even in a man that lied to the American people while he was in office. Through my love for God, I came to see the great accomplishments of President Clinton and became extremely cautious about passing judgment on others.

Amusingly, I had a connection to Monica Lewinsky. While living in California, Monica was employed with one of the Bigsby divisions before her involvement with Bill Clinton. She worked at the Knot Shop in the Century City shopping center in Los Angeles, at the same time that I worked at the company—leading their visual merchandising and store development department. Supposedly, a famous necktie that Monica gave to President Clinton, referenced in the news stories at the time of their involvement, was purchased from one of the Knot Shops. I found this to be a strange coincidence, but perhaps this was not a coincidence at all. Was Fate telling me that the similar situation between President Clinton and Alex's behavior could be taken personally because of our close six degrees of separation?

After being in California for six months, Alex's lavish stories to cover his infidelity continued. Since I worked from home, I did the laundry. Frequently, I would throw a load of clothes in the washer while I was working, a simple task when you have the luxury of working from home. Alex was still going to his therapy sessions twice a week. I was aware that Alex could and probably would act upon his addiction while he was trying to get himself under control, a natural process when trying to overcome an addition of any kind. I kept a watchful eye as he dealt with his addiction through his therapy treatments and looked for any potential signs that he was swerving off track and might be back to his old tricks and cheating ways.

As I was doing the laundry, I checked his underwear for semen stains. Being a guy, I understood that oftentimes men usually leak additional semen after they have ejaculated. If Alex had been cheating on me again, I might find semen stains in his underwear and, as I looked, I found exactly what I hoped not to find—semen tracks in several pairs. I was trying to be a realist when it came to Alex attempting to get his addiction under control and I was trying to be a supportive partner, yet I was still pissed off, frustrated, and disappointed—even as I knew that his recovery would most likely be a process that would play out over time rather than a quick cure.

When Alex arrived home that day, I confronted him with my underwear discovery and, as usual, he maintained his innocence. I stopped him in his tracks, no pun intended, and explained to him that my finding semen stains in his underwear was not up for discussion. I wanted him to know that I was aware of what he was doing and thought that by confronting the issue and letting him know he was not fooling anyone other than himself, he would stop doing whatever he was doing. By now, I had become very sensitive to listening to my intuition. I did not need to know the exact details regarding his actions that were causing his pecker to drip in his under garments; the larger picture was good enough for me. In my heart and mind, I now knew without a doubt he was still operating under his own rules and not honoring the conditions of our relationship.

A few days later, Alex came home with a prescription from his doctor to treat a urinary tract infection. Alex claimed that the so-called semen that I accused him of having in his underwear was not semen at all and claimed that the discharge that I found in his shorts was related to his urinary infection. If this was my first time at the rodeo, I may have bought into the possibility of his elaborate story. However, I had now become a full-fledged cowboy and I did not believe a word of his bullshit story, not for a minute and not even with the prescription from his doctor.

Afterwards, I started to lose control. How far would he go to lie? I was angry about the extent that he had gone to make me think I was crazy and his retorts that I was falsely accusing him. I was seriously showing signs of coming unglued and Alex finally realized he had gone too far. I was still using Tina and there was no calming me down. I could not hear any more of his bullshit stories. It became clear to me that I was either absolutely nuts in my suspicions or I was absolutely right on target. But I'm nothing if not stubborn—and I knew in my gut I was right about this situation—and my intuition was telling me that I was being played. I did not back down from my position and I verbally attacked Alex as aggressively as he had tried to prove me wrong.

The following day, after my meltdown, Alex made an emergency appointment to have a couple's therapy session with his therapist. I had not been a part of his therapy sessions nor had I ever met his therapist. The evening was going to prove to be a very interesting and informative night. As we arrived at the therapist's office, Alex acted like a hurt puppy, showing signs of being very sad and looking to be consoled by someone. I, on the other hand, felt like a bulldog ready for a fight and, if cornered, I was going to bite someone's head off. As the session progressed, I was so angry that I do not recall everything that took place. I do remember that I was very accusatory of Alex and talked about how I believed he was still going to great lengths to tell deceitful stories to cover his actions. Alex cried and cried, though by this point his crocodile tears no longer had an effect on me. I was relentless in my pursuit to beat him down and prove that he was cheating and lying to cover up his actions. After months of seeking professional help to get his addiction under control, it seemed as if nothing had changed. As I fought to get the truth, his therapist came to his rescue, interrupting one of my angry rants, and said, "I'm not sure if Alex is doing what you say, but if he's doing what you're accusing him of, his lying to cover up his cheating is not a secondary situation to the sex addition; the two behaviors go hand in hand." What the fuck?

If his therapist didn't truly know what Alex was doing after months of therapy, twice a week, thousands of dollars later, then I felt the situation between us to be hopeless. Was it all an act on Alex's part? Had he been lying to the therapist all these weeks and months? Was this just another game that he was playing to keep me in check? I thought Alex was truly serious and really cared about getting his addiction under control. Was this the ultimate betrayal, the last straw? Was the semen-stained underwear going to be the situation that would finally break us up for good?

The therapist's statement that the lies were not a secondary situation to the sex addition—and that both behaviors went hand-in-hand, absolutely frightened me to the core. All that time, I believed he was telling lavish lies to cover his infidelity, but according to the therapist this was not the case.

There *was* a secondary motive to his addictive sexual behavior and its real power over Alex came from the manipulation that he got from controlling the situation. The lies that he was telling me, to convince me that he was not doing what I accused him of doing, was about control. I was speechless and I had no fight left in me for a science project of this magnitude…I was in over my head and I was done. Session over!

As I see it, one of the greatest gifts that God gave me would also be one of my greatest weaknesses. I'm able to forgive and move on from a situation—even after I've been lied to or mistreated. In my past relationships, people have taken advantage of me in many circumstances because they know that I'll get upset and will probably confront the issue with them and, if they show signs of remorse, I will forgive and move past the incident. I understand that this is the way we are supposed to conduct ourselves through the teachings of the Bible. But some people have used my forgiving nature to manipulate me when it comes to their wrongdoings, while having no genuine remorse in their heart for their actions. As a result, over the years, I've learned to be a forgiving individual, while struggling to ensure that I'm not deliberately being manipulated. Alex keyed into my forgiving nature early on in our relationship and began to exploit it to his advantage. But, what doesn't kill you will make you stronger and even though the years I spent with Alex would encompass much heartache, I loved deeply and experienced much. However, three and a half years into our relationship, I realized I had followed him all the way to the gates of hell.

8 | PIT BOSS

Papi was nearing three years of age and Puckles was two when Alex and I moved to San Rafael. The little guys were crazy about him. When he arrived home from his day at the office and hit the open button on the automatic garage door from his car, the dogs would run downstairs to greet him. They were always hard at work sleeping under my desk—until they heard the garage door open or until they heard me say "daddy's home." They would immediately jump up from their slumber and start barking as they ran down the stairs to greet Alex. They loved their daddy Alex and Puckles especially was crazy in love with him. Papi was a little less enthusiastic about Alex, although both dogs showed him great affection. Possibly Alex was holding a small grudge against Papi for having pissed on him while we were living in Chicago. Or possibly Papi was smarter than I was and could see Alex for who he truly was. Papi and Puckles slowly became the object of my affection, as Alex and I grew further apart. I came to adore my little boys as they loved me much and it was reflected in their behavior.

The evening that proved to be the end of my relationship with Alex would consist of a chain of events that took the love that I had for him and turned it into contempt. He had been traveling for a few days on a business trip in the southern part of the United States, when he arrived home at five o'clock in the evening on a Friday. Rick was still working as a member of Alex's team and he happened to be working on assignment at a location near our house. I called him and invited him to stop by our home on his way back into San Francisco to have dinner. Since Rick and I were best friends and Alex was Rick's immediate supervisor we were very close and got together regularly. Rick accepted my invitation for dinner and came by the house from his client's location. The memories of what happened next are burned into my mind and I can recall the events as if they took place yesterday.

Alex had begun to prepare dinner by the time Rick arrived. The three of us had some wine and chatted about our week's events while Alex finished preparing dinner. We sat outside on the new patio that we recently had installed and we had more conversation and more wine while we enjoyed our dinner and evening. After dinner, Alex decided he was going to get into the

Jacuzzi. He took off his clothes, down to his underwear and got into the hot tub. Shortly after, I went into the house and changed into shorts and I joined him. Rick did not get in the Jacuzzi, although he stayed for a while longer. We had more conversation and more wine. At the end of the evening, Alex got out of the Jacuzzi and went into the house to use the powder room on the first floor adjacent to the kitchen and family room where he took off his wet underwear. He grabbed a towel from the bathroom to cover himself and headed upstairs to retire to the bedroom for the night. Rick helped me clean up the dishes from dinner before heading home. I took the dogs outside for a quick walk by the bay before heading to bed myself. Upon my return, I came into the house, turned off the downstairs lights, set the security alarm, and headed up stairs to join Alex.

The following day, I woke up and was out of bed before Alex. I thought I would leave him to sleep a while longer since it was a Saturday and he had been traveling the prior few days. When I walked downstairs and got Puckles and Papi ready for their morning walk, I happened to glance toward the powder room from where I was standing in the kitchen. I noticed stuff on the floor that looked like pieces of paper towel or toilet paper. I walked over to get a closer inspection. I realized it was tissue paper of some kind or a paper napkin that had gotten wet and was now in little pieces all over the bathroom floor. When I looked in the sink, I noticed that Alex's underwear from the previous evening was sitting, still wet, in the sink basin. I grabbed the underwear and, upon taking a closer look, I also found remnants of wet paper in his shorts and in the sink. I knew immediately what had taken place. Alex's was back to his old bag of tricks, although this would become the last trick that he would play on me. I cleaned up the mess and went to walk the dogs for their morning bathroom run. During my walk along the bay, I had an epiphany and realized I could no longer live under these conditions and if I didn't do something about it immediately, eventually someone would be looking for me at the bottom of that same bay.

As I walked the babies, I came to the realization that Alex was never going to change his lying and cheating behavior. I was now left to decide which direction I was to turn. I began to cry as I was feeling extremely defeated and very sad for myself. All the effort that had gone into attempting to get our relationship on track was in vain. The large sum of our money that had been spent to support his recovery therapy for his sex addiction was also spent in vain. He was no closer to resolving his addiction then when he started seeking professional help. I had hit my limit of no return. I could not stomach another day of bullshit from this man and recall thinking that I was going to die if I stayed in the relationship any longer. I was suffering greatly from having to deal with the man that I loved lying to me to cover his dishonest ways. I was living on the edge of a disastrous outcome if I didn't put an immediate end to the madness. I was dangerously close to a mental breakdown that could easily be triggered by hearing one more little lie from Alex. This Humpty Dumpty couldn't survive another lie; otherwise I would never be able to put myself back together again. I felt truly unstable, although I now had to try to pull it together and use every ounce of energy I had left to deal with Alex and the tissue issue when I arrived back at the house. I thought that I would rather be homeless, pushing a shopping cart down the streets of San Francisco, than live in this disrespectful and messed up environment for another day. Later in life, when I reflected back on this day, I was grateful that God had another plan for me and it didn't include me becoming homeless and pushing a shopping cart.

By our standards, we had purchased a very expensive home and the mortgage payment was equally as expensive, over five thousand dollars a month. We owned three cars, a Jeep Cherokee, the E320 Mercedes that Alex leased and gave to me to drive, and a BMW sportster convertible that I leased and gave to Alex as a present. We also had credit card debt of thirty thousand dollars. We were very much financially tied to one another and a clean and speedy split was not going to be in the immediate cards. Alex and I were grossing over two hundred thousand dollars a year annually between the two of us, although our expenses were in line with our income. Our lifestyle was based on dual incomes to support and maintain it. A separation was going to be difficult and would result in a financial hardship for me, as Alex was then the main provider in the relationship. We had mutually agreed that he would be responsible for the bulk of the living expenses until I re-established myself professionally on the West Coast. I had given up my vice president position in Chicago and a six-figure income to build a life with him in the bay area. My base salary was fifty thousand dollars a year, which was substantially less than what I had been accustomed to earning. The upside to my current position was that I had the opportunity to increase my base salary substantially with the commission structure in my employment contract. However, building a new sales clientele normally takes one to two years and you need to be focused to build the business. Unfortunately, my focus had become my relationship and the screwed-up behavior that surrounded it.

As I walked back home, I thought...when it rains it pours. In my case, it was happening literally and figuratively. El Niño was raining buckets on California and Alex's rain of bullshit seemed to have no end. Would Humpty Dumpty fall and drown in the financial calamity of it all or would he float away, unbroken, to a safe place despite the reign of terror that was now engulfing my existence?

As I reflect on sex in a relationship, I believe that the mutually-agreed-upon rules that are set by two individuals in the beginning of their commitment are certainly that...rules that both individuals must follow and conduct themselves accordingly. Whatever the specifics of their commitment – whether it's a monogamous relationship, occasionally open to others, takes a 'whatever and whenever' approach, or follows a 'don't ask and don't tell' policy – I believe the key to the success of the arrangement is based on both parties honoring the agreement at all times. Unfortunately, in my case, Alex's approach was 'do as I say and not as I do'.

I had certainly been exposed to temptation during my relationship with Alex. I had traveled to Washington, DC for an installation project for an international accessory client that was based in London. I had to install a new store fixture program in one of their stores in the capital. I was scheduled to perform the installation over the weekend and, since Rick and I had worked together in the past, I contracted him to join me to help get the fixtures installed.

After we completed our work and had a successful installation, Rick and I decided to check out the local gay scene on Saturday evening, prior to retuning to San Francisco on Sunday. We went to Tracks, a great gay club, which I frequented in the past when I happened to be in the DC or the Baltimore area. It was huge, with numerous rooms and a large outdoor patio space with a sandy area where you could play volleyball during the summer months, certainly very popular on warm evenings, and it also had several dance floors and many bars spread out across various areas of the venue. After many drinks, I took off my shirt and Rick and I hit the main dance floor to join the wondrous cloud of lovely shirtless men dancing. To my amazement, a man of immense beauty and amazing stature emerged from the sea of men surrounding us. He was stunning, with a beautifully handsome face and an equally amazing body. Whoever said God does not tempt us, never met this man. Possibly he was an angel from heaven sent to seduce me into his lustful splendor. I now had a dilemma. The gorgeous man was expressing his interest in me and, as I was very interested and extremely attracted to this vision of a man, every desire in my body was telling me to accept his advances. I was overwhelmed with lust and wanted to experience every inch of him. As he flirted with me, I wondered how Alex would feel if he found out that I had cheated on him…so I did not accept or reciprocate the advances from the interested Adonis. This was the difference between Alex and me.

I was certainly not above cheating on Alex and enjoying this beautiful man for all that he had to offer, although I was above making the conscious decision to hurt Alex in this way. A successful relationship is based on what you're willing to sacrifice of yourself for your partner. In this case, my dick wanted to come out and play, although it wasn't in control of making my decisions; I was. At the time, it seemed to register as a major sacrifice on my part to pass up such an opportunity with this handsome stranger, in light of Alex's behavior, although, despite all his lies, he still meant more to me than my sexual desires that this man could fulfill this evening. Even after all the bullshit and lies that had transpired between us, the immense love that I had for him overrode any sexual desire that the world had to offer. I was able to respect the boundaries that Alex and I agreed upon—and cheating on Alex was not a boundary that I was willing to cross. Even though I had traveled across the entire United States and was standing in a place where temptation was staring me in the face, I didn't let my dick rule my actions. I was not willing to gamble the morality of our relationship on a one-night stand, although I certainly wanted to do just that at that moment in time.

As I continued walking back to the house to confront Alex about the tissue I found in the bathroom, I recall knowing right away what the tissue was all about upon seeing the pieces of wet paper. Some weeks earlier, I had confronted Alex about the semen stains that I found in several pairs of his underwear when I was doing laundry and he had explained away the accusation as being part of a urinary infection. A few days after that confrontation, Alex had come home with the prescription from the doctor to treat his so-called infection. I certainly understood that after a man ejaculates, additional semen may flow out afterward. Usually the additional discharge takes place for a few minutes after they've gotten off. During my single years, I often placed tissue in my underwear to catch any drips of post coital cum so that I didn't have a stain or a disgusting wet feeling in my underwear. Based on my own experience, and on my previous finding of semen stains in Alex's underwear, I knew exactly what he was doing. As I had done, he placed the tissue in his underwear to catch any semen after he had sex on his way home from the office on the previous evening. He was trying to hide any evidence that he had gotten off prior to coming home. When he arrived, he had forgotten that he placed the tissue in his briefs. The wine that we were drinking at dinner probably made him forget. After dinner, Alex had taken off his clothes down to his underwear and gotten in the Jacuzzi, resulting in the wet tissue that I later found on the floor, with the remaining tissue still in the underwear that he threw into the sink. It's laughable. Alex thought he was so slick in covering his tracks, but it just goes to prove that Fate had another agenda for Alex and it didn't include allowing him to lie to me any longer.

Upon finishing my walk with the boys, after much soul searching about what I was going to do with this new evidence, I came to the conclusion that I was done with the relationship. I felt like I was standing in a valley of bullshit that was neck high and if I didn't end my involvement with him, I was soon going to suffer unbearable consequences. Whatever the outcome of my decision to seek a better life, I needed to get out of this relationship. At this point, I believe there was an intervention from beyond and my story became larger than myself. When I opened the door from the garage that led into the house, I could see Alex standing next to the island in the kitchen. It was strange to see him out of bed and in the kitchen so early in the morning. He looked like he knew something was up, although, how could he know what

I found on the bathroom floor? From where I was standing, I could also see the television in the den and could see and hear Cher talking about *Believe*, her new album that had just been released. As I entered the house, I heard her say "if you believe in yourself, there's nothing that you cannot achieve." This message coming from the television sounded like an angel declaring words of wisdom. It seemed as if God was using Cher's voice at that exact moment to send me a message that I needed to hear – via someone that I would embrace as inspiration – so that I would do what I needed to do to return sanity back into my existence. I did believe in myself at one point in my life and then Alex fed me so many lies that I was no longer confident that I could make the correct choices for myself. At that moment, Alex evoked an image of a poltergeist of lies and deception. He would soon try, once again, to prevent me from making the healthy choices that I needed to make to get my life back on the right track. As Cher began to sing, she sounded like an angel sent through the television, encouraging me to exorcise Alex from the kitchen and from my life.

I wanted to believe in myself once again and have the opportunity to be happy—and I embraced Cher's words of encouragement. I knew deep down in my heart that I deserved a better life partner than the one that had been lying to me. While I now believe that God speaks to us in many ways, I was then faced with answering the single most important question of my life at that moment on my own. Was I going to believe the words that had just come from the television? In my mind, the timing of hearing Cher's words that day and at the exact moment of my walking back into the house was not a random coincidence. I had not begun – nor was I thinking about – seeking a relationship with God during that time so I believe God knew that I was not listening for his voice to guide me to a safe place. But He knew I would listen to Cher…so, in my mind, the timing of Cher's album release combined with her interview at this exact moment was like receiving a prophecy. The words that I heard through the television were instrumental in inspiring and motivating me to believe in myself at a time when I was lost and confused and when I really didn't believe I was strong enough to pull away from Alex on an emotional and financial level. This brief incident with Cher was the beginning of several messages that I felt God delivered to me, using the success of her career, at a time when I needed the inspiration the most. Without ever knowing, Cher would eventually lead me to seek out BoBo once again and begin a relationship with Him.

I believe that Cher's inspirational words are a perfect example of how influential and successful people can be a positive influence on an individual's life. This is especially true for people that are seeking a role model, and who do not have a relationship with God. A spiritual journey may take someone decades – in my case it took almost a half a century – before I found my way to the promise of what God had to offer. At the time of hearing Cher's words,

I had followed Alex to the gates to hell. I now believe God will use all things to rescue us from entering through the gates of our own hell; we just need to ensure that we're listening for his voice or, in my case, that of his messenger, Cher. I'll forever be grateful to God for sending Cher to intervene on His behalf.

Upon removing the dog's leashes, as I began to put them away in the closet, Alex asked me what I wanted for breakfast. I responded that I wanted nothing from him. After my rude retort, he asked me what was wrong, as he deduced from my demeanor that I was upset about something. I was quick to confront him about the tissue that I found on the bathroom floor and in his underwear. I don't remember the exact story he came up with to explain the tissue, but I recall it was another bullshit fairytale. I called him a liar and walked up stairs to make the bed. He followed me, maintaining his innocence as I continued to accuse him of cheating once again. After repeatedly stating that I was done with him cheating on me and all the bullshit that accompanied the web of lies that he told to cover it all up, I asked him to stop professing his innocence as it was an insult to my intelligence. As he continued, I become increasingly angrier every time he insisted he had done no wrong.

Alex then did something unusual. He changed his story, which is something that a professional liar never does. Changing the original version of his story was a sign of weakness in his so-called truth about how the tissue had gotten in his underwear. This would be the first time in three-and-a half years that Alex ever changed his story from his original telling. He finally realized I was not bluffing about leaving the relationship, so he felt compelled to give me a different variation that I could sallow as the truth. He confessed that he masturbated in the bathroom at work before coming home and used the toilet tissue in the bathroom so as to not leave a stain in his underwear. This new version was a good attempt on his part to tell a story that I would buy into, although I did not believe it for a minute. I stayed strong and this was the end.

I always sincerely believed that he was truly in love with me, but I would not come to fully understand the depth of his love until we were living apart and in different cities. After he and I broke up, I realized that even though he may have loved me deeply, he didn't love me enough to change his behavior. In the final months of our relationship, I had come to realize that his infidelity was secondary to the web of lies that he had been spinning. The many lies – and the grand nature of those lies – that were being fed to me regularly had taken a major toll on my emotional well-being. I had begun to question the intentions of everything and everyone with whom I came in contact.

A day after our confrontation, he left for another business trip and our relationship would be officially over. Several months later, Alex finally admitted what took place. Upon returning from his trip, before heading home from his San Francisco office, he decided to stop off at a gay adult theater in Nob Hill. He got his rocks off in the theater and that's where he put the tissue in his shorts to hide any resulting evidence. To the end of our relationship, Alex's behavior was representative of a child's schoolyard rhyme… "Liar, liar, pants on fire; Alex's nose was a long as a telephone wire."

My life became very complicated after Alex and I broke up. I finally understood why people stay in bad relationships. In many circumstances having to go through a painful breakup is almost worse than staying together. I also learned that sometimes we need to go through some tough times to have hope of achieving something better for our lives. "Do you believe in life after love?" Yes, Cher, I do…and there is life after love, although life without love is hardly a life at all.

For all the craziness that transpired between us, the love that I had for Alex would be an invaluable life experience. Despite it all, Alex had many attributes that I loved very deeply, though some that I certainly could have lived without. In his defense, I had my own shortcomings and could have worked on becoming a better person while we were together. Although, there was a big difference between Alex's behavior and mine—I was not lying or cheating on him even when given the opportunity to do so. The fact that Alex was having sex outside of our relationship did not make him a bad man; it just made him a bad choice of a partner for me. His behavior was contrary to what I wanted in a monogamous relationship. I wanted a relationship with Alex, minus the cheating and the lies to cover it up. Was I asking too much of him? Yes, because Alex was not willing to overcome his addiction to achieve what we both agreed upon. As a wise woman once sang, "'Coz when love ain't blessed. And it's laid to rest. It can leave a mess."

After Alex left the house for his business trip, we would not see each other for three months, even though we both continued to live in the house in San Rafael. When Alex was traveling on business, I would stay at the house. When Alex returned home, I scheduled sales meetings in other states and would be in the car in route to catch my flight shortly after he landed at the San Francisco airport. As I returned, Alex would be on his way back to the airport. Somewhere along the freeway, we would pass one another. After three months of this back and forth, I received an email from Alex informing me that he was moving out of our house and out of the Bay area. He had requested a transfer to his company's office in Los Angeles and his request had been approved.

Like so many things that took place between us, he did not give me a heads-up nor did he discuss his decision with me prior to making it. I had two days to get our financials in order—in preparation for an in-person meeting between us, before he departed to Los Angeles. We needed to discuss and settle our finances, including selling the house. Since we only lived in the house for a year, most of our cash was tied up in the down payment. Now, it needed to be listed with a realtor and placed on the market. We needed to time the sale of the house two years after we had bought it, otherwise we would be required to pay capital gains on the income that we would potentially net on the sale. As we met, I thought how Fate had a strange sense of humor. I was the one that had hoped to eventually move to Los Angeles with Alex, but that was no longer a possibility. The sex-addicted nut was flying off to the Land of Oz to taste the many beautiful and delicious fruits that LA had to offer, while I was left to clean up the mess that he had created for the two of us.

But I had a card up my sleeve.

I gave up my career in Chicago and decided to follow Alex to the bay area under one condition. I asked Alex for a written financial agreement that would protect me financially if our relationship failed. Prior to moving to San Rafael, I approached an attorney who put together a legally binding document that required Alex to cover certain expenses for a period of one year, should we break up. Alex, who wanted me to move to California with him, agreed and signed the document. I was very much in love with Alex and wanted our relationship to work, but I was skeptical that he could curb his bad behavior and something told me to get an insurance policy for myself.

It turned out to be a prophetic and wise decision, as I was very concerned about making our financial ends meet once we split up. We would soon be living in two different homes, in two different cities, with twice the monthly expenses. It wasn't just going to be a financial burden…it was also going to be an emotional roller-coaster ride. I was now damaged goods, daily sorting through the lies in my mind that Alex told while we were together and trying to make sense of them. I started drifting aimlessly in the valley of deceit that Alex had created for me and soon I would descend recklessly into an abyss of self-medication to get me through the days, nights, weeks, months, years and decade that lay ahead of me. Alex's dishonesty really messed me up and it would take almost a decade and two therapists before I would stop living in a paranoid state of mind.

But God works in mysterious ways. I believe our subconscious takes over when our mind has hit its limit of what it can handle…and I wonder if this is part of what they mean when they say that God works in mysterious ways. Does God play a role in our subconscious? Is our subconscious a safety mechanism that He has built into us for our own safety, allowing him to guide us to a safe place when we are not capable of looking after ourselves? In the year to come, I believe God worked overtime to get me to a better place, although I wasn't even conscious that He was there and working in my life. In the midst of my being lost, paranoid, and doing drugs, prescription and illegal, to numb the pain to get me though the day, God was present and – unbeknownst to me – he was building upon that early foundation that had been laid by my parents and grandmother. At this time in my life, the concept of God was certainly a simple concept for me to understand, although the reality of God, and how he could be present in my life, was impossible for me to comprehend from where I was standing.

In my efforts to hold myself together emotionally, I was terrified that someone with whom Alex had a sexual encounter might want to take out his frustrations on Puckles, Papi or me, as a result of their being used by Alex. I was overly protective of the boys, as I was afraid of the unknown. I didn't know how many individuals Alex was having sex with – while we were together and living in the Bay area – nor did I know who these people were…and I didn't know what they knew about me. I didn't want to get caught back up in a situation where I would ultimately end up being hurt or having someone potentially try to harm Puckles and Papi to get back at Alex for hurting them, as he had hurt me. I suppose I was paranoid that another shoe was yet to drop. Like the nursery rhyme about the "Old Lady that lived in a shoe and had so many children, she didn't know what to do," I lived with an old whore that had so many tricks I didn't know what to do.

Music had a big influence, and was of great comfort to me, in the darks days that followed. I found great solace in hearing beautiful women sing ballads that encouraged my heart. They sounded like angels from heaven, sent to comfort my hurting soul.

Well there's a bridge and there's a river that I still must cross
As I'm going on my journey
Oh, I might be lost

And there's a road I have to follow, a place I have to go
Well no-one told me just how to get there
But when I get there I'll know
Cuz I'm taking it

Step By Step, Bit by Bit, Stone By Stone, Brick by Brick
Step By Step, Day By Day, Mile by mile

And this old road is rough and ruined
So many dangers along the way
So many burdens might fall upon me
So many troubles that I have to face

Oh, but I won't let my spirit fail me
Oh, I won't let my spirit go
Until I get to my destination…

Whitney Houston

I was so entrenched in what I needed to do to maintain our financial responsibilities that it was a daily battle for me just to make it out of bed and to work on time each morning. With the layers upon layers of emotional baggage that I carried out of this relationship, I leaned on my friend Tina once again to comfort me through these troubling times.

After my breakup, I learned one very important lesson. As I attempted to rebuild my life, I could not look past the immediate tasks at hand and focused on the immediate things I needed to do. I felt that if I looked at everything that I needed to accomplish to financially separate us, it would have overwhelmed me. Rebuilding a life that did not include Alex was a devastating reality that I had to overcome—and there were times when I would've preferred to die in San Rafael than endure all the tribulations that need to be conquered to recreate my professional, financial, personal, and emotional life. Before it was all over, I would consider putting an end to my misery.

I stood at the top of the stairs on the second floor of the house in San Rafael and thought of the effort that it was going to take to unwind us financially. Since Alex had ran off to Los Angeles, it was now my responsibility to list and show the house, which was now up for sale, ensure that we paid our credit cards until the house sold, sort out the finances on the three cars that we owned, divide the furniture, and pack my belongings to move to a new place that I was yet to find. I felt like I was climbing an enormous mountain and needed to find a way to get myself out of the valley of depression that was engulfing me and to the top of that mountain.

In my depression, the terrain ahead of me seemed overwhelming and treacherous. I worried that my footing could give away at any time and I would find myself falling toward financial disaster that would place me in bankruptcy. At the top of the stairs, I decided that I would rather take an alternate route out of the valley, which seemed like a viable solution to the problem. I would rather kill myself than go through the pain of climbing out of the valley and conquering the mountain of troubles that I faced. It seemed such a simple and swift answer to a very complicated problem. But I failed to consider what would happen to Puckles and Papi if I were not alive to care for them. I thought that Alex would probably get custody—and I knew he didn't want them, nor would he take care of them. He probably would've given them away to another home. What was I to do? I loved these little guys; they were my little boys and if I was the responsible father I always considered myself to be, I would be compelled to put my crap aside for the moment and take care of them in the best manner possible. Their well-being was now dependent on me getting my shit together and being there to care for them. So, I concentrated on one task at a time and realized that with each task completed, I would find myself a little closer to my salvation on that mountain. Had I focused on the larger picture, I would've never taken the first step to attempt to rebuild my life.

I know that God knew I was not listening for his voice, nor was I seeking his guidance, but He knew that by placing these much-loved dogs in my life, when he did, He would prevent me later from going over the edge and hurting myself. As I stood at the top of the stairs, I decided I had to go on, not for myself, but for these little guys that loved me and were depending on me. Puckles and Papi saved my life that day and I'll forever love them for that along with a million other reasons. They were not only my best friends, but I believe they were sent by God through Alex to be my savior in my time of despair. God used the person that I was going to end my life over to bring Puckles and Papi into my life to keep me from hurting myself. Assuredly, God's ways are not our ways.

Without ever realizing it at the time, Fate would use my experience with Alex as a teaching moment. Over a decade later, I would realize that the conditions I endured during the Alex years were for a much greater cause. There was a larger plan for all that pain and betrayal. I began to understand that the journey with him was not without purpose and now believe it was Fate that brought us together. Eventually, she would lead me to a specific point in my self-discovery, utilizing the demons that had been unleashed by the lies and self-doubt of my relationship with Alex. These demons would ultimately bring me closer to something that I had no idea I even wanted.

9 | PLAYING THE WILD CARD

I'm certainly no prude by any stretch of the imagination, although I believe there is a time and a place for everything. The sexual insanity that surrounded my relationship with Alex, and the ensuing consequences, resulted in my becoming much more conservative in expressing my sexuality. The gay male testosterone that surrounded any potential relationship with another man now turned me off. I was paranoid that I would meet or hook up with someone that Alex had screwed around with while we were together. I became leery of people and had issues in differentiating an individual's motives. I isolated myself from any sexual encounters with men to protect myself from any further emotional damage, afraid that any sexual energy might manifest into something more.

Even though sex was a turn off at this time, I became a wild card nonetheless. In my free time, when I was not working or at the gym, I was frequenting gay bars and clubs to numb my pain. I just wanted to get high and loose myself in the music and enjoy the DJ's performance at whatever venue I happened to be at that evening. For the next five years, I would spend the majority of my free time with hundreds of other gay partygoers in any of San Francisco's clubs and danced my grief away with my numerous and anonymous shirtless friends until the wee hours of the morning. Partying in San Francisco became a lifestyle for me. I was missing Alex so much and I was trying to forget him and trying to drown the demons of self-doubt and paranoia that occupied my mind—working overtime to distract myself so I didn't have to deal with my heavy emotional baggage.

Shortly after we split, the New York-based start-up company that I was working for began to experience cash flow issues. My business expense reimbursements and paychecks began to show up late, which I was not in a financial position to handle…so I began to look for other work. Interviewing for a new job is a difficult experience and when you're seeking a position in the six-figure range it becomes even more difficult due to the intensity of the interview process. I now found myself having to interview with potential new employers even as I was broken-hearted, self-medicating, under financial duress to meet my obligations…and partying way too much. I had to pull my shit together to present myself in a positive manner, which was almost more than I could handle.

Once again, I believe God showed up on the scene at the right time. My subconscious took control of my body and allowed me to get my act together enough to make a positive first impression on a potential employer in the Bay area. Shortly after completing a second interview with the same company, I was offered a position, which I accepted. My new job in sales had a huge positive impact on my life and took some of the financial pressure off my plate. Securing a new position during this difficult time was nothing short of a miracle and was another representation of God's grace in my life.

Despite this good news, I was an emotional mess – by any definition of the word – and I constantly found myself in a chaotic state. I worried about meeting my monthly obligations and so my focus became to survive financially. I had no time to work on my emotional problems; I needed to focus all my energies on becoming successful in my new job and selling the house in San Rafael. Since Alex had moved to Los Angeles, I was left to maintain the house and keep the landscaping in a presentable manner for any possible real estate showings—which was made more tedious by my constant partying.

I was also left with the responsibility of cleaning up our financial mess and I was keen to not lose any money on the assets that we gathered in the three-and-a-half years that we were together. I was envious and resentful that he was able to move to Los Angeles and begin a new life while I was still living in the shadows of the one we had together. Once he arrived in Southern California, he spent ten thousand dollars to have his teeth veneered. Shortly after improving his smile, he traded in the BMW 4-cylinder convertible that I bought for him and purchased the same car in a newer 8-cylinder model, a much more expensive car than the one I had bought for him. I found myself conflicted with mixed emotions over Alex's new life. On the one hand, I was broken-hearted and missing him with every breath I took, but on the other hand…I was jealous of his new life. He was living large in the Land of Oz and spreading his seed, while I was left to orchestrate and finalize our separation in a city that I had moved to because of him.

After I started my new job, I commuted fifty miles every day from San Rafael to San Carlos south of San Francisco. I would wake up at five thirty in the morning to get ready for work, walk the dogs, and make it to my new office by eight o'clock in the morning. Brad, who was the owner of the company and a few years younger than myself, was a stickler about arriving at work on time. I genuinely enjoyed working for him and having the opportunity to get to know him. While employed with his company, I would often make a joking reference to my friends that Brad was the closest thing I had to a new boyfriend at the time. He was very handsome and we shared many of the same interests…he dressed very fashionably, wore Chrome

Hearts jewelry, and drove expensive cars. What more could one want in a man? He was married to a lovely lady and they had two children. Over the three years I worked for Brad, I became increasingly fond of him.

When Cher sang "...when love ain't blessed and it's laid to rest it can leave a mess", she was not kidding. Alex and I had lived in the house in San Rafael for a year when we placed it for sale and, it being new construction, a number of issues came to light. The recessed interior sprinkler heads in the ceiling had been recalled by the manufacturer and they all needed to be replaced. Some heads were screwed on so tight that they had to cut holes in the drywall of the ceiling to remove them, requiring the drywall to be patched and painted. The limestone flooring in the kitchen and family room began to show signs of cracking. The contractor determined that all the deficient limestone that was installed in these two rooms needed to be jack hammered out and replaced. The shag carpet in all the rooms on the second floor was determined to have dry rot and all the wall-to-wall carpeting needed to be torn out and replaced. The house, like me, felt like it was falling apart.

In California, when reselling a house, you need to disclose all known issues when you list the home for sale, so these problems required immediate attention if we were going to get the most value from the sale. My hands were full. I found my new daily commute to be difficult and I struggled with trying to keep myself together emotionally and fix the issues with the house—all while trying to make a success of my new job. I was pissed that Alex had ran off on his responsibilities and became even more angry with my having to clean up the mess on my own while the sex-addicted playboy made his debut in Los Angeles.

Shortly after Alex moved to LA, a friend of mine sent me one of the gay rags, a local weekly magazine, from the West Hollywood area. It had a four-page spread, which included pictures of Alex sporting his new ten thousand dollar smile. The story detailed his arrival in the Land of Oz and his interest in getting acquainted with any curious fruitlets that had an interest in meeting him. I was not happy with the situation at all. I was putting forth all the effort to manage the repairs on the house to net us the best resale value as possible, while Alex was being featured in a photo spread of new hookers in Los Angeles.

A few months after seeing his photo in the gay rag, I discovered that he had been hooking up on a regular basis with a specific man when we lived in Chicago, prior to us moving to San Francisco. Even though I was pissed to have confirmation of this affair while we were together, it came as no surprise, as I always felt that Alex was seeing someone else while we were living in Chicago. Right after we broke up, Alex immediately turned to this guy for comfort. He had kept him on the hook until he moved to Los Angeles, but shortly after arriving there, he dumped the guy in the Midwest for a younger and more attractive model on the West coast. Imagine that.

A year after we split up, when the house in San Rafael sold, Alex bought a condo in West Hollywood with his new boyfriend. It would be seven years after Alex and I separated – and two major moves to other cities – before I would even consider dating again. In contrast, less than a year after our breakup, Alex had at least two boyfriends, that I knew about, and purchased a home with one of them. He certainly seemed to recover quickly from our split, but I wondered if he was just masking his insecurities by having someone at his side at all times. In either case, I was a tragic mess. I was extremely sad, but I was also majorly pissed off because it seemed that in a very brief time Alex had forgotten about me and the boys—and the life that we had together.

Looking back, I now realize that you certainly don't get to choose the person you fall in love with, but you do get to choose with whom you breakup. Even though Alex broke my spirit and made me lose my confidence, I was sure that I made the right decision in severing our relationship to pursue my own happiness. Much like the nursery rhyme where "all the king's horses and all the king's men couldn't put Humpy Dumpty back together again," I wondered if I could ever be whole again. I would come to learn, that, unlike Humpty – even when all else has failed – someone has the power to make people whole once again and could and would do just that, although, in my case, I would need to wait almost two more decades before having the opportunity to meet Him.

On the afternoon that Alex left forever, the only way I could accept that reality was to convince myself that we had to separate to sort through our problems. Like so many straight couples do, when they are having large issues in their relationship, they sometimes separate for a period in the hopes of resolving their problems and reuniting later. Today, when I look back, it seems that my subconscious knew that it was over between us, although my heart was not able to accept the reality of our breakup, so it created an illusion of a possible reconciliation.

On his way out the door that afternoon to his new life in Los Angeles, Alex said, "if you and the boys ever need anything, feel free to call me or call my office and I'll be sure to get back to you immediately." I've never forgotten those words. He also told me that he had received an increase in his salary now that he was moving to Los Angeles and would be making one hundred seventy thousand dollars a year. He was always impressed by the amount of money that he made and I was proud that he had achieved such a level of success while we were together. Money can't buy you happiness, and it certainly didn't buy it for us, although, for a time, it masked and diverted attention from the problems in our relationship. I had distracted myself by buying a larger and more expensive home, more expensive cars, and extravagant vacations, among other indulgences. I came to see money like air…the more you have, the easier it is to breathe—and after our breakup, I had become short of breath, as the majority of our household income left when Alex departed for the Land of Oz.

I believe most of us can probably agree on common adages that apply to life. I don't mean just typical statements that we've all heard before like "we all must pay taxes" or "we will all die one day." I'm referring to the fact that "life is not free." No matter how we pay our way through life, we must all pay our way by one mean or another. Now, when money seemed as necessary as precious air, Fate once again entered the room and began to perform mouth-to-mouth resuscitation—to give me enough additional cash to recover financially and lead me to economic freedom from Alex.

When Tim and I lived together, he would on occasion wake me up in the middle of the night and tell me that he loved me, give me a kiss, and then he would go back to sleep. Almost always, I too would fall immediate back to sleep upon hearing his words of love and receiving his kiss. When I woke up in the morning, I completely forgot about Tim waking me up in the midst of a sound sleep, but sometime during my day I would recall what he had done and it always brought a smile to my face. It still does. It was a lovely little gesture on his part that, while annoying in the middle of the night, was like a morning glory flower that blooms at dawn for one day.

One evening, after I had come home late from a night of partying, I called Alex in Los Angeles to wake him up and tell him that I loved him, as Tim had so frequently done with me. I was feeling melancholy and thought that it would be a wonderful act of love that I could share with Alex, giving him the same experience that I had felt when Tim bestowed this loving gesture on me. I called Alex at three o'clock in the morning. He did not pick up, but I left him a phone message explaining how Tim used to do this exact thing and I now wanted him to feel the same joy that it had brought me.

Several weeks later, I received a package in the mail from Alex. It contained a hand-blown, cobalt glass vase created by a designer in Australia. It turned out that he had left for vacation to Australia on the same day that I left him that message. He never returned my call, but he made the effort to buy me an item that he knew would appeal to me and had it sent to California, from the other side of the world, while he was on vacation. He had apparently received my message and I felt that this was his way of telling me that he too loved me. Now, many years after he sent me the vase, I look at it as I write this story and experience a similar feeling that I felt when Tim woke me up to tell me that he loved me. In some way, I still love Alex, or at the very least I'm in love with the idea that we both truly loved one another at some point…and maybe it took us breaking up to realize how much we really did care for one another.

One year after our breakup, we finally had an offer on the house and, shortly after receiving the offer, we were finally financially free from one another. With the proceeds from the sale, we paid off our mutual credit card debt and settled the dual legal ownership of the vehicles. It was a long drawn out process, which took every ounce of energy that I had and it seemed nothing short of another miracle. Now that the house was sold, I took residence south of the Golden Gate Bridge, in San Francisco, and said bye-bye to Marin County and hello to San Francisco.

For all the craziness surrounding Alex's behavior, his sex addiction, and the web of lies that he spun, I do give him credit for one main thing. He absolutely, without exception, lived up to his commitment in honoring our financial agreement until the house was sold. He paid out sixty thousand dollars in the year that we were separated, which went toward paying the mortgage on the house and its upkeep, as well as the payments on the Mercedes.

Timing once again played a very important role in my life. It had been extremely difficult for me to manage all the repairs on the house, keep it presentable for showings to potential buyers, maintain the grounds on the weekends, manage the hundred mile commute each day, while mustering the energy that went into building a new sales clientele at my new job—and mending my broken heart. Certainly, the expression "what doesn't kill you, makes you stronger" applied in my situation. I had endured about as much as I could handle and just when I believed I could take no more and I was losing hope of selling the house for a profit and minimizing my daily commute, Fate showed up with a cash buyer in tow and salvation arrived in the form of a check from the buyer's mortgage company. Once again, I could breathe easily. I was thrilled that we were finally free from one another and the timing of the sale generated the biggest return for us, as we netted one hundred and sixty thousand dollars from the sale and because I had occupied the house for two years, maximizing our capital gains and minimizing the tax that needed to be paid on those gains.

As I was getting ready to move out of the house, I found out about one final and outlandish story regarding Alex's sexual shenanigans, while we were together, that further illustrates the great depths of the poor behavior that he engaged in to feed his addiction. About a month after Alex and I had placed the house in San Rafael under contract, we had to choose the finishes for the house. When we arrived at the model home that also served as the design center for the complex, we were met by our relator, a very stylish older woman, and her gay assistant, who was about my age or just a little younger. At some point, as we were walking the house with the relator, she and I made it to the upstairs master bathroom where we discussed the tile finishes, bathroom fixtures, and the glass shower doors, which took a considerable amount of our time. Alex and her gay assistant were nowhere to be found and I didn't give it much thought.

It turned out that they were downstairs in the powder room on the first floor of the model home, where the realtor's assistant was giving Alex a blowjob, while I was upstairs choosing finishes for our new home. I expect that if you asked Alex about this incident, his reply would echo President Clinton's famous reply that he "did not have sexual relations," as a blowjob was not considered to be having sex in President Clinton's or Alex's vocabulary. In either case, President Clinton was Hilary's problem and thank God and all the angels in heaven, Alex was no longer mine.

Today, I can laugh about the messed-up behavior that engulfed my relationship with Alex and the various messed up situations in which I found myself. Then, I would spend the next five years in San Francisco trying to rehabilitate myself back to a point where I was able to stand on my own two feet without looking over my shoulder every time I sensed fear in the air. I feared anyone that would potentially play me for a fool again. I became very confrontational with everyone that I suspected of foul play. This behavior lasted for many years and became a stumbling block for me in my professional career. I was now an angry bird attacking anyone that seemed to be a possible threat to Puckles, Papi, or me.

Shortly after moving to San Francisco, I met Danny, who was the first man I had sex with after my breakup. Having sex with Danny was a big deal for me at the time and I'll always remember him for being so kind to me when I was so emotionally fragile. Danny was Hispanic, very cute, and younger than me. He was looking for a boyfriend when we met and I was certainly not in a position to offer him a healthy relationship due to my emotional baggage. We hooked up on several occasions for fun, but I always kept my distance to refrain from getting emotionally involved. I was leery of most gay men and questioned their true intentions. He and I eventually drifted away from one another, although on occasion we would run into each other when we both were out clubbing.

One Saturday evening, I ran into Danny at Club Universe, my favorite gay dance club in San Francisco that I frequented. It was my home away from home every Saturday evening and sometimes on Sundays. I loved Club Universe. It was an amazing venue in what was then the city's warehouse district. It was a joyous place where I could escape and lose myself in the rhythm of the dance music that played until the early hours of the morning. All good things frequently come to an end and the club is now gone and, if it still stood today, its backside would be across the street from AT&T stadium. While the club is no longer in existence, the outstanding memories and the phenomenal times I spent there will stay with me for the rest of my life.

Danny had met a man that he had been dating for some time, but on this occasion, he was out alone and I suspected they might have had an argument. He approached me on the dance floor and while we were both high, we were very much coherent and embraced one another with a big hug. He began to tell me about an argument that he and his boyfriend had that night. Danny believed that when a couple is in a relationship the love that they have for one another should be unconditional and the boyfriend disagreed with his philosophy. I thought that Danny must have done something inappropriate and was looking for his boyfriend to forgive him. Based on what I had been through with Alex, I felt like I could offer Danny some advice when it came to boundaries surrounding relationships.

I probed his definition of unconditional love and posed a question to him. If he and his partner had children – I asked him – and his partner intentionally harmed their children in some physical way, would Danny still love him unconditionally? Danny replied that yes, he would, without a doubt. I then corrected him on his answer. I told him that I concurred with his belief that there're truly no limits to the level of love that we can experience with another, although there are certain boundaries within that love that should not be crossed. Intentionally harming one's children was one of those boundaries that should never be crossed—and that should be a condition of any relationship involving children, one that must be honored. Danny went on to reiterate that he would still love his boyfriend unconditionally even if the boyfriend harmed their children. Even though I was high, I felt that Danny's thought process was fucked up. I knew he was not a bad person, he was just looking for a way to justify his poor behavior with his boyfriend. At that moment, I walked away and left him standing on the dance floor alone after our conversation ended abruptly. I never saw or spoke to him again.

I recall being very upset over my encounter with Danny and I relayed the conversation that had just taken place to Rick, who was out with me, as he was most of the time. As always, Rick indulged me and listened to my ranting and raving over Danny while nodding his head as if he agreed with what I was saying. He was high himself and the music was so loud in the club most of the time that he really could not understand me or hear me clearly. Although, being the good friend that he was he would politely nod his head, as if he agreed with whatever I was telling him. I was still dealing with my many demons and this frequently resulted in a confrontation with someone at the club, on many of our nights out. Today, Rick and I laugh about these evenings and we mostly remember the fun we had.

On the night I saw Danny for the last time, I believe I experienced a spiritual encounter of some kind. I had been coming to Club Universe every Saturday night for years—when something happened that never took place before that night or since. I was a regular at the club and I was extremely familiar with the lay of the land and the things that management would allow to take place inside and outside the club. Rick and I left the venue that night at three o'clock in the morning and I saw a flower stand outside the club's entrance, as we exited. It consisted of three rows of buckets. There were about five or six buckets in each row and each bucket had its own type of flower, with fifteen to eighteen different types of flowers or bouquets.

The flower stand had never been outside the club prior to that evening nor did it ever show up again in the years that I patronized the venue. I approached the flower stand and discovered that the flowers being sold were to generate money for abused children. Seeing this stand at the club and its timing blew my mind at that moment and the situation still amazes me to this day. Some will argue that this was a simple coincidence and nothing more. However, I would have to say, it was not a coincidence in any way, shape, or form. Possibly it was a happenstance and I happened to be standing exactly where God wanted me to be standing, at the exact time he wanted me to be standing there. I wholeheartedly believe that some divine presence was sending me a message of confirmation, as if heaven was in agreement with my belief that true love is not without conditions.

One evening, while living in San Francisco, I had a dream that I lost my wallet and a car hit Papi. While I would consider both of these situations to be a nightmare, Papi getting hit by a car would be my ultimate nightmare. The following day, as I walked Puckles and Papi to the park for one of their daily walks, Papi suddenly began to chase after another dog, running into the street, where an oncoming car hit him. Papi suffered no major injuries, but this incident proved to me that there is certainly more to our dreams than we can logically explain.

As if this incident was not enough drama for one day, later that afternoon, I took the boys to Dolores Park. I didn't lose my wallet, as I had dreamt the night before, although I did lose something of great importance to me. While playing with them, I somehow lost my cellular phone chasing Puckles in the park. I was somewhat astonished that both situations that I had dreamt about the previous evening took place the following day.

On another occasion, when I was employed with Brad's company, I also dreamt that Brad's father, who I had recently met, had a heart attack. The following morning, when I arrived at the office, Brad informed me that his mother had a heart attack the previous evening. Initially, I thought Brad was messing with me. How could he have known about my dream the night before? I wondered if my dream took place at the exact time she was experiencing her heart pains. These dreams unnerved me and had a profound effect on me. Did these events have a greater meaning? Is there a divine connection to our subconscious when we're dreaming? In other words, does God speak to us when we're sleeping? Was my dream a vision from heaven? I can only hazard to guess.

Martin Luther King Jr. famously stated that he had a dream. I was only three years old when he declared these words on the steps of the Lincoln Memorial in Washington, DC. Thirty-seven years later, I would hear his voice proclaiming that dream when out partying at Club Universe. As the dance music played, the club's DJ began to interject the "I have a dream" portion of King's speech into the music. Hearing Mr. King's booming and recognizable voice in the club when he proclaimed "I have a dream" was unforgettable. The style in which the DJ mixed his inspirational words with the music was truly a spiritual experience. The phenomenal performance by the DJ left an everlasting impression on me and to this day, when I recall the experience, it still brings a smile to my face. The power of Mr. King's words, as he proclaimed his dream for a better life, combined with Cher's message to "Believe" were just the words of encouragement that I needed to hear during that time.

I was trying to embrace my own dream of a better life, but the tribulations of my relationship with Alex made it difficult. Prior to meeting him, I naturally believed in the goodness of the human race, but after we split up, I became very leery of individuals and got *spooked* easily. I no longer trusted people and I suspected everyone of potentially having bad motives. I no longer trusted my gut. My overly sensitive nature to being wronged affected all aspects of my life and, as my intuition was on overdrive, I eventually began to ignore it deliberately. I was experiencing a great deal of self-doubt and I became more and more confused about my feelings. I needed a place to escape and seek refuge…and Club Universe became that place where I could seek solitude, which is certainly a contradiction since I was surrounded by hundreds of other gay men.

In a church, a temple, or a mosque – even though many others may surround us – we can focus our attention on God and not on our surroundings. By focusing on God in a crowed place we can perceive to experience a feeling of solitude, even when we are not alone. In this way, Club Universe was like church to me. It provided me with a spiritual experience, with the DJ controlling the room, much like a priest does in a church. The music that the DJ spun was the sermon that was being preached that evening and I experienced a heightened spiritual awareness on my many evenings there, depending on the DJ's performance. Every Saturday evening, which would turn into Sunday morning, you could find me at the club. I was desperately searching for a place within myself where I could come to terms with what had happened and achieve some peace of mind. Ironically, I found my peace and solitude in the loudest place imaginable—a place where I obtained solace from hearing the beautiful words of wisdom spun by a DJ and from the energy that was being generated from the crowd within the room in response to his performance.

The club was an unconventional means of discovering a relationship with God, but I believe He is frequently found in unconventional places. My life was in disarray and I was not focused nor was I seeking a relationship with Him; I was just trying my best to keep my head on straight while attempting to mend my broken spirit. At Club Universe, I can emphatically recall experiencing a presence surrounding me on many of my party nights. Even though I couldn't see or touch what I was feeling, I felt its presence. If I closed my eyes and reached out, I felt like I could touch whatever it was, it felt that close to me, although I could not see it and it was always just out of reach.

I like to think that I experienced God's presence for the first time on the dance floor at Club Universe. I sensed that the shaman DJ was able to somehow manifest His presence within me, or around me, with the words of encouragement and love that were streaming out of the speakers. The voices sounded like angels singing from heaven. While this may rile church goers and cause them to get their panties in a bunch, there is little to no difference in a DJ's performance compared to the faith music that is performed in churches. Does it not make sense that God would be found in a club filled with lost souls? Is it a coincidence that in New York and in London, I had danced at Limelight, which were former churches that had been converted into dance clubs? One year, I even spent Christmas Eve dancing at the Limelight in New York. Was all this just another coincidence or was this all a means to a greater encounter that would come to fruition many years later?

I now believe that God has no boundaries when it comes to reaching out to his creations and I believe He will show up at the least likely places and at the least likely times to let His presence be known, and yes, I also believe this includes dance clubs around the world.

I envision a place where the birds and the bees will love the flowers and the trees, the outside comes to live inside and the inside comes to live outside, dark becomes the light and light becomes the dark, in the end, I dream of a place where we can all dance together, inside the house, a place where we all can play and live together, outside the house, for love is where the dog lives.

A PARABLE | FOUR-OF-A-KIND

King of Hearts

I believe God represents love and with love comes hope. Hope to the poor that God will provide a way for a better life when there seems to be no other way for an improved existence. Hope to the sick that they will get well when doctors tell them that they will not. Hope to the lonely that God will send them a friend or a person to love them, when they have no one in their lives to show them love. God offers hope to the soon-to-be-new parents that their child will be born healthy. God allows me to have hope that I'm capable of telling a story that will engage your curiosity, when I've only read one book in my entire life.

Hope is a wonderful thing; it offers possibilities when there seem to be none. These possibilities can manifest into opportunities that can become our successes and ultimately bring us to a place where we can achieve our dreams and our goals. Without Hope to comfort us, where would that leave us? Certainly, if Hope was a person and had a gender, I believe it would be a woman, much like Fate, who could be her sister.

It's important to me that people who read my story are open to the idea that God is current and not just view Him as someone that they read about in antiquated stories from thousands of years ago. Through many adversities that I've encountered, I've come to believe that God is as relevant today as ever. If I'm correct, then He must have been the one that took a depressed, emotionally-abused, self-medicating, broken, angry, messed-up wretch like me and was able to delicately and forcefully unveil the ultimate purpose that was intended for me. By unconventional methods, God revealed His presence, which captured my mind and my inner spirit and led me to pursue something that I didn't even know I was interested in pursuing. He enlightened my spirit through an encounter with Hope for a better life—while Fate brought my friend Lance and I together for a much greater cause then either of us realized.

King of Spades

After I wrote chapter eight in this book, I began searching for the name of chapter nine. All chapters are named after a playing card, some type of card game, or gambling expression. I thought about the Four Horseman that are mentioned in the Bible, which led me to the gambling expressions known as *Four-of-a-kind* or *Four Kings*, before ultimately settling on *Playing the Wild Card.* The day after deciding on the name for chapter nine, I went to a theater with Lance to see the movie *Now You See Me.* This was the only occasion I went to the movies with him during the time we knew each other. A few weeks after seeing the film, he would be murdered. As I began to write chapter eleven of this book, Lance had died. Chapter eleven is devoted to Lance and tells the story of how I came to know him.

In my mind, the movie *Now You See Me* has great significance and I associate it with the common expression that goes "now you see me and now you don't." A few weeks after viewing this movie with Lance, I wouldn't have the opportunity to see him again, at least in this life. Connecting the title of a movie to Lance's passing may seem like a stretch of the imagination and I would have to agree with you—if this was the only unusual situation that occurred shortly before his murder. It was not; it was only the beginning of many unusual and coincidental circumstances that depict a pattern that – in the final analysis – will show that there was more to Lance's life path than can be explained by ordinary means. For those of you who are not familiar with the film, it's about four magicians that come together to form a single act in Las Vegas. I had seen the trailer advertising the film prior to seeing it in the theater, although I had no idea that the name of their act was The Four Horseman until I saw the actual movie. Even though I didn't end up using The Four Horseman as the title of chapter nine, this coincidence felt like something was telling me that this story was on the right track.

King of Clubs

There is another movie, *The Truman Show,* to which I also relate. In the movie, Truman is a man whose life seems to be real on the surface, although he feels like there's more to his life than what meets the eye. As he goes about his daily routines, he begins to experience coincidental events that begin to unnerve him. In actuality, Truman lives in a large movie set with hidden cameras everywhere, watching and recording his every move. Truman thinks that he is an ordinary man living an ordinary life and has no idea that he's being filmed and his life is being viewed by a TV audience. Truman becomes unhappy and feels like there's something that he's missing. He begins to yearn to see more of the world. Eventually, he begins to pay closer attention to his surroundings, which leads him to discover that he has been living in a world that is a lie.

Until I began to pursue a relationship with God, my life seemed like one never-ending lie. As early as I can remember, I was attracted to the same sex, although I had to convince the people around me that I was attracted to the opposite sex. When I finally was able to embrace that I was gay, I became positive and had to act like I was negative. When I fell in love with the man I believed to be my soul mate, he cheated on me and did it so frequently that I began to lie to myself about what was going on. The shame that I felt from being gay, then being positive, and later having a partner that lied to me consistently, led me to live a life shrouded in lies. Until one day, I turned away from living that never-ending lie and embraced a story that required a great deal of exploration on my part to discover the truth. In my pursuit to find that truth, I would need to love again. How does a broken-hearted man that is lost, wondering aimlessly in life, find a place within him to love again?

When I saw *The Truman Show* for the first time, I related to Truman's life. When I lived in San Francisco with Alex, and for many years afterward, I was a paranoid mess. Much like Truman's story, I too felt that someone or something was watching me, although I attributed it to feeling that I was messed up. Yet, I could not escape that feeling that someone or something was lurking in the shadows. I often wondered if the HIV medication that I was taking was interacting with the recreational drugs that I was ingesting—creating paranoia. Was I experiencing a chemical reaction that was feeding my paranoia or was it something else? Several decades later I would come to understand that I was not paranoid. I now know and believe that the thing that I felt surrounding me was something greater altogether.

King of Diamonds

In another great movie, *The Game*, a rich man, who is a banker, is an arrogant and self-centered ass that lives in San Francisco. For his birthday, his wealthy younger brother buys him an experience called *The Game*, which consists of an elaborate sequence of events that takes place over several weeks and months, with one twist after another.

The intricate trail of coincidental circumstances that are part of the game eventually lead him down a masterful road of manipulation, which begins to screw with his mind. He doesn't know the ultimate goal of *The Game*, but while playing it, he becomes very concerned for his emotional and financial well-being. The birthday boy cannot discern what is real and what is not, because of the lies and manipulative behavior that he has encountered. He becomes confused and ends up not believing anything that anyone tells him, especially those closest to him, and he begins to second-guess every thought he has and every decision he makes. At the end of the movie, in his confused state, he ends up shooting his younger brother. Once he realizes what he has done, he jumps off a building in the hopes of ending his life for mistakenly killing his sibling.

It turns out that the entire movie was a set-up. The man lands on an airbag that breaks his fall, which was anticipated and manipulated by the organizers of the game. Once the organizers rescue him from his jump, his brother is seen to be alive. The man's outlook on life is renewed due to the horrific chain of events that he had just endured and brought to fruition by his exhausting efforts to seek the truth—and by ultimately receiving the good news of that truth.

All three movies revolve around a feeling or intuition felt by the characters that there's more than what meets the eye. Even though the reality of the circumstances in the movies would suggest that they're being overly sensitive, their perseverance allows them to seek out the truth of their situation. Without their undeniable determination to seek their own answers, they would have never found their own truth.

I spent years looking over my shoulder, and countless hours, days, and months contemplating that there was more to my life. I felt that I was missing something of significant importance. My broken relationship with Alex exacerbated this feeling and I was afraid that there was yet another deceptive chain of events on the horizon. I was working overtime to protect the dogs and me, although I had no idea from who or what I was protecting us. I don't know why I never turned to God. For whatever reason, this was a road that I was meant to walk alone. I was focused on protecting my little family and identifying the evil in my life—and I was not able to look past myself.

While the movies stand on their own merit, I connected to their various stories because of what I myself had experienced and because of the curious timing when I saw these movies. Since movies are a visual telling of a story, is it possible that the films have a deeper message for certain individuals? I think they do and that's what makes them good stories.

I find it ironic that many religious leaders have referred to Hollywood as sin city and have discounted the presence of God within the filmmaking industry. But isn't God's presence everywhere? Is Hollywood a place where heaven and art meet for God's voice to be heard? I've read that God stated that He will reveal himself to the world through His people. If He truly said these words, then does it not make sense that we can see Him in extraordinary stories told by ordinary people, including those told by filmmakers? If we happen to take the time to seek his voice, might we hear it in the oddest places, even in our favorite film or television programs?

Heaven Is for Real is another great movie, based on a true story, which tells the tale of a young boy who visits heaven as part of a near-death experience. The boy tells his family of his journey to heaven, describing the angels and an encounter with Jesus. The boy's father, who is a minister, shows him pictures of Jesus from various religious books and asks him to identify which one of the pictures represents the Jesus that he met. The boy does not identify any of the pictures that his father shows him as the Jesus that he encountered.

However, at the end of the film, the boy sees a picture on his father's laptop of an image of Jesus, with blue eyes, painted by a little girl.

The little girl, Akiane Kramarik, is a child prodigy and an amazing artist. Interestingly, she didn't have any formal art training, her talent is innate and God-given. The little girl grew up in an atheist home and, at four years of age, she had an encounter with Jesus. Without faith or religion in the home she was raised, she still entered into a personal and loving relationship with Jesus and produced an image of him that the little boy in the movie identified as being the Jesus that he met while he was in heaven.

"I tell you the truth, unless you change and become like little children, you will never enter the kingdom of heaven"

– Matthew 18:3.

10 | WHAT'S THE DEAL?

After Tim and I split up, my insecurities intensified due to my health status and this fueled feelings of being less than worthy of another relationship. After Alex and I became boyfriends, and upon discovering his infidelity, I feared his sex addiction would lead him to find someone that he wanted to be with more that he wanted me. My feelings of unworthiness were exaggerated by his unfaithfulness. When we lived in Chicago, before moving to California, we went to the White Party in Palm Springs. Prior to meeting Alex, I had gone to the party on many occasions. It was my first gay circuit event that I attended after splitting up with Tim many years earlier. It was not only the first time I traveled to a gay circuit party, it was also the first time I attended a circuit event alone. The White Party was then held on Easter weekend. I loved going to this event each year and always looked forward to attending the festivities. I had a fantastic time whenever I went and going to this party every year made me fall in love with Palm Springs, which became one of my favorite places to visit. During the early years of my travels to this party land, Sonny Bono was the mayor of this lovely desert oasis.

On the Easter weekend that Alex and I went, we were joined by several of our friends from Chicago. Typically, on the Sunday of the three-day weekend, the organizers would turn the tennis courts at the hosting event hotel into a dance floor for an afternoon tea dance. During the tea dance, Alex and I met another couple from Los Angeles on the dance floor. Michael and Alex, the LA couple, happened to be friends of a mutual friend of ours from Chicago. Initially, I did not take a liking to them, as they were loud and obnoxious, which distracted me from enjoying the music and my party favors. However, we danced together and exchanged pleasantries – and one thing led to another – and we eventually exchanged phone numbers. Alex and I frequently traveled to LA for fun and thought it would be nice to look them up the next time we were there. The other Alex was also Latin, like my Alex, though he was Argentinian. His boyfriend Michael was a white boy like me. As I spoke and engaged with them, it felt as if I was looking in the mirror, seeing a reflection of me and my Alex. I sensed an evil eye looking back at me. I would later come to learn, through many painful experiences, that there was in fact an evil eye staring at me when we met and I initially saw the similarities between us. It would take several years before I figured out that one half of the couple from LA was actually wicked, though the one I initially thought to be evil was the wrong one. One half of the LA couple was as calculated and malicious as one could imagine.

Several months later, we received a call from Michael saying that he was going to be in Chicago for a work-training seminar. Being the good hosts that Alex and I were, we invited Michael to stay with us over the weekend that he was going to be in Chicago so we could take him out to dinner and introduce him to some of the local gay clubs and bars while he was in town. His boyfriend Alex did not join Michael on this trip since it was work-related. During the time I spent with Michael, I never got the impression that my Alex had any sexual interest in him, nor did I get a feeling that Michael had any sexual interest in Alex. As our friendship with Alex and Michael grew, Alex and Alex ended up becoming close friends and Michael and I developed our own close friendship with one another. We were a walking cliché where the two Hispanics bonded with one another, as did the two white boys.

Over time, Alex and Michael became our close friends and I eventually confided in Michael about Alex's sex addiction. In turn, Michael confided and revealed to me that LA Alex had experienced a similar problem, although had seemed to have the situation under control. I thought this to be good news since LA Alex could be a positive role model for my own Alex. LA Alex did in fact seem to have a positive message to share with Alex and reinforced the importance of getting his situation under control and not to let his addiction dictate his life — and ultimately let it affect our relationship. Somewhere in the years when our friendship grew, LA Alex supposedly began to have sex outside of their relationship once again. With this in common, the friendship between Michael and I seemed to bond to a deeper level over our spouses' infidelity, a classic case of misery loving company. Since I had issues with people lying – and infidelity usually encompasses lying – I put some distance between LA Alex and me when we were together and, as a result, I was not close to him on any level. In retrospect, this was a mistake on my part. I staked a position after hearing only one side of LA Alex's infidelity story. I've certainly come to learn over the years that there are two sides to every story...and then there's the truth.

Several months after Michael's visit to Chicago, my Alex had a business trip that took him to New York City. He needed to be in New York on a Monday morning for meetings and would need to stay in the city for the entire week. We decided to take advantage of his business trip and use the opportunity to enjoy the weekend in Manhattan. We flew out together on Friday afternoon and I planned on flying back home on Sunday since Alex would be occupied with work during the week. As we approached our hotel, Alex seemed preoccupied, fidgety, and emotionally distant. When we arrived at the hotel, he lit up a cigarette upon exiting the cab, which was unusual since he only smoked when we were partying and he was high. His sudden need to have a cigarette made me uncomfortable. I felt that he had something other than our time together on his mind and I felt estranged from him the entire weekend.

I was not sure what was on his mind, but due to his demeanor, I allowed him to have some space to deal with whatever was preoccupying him. We managed to do some of the usual things that one does when in Manhattan…sightseeing, shopping, dinner, and dancing. When Sunday came, Alex began to cry as I was leaving him to go back home. I was troubled and not sure why he was so sad. I was filled with anxiety on the entire cab ride to the airport and on the flight back to Chicago. Alex's actions when we arrived, combined with his strange behavior when I left him at the hotel, unnerved me. As we did not carry cell phones then, I would be out of contact with Alex for six hours until I arrived back home that evening. Once I got home, I called him. We spoke, I let him know I had gotten home safely, and wished him a goodnight. I went to bed without knowing that there was a rat lurking in the shadows the entire time I was in the Big Apple.

The following morning, I had this undeniable sense that Alex was up to something. Even though I knew he was supposed to be at a business meeting, I felt the need to call his hotel room. It was nine o'clock in the morning in New York and the phone in his room just rang and rang with no one to answer it. As Alex did not answer the phone, I hung up and immediately called the hotel again and requested to be connected to his room. This time he answered the phone.

I wondered why he picked up the phone a few minutes later when I placed the second call to his room. In my gut, I knew that he was up to something, although I didn't know what. When I asked him why he did not answer the phone on my first try, he replied that he had just returned to the room from a meeting when he heard the phone ringing and picked it up, but I had already hung up on my end. He explained that he went to his meeting in downtown Manhattan and the person with whom he was meeting was tied up for the day, so he decided to return to his hotel room and arrived just as the phone was ringing. His story was not plausible. How could he be staying in midtown and travel over fifty blocks south to his destination downtown, get out of the cab, walk to the building, ride the elevator to meet the client, discover that the meeting was canceled, travel back down the elevator, hail a cab again and then travel more than fifty blocks north to his hotel, in an hour's time, in rush hour traffic? This would be an impossible task to complete in Manhattan even for the amazing Alex. I knew he was lying to me, although I wanted to know the exact reason why he was lying.

Speculating what Alex was up to was driving me crazy. I pondered what the overly active sex nut was up to—and thought of two scenarios. I considered that Alex was having another random sexual escapade. I also contemplated that he was using his company business trip as a charade to cover a premeditated affair. This seemed the more likely scenario. If true, then who was he having an affair with in New York? My inquisitive and suspicious mind wanted to know. When I spoke to him after he answered the second phone call, I went off on him and explained very firmly that I believed he was lying to me about what was taking place with him in the city and that I was not happy about the situation. He maintained his innocence, of course. Our terse conversation was brief and we hung-up quickly. When I arrived home from work that night, I found a message from Alex on our answering machine, so I called him back. Our conversation was one-sided with me inquiring about his whereabouts that day. He told me that his meetings for the rest of the week were going to be held in his company's New Jersey office, so he had decided to change hotels and was no longer staying in Manhattan.

Alex was a stickler for expensing all his travel-related costs so I inquired how he got to the New Jersey office from his hotel in Manhattan. He responded that he took a cab and I assumed he must have gotten a receipt for the cab fare. I had learnt that compulsive liars rarely veer from their normal actions and, if they do so, there's usually a specific reason why. They know that any unusual behavior may result in drawing unwanted attention, or possibly having people question their intentions, so they usually operate in a preconceived manner. When I asked him if he had a receipt for his cab ride, he told me that he did not; he forgot to get one from the driver. Under normal circumstances, forgetting to get a receipt for a cab ride so the fare can be expensed could be something that might happen, although this was Alex's second shady story this day. First, his meeting is canceled for no apparent reason and secondly the cheap-ass that normally expensed a cup of coffee back to his company forgot to get a cab receipt for a ride that cost a hundred dollars. I lost my patience and became a raving maniac on the phone. I told him that he was a liar and I didn't believe a word of his bullshit stories and I had just about had enough of him and his deceitful behavior. I was so angry that if he had been standing at arm's length, I would have physically hurt him. There was no way for me to get my hands around his lying Puerto Rican neck at the immediate moment and thank God that there were hundreds of miles and several states between us.

During our conversation, Alex back peddled and tried to use his typical bag of tricks to get me to calm down, although it did not work on me. I had listened to just about enough of his shit and then I began to feel ill. The conversation had become tiresome and his behavior seemed like it was never going to change. I didn't know exactly what he was up to on this trip apart from work-related activities, although I felt he was up to no good. It really didn't matter to me anymore. I didn't need to know the dirty details of the situation because I knew it was a different telling of the same old messed up story. But, as the expression goes, good things come to those who wait…and wait I would.

On the following Tuesday afternoon, I received a call from Alex that he had cut his business trip short and was flying back home on Wednesday rather than Friday as he originally planned. He indicated that he was coming back home to deal with my emotional meltdown and asked me if I would pick him up at the airport. I was unsure why he would ask me to pick him up since he knew I was very upset with him, but I reluctantly agreed. When I arrived at the airport, I did not park the car; I waited for him curbside. He emerged from the terminal and entered the car. We did not say a word to one another the entire ride back to the city. I did not want to give him the impression that he was out of the doghouse. I was still fuming over whatever took place in New York after I left him in the city.

When we arrived home, I stopped at the security gate of our housing complex to wait for it to open so I could pull into the driveway and park the car in our garage. At that moment, Alex decided to open his mouth and speak for the first time since he got into the car at the airport. I was not interested in whatever words came out of his mouth and didn't want to hear anything that he had to say. As the gate opened slowly, Alex began to tell me another bullshit tale…and I lost it.

I leaned over to the passenger side of the car and grabbed him around the neck. I began to bang his head against the passenger window of the Mercedes. He had pushed me to a breaking point. I exploded with frustration and anger. It was my love for Alex that made me react. At that moment, I realized love had an ugly side and this is especially true when it resides in a deceitful environment. I didn't hurt him, but he certainly got the message that the situation between us was out of control and becoming volatile. The lies and the suspicious and unexplainable situations were affecting my disposition and the love that I had for him. I was becoming increasingly weary and easily agitated over his actions. This was the first and last time I ever laid my hands on Alex. In the heat of the moment, I reacted when I should have held my temper for a few more minutes when I would've been out of the car and he would've been out of my sight. From that day forward, Alex was a little afraid of me, although not enough for him to curb or clean up his behavior.

As with many of the inexplicable situations surrounding Alex, this latest event seemed to be no different. I never received a satisfactory explanation from Alex over his whereabouts other than him sticking to his original story. Again, I was left with two options to explore. I could have left him and abruptly ended the relationship over what was still a hunch. My second option was to let the situation go and try to move forward with building a more solid foundation. This seemed like a better choice since it was still relatively early in our relationship and I still had hope that we could make our relationship whole. Most of the time, when I was dealing with his lies, I felt like I was moving backward and most of the time when it came to dealing with Charlotte and the web of lies that she was spinning, I was clearly not sure what I was doing—and so the carousel continued to go around and around.

About a year before Alex and I eventually broke up, Michael and his Alex also split up in LA. I liked Michael very much and, as we considered each other good friends, he confided in me and told me all about their breakup. I related to Michael's plight and naturally gave him my sympathy because I had no compassion for liars. LA Alex tried on several occasions to speak with me and share his side of the story, but I would always brusquely cut him off, as I was not willing to listen to yet another set of lies. This was a big mistake on my part and I would come to regret this decision. By not hearing what he had to say, I only heard one side of a two-sided story and Michael's version became the truth of what transpired between them. Did Michael give me an accurate version of their breakup? I never for a moment thought that Michael would have any reason to lie to me. Why, I thought, would he tell me anything other than the truth when telling me the story of why he broke up with his boyfriend?

After they split up, Michael moved into a one-bedroom apartment in West Hollywood on his own. We remained friends, and later, when I was still living in San Francisco and newly single, we would meet up on occasion. He would fly up to San Francisco and we would go to large gay circuit party events, such as gay pride in June or Magnitude, which always took place the same weekend as the Folsom Street Fair, in September. Intriguingly, whenever we were together and out partying, Michael would always spook me in some way. It never failed. As time progressed, an undercurrent and an underlying feeling that all was not right with our friendship began to linger right beneath the surface.

One time, when we were out together at Club Universe, it all seemed to catch up with me. I had begun to feel that Michael was someone other than who he presented himself to be. When I was high and in Michaels's company, a feeling would overtake me and I would suddenly have this undeniable sense that Michael was an evil lying piece of shit that could not be trusted. I only had this impression of him when we were out partying, so naturally I struggled with this perception as I thought these feelings were driven by the party drugs we were all taking. This was not the first time nor would it be the last time I would have these feelings about Michael and his behavior, although it would be a defining moment for me as I finally had enough.

I turned to Rick, who was out partying with us, and asked him whether Michael was a friend or foe. Rick, always looking for the best in people, responded without any hesitation that Michael was a friend. Shit! I was sure that Michael was an evil foe, but based on my recent history, I was confused and not sure of myself and so I questioned my intuition. Since I was on shaky ground, I turned to the person I trusted most in life and leaned on him for guidance. Rick's answer was not what I wanted to hear, but I reluctantly accepted his assurance and went against what my gut was telling me. At that exact moment, I had confirmation that Alex's cheating had indeed become secondary to the lies that he had been telling me for so long. The constant lies and the uncertain environment they created, left me in a state of confusion that affected my ability to assess a situation properly, including my conflicted feelings about Michael.

When he was back in LA, Michael and I would speak on many evenings, as I commuted fifty miles from my office in San Carlos to my house in San Rafael. During the hour or so it would take me to drive home, we had plenty of time to trash the ex-boyfriends. Michael worked from home and seemed to have a lot of free time on any given day. He was usually available to talk when I called, but one thing always struck me as odd…and while it may have been nothing, my intuition would tell me otherwise. He would always, without fail, place me on hold for a minute when I called, before coming back on the line to begin our conversation. I realized that since he worked from home, he may have had other people on the other line when I called, although he put me on hold so regularly that I began to think he was taping our conversations. In these situations, my gut and intuition were telling me that he was up to something, although when I looked at the situation in a logical manner, my mind was in disagreement with my intuition. His regular habit of putting me on hold before all our conversations is something that has stuck in my mind throughout the years. Was it real or was it Memorex? I wonder if Monica Lewinsky's intuition ever told her that Linda Tripp was taping their conversations. I never confirmed that Michael was actually taping our calls and to this day I'm not one hundred percent sure what he was up to, if anything, although I finally saw Michael in his true light several years later at the Limelight in New York on a Christmas Eve.

Michael had told me that he and his Alex were having difficulties because Alex was having sex with other men while they lived together in Los Angeles. Shortly before they broke up, Michael, who was raised in the New York area, traveled to the East Coast to visit his family when he met an Italian man in New York City. LA Alex was to meet Michael in Manhattan on the weekend that Michael was visiting his parents, but his arrival had been delayed. Before LA Alex arrived, Michael met the Italian man when he was working out at a gym in Chelsea. Shortly after meeting the Italian, Michael and Alex broke up, and Michael began a long-distance relationship with the Italian who lived in Manhattan.

Several years after Michael and the Italian met, during one of our conversations, Michael divulged the portion of the story when he and the Italian met and hooked up, in the period when his Alex had been late in meeting him in New York. Michael slipped up by telling me this part of the story. Several years had passed, but I still made a connection between Michael's story and the weekend that my Alex and I had spent in New York, when he had been acting suspiciously. I suddenly realized that Michael's tale of meeting up with LA Alex in New York City had very similar pieces that coincided with my Alex's escapades in Manhattan several years earlier.

My mind began to go into hyper-drive. Was there an affair going on between my friend and my lover? Could they have been having sex without me having any idea that they were seeing each other? Is this the reason why my Alex began smoking when we arrived at our hotel in New York and why he seemed so anxious that weekend? Could Michael have been in Manhattan, waiting for my Alex to arrive? Is this why Alex began to cry on Sunday when I left New York City to go home? Was my Alex contemplating leaving me for Michael? I had unexpectedly decided to join Alex for the weekend in New York and my presence would have made it impossible for my Alex and Michael to meet up until I left. This could have possibly pissed off Michael. When Michael met the Italian at the gym in Chelsea, was this a slap in my Alex's face for him not telling me that he wanted to be with Michael?

If any of these suspicions were true, was my hunch that Michael was taping our calls when we were trashing our ex-boyfriends viable? Was he taping our conversations and replaying them to my Alex to hurt him and get revenge on me? While these bizarre and twisted scenarios seem far-fetched, they made sense to me based on Alex's previous track record. Could my Alex and Michael have been conspiring for years? If I'm correct, how sick and screwed up were these two individuals? Could this be the reason that I suspected Michael of being an evil, twisted, lying, fucked up person when we were our partying together? Were the drugs taking me to a heightened state, allowing me to see the real lying boyfriend thief for who he was and not who he pretended to be?

When I look back on that day when I met Michael and LA Alex on the dance floor in Palm Springs during tea dance, I've come to the realization that I was not only looking in the mirror when I met them for the first time, I was also looking directly into the eyes of evil. In the end, I only have my intuition that Michael was messing around with my Alex, although I have come to believe that we need to listen to that little voice within ourselves and that voice tells me that Michael was not the friend that he presented himself to be.

Before I heard that little voice inside me that made me see the truth about Michael, I traveled to New York one year to celebrate Christmas in the Big Apple. By this time, Alex and I had been broken up for a few years, and Michael had moved from Los Angeles to Manhattan to live with the Italian and they had been living together for some time. I went to New York with Manuel, a friend of mine from San Francisco, with whom I had a slight romantic interest. Manuel had recently broken up with his boyfriend and was feeling a little melancholy, so I decided to invite him to join me to cheer him up. Manuel had never been to New York and was excited to experience the city and I was equally as excited to have the opportunity to introduce him to the party scene, especially during the most festive season of the year.

In addition to showing Manhattan to Manuel, I also wanted to spend time with Michael during Christmas since his Italian boyfriend was traveling to Italy. Michael was also feeling melancholy, as he was going to be alone in New York for Christmas. As it turned out, I willingly, but unknowingly, traveled cross the entire country to catch Michael in her own web of lies on the night that Christ was born.

On Christmas Eve, myself, Michael, Manuel, and Teddy – another friend of mine that also lived in New York – went to Limelight. Once we got to the club, we settled into a spot near the dance floor where we could view all the shirtless sugar plum fairies dancing and drinking holiday cheer wishing that Santa would deliver them a nice package that they could take home that night. We drank and we chatted and we danced as the evening wore on. Teddy and I ended up hanging together for most of the time, in the early part of the evening, while Michael and Manuel went deeper into the cauldron of dancing men. As we looked about for them, we saw that Michael had his hands down Manuel's pants. This would be my first actual proof that Michael was not the Mother Teresa that she claimed herself to be. Michael's Italian boyfriend, with whom he was living, was in Italy visiting his family for Christmas and to my knowledge they did not have an open relationship. The little rat may have been blinded by the strobe lights flashing on the dance floor, but he was certainly stirring about and using his little hands to feel for the goodies hanging between Manuel's legs. I'm no stranger to having a good time, or looking for a hookup, but Michael was in a relationship and Manuel was someone that he knew I was romantically interested in. Here it was at last, Michael showing himself for what he was and proving the adage that when the cat's away, the rat will play.

Shortly after we saw the groping incident on the dance floor, I suggested that we all go to the back lounge area of the club. We were high and hanging out and lounging on one of the sofas sounded like a good idea to me. Somewhere between walking from the dance floor to the lounge area in the back, we lost Michael, or perhaps Michael made sure he lost us. I was somewhat relieved to have a moment to hang with my other two friends and enjoy the Limelight without having to deal with Michael's shenanigans. We sat on one of the sofas, chatted, and amused ourselves by watching the little Christmas elves running amuck as they were being cruised by the intoxicated sugar plum fairies who were looking to take an elf home so they could unwrap their package in their bed that night. At some point, I realized that more than an hour had passed since we had seen Michael, so, since it was Christmas

Eve, I decided to be a good friend and go look for him. I spotted the cheating bastard putting on his jacket in the coat check line at the entrance to the club. When I asked where he had been for the last hour or so, he replied that he had been looking for us without success. Instinctively, I knew at that exact moment that he was a nothing but a liar. The lounge area where we had been sitting for the last hour was directly in the path between the front and back bars. If Michael had actually looked for us, he would have had to walk right past us and I would have seen him since I was keeping an eye out for him. The cheating rat must have lured an unexpected elf into his trap and was now leaving with his prey. I finally realized without a doubt that Michael was not the person that he claimed to be and that my friendship with Michael had come to an end. God had rewarded my act of giving, when I had sincerely traveled to New York to spend time with my friends this holiday season. My act of kindness was met by Fate unveiling the truth about Michael that I had longed to know all those years and had bestowed on me the greatest gift…the true meaning of friendship or – in Michael's case – the true meaning of what friends are not. Merry Christmas to me indeed and to all a goodnight!

I had long felt that another shoe was yet to drop and that I would eventually learn that Alex had messed around with someone close to me. I now believe Michael and Alex had sex when we were together. Michael had pretended to be my good friend all those years, when in fact he was carrying a grudge that Alex never tossed me aside for him. This was the evil that I always sensed coming from him and that I picked up on when we were partying together. There was certainly more to Michael than the untrained eye could see…he was a lying fag by day and a cheating creeping rat by night.

My Christmas holiday in New York brought me unexpected clarity to a long drawn out conundrum. The riddle surrounding Michael had finally been answered and what a relief it was. However, when I traveled back to San Francisco from New York, I felt a profound sense of loss. I was now associating the city that I loved for so many years and that I had hoped to live and work in one day with the behavior that had transpired between Michael on Christmas Eve at the Limelight. Unfortunately, in my mind's eye, Michael living in New York now overshadowed any affection that I had for the Big Apple, at least for the moment.

The funniest part of this story is that my Alex and Michael were made from the same mold. They certainly should have been together, although I now understand that this was not a possibility, as they both knew that they could not trust one another; two peas in a pod.

11 | FOR THE LOVE OF THE GAME

Artificial Intelligence is another movie that speaks to me. This film takes place in the future where robots live amongst mankind and appear to be human. A husband and wife purchase a little boy, who is a robot that looks very much like any other young child. The couple tried to have children the natural way, but they had no success in conceiving. Their new little robotic son is programmed to love. His main purpose is to be a child and to love his mother, which he does with all his being, as this is how his creator created him. The mother shows much affection toward the boy and they spend their days together and build an everlasting bond.

Several years after "adopting" the boy, the mother becomes unexpectedly pregnant. As her newborn baby boy grows up, he reaches the same age as his artificial brother—and becomes jealous of the relationship between his robotic brother and his mother. The biological son sets up his brother to seem as if he is the jealous one, out to hurt him. After several frightening incidents, the father insists that the mother take the boy back to the factory where he was made and have him disengaged, or put to sleep, as he is fearful that he will harm their son. Reluctantly, the mother agrees. As with any loving mother, she realizes on the way to the factory that she can't and will not have the boy – whom she has come to love – disengaged. She stops the car and leaves him and Teddy, his stuffed toy bear, in a forest near the place where he was made. Teddy was created to be the little boy's companion and best friend and he loves the boy very much. He walks on two feet and talks as if he was human, although he is a robotic teddy bear.

The story is about the loving bond between a young boy and who he believes to be his mother and his everlasting friendship with Teddy, who stays by the boy's side through the entire story, as they try to return home. To me, the movie represents the perseverance of friendship and the lengths that pure love will endure for one's creator.

David, the little boy, and his teddy bear search for days, which turn into months, trying to get back to David's mother. Along their perilous journey, they come across the fairytale story of Pinocchio. They learn that a Blue Fairy in that story has the power to make Pinocchio into a real boy. David then seeks to find the Blue Fairy to make him into a real live boy that his mother will love, just like her biological son. He comes across Dr. Know, an animated computer program that tells David that he can find the Blue Fairy in Mecca, a restricted area, which is at the end of the world in a lost city that is located in a sea where the lions weep.

David, who is programmed to believe he is special, accepts the challenge and seeks the assistance of the Blue Fairy. After many travails, David finds a statue of the Blue Fairy, which is located deep under water in the foretold area. David begins to pray over and over again to the Blue Fairy to help him find his mother…night after night, month after month, year after year, decade after decade, century after century—until his world freezes into a new ice age and time appears to stand still. Endless time passes and David and Teddy find themselves so far in the future that humanity has ceased to exist.

An advanced alien race finds David and Teddy encased in their frozen world. David is the only representation of the human race that is left on earth. Once David and Teddy are brought back online, David immediately wants to continue his search for his mother and what he believes to be his creator. As the alien race observes David and attempt to learn about the humans that once inhabited the earth from him, they can't help but notice the unrelenting perseverance of this boy to reunite with his mother. The aliens develop compassion for him and come to the conclusion that they must give David what he so longs for and seeks. Being an advanced race, the aliens recreate David's home from his memories and recreate his mother from DNA taken from a lock of her hair that Teddy has carried with him through time. David, being a robot, did not require sleep and he and Teddy spend an entire wonderful morning and afternoon with his mother, as they had always done when they all lived together. Their evening, however, would be like no other evening that ever had taken place when they were together. David was so happy and had so much peace since finally being reunited with his mother that on this particular evening, when night came, and his mother fell asleep…so did David—for the first time ever.

Come away, O human child!
To the waters and the wild
With a faery, hand in hand,
For the world's more full of weeping than you can understand.
The Stolen Child

W. B. Yeats

I believe that sincere and pure love will give a sense of peace that defies all logic, just as David experienced. In our modern world, we frequently experience an existence that offers very little peace or tranquility and possibly, like David, this is why we have such a yearning – and search so desperately –

for a love that gives us a sense of fulfillment that can't be achieved by any other means. I often felt like someone was watching over me for years, as the aliens watched David, wanting me to have that same type of love, and experience peace. I never made any real connection to these feelings until I saw ***Artificial Intelligence.*** Today, I believe it was God's presence that I felt and it was He that wanted me to experience the love and peace that comes with knowing Him. While I would not experience tranquility for years after seeing this movie, I felt the presence of something wanting me to have peace at a time when I had not yet developed a relationship with Him.

I find the movie to be an amazing love story as it pertains to the love between a child and his mother and his best friend, something to which we can all relate. Like David, I had my own love story involving a great and dear friend that I met fittingly in the city of angels, for an angel he has become.

Over a half of a century ago, I was born in the county of Los Angeles. My parents moved from the West Coast to the Midwest when I was just a baby and ever since I was a young man, I had the desire to return to LA to live and work. On April 13 of 2011, my wish came true and I moved from Palm Springs to the downtown area of Los Angeles. After living there for a year, I met a very attractive young man named Lance, at Gold's gym near my loft. My relationship with Lance should've been told toward the end of this book, but a set of tragic circumstances came into play that would place his story and the tale of our friendship exactly at this place. On the evening of Thursday, the eleventh of July in 2013, after Lance and I finished working out together, I would see him for the last time for he tragically passed away that night. I've since come to believe that his passing was not a random occurrence and that his story has been placed in this chapter by a divine set of circumstances.

It all began at the gym in the month of October the year before he died. One day, I noticed a handsome young guy working out by himself. He had dark hair, dark eyebrows, weighed about one hundred and forty pounds, and was approximately five feet, nine inches tall. He looked Caucasian, with a very light tannish color to his skin. I would later come to learn that his mother was from Colombia and his father from the Netherlands, which turns out to be a wonderful mixture if you use Lance as the standard of measure. His mixed European and Hispanic background was a major contributing factor to his handsome demeanor. I guessed him to be about twenty-six years old. He had a certain flair about him…confidence with a hint of shyness. He was very manly in a boyish way and I came to know him as a unique individual. Not only was he good looking, he also had a very distinct way that he carried himself and an equally interesting walk. In fact, it was that distinct stance and unique gait that first caught my eye. He carried himself like no other man in that gym.

Over the next several weeks, I came accustomed to Lance's workout schedule. He usually arrived at the gym around three o'clock in the afternoon – sometimes earlier – and on rare occasions he would arrive a little later. Once I got a handle on his schedule, I adjusted mine to align with his. Even though I was fifty-two and had previously lived in Manhattan, San Francisco, Chicago, and Palm Springs, I was still somewhat reserved when it came to making new friends and being the first to engage an individual in conversation. My encounter with Lance was no different. I wanted to introduce myself to him, although my shy nature prevented me from doing so. Each day, I would look forward to going to the gym to work out and, as a bonus, I could see Lance and admire him from afar. Was my interest in meeting Lance the silly admiration of a middle-aged gay man for a younger handsome man? Or did I subconsciously recognize the deep friendship that the two of us would eventually develop?

After three or four weeks of working out near Lance and making casual eye contact on various occasions, I finally decided to make my move and introduce myself to him. Fate once again stepped in and set up the ideal set of circumstances for my introduction. In my mind's eye, I can recall the moment as if it took place today. As I finished my work out, I walked to the locker-room to change out of my gym gear and into my street clothes. I passed Lance working out on a lower back machine close to the men's changing area. The lower back machines were at the rear of the gym, somewhat isolated from the rest of the workout area. This ideal situation allowed me the opportunity to approach Lance without anybody in the vicinity being able to eavesdrop on our conversation. I certainly would not have said anything inappropriate, but this scenario allowed me to comfortably approach Lance and speak with him without an audience nearby. As I was changing my clothes, I convinced myself that if Lance was still working out in the same area, I would engage him in conversation.

As I left the men's changing area, I reached into my gym bag for a business card and placed it conveniently in my pant pocket. I had already imagined this potential encounter many times prior to this day. As I approached the area where Lance was working out, I suddenly began to feel very anxious. When I reached the machine where he was exercising, I extended my hand and introduced myself. I asked him if he worked downtown, which I assumed he did since he was at the gym at the same time each day. He answered that he worked nearby, as a server at California Pizza Kitchen in the financial district. I reached into my pocket for my business card and handed it to him. I then asked him if he would like to work out together sometime and, if so, he could reach me via my cell number that was printed on my card. Lance seemed to genuinely welcome my suggestion and answered that he would be interested in working-out together sometime. I wished him a good evening and headed to the exit. As I remember it, the entire exchange took less than one minute—but the resulting friendship will be remembered for a lifetime.

Being somewhat shy, I've always had a major issue with approaching people that I didn't know. It's possible that my reluctance to approach strangers and engage them in conversation is linked to a potential risk of rejection. Even at the age of fifty-two, I still had some of my teenage insecurities that carried over into my adulthood. I was also afraid that someone might get the wrong impression of my intentions and think I was hitting on them for a sexual encounter. Having been in sales for many years, I've been able to overcome my shyness in my professional career when seeking new business clients. This boldness, however, did not find its way into my personal life and I regret the missed opportunities where I might have developed some great relationships had my shyness not prevented me from doing so. When it came to meeting Lance, I decided that this was not going to be the case. There was something about him that was drawing me in his direction. I worked out alone and had been thinking about looking for a workout partner prior to seeing him at the gym. Our schedules certainly seemed compatible, allowing us the chance to train together, if he was interested. As I continued walking home, I was pleased that I had finally had the courage to approach him and introduce myself.

Four days later, on Tuesday, the thirteenth of November 2012, I received a text from Lance stating that he would be at the gym at three o'clock in the afternoon that day, if I wanted to work out with him. I texted him right back and accepted his invitation. We met at the gym and I quickly found out that he was twenty-one and just a few weeks away from celebrating his twenty-second birthday. I had thought he was in his mid- to late twenties when I initially saw him and when I told him that I assumed he was older, it brought a smile to his face. He was a baby, at least from the point where I was standing, being thirty years his senior.

Lance too was somewhat shy and in the early days of us working out together he was a little on the quiet side. Having been a salesman, I could certainly keep a conversation going with very little input from anyone, which became the case when engaging Lance in conversation during the first few months. As our friendship grew, he began sharing more stories about his life, his immediate family, and his friends.

Prior to meeting him, I had been going to the gym three to four days a week. Once we became workout partners, we began working out five days, Monday through Friday. My interest in working out more was driven by my desire to see Lance each day. I didn't have any friends that I hung out with on a regular basis in LA, although I knew quite a few people there. Having the chance to develop a new friendship and have someone that shared my interest in getting in shape was very welcoming. When I originally joined the gym, a year before, I had thought I needed to lose ten to fifteen pounds. In reality, I needed to lose forty to fifty pounds that I had gained while living in Palm Springs. At the time I met Lance, I had lost nearly thirty pounds and needed to lose another ten to twenty to achieve my ultimate goal. The weight loss was a little tricky. I wanted to gain lean muscle mass in all areas of my body, while trimming down the fat. Ultimately, I wanted to gain muscle while losing my chubbiness. I tried not to get caught up in what I weighed. Once I lost the initial thirty pounds, my focus became how I looked in the mirror rather than what I weighed on a scale.

Lance originally joined the gym with Richard, one of his closest friends. They had planned to be workout partners, but at the last minute, Richard's work schedule changed and he was unable to work out at the same time as Lance. If it were not for the last-minute change in Richard's schedule, Lance and I probably would've never had the opportunity to become friends and, once again, I believe that there were unseen forces that brought us together.

After a month of lifting heavy weight at the gym, Lance mentioned that his palms hurt from the weights rubbing against his skin. I asked him if he had workout gloves because I had previously seen him wearing some type of hand protection in the gym before we began to train together. He replied that he bought workout gloves on eBay, but they were too thin and didn't give him the protection he wanted, so he stopped wearing them. I too needed gloves for working out and had been thinking about purchasing a pair for myself. So, one day, a few weeks before Christmas, I stopped by the pro shop in the club and bought leather workout gloves for the two of us. A few minutes later when I saw Lance in the locker room, I said that I had a present for him and handed him the gloves. He thanked me politely. He was still getting his gym clothes out of his backpack and as I was already in my gym clothes, I told him I would meet him on the gym floor.

When Lance caught up with me, he seemed to be in an exceptionally good mood. I had only worked out with him for a month and he seemed to be happier than ever before. Later that same week, on the Friday after giving him the gloves as a Christmas present, he and I went out for drinks after the gym, which become a regular ritual of ours. These Friday drinking excursions were our reward for working out all week. On our first outing, Lance brought up the workout gloves that I had given him. He told me that my gift made him happy, as no one had done anything like that for him before. I believe he was expressing that nobody that he barely knew had done such a thing for him before. I was pleased that my small gesture could bring him some joy, especially so close to Christmas. I found it interesting that I could perfectly tune into his happy demeanor after giving him the gift. It was such a joyful moment for me to have been able to bring a moment of genuine happiness to Lance, certainly proving the adage true that it's better to give than receive. While the smile on his face that day was the result of a small gesture on my part, the real gift was mine and greater than I could've imagined at the time. When I recall Lance's smiling face, it's an especially meaningful moment for me considering what would happen a mere seven months later.

That same Christmas of 2012, Rick and I traveled to Spain to celebrate the holiday season in Barcelona and Madrid. We arrived in Barcelona on Christmas Eve and that night we went to an old Gothic church that celebrated a beautiful and very famous midnight mass that alas was celebrated in Catalan, which neither of us understood. Regardless, the service, the music, and the incense brought us closer to Christmas, which was the main reason for going to Barcelona on this trip, along with visiting the church of the Holy Family, the Sagrada Familia. I had seen the dedication of the basilica on television several years earlier when I lived in Palm Springs and ever since that moment when I saw this architectural masterpiece, I had longed to visit Spain and see this phenomenal work of art and tribute to the Holy Family by the amazing and talented architect Antonio Gaudi. It was as glorious as I expected and I hope to visit it again one day when it is completed.

I returned to Los Angeles and went back to the gym on Wednesday the second of January in the new year. Lance inquired about my trip to Europe and I told him that I went to visit the church that Gaudi had designed as a tribute to The Holy Family, although it was still under construction. I explained that the structure was the most wondrous church that I had ever visited and he told me he was familiar with the project, which was not surprising as I found him to be a very insightful; he was always watching documentaries and was hungry to learn about life and what the world had to offer.

A few weeks later, after the gym, during one of our Friday night drinking adventures, I asked Lance if he was straight or if he was gay. Up to this point, neither Lance nor I had spoken about our sexual preference. Lance responded that he was straight, then asked me if I was straight or gay. I responded that I was gay and he replied that "he was down with that." Since there was a thirty-year gap between us, I assumed that his response that 'he was down with that' meant he was OK with me being gay.

On the outside, our relationship certainly seemed unusual. I was gay with a long history behind me and he was straight with all his life ahead of him. I didn't feel as old as I was, and even though I thought he was older when I saw him from afar, as I got to know him I learned that Lance was quite boyish, which made him seem younger than he was. In addition to being young and good-looking, I came to know him as being extremely kind, inquisitive, and beautifully well-mannered.

Before we met, when I first saw Lance in the gym, I cruised him on several occasions. After we became friends, I discovered that he was nearsighted and could not see things clearly that were a distance away. He normally wore contacts, but had lost them and he had been wearing glasses until he could buy new ones. Sometime between losing his contacts and the first time I saw him in the gym, he damaged his glasses roughhousing with a friend and no longer had contacts or glasses. I believe there was more at play than Lance not being able to see things clearly. I think he could somewhat tell – from a distance – that I was looking at him, but without his contacts or his glasses, he was not able to ascertain why I was looking in his direction. On several occasions, he would walk over to where I was working out, trying to understand why I was staring at him. I have to admit that part of my boldness in introducing myself to Lance was driven by a hope that he might have been gay, but I now believe that something brought us together and used his nearsightedness as a means by which to make that happen. I now know that God works in mysterious ways and Lance losing his contacts and damaging his glasses prior to us meeting is another in a long line of circumstances, perhaps driven by unseen forces that brought two unlikely people together to create a new friendship. Lance was once blind, but now it is I that sees clearly.

Among his interests, Lance was very keen on joining the U.S. Armed Forces. He was studying diligently for his military exam and wanted to become a Marine. He was very passionate and committed in his pursuit to be accepted into the military. Before we met, he had taken a practice test for the Marines and hadn't scored very well on his initial test. This discouraged him somewhat and it also made him a little insecure about taking the actual exam. From what I gathered from our conversations, a high score on the test would have allowed him more options when it came to deciding which job he wanted to perform within the Marine Corps. A low score would have limited his choices, hence his dedication to studying for the test. Over the next seven months, Lance talked about the military and his interest in pursuing a career in it. I asked him why he opted for the Marines as his number one choice and he replied that it was due to its status amongst the various arms of the military. He believed that the Marines were a noble choice for him because they had a presence that separated them from the rest of the branches. He also wanted to be part of something that focused its efforts on making the world a safer and a more compassionate place. He continued to study for his entrance exam the entire time that I knew him. As July of that year drew closer, he became more determined to finalize his studies, so he could take his entry exam and become a military man. He wanted to be a Marine more than anything else in life and it still saddens me to think that he never had an opportunity to fulfill this dream.

One time, Lance and a few of his co-workers went to a club in West Hollywood after completing their shift on a Saturday night. Lance worked with a gay woman at the restaurant and she and a few other colleagues were getting together at a gay bar on the Santa Monica strip to celebrate her birthday. Lance ended up joining them and that would be his first time at a gay club. During our workout on the following Monday afternoon, Lance couldn't wait to tell me the story of his adventure in West Hollywood. He was excited to share his story with me and let me know that he was OK with the experience. I found it adorable when he told me that he had never received so much attention from so many people in one evening. While his new popularity happened to be driven by gay men at the club, this didn't seem to lessen the impact it had on his ego. Being so handsome, I certainly knew why he would be such a big hit amongst the gay crowd. Even though men – and not women – were hitting him on, it still fed his ego in a positive way and it made me feel good that he was genuinely charged that he was such a big hit.

As the months went by, Lance and I became closer and our friendship grew. The amount of social time that we spent with one another also grew exponentially. We not only hung out on our typical Friday nights after the gym for cocktails, we would occasionally hangout on Saturday nights too. One Saturday in May, for my fifty-third birthday, I invited Lance to go with me to West Hollywood to celebrate at the Abbey, a large and popular gay club, frequented by a mixed crowd—a place where all sexual preferences are welcome and mix equally together.

We took the train from downtown Los Angeles to Hollywood. Our first stop was the W Hotel at Hollywood and Vine where we had a drink, before heading over to the Abbey in West Hollywood. Once at the Abbey, drinks became many and before long the G-string wearing male dancers came on stage along with one bikini wearing female, gyrating to the music. There was something for everyone at the club that night. At one point, two girls began to kiss at the bar next to us. Lance saw the girls kissing, leaned over to me and declared, "I love this place!" I never really understood a straight man's fascination with seeing woman on woman action, which probably explains why I'm gay. His comment, however, certainly made me feel good. I was happy that he too was enjoying himself.

Since it was my birthday, Lance kept handing me single dollar bills so I could place them in the G-strings of the male dancers. We went through forty dollars in singles that night, distributing them between the male dancers and the single female dancer. At one point, I managed to get Lance close enough to the dancing woman on stage. As I was stuffing singles in her bikini, she grabbed Lance and pulled his face to her chest, rubbing her boobs all over him. Lance was very cute and a little shy about the experience, but later in the evening, on our way home, he verbally expressed his enjoyment and went on and on about his titty moment. Straight men—so easily amused.

Despite the age gap between us, we always seemed to genuinely enjoy our time together. I enjoyed spending time with him and derived pleasure from exposing him to new experiences. One Thursday after the gym, Lance and I went to Coco Laurent, a French restaurant on Seventh Street in downtown Los Angeles. We sat outside on the patio and had appetizers and drinks. Lance had never drunk champagne, so I ordered a bottle for us. He asked if champagne tasted like wine. When he experienced wine for the first time at the restaurant where he worked during a wine tasting seminar, he hadn't liked the taste of red or white wine. As we waited for the champagne to arrive, I reflected on my own youth and recalled the time when I was in my early twenties. At the time, I too was still experiencing new things that would shape me into the person that I would eventually become. Although, it wasn't until I was forty and living in San Francisco that I developed a true appreciation for drinking champagne. In this instance, Lance was ahead of me by nearly twenty years. When the bottle arrived, the server poured us two glasses. Several hours – and two bottles later – Lance had thoroughly enjoyed his first taste of champagne and it continued to give me great pleasure to be able to introduce another new life experience to my good friend.

In the eight months between the thirteen of November of 2012 and the eleventh of July of 2013, Lance and I devoted much time to our workout regimen. We continued to hit the gym each day, working out for about an hour and a half. We both were committed to the gym and encouraged each other to become the best we could be. Motivation is a key factor in hitting your personal goals in life and the gym is no different. Anyone who has started a gym membership to improve his or her body will tell you it's a process. To become successful in achieving your goals, your workout must become part of your daily routine. You must change your lifestyle and incorporate the gym into your day, as a priority, which is certainly not as easy as it sounds and probably the reason why so many people end up quitting the gym after a few months. Having a workout partner, whose company you enjoy, can be the difference between being successful at the gym or quitting. I'm grateful that Lance accepted my invitation to become his workout partner, which in turn allowed me the chance to become his friend. He not only helped my commitment to get my body in the best shape possible, more importantly, he allowed me to be part of his life. He befriended me at a time when I needed a positive influence and by doing so he had a major impact on developing me into the person I'm today and, more importantly, the person that I hope to become and for this, among many other reasons, I'll be forever grateful to him.

Going to the gym and staying in shape is of great importance to me. It's a lifestyle…the more quality time you spend exercising and the more effort you place on working out, the better the overall results, and the happier you'll be with the outcome. In order to achieve your physical goals, you also need to concentrate on your diet. Eating nutritious and well-balanced meals will have a direct effect on the level of your results. As Tim used to say…one-third workout, one-third diet and one-third rest, to achieve maximum results.

I believe this same discipline applies to developing a relationship with God. The effort you put forth will dictate the type of relationship that you have. I've come to view my relationship with God as a lifestyle and not something that I do on a Sunday by going to church. I think everyone needs to find their own unique spiritual path that allows them to have a fulfilling experience. For me, this relationship has been a long and ongoing process and I feel that I have a meaningful connection with Him after putting forth sincere effort.

I came to know that Lance believed in God. One day, while we were working out at the gym and happened to briefly touch on the subject of religion, he indicated that Jesus "died for us." We also had a brief conversation about God one evening when we were out having drinks at the Standard Hotel in downtown Los Angeles. We were at the rooftop pool bar and Lance made a passing reference to "his" God. This comment caught my attention and I replied that I believed that there's only one God. He agreed and told me that he too thought there was only one. I think he was trying to be politically correct when he referenced his God, so as not to offend me in the event I believed differently. Even though Lance and I never spoke in great length about our specific beliefs, we both understood one another on this topic and accepted that there was only one God.

Frequently, I was asked by various people if we were brothers or boyfriends, and at one restaurant in Beverly Hills, the hostess asked Lance if I was his father. Looking back, I find it interesting that we were very seldom pegged as just being friends. Strangers seemed to usually perceive us as having a special bond and naturally assumed that we were somehow linked to one another. I would've been honored to have been Lance's father, as he could've been the child that I had always hoped to raise. I also would've been thrilled to have been his older brother as he could've been the little brother that I always wanted to hang out with, but never did. But in the end, Lance was – most of all – simply my friend. Now that he has died, I've come to believe that God placed him in my path, knowing I needed the positive influence of this very special human being and that I would be forever changed by our bromance.

Lance had only read one book in his life, *A Child Called It*, written by Dave Pelzer, which I found amusing as I too have only read one book in my life, *Old Yeller*, by Fred Gipson. On the night that we went out to celebrate my birthday, when we were having cocktails at the W Hotel in Hollywood, I told Lance that I was writing a book. I could see in his facial expressions that he was surprised that I was writing the story of my life. I could also tell he was sincerely happy to hear that I was working on something that I was passionate about—and I found his enthusiasm very encouraging. Lance never realized how much of a positive influence he had on me. I worked from home and I had little personal interaction with people. The time I spent with him at the gym was instrumental in helping me make a personal connection with another person, after a harrowing time in Palm Springs. Without knowing it, Lance helped me to believe in myself and to trust people once again. He showed me that love can happen at the most unexpected time between the most unlikely people. My admiration for him is unbounded and, one day, I hope to be able to honor his life by establishing a nonprofit organization that will have a positive impact on the world. By building this legacy, I hope to show the love that I have for him and, more importantly, the love that Lance exuded wherever he went, without ever realizing it.

On Thursday, the eleventh of July, Lance and I stopped by Salvage, our usual watering hole on Seventh Street in downtown Los Angeles for a few drinks after the gym. Lance had five cocktails and I had three. We arrived at the bar at four thirty in the afternoon and left at twenty minutes after six. Aston and Bentley were being groomed and I needed to pick them up before seven o'clock. The walk from Salvage to the pet groomer's salon took twenty-minutes. As Lance and I left the bar, his intention was to head home for the night. We arrived at the Seventh Street and Flower metro stop, which is where Lance would've jumped on the train to head home. I suggested that he walk with me and catch his train at the Pershing Square Metra station at Hill and Fifth Street. The Pershing Square stop was in same direction that I was walking and Lance agreed to catch his train at that station. As we walked together, we chatted though I do not recall our conversation. We just genuinely enjoyed each other's company and it didn't matter what we were discussing; just spending time together was gratifying enough.

We arrived at the corner where Lance should've turned to catch the train at the Pershing Square station, but he kept walking with me and neither one of us said anything. We just kept walking. It seemed that he decided to spend more time with me that evening and I was happy to hang out with him for a while longer. Once we arrived at the groomers, Lance asked the woman at the front desk if he could use the restroom. I paid my bill and, when Lance returned, we headed to my apartment around the corner to drop off the dogs.

Lance and I had decided to have one more drink at a neighborhood bar next to my apartment building, on South Spring Street between Seventh and Six Streets. At the bar, Lance decided to open up to me in a way that he had not done in the eight months that I had known him. By now, I had four drinks and Lance was working on his sixth cocktail. We had been drinking for a four-hour period, so we were feeling pretty good, although we were definitely not drunk. He told me that when he was in his early years of schooling, he had been pegged as having special needs, with having a learning disability, specifically. I chuckled a bit when Lance told me this story, because he would be the last person I could imagine with a learning disability. He was a charismatic individual that elicited comments from strangers – whenever we were out – who were taken by his beauty and felt compelled to comment on it—and having a disability did not feature in his makeup. We had spoken extensively over the past eight months…covering a wide range of topics, including current events, relationships, the U.S. military, our personal lives, music, movies, and food—to name a few. At no time, did I ever get the impression that he had a learning disability. When he divulged his so called special needs that his teachers had diagnosed when he was a child, I could not stop from smiling. He was so well-adjusted and the opposite of what I believe one would be if they had a learning disability that I found it difficult to picture it. I believe his teachers were correct in their assessment that Lance was special, just not in the manner that they had originally thought.

In hindsight, Lance is a perfect example of how a perceived weakness in life can become our strongest characteristic. Due to his so-called disability, he developed a compassion for others and became a very patient person when dealing with people that had challenges. He always was willing to give people the benefit of the doubt and I believe this characteristic was driven by the lack of patience that his teachers had shown him over the years. He became very tolerant of people's shortcomings and was always willing to assist those in need. Lance used his early experience in life as a learning platform to become a better person, a standard to which we should all aspire.

After Lance and I finished our drinks, I told him I would walk to the Pershing Square station with him, which was four blocks away. We began walking on Spring Street toward the train station and after one block, between Fifth and Six Streets, Lance turned to me and said that he decided he was going to walk home, instead of catching the train. It was not unusual for him to walk to his apartment from my place, which he had done on several occasions. The walk was a forty-five-minute trek for him.

We said our goodbye and hugged twice. Every other time, after the gym whenever we finished working out, as we parted ways at the train station, we always shook each other's hand and wished one another a good night. For some reason, on this evening, something was different. Instead of shaking each other's hand, we hugged one another twice. This was the last time I would see Lance alive. I left him at eight o'clock that evening and, sometime between then and midnight, Lance was murdered on his way home to East Los Angeles. At some point, as he walked from downtown LA through little Tokyo and the Art District toward his home, he encountered evil. When Lance was crossing over the First Street bridge it's believed that he had an altercation with someone and that someone threw Lance off the bridge that leads from the Art District into East Los Angeles. As Lance was thrown over the railing of the bridge, he fell and hit his head on the concrete pavement below and eventually bled out. This tragic event ended his life.

Three or four months before his untimely death, we had been out one Friday evening. That night, Lance had also walked home from where I lived on Seventh and Spring, as he had frequently done before. The following Monday, Lance told me a story about his walk home. He related that when he came to the same First Street bridge, that connects the Art District and East Los Angeles, he had stopped on the bridge to rest for a few minutes before walking the rest of the way home. As he was leaning on the balustrade of the bridge, passing cars began to honk their horns. He said he didn't know why they were honking at him, but felt that they had done so because they must have thought he was going to jump off the bridge. In hindsight, I can't help but wonder whether this was a premonition of what would come to pass several months later, when he was maliciously thrown to his death off that same bridge.

The day before Lance died, we went to Home Depot after the gym. On the way to the store that Wednesday, we crossed over the Seventh Street bridge, at South Figueroa Street in downtown Los Angeles, which spans over the 101 Freeway. As we crossed the bridge, Lance described how, when he was in school, a person tried to throw themselves off that same bridge. The following day, he himself was thrown off another bridge on the other side of the city. This incident on the bridge, together with the other bridge story that Lance shared with me, seemed to me to be very strange set of coincidences. It's as if the universe was trying to send me a message—and the fact that I heard these premonitions directly from Lance makes them all the more foreboding.

I've struggled with why God didn't protect Lance from harm and this tragedy has certainly tested my faith and my belief in Him. How could He let this happen to my dear friend? I understand that there has been and will continue to be many things that happen in life that I'll never be able to truly understand, including the reason why my good buddy Lance died in such a manner. I will just believe that Lance must have encountered something evil on that bridge that night—an appalling example of a random act of senseless violence. Like many people of faith, I take solace in knowing that Lance's time here on earth was for a much greater cause than I can possibly imagine and believe that God has a greater plan for his life's legacy than his family and friends can begin to comprehend.

In addition to these bridge incidents, there are several bizarre numerical coincidences, related to Lance's death, that I have observed. When I moved from Palm Springs to Los Angeles, I signed a new rental lease for my loft at 650 South Spring Street (6+5+0=**11**). The start date for that lease was April **13**, 20**11**. The night that he died, before we said goodbye, he had been in my apartment as we dropped off the dogs after picking them up from the groomer's. At the end of our evening and as I was walking with him to the Pershing Square train station, we stopped and parted ways on Spring Street between Fifth and Sixth Streets (5+6=**11**). It was here that Lance turned to me and said he was going to walk home so he could save the train fare. My apartment building's address, where Lance was inside on the night he died, not only adds up to the number **eleven** – the day of the month that he passed away –the building also happened to be at the corner of **Seventh** and Spring Streets—and Lance died in the **seventh** month of the year. My apartment in that building was on the ninth floor and its unit number was 9**13** (9+1+3=**13**).

I was informed that Lance had passed away two days after he died, on the **thirteen** day of the **seventh** month.

After I learned of his death, and I turned and turned the night's events over and over in my mind, I began to wonder what ties we had to the numbers **eleven** and **thirteen**. I realized that Lance had texted me for the very first time in November, the **eleventh** month, on the **thirteenth** day of that month to invite me to work out. I began to see a pattern to these two numbers. Lance's birthday was on the twenty fourth of November, **eleven** days after we began to work out together. The lease on my apartment was scheduled to expire on the twenty fourth of July in 2013, but due to certain circumstances, the lease was adjusted to expire two weeks earlier and it now expired on the same Saturday when I was informed of Lance's death, the **thirteenth** day of the **seven** month. I began to write my memoirs in January 20**11**, while still residing in Palm Springs, and I dated them on the **thirteenth** of May of 20**13**, while living at 650 Spring Street in Los Angeles when Lance was still alive.

While I might lose you in the midst of all these dates and numbers, I share them for two reasons. The numbers **eleven** and **thirteen** depict a pattern that keeps repeating in my relationship with Lance—and I've come to believe that the number eleven and thirteen that surround his life and passing is an intricate pattern of code from an inexplicable place. In Numerology, the number eleven is a master number—something above and beyond the mundane. It's believed to be the link between mortal and immortal, between man and spirit. Individuals associated with the number eleven, like Lance, are believed to be very intuitive and spiritual messengers. The number thirteen represents the number of God. It's derived from the number six, which represents man, and the number seven, which represents creation (6+7=**13**). I now believe God created a path for us to meet. My journey from Palm Springs to Los Angeles was specifically designed to bring us together. This is why the buildings address where I lived and unit number are representative of the day and month that Lance and I began building our friendship.

One month after Lance died, on the **eleventh** of August, I traveled from Chicago to Los Angeles for his memorial service, held by his family. He was cremated and laid to rest at Forest Lawn in Long Beach, the same city where I was born, in crypt number 2018 (2+0+1+8=**11**). Even in death, I find his final resting place to be another coincidence that links us together.

I traveled back to Chicago and landed on the **thirteen** of August, exactly one month from the date that I was notified that he had died. Interestingly, in the year 2018 (2+0+1+8=**11**), the same number as Lance's final resting place, I will be fifty-eight years old (5+8=**13**). When he passed away, I had just begun to write chapter **eleven** of this book, which was not originally intended to detail my admiration and love for him, nor his death. After I learned that Lance had died, I read an article on the internet that his body was discovered on the morning of July 12 by bridge workers who happened to be walking under the First Street bridge. The article was written by a reporter whose last name was Lloyd, same as mine albeit with a different spelling, and the article was written on **thirteenth** day of the **seventh** month of 20**13**—exactly eight months to the day after our first workout and the day Lance and I began our friendship.

Most people are familiar with the famous picture of the three firemen raising the American flag at ground zero after the World Trade Center towers came down. In the eight months that I knew Lance, we only took three photos together. The pictures of us were taken on the rooftop of the Standard Hotel, in downtown Los Angeles, at the pool bar. There are two American flags in the background. When looking at the pictures in detail after Lance died, I realized that the stars, in the upper left of the American flag, representing the fifty states, are laid out in nine vertical rows and eleven horizontal rows. I noted that this numerical sequence in the flag – the numbers nine and eleven – curiously ties the nation's flag to September 11. More coincidently, the number thirteen, God's number, is also represented by the number of stripes on the flag, which add up to thirteen (6 white stripes + 7 red stripes=**13**).

My life has been riddled with such coincidences and I've come to believe that these so-called coincidences in life are not that at all and I now pay close attention to these situations. In Lance's case, I've come to believe that "something" is reaching out in my direction, trying to give me some comfort in dealing with his life coming to such an abrupt and violent end. I once heard Joel Osteen, a famous preacher, say that "the people that God places in your life are not there by accident. It's not a coincidence, they're a gift from God." This is how I view Lance.

On the evening of Wednesday, the third of July, Lance and I went for a drink after the gym and he told me that his sister had gone into labor that afternoon. Sometime after midnight, on the Fourth of July, his sister had a little baby girl. The following Tuesday, Lance walked with me to my apartment building to pick up a gift that I wanted to give him for his newborn niece—a large white teddy bear. Curiously, at the time, I had begun to write this chapter and was in the middle of writing the story about David and his teddy bear. I would not make the connection between what I had wrote and my gift for Lance's newborn niece until after his death

Seven days after Lance's new niece was brought into this world (fourth day + seventh month=**11**), Lance left it on the eleventh day of the seventh month. At Lance's memorial service, the officiant stated that "through knowing Lance and having the privilege to experience his love, we encountered the face of God." By knowing and loving Lance, I do feel as if I have looked directly into the face of God and I came to see that it's not about Lance's death or the sad circumstances surrounding it. It's about his life. While I may never understand the true meaning behind his passing, I believe that God has a plan to utilize the relationship that Lance and I developed with one another for a greater good. Lance changed me as a person and impacted my life. I'm grateful for our time together and cherish the memories of our friendship. Like the fair youth on the Arcadian urn, he'll remain forever young and handsome—an archangel in the eyes of those who knew and loved him.

12 | IT'S NOT ABOUT WINNING OR LOSING; IT'S ABOUT HOW YOU PLAY THE GAME

After living in San Francisco for six years, I became interested in exploring other careers outside of California. I had managed to become quite successful working for Brad, selling retail store fixture environments for his company, in San Carlos. My success was not immediate, it was built over several years of consistently developing new business for the company. Looking back on the experience, I certainly have regrets. I allowed circumstances and people within the organization to come between me and Brad. The time that I spent partying on the weekends – and the drug use that went with this behavior – was also a contributing factor to my strained relationship with him and his company. In general, my late-night partying had a profound effect on my disposition, which regrettably effected how I interacted with Brad and ultimately had a negative impact on our relationship.

I earned about one hundred and forty thousand dollars the last year that I worked for Brad, a very good salary. While I've come to believe that "money can't buy you happiness", it can certainly offer you relief from living a painful existence. Someone who had money – and happened to be unhappy in life – must have been the type of person who originated this saying. A less fortunate individual, who never had money and was suffering financial duress, would never make this type of claim. Money can be like comfort food, it's so comforting to see a plethora of dollars in one's back account, especially when you have none.

My decision to move to San Francisco from Chicago had been driven by my relationship with Alex. Since I was born in Long Beach, I was more familiar with the Los Angeles area and would've preferred to reside in the southern part of the state. The LA boys, with their blond locks and their shaved bodies, combined with the glitz and glamour of Beverly Hills were more my style than the jean and T-shirt wearing hairy bears of San Francisco, although who doesn't love a hot grizzly bear to keep them warm at night. I followed my heart when moving to San Francisco, but after my breakup with Alex – and after spending six years in the bay area – I thought it was time for me to make a break from the bears of the redwood forests of Northern

California and decided to pursue my life-long dream of living and working in the Big Apple. San Francisco…darling, I love you, but give me Park Avenue, or at least the gay boys in Chelsea.

Ever since I was a young man, I had dreamt of working and living in New York. A year after the World Trade Center towers came under attack, my dream would come to fruition. I interviewed for an account executive position with an Italian manufacturer of retail store merchandising systems that had an U.S. sales office in New York. This company was a direct competitor with Brad's company, which made me a desirable candidate for their operation based in Manhattan. After September 11, the sales for the Italian company dropped from three million dollars for the Northeastern territory to just over a million. If I were to be offered the position, it would be my responsibility to jump start the territory as fast as I could and build a solid client base – in the first year of my employment – that generated three and a half million dollars in sales. Certainly not an easy task, although I was confident that I could accomplish the target and hit the aggressive projected sales goal.

After several months of conversations, interviews, and negotiations, I was offered the position at a salary of one hundred and ten thousand dollars, with a guaranteed commission of thirty thousand dollars for my first year of employment. I would have the opportunity to earn an additional six percent on sales over one and a half million dollars. To the average individual this may sound like a large salary, but it was not uncommon for New York. My rent in the city cost me forty two hundred dollars a month for an amazing two bedroom, two bathroom apartment on Tenth Avenue, at the corner of 42nd street, adjacent to the Lincoln Tunnel, in a newly constructed high-rise. I also needed to continue to pay the twenty two hundred dollar monthly mortgage on the condominium in San Francisco that I owned, until the unit sold. With the two dwellings on my plate, this monthly outlay of $6,400 in rent and mortgage was certainly a large expense, but I was counting on selling the condominium in San Francisco in a short time. Unfortunately, a quick sale on the unit was not in the cards.

I arrived in New York and took possession of my new apartment, on the 34th floor, the day before Christmas Eve in 2002. The following morning, I awoke to a major snowstorm that had arrived in the middle of the night. It had been over six years since Puckles and Papi had lived in a city where snow fell in the winter. I got the boys ready for their morning walk and we left the apartment and headed toward the elevators. We traveled down to the lobby and when we approached the exit of the building, the boys stopped dead in their tracks when they saw what awaited them outside. I had to carry them two blocks to the Jacob Javits Convention Center where there was a grassy area where they could do their business. They were not featuring the snow whatsoever and I also had to carry them back to the apartment. It was freezing that Christmas Eve, with snow blowing from every direction. The boys must have wondered "what has this crazy bitch done to us, by moving to such a cold and snowy place?"

I too was wondering if I had made the right decision to move to New York. It was too late to rethink my decision. There was no turning back. Our belongings had been packed and loaded on a moving truck that was making its way across the country to meet up with us. I had resigned from my position in San Francisco and had placed my California residence on the market. Would my decision become the fulfillment of my life-long dream of living and working in Manhattan? Or was it going to turn into a nightmare for me and the boys? Only time would reveal what life had in store and what I would encounter in New York at 42nd Street and Tenth Avenue, in apartment 34J.

As fate would have it, the president of my new company, to whom I reported, had studied at a seminary to become a priest. Before taking his vows, he decided not join the priesthood. Later, I would look back on my life in Manhattan and realize that it was perhaps not a coincidence that brought this would-be-Father and me together—and have since come to believe Fate was involved in bringing me to this specific company and supervisor.

It was a time of great unrest in New York, as the 2002 Christmas season ended and the New Year began. The average New Yorker was feeling anxious. Talk of war with Iraq was brewing and adding more unease to an already anxious environment. The aftermath of September 11 was still lurking in the air; it had been a little over a year since the attack on the World Trade Center. Perhaps it was the mood of the city, or just my own baggage that I was carrying, but like most New Yorkers, I had my guard up. My anxiety was not attributable to the fallout of September 11 or the talk of the coming war with Iraq, I was outfitted for a different type of battle. I had declared war on anyone that would attempt to get in my way to become successful in my new position or who would even think of messing with me in any way, shape, or form. After leaving California and the messed-up behavior engendered by Alex, I was not willing to entertain any additional mind games or people's alternative agendas. I was a military of one with Tina at the command center. The casualties would be enormous.

My office was in Chelsea on 25th Street, between Sixth and Seventh (6+7=**13**) Avenues. Every morning when I left my luxury apartment and jumped into a cab in front of my building and headed to the office, I felt like I was living my dream. In the beginning, it was exciting for both my professional and personal life. There was never a dull moment in the city. Every day, an adventure lurked around every corner. But like anyone who has lived in other parts of the country – and who has moved to Manhattan will probably tell you – the honeymoon doesn't last long. The reality and the hardships of living in the city hit you fast and it hits you hard. I hid my drug use, which was easy to do amid the crowded city. I began to drink more. In a short time, I discovered that there were bars on every street and in most corners of the city. I soon came to understand that if I was going to make it through the stressful days, weeks, months and years of living in New York, I would need to fortify myself and have a drink or two during the day at lunch – and possibly a few at the end of my day – to make the overwhelming hardships of life in the city a little easier to manage—or so it seemed that way at the time. I would later realize that I moved to New York too late in life. If I had been in my thirties, rather than my forties when I moved there, I probably would've enjoyed the crazed and fast-paced life more than I did at forty-one. Was I too old or was I just unwilling to become part of the rat race of the Big Apple? Did I just need time to adjust to the fast and crazy life in the city? Would I eventually realize that the rat race was exactly what I needed to overcome my feelings of loneliness?

After leaving my office one rainy evening, I walked northwest on Twenty Fifth Street and made a right turn on Seventh Avenue, heading toward my apartment. It had been a very trying day and I thought I would grab dinner to take home from a little market on Seventh Avenue. If you've never been to New York, these city-wide markets sell a variety of prepared cold and hot foods available buffet-style. You fill a plastic container with your selections and these are weighed and priced by the pound. I then noticed a man who seemed like he might be following me. In New York, it's always good to be aware of your surroundings and who may be lurking nearby. In a city of that size, there are so many people on the street at any given time that inevitably there's bound to be someone behind you that seems like they could be following you.

In this instance, I had an overwhelming sensation that I was being followed. I was not being paranoid and I only noticed the man because it was raining. When it rains in New York everyone is running to catch a cab, if they can find one, or running to a train station, or just running to get out of the rain. The man kept an even distance between us the entire time we walked up Seventh Avenue. When I walked into the market to get my dinner to take home, he followed me into the store. I took a plastic container and began to walk around the buffet, selecting and filling my container with my favorite foods, while keeping one eye on the man that had been following me on the street and into the market. I was careful not to make direct eye contact with him because I didn't want to offer him the opportunity to engage me in conversation. When I reached the cashier to pay for my items, he followed me again and stood directly behind me in line. I had not seen him pickup any items in the store.

I was not going to turn around to see what he may have been holding, if anything, or what he was going to buy. I really didn't care if he was purchasing anything, I just wanted to see if my suspicions were correct. The cashier took my container and placed it on the scale and told me the price for the food. The man behind me then began to talk, although I was not focused on what he was saying. I just wanted to pay for my food, get home and out of the rain so I could enjoy the rest of my evening with Puck and Papi.

The man behind me kept uttering something over and over again and, as I began to concentrate on what he was saying, I noticed that the cashier was becoming fidgety and showing signs of being nervous. I then heard the man behind me voice what the hell was in my container that was so expensive. Upon hearing this, the cashier took my plastic container and re-weighed it. He then told me that my food was now eight dollars less. I turned half way to the man behind me, so as not to give him my full attention, and I thanked him for his intervention. After I paid, I headed out of the market with my container of food and continued up Seventh Avenue toward my apartment. The man that followed me into the store was no longer in pursuit. I continued to walk home. I wondered if the mysterious man could have been an angel. This was certainly debatable, although in the days that followed, I would realize that he must have been an earthly angel, if not a heavenly one. The real question to be answered is who or what sent him.

I had been traveling to New York since I was twenty-five. I knew New York was an expensive city, but I soon realized why it was more expensive than it should have been. Over the next several days, I began to pay close attention to what I bought and the cash transactions in which I engaged. I discovered that I was being consistently short-changed and being taken advantage of when paying for things.

The morning after my encounter with the stranger, I hailed a cab outside my building to go to my office. Once I arrived, the cab driver said the fare was six dollars. I handed him a twenty and he handed me my change. Normally, I would just take my money and shove it in my pocket, as I exited the cab, without ever counting it to ensure I had received the correct amount. However, due to what took place the prior evening, I counted the money and, to my amazement, I discovered that I received change for a ten-dollar bill, not a twenty. Was this another random coincidence or was there more to this new awareness brought on by my follower from the previous night? Over the next several days, when I handed a twenty-dollar bill to various people – at different venues around the city – to pay for items that were less than ten dollars, the money that I received back was incorrect for three separate transactions. I was given change for a ten-dollar bill, instead of the twenty-dollar bills with which I paid. No wonder the city seemed so expensive to me. I was being consistently short changed by many people. I wondered how many times I had been taken advantage of when visiting Manhattan over the years. The circumstances surrounding the man that followed me into the market that rainy evening after work seemed like more than a bizarre incident and more, in its' simplest form, like a guarding angel sent to awaken me to the realities of life in the big city.

I had now been living in New York for three months, making it through one of the coldest winters there in twenty years. Spring was in the air, although the anticipation of the warmer months was accompanied by overtones of anxiety from the lurking war with Iraq. In March of that year, I was Chicago for a retail tradeshow when the war with Iraq became a reality and I returned to New York on the day that the U.S. declared war. The tension in the airport was enormous and it felt like my flight would not make it safely to its destination. I trusted that Fate would have her day, so I boarded the flight and left it to her to land the plane safely back on the East Coast, or not.

My flight landed without incident in the air or on the ground. Once I arrived in the city, the military was present on every major street corner. I had not experienced anything like this before. It was like something you see in a movie. Military personal were carrying machine guns and they were on the streets and in every train station above ground, as well as the subway stations below ground. Civilians were extremely serious and intense. Military war planes circled the city at all hours of the day and night and there was a defining visual feeling that a potential war could encroach on the city and become a reality at any moment. The heavy military presence was a precautionary measure implemented by the U.S. government to protect the city and ease the tensions that were still lurking from the September 11 attacks and the potential possibility of reprisals in retaliation for America attacking Iraq. I was living in what resembled a war zone, which was symbolic, as a war is what I would find myself fighting in a short time. My own war, however, was a personal one and it involved battling and trying to conquer my fears. My immediate battle was to defeat my professional fears. I needed to overcome my fear of failure. If I didn't conquer this fear, it could impact my ability to reach my target sales goals, which in turn would prevent me from meeting my financial commitments.

As the anxiety in the city rose in the days and weeks following the onset of the war, my disposition was beginning to reflect the uncertainty that was mounting in the city. When I had arrived, I had zero debt and six months later, I had accrued a debt of forty thousand dollars. I was bleeding financially, stemming from not being able to sell the condominium in San Francisco at my desired price. Carrying the mortgage on the condo, and its associated monthly expenses – on top of my rent in New York – was more than my monthly paycheck. I needed to do something to stop the profuse financial outlays, but what avenue could I take to relieve the hemorrhaging? I could apply a tourniquet, such as renting the unit, to slow the bleeding or I could amputate the property from my responsibilities and sell it at a loss, a more dramatic solution.

As most things in life, timing is usually essential to a successful outcome and this is especially true when selling real estate. Selling a property in one of the hottest areas of the country would require placing the unit on the market at the correct time to maximize the profit I was expecting. The economy in San Francisco had begun to slow and this was going to impact the sale of my unit at my price. Fortunately, I had bought my amazing thirteen-hundred square foot condominium on the top floor of a newly constructed building at a reasonable price, for San Francisco, during a dip in the market following September 11. I had only lived in the unit for a year when I decided to take the new position in New York and I needed to sell it because I was not in the financial position to maintain two homes in the most expensive cities in the country. Unfortunately for me, the time to sell it was not ideal. A few months after placing the unit on the market, I came to realize that a quick sell of the property was not going to be possible.

Six months passed and I still had not received a serious offer for the condominium. In the time the unit had been on the market, I only received one offer of less than four hundred thousand dollars, when I had anticipated an offer closer to the five hundred thousand dollar range. The low offer would've only paid off my mortgage and the relator's fee. I could've dumped the property for what I owed and forfeited my original down payment, but I would've been free and clear of the financial responsibility. However, this option would've left me forty thousand dollars in the hole, the debt I had accumulated maintaining two homes.

I needed to make a decision. The situation was adding a tremendous amount of stress that was weighing on me. I certainly could've taken the single lowball offer, dump the property, and been free of the financial burden. However, if I had learned one lesson in life so far, it was that the easiest solution to a problem is not always the best solution. My subconscious told me that I needed to wait and explore all my options before making a final decision on how best to proceed. Anticipating the future highs and lows of the real estate market in San Francisco was going to be critical in making a profit or a loss.

With the war in Iraq now in full throttle, the military on every street corner provided anxious New Yorkers with calming signs of strength and support. I too was feeling anxious, albeit more for the financial calamity that had engulfed my life. My debt was rising daily. The more it rose, the more stress I experienced. It was becoming all-consuming. I was not sleeping at night and the situation was getting the best of me. I needed to come up with my own defensive plan quickly. My financial affairs were worsening by the day and required immediate attention. I had to strengthen my financial position sooner rather than later or otherwise I could soon be facing potential bankruptcy, a financial disaster for my creditors and myself.

If I had a crystal ball, I wonder what it would have told me about the real estate market in San Francisco. Would it have advised me to hold out for at least another year or possibly two before selling? Would the real estate market rebound and, if so, when? If I held onto the condo, could I sell it at a higher price later, allowing me the option to pay off the debt that I was now carrying? I decided to listen to my gut and wait to sell—and allow Fate to intervene. The solution was going to be very complex, although worth the wait.

My apartment in the city was on the thirty-fourth floor of a forty-five-story building. From my bedroom window, I could see the steeple of a church opposite my building. I was literally across the street from a house of God and, at the time, the proximity of the church to my home seemed like yet another simple random coincidence. Was it a coincidence? Or was it happenstance *and* confirmation that I happened to be standing in the exact place and time that I was supposed to be there? I now believe the situation that led me to reside next to a church in Manhattan was not a coincidence, but a visual for me to take notice and a sign that God was close by.

After becoming positive, something had drawn me to visit the great cathedrals of Europe. I had visited Westminster Abbey and St. Paul's Cathedral in London. I traveled to Notre-Dame, Sacré Coeur and Sainte Chappelle in Paris, where I saw the Crown of Thorns. I visited Il Duomo in Milan and Florence, St. Mark's in Venice, the Dom in Berlin, and St. Peter's Basilica in the Vatican, where I was amazed by this seat of the Roman Catholic Church that I always admired. I marveled at seeing a relic of Jesus' crib at Santa Maria Maggiore in Rome. I prayed to God many times, in front of breathtaking gothic and baroque altars, over many years, in these and other churches—to keep me healthy. I was carrying the HIV virus and I had no idea how much longer my luck was going to last before I became ill. I thought that it couldn't hurt to ask God to keep me safe, even though I had no relationship with him. Over twenty-seven years after contracting the virus, I'm healthy and here to tell you that God not only heard my prayers, he answered them.

Moving to New York when the city was unsettled seemed very much like a deliberate maneuver by Fate to envelop my existence in a volatile environment so I could see the world in a different light. I too was in a state of unrest and the military presence in the city would open my eyes to the harsh realities of the world that I never paid attention to before. I still had not begun to notice God, but my time in the city was monumental to my overall spiritual development. It wasn't until I began to reflect upon my life and experiences that I realized God had been trying to build a relationship with me my entire life. Today, I see the financial pressures that I was facing – together with the potential hostile environment in the city – as lost opportunities to interface with God—and I have since come to believe that many of the coincidences in my life were in fact God reaching out to me. Each coincidence built upon the other, like floors in a high-rise. Each floor

I've encountered leading me to a heightened awareness. I hope to eventually reach the ultimate floor where everyone wants to dwell—the penthouse in the building with the best views. It wasn't until several years after living in New York that I would find myself reunited with BoBo, my long-forgotten childhood friend.

13 | YANIV

I had been living in New York for six months when I took the San Francisco condominium off the market. I decided to listen to my intuition and followed the advice of the silent voice that I was hearing. I was not exactly sure who was speaking to me. Possibly it was Fate who was whispering in my ear. I refinanced the apartment and secured an interest-only loan, which resulted in a much lower monthly payment. Rick was still living in San Francisco and being the good friend that he was, I was able to convince him to move into the unit and rent it for sixteen hundred dollars a month. In doing so, Rick would cover the expense of the refinanced mortgage and the monthly assessments with his rent payment. He lived just a few blocks from my place and by moving and renting my unit, he would save a few hundred dollars a month and would be doing me a great favor, a win-win for both parties.

I believe sincere friendships are a key element to achieving success in this life. I also believe God did not create us to go through life alone. A man or a woman without a good a friend in this world is someone that might not have a chance to become successful. If there's another thing that I've learned in life…it's that at some point in our journey we will find ourselves in a position where we need a friend to lean on to comfort us and, more importantly, offer us support during our challenging times. Whether this support is emotional or financial, it usually has a far greater effect on the person in need than one can imagine. I've also come to discover that when an individual is doing well financially, they'll usually have all kinds of people that want to be their friend. In one of her hit songs, Cher asks, "when the money's gone, will you be my friend?" To me, the true test of friendship is those individuals that are still around – and are part of your life – when the money's gone and you have nothing to offer other than yourself. Rick is one of these individuals and he has been part of my life through thick and thin. He has joined me in celebrating the good times of my life, but – more importantly – when I was broke and had nothing to offer other than my friendship, he was a reassuring and constant presence in my life, lending his financial support and emotional comfort in my time of need.

At last, my financial hemorrhaging had finally come to an end. Would I recover from the loss of the forty thousand dollars of debt that I incurred in my attempt to shore up both residences? Only time would bring the answer to the forty thousand dollar question.

God will never put more on your plate than he knows you can handle, goes the expression, which is very true in my case. After I got my financial situation under control and stabilized the debt that I was incurring by maintaining two homes, a work associate informed me of a rumor that was circulating in the office. She told me that she had heard that I had a drug problem. Today, I can find some humor in this anecdote. Getting people to talk about you in New York—whether in a good or a bad way is a complicated matter. There's a great deal taking place on a single day in the city and my life being the topic of conversation is definitely saying something. Growing up in a small town and finding my way to live and work in New York was a major accomplishment. Having people in Manhattan talking about me was more than I would have expected—and a far cry from the little skinny poof that was bullied in grammar school by his classmates and labeled a pansy. However, had someone told me that this rumor was circulating within my industry and city, at a time when I was under financial duress, I would've lost all my marbles and gone on a crazed hunting expedition to confront the gossips with loose tongues.

After being told of the rumor, I went back to my office and immediately asked to speak to my assistant. I started by telling her that I would appreciate if she answered the question that I was about to pose to her with the candid truth, as we were a team and I believed I deserved a truthful answer. She nodded her head in agreement with what I was asking. I inquired whether she had heard that I had a drug problem. Without hesitation, she replied yes, she had. I then asked her when she heard this rumor and she explained that she heard it prior to my arrival in New York. I was stunned. The story had been circulating on the streets for six months after I arrived and before it had been brought to my attention. My longtime affair with illegal drugs had finally caught up with me. Unbeknownst to me, the rumor had also reached the ears of the president of my company. To my amazement, I discovered that the would-be Father was watching me, or as he might prefer to tell it, he had me under close observation.

I began to take a closer look at my work environment. I realized that almost all my co-workers had heard the rumor and judged me without ever having a conversation with me. I felt that if the company had invested ten thousand dollars to move me across the entire United States, then they would certainly confront an employee rumored to be using illegal drugs. I was wrong. Instead, I found myself isolated from my co-workers. They had made up their minds about me and were looking for signs of my being high at work. Worse yet, the would-be Father was deliberately speaking to me in a confrontational way to see if I would react erratically. He was aggressively challenging me on several areas, including building my sales territory.

One day, we had a confrontation that changed the dynamics of our relationship and would be a defining day. We were attending a retail tradeshow convention in Chicago and were standing in the company's booth with co-workers and customers. The director of purchasing was being a bitch to me and I was upset that she was being rude and treating me badly. She and I had a history of butting heads because I was bringing custom projects to the company and she was consistently falling short of the client's expectations, which precluded my territory from securing the sale. I was expected to grow the business substantially in a years' time and I needed the support of the entire company to make it happen. I finally had enough of her hostile behavior. I, of course, was using Tina, as I had done regularly since I started working for the company—and she wasn't going to let me take any prisoners. I lost my temper and flipped out on her and the Father in the booth, in the middle of the convention floor. After a heated conversation, I asked the aspiring Father to fire her, or let me go back to my hotel room as I wouldn't stand in the same booth with her. Subsequently, I was sent packing to my room at the hotel. For some unknown reason, I was wearing a rosary around my neck that day—as if a heavenly body had armed me, as if it knew, in some strange way, that I was going to engage in battle that afternoon.

While I was certainly using drugs, I was also consistently going to work punctually every day. I was normally the first person in the office and opened the showroom each morning. I was also the last person to usually leave the office and closed the showroom nightly. I was hired to bring in three and a half million dollars in business that year. By June, my assistant and I had one million four hundred thousand dollars in sales and we were on track to make our sales goal. I certainly understand that it's not acceptable to do drugs and go to work, but in my defense…I was trying to maintain my work commitments even as I was dealing with the demons that had been chasing me for years and had followed me to New York. Much like the apple that proved to be Adam's demise, the Big Apple was looking as if it was going to be my demise too.

Amidst all the crazy events, a wonderful relief to the overwhelming stress took place. The same woman that happened to be on the television that morning in Marin County when I walked into the house, after walking the dogs and after deciding to leave Alex, was in the city performing at Madison Square Garden. Yes, Ms. Cher was in town for her 'farewell tour'. This would be the third Cher concert that I would have the pleasure to attend in the last few years. I had previously seen Cher perform in concert in Oakland and in San Jose, California a year or two earlier. Interestingly, she was performing on two nights: Wednesday, June 11 and Thursday, June 12 of 2003. I don't recall which day I went to see her, but would it not be beyond coincidental if it were on the **eleventh** of June? The woman that I believed God placed in my path to give me those essential encouraging words that would inspire me to go the distance in my pursuit of a better life than the lie that I had been living in California, was now performing in my city. Once again, I was in desperate need of her comfort and support. God clearly knew that I still did not have a relationship with him, so he again sent a voice – Cher's in this instance – to encourage me, until the day when I would begin to seek a relationship with Him and begin to listen for His voice and receive His words of encouragement.

Do you believe in life after love? As Cher sang these words, I was encouraged that I'd get through those difficult times. I did not need Alex anymore, although I was still licking my wounds from the aftermath of our relationship, even six years later. The real question was whether I was strong enough to make it through to the other side. If I did make it through the trials and tribulations, would I love again? Would there be life after love? While I didn't realize it, it seems that there was a plan and Cher was going to be an integral part of it. I heard on several occasions that God will reveal himself to the world, through his people…and I love to think that Cher is one of God's messengers, whether she realizes it or not. I created trouble for myself at work and I was possibly going to be unemployed shortly, but I had my own Sybil to prophesize to me and let me know it was all going to be OK.

Each day that I walked through the streets of New York, I feared evil. Like the military presence, I was mentally armed for any potential encounter with evil and ready for battle. I was still fighting the demons of insecurity and self-doubt that had been unleashed by Alex's lies. When there's fear in your heart and battle on your mind, there's little room for God. I believe He had begun to fight for my existence without me ever making a conscious effort to embrace His authority over the demons that tormented me. This is probably why, for no apparent reason that I can recall, that I took a rosary that I bought at the Vatican many years earlier and was now wearing it around my neck every day. I think subconsciously I was hoping it would offer me divine protection.

Looking back, the individual pieces of my life seemed to be laid out before me, like a jigsaw puzzle poured out of a box onto a table. To make sense out of the individual pieces and to have the satisfaction of seeing the completed picture I would need to rely on my determination to bring the pieces together. What I did not know at the time was the enjoyment that would follow in being able to make sense out of my life's random coincidences, but this was not going to be possible without a relationship with God. Once I added God to the equation, things began to relate to one another and the puzzle pieces would begin to fit together. First, a few came together, then a few more, until eventually I was able to see a glimpse, and then an outline of a picture. As the picture evolved, each coincidence had more meaning than I had previously thought and soon the outline was transformed into a plan that I believe God has intended for my life. But, I would need to wait five more years and suffer through many more life lessons before I could establish a meaningful relationship with Him. Somewhere in my subconscious, however, the process had already begun. I struggled with the meaning of my life for years before the conscious part of my mind would eventually catch up with my subconscious.

Timing is key in most aspects of our life and having a deep relationship with the God is certainly contingent on developing a connection when the time is right. I believe that when one is at the furthest point of a ridge, lost, lonely, sad, and broken – and about ready to fall off a cliff – God is there, standing by our side. If we're ready to begin to listen for the voice within us…no matter where we are in life, no matter what roads we've traveled, no matter how many wrong turns we've taken, no matter how far we've gone in the wilderness, no matter how lost we may be in the desert, no matter how close one might be to stepping off that cliff, once we listen to our inner voice, God will turn-on our spiritual navigation. He will re-calculate our position and, if we're willing, we can begin the journey home. The road can and, most likely, will be long and it can be perilous, without shortcuts, but I've found it's certainly worth the effort and dependent on what you're willing to put forth.

My spiritual compass was nonexistent in New York. I was lost on my journey. I had traveled across the country in search of a better life and found myself feeling unhappy and empty. I was still naïve to the under-handed ways of the world. My life-long dream to live and work in the city had become a daily fight…a fight for financial survival and for my career. The dream had turned into a living nightmare. Was evil going to win? Were the drugs finally going to become my demise? Could I hold onto my dream of a better life, or would I fold my cards and leave Manhattan in defeat? After I lost my cool that day on the convention floor with the wannabe Father, my days of working with the Italian company were numbered and management wanted me out. Before I lost my job, however, Fate unveiled a new plan that did not include being employed by the Italians any longer. She sent wise Jewish gentlemen to my rescue, who came offering salvation in the form of a new job offer.

My new job as a creative director for a family-owned visual merchandising company was also on west 25th Street. Only Fate could've orchestrated such a simple solution to such a complex problem. Not only did I get a new position, my salary also increased. Coincidentally, as concentrated as the city can be, with all the companies located there, I literally relocated just across the street from my former employer. I worked for the Bernstein's for the next year. I developed two new product lines for the company and remodeled their Manhattan showroom, a tremendous achievement. Now, in addition to fulfilling my dream of living and working in New York, I also achieved a career goal of working as a designer in the Big Apple.

While my professional life seemed back on track, my personal life was less so. I had become increasingly paranoid of people and their intentions. I still carried the emotional baggage from my time with Alex and had become leery about getting involved with people on a personal level. I was becoming increasingly weary that anyone that I befriended could deceive me, as Alex had done. I became very intolerant of liars and became short-tempered and confrontational when encountering them and their games. The war-like atmosphere in the city seemed to add to my aggressive demeanor, and I was ready, willing, and looking to confront trouble. I now see and understand that my drug use affected my behavior. I was a sad person living in a scary environment and – to compensate for showing any possible signs of weakness on my part – I became edgy, easily riled, and willing to confront anyone at any time. I was a walking time bomb, ready to go postal on anyone for any reason that didn't resonate well with me. I feared that someone was going to hurt Puckles and Papi, the most important things in my life, and this further contributed to my hostile temperament.

Throughout my entire adult life, I had looked for a man with whom to build a life and love me and, more importantly, not lie or cheat on me. Unfortunately, to that day, I had never found such a man, although God gave me the second-best thing, my two little dogs, Puckles and Papi. They loved me unconditionally and they made me feel loved. They saved my life that day back in Marin County when I was ready to give up on life and end it all. That same day, they motivated me to take a second gamble at life even while knowing that it was going to be an uphill battle to mend my state of mind and my broken heart. In return, it was now my responsibility to love, support, and protect these little guys and I took that responsibility very seriously. I now realize that I was overly protective of them, due to my ongoing paranoia fueled by my drug use. A large portion of my fears was also driven by survival and had anything happened to Puckles or Papi on my watch, I would've crumbled like a cake left out in the rain.

One evening, after a late night of partying, when I was still high, I had a conversation with Puckles and Papi. Though I was high, I often talked out loud to the boys when I was sober too. That night, I told them that if they were ever to get separated from me that they were to wait with each other in the same area where we got separated, until I returned for them. They looked at me intently and hung on my every word. It was not unusual for me to let Puckles off his leash during our walks. He was very good about staying close by and I was very confident that he would not run off. He loved his daddy and always stayed close to me. Papi, on the other hand, was easily distracted and, if he saw another dog, he would take off running without a second thought—so I never allowed him off his leash during our walks. He was hit by the car in San Francisco because he was running after a dog that he saw on the sidewalk and I made sure that never happened again.

The day after my conversation with them, Puckles got separated from me and Papi during our afternoon walk. We were taking a stroll on 42nd Street, halfway between 10th and 11th Avenues, when I left Puckles off his leash to do his business. I always kept an eye out to ensure he was nearby and following us when he was unleashed, and he usually followed us without fail. Plus, he had abandonment issues and stayed nearby at all times. Once they did their business, we headed back toward our apartment. As we walked home, I looked down and saw Puckles walking alongside me. As we reached the corner of 42nd Street and 10th Avenue, a friend of mine noticed us as he was driving past. He stopped and I approached his car. He told me that he was seeing a friend in the area and I informed him that my building had a parking garage one street over, on 41st Street between 10th and 11th Avenues. I told him I would walk over to the garage entrance and met him there to talk a bit more. When I reached the parking garage, I looked down and realized Puckles was no longer by my side. I had been distracted by seeing and talking to my friend and had failed to check that Puckles was still following us. I freaked. Puckles was nowhere to be seen. I immediately ran from the garage entrance to the corner of 41st Street and 10th Avenue in search of him. I looked anxiously around in all directions and saw little Puckles standing a block away, on the corner of 42nd and 10th. Even a city block away, I could see that he was looking around for his daddy and Papi. He could have easily walked into the street and been hit by a car, but he was waiting as instructed the day before. I yelled his name at the top of my lungs, like a crazed father calling his son to safety, and he heard me. He saw me and Papi and began to run toward us. We too ran toward him and we met in the middle of 10th Avenue. I was never so happy to get my hands on that little dog. By the grace of God, he was unharmed.

This became a defining spiritual moment for me. I believe it was no coincidence, or the ranting of a druggie, that I engaged with the dogs the previous evening, telling them to stay put in the same place if we were to ever get separated. Was Puckles so smart that he understood what I was saying the prior evening? While I would like to think so, instead I believe that it was the hand of God that kept Puckles safe by keeping him standing on that corner looking for me instead of walking out into traffic or in the wrong direction. It's as if God spoke through me, foreshadowing the events that were going to take place…His way of getting his point across that He had safety controls in place, even though I was out of control and felt unsafe and alone, and extremely afraid.

If a car had hit Puckles that day, I would've never made it out of New York with my sanity intact. The tragedy would've destroyed me and I would never have been able to recover. This event gave me a glimpse of God's authority in my life and my curiosity was peaked. In retrospect, I came to believe it was nothing short of a miracle that Puckles remained at the corner of 42nd Street and 10th Avenue, awaiting his daddy to return to the place where we had been separated. I came to refer to this event as "the miracle of 34J," because we were living in that apartment number and Puckles had been a Christmas gift from Alex to me many years earlier.

Puckles was born in Rockford, Illinois. I had wanted a pug, and when I went to pick one out of a pug litter, I originally selected a black puppy. Since the puppies had recently been born, I needed to wait several weeks for them to get old enough to be weaned off their mother's care. One evening, while I waited for the puppies to grow, the owner of the pug litter had to work the night shift. If you let the mother stay in the same cage with the puppies when they're very young and not feeding, there's a chance the puppies could accidently get suffocated by the mother if they were left unattended. To prevent this, the breeder asked a friend to go to his house that night and place the mother in the cage with her puppies so they could feed. The friend had gone drinking after work and stopped by his own home before going to the dog owner's house. Tragically, the friend fell asleep and never made it. Half of the puppies died that night from starvation. The black pug puppy that I had selected from the litter was one of the ones that had passed away. Puckles, a puppy who was the runt of the littler, had survived the starvation ordeal, and seeing his determination I decided to adopt him. He was fawn-colored, not black as I originally had wanted. Little did I know on that snowy Christmas Eve, traveling to Rockford from Chicago in a snowstorm – to pick up my pug – that I was going to bring home a kindred spirit. He was tough and survived against all odds in Rockford and, many years later, he would show his street cred again and survive the streets of New York—a survivor just like his daddy.

Since I stopped working for him, Gene had lost all three of his retail companies. When I worked for Bigsby, my relationship with him was always dysfunctional, even as the company and my professional career managed to thrive. The difficulties in my relationship with Gene became overshadowed by the creative energy that I was able to extract from my position and the achievements that I was able to ascertain while working for this man. During the years after I worked at Bigsby, I came to look back fondly on my time spent working for his empire. Gene was now working for the third largest real estate holder in the United States, after the U.S. government and the Catholic Church. Equity Office Properties' commercial real estate portfolio was comprised of over seven hundred office buildings across the United States. Gene was hired to develop the buildings' first floor experience, a huge undertaking to develop the lobbies and first floor retail spaces of these properties. Gene's main objective was to elevate the first floor experience to a hospitality environment, much like a hotel rather than a standard office lobby. He was to create a welcoming atmosphere to entice and engage the properties' customers and their clients to spend more time in the building lobbies. This new venture would allow Gene to elevate the company brand and create a wonderful opportunity in senior management for himself—and an equally amazing opportunity for the team that would support his efforts. The Mad Scientist was once again in the laboratory creating his retail concoctions and soon he would be looking for a creative assistant.

During my short tenure with the Bernstein's, I achieved a lot for the company from a creative standpoint, although it generated much resentment and jealously from others within the organization for what I accomplished. Change can be difficult for many people and I brought a great deal of it to the showroom in quick succession during a very brief period. This rapid change was viewed by some of my associates as a threat to their abilities and their position within the company—and they reacted adversely.

One evening, the Bernstein's held a party to unveil the remodeled showroom and the newly developed product lines that I had created to the retail industry. A few days earlier, a group of my friends from San Francisco traveled to New York for the debut of my work at the opening party. In addition to them, the guest list was comprised of retail clients and creative staffs from the large department stores and specialty retailers…from Canada, the U.S., South America, and some from Europe. Bernstein was debuting and promoting two new display fixture lines that I designed and a new mannequin line that had been sculpted by the in-house company designers. On the day of the launch party, a huge snowstorm hit the city, the largest blizzard the city had seen in over twenty years. Airlines canceled most flights coming in and out of the New York area. The snow fell steadily all day and with the ever-thickening clouds a silver lining was forming. Later that night, amidst the mountainous snow that had accumulated, I would see that silver lining.

Months earlier, when I was still working for the Italians, across the street from the Bernstein's showroom, I met a man in the building's elevator that had an entertainment company in the same building. I ended up befriending him and his girlfriend, one of the entertainers that he represented. Over several months, we got to know one another and, on several occasions, they invited me to a few venues where their entertainers were performing. Several months later, at a party in the Hamptons, we discussed and agreed to have three of his entertainers, who were singers, perform at the Bernstein opening party free of charge. I was very appreciative of their kind gesture and their overwhelming commitment to our newly formed friendship.

Up to the evening of the event, I had been working many long nights and weekends for several months to get the showroom ready. I worked twenty-four hours straight on the day leading up to the party and I was exhausted. The opening event was very important to me because it was intended to showcase the product lines, which I designed, to my peers in the retail design industry. My exhaustion, compounded by the random snowstorm that had engulfed the city that afternoon, and the difficulty in getting a cab in the foul weather caused me to arrive late to the party. Prior to my arrival, an associate of mine with whom I worked, decided to take advantage of my late arrival and changed the arrangement of the entertainer's schedule. When I arrived, and saw that she had changed the program to feature her boyfriend, who was a musician, instead of the entertainment that I had arranged, I was extremely upset with her. We had many planning meetings prior to the event to ensure everyone was on the same page and we had collectively agreed to the party details. A woman of dubious character at the best of times, she opted to take advantage of the situation for her own benefit. She was feeling threatened by my success that was being highlighted by the evening's event. Since I had worked so diligently to deliver a fantastic debut for the company, with the assistance of my friends who helped me out of kindness, I was not appreciative of anyone trying to steal my thunder, least of all someone who was feeling threatened due to their own insecurities. I was also extremely protective of the entertainers because they were doing the company and me a big favor by performing for free. My associate was a tall lumbering woman with red hair and a pendulous gait, much like a penguin. I was not featuring this 'Big Bird' and I let her know of my dissatisfaction as soon as I arrived.

The lack of respect for my efforts to deliver a beautiful new showroom and launch, added to my exhaustion and pushed me over the edge. Big Bird sensed my displeasure and approached me to justify her actions. In no uncertain terms, I told her to stay the fuck away from me. The confrontation between Big Bird and I got out of hand and our formerly favorable working relationship became very hostile. The reason I found Big Bird's behavior so disconcerting was because she acted out of spite. She was a well-established individual in the creative field, who previously had her own company, but had lost that business as a causality of the poor economy from the aftermath of September 11. She was unhappy with her own life and her behavior reflected that. As I reprimanded Big Bird for her inappropriate actions, I had some satisfaction in slamming the door to her cage in her face. This only added fuel to the fire burning within an already pissed off and bitter bitch, with a loose tongue, who would be spreading all types of vicious rumors about me in the coming weeks. What should have been a joyous occasion became an ordeal.

After the party ended, Rick and two other friends who had traveled from San Francisco, accompanied me to a competitor's party that was taking place later that night in a different part of the city. If nothing else, it would allow me to forget the night's frustrations and provide free food and liquor on a cold and snowy winter night. As Fate would have it, I ran into Gene at the party.

Gene had been in the city touring Equity properties and was supposed to fly out that evening, but the blizzard that had crippled the city changed his plans. The snowstorm stranded him and caused his flight back to Chicago to be canceled. Rick, being the good friend that he was, entertained my other guests while Gene and I caught up and had an in-depth conversation. Gene inquired if I would be interested in relocating back to Chicago and joining his team as head creative director for his department. I was immediately intrigued. We spoke in great length about his creative direction for the position and the longer we spoke the more interested I became. I convinced Gene to accompany me back to the Bernstein showroom. What better résumé could I possibly offer him than an entirely remodeled showroom in Manhattan and two new product lines that I created? It was an outstanding opportunity for me to showcase my talents and sell him on my expanded capabilities. Gene had been a big fan of my creative talent while I previously worked for him, although many years had now passed. Even as he was interested in my abilities, I needed to ensure that he saw the difference between the young designer that once worked for him back in Chicago and the seasoned creative director that now stood before him in Manhattan.

It was now past midnight and over twenty inches of snow had fallen within a 24-hour period and cabs were still difficult to come by, but Fate had been working overtime. My friend Teddy, who had attended the Bernstein event, had driven his own car and had given us a ride to the competitor's party. He volunteered to take Gene and I back to the Bernstein showroom while Rick stayed behind and entertained the troops. When we arrived at the showroom, the lights were still on, as the maintenance staff was still cleaning up. Gene stood on the sidewalk in front of the building staring through the main window into the showroom and asked, "is this all your work?" I replied that yes, it was, except for the mannequin line, which was developed by the sculptors for the company. He commented that it was very impressive and we walked inside so he could take a closer look.

We toured the showroom for an hour and, after we were done, Teddy – who was waiting patiently – drove again and together we dropped Gene off at his hotel. As Gene exited the car on that monumentally snowy evening, he said that he would be in touch with me shortly. I bade him a good night and replied that I would look forward to hearing from him. I had a very good feeling that he was not only impressed with what he saw at the Bernstein showroom, but that, more importantly, he realized that I was not the same creative individual that worked for him in the past. He could see my professional growth since leaving his employ and he could see that I was now an accomplished designer that had achieved a great deal in a short time of living in New York.

Those who interacted with me daily in Manhattan began to find my behavior exhausting. I had always been very intense and, after the Alex ordeal, I had developed a very sharp edge to my intensity. One person that I met during the Bernstein remodel even went so far as to tell me that if he was going to be in a street fight, he would want me on his side because I could be so mean. Much of my edginess and the abrupt shortness of my demeanor was brought on by my drug use. Tina will have that effect after using her for a long period. The lack of sleep that she enables will cause you to become intolerant and short tempered. After working on the showroom remodel around the clock for six weeks straight without a day off, I had hit my limit. I turned into an unhappy bitch that was angry about the everyday things that were associated with living in New York, especially my work environment and relationship with Big Bird. My unhappiness was, in part, a result of feeling less than appreciated by my coworkers. The Bernstein corporate office executives in Port Washington were not thrilled with the hostile environment in their New York showroom. Big Bird tried to get me fired by speaking untruths about me, but I overcame the lies that she was spreading about me and to damage control the issues that I created.

Christmas of 2003 came and went and the New Year was rung in by a call from Gene. He had kept his promise that he made on that snowy night in early December when he said that he would be in touch shortly. He had received approval to offer me a position to join his creative staff in Chicago. As always, Gene was a negotiator and he presented an offer that was less than what I would consider to pick up my life again and relocate back to Chicago. Even though I was unhappy at the showroom, I was working toward a reconciliation with my co-workers, although this did not include Big Bird who was conducting herself more like a Looney Tune cartoon character than a colleague. Toward the end of the year, the Bernstein CEO had informed me of his master plan for the showroom, which involved placing it under my supervision. He proposed that I would not only be the creative director for Bernstein on a corporate level, but I would soon also be the showroom manager. I was very happy to receive the news that showed the executives at Bernstein appreciated my efforts and believed in me by adding showroom manager to my existing responsibilities. The existing manager of the showroom was one of the individuals that felt threatened by me and he and Big Bird were creating as many issues for me as they could. They had joined efforts and were determined to get me out of their way by any means necessary.

Gene was persistent in his pursuit to have me join his team. One day, after several phone calls to secure the correct deal and after weighing it against my current hostile work environment, I began to consider Gene's offer. I shared my concerns with him about his management style and he assured me that he wasn't going to micromanage me or his staff, as he had done in the past. He reiterated that he had much to accomplish in a short time in his new position. He reassured me that he was going to be preoccupied with the larger picture and that he needed someone that he could trust, like me, to head-up the creative execution for his newly formed department. Toward the end of our negotiations, on his fourth attempt to secure the deal, he presented a revised and attractive financial package that I could not decline and I finally accepted the offer to join his team as director of interior lobby design and visual merchandising for Equity Office Properties.

While incredibly excited for my new opportunity that would remove me from the complications of my life in New York, I had mixed feelings about leaving my job. Mitch Bernstein always believed in my abilities and had allowed me the chance to work at his family's company. His business partner Roger, who was also the CEO, supported my creative vision and it was a pleasure to be part of his team. To this day, I am grateful to them for being so kind and supportive and wish we could have worked longer together, under different circumstances. Ironically, Big Bird left the Bernstein's employ six months after I resigned and moved back to Chicago. Had I known that she was going to fly the coop, it certainly would've had an impact on my decision to leave the Bernstein Company and New York City.

I told my father of my new position and for the first time in my adult life he told me that he was very proud of me. In some way, this felt like my own Bar Mitzvah. I was no longer thirteen, nor was I Jewish, but hearing my father tell me that he was proud of me certainly made me feel like I had finally entered into manhood. Gene's determination and persistence in securing my talents to join his team with the third largest real estate holder in the U.S. – combined with my dad's praise – left me feeling like I had achieved the level of professionalism in my career that I had always hoped to ascertain. I was now employed with a major corporation with a large six figure salary, plus a fifteen percent incentive bonus target. My job offer also included health care, life and disability insurance, and stock options. I certainly felt like I had traded up from sharing a showroom with Big Bird to being employed by the proverbial goose that laid the golden eggs.

In March of 2004, I left New York and headed back to the Midwest. In doing so, I made a promise to myself to stop using drugs. I left Tina behind and she wasn't invited to join me in Chicago. For the first time in fourteen years, I finally made the conscious effort to stop self-medicating and recreate a sense of purpose for my life. I was thankful to Gene for allowing me the chance to be a part of his team and grateful to be back in a city that I once considered home.

On November 27 of 2013, the day before Thanksgiving and the day before Hanukah that year, I completed the first draft of this chapter. This was the first time since 1888 that Thanksgiving and the first day of Hanukkah fell on the same day—a phenomenon that will not take place again for another seventy-nine thousand and forty-three years. As I wrote the chapter, and thought of *Thanksgivukkah*, my mind wondered to a small Jewish girl who I encountered many years before.

Rick and I had gone on vacation to Amsterdam in April of 1995. On our first day in the city, we were out and about taking in the sights, and we went to see the house where Anne Frank lived in the attic when she was hiding from the Nazis before she was eventually discovered. As we approached the house, we came upon a statue of Anne Frank. Rick and I walked toward the statue and reflected on the impact that the little girl had on humanity. After taking a few pictures of her statue, we walked over to the house where she hid and we went on our way to see more sights. Eventually, we made our way to lunch. After finishing our lunch, we went to the Rijksmuseum where Rick excitedly led us to see *The Night Watch* painted by Rembrandt, which he longed to see. As we stood in front of the painting I had to admit that I was very taken by this beautiful masterpiece. Rick was enthralled and I commented to him that a dog in the painting looked as if it was never fully completed, which he explained was due to damage that the painting had seen over the centuries.

That evening, we went to the Roxy, a large gay club to hang and socialize with the locals. At one point, Rick turned to me and said "bitch, take your shirt off, we're not getting enough attention." I honored his request and quickly removed my shirt and hung it off the waistband of my pants. At the time, I was in peak physical condition and very muscular from going to the gym. Shortly after standing in the bar naked above the waist, the removal of my shirt had caught the attention of the locals and soon a handsome Dutchman approached us. After the usual chatter, he asked us what we did that afternoon. I told him that we had gone to the Rijksmuseum where we had seen *The Night Watch*. He seemed impressed by my presumed interest in culture and asked if we had noticed the unfinished dog in the painting. I replied, yes, we had, and I could not help but smile as I did notice what seemed to be a less than finished dog in the painting.

After many cocktails and conversation, the handsome Dutchman inquired if I would go home with him. I was much more adventurous then than I am today and this confidence could have been attributed to my youth, my being in good shape, or from naiveté. Whichever the case, like any respectable gay man on the prowl in a foreign land, I said yes. He told me that he didn't live very far from the club and it was just a short cab ride to his place. I said goodbye to Rick, told him I would see him in the morning, and off I went with my gay Dutchman.

Back then, many hotels in Europe had actual keys for the rooms and not the electronic key cards that are common today. In the hotel where we were staying, we had to leave our room key with the front desk whenever we left the hotel. As a result, I had nothing on me with the hotel's name or address. After we jumped in the cab, I realized I was a little more intoxicated than I had thought when I was in the bar, so trying to pay attention to where the cab driver was driving was more complicated than I had thought. Once we arrived at his place, I totally forgot about how I got there. We started making out and I quickly began entertaining my new Dutch buddy.

The next day, I was sporting a mean hangover. When I awoke in a stranger's house and bed, I felt a little uncomfortable. I thought it be best if I got out of his way as quickly as possible and began my walk of shame back to the hotel to meet up with Rick. It was now early in the afternoon and I was sure that Rick was wondering what the hell had happened to me. In my haste to get out of the trick's house, I failed to get directions back to my hotel.

I didn't remember the name of the hotel, so I'm not sure my trick could've given me directions to it, even if I had asked for them.

As I left his apartment and started walking, I realized I had no idea where I was or where I was going. Nothing looked familiar. I thought that the cab ride didn't take that long to go from the club to his house…so I certainly couldn't be that far from the club where I hooked up with the Dutchman. I told myself that if I could find the bar, I surely could make my way back to the hotel from there. That sounded like a logical plan. After several attempts to find my way back to the club, with no luck, I became increasingly anxious about being lost in a foreign city. It was getting late and I was starting to feel like I was screwed, which made me laugh—as I expect that's how my Dutch friend was feeling too. I kept on walking and looking for anything that looked familiar. Just as I was starting to panic, I came across the little statue of Anne Frank that Rick and I had seen the previous day. That was the sign I needed and I realized that I could make my way back to the hotel from this landmark.

That day back in Amsterdam, little Anne Frank seemed to appear out of nowhere and saved me from a whole lot of anxiety. I'm not sure what I would've done had I not stumbled across her when I did. It was hard not to see Anne as my guarding angel that day. She guided me back to the house where she took refuge and from there I found my way to our hotel. Had Rick and I not visited her on the previous day's sightseeing tour, I would've had no way of knowing how to find my way back to the place where we were staying. I recall that afternoon often and I am still grateful that Anne Frank came to my rescue, like an angel from heaven, that day.

14 | THE SEVEN OF SWORDS

I believe in psychics and wonder whether it's possible that some of them are spiritual messengers. Psychics can certainly be seen as an unconventional means of hearing heavenly messages, but is it possible that there are legitimate psychics in the world that relay communications from heaven? Does God speak through some of them? While I don't recommend going to a psychic in place of building a relationship with Him, I've visited a few mediums in my lifetime.

When I lived in New York, I went to see a psychic during gay pride weekend in 2003. She told me an evil presence had been influencing my life. She went on to explain that this presence was no longer fastened to me. The weird thing was that I had been having this same feeling prior to her relaying this information. At no time during our session did I give her any details about my life or the feelings that I had that there was an evil presence in it. During a large portion of the time when I was with Alex, and after we split, I felt that evil was lurking in the shadows. I was afraid that another shoe was yet to drop once we split. I often wondered if my feelings – and the psychic's sense of evil in my life was about Alex and his possible and most probable relationship with Michael. I don't believe Alex was evil, although much of his behavior had a negative effect on my overall well-being. I now believe Michael was that shoe that I feared was yet to drop. More importantly, I wondered if the psychic was referring to the shit that Michael might have done after the alleged affair came to an end, when he was supposed to have been my friend.

I left San Francisco because I moved there for Alex. As our relationship ended, I wanted to pursue a dream that was more in line with what I was interested in before I met him. My decision to move to New York was in pursuit of this lifelong dream to work and live in that city. As I look back, my move there was the beginning of a pattern that I followed for many years—running away from my issues.

I tried to escape from my problems when I moved to Manhattan because I thought it easier to run rather than confront and deal with my emotional scars, but my New York experience was fulfilling in some aspects. I accomplished much professionally in a short time and was able to complete and achieve a lifelong dream for which I'm forever grateful. On the other hand, my time there was not without difficulties. I regret that I was not able to fully enjoy all of what the city had to offer due to my heavy mental state of mind. The war-like presence that engulfed the city during the time that I lived there added another layer of emotions to an already complex emotional situation. I am grateful to all the military men and women that patrolled the streets, the subways, and the skies of Manhattan during the initial months that followed the announcement of war on Iraq. The heavy military presence in an urban city was certainly an unusual sight, but I still believe their presence was much appreciated at the time and I am still thankful that they kept the city and its people, which included me, safe. Yet, I was a runaway from the west coast who was afraid of failing on so many levels, trying to be a tough guy in a potentially volatile environment.

It saddens me when I think of the number of people who were aware of my rumored drug use while living in the city and the numerous people who were whispering to one another about me behind my back. No one person ever came forward to offer support or to just express genuine concern for my well-being—a perfect example of people judging from afar, rather than drawing close to an individual in need…and extending a helping hand. My issues, combined with my financial problems, created a level of stress that I was not equipped to handle. I opted to avoid dealing with my problems and my drug use increased—and this bad behavior only added fuel an already out of control situation. So, my leaving the city came at a good time.

In March of 2004, Puckles, Papi and I moved back to Chicago. I left Tina in the streets of New York and was happy to have the chance to have a clean slate in the city that I called home for much of my life. I found Chicago to have a comforting familiarity from having previously worked and lived there and its' suburbs for decades.

Now that I was back in the windy city, I needed to find a new home for us. I rented an apartment in downtown Chicago until I could decide exactly where I was going to live for the long haul. After several months of looking, I decided to buy an apartment in a newly constructed high-rise just a few blocks from my new office. The building was across the street from the historic Old Saint Pat's Church, slightly west of what is considered the Loop area of Chicago. In New York, I had lived across the street from the Croatian Church of Saints Cyril, Methodius, and Raphael—near the Lincoln Tunnel. Was this another coincidence or was this God's way of letting me know that he had followed me from New York and was nearby and watching over me? Today, I know the answer to my question.

I started my new job with Equity Office Properties immediately after arriving in Chicago. I began a new chapter in my life and it didn't include Tina or rumors of drug use. One of the big factors that resulted in my using

Tina on a regular basis was Alex's promiscuous affairs and the behavior that accompanied his actions. I turned to drugs to have the physical energy to get out of bed every day and deal with the emotional turmoil taking place. In moving back to Chicago, I decided to make a clean break from Tina and go cold turkey. It was a perfect opportunity for me to begin a new clean lifestyle. For the first time in fourteen years, I was no longer using drugs for recreational use. I started to clean up my behavior and my life. My new position was the first one I held outside of the retail industry in the entire time that I had been working as an adult. I realized the commercial real estate industry would be less forgiving of a lapse in judgment, when it came to partying, than the retail industry. Needless to say, staying away from drugs was not only a choice that I needed to make, it was also going to be a pre-requisite to keep my position and achieve success with this company. But like most people that stop drinking or doing drugs, I replaced one bad habit with another. I took up smoking cigarettes, which I saw as the lessor of two evils.

I believe it was divine intervention that brought Gene and I together that snowy evening in New York. I ended up in the city at the wrong time in my life. I was in a bad state of mind and between the ominous environment and my self-medicating, this scenario became a lethal combination. I was financially over-extended for most of the time that I lived there, which had further fueled my anxieties. New York is an amazing place, but if you're not in tune with the city and it's not in tune with you, it can and will be a lonely and painful experience. I was lonely as I was not able to build any sincere friendships, except for my lovely assistant Emily with whom I worked at the Italian company. I now know I needed to leave the city when I did because I had to clean up my act and begin a healing process to build a better life for myself. I also believe God knew I needed a familiar place where I could surround myself with loving family and friends so I could begin to heal emotionally. Chicago, near my parents, is where He knew I would feel safe. I believe God sent Gene, as unlikely an angel as possible, to bring me back to a safe place. Even though we had somewhat of an estranged relationship at times, God knew He needed to send a familiar face if He was going to be successful in His attempt to get me out of New York. He knew Gene was a big fan of my creative abilities and that he was a fantastic salesman. If he wanted something from you, he had the ability to sell you on the idea. God sent his best man and because of this, I believe there's a message here for all of us...God will in fact use the most unlikely people and the most unlikely circumstances to get His work done. In doing so, we will realize that certain situations that take place in our lives could only have been orchestrated by Him.

Now that I was living drug free, I focused my efforts on decorating my new home and becoming successful in my new position. I felt I would work with Equity for many years to come so I decked out my newly constructed condo with marble floors throughout and spent a considerable amount of money upgrading the finishes in the kitchen and bathrooms. I still had a condominium in San Francisco that I was renting to Rick, which I decided to place back on the market. This time the unit sold for well over a half of a million dollars, a perfect example of how being in the right place at the right time drives so many of the successes in our lives. The final sale price was considerably higher than my original asking price just eighteen months earlier. With this windfall, I was now able to pay off the forty thousand dollar debt that I incurred while living in New York and holding up two residences. I also placed a substantial down payment on my new home and had enough cash left over to place a sizeable down payment on a lease for a brand-new BMW 545i. With a beautiful place to call home – only a few blocks from my office – and a brand-new car, it was time to get entrenched in my position and settled in for the long haul.

My first few months were spent getting acquainted with the company and its' portfolio of properties. Gene, who again became my immediate supervisor, greeted me with open arms. We spent our time together in the early months traveling, familiarizing ourselves with many of the properties in various markets. Each market had its' own distinct needs and any upgrades to the building lobbies would need to be unique. We needed to select six properties out of the entire portfolio to participate in a pilot program. If the pilot proved to be successful where we tested the concept, and well received by Equity's executives, we would receive funding to design and upgrade the first floor experience of one hundred and seventy five properties.

As a designer, my creative talents were strongest in the space planning and visual merchandising fields. I was not very proficient in constructing formal communications. In my new role, I would need to articulate positive and exciting directives that showcased my creative vision to the building managers for their individual properties through email. Since Equity had a large portfolio, email communications, which I did not enjoy writing, became an integral part of my responsibilities...something that I was also not accustomed to doing. I would've preferred to pick up the phone and have a conversation with whomever I was dealing with at the time. However, as we began to get our pilot program off the ground, I was dealing with numerous people—so a simple phone call to one person was usually not an option. I needed to sharpen my written communication skills in a professional, positive, and precise manner. I had to master the art of corporate communications – via email and personalized presentations – and do it quickly.

I was not in Kansas anymore and keeping my position depended on my ability to click the proper letters on the keyboard and form precise and interesting communications that detailed my creative intent for the projects at hand, while engaging the email recipients. This was an overwhelming task that I had not planned to perform when I signed on for the position. I was creative and considered myself a right-brained type of a person. I was never a good speller and I had always shied away from having to write. I understand that left-brained people are considered to be less creative than their right-brained counterparts, but they are usually much better at spelling and writing. Could I train myself to become a left-brained thinking individual and still be an effective right-brained creative person? Is it possible for someone to be highly creative and articulate the specifics of their designs in writing? Even if this could be done, I really had no interest in developing my corporate written communication skills; I was a designer not a writer.

Within a short time, I eventually came to the realization that I would need to improve my writing skills if I was going to stay employed on this project and get the executives of the company behind the program. I began to concentrate on developing my story telling and writing abilities to be successful in my new position and possibly for another project that would not come into play until many years later—a precursor for a project I was yet to embark upon, writing this story.

Life in Chicago was good. I was enjoying my new home and my new job and by all accounts I should've been genuinely happy. There was certainly no cause for me to be unhappy. One morning, for no apparent reason, when getting ready for work, I stood in my bedroom in front of my dresser, and a sensation overtook me. For no logical reason that I can explain, I uttered out loud, "I'm supposed to be doing something else with my life." Why did I have the need to speak this thought out loud and to whom did I think I was speaking? For some reason, I had an overwhelming feeling that I should be somewhere else, doing something different. The question of what was I supposed to be doing with my life would remain a mystery for many more years. At that moment, I certainly felt like I was in the wrong place at the wrong time doing the wrong thing, which was inexplicable to me. This strange and unusual revelation would finally make some sense to me four years later.

Since Equity was proving to be a fantastic place to work, I decided to entertain the possibility of purchasing a second home near Chicago that offered warm weather all year around. Since Florida is a short plane ride from Chicago, I thought the sunny beaches of the sunshine state could be a place where I might flock to during the winter months. Even though I grew up in the Chicago area and had lived through the cold winter season that seemed to last forever, it did not stop me from disliking the extreme winters.

I'd been to South Beach several times for the White Party in November around Thanksgiving. This party was one of the very first fund raising events designed to raise money and awareness for the AIDS community. The party always attracted a who's who of the gay community, who came from coast to coast to enjoy the extravagant affair. Since I had vacationed on an annual basis in South Beach for numerous years, I was acquainted with how instrumental the gay community was in developing the city into the popular destination that we know today—one of the hottest areas to live in or to spend some quality vacation time. During my yearly junkets, I had become familiar with the surrounding adjacent areas. Over the years, it moved away from being an affordable sunny place where the gays lived and vacationed, to one that became populated by expensive restaurants and luxury hotels, and a very popular place with the affluent straight crowd. By 2004, South Beach was no longer considered the hot gay spot and the gays began to retreat to Fort Lauderdale, a beach town north of Miami, in a formerly popular area of the Sunshine State with the fags before they migrated to South Beach. The local gays now returned to the place from whence they came.

One weekend, I flew down to Fort Lauderdale to spend a few days looking at properties. I booked a hotel room at a gay resort as I thought it best to check out the gay scene by staying in a gay nesting place. It turned out that I was several years late in following the migration wave back to Fort Lauderdale. After looking at a few properties, I immediately realized that I was too late to the game. The housing market was on the rise due to the number of homos who were settling or resettling in the area—and buying a second home there was now out of my financial reach. I decided to look at properties in the towns adjacent to Fort Lauderdale and settled on Wilton Manor. I had been told that Wilton Manor was extremely gay friendly and still affordable, although it was a little further away from the beach than what I would've preferred. On the third and last day of my search, I found a place that was in my price range that I liked, although it did not have an in-ground pool and the house would require some work to make it feel like a place where I could reside. It had a large back yard and plenty of room to eventually add a pool should I decide to do so later. After much internal debate, I asked the real estate broker to fax me the purchase contract to my office. I was returning to Chicago that night and would be back in my office in the morning. I had found what I came seeking, a place that I could call home during the winter months. I thought I would soon become one of Florida's newest gay snowbirds…flocking there every winter. Fate, however, had another plan and it didn't include buying a home in Wilton Manor.

By most accounts, life was going well for me. I was moving in a positive direction for the first time in many years. I had been drug free for six months and, most importantly, Tina had not come to visit since I moved back to Chicago. For the first time in almost a decade, I regained my interest in dating and began to entertain the idea of going out on a date with another man. It had taken many years and two different cities before my battle wounds from my failed relationship with Alex began to heal and I was ready to entertain the concept of trusting my choice in others once again. I had reached a huge milestone in my recovery. I was finally able to start to rebuild my trust in humanity and other single gay men, although, I still proceeded cautiously – and with some reservations – with people outside of my immediate circle of friends and family.

On Monday morning when I returned to my office after spending the previous weekend in Florida looking at properties, I received the fax from the real estate broker. The broker sent the purchase contract for the property in Wilton Manor for which I had expressed interest. Then things became interesting. For no apparent reason, I decided to google Alex. I had lost all contact and any trace of his whereabouts. I did not know where he lived and I had not spoken to him in many years. The last I heard, he was living back in San Francisco. Once I googled his name, I was absolutely astonished by the results. I saw that his last and current residence was in Wilton Manor, Florida. I was gob smacked. The odds that Alex would be living in Wilton Manor, at the same time I expressed interest in buying a second home there, were unbelievable. In the ninth hour of reviewing – and just before signing a contract to buy a house in Wilton Manor – I found out that Alex was living in that same town. I was still harboring ill feelings toward him for all the untruths he brought into our lives. I had not been able to forgive him nor was I interested in extending forgiveness. I immediately called the real estate agent and let him know that I would be passing on the property and more specifically, on Wilton Manor.

My decision to google Alex's whereabouts came out of left field. Or did it? Shortly after the Wilton Manor incident, I began to revisit certain aspects of my life. I started to give sincere consideration to the concept of a higher power. I felt something prevented me from making a mistake by buying property in an area of the country that would have given me much grief upon discovering that Alex lived there. I began to take notice of the random, but curious chain of events around the Florida incident and similar ones. The Wilton Manor incident was a turning point. I realized that the coincidental situations that had been taking place for years were not random at all. I finally saw a pattern to these mysterious events. My apophenia finally led me to ponder the idea that God could be present. This epiphany would be the start of a long-awaited journey to believe in something greater. But seeking out and believing in God would have no value if I were not able to comprehend the world as being created by one God. With very little knowledge of religion, making sense of how one God fits all races and religions was an undertaking that I was not equipped to take on at that time. My relationship with God and, more importantly, my understanding of Him would need to wait, as my darkest hour was fast approaching.

I had been employed with Equity for a year when my working relationship with Gene took a turn for the worse. A leopard truly never changes his spots and in Gene's case this proved true. All his promises to allow me to manage my own department and make my own decisions to execute the designs for the lobby upgrades came to naught. He micro managed every detail of the final stages of the program, which drove me absolutely crazy. I had spoken with him about his management style before I left New York and had expressed my concerns about it—and he had assured me that it would not be an issue. However, Gene was notorious – throughout his career – for consistently changing his mind on design projects and micro managing the details all the way up to the end. This 'perfectionist' behavior usually resulted in frustration from those working with him and the projects ultimately ending up over budget and late. Prior to accepting his employment offer, he promised he would not hold my hand once a project was approved by corporate and signed off by him. Without his consent on this condition, I would've never accepted his job offer. He was certainly the "idea" man and a genius when it came to seeing the big picture, but his biggest downfall was that he didn't allow his direct reports to do what he hired them to do on their own. This would be especially true when it involved a written document. He would tweak the words continuously, which drove his communication team insane. He displayed this neurotic behavior when he owned Bigsby and it frustrated the various departments under his supervision. Unfortunately, he brought this management style to Equity and it consumed the overall team and – more significantly – the design department managed by me.

I finally confronted Gene. There was a great deal at stake. It was imperative that The Retail Group, our department, be successful in implementing the pilot to receive the additional funding. The team needed to hit a home run. The future of The Retail Group depended on it. Gene had recruited me to become part of his team because of our previous working relationship. Based on his knowledge of my creative abilities, he knew that I would be a great candidate to assist him in his efforts and ensure that he would be successful in his endeavors at Equity. What Gene didn't realize was that I was no longer the intimated young designer that worked for him almost a decade before—having become more established in my design career and matured since then.

During our discussion, he reiterated that the pilot program was essential to our future and he was not going to allow me or anyone else to screw up the success of the department. What he was really conveying, without being man enough to say the exact words, was that he wouldn't allow me or anyone else to stand in the way of him becoming successful at the company. I forcefully reminded him of our conversation prior to me accepting his offer. I reiterated that I did not agree to work for him under the conditions that he was going to hold my hand on every design decision I made. He replied that he could not believe that I was going to fuck up the best employment opportunity that I ever had because of my ego. I stressed that he recruited me because of my creative talent and that he knew I would do everything in my power to ensure his success and that of the entire five-person department.

Our conversation and relationship quickly soured. Our situation suddenly went from being nurturing, with mutual respect, to one that became confrontational and hostile. There were no exceptions to his management philosophy of his way or the highway. His true colors were now in clear view. His face became beet red. He was pissed off that I had called him out and confronted the issue.

Gene was correct. Equity was the best career opportunity that I had up to that point. But he was incorrect that I was going to fuck up my opportunity. That couldn't be further from the truth. During the installation of every lobby upgrade for the buildings in the pilot program, I traveled to each location to ensure the design was executed correctly and to ensure the property management team was pleased with the results. Their support and approval was critical if we were to obtain the funding for the rollout of the upgrade program to the additional buildings in the portfolio.

After I successfully managed the execution of the pilot, The Retail Group received the funding to proceed with rolling out the program to the additional properties. I had accomplished what I was hired to do and had ensured the success of the team and the program. However, shortly after we received the funding for the expansion, Gene called me into his office and informed me that he was re-organizing the department and he was going to outsource my job. By all accounts, he should've been pleased with my efforts. But now, after I had ensured the pilot's success, my services were no longer needed. I was speechless. Someone who I knew for decades that I trusted betrayed me. I had been fed a bunch of lies and my design talents had been used without any regard for my well-being. Now that Gene's program was funded, I became expendable and was tossed to the unemployment line.

Losing my job became a trigger that led me down the wrong path. Addicts are frequently pushed to repeat the behavior of their addiction if they suffer a hardship, like losing one's career or being betrayed by someone they trust. I was certainly no different. I ran to seek comfort from my old friend Tina, who once again became a guest in my house. My poor choices were building upon each other—one bad decision was leading me to make another. This behavior would bring me to my lowest point. I was en route to a very dark, lonely, and dangerous place, where even my shadow would leave me. What I didn't know at that time was that God would be awaiting my arrival in that place.

Six months after Gene eliminated my position, the Mad Scientist was fired from his position as department head of The Retail Group. I later discovered that his executive counterparts – other senior regional vice presidents – did not consider Gene a team player. Gene saw himself as a superior to the other regional leaders in the territories and this behavior eventually cost him his position. Due to his own bad behavior, Gene knew he was on rocky ground when he eliminated my role and by removing me from the equation he thought he would be able to stabilize his own position. Since the pilot program had been designed, executed, and approved for additional funding, I certainly could've overseen the program—had Gene been fired while I was still employed with the company. With me gone, Gene thought he was indispensable. The Mad Scientist had miscalculated his equation and joined the same unemployment line to which he had sent me several months earlier.

The aftermath from Gene's betrayal, combined with the humiliation of losing my job and the pressures of how I was going to meet my financial responsibilities now that I was unemployed, depressed me. I asked my doctor whether I would be a good candidate to go on anti-depressants, which were not widely used like they are today. My doctor prescribed the medication, which I began to take daily combined with my HIV drug regimen. Most of my adult life, I had experienced bouts of heavy emotional days—dark days that were accompanied by random mood swings. On these occasions, when I awoke in the morning, I was afraid to open my eyes, as I feared the worse. Often, I would awake with a miserable disposition for no apparent reason. Sometimes it would last for several days, if not weeks. I felt helpless and in despair. The happy drugs didn't make me happy, but they did strip the dark layer off my day. It was like someone took a can of *bitch-be-gone* and sprayed it on me. The depressing layer over my life seemed to vanish. Were these anti-depressants a cure? Or were they just another quick fix, masking deeper and more complex issues? In either case, the medication provided relief to a problem that required immediate attention.

I was terrified that I was not going to secure a new job at the salary that I required. I needed a certain income to hold up my financial commitment on my new condominium. I had dumped all my cash reserves into the down payment and the condo upgrades. The apartment was only a few blocks from the Equity office as I wanted to be able to walk to work. More importantly, I wanted the walk to be quick because the winter months were so unbearable. Now that I had relocated from New York to Chicago, sold my condo in San Francisco, purchased a beautiful and lavish new home, I was tormented by how I was going to maintain it all now that I was out of a job.

A few months later, I was offered a sales position by a vendor with whom I had done business while working at Equity. The company handled the freight and warehousing of the design elements of my projects around the country. I was fortunate to have received a generous six-month severance package – my full salary and medical coverage – so I was still in decent financial shape when the new job offer came my way from the logistics company. I had been very concerned about how I was going to secure a six-figure position without having to relocate yet again to another city—so the new job brought me much financial and mental relief. While I had previous business development experience, I was not thrilled about the idea of re-entering the selling arena. Sales, otherwise referred to as *developing new business opportunities*, is not easy. Pounding the pavement for potential leads requires much effort upfront with little result in the first twelve months. Over the years, I've come to realize that if you can stay focused and put in the time to seek, secure, and build sales contacts, you will more than likely produce results, but then only over time. It takes a solid year to see a positive outcome from your efforts and you'll normally start reaping the fruits of your labor within a two-year period. But even while selling is certainly tedious, the results can be very lucrative.

The main reason I agreed to move back to Chicago and suffer through the hateful winters was for the career opportunity at Equity. I was thrilled to have been offered a new position with the logistics company with a six-figure salary without having to relocate to a different city, but I did not love being stuck in a place where the winters were extremely harsh and the summers very humid. I was shackled with golden handcuffs. I had an elaborate and expensive apartment that tied me financially to Chicago. I didn't have many choices so I did what any responsible person would've done…I took the job offer and hoped for the best—even as I was unsure that I could build a new customer sales base for a new company in an industry with which I was unfamiliar.

After a short break from having survived the Alex and New York years, I was once again feeling physically and mentally exhausted following Gene's actions. It felt like yet another failed relationship where I was left to pick up the pieces, which had a negative effect on me. Did anyone really care about me, other than me? I'm not sure I even cared about me. Somewhere around this time, I began to notice that my feelings of paranoia, in place since my breakup with Alex, had begun to change. Instead of just being fearful that someone was out to get me, although my distrust of people was still very evident, I began to feel like there was more to my feelings. I began to think that if someone wasn't out to get me, then certainly *someone* was watching me. From feeling fearful and distrustful, I began to sense the presence of something greater and it didn't answer to the name of 'psychiatric disorder'.

15 | BABY NEEDS A NEW PAIR OF SHOES

After working at Equity for a year, I convinced Rick to move from San Francisco back to Chicago. His family lived in the city and it's where he had grown up. He was born in Mexico, but his parents had immigrated to the U.S. when he was a young boy. Since I was instrumental in getting him to relocate to San Francisco when Alex and I moved there, I thought it only fitting that I convince him to come back to the city where he grew up. Rick and I had a rare friendship and I wanted to have my best friend in close proximity. He ended up buying a condominium in the West Loop, just five blocks from where I lived. Now that we both were in the same city once again, we began hanging out. Occasionally, we would patronize the bars in Boystown. We decided not to take a trip down memory lane and never reunited with the original group of friends that we hung out with prior to leaving Chicago almost a decade earlier—both of us feeling like we had outgrown those relationships.

There was a park kitty-corner from my building and across the street from Old Saint Pat's church. It was a convenient location for Puckles and Papi to do their business and have some playtime. By all means, I should've felt settled. I had secured a new position making a good salary and had a great place to call home. But I was feeling betrayed and unsure of myself — and anxious over what my future held. I'm not sure what I was looking for and seemed to blame my unhappiness on Gene and his decision to eliminate my position at Equity, which resulted in my having to reinvent myself professionally once again.

I decided to seek professional help to deal with my issues, the second time I had done so. The first time I went to see a therapist was in New York when I had created problems for myself. My father had encouraged me to seek some professional assistance. He knew I was under a tremendous amount of stress, but he didn't have a clue that I was self-medicating. He told me, "If you don't take the time to take care of yourself, you'll be of no use to anyone." Simple words to live by, although difficult ones to follow when there are many issues at hand and very little free time to address them. Up to that point, I was dealing with my emotional problems in the same manner that so many people do. I buried them deep inside me and kept busy. I decided to follow my dad's advice and went to see a therapist once a week on the Upper East Side. Seeking professional help was the best advice he ever gave me — and his recommendation had a huge impact on my healing process. A year later, while living in Chicago, I could hear my dad's voice telling me that if I didn't take the time to take care of myself, I'd be of no use to anyone. I decided to follow that advice once again.

There was one question that kept nagging me. Why did I keep investing in people that either lied to me or used me, or both in many cases? After Gene fired me, I began to think there was something seriously wrong with me. When it came to men, I always invested my time, my energy, and sometimes my love in those who had very little to no consideration for my well-being, although they always told me they did. Why was I not able to see through the bullshit artists of the world? Could a therapist help me get to the root of my problems so I didn't keep repeating the same mistakes over and over? Or was I bound to relive them time and time again until the end of my time?

Since I was eighteen years old, when I was a shipping and receiving manager, I always reported to a male supervisor. After I stopped working at Equity and went to work for the logistics company, I reported to the owner and president of the company, a woman. I'd always interacted with women at a higher level, of course, but this would be the first time I had a female boss. After being betrayed by Gene, I welcomed the opportunity to work for one. She had been married twice and had three children with her first husband. Her first husband, who happened to be named Alex, owned an installation company and did work with her company. He was a great all-around guy and I ended up building a wonderful working relationship with him. Her second and current husband also did work for the company, but he was very much an asshole. As they were both vendors who transacted business with the logistics company, I worked with the two of them.

Why Madame President ever left such a wonderful man like Alex for an asshole escaped me. Besides, Alex was extremely well hung and who doesn't like a great guy that is well endowed? How in the world that I know this very personal point? Alex told me once when we were together in New York on a business appointment. During a conversation with him, Madame President's current husband's name came up and I joked that he must have a big dick, as that would be the only reason why Madame President was attracted to him — because it certainly wasn't his personality. Without missing a beat, Alex indicated that he had a much larger dick, which made me laugh. Perhaps the second husband had dick envy that manifested into him acting like an asshole.

Throughout my life, whenever I interacted with a lesbian I always thought, for some odd reason, that these women were not very fond of me.

The vice president for the organization was a lesbian and, like most of the other lesbians that I had previously encountered, she didn't like me very much either. The other employees were all straight women so I was the only male employee. I felt that my being a fag bothered Madame President's second husband, although Alex had no issues with my sexual preference…being more comfortable with his manhood then Madame President's second husband. I guess being well hung can help a man's self-confidence.

I was excited and appreciative to have secured a job with a good salary, but I was extremely anxious about developing a new sales clientele from scratch. I knew how lonely a one-person office can be when you're cold calling or working leads electronically for eight hours a day, every day, for weeks and months on end. To complicate matters, I wasn't in a healthy emotional state of mind to take on this challenge. But I didn't have a choice. It was the only job that I had been able to get and I had financial responsibilities that I needed to meet.

I had a lot of work to do before I could begin selling. The company didn't have an office in Chicago and I needed to set up a home office in my apartment, just as I had done when I lived in Marin. I needed to hire and manage a contract graphics and web designer to develop a new brand identity for the company, which also fell under my responsibilities. I needed to revamp the company's website to update its image so that I could successfully introduce the business and its services to new clients in the retail, banking and hospitality industries.

Despite my anxieties, I shouldered on and did the best I could, or so I thought at the time. I had begun to see the therapist to help get my emotional state under control, but I knew in my heart that the new job was going to be a tremendous and stressful undertaking. I really didn't want to take on the overwhelming job of building a business from the bottom, on my own, out of my home. Gene had not only selfishly used my design talents to secure his success, he had left me in a vulnerable position. I was now forced to work in a field where I had absolutely no interest in developing a career path and in a place where I was left alone without an opportunity to engage in face-to-face interaction with other co-workers. When fighting depression, being isolated is not the most opportune place for one to attempt to develop a new sales business and this isolation was certainly not going to be a healthy environment for me.

Since Rick was back in Chicago, I hired him to assist me in rebranding the logistics company. When I worked at Bigsby, the graphic design department fell under my supervision for a period. During this time when we worked together, Rick asked me for his first Mac computer and began to learn graphic design. Gene had recruited a woman named Heather to manage the branding for the Knot Shop division at Bigsby. She had been the head of the graphic design department for H_2O, a Chicago-based retailer. Rick worked with Heather and he learned a great deal from her. Under her supervision, he honed his graphic design and communication skills. He was very inquisitive and his devotion to learning as much as he could in the new digital space enabled him to advance his career when he went to work with Alex and later in life.

Rick and I rebranded the logistics company. We developed a new logo and Rick redesigned the companies' complete brand collateral, including promotional materials that I used to solicit new business. We worked closely together to develop and launch the new company website. We were not only best friends; we were also colleagues who worked together at several different companies on many different projects. He and I had an unusual relationship. We were very different in many ways and often we didn't see eye to eye, but we always had each other's back, no matter what the circumstance. We were more than best friends and we protected each other, much like brothers who safeguard one another.

After the rebranding projects were completed, a few months into my employment, I flew to Atlanta, Georgia to meet with Madame President. I had met her on one other previous occasion. I interviewed her in Chicago before contracting her logistics company to handle the freight for the lobby upgrades at Equity. I was grateful to her for giving me the opportunity to work for her company. She did all the business development for the organization before I was brought on board to expand their business model. Prior to my arrival, their largest client was a discount retailer with whom Madame President was employed before she and the Lesbian opened the logistics company. Madame President told me that she owned ninety percent of the company and the Lesbian and one other employee owned the remaining ten percent. Our meeting was supposed to last for two days, although we completed our time together in one. During a meeting over lunch, she mentioned that she hoped that, someday in the future, I would buy her out of the logistics company. I was flattered that she expressed that much confidence in my ability. It was the highlight of our time together. While in Atlanta, I also learned from her second husband that the Lesbian was jealous that I was spending time with Madame President. From what I was told, the Lesbian was very possessive of Madame President and didn't like anyone from the company spending any quality time with her. I remember thinking that the Lesbian sounded like she was an insecure individual and the last thing I needed was a dyke up my ass…horrifying.

Since our meeting only lasted one day, I decided to check out the local gay scene. I ended up drinking too much and found myself looking for dick in all the wrong places. My evening ended with me in a towel at a gay bathhouse in Atlanta. When I went to these types of places, I usually didn't spend much time in the venue. I was there for one reason and one reason only and I usually got my business completed and was out the door as quickly as possible. In this instance, I met a local at the bathhouse and we had sex. I seemed to have made an impression on him, as he wanted to exchange numbers in case I ever made it back to Atlanta. So we did. The next day, I spent most my day in bed recovering from a hangover and from being out to all hours of the morning. I flew back to Chicago the following day.

That summer of 2006, the seventh Gay Olympics, a week-long sporting and cultural event organized by the gay community, were held in Chicago. Rick and I went to the opening and closing ceremonies and we also went to a few of the sporting events throughout the city, including the bodybuilding contest, which was a great thrill as I find body builders to be so hot. Tim had been an amateur body builder and I can appreciate the amount of effort it takes to build one's body to the level to compete in this type of sport. At the closing event held at Wrigley Field, I saw and heard a guy outside of the stadium, pontificating about prostitutes and Jesus. Tina was visiting and staying with me during the Gay Games so I was off my own game. I had begun to ponder the concept of a spiritual presence in my life, but I had not been able to get my head to fully embrace it. I did consider that Tina was messing with my mind and I thought that my peaked curiosity in a spiritual presence was nothing more than me being high. In either case, I had the impression that the guy preaching outside of the Gay Games about prostitutes and Jesus was preaching directly to me for a personal reason.

The Games were originally awarded to Canada, but at the ninth hour they were pulled from Montreal and moved to Chicago. I thought it very strange that the games got re-routed to Chicago at the last minute and I felt that there was more to the story. I'm not sure why I felt this way. It could've been Tina's presence that was making me have these unsubstantiated feelings. After the Games, I never thought about my feelings surrounding the games and the change in cities again until I began writing this chapter. Whatever was driving my thoughts at that time obviously left a strong enough impression on me that it stayed with me all these years.

When I lived in New York, I met two lovely men, Marcus and Fabio, who were male escorts. They were Canadian and lived in Toronto most of the time, except when they came to Manhattan to "work". To my knowledge, they were not boyfriends, just good friends. Marcus was a fair-skinned blonde in his mid-twenties and Fabio was swarthier, with a darker complexion and dark hair, also in his mid-twenties. Both were extremely handsome and very sweet, nice guys. I had sex with both of them at the same time, and separately, although for some reason I was more drawn to Fabio. Tall dark and very handsome always gets my undivided attention.

Before moving to Manhattan, I had developed several long-term professional business relationships with a handful of individuals in my field. Unfortunately, for some reason, these people were not particularly friendly once I arrived in the city. I don't know what issues they had with me, which never came to light, and I guessed they may have been jealous or resentful of my living environment. This was somewhat unsettling to me, because I had hoped to nurture these professional relationships – that I had developed over the last two decades – into serious friendships when I moved to the city. I had rented a fabulous seven-room corner apartment in a brand-new luxury high-rise building, while my acquaintances were crammed into one-bedroom apartments with their partners or, worse, living in a studio by themselves. It was laughable, as they were jealous over something that caused me much heartache. I could barely pay for that lovely apartment and I was only able to afford it if my condominium in San Francisco sold — and it didn't sell until after I left New York. I felt more love and received a warmer welcome from the two Canadian hookers that I hung out with for several months than I did from my business associates that I had known for decades. I often wondered if God sent those two young men to love me, even if it was only for a few hours at a time and I had to pay for it, when the people that I had known for ages wouldn't give me the time of day.

As I heard the man yell about prostitutes and Jesus on the sidewalk outside of Wrigley Field, I thought how strange it was that he was talking shit about hookers at the closing ceremony. I then recalled the decision to move the games to Chicago after I moved to the Windy City, rather than hosting them in Canada, as originally planned, which seemed to be a strange coincidence. Had I not moved to Chicago when I did, I would not have attended the Gay Games. Naturally, I connected the dots and thought about my relationship with the Canadian hookers in New York. I sensed that these types of situations all related to one another. While I believe most people would think that these are nothing more than random and unrelated to one another, I've come to believe that there's no such thing as a random coincidence. I once heard that a coincidence is nothing more than God's way of being mysterious. I like to think that God had the three of us on His mind when the shouting preacher got me thinking about Marcus and Fabio. I hope they are doing well and that life has treated them with kindness. Perhaps someday we'll meet again for something greater than when we initially met in New York, when they helped ease my loneliness.

Those who feel like they're not worthy of God's love, or have done things in their life that they regret, should come to learn, as I came to believe, that His love knows no boundaries. Mary Magdalene's story is such a tale of compassion and acceptance and I like to think that my encounter with Marcus and Fabio was too. For those who would judge me for building a relationship with these men, or to those who would judge Marcus and Fabio for being hookers, I say don't judge and you shall not be judged. A harlot was brought before Jesus and through the love of God she was transformed and has become a saint of the church. If God is for us, who can be against us?

Nobody and certainly not the people who would pass judgment on others.

After the closing ceremony of the Games at Wrigley Field, a dance party was held at the Uptown Theater, which Rick and I attended. Like most large gay dance parties, this event was chockfull with hundreds of gorgeous gay men from Chicago, its surrounding towns, and from states around the country and other parts of the world. Amidst the massive crowd, Rick and I saw my ex-lover Matt, with whom I lived for less than a year, who was terrified that he was going to contract the HIV virus from me. Our relationship had not been a good fit for either of us and a decade had passed since Matt and I had been boyfriends. I quietly wondered whether he was surprised that I was looking so well. I'm sure he was shocked that I wasn't dead and he had to be somewhat amazed that I was still in good physical shape and looked so healthy. We exchanged eye contact from a distance, but didn't approach one another at the time of our initial sighting. He was with his circle of friends and I was hanging out with Rick.

A few hours into the party, a hot guy came up to me and introduced himself. After he and I exchanged pleasantries for a few moments, he walked away. Shortly afterward, Matt approached me and stated that he saw that guy first and had been cruising him. What the fuck? Was I back in high school? I had not spoken to Matt or seen him in ten years and up to this point in the evening he had not found the time to approach me and say hello. When he finally decided to come up to me, this is how he greets me? Matt was always selfish when we were together and it seemed that he had not changed a bit. He was more interested in a potential trick that he was cruising that night than he was in the man who he lived with and was his boyfriend for a year. I was so pissed off that I could've decked him at that very moment. I informed him that the guy that he was cruising came up to me and if he wanted to be introduced to the trick then he should approach him directly and leave me alone. Instead of Matt being happy that his ex-boyfriend was well, he was more focused on getting laid by a stranger in the crowd. Matt's behavior confirmed why he was an ex and not my current boyfriend.

Matt's conduct unleashed an array of emotions in me that resulted in an emotional meltdown on my part later that evening. I was now pissed off. I was hurt, disappointed and once again feeling like nobody really cared about Darrel Loyd, other than Darrel Loyd. I may be a lot of things, but to enter a competition with a friend or an ex-boyfriend over a guy that I happen to see, meet, or cruise in a dance club is not who I am. Now that I was feeling overly sensitive about being reprimanded by Matt, Rick and I continued our evening from the opposite side of the dance floor from where Matt and his friends were partying.

Several hours later, after more drinks had been consumed, Rick and I were dancing on the edge of the dance floor. I spotted two beautiful men who were dancing near us, who were not together. After the incident with Matt, I was being very cautious. I was now observing Rick to see if he was interested in either guy before I decided which one to make a move on. I'm not trying to depict myself as such a gentleman or a good friend, I just didn't want another confrontation over a potential trick this evening. I was doing drugs, and Rick was not, so I was in a different mindset than him, although he was certainly a little over-served by this time. I observed, or at least it appeared to me, that Rick was cruising both of the guys that I was interested in meeting and they were all flirting with each other. What? I watched Rick's behavior and the other two guy's body language for a while before I had enough of the situation and just lost my cool. I pulled Rick aside and yelled at him "just pick one!" Rick must have thought I was crazy and off my rocker. Being single and not knowing that I was interested in either of them, Rick replied "why should I pick just one?" This exchange soured our mood and we walked off the dance floor. Being angry, I went off on Rick and I attacked him and, for some reason, I accused him of being a liar. Rick who had been so loyal for so long was wounded deeply and finally had enough. He turned away and left the club.

We had been extremely close for fifteen years and due to an unforeseen set of circumstances put into play by Matt's inconsiderate behavior, I told off my best friend over a potential encounter with a trick. In my defense, I had become extremely angry over the way that Matt treated me earlier that evening and I was devastated that he had more interest in a stranger with whom he wanted to have sex than he was in someone who had loved him. Between the feelings of being mistreated by Matt combined with the booze of the evening and the drugs from earlier in the day, it all fueled my insecurities and when I finally reacted, the lethal combination resulted in the end of a friendship that I cherished.

By this time – ten years after Alex and I had broken up – I had overcome my reservations of dating and had started to entertain the possibility of becoming romantically involved once again and sharing my life with another man. But it seemed like nobody cared about my feelings or what I had gone through to get to a place where I would consider dating again. It felt like a lifetime had passed since I had been in a good mental state where I would even consider cruising another guy for a date or a hookup. After my breakup, I had frequented various houses of ill repute where I looked for anonymous sexual encounters. In these venues, I didn't have to worry about getting emotionally involved or that someone would lie to me or deceive me. Since the encounters never went any further than the immediate need at that specific moment and place, I felt safe for some odd reason. I guess the word anonymous says it all.

I pouted about the little regard that Matt had for my feelings and had certainly over-reacted by going off on Rick, although I felt he might have been a little more sensitive to the situation, especially since he knew what had taken place between Matt and I earlier that night. In his defense, he was single and certainly could flirt with anyone he wanted, although I followed the gay male bro-code that states you must call it first before it can be yours. Maybe that explains Matt's behavior that night. But I was feeling sorry for myself and disrespected so I lashed out. Something had snapped. I was now going to do whatever I wanted with whomever I wanted and nobody was going to tell me that I couldn't cruise another individual. I was not going to worry about being the better person any longer or be concerned about hurting someone's feelings. My new bro-code was hos before bros.

After that night, I was so angry at the world that I did something only a screwed-up person would do — I called the guy that I met at the gay bathhouse in Atlanta and scheduled a trip to visit him for a weekend of drugs and sex. This would be the beginning of an out of control Darrel Loyd that would last four to five years of sorrowful behavior on my part that I would come to regret.

I'll spare myself the embarrassment of describing the details of that sordid weekend and focus on the low points and so-called highlights of the two-day affair. Before traveling to Atlanta for my scheduled sex party, I had always snorted Tina, but that was about to change. Up to that point, I was always interested in going to the clubs to dance and hang out with my friends when doing drugs, but I was introduced to smoking Tina in Atlanta. Inhaling Tina is a very different high than you get when you snort the drug. I learned that weekend that people who partied on Tina while having sex usually smoked it.

My host invited some really hot guys to his place. We partied and people got naked. I was introduced to a gay sex site on the internet called Manhunt by my fellow naked partygoers. Manhunt was a place where many positive men hooked up with other positive men for sex, revolutionary at the time. There wasn't a whole lot of sex taking place at the sex party, mostly because the guys were bottoms with no tops present. Some guys were naked, watching porn on the bed, while others were logged onto Manhunt cruising for other guys. I was totally out of my comfort zone. The night turned to day and the next day we were still getting high and hanging out. When the evening came, we decided to go to a gay club. I was becoming a little sketchy and felt unsafe. I had not slept in thirty-six hours and had very little to eat in that time, if anything. I knew very little about my host, as I had only met him one time before at the bathhouse and that encounter only lasted a short time.

When we arrived at the club, I was certainly over my normal limit on the amount of drugs I considered safe to consume in a specified amount of time and I was not feeling good about the situation or myself. However, in the midst of my screwed-up behavior, I was still able to ascertain that I was out of control and not feeling very happy about my actions. Shortly after we arrived at the club, I separated myself from the group and deliberately got lost in the throbbing music and the crowd of gyrating men on the dance floor. The longer I stayed the more it felt as if the walls were closing in on me. My self-respect had caught up with my behavior and it was not happy. As this realization hit me, I impulsively left the club and the people with whom I had come to party.

Since I had been to Atlanta on many other occasions, I was familiar with the city. I decided to check myself into a nearby hotel for the night. I was in a desperate state and had to get away from the sex and drug-fueled environment where I was staying. I needed a solid night's sleep to get my mind thinking properly and the only way that was going to happen was if I checked into a hotel alone. I had left the club and headed to a hotel because I was not feeling safe in the environment where I had placed myself, but I had definitely lost my way and my moral compass was beginning to show signs of rebooting.

When I arrived in my room, I locked the door behind me and placed a chair in front of it and under the door handle. I'm not sure what I was afraid of, although I was afraid of something. I felt like a little boy in a grown man's body and all I wanted at that moment was for someone to hold me, tuck me in bed, and tell me that everything was going to be all right. I looked for a Bible in a drawer of one of the nightstands. For those of you too young to know what I'm referring to…there was a day when hotels placed a copy of the Bible in a drawer next to the bed. I took the Bible out of the drawer and held it in my arms while I laid on the bed. I asked God to keep me safe and shortly afterward, I fell asleep. Gideon International, a Christian association, has placed more than 1.8 billion Bibles in hotels throughout the United States and in over 190 other countries, as they did in my hotel room in Atlanta. This project has been so successful that other religions have started providing literature to hotels. As a result, you may find the Quran or the Book of Mormon next to your Gideon Bible at your next hotel stay. If I knew then what this little book represented and the power within it, I would've taken it and kept it with me for the rest of my days. That little Gideon Bible did what no man could do. However, I would need to wait years to be enlightened as to what transpired in that hotel room in Atlanta that night.

I made it back home to Chicago safely and while my moral compass was resetting itself, I had lost my dignity along the way. I was ashamed of what I had done, although a part of me was still intrigued by the introduction to the party-and-play (PNP) men that I met on Manhunt. PNP represents those gay men that party (do drugs, usually smoking Tina), and play (have sex).

Alex's sexual antics had engulfed our relationship, so sexual intimacy had become a stumbling block for me, but a part of me was intrigued by the notion of letting one's dick do the thinking for them. Like Alex, and so many other guys that allow their dick to rule their lives, I too had become somewhat captivated by this idea. I figured that since I couldn't find a monogamous partner, I probably should join the crazed dick train. I always found my idea of wanting a loving monogamous relationship with another man, adopting children someday, and raising our family and dog in a beautiful home an interesting one, since I always ended up getting into relationships with men who lied and cheated and who had their brains in their crotch, which was the opposite of what I thought I wanted. This contradiction would haunt me until I ended up in a desert valley staring at a mountain seeking the answer to this paradox.

I had been working for the logistics company for eight months when I returned from Atlanta. When I worked from my home office and connected to the company's servers, it was done through their IT department. I was still a novice when it came to computers, their operating systems, the internet, and all the technical mumbo-jumbo that goes with running a remote home office. The logistics company was a Windows shop, but because I was an Apple user, I made the request to work using my own equipment. Madame President approved the request, although I still had to connect to the logistics company server to access their network via their router. I didn't realize that when I connected my computer to the logistics server, they were able to track my computer and see whatever websites I visited – no matter if it was during working hours or after. I was not informed that this would be the case, nor did I think that they could do this from a remote location. My naiveté resulted in my privacy being invaded. It seemed that when it came to snooping or checking up on me, Madame President and the Lesbian were masterful.

I became engrossed with Manhunt.com and with searching the site for hookups with other men. I was only interested in meeting or hooking up with other gay men that were positive. It was less complicated and Manhunt seemed to me to be the first online gay sex site where men actually revealed their HIV status in their profiles. In this forum, I could simply share my status and no longer had to worry about how or when to tell a potential suitor that I was positive. After all these years, I finally had a place where it was acceptable to be openly positive and where I would be welcomed rather than shunned for my health status.

One can easily get distracted working from home, especially when your main duties are searching for potential business leads and developing these into sales. One entire week, I got sucked into Manhunt when I was supposed to be working. I was consistently searching for men to meet — not a good idea when the Lesbian was monitoring my computer activity. After messing around on Manhunt like a kid in a candy store, I felt guilty for not working even as I was earning a salary. On Friday of that week, I informed the Lesbian that I would be recording two days off that week. I then worked Saturday, Sunday and Monday, which was a holiday, to makeup up for the time that I spent on Manhunt. By using the two vacation days and working the entire holiday weekend, I was innocently trying to rectify the wrong that I had done.

I was not aware that the Lesbian had any idea that I was hunting for dick during work hours.

Prior to starting my job, I had worked with Rick to develop the company website and brochure. I didn't pull a salary or receive any compensation for this time — giving my time and creative efforts to the company at no charge for several weeks. While I felt that I gave much to the company and didn't receive compensation for every hour worked, I certainly understand that I was wrong to hunt for dick during work. But what was done was done and all I was able to do once I stopped thinking with my dick was to attempt to right the wrong. I took the two vacation days and worked the holiday weekend to make up for my mistake and ease my guilt. We all do stupid things from time to time and I feel we should not dwell so much on the stupid, but focus on a sincere effort to atone. We should also not underestimate the power of admitting one's mistake while attempting to rectify a situation. At the very least, I realized my behavior was inappropriate and I tried to make it right.

In my first calendar year with the logistics company, I sold over a half-million dollars in services. The second year, I sold over $1.4 million. I was well on track to build the business model that I was hired to develop. Building something from scratch is never easy and to bring this level of new business to a company in a field that was unfamiliar to me was not without difficulties or distractions. But by the grace of God and with much help from Emily, my former assistant in New York who sent many business opportunities my way, I was able to build a solid client base in a relatively short time.

I appreciated Emily's devotion to our ongoing friendship and most importantly for supporting me when we worked together in New York. Her friendship is still very important to me and I'll forever love her for being a genuine person and standing by my side when most of the people in our industry were talking shit about me. She was, and remains, a fantastic friend, a lovely lady, a beautiful person and a wonderful mother to her little girl. She was twenty-one years old when I arrived in New York and even though there was a twenty-year difference in our ages, we bonded with one another quickly. We were the New York team that was admired by many and envied by some. I once told her that she was the female version of me, minus the drugs. It was this mirrored vision that allowed us to embrace each other's shortcomings while bonding us closer together. Later in life, Emily married for a second time. Her second husband was a lovely and handsome Muslim man from Algeria. Emily and I like to refer to him as the Arab, due to his being dark complexioned and so good looking. If Emily is the female version of me that would make me the gay male version of her and so perhaps there's still hope for me to marry my own very handsome Arab with a dark complexion.

On Friday, June 28 of 2015, as I wrote these words, the United States

Supreme Court ruled that same sex marriages were legal in all fifty states in the U.S. With this landmark ruling, my American gay dream can now simply be referred to as my American dream. Now all I need is to find an honest man that wants a family, who will love me with all his heart and who I can love back. What's not negotiable is that no matter where he lives or what race he may be, he too must love God. If there's such a man in this world for me to marry and if he just so happens to be someone other than an American, then possibly my American dream is nothing more than simply living the dream.

I frequently traveled to San Francisco to meet with clients. During one of these business trips I met a guy on Manhunt named Philven. His mother had liked the name Phillip and Steven so she combined the two and that's how he was named. His mother must have had a premonition when she named her child. I would eventually come to know that Philven conducted himself like he had two different personalities within him. When he came to my hotel to hook up with me after we connected on Manhunt, I had to meet him in the lobby. My hotel in San Francisco, and the floor where my room was located, was off-limits to the public and one needed a keycard to activate the elevator to access the floor where I was staying.

As I left my room and got in the elevator to walk to the lobby to meet Philven, I had no idea my life was about to change. When the elevator stopped at the ground floor and the doors opened, I was not aware that by walking out of the elevator and introducing myself to Philven I would open Pandora's Box again. What was intended to be a casual one-night stand would end up costing me a great deal.

I noticed Philven right away standing in the lobby. He was tall, standing six feet and two inches in height. He was a bit thin for his size, nicely dressed and wore a very stylish pair of gym shoes. He looked good so I invited him to my room. He was British and had a fantastic accent that I thought was extremely hot and very much turned me on. Once we arrived upstairs, we both got naked right away. I quickly glanced at his dick while he was undressing. I had never seen a guy so hung before. He definitely had my attention and curiosity. One thing led to another and the dastardly deed was done. It had been years since I had had another man in my bed overnight, but I decided to invite Philven to spend the night. Before falling asleep, he told me that he had a twin brother that was also gay. He went on to tell me that his twin and his brother's lover had apparently died in a car accident in London. It turned out that his brother and his lover were driving to the home of Philven's parents where Philven's twin planned to come out to them and introduce his boyfriend. On their way, they were involved in a car accident and both were thrown from the car and were lying in the street close to one another. The brother was killed immediately. The boyfriend was apparently able to crawl his way to Philven's brother's lifeless body lying on the road.

The boyfriend then put his hand on Philven's brother's arm before he too passed away. Philven told me that a policeman arrived on the scene, who also happened to be gay. The policeman saw both of them lying dead in the street and realized that he knew his brother and his boyfriend. He then removed the boyfriend's hand from the brother's arm before the paramedics arrived on the scene. I asked why the policeman removed the boyfriend's hand and he replied that the policeman knew that Philven's parents didn't know that his brother was gay and he didn't want them to find out this way. I was overcome with sadness over the story and thought how tragically romantic the tale was.

The next morning, Philven spotted a Dolce Gabbana suit hanging in my room that I was wearing the previous day when I was running around San Francisco for my meetings. He told me that he seen me at the corner of Howard and Beale Streets, as I was crossing the street. I had been at the Starbucks at that intersection the previous day and had walked across Howard and then across Beale as I walked to the Embarcadero for a client meeting. The suit had a very distinct look, but I thought it interesting that he didn't remember my face, but he remembered the suit. Does the suit make the man in my case or did I make the suit? In this incidence, it was obvious. It was all about the suit and that's why I had bought it when I came across it in a store in New York.

As I wrote the above paragraph, I happened to have patronized the same Starbucks where Philven initially saw me crossing the street. This doesn't necessarily have anything to do with this narrative, although I think it's a perfect example of a coincidence that confirms I'm exactly where I'm supposed to be in writing this story — another marker to let me know that I'm standing or have arrived exactly where I'm supposed to be in life at the exact time I was expected to arrive. It's like traveling on a highway and passing a mile marker that's been placed on the side of the road by the highway transportation authority to help you identify your exact location — in case of an emergency and when you need to let someone know where you are on the highway.

Philven and I exchanged phone numbers and we went our separate ways. Four weeks later, I was required to return to San Francisco for follow-up meetings. I had not spoken to him since we said our goodbyes in the hotel a month earlier. I called him and indicated that I would be back in the city in a few days. I asked him whether he was interested in making plans to have dinner together on the evening of my arrival. He was very interested. We hooked up, had dinner, fucked, and he spent the night with me in my hotel room again. The next day, we made plans to get together later that evening when my meetings were over. When I arrived back at the hotel, Philven was waiting for me in the lobby. He had brought Tina with him.

That night we smoked Tina and had sex for hours. I was now in lust. As we spoke, I found out that Philven was escorting to support himself while he was living in San Francisco. He was a British citizen who had entered the United States on an education visa and said he had enrolled in a college in Los Angeles to earn a Master's Degree in Finance. I went back to Chicago, but not before inviting Philven to come visit me. The sex we had was pretty amazing and I was definitely letting my dick do the thinking for me.

Upon returning to Chicago, I had a routine medical checkup with my doctor. Being positive, I had quarterly labs to monitor my HIV viral load, T-cell count, and overall health status. Through these tests, the doctor ensured that the medications I was taking were being effective in fighting the replication of my HIV cells. When I got my results, I was in for a weird surprise.

When I first was diagnosed as being positive, my T-cell count was in the six hundred range and over the years of bad relationships, poor life choices, alcohol abuse, and drug use – combined with my late nights clubbing – my T-cells had deteriorated, dropping to the high three hundreds, which had become a concern. If the T-cell count of an HIV-positive person drops below the two hundred range, they're considered to have AIDS. When my medical results came back from the lab, my T-cell count had jumped from the three hundred range to the nine hundreds. My T-cells had never been anywhere close to this number before. My HIV medications had not changed in several years so the enormous change in my T-cell count was not due to any medical reason. While I was thrilled with the news, I pondered what I had done that made my T-cells increase so dramatically.

From this point on, my T-cell number stayed in the nine hundred range and over the years my count would climb even higher to the fourteen hundred range. An average person, considered to be in good health, has a T-cell count that can vary from five to fifteen hundred. I was now on the high-end of the scale and feeling very much relieved. I was in the safe zone and I now had some wiggle room if future labs took a decline for whatever reason. Prior to this miraculous change, I had been dangerously close to the two hundred or below number, which was more of a mental obstacle for me than a physical one. I felt and looked healthy, but dropping below the two hundred count would've added more stress to my already stressful life. What had taken place that caused such a drastic change in my health condition when it had been deteriorating for years? I would need to wait several years before this perplexing question would be answered.

Philven came to visit me in Chicago in the fall of 2006 and stayed for one month before returning to San Francisco. I always had a habit of getting involved with lovers too quickly and Philven was no different. My first gift to him, the first of many, was a pair of Kenneth Cole shoes. I love a man that wears stylish footwear and believe that you can tell a lot about him by the shoes he wears and their condition. To me, a well-dressed man with bad shoes is like a very sexy man with a fantastic body and discovering he's a bad kisser or, even worse, a bad lover. It's just a big fat disappointment. As the month went on, we got acquainted and we fucked a lot. I got caught up in the sex and my dick guided my judgment. This was the first time I had entered a relationship based solely on sex, which was not a good idea. I began to further comprise my morals. I thought back to Alex's adulterous relationship with me and entertained and acted on the idea of having a three-way with Philven and another guy. If we both slept with another man, I felt that there would be no need for him to cheat on me—and tell me a bunch of lies to cover it up, as Alex had done.

After Philven left Chicago, we spoke and made plans for me to take him to Las Vegas for us to spend Christmas there that year. He came back to Chicago in November and we both left for Las Vegas a few days before Christmas. Prior to leaving, I got tickets for us to see *Love*, a Cirque du Soleil show with songs by the Beatles, at the Mirage hotel. This was the only time I ever bought tickets on my own to see a theatrical production, but I was starting to fall in love, or so I thought. Even though it was still early in our relationship, that little voice inside of my head began telling me that Philven was not entirely truthful or that he was not as forthcoming as to who he was or what his real intentions entailed. On our flight to Las Vegas, I caught him shaking his head to one of the flight attendants as he approached us while we were seated on the plane. I never knew what that was all about, but I figured that he and Philven must have connected at some point and Philven didn't want me to know that he and this flight attendant had hooked up. It was little signs such as this that made me start to think that Philven was already hiding things from me.

When I met Philven I believed good people came in all shapes and sizes, from different ethnic backgrounds, countries, religions, and sexual preferences and from all professions. Even after all the craziness I've been through, I still believe this to be true. If the movie Pretty Woman could have a happy ending, then why couldn't the British escort and I live happily ever after?

Before leaving for Las Vegas with Philven, I leased a new 2006 XJ8 Jaguar automobile. I love expensive luxury cars and I appreciate their beauty and fine craftsmanship. I had leased a BMW 545i when I relocated back to Chicago from New York and I had decided not to lease another BMW because a saleswoman at the BMW dealership and I couldn't agree on a fair price. Additionally, during our negotiations, she haughtily told me that maybe my next car shouldn't be a BMW, and so it wasn't. The Jaguar dealer had to obtain the car, for the price that I was willing to pay, from a dealership in a different state. The car was expected to arrive sometime around Christmas so I informed the salesman that I would pick it up when I returned from celebrating the holiday in Las Vegas. The Jaguar represented a level of success that I had achieved. I had never thought in my wildest dreams that I would one day be able to afford a car of this magnitude when I was young growing up in Mokena. The anticipation of the car's arrival made the 2006 Christmas season even more exciting.

Christmas came and went and the New Year dawned. With Philven living in San Francisco and me living in Chicago, it would've been difficult to attempt to build a relationship—so we were going to try to live together in my place and see if we were interested in becoming boyfriends, the next level in our relationship. Philven went back to San Francisco to take care of some personal stuff and a month later returned to Chicago. this time bringing all his meager possessions with him. Initially, we had an understanding that he would live with me for a couple of months. During this trial period, we would determine if we were compatible and wanted to become permanent boyfriends residing under the same roof, mine. I told Philven that I didn't want him escorting and that I would cover his living expenses as we began to build our relationship. This sounds like a bad idea, even now, but I've always believed in the goodness of people and their circumstances don't necessarily determine who they are or who they will become. If a person's current circumstances defined their entire life, then I would've stayed a screwed up, scared, mean, self-medicating mess.

After a month of observing Philven lay about the house watching television or surfing the internet, I decided to have him help me with some of my work. I was becoming extremely busy with managing the projects that I was bringing to the company and I frequently worked late. Since Philven was doing nothing, I made a financial deal with him. I offered to teach him the logistic business so he could assist me. If we were successful in generating sales for the company together, we would split my commission for those projects. My yearly base salary of one hundred and twenty five thousand dollars was supporting us. The first million of invoiced business went to cover my base salary and I received ten percent commission on everything after the first million and up to the second million. All sales above two million were to receive a commission of six percent. While this could be lucrative, it was not easy to book and invoice sales in the millions in a single calendar year, although possible. There was certainly a financial upside to Philven learning the business and helping me increase my sales. Plus, I was trying to make an honest man out of him.

Before we started to work together, I spoke with Madame President and cleared the deal that I had made with Philven. She agreed with the arrangement and approved his becoming my assistant. She had the Lesbian issue him a company email address and sent an email welcoming him to the company. It was a great deal for her, as she now had two people working on developing her business for the price of one, as Philven would only be paid by me when I hit my sales goals and received commissions.

Before meeting Philven, I had installed and signed up for Yahoo Instant Messenger. I met a guy online from Saint Louis and from time to time, I would instant message with him using Yahoo. After meeting Philven, and from trying to eliminate work distractions, I deleted the application from my computer. One day as we were working, for no apparent reason, I decided to reinstall the Yahoo Messenger application and to my amazement the guy from Saint Louis immediately popped up on Yahoo texting me when I launched it. At that exact moment, Philven shut his computer and got up from his side of the desk where he was supposed to be working and walked away from the office. I then noticed that the Saint Louis guy's message looked like he was in the middle of a conversation. I pinged him back and asked him who he was chatting with and he replied, "You, Darrel!"

What? How could he be talking to me? More importantly, who or what drove me to re-install and launch the application at that moment after I had deleted it from my computer? This unexplained event was one of the defining moments where I now know for a fact that Philven was able to connect to my computer remotely. I later came to learn that Apple computers have a pairing capability that allows another user to wirelessly pair with your computer if they are near your terminal and the pairing application is open. This is only one of several options that Philven could've used to connect to and monitor my computer. By doing so, in this case, he was pinging the Saint Louis guy on Yahoo Messenger and impersonating me in the process. This incident made me realize that the client information that I stored on my computer was not necessarily safe. For the first time in my career, data that had a direct impact on my salary was in an electronic device and I had little knowledge about how to keep sensitive client information safe, other than relying on the logistics IT department to ensure it was secure.

The more Philven became entrenched in my life, the stranger things became. One day, Philven made lunch for the two us and for Puckles and Papi. Philven and the boys were in the den waiting for me to finish up in the office so we could have lunch together. On my way to the den, I stopped at the laundry room to put a load of clothes in the washer when I had an overwhelming premonition. I stood at the washer when a thought overtook my mind. For no apparent reason, at that moment, I thought that Philven was slipping out of the house at night after I fell asleep and was meeting up with guys for sex. If this was true, then he must have been meeting guys on hookup sites when he was supposed to be working. I had taken an area off the kitchen and converted that space into my home office. I took my dining table and transformed it into a workstation for Philven and me. The table was large enough for the two of us to work directly across from one another, but with this seating arrangement, I was not able to view Philven's monitor from where I sat. I had no idea what he was working on at any given time and naturally believed and trusted that he was working when he was sitting at his side of the desk.

A few months earlier, I had confided to Philven that I had suspicions that Alex had once slipped out of our hotel room in the middle of the night while we were on vacation in Miami for a circuit party. We were there during Thanksgiving and were joined by several of our friends. One night, after being out partying with these friends who were staying in different hotels nearby, Alex and I returned to our hotel. Before going to bed, he and I took a sleeping pill to get a good night's sleep. We had taken ecstasy earlier at a dance club and if we didn't take a sleeping aid, we wouldn't have been able to get a good night's rest. When I awoke the following morning, I had an overwhelming feeling that Alex had slipped out of the hotel room that previous night after my sleeping pill kicked in. Alex had pretended to take his sleeping pill, when he had not. He waited for me to fall sound asleep and out the door he went into the darkness looking for a sexual encounter. All I had to go on was an unsubstantiated hunch that my adulterous husband was up to no good while I was sound asleep. Later that afternoon Alex and I met up with our friends. I had not mentioned to anyone that I believed Alex slipped out in the middle of the night when I was sleeping. However, at lunch, a friend of Alex pointedly stated that he didn't understand why men who are involved in a relationship with a handsome man would sneak out on their boyfriends in the middle of the night looking for dick. It was no random coincidence that Alex's friend made this statement on the same day that I was having these feelings. It turned out that the friend, who was with us the previous evening, was cruising the streets of South Beach for a possible hook up after we left the club, which in his case was fine because he was single. I was freaked out! He must have seen Alex trolling for random dick. Otherwise, how could my unsubstantiated thoughts of Alex slipping out of our hotel room be voiced out loud by someone who had no idea what I felt had taken place? I had not spoken to anyone about my premonition. I wanted to reach over the table and grab Alex by the neck and choke him until he passed out from my blocking oxygen to his brain—or lack of oxygen to his dick, since it was doing the thinking for him. Instead, I sat in my chair freaking out over what had just gone down. Was the incident with Alex those many years before a precursor for what was yet to come?

Now, that same gut feeling that I experienced in Miami had come around again. I was able to shrug off the feeling and headed toward the den to meet Philven and the boys for lunch. Once I sat at the table where Philven had placed my food, I heard a woman's voice coming from the television. The Jerry Springer show was on and a woman was telling a story about how her husband was stepping out on her in the middle of the night after she went to sleep. How could I have the exact same thoughts about Philven just a few minutes before and then hear a person on the television repeat those same thoughts? I was a little freaked out by the coincidence. Was I standing exactly where I was supposed to be standing, at the exact moment, to receive confirmation that my premonition was in fact coming from a spiritual place? I was a little frazzled by the incident and was now left with figuring out how to deal with this information. Why were these circumstances lining up in my life and what did they mean, other than the obvious fact that I had poor judgment in choosing a mate?

Between premonitions that were mounting on a regular basis, the logistics company monitoring my computer, and Philven's unsubstantiated but dubious actions, I was feeling suspicious and that someone was watching me. The poor life choices that I was making, combined with Philven's behavior and that of the logistics company, were beginning to increase my feelings that I was being watched. I felt like I was heading the wrong way down a one-way street. I was traveling at a dangerous speed unable to read the signs placed before me. The premonitions were increasing as if something or someone was showing me many cautionary signs. But I was too distracted and confused to decipher the real meaning behind what was flashing before my eyes. I'm a Taurus and I was possibly being stubborn or I didn't want to acknowledge the signs for what they really represented. A head-on collision was inevitable.

I became angry and I started to care less if I lived to see another day. I began to realize I was in yet another bad relationship and was feeling paranoid. I now understand that these feelings were not paranoia at all, they were gut feelings that were being substantiated by dubious actions. I couldn't prove that Philven was lying to me or that he and the company were snooping in my terminal, but I felt someone's presence invading my proprietary information and privacy and I was becoming increasing hostile over the situation. I was extremely anxious about protecting my electronic client information. Had either of them asked me or told me that they were the ones accessing my computer and its information, I would've appreciated their candor and my anxious behavior and the exhausting energy on my part to protect this data from an unknown intruder, could've been avoided.

My anger boiled over on August 1, 2007. I started to rant and went off on a hateful tangent, wishing that the bridges in America would begin to fall without warning and for no apparent reason. That same day, a bridge in Minneapolis, Minnesota fell without warning, killing thirteen people. I've never forgotten what I said in anger and what took place later that day. I certainly don't believe my words had anything to do with the bridge falling in Minnesota, although from that day forward I would not speak of such things in anger again.

The same year as the bridge incident, little Papi became ill. One Thursday, he was not quite himself and started to feel progressively worse. He was a little barking monster, but despite this oftentimes annoying trait he was such a lively dog that it saddened me to see him that way. We took him to the vet on Friday and it turned out that he required emergency surgery that day. He survived the surgery, but because he was eleven years old, the anesthesia caused his kidneys to begin to fail. By Monday morning, his kidneys were beginning to shut down and I needed to make the decision to put him to sleep. After Alex and I had split up, Papi had become sick when I was still living in Marin, and he was diagnosed with having anemia. His body was consuming his red blood cells. The veterinarian placed Papi, who was three years old at the time, on Prednisone and told me then that he would probably not live to celebrate his seventh birthday. The little guy ended up beating the blood disease a few years after being diagnosed and he lived a long and full life, endlessly loyal through eleven years. He was a wonderful friend and companion who loved me unconditionally when I felt like nobody else cared about me. To this day, I believe God sent Papi into my life when he did, so that he, and eventually Puckles, could save me from my lonely self.

Upon reaching the decision to put Papi to sleep so the little guy would not suffer anymore, I reached out to Rick so he could say goodbye to his little friend. Papi had always loved Rick and had such an extreme affection for him that I often wondered if he loved Rick more than he loved me. Rick and I had not spoken since the closing night of the Gay Games when he walked away after that night's unfortunate events. Because they had been so close, I made a point to invite Rick to meet me at the veterinarian's so he and Papi could say goodbye to one another. Rick came, of course. It was heartbreaking to see Papi so ill. He seemed to be entirely out of it and unresponsive, but as Rick approached him and called out his name, he wagged his tail for the first time in days as he recognized his old friend. Good to the last, Papi was instrumental in bringing Rick and I together for one last encounter. This would be the last time I would see or speak to Rick for four years. In some odd way, the disagreement that resulted in us becoming estranged was not without reason or purpose, but I would not discover its purpose until the end of those four years.

I've come to understand that not all things that take place in an individual's life are meant for that specific individual. In other words, I believe God may use one person's circumstances to get his voice heard by another. I had a former landlord who had a poodle from the time it was a puppy. The puppy grew up and lived a long and full life before it eventually died from old age. Needless to say, this individual was very distraught over the loss of her best friend and companion of many years. She had a girlfriend who had a premonition that the poodle would be reincarnated and was concerned that my former landlord would not be reunited with the reincarnated puppy. When I heard this story, I thought how ridiculous it sounded and whether these people didn't have more important things to be concerned about in their lives than the reincarnation of a poodle. Later, I came to wonder whether this story was meant specifically for me to hear.

I had Papi cremated and his ashes placed in a wood box with a small Schnauzer mounted on the top of the box. His name was engraved on a bronze nameplate adhered to one side. To this day, I keep him on my desk to remind me of the great love that he gave me. On the day that I went to retrieve his ashes, Philven and I went to get the Jaguar out of the garage where I had parked it a few days earlier. Upon walking up to the car, I noticed that it was parked a bit askew. Since it had been such an expensive purchase and my new baby, I was very particular in the way I parked it in the parking spot allocated to me in my building.

My drug use was increasing so I had prescription sleeping pills at the apartment so I could jack myself up during the day, and if I was unable to sleep at night, I had sleeping pills to help me go to bed. Philven prepared dinner and – as I had told him the story about Alex slipping out of the hotel room in Miami – he decided to take that concept to a whole new level. He began to grind up sleeping pills and then mixing the resulting powder in my food. By doing so, he was ensuring that I would sleep through the night without waking up. After dinner, I would almost immediately go to bed and he was then able to comfortably make his late-night rendezvous with his internet butt buddies. To add insult to injury, Philven was not only slipping out of my bed and my apartment in the middle of the night after he had drugged me, he was also taking my brand new very expensive Jaguar out of the garage without my permission and driving my baby to some unknown tricks' place. I eventually found an email from one of his late-night adventures confirming my suspicions. Philven's behavior only got worse and his actions eventually made Alex's behavior look like child's play, which was not an easy feat. It was a tragic nursery rhyme where a little piggy went to a tricks house, while this little piggy stayed home and slept, and the first little piggy went wee, wee, all over town with his weenie. Fucking unbelievable! I now understand how the expression "men can be pigs" came to fruition.

What was wrong with me? Why did I keep getting involved with people who conducted themselves with absolutely no honesty or moral foundation? Why was I so fucked up and why did I keep getting involved with people that took advantage of me? Did I really think so little of myself and have such disregard for my own well-being? I thought I wanted to be loved and treated well, but was I wrong and did I like being used, abused, and treated like scum that you might find on the bottom of your shoe after walking the streets, which you eventually scrape off and toss back in the street?

Philven supposedly enrolled in school in LA to earn a Master's Degree. He had a Master's Degree all right, although it was not in Finance…it was in fine arts— he was the finest con artist I ever met. I soon came to understand that Philven had no interest in being an honest man or making an honest living. He was a liar who used people for his personal gain and, while there were many "happy endings" during the time we spent together, a permanent happy ending was not in the cards for us. Philven had himself been used throughout his life and so he had adapted to use people before they could use him. I like to think that he was the way he was because of what he had been through and that he did not chose to be the despicable person that I eventually came to know. Possibly there was some deep emotional issue that drove his fucked-up behavior. By the time we were through, Philven, my so-called boyfriend, would show me more disrespect and unkindness than any another human being ever has. Before all this would be clear to me, I fell in love with him. I would rearrange my entire life to make him feel like an equal—my first major mistake. I now understand that I couldn't just make him an equal, this was something that needed to develop over time. I've come to believe that a partner must find their role on their own. A counterpart that graciously compliments its equal is not something that can be forced, given out of sympathy, or offered up in the name of love…it must develop and usually in a natural and organic fashion. In my eyes, Philven never deserved to be my equal, but this was my mistake, not his.

16 | JOKER'S WILD

A few months after Papi died, in late October of 2007, I sold my condominium in Chicago with the hopes of being able to relocate back to California. In preparation, Philven and I traveled to Palm Springs on two occasions to view various houses in the desert resort cities of Palm Springs, Cathedral City, and Palm Desert. On our second trip, I had a premonition, one morning after Philven and I looked at potential homes. I awoke and immediately had an overwhelming sensation that Philven had slipped out in the middle of the night while I was asleep. Up to that point, I only suspected Philven of sneaking out for late night rendezvous — except for one email that I found on his computer in Chicago, where Philven stipulated that he could only meet up "late at night."

The evening before, Philven was very helpful in reminding me to take my HIV medications before going to bed. I wondered if he could have switched out one of the HIV drugs in powder form, in a capsule, with a crushed up sleeping pill. This would've been the only way that he was able to get out of the hotel room at night without risking that I would wake up and catch him in the act. I felt so fucking messed up that I was even experiencing these feelings of betrayal, at that level. How fucked up was I? Or was Philven the fucked up one? Were my feelings valid or were they an aftermath of the insecurities left behind from my failed relationship with Alex? Once again, I was experiencing the same emotions of betrayal, as I was buying a home and thinking of living in that home with a boyfriend, just as I had done with Alex. Was my premonition real or was it Memorex?

Soon, I would be facing my darkest days without Rick, my best friend, or Papi, my little protector, by my side. In a short time, I would find myself surrounded in what seemed to be a morally-barren battlefield. In the desert valley of California, I would encounter my worst fears and would need to decide if I was going to allow my fears to rule my life or if I was going to declare war on evil and finally conquer my fears and self-doubt. Would I submit to evil and submerge myself into an abyss of hatred or would I begin to be governed by God's compassion and love?

In Palm Springs, I found a home that fit my budget, in a neighborhood that Philven and I could agree on, north of the airport. The house was close enough to the airport to see the planes landing and taking off, but the flight patterns weren't directly over the house so we wouldn't have to endure the overwhelming noise that the jet engines create when flying directly overhead. The house was unoccupied, had been recently renovated, and the landscaping was in decent condition. I wanted a house that I could gut and design and build to my specifications. The house, on Whitewater Club Drive, had great bones, although it needed a substantial facelift for it to become my dream home. It was a Meiselman – after the builder – and a classic mid-century modern home. Meiselman houses have the master suite on one side of the house with the second bedroom on the opposite side, allowing for privacy for both bedrooms. The homes were constructed in the 1950s and the 1960s and less than two hundred of them were built, making this Meiselman home a rare desert find.

Why didn't I leave Philven in Chicago when I sold my condominium and relocated to California? I should have sent him back to the street corner where I found him. In retrospect, I believe I was too afraid to make the transition to Palm Springs on my own. I felt like I would rather be badly accompanied, as Rick's father used to say, than move to the desert by myself…a bad choice on my part.

This was my second move to California with a boyfriend in tow. Similar to my relationship with Alex, the down payment for the Palm Springs home was generated by the sale of a condominium in Chicago, but, unlike my relationship with Alex, I was the sole owner of the house on Whitewater Club Drive. Philven's name was not listed on the title of the house nor was he listed on the loan. Not surprisingly, he had several delinquent credit card accounts and I was not willing to add him as a co-owner in case his creditors came looking for him to legally pursue him for his outstanding debts. I was always very conscientious, throughout my adult life, about keeping my credit report in good standing, which is something that my father instilled in me as a teenager. When I bought the Whitewater home, my middle credit score rating was seven hundred and seventy, which is considered to be very good.

I contracted a local architect to draw up blueprints to expand the square footage of the house and update the electrical system, plumbing, roofing, flooring, and bathrooms. I had the architect reconfigure the kitchen and laundry area and added a powder room at the main entrance. I had him tear down the existing carport and replace it with an enclosed addition that we could use as a home office. The house was to undergo a major demolition to remodel it to become the dream home that I always wanted, while maintaining the integrity of its mid-century modern style.

Even after all the shit I had been through with my previous so-called lovers, I was still a hopeless romantic. I was still looking for my happy ending like one finds in a fairytale.

After selling the condo in Chicago, on my way to the airport to catch my flight to California, I thought that God must have played a role in getting me to live in the desert. I began to think He wanted to isolate me from my family and friends for an unknown purpose, as if He required my undivided attention. I had no real basis for these thoughts and they left my mind as fast as they entered it. After we arrived in Palm Springs, Philven, Puckles and I moved into a temporary residence as we waited to close the home sale and for the architect to finish the blue prints for the remodel.

The excitement of living in a sunny and warm environment all year round was certainly a welcome change from the cold winters in the Midwest. I quickly discovered that the desert cities of California were notorious for the manufacturing, distribution, and use of Tina. I also discovered that an enormous number of gay men, previously diagnosed with HIV or AIDS in the early days of the epidemic – who also went on social security disability because there wasn't any treatment for the disease at the time – had moved to the desert region of California or to Florida. Many of these men were not only living on social security disability benefits, they were also partaking in illegal recreational drugs while filling their days with fucking. Over the years of doing drugs, I've come to see that the majority of people who use Tina become shady characters and their drug use usually leads them to develop deceitful behaviors. Many people that I encountered in Palm Springs fit this profile, although there were certainly a few that were the exception. Even though I had used illegal recreational drugs for almost twenty years, I was never one of these people who used other individuals for their benefit, or told lies to deliberately fuck with someone's mind, and then used my drug use as an excuse for my behavior. I'm not trying to paint myself as a Saint. I've certainly told my share of lies, but I try very hard to no longer partake in this type of behavior. I'm also not the type of person who's clever enough to manipulate someone. My mind is simple and it doesn't operate in a manipulative way to get people to do something for my own gain. I've always been more direct when interacting with people and, if there's such a thing as a respectable drug user, then I would say that I was as close to respectable as one can be when using illegal substances on a regular basis for decades.

I can't speak for others, but my own drug use was being fueled by my insecurities, my inability to connect with good people, and from being terrified that someone with whom I was close would use me once again. I was overly sensitive to being mistreated and my drug use was a means of numbing my insecurities. This had a direct effect on my inability to identify the type of people that I was trying to keep out of my life. Now, my worst fears had been set in motion by allowing Philven to become part of my circle. In my new desolate crystal valley, Philven, Tina, and their evil followers were going to use everything in their power to destroy what I believed to be good. I expect that God knew I would eventually be brought to my knees and I would surrender to His will. In doing so, He would help me cut through the overwhelming darkness of my past and present—a dark void filled with angry tantrums, debilitating sadness, and pathetic and poor choices. He eventually led me to a place where I would be able to see the light of day, but it would get a whole lot darker before I could see a hint of light in the very far distance. The battles would be many and the struggle would last for more years than I care to remember, but, by the grace of God, I was eventually victorious over the hold that evil had on my life. To my amazement, my life purpose was revealed to me in that desert valley where my heaven and hell collided at 1780 North Whitewater Club Drive.

The time I spent in Palm Springs was the most difficult period of my life, while simultaneously the most spiritually gratifying. I lived there for three and a half years and during that time my Tina use increased. I was high on many occasions, but not always. I'll let your imagination guide you – on whether I was high or not – as I relive the events that I encountered in that desert valley where Tina called home sweet home and where God revealed himself to me.

When I lived in New York and then when I moved to Chicago, I resided next door to a church in each city. I came to see it as God's way of letting me know that He was close by and that He was watching over me. In the Whitewater house in Palm Springs, I was no longer living next door to a church, but I felt God was still close and seeming to draw nearer. The previous owner of the home was an Asian minister, though I never knew which part of Asia he was from. When I learned about him later, a joke came to mind:

Knock! Knock! Who's there?
It's the Vatican.
The Vatican who?
The Vaticinator that sold a house to a lost soul so he could be found.

On the first day that Philven and I met, he had told me the story of his twin brother who died in England. After moving to Palm Springs, I noticed a marked change in his behavior within days of our arrival. It was such a drastic departure from the person I had come to know that I thought his twin had changed places with him mid-flight from Chicago to California. It was crazy that I thought that, but this scenario made more sense to me than what was about to be unveiled. I naturally wondered what had taken place in Philven's life – that I didn't know about – which could have resulted in such a radical change in his behavior, as I was unaware that anything had happened in the time we had been together. I recalled the initial conversation with Philven about his twin brother and since he had planted the seed, and was now acting so drastically different, I came up with the scenario that Philven's twin brother was not dead after all...they must have changed places with one another. This seemed to be such a viable option, explaining the radical transformation in his behavior. Something was undeniably different. It seemed to me that Philven was not Philven at all. The person that I met in San Francisco and that I got to know in Chicago wasn't the same person that now stood before me in Palm Springs.

He became very distant and had emotionally checked out once we arrived and settled into the temporary residence. In Chicago, Philven was always very helpful in cleaning the house and making sure it was tidy. Once we were in Palm Springs, he never lifted a finger to assist in the household duties and I was left to complete these chores on my own. My plate was full with work. I was also working closely with the architect on the final design for the home and was knee-deep in paperwork, attempting to lock in the financing for the closing of the Whitewater house. I budgeted enough cash in my financial reserves to carry the mortgage on the Whitewater house, while it was being renovated, and to pay rent on the temporary residence for six-months. We needed to be out of the rental property by the end of March of 2008, as I was not in the financial position to carry the rent and a mortgage longer than the budgeted time. I always tried to be very conscientious and made it a priority to uphold my responsibilities at all times in my professional and in my personal life.

While staying at the rental property, oftentimes Philven became ill and said he had the flu, or at least that's the story that he claimed, to explain away his unhelpful behavior. He never appeared particularly unwell, or threw up, or went to a doctor to seek treatment. His so-called illness lasted for several months. One night, for some unknown reason, I had a dream that he was moving back to Chicago. In the span of a short time, he had moved from San Francisco to Chicago to Palm Springs so it made no sense to me that I dreamt about him moving back to Chicago after we moved to the desert as a couple. Several weeks later, we met with the architect to see the final design for the remodel. After the meeting, the architect turned to Philven and asked him when he was moving back to Chicago. What the fuck? The architect knew we were partners. Why would he ask such a question? I had not told anybody about my dream. Philven seemed unnerved by the question and brushed it off by replying that he was not moving back. The architect's question, however, shook me to my core.

Several months later, I had an epiphany. Philven didn't have the flu when we arrived, as he claimed nor was he ever physically ill. It turned out he was feeling the blues from being lovesick. The slime ball must have met someone in Chicago and it was possibly the same person who sent the email I found—the one where Philven told him that he was only available for a late-night hookup. He was feeling lovesick because the other man in Chicago must have changed his mind about Philven after we moved to Palm Springs, and he no longer wanted to pursue their affair. This action drove him to pretend being ill for months and the question posed by the architect. Palm Springs is a very small town and I expect the architect heard a rumor that gave him the impression that Philven was leaving once the house was completed. How fucked up was Philven? I had sold my condo in Chicago to purchase the Whitewater property. I was remodeling the house for us to live in as a committed couple—while he was screwing around with another man the entire time. Looking back, I'm sure it would've been emotionally devastating to have Philven betray me on such a level at the time, when I had so much on my plate. Although, had he left me high (pun intended) and dry as he had planned, it probably would've saved me a whole lot of hardship. He did not leave…so God clearly had another plan to end my cycle of pathetic behavior when it came to me attaching myself to the wrong type of man. That plan, to mold me into a more spiritual individual, had many points where I seriously believed I wasn't going to make it out of that desert in one piece. As the saying goes "what doesn't kill you will make you stronger," and so it did.

We arrived in Palm Springs in October of 2007. One day, sometime before Thanksgiving, we were walking down Palm Canyon Drive, the city's main thoroughfare. It's lined with many retail shops, several hotels, and numerous restaurants. Walking down this street, I thought I saw a puppy pop his head up in a storefront window, on the opposite side. I crossed the street to get a closer look at what seemed to be a Schnauzer puppy jumping around in the window. We saw that the small store sold cat and dog accessories and Philven and I went in to get a closer look. We found that the owners were also selling two litters, from the same mother, of miniature Schnauzers. There were only two puppies left from the first litter and the rest of the puppies were from the most recent litter and were much younger and more popular than their older siblings, which was not surprising as most people are naturally drawn to younger puppies because they're so damn cute. The older two puppies from the first litter were also very cute and were only three to four months older than their younger siblings.

Puckles had become very depressed after Papi died. I could tell he was very sad by the change in his disposition and in his behavior, which became noticeable in the month after Papi passed away. His companion that he had grown up with and known his entire life was suddenly gone and I'm sure he had no idea why. After seeing the miniature Schnauzer puppies, Philven and I went home to get Puckles and brought him back to the store so he could meet and interact with the Schnauzers. He seemed genuinely interested in the two older puppies and they seemed to make him happy. He appeared to be very welcoming of them and I felt this was because they reminded him of Papi. Even though the puppies were very cute and Puckles seemed thrilled to meet them, I was not sure about taking on the responsibilities of getting a new dog. We were in the initial bidding process of securing a general contractor to manage the home remodel and I thought that the amount of time that a new puppy required would add stress to an already stressful environment. After much debate with Philven about getting one of the Schnauzer puppies as a new companion for Puckles, I gave in to his request. Instead of buying one of the older puppies, I purchased them both. I couldn't separate the two brothers and could not bring myself to leave one behind. I thought they would miss one another greatly if they were separated at this point in their lives. That November, as I added the two new puppies to our family, I closed escrow on the Whitewater house.

Around this time, shit hit the fan with the logistics company. I started to get push back from the Lesbian over Philven being my assistant. Over the past eleven months that Philven had been assisting me, I had trained and educated him in the industry of retail and commercial installations and began introducing him to my clients. Since I was responsible for him, I managed him very closely. He appeared to be very eager to learn and help me in growing the business. I soon learned that first impressions are not always lasting impressions.

I discovered the Lesbian had been trying to convince Madame President to let me go for months. She was trying to leverage the fact that I had not hit my sales goals, by September 2007, to convince Madame President to fire my ass. Anyone who has been in sales understands that it usually takes two years to develop and establish a profitable client base from scratch and one only begins to see substantial business generated after this investment in time and after much effort. The general rule when one is attempting to build a sales business is that if you sell at least five hundred thousand your first year and at least a million in your second year, you're doing very well. In my first full calendar year, I didn't have a sales goal assigned to me, yet I sold over half a million dollars in services. For my second year, my sales goal was $1.2 million and by the end of that year I hit $1.4 million. With these results, it was hard to see what the fuck more the lesbo wanted from me. What was apparent was that the Lesbian was very insecure. She was threatened by anyone who got the attention and praise of Madame President and assumed that any person who caught her interest was a potential threat to her own position. This type of individual can be very detrimental to an organization. They'll risk a company's success to ensure that management perceives that they can't survive without them. Up to now, she had not been successful in driving a wedge between me and Madame President, so she tried to use Philven to create that wedge. However, Philven was not on the company payroll and I was not letting the Lesbian bully him or me, but she began her attack on him nonetheless. The more intense she attacked, the harder I defended Philven. In retrospect, Philven probably did not deserve to be defended, although it was not the Lesbian's call to bully him—and so I did what I would do for anyone…I pushed the bully back.

One evening, while Philven and I were still living in Chicago, Madame

President had the Lesbian cut our access to the company server. After I awoke the next morning, I signed on to the server to access my email, but I was unable to login and neither was Philven. I learned later that day that Madame President had been drinking the night before on a business trip with the Lesbian and, at some point during their evening, Madame President sent me an email with a new login password explaining that she locked us both out of the server. She wrote that she no longer wanted Philven to have a company email address, which he had been using. She must have known that I had given access to Philven to see my company email account, otherwise she wouldn't have changed my password too. In her drunken stupor, she failed to realize that, by changing my password before notifying me that she was going to do so, it would lock me out of the system and I wouldn't be able to read her email where she explained her intentions. After many failed attempts to log into the system, I called Madame President to find out what the fuck was going on. She didn't answer her phone. I then called the Lesbian who did answer. The Lesbian told me that while Madame President loved me, she didn't like Philven. She also stated that Madame President didn't feel that she owed me an explanation as to the reason and I shouldn't ask. The Lesbian then read me the email that Madame President had sent the previous evening. Since I was an officer of the company, I felt that if she had proof or speculation that Philven was doing something inappropriate, within the company parameters, she should inform me.

I was thrown for a loop by Madame President's behavior and abrupt decision to lock us out of the server. It made me question her intentions and clouded my ability to see the actual issue that she had with Philven. My work arrangement with him was separate from our personal relationship so I thought the circumstances surrounding her sudden move to eliminate him from being my assistant to be contradictory, as she had welcomed him in the beginning. A few hours later, our server access was reinstated. I never received an explanation as to why we were locked out. Several years passed before I came to know that Madame President had the Lesbian monitor his internet whereabouts when he was supposed to be working and didn't like what she found. Philven was doing God only knows what on his computer when he was supposed to be working. I now believe he was searching for sexual hookups. Regardless of what they may have discovered, I found their own behavior to be screwed up. They could have confronted me and clued me in on the information they had in their possession. However, Madame President and the Lesbian didn't want me to know that they had been monitoring our computers during – and more importantly – after work hours.

We should never have allowed the situation to get to this point. The relationship between me and Madame President became strained due to Philven remaining my assistant and from the snooping by the Lesbian.

Madame President was also unwilling to come clean with their findings, which created an uncomfortable working environment for all. The Lesbian would use this opportunity and take advantage of the circumstances to drive that wedge deeper between Madame President and me. It was unprofessional and it bordered on children's play.

I see London,
I see France,
I see Philven's underpants getting bunched up in a knot from a Lesbian that was giving him a wedgie.

One Saturday evening, during the week of Thanksgiving in 2007, Philven and I went to The Parker, a local upscale hotel in Palm Springs, to celebrate the closing of escrow on the Whitewater home with our real estate broker. As we were having cocktails, I received several unpleasant emails from work. I had been drinking for several hours, so I emailed my project manager who worked from his home office in Tucson, Arizona. I drunkenly inquired if he wanted to come work for me at a company that I referred to as "ILD." The logistics company name was a three-letter acronym that represented the short name for the company, so I thought it fitting that I too have three letters to represent my fictitious company's short name. I made it all up on the fly, in my intoxicated state. I thought the email was funny and it gave me the opportunity to blow off some steam in response to the curt emails from the logistics company. In my mind, ILD stood for "I Lost Darrel." Since my relationship with Madame President was becoming increasingly confrontational, combined with the bullshit antics that the Lesbian was pulling on a regular basis, my patience had worn thin. I intended the email to my project manager to be personal and a joke between us that we could have a chuckle about. Since I just purchased the Whitewater home and was looking to begin the remodeling in a few weeks, I knew the best I could do about the mounting hostile situation was to make light of the attacks and keep a low profile. Blowing off some steam seemed like an innocent thing to do at the time, especially after consuming several cocktails. My project manager did not understand the nature of the email, but on Monday morning I told him that I had been drinking and explained the email away. A few days later, since I was having issues with Madame President being less than happy with my performance, by which I mean Philven, I inquired if she would be interested in selling me the portion of the business that I had so far developed. Once the deal was completed, we would then go our separate ways. She replied that she would be interested in hearing my offer.

In December of 2007, two weeks before Christmas, I hired a general contractor to begin demolition on the house. By the time of Jesus's birthday, on the twenty fifth of December, the house was totally gutted and looked as if a bomb had hit it. The carport had been demolished and the entire frontage had been removed. I was expanding the main portion of the house by four feet and planned to maximize the additional square footage by installing sliding glass doors in the new front of the house. The design intent was to have the option to open the kitchen, dining area, and the living room to the pool, when entertaining guests. When the house was built, it was positioned on the back of the lot, so the pool was situated in the front of the house. The unusual arrangement of the pool was one of the main reasons I had been so attracted to the property.

One day, Philven decided to come clean and confessed that he had lied about having a twin. He told me that he had done some inappropriate things in his past and his therapist in San Francisco, who he was seeing when he lived there, had told him it might be best to project that "not so appropriate" behavior onto a twin brother and then kill that twin off. This, he explained, resulted in his telling of the fabricated car accident story that ended with the death of his gay twin. What the fuck? I was living with a drama queen who thought she was the lead star in a European melodrama. Philven instantly resurrected the dead when he told me that outlandish story. I saw my relationship with Alex flash before my eyes. I had another fabricator of lavish stories on my hands. Alex as well as Philven created these fucked up stories whenever it suited them. From that point forward, I never really knew what to believe when it came to Philven and his stories and I quickly pivoted to not believing anything that came out of his mouth.

The temporary rental property, a two bedroom and three-bath bi-level condo that we lived in for six months as the new home was being readied, was several miles away from the Whitewater home. Most of the people living in the complex were single gay men or gay couples. Our place was next door to a gay couple, who seemed like nice guys and who had relocated from Los Angeles. They were closer to Philven's age than mine. A few months after we arrived, they invited us to a Christmas party at their place. We went and, when we arrived, I immediately felt a little uncomfortable. All the guests were gay men and, even though I was a homo, I was still uncomfortable walking into a room full of gay men, especially when they're mostly west coast fags. I had several drinks to relax. As I became less inhibited with the gayness of it all, I began to mingle. Right after I started being friendly, I thought it strange that Philven wanted to leave. It was even stranger as we lived right next door. What was the rush to go home? We left and when we arrived back at our place, thirty seconds later, Philven poured us both a drink. I had one or two more cocktails and I ended up falling asleep on the sofa where I was sitting. When I awoke the next morning, I was still dressed in the same clothes that I was wearing the night before. I had passed out on the sofa after drinking the cocktails that Philven made once we returned home.

As I recall the events of that night, I wonder if that was one of the times when Philven may have drugged me and gone out looking for dick. This would explain why he wanted to leave so quickly after arriving at our neighbor's event. This would be typical of him and he may have headed right back to the neighbor's Christmas party to hookup. How could this happen? Surely someone would tell me that Philven returned to the party. I don't believe this would necessarily be true. Being "discreet" is probably one of the most interesting and most fucked up factors in gay culture. There are many gays who cheat right under the nose of their boyfriends and nobody ever clues in the boyfriend that he is being cheated on. I don't understand this type of behavior and can only remotely give credence to this conduct, but for one factor. Since the gay culture emerged from centuries of having to lie to keep their sexual encounters a secret, especially within mixed companies or crowds, the gays have come to accept this behavior as being acceptable from those within our community. Being discreet was the only way to keep oneself from being outed and I feel it's difficult to eradicate this behavioral pattern—in a community where that conduct has been so entrenched for centuries. To this day, many fags accept and practice "discretion" or a "don't ask and don't tell" policy. This behavior can also take place when a so-called straight guy, who's married to a woman, is fucking around with another man. Some poofs might be aware of the situation and they would stand in the room with the wife and never clue her in to the fact that her husband sucks dick. In my eyes, the gay culture has failed to fully emancipate itself from this hideous conduct. I'm no saint and I've made numerous inappropriate judgments in my life and accept that I might make more, but I've learned a lot from my mistakes and, hopefully, as I continue to spiritually evolve, I will make fewer misjudgments. One thing I learned in Palm Springs is that even though I was gay, and might be referred to as a homo, a pansy, poof, faggot, butt buddy, cocksucker or a dick licker, I was not like most of the gay rats I encountered in that desert. Even though I was one of them, I was not like them.

As children, we're taught that we should always listen to our mothers. My mother always told me, my father, and my brothers that the less people know about you, the better off you'll be. When I was a young boy, growing up, I never agreed with my mother on this point. I had nothing to hide, so why did it matter what people knew about me. How could people hurt me with the truth? What I didn't realize is that people are sometimes jealous of others and of their successes. I was proud of what I was able to achieve and I was always willing to share most aspects about myself with most people. What did it matter if people at work knew that I went out clubbing the night before coming into the office? I later realized that people would use this type of information to start rumors about me. Since I told them that I was out partying all night, they embellished the story and added that I was probably doing drugs and, more than likely, I did more drugs to make it to work. Even though they might have been correct on occasion, if I hadn't revealed that I had been out partying the night before, they would not have had the information to put one and two together. People can and, in many cases, they will use a situation and the details surrounding that situation against you—and usually for their own benefit. I realize that I can't stop people from talking shit about me, but if I had listened to my mother, I could've stopped myself from giving them ammunition to fuel the fire. I would finally learn later in life that my mother was right all along. The less people knew about me, the better off I was. When I told Philven the story about Alex drugging me in a hotel room in Miami, it would give him the idea to do the same thing to me so that he could slip out of the house and look for dick in the darkness of night. Always listen to your mother, because mother always knows best.

In January of the New Year, Philven and I hooked up with a random guy with whom we connected on Manhunt.com. He was a local who partied and played. We invited him to the rental condo to smoke Tina and to have a three-way. When he arrived, he was a mess. His behavior made it appear as if he had injected Tina prior to coming over, which renders a much more intense high than snorting or smoking the drug. This is how I explained his messy and incoherent behavior. He seemed to be having some personal problems, which added to his disjointed disposition. He told us a story about an escort who was staying at his place. As he related the story, Philven interjected and asked this relative stranger, who we had just met that evening for the first time – at least it was the first time for me – if he would let him stay at his house. This was an odd question to ask and I wondered why Philven would pose it. Perhaps he asked it, because he too had been an escort. The guy firmly replied that no, he would not let Philven stay at his house, and his response totally pissed Philven off.

In many situations with people that party and play, the drugs usually get the best of the situation and very little sexual interaction ends up taking place. Manhunt guy seemed to be dealing with some emotional issues and as I was carrying my own emotional baggage, we ended up chatting with one another rather than having sex. At some point in our drug-induced conversation, Manhunt guy mentioned that he had met Philven before. I found his comment very interesting, and disturbing, and I wanted to know more. Philven jumped into the conversation and emphatically stated to Manhunt guy that no, they had not met before. He then inquired when he thought they had met. Mr. Manhunt replied that he encountered Philven at a gay resort called CCBC, which is more like a sex club than a resort. Philven knew that I had been suspecting him of cheating for some time and was watching him closely. He proceeded to ask when he thought they might have seen each other at the gay resort. The conversation then took an interesting and intriguing turn. Mr. Manhunt replied with the exact month when Philven and I came to Palm Springs to look for a house. It was the trip where I thought Philven had drugged me and slipped out of our hotel room. Seven months had passed since then and here was a random guy that we meet on a sex site—who just so happened to guess the exact month when we had been in Palm Springs. The guy couldn't have been lying – he had no reason to – and he wasn't making a joke. This wasn't a random coincidence of any kind. Something or someone other than Manhunt guy was trying to clue me into Philven's late night activities. Philven had likely drugged me the night he slipped out of our hotel room looking for dick and now that dick had come forth with the truth that corroborate my suspicions. I now had confirmation that I had gotten myself involved with another asshole that couldn't contain his pecker. This shit was too wild for daytime television and was certainly something that you just couldn't make up. At that moment, I realized I was not involved with a European melodrama soap opera queen as I had thought. I now knew for a fact that I had gotten myself involved with a devil or what seemed to be possibly Satan himself.

Many of my issues at work and at home were fueled by Philven. I should have cut him from the logistics business before it got to the point of no return, a truth I now know to be the case. I believe God was trying to give me insight into the behavior from the Devil, aka Philven, but I ignored the warning signs. Unfortunately, I was blinded by the lustful nature of our relationship. In that desert valley where the Tina users were many and where his huge-cock was the one-eyed serpent, I found myself tempted by it and succumbed to lust. What I didn't realize is that God had been intricately, delicately, and forcefully positioning me for the battle that was yet to come, one that would cost me more than I could have ever imagined. On many occasions while living in that desert, I contemplated if I was going to make it out of that desolate place alive. At one point, in the midst of my battle, I would attempt to take my own life hoping to end the madness. But God had another plan and it didn't involve my being buried in that ground. I needed to overcome the hateful existence that I created for myself and that I allowed others to create around me. In that cracked-out, lifeless place where many Tina users and sex addicts prey, I finally came face-to-face with my fears. Eventually, I needed to embrace those fears before I could be released from my prison and, even though I bet it all in that desert valley and ended up losing most of my possessions, I gained more than I could've ever imagined. What the Devil and his drug-fueled Tina followers thought to use to destroy me – the lies, the deceit, the disrespect, the lack of morals, and other foul conduct – God would use to finally put an end to my fucked-up behavior and delivered me from the hellish existence where I had immersed myself.

Philven heard my proposal to Madame President about buying the portion of the business – at a fair price –that I developed. I had told him that we might possibly start our own company if things with Madame President couldn't be resolved amicably. This comment was a big mistake on my part. Philven became relentless in his efforts to get me to break away and start a new company with us as co-owners. I knew that there was no way I was going to be able to remodel the Whitewater home, to the tune of two-hundred thousand plus dollars, and simultaneously start a new business. If I were to go off and start a new company on my own, it would need to happen later and most definitely after the remodel of the house was completed, and the home had been refinanced. The remodel was scheduled to be completed in early March and I was not reneging on my suggestion to open our own business, I was being a realist. I knew it had to be a transition rather than an emotional and abrupt decision. Being a business owner is also much more difficult than Philven had considered, although he was soon going to find out firsthand what adult responsibilities entailed.

Before moving to the desert, Alex, Madame President's first husband and father of her three children, died suddenly from a heart attack. He was a great man and one of the main reasons I was becoming successful at the logistics company. We had partnered on numerous projects that I brought to the table. Madame President owned five percent of her ex-husband's installation company and five percent of her current husband's installation company. When bidding my clients projects, I usually requested quotes from both of these family vendors, as well as outside contractors. I was on track to build a solid and successful business relationship with Alex and his company and he seemed to appreciate the opportunities that I was able to secure for us both. He was always interested in listening to what I had to say and, more importantly, he was supportive of my efforts to secure business for Madame President's company and his own. I believe we were the perfect example of how the right people, from entirely different worlds, can come together to build a successful and lucrative partnership while enjoying working together.

When my position was eliminated at Equity, I had begun to see the therapist to help me deal with my anxieties, my feelings of being betrayed by Gene, and the difficulties I knew lay ahead. I also needed to overcome my fears about taking a new job in an unknown industry. At the same time, I went to a psychic to get a reading from her on my new career path. She informed me that the logistics company would have two entities and one of those entities would be welcoming of my efforts and the other entity would be less so. She explained that the main reason behind the split in support within the structure was going to be a direct result from my being a homo. Alex had no issues with my lifestyle, but Madame President's current husband and his company's executives were less than accepting of my interest in dick. After Alex died so abruptly, this became a problematic situation that I wouldn't be able to overcome. After his death, I was instructed by Madame President to transition all the current business that I was conducting with Alex's company to her current husband's company. This was the beginning of the end. The psychic was correct. The homo's projects were not welcome at the company of Madame President's current husband, the asshole.

Early in that same January of 2008, I was compiling the specifics of my financial offer to Madame President to entice her to sell me a portion of the business. That month, Philven sent me an email from his logistics company email address to my work email account indicating a website for me to check out. He noted ILD in the subject line. When I saw the email, I immediately deleted it and told him not to reference ILD on the logistics company server. I thought that Philven deliberately referenced ILD in the subject line to get shit started between the logistics company and me. I saw this as a passive-aggressive attempt on his part to get me fired so I would be forced to start a company where he and I were the owners, as he had been pressuring me to do.

A few weeks later, on a Saturday morning, Madame President heard a rumor that I was going to start my own business and therefore steal clients away from her company. Upon hearing it, Madame President called me in Palm Springs and fired my ass. Earlier that same morning, I had tried to log into the logistics server to check my emails and I had not been able to log into my account. I immediately thought I had been locked out again by the Lesbian. I had Philven check his work email account and he could log in and access his emails. I naturally just assumed that the company was having some type of IT issues on their end. I decided I was being paranoid about the situation, so Philven and I left the house to run errands. While we were out, Madame President called me and delivered the news that she heard a rumor that I was going to start my own business and asked me if this was the case. I answered that yes, it was something that I was considering. Otherwise, why would I've inquired if she was interested in entertaining an offer from me to buy the portion of the business that I developed, if I was not planning to start my own company? When we returned to the house, Philven checked his email and he was still able to access his work account. What the fuck? One of the reasons that I was fired from my position was because Philven was my assistant, which remained a bone of contention. When I got fired from the company, Madame President and the Lesbian took down my sever access, but they left Philven with access to the server—and he wasn't even a company employee.

I wanted to kick Philven in the teeth for sending me the email with ILD in the subject line. I felt like he had done it on purpose to get me fired. Since Philven was still able to log into the server, I had him check my work email account from his computer. He could see that Madame President appeared to have given her husband access to my work emails. Her husband, or someone else, had apparently looked through my emails and sent Madame President an email from my account that stated that I was attempting to fuck her over and steal her business. I'm not sure how he determined that I was trying to screw her, unless he found the deleted email referencing ILD that Philven had sent me, although I had deleted that specific email.

Several weeks prior to my getting fired, Madame President was pressuring me to consider releasing my project manager from his position. We worked very closely together before he joined the logistics company and he was doing a fantastic job. I had recruited him from Alex's company, after Alex died. I had planned on taking him with me if and when I made my offer to Madame President and if and when she accepted said offer. In the same email that the husband wrote to Madame President, the one where he indicated that I was out to steal clients from her company, he made a reference in the email to "fuck him and fuck him too." While I initially thought the reference was to Philven and me, I came to believe the asshole was referencing to fuck my project manager and fuck me. I immediately called my project manager in Tucson who informed me that his email account had also been taken down. Madame President and the Lesbian were so concerned about locking us out from the server to protect their company that they overlooked the wolf that was lurking at their backdoor. The wolf had deliberately manipulated them both to get what he wanted and he of all people still had access to their server. Fuck me was exactly what I was thinking and, for the first time ever, the asshole and I were in agreement.

The person who heard and relayed the rumor to Madame President was a vendor of an existing client who I solicited and whose business I brought to the logistics company. Of course, he did not know the entire story about what was taking place between Madame President and me before he decided to repeat the rumor. I was putting a financial offer together, to present to Madame President, when he repeated an inaccurate version of what he thought to be the truth. The rumor had me breaking off from Madame's President's company, which was accurate, but it inaccurately relayed that I was ***taking*** the client base that I developed, rather than indicating the fact that I was looking to ***purchase*** it. One word changed the entire premise of the story from a positive to a negative.

In this case, justice, which is complex and can be delivered in many forms, would prevail. Several years after I was fired, the individual that repeated the rumor that ended up getting me dismissed received an employment offer from Madame President's current husband to join his company. He had become acquainted with Madame President and her husband through me after I closed on a large sale for the logistics company where he was employed and where he was my contact. This individual, and a colleague that he came to know after he started working at the husband's company, eventually started their own business and took clients with them when they left the husband's company—a perfect example of divine justice prevailing. The person that screwed me over by repeating hearsay that I was trying to steal business, which was not the case, fucked Madame President and her husband in the end. Karma is indeed a bitch. Madame President's husband was simply an arrogant asshole that got fucked at his own game. His employee, who they chose to believe, did to him exactly what he falsely accused me of doing. I had to wait several years to see Karma catch up with both of them, but I didn't have to do a thing to see justice come to pass.

After Madame President fired me, I needed to make several crucial decisions quickly. Was I going to start my own business or was I going to look for a job with a new employer? Should I throw all caution to the wind and continue remodeling the house even though I had no immediate means of income? Should I halt the construction and board up the house until I was in a better financial position? I narrowed my decisions down to two options. If I opted to open my own company, I would stick to my original plan to remodel the property. If I decided to secure employment with a new employer, I would postpone the remodel and board up the house until I was earning a salary. These options gave me the answer on how to proceed. I had moved to Palm Springs with a dream to buy and remodel a mid-century modern home and to abandon that idea after the house had already been gutted would have been crushing. If I stopped the remodel, I would have felt like a complete failure, so – against all odds and with no savings or current employment – I decided to stick to the original plan and move forward with the remodel. Palm Springs was not a place that could offer me an opportunity to obtain work in my current field of expertise. Since I was unemployed and needed to earn as much money, as quickly as possible, I reluctantly agreed to establish a business agreement with the Devil.

The additional pressure that I felt from being abruptly fired was overwhelming and almost more than I could bear. I wanted to kick Philven to the curb for what I felt he had deliberately set in motion for personal gain. What the Devil didn't realize was the amount of effort that would be required on his part for us to start our own business. I also never thought that by agreeing to become business partners I would be putting myself in financial harm's way. By the end, I would find myself betting everything that I owned on the business. I named it ILD International, which was an acronym for I Lost Darrel, for lost I had become. However, my days of wondering aimlessly through life were about to change. I had been lost and soon I would be found.

I was somewhat of a novice when dealing with computer or internet issues, but shortly after getting fired, I learned much about the technical aspects of running a business. My technology expertise began after I inadvertently connected my personal Apple email account to the logistics company server. After being let go, and before I could establish a network for ILD, I used my personal email account for my newly developed business. In doing so, I failed to disconnect the logistics company security router from my internet provider and the logistics company captured numerous personal emails before I disconnected the account from their server. Those emails contained several conversations with guys from Manhunt where I discussed having party and play three-ways. Madame President and the Lesbian were now in possession of emails that proved my illicit drug use and my private sexual encounters. This was not information that I wanted anyone to know. I had fucked myself in a big way. The worst part is that I was not immediately aware that I had inadvertently connected my personal email account to the logistics server and it took me a month to become aware of what I had done and correct the situation.

It wasn't a coincidence that I named my new company ILD. Something was pulling at me to use these three letters for the company name. I knew future and former clients would inquire what the letters represented. I struggled to come up with the words that would best represent the new company and the services that it would offer. One morning, after days of struggling to compile a list of services that represented ILD, I awoke and three words formed in my mind. Installation, which would be the main focus of our business, logistics, which would be our secondary focus, and design, which was a service that we would offer although we would promote it the least. We intended to concentrate our efforts on the installation piece of the business, as its core function. The random letters that I had pulled out of thin air several months earlier for a made-up company, while intoxicated, ended up being the exact name of our new business. The letters seemed to be the three in the alphabet that best represented the short name of our company. In a situation where I had very little choice other than to make a pact with the Devil, I still found inspiration in the naming of our new business.

I contacted Anthony, a lawyer in Chicago who I knew when I worked at Bigsby and who had prepared my prenuptial agreement with Alex. Anthony had an identical twin brother named John, who was also an attorney. They had established their law practice together and their firm had also represented my interests on a several escrow closings when I lived in Chicago. They now established our new limited liability company for the Devil and me in California. We had decided to add the word International after ILD to give the perception that the company had a larger presence than it did when it was established. Since Philven had a fantastic English accent it seemed fitting to imbue the company with what I optimistically hoped to eventually have an international presence.

Philven had presented himself with the Master's degree in Finance so I agreed that he could be Chief Operation Officer. Since the success of the business was contingent on me leveraging my former client relationships and developing new business, we mutually agreed that I would be the company's Chief Executive Officer. Now that Tweedledum and Tweedledee had grand titles, we also agreed that Tweedledee, Philven, would handle all the operational functions needed to run the company, including financials, legal, taxes and all IT-related operations. Tweedledum would handle sales, client relations and project and vendor management. It felt like two inexperienced children were thrown into a grown-up world overnight, and rather than

Tweedledum and Tweedledee, a better comparison would be that we were more like the lead characters in the movie Dumb and Dumber.

When we established the company's email account, the login information and password were sent to my personal Apple email account, which was the beginning of a huge problem. I still had the logistics security router connected to my internet service and the logistics company captured the login information to our network account, as well as our ILD email accounts. Several days after establishing the network, I figured out the connection issue and I immediately disconnected the logistics equipment from ILD's internet provider. Tweedledum and Tweedledee never figured out that we may have inadvertently allowed those initial emails to be captured by the logistics company server—not even after I realized that the email containing our network login and password information had been deleted from my Apple account. I told Philven and the IT person – who helped us establish ILD's account – that the email containing the login credentials, which was sent to my personal email, had mysteriously disappeared from my computer. They laughed and told me I probably deleted it by mistake. I knew I had not deleted the email, but I had so much on my plate at that moment that the last thing I needed was to freak out over a missing or deleted email.

Two weeks after I was fired, ILD International was born. The new company had a name, a logo, a web site, and official company email accounts for its two employees. As I was entirely engrossed in securing business for ILD, I was not involved in setting up the company. Instead, Philven worked with the attorneys in Chicago to legally establish it. When they filed the papers for the limited liability company, Philven took it upon himself to divide the company equally between us. Since I was preoccupied with nurturing the budding business, I was unaware that Philven and the attorneys split the company fifty-fifty. Many months later, when I tried to partner with Philven on managing the business, I realized he wasn't going to agree on much with me and it really didn't matter if he was a fifty percent owner, or if he just owned forty percent…he wasn't going to be a team player on any level.

In the first month of being in business, we were fortunate to receive several bid requests from former clients for upcoming projects. Over the next few months, we began to obtain business from many of the clients that we solicited. I contacted Emily, my former assistant in New York, as I knew she would continue to be a good friend and support my efforts now that I was self-employed. When I worked with the logistics company, she was instrumental in sending me projects to bid on for most of her clients. I now began to campaign to get her employer to allow ILD to bid on their client projects, as I had done in the past.

Around this time, Philven received an email from a client in response to a project quote that he had requested from us. In the email, he indicated that Madame President had contacted him about the same quote that we sent. In that communication, Madame President inquired if he wanted her logistics company to handle the project that ILD quoted. This was proof that she and her company had access to our email and were reading our client communications. The logistics company had definitely obtained our network credentials. Philven and our IT person had dismissed me when I told them that the email with that information had gone missing, and assumed I must have deleted the email, but I knew that I had not. Madame President and the Lesbian had hijacked our email correspondence. The irony was rich. Madame President claimed that I was conspiring to steal her clients and business away from her, which is why she said she fired me, but she was doing exactly what she had accused me of doing.

Was I being stupid by inadvertently connecting the logistics security router to my personal Apple email account? Was I an even bigger idiot by neglecting to disconnect my personal email account from their server immediately, after I had inadvertently done so? Perhaps not. Madame President and her husband scheduled a meeting in New York, with Emily and her boss, to solicit the continuation of the business relationship that I had originally developed between the two companies. Emily's boss, who was the company president, was hesitant to allow Emily to just transfer her clients' projects from the logistics company to ILD. Not surprisingly, he saw ILD as a new company that needed more time to get established before he would entertain the idea of transferring their business to us. However, on the day of the meeting, Madame President showed up and imperiously informed Emily that her logistics company had decided not to continue doing business with her employer. She then pivoted on her heels and abruptly left the New York showroom as quickly as she arrived. By firing Emily and her company as a client, she walked away from a substantial amount of business. Her reason for doing so was because she knew, from reading my ILD emails, that even though Emily and her boss were not willing to give us their business at present, it was something they would consider after ILD got more established. Madame President's ego had been bruised, by reading the communications between me and Emily, and her arrogance got the best of her and the situation. Her walking out of the meeting allowed Emily to convince her boss to let ILD replace the logistics company as their installation vendor. Ironically, this chain of events was undoubtedly the reason ILD became a success practically overnight. Madame President had improperly and nefariously accessed our email, and she had not liked what she read between me and Emily, but we now had a major international client with immediate business needs in many states in the U.S. Overnight, ILD went from having very few business opportunities to enjoying a plethora of new business. From this situation, I came to believe that God used my stupidity and proved once again that if God be for us, who can be against us? Nobody, not even the she wolf in sheep's clothing that read proprietary emails that pissed her off and caused her to do something that she would've never done—had she not read emails that she had no authority to read. My stupidity, combined with Madame President's determination to fuck me over because she wrongly thought I was trying to fuck her over, ended up being my saving grace.

In spite of this, I was upset with how things had come to pass. How did the situation deteriorate so quickly? I would have preferred if Madame President called me out on my shit and then flew to Palm Springs, or had me fly to meet her, for a face-to-face discussion, before abruptly telling me that she didn't believe me, that our arrangement was no longer working for her, and then letting me go. Her concerns about me trying to start my own business had merit, but I did ask her if she would be interested in me making her an offer, for the business that I developed, and she had expressed her interest in hearing my proposal. But before I could get my shit together to approach her with a dollar figure, the situation got out of control quickly and definitively—and she reacted. Even now, I appreciate her concerns, but I still have an issue with the harsh way she handled the circumstances.

My bitter parting with Madame President mirrored my experience with Equity. I had moved back to Chicago, and bought a home in a city that I had no interest in living in – with the most extreme winters – because of the position and financial package I was offered by Gene. I understand that business conditions change and agreements must be altered to maintain profitability and I don't fault Gene for eliminating my position at Equity after I executed the program to a level of success that he needed to ensure further funding. But I do hold Gene responsible for the way that he handled the situation. The history that we had together, and the fact that he recruited me, should've pre-empted his abrupt delivery that he was eliminating my position. I would have preferred if he called me into his office, told me he needed to make a change, and thanked me for my efforts and my part in making the program a success. He could have acknowledged that I had moved from New York to Chicago for the job and offered me six months to find a new one and be eligible to receive my annual bonus. As long as I maintained my responsibilities, I could stay the entire six months or leave at any time, if I found a new job. Instead, he chose self-preservation. Offering his compassion, based on our history, combined with the generous severance package I received, would have been the right thing to do.

Just like Gene, the situation with Madame President could've been handled better. Madame President could've still cut my network access to protect her interests, but instead of immediately firing me, she could've taken the time to meet me in person for a heart-to-heart discussion about what took place and where we went from there. I take responsibility for adding undue stress onto Madame President by insisting that Philven work with me, but if she had taken the time to have an honest conversation with me, the outcome might have been different. Although, with the Lesbian trying to get me fired for a year – as confirmed by the company controller – the end result might have been the same. If we could have come to a mutual agreement that would've satisfied us both, it would have prevented the collision that would come to pass and which would cost us both more money than we could have imagined.

Much like Alice in Wonderland, I too had fallen down a rabbit hole. After Madame President fired me, by the end of my three and a half years of hard labor in the desert valley, I found myself peering through a looking glass and catching a glimpse of a stranger's reflection. Even though I didn't recognize the appearance of the person that I saw, I eventually came to realize that I was the man whose reflection I was seeing in the mirror. Just like Alice, I had no idea who I was and I would need to have more encounters with numerous evil queens before I could claw and eventually climb my way out of the low-lying place where I had fallen.

17 | EYE OF THE TRUTH

Once upon a time, there was a slight little boy with piercing blue eyes and very long eyelashes. He was born in a land where wishes are free and dreams come true. The boy was different than most other boys that he knew, although he had no idea why he felt so different. He had two brothers, one older and one younger, but he was never able to emotionally connect with them and so he became a loner. Just like David from the movie ***Artificial Intelligence***, this little boy also had a best friend named Teddy, who was the family dog. Teddy was his companion from the time he was a little boy until he grew to be a teenager.

As he transitioned into his teenage years, the boy became very shy and introverted. This shyness caused him to become nervous when speaking with others and he stuttered on occasion. He was not very athletic and during gym class at school he was always the last one to be chosen when the other kids picked their teammates to play games. Being the last kid to be selected, waiting anxiously for someone to call his name, exaggerated his feelings of being different and he became even more introverted. Some of the boys at school called him names. On occasion, they shouted derogatory words at him, calling him a pansy, and at other times they referred to him as being a little girl. They nicknamed him Darlene. Being a pretty blue-eyed teenage boy with long eyelashes didn't help and he began cutting his lashes to avoid drawing attention to his eyes. He picked up the habit of not looking at people in the face to keep them from commenting that he was so pretty—the last thing this young boy wanted.

As the teenage boy grew to be a young adult, he began to understand why he was different than most of the other boys. He realized he wanted what most little girls want as they grow up and become young women. Like most girls his age, he too wanted a Prince Charming of his own. He wanted his Prince to love him, protect him, and marry him just like the other little girls dreamt. He wanted to create his own family that loved him as much as he loved them. He and his new family would live happily ever after in a house and in a land that accepted people like him. This boy is now decades older and I'm now a middle aged gay man.

In my ideal storybook ending, my Prince Charming would ask for my hand in marriage and proclaim me as his husband to everyone and to God. I would be his equal partner in life and we would build a home and raise our children. Just like any little girl or boy hoping to find their Prince Charming, I too long to achieve my fairytale life and live happily ever after with a man who is a loving, kind person and, most of all, a nurturing father – the most important part of my fairytale – but my tale to find my Prince Charming was about to become a nightmare and not the fairytale of which I dreamt.

While living in the rental apartment, I worked diligently every day to protect my dream. During that time, I became very concerned and even more paranoid about the proprietary ILD information stored on my Apple computer. I was constantly changing my computer login password to keep anyone from accessing the information. I quietly thought to myself that by changing my password I was sending discreet and personal messages high into the clouds. I was not sure who was the recipient of my messages, but I felt as if someone would hear my SOS distress calls. The new passwords that I came up with were always associated with the words that referenced a place of belonging...*on the road again*, *coming home*, *bring me home*, *take me home*, and so on. I was curiously sending messages about finding a place of belonging when I had just recently arrived in the desert and bought a new house. Where did I think I was going or where did I think I needed to be? Could I've been subconsciously sending messages into the clouds for God to know that I was lost and needed help? Just like ET in the movie, I believe, without realizing it at the time, I too was trying to phone home.

Shortly after being fired, I went to the Whitewater home and found my last paycheck from the logistics company in a pile of construction debris. They had mailed a paper check for my final earnings rather than deposit the funds into my checking account, as they had always done in the past. The envelope containing the check had been delivered to the Whitewater address and thrown over the fence, where I happened to randomly come across it when cleaning the yard. I saw the envelope in the pile of debris and felt like I had been thrown out with the previous day's trash. I was owed three weeks' vacation pay and that amount was not in the check. The logistics company didn't offer me the opportunity to extend my medical coverage and, by the end of that month, I was going to be medically uninsured for the first time in my adult life. I had worked the last twenty years to ensure I had medical coverage to pay for my HIV medications, doctor visits, and labs, but now, due to Madame President's abrupt decision to fire me, I wasn't going to have medical coverage or any way to refill the medications that cost six thousand dollars a month. Rome was burning all around me and my Armageddon was fast approaching, but God had a plan. Without me ever realizing it, He suited me up with all the armor that I needed to fight and overcome Goliath and the numerous other giants that I would soon face.

It was my responsibility to buy new sinks for the three bathrooms and kitchen for the contractor to install. I found a retailer in Palm Springs that sold amazing tile and spectacular modern sinks for the home. The store owner told me that American Express was reducing credit lines to some of their existing customers. Some of these clients tried to purchase products from his store, but their purchases were declined. When they contacted American Express, they were informed that their credit line had been significantly reduced, resulting in the declined sale. American Express' actions were a direct result of the company reacting to the forthcoming financial crisis that was yet to peak in the latter months of 2008. The store owner's story caused me concern, as I had several credit cards that were issued by American Express and was planning to leverage my open credit on these cards for the remodel. I had a Gold American Express that had no limit. I also had three other cards issued by American Express…an Optima Platinum card with a thirty five thousand dollar credit line, a Starwood Preferred Guest card with a twenty two thousand dollar credit line, and a Bank of America card. I had other major credit cards…a Chase Visa with a thirty five thousand dollar credit line and a Diners Club International card, my favorite, with a credit line of over twenty thousand dollars. With all the available credit I had, I planned to leverage it in the coming year to weather my financial storm. I'm certainly not the sharpest tack in the box and I will never debate that with anyone, but I believe God has equipped me with good intuition, common sense, and a talent for doing the right thing in business. I had no malice in my heart when I was planning to leverage my credit cards to get me through the rough patch. I needed a temporary solution to overcome a difficult situation and I see using one's credit to get them through a financial pinch as the reason why a person has credit in the first place.

The financial burden of maintaining the new mortgage and the rent on the temporary residence, for six months, was something for which I planned, but the unexpected financial pressures of starting a new business, on top of the remodel, was something new—and it quickly became overwhelming. My savings account was emptying fast and soon I would be two hundred thousand dollars in debt. I carried the majority of the expenses for the remodel on credit, while awaiting the construction to be completed. Once the remodel was finished, I planned to refinance the home so I could roll the incurred debt into the new mortgage. However, the global financial crisis of 2007 and 2008 had another agenda.

I've done many fucked up things and I'm not proud of that behavior, but my actions usually hurt me and not others. In my lowest point, when my boyfriend and business partner was lying to me, I tried to be honorable and maintain some sense of integrity in how I conducted myself. The pressures I was experiencing caused me a tremendous amount of emotional duress. At times, I felt I was going to be crushed under all the pressure. One day, I awoke and wondered if my current financial situation was indicative of how people lost everything that they worked their entire life to achieve. I was afraid and terrified that I was going to end up bankrupt and, worse yet, homeless. A cracked-out Humpty Dumpty sat on a wall trying anxiously and diligently to keep the repo man from taking his property out from under him—and he was fearful that he was going to fall to his demise if the repo man was successful.

The U.S., the rest of the world, and I would soon be facing a financial meltdown with few equals in history. The unfolding crisis would develop into the perfect storm that would drown my American dream, as well as the dreams of many others, and transform them into nightmares. For many of us who owned property, caught in the midst of the disaster and not in a financial position to weather the storm, it proved to be tragic. We ended up becoming a casualty of the greed on Wall Street. Many people not only lost their future financial stability in the midst of the crisis, but they also lost their jobs and, in many cases, they lost their homes, which tore lives apart.

I came to learn that Cher put her Hawaii and Malibu residences up for sale during the most challenging economic downturn in the real estate market since the great depression. I'm certain that Cher is financially savvy, so why would she try to sell two major properties at the bottom of the real estate market? What did she know that most people didn't? She ended up auctioning off her property in Hawaii, which was sold to the highest bidder. It seemed that Cher was cashing out. To my knowledge, Cher never sold her Malibu home, a picture of which I used as my computer screen saver while I was living in Palm Springs. It allowed me to fantasize about buying her home and having a better life than the one I was currently living, which allowed me to mentally escape from my miserable situation even if just for a brief moment each day.

From the moment I arrived in Palm Springs, I felt as if I was riding an amusement park merry-go-round that never stopped going in circles. I realized I had repeated the same mistake of getting romantically involved with a compulsive liar that was cheating on me. I also got myself involved with yet another employer who seemed more interested in what they could get out of me, rather than nurturing an honest and equally beneficial relationship for both parties. The longer I lived in Palm Springs, the faster the merry-go-round seemed to turn. Although, amidst the turmoil, ILD had picked up momentum—much needed good news in that dusty desert.

Shortly after ILD was launched, I received a call from a client in Boston, Massachusetts requesting a meeting. I bought plane tickets for Philven and me to go meet with the customer. The tickets were on Jet Blue, as they had a hub in Long Beach and they offered the cheapest flights to Boston nonstop from Southern California. I needed to watch every dollar very closely and stretch each one as much as possible. Jet Blue didn't fly out of the Palm

Springs airport, so I decided we would drive two hours to Long Beach to catch our flight. It wasn't about convenience anymore, it was about saving as much money as possible. When I booked the flights online, an offer popped up on my screen to charge the tickets on a Jet Blue American Express account. I never thought for one moment that by clicking yes and opening a new account with American Express, to defer my payment for these tickets, it would send the merry-go-round that I had been riding into hyper-speed.

By the time we landed in Boston, American Express placed all my accounts on hold. My mojo was all fucked up. I could not seem to catch a break. The merry-go-round that I had been riding longer than I care to admit suddenly came to a screeching halt and shit began to fly in every direction. I cussed American Express with every curse word I could think of. When I filled out the application to defer the payment on the airline tickets, I listed my employer as ILD International. By answering truthfully, I didn't realize I was going to be punished by a creditor with whom I had done business for decades. The information on the application triggered something at American Express and they froze all my credit card accounts. There wasn't anything in their actions that was American from where I was standing. I was out of town and I was now fucked. Is this what America had become? It seemed that American Express had adopted a *fuck-them-over* before they have the *chance to fuck-us-over* philosophy. I have nothing but sarcasm for this company and how they treated me at a time when I needed them the most. Once I learned that my accounts had been placed on hold, I called who I came to see as the Anti-Christ to inquire why they froze all my accounts. A representative informed me that they couldn't find ILD International listed as a company on some fucking list and, as a precautionary measure, they froze all my accounts. I provided the representative with the information needed to verify that ILD International was a legally established LLC with the Federal and California governments. After they received this information, they requested that I fax them my personal federal tax returns, with my annual income statements for the two previous years, before they could determine if they would release my accounts. I was out of town for a week on business and the assholes wanted tax returns that I would not be able to provide until I returned. I had been their customer, in good standing, for decades, but none of that seemed to matter. I now stood on the streets of Boston with my dick in a vice-grip without a way to pay for my traveling expenses and, rather than help me, the representative tightened the grip—and could have cared less about the situation in which American Express stranded me.

The financial sector was clearly aware of the housing market collapse many months before it trickled down to the news networks and before peasants like me became aware of what was taking place. These assholes were monitoring accounts and cutting the credit lines of long-standing customers almost a year prior to the banks failing. It was a calculated move to mitigate their upcoming risk. I can't fault American Express for looking out for its own financial well-being, but they were pushing the financial crisis further into the abyss, where it finally ended up, by reacting so aggressively to the situation. I joke when I refer to American Express as the Anti-Christ, but they seemed to show no understanding, forgiveness, or compassion for their customers as exemplified by the way they treated me. I told them I was stuck in Boston with no credit and that I needed to pay for my hotel. The representative replied that my situation wasn't their problem. They didn't care about the credit issues that they caused me by freezing my accounts. Their only concern was receiving the documents that they requested. Perhaps the Anti-Christ is not a person after all...maybe it's a corporation.

Once I returned to California, I faxed my federal tax returns and W2 forms for the past two years to American Express. These showed total income of $169,980 dollars for 2005 and $124,999 dollars for 2006. Once they received the documents, they released my accounts, but reduced the available credit at my disposal. The lower credit lines were just above what I already owed on each of my accounts. I had been using my open credit to purchase lumber, windows, doors, roofing materials, concrete and all the other items that the contractor needed for the remodel. American Express compromised my financial situation by reducing my credit lines and their actions lowered my credit score.

I didn't know how I was going to finish the remodel, or refinance the house, without any available credit and with a declining credit score. Refinancing a remodeled home is challenging in the best of times, much less in the circumstances in which I now found myself. The appraiser for the financial institution that is funding the refinance on an existing mortgage requires the construction to be entirely completed before they can assess the value of the remodeled home. It's a catch-22 situation, as they will not consider funding a refinance on a remodeled property until the remodel has been fully completed and the property has been reassessed.

The fucking funny part of the story with my good friends at American Express doesn't end there. Several years earlier, when working at Brad's company in San Francisco, I had a project with a design firm in New York to supply and manufacture a fixture program to house and display photographs from American Express' *"Rewarding Lives"* campaign. After the project was installed, I visited their corporate office to view the project that included an exhibit of images shot by Annie Leibovitz, which were conceived to welcome American Express employees back to their corporate office at the World Financial Center in New York after September 11. The campaign eventually traveled the country and I saw the exhibit again when it made its way to San Francisco. Not only was I a loyal customer, I also did work for them and supported their efforts. Now it seemed as if a cruel joke was being played at my expense.

The comedy continued. Shortly after the standup comics at American Express reduced my credit, they sent me two letters informing me that my credit line on two accounts had been increased. In a letter dated February 22, 2008, they stated that my credit on the Starwood Preferred Guest credit card that they issued had been increased and my new credit line was now two million three hundred ninety thousand dollars, with a cash advance limit of twenty thousand dollars. My prayers had been answered. When I called American Express about the letters, they explained that a computer error had generated the letters and sent them out. Fucking unbelievable. The jokers blamed their error on a random computer glitch. Were the computers running their organization? Were my credit lines pulled in the first place because of a similar glitch? Decisions impacting my life were being made by a fucking computer or server. These machines might as well have generated and mailed the letter below. It would have been more reflective of the situation.

Dear longstanding customer,

Your open credit lines have been dramatically reduced and, by the way, the letters that you received from American Express informing you that your credit lines had been increased was our bad. Asshole, we were just kidding when we sent those letters informing you of a credit increase. You have absolutely no open credit available with American Express. Have a good fucking day and thanks again for being a loyal customer these past decades. Although, honestly, we really don't give a shit how long you've been a costumer with us.

Sincerely, we couldn't care any less than we already do about you and your situation.

AmEx

P.S. Dickhead, good luck finishing your remodel with no available credit.

Today, I can find the humor in the story, but at the time I was not laughing, I was crying. When it rains it pours, though in Palm Springs it very seldom rained and my life was about to get a whole lot drier and more difficult. It seemed as if Lucifer was turning up the furnace, transforming my life into my living inferno. Having lived through that nightmare, I came to learn that if God is for me, who can be against me? Nobody, not even the financial institutions, insurance brokers, medical and pharmaceutical companies, Madame President, her relentless and belligerent Lesbian, or Lucifer himself, for that matter.

The construction of the Whitewater home was completed in April 2008. The remodel took six weeks longer than expected, costing me additional money that wasn't in my original budget. At every turn, there seemed to lurk unforeseen situations that cost me more cash than I had to spend. For months, it felt as if Wall Street, American Express, and other financial institutions were in control of my destiny when in fact they were nothing more than a thorn in my ass. Unbeknownst to me, God was in control all along. I see that now. To paraphrase a line from the Bible, greater is He who is in you, than American Express who is in the world.

Philven and I moved into the house during the same weekend as Palm Spring's annual White Party. I had no idea when I stepped through the gates of the Whitewater property that I was entering the grounds where my world would implode. I had lost my spiritual footing when I went from being a child to an adult, but in that house, bought from a man of the church, God would begin to resurrect my faith that was established when my parents and grandmother took me to Sunday church. Today, I can barely remember the person I was before I entered the Whitewater home and encountered a chain of events that would change me forever.

The day of our move, I saw the construction workers carrying what seemed to resemble a very large wooden cross, ten to twelve feet in height, off the property, just as the movers arrived with our household items. The scale of the wooden structure combined with the fact that I purchased the house from a minister, were two circumstances that have stuck in my mind, to this day. It turned out that during the remodel, the electricity had to be disconnected from the utility company and a temporary hookup needed to be put in place so the construction workers had access to electricity. They built what resembled a large wooden cross to run the electrical wires from an adjacent electrical pole over to the house. I expect this is a standard construction practice. These two situations were the first two of many circumstances that would manifest over the time when I lived in that house. The preponderance of these events would eventually drive me to question the significance of these and other similar occurrences.

Before I arrived in that desert, I had felt an unexplainable presence of some kind for several years. These feelings that most people in my life described as paranoid delusions seemed to get stronger as I entered the desolate valley—and they became overwhelming once I moved into my new place. Could I have been living in a house with a spiritual presence of some kind? There was certainly something different and special about this ten thousand square foot lot surrounded by a five-foot high cinderblock fence that I now called home. I lived in that house for three years and, at some point in that time, I came to believe that I might have been mistaken when I thought the house was going to be my refuge from the world. I began to ponder if I had entered into my own underworld. Since I had walked through the gates that led to the yard of my new home, with whom I believed to be the Devil, did I sense an evil presence? Would the house that I bought and built to be my castle become my prison?

I had to battle every day for many months to find a financial institution that would consider my application to combine my existing balance on the property with the two hundred thousand dollars I spent on the remodel. The financial crisis had been brewing for almost a year and obtaining a mortgage had become grueling. I quickly learned how screwed up the process had become. The longer it took to secure a loan, the lower my credit score became, which complicated the process further. The large debt I was carrying was having a direct effect on my credit score that then affected the type of loan I could obtain. I was caught in the middle of a fucked up financial calamity that consumed my days. I wanted to mentally escape from it all and my drug use increased accordingly.

Two weeks before the banks in the U.S. started to fail, and one week before I was finally approved to refinance the house, I voiced to my mortgage broker that America was headed for bankruptcy due to the fucked-up behavior that I was experiencing from the financial institutions with whom I was dealing. The large number and different types of documentation they requested to process my loan application was ridiculous. These so-called financial experts went from giving a loan to anyone, without proof of employment or income, to asking for documented trivia that didn't make any difference in my ability to repay my loan. These masters of finance now judged a person, and their perceived worth, by a credit score, a set of numbers on a piece of paper. Shame on them. Years later, I am still angry about these bastards who fucked the people with their lack of morals, honor, and integrity. After I lost my job and opened my own company, the credit card companies, with whom I had done business for decades, began treating me like I was a piece of garbage. For years, creditors had been consistently sending me offers for additional credit or for very low- to no-interest rates. These companies acted as if they were my best friends and closest allies. Now, the history that we had together and our relationship, built over years, didn't make one fucking difference to them, on any level, once the financial crisis hit. It was a financial war, with them and their system against people like me.

In the meantime, cracked-out Humpty Dumpty sat on his five-foot cinder block wall and he was one pissed off and fearful customer. Two weeks after I voiced that financial institutions would begin to fail, Lehman Brothers filed for bankruptcy protection on September 15, 2008. Many other financial institutions failed in the days and weeks that followed. My prediction that the financial sector would begin to collapse seemed to be coming to fruition. While I had voiced the sentiment out of frustration, it seemed like more than a random utterance. I didn't follow the news closely at the time, so where did this come from? Was it God's way of letting me know that he was watching over me and assuring me to remain calm?

On September 29, 2008, the U.S. Congress failed to pass TARP, a bill to bail out troubled financial institutions. Investors around the world reacted and the Dow lost 777 points in a single day, which erased 1.2 trillion dollars in stock market value. People who had invested the majority of their retirement savings in the stock market saw their 401(k) drop in value. When the U.S. House of Representatives failed to come to an agreement that day, they adjourned to observe Rosh Hashanah—and the American people lost over a trillion dollars. This was ironic, as most of the members of Congress are not even Jewish, and I often wonder if any of them have asked for God's forgiveness for not working late that day. Had they passed the TARP bill, they might have prevented the stock market from dropping so steeply and saved the country and its' people a tremendous amount of money. Sloth, or laziness, is one of the seven cardinal sins and the laziness, or unwillingness of the House to work late and through their differences – to pass the bill – impacted many people's lives in such a harsh way. The ministers in America that preach prosperity must have had a meltdown too that day, when the House and Wall Street financially raped God's good people, whose donations they craved.

I obtained the mortgage refinance, in spite of all the obstacles, at a higher interest rate than I would've preferred. I paid off some, but not all the outstanding balances on the credit cards, and rolled those payments into my new mortgage, which came with a lower interest rate. By paying off the outstanding balances on these credit cards, I would free up my credit lines, which would increase my credit score. With a higher credit rating, I could eventually refinance the house for a second time and secure a loan with a better interest rate. It was an intricate plan to maneuver my financial situation. I had to learn to play their game by their rules. My new mortgage company sent checks to my creditors to settle the roughly $140,000 dollars of the $200,000 in debt I was carrying from the remodel. Chase and American Express then reduced my credit lines to a few thousand dollars for their cards. Their actions didn't lower my credit score, but it didn't help. My rating remained the same, crushing my hopes of raising it and my plan to secure a better mortgage with a lower interest rate. My efforts to maneuver through the complexities of the financial markets were in vain. These creditors delivered the final blow, which resulted in my having to do something that I thought I would never do.

Five years later, in 2013, JP Morgan was fined thirteen billion dollars for packaging bad mortgages as good investments and selling them off to investors. In doing so, they became a major contributor to the financial crisis. They were fined for their unethical, if not illegal conduct, after the fact—and after many families had lost their homes.

When working for Madame President, I had booked less than six hundred thousand dollars in sales by September of 2007, against my goal of 1.2 million dollars. In September, just before arriving in Palm Springs, Madame President noted that I was nowhere near making my sales goal for the year, a comment I have never forgotten. While she was correct, I had quoted several large projects and it was still possible for me to make my goal. The following month, right before arriving in Palm Springs, I landed a half a million dollar sale and ended the year with $1.4 million in sales. I not only hit my goal in the last three months of the year, I exceeded it. In the two years I worked there, I pushed everyone in the organization very hard, in my attempt to expand the logistics company's customer base and increase their revenue, although I drove Philven and myself the hardest. Until I opened my own company, I had never worked as intensely as I did for Madame President. If it weren't for the Lesbian and Philven plotting against me, I probably would still be employed with her company. I acknowledge and understand I had many areas where I needed to improve, but my actions were always well-intended and in line with bringing as much revenue as possible to making the company more successful. I stuck my neck out financially and went forward with the remodel because in January of 2008 when I was still employed with the logistics company, I was forecasted to earn approximately three hundred thousand dollars that year, based on the verbally confirmed projects that I had in the works. I've learned that money and greed can influence people to do things that they would not normally do. After being let go, I wondered if Madame President's decision to fire me was fueled by the fact that she wouldn't be required to shell out around three hundred thousand dollars in salary and commissions if I was released from my position.

Madame President received a verbal commitment from one of my clients for a two million dollar deal that I brokered in 2007, to be executed in 2008. I was fired in January 2008 and I believed I was also owed commission on that sale. I received an email, which I still have, from Madame President congratulating me on this multi-million dollar project. If I was not legally owed the commission on that sale, what was stopping Madame President, or anyone else in any other organization, from firing a salesperson – who brought a large sale to the company – before they paid out their commission? If this is allowed, a company could reap the benefits of a commission-based employee without ever having to pay their commission for any sales they earned, but had not yet received. This behavior seems not only unethical, it's also illegal and a very unfair practice…and there are laws to prevent this type of conduct, as there should be.

I had so looked forward to moving into the Whitewater home, but after doing so, all hell broke loose. I was negotiating with Madame President to have her company extend my healthcare coverage – pay out my outstanding vacation pay, reimburse me for five thousand dollars in outstanding expenses, and pay me forty thousand dollars in outstanding commissions I had earned in 2007. I desperately needed what was owed me. It was literally a matter of life and death. Without medical coverage, I was not going to be able to refill my HIV medications and my health would decline. I needed my commission payment to see me through my living expenses until my new company turned a profit and could help cover some of the remodel costs. I contracted Anthony and John, the twin lawyers who helped to legally establish ILD, and they reached out to Madame President to negotiate a settlement.

During the negotiations, I requested that the logistics company convert my healthcare policy to COBRA, which is a private plan, reimburse me for outstanding unpaid expenses, and pay my 2007 commissions, and I also requested that they pay me the two hundred thousand dollars' commission that I earned on the two-million dollar sale in December of 2007. After several months of back and forth between our respective attorneys, I received an offer to settle the dispute. Madame President offered to pay me nearly forty thousand dollars, which included commissions for 2007 and a portion of the outstanding expenses. They had already sent me a check for my vacation pay and had continued to cover my medical coverage for six months. I needed money desperately, so I agreed to the terms. By doing so, I sacrificed the two hundred thousand dollars that I believed was owed me and accepted an offer of thirty nine thousand dollars for commissions plus a portion of the outstanding expenses.

Several weeks went by and I never received payment. I'm not sure what the fuck happened between the time Madame President's attorneys offered to pay the accepted amount and the time my lawyers contacted them to follow up. Once my lawyers contacted her attorneys they relayed that the logistics company would rather pay the thirty nine thousand dollars in legal fees than cut me a check. What the fuck was going on with Madame President? Was she just fucking with me when she made me the offer or was the Lesbian so far up her ass that she was controlling her like a hand puppet? I was outraged and pissed off that even now I have a hard time putting it into the right words. After months of negotiations and agreeing to forfeit two hundred thousand dollars, Madame President betrayed me again. I had an email from her attorney confirming that she agreed to pay me the thirty nine thousand dollars, but this confirmation was not worth the paper on which it was written.

I was in a hateful mood and sent an email to Madame President to let her know how pissed off I was. I wrote that I would come after her for the money that she owed me. I stated that I would slap her and her company with a discrimination lawsuit for the Lesbian's scheming actions to try to get a gay man fired. I mentioned that I would sue her and her organization for wrongful termination. I was so livid that I don't recall what else I put in the email, but it was strongly worded and threating in tone. It was my last attempt to get her to release the money that she had agreed to pay. Like many rich people, she thought her money allowed her to fuck over the little people whenever it suited her to do so.

Several weeks after sending Madame President my threating email, I was served with a lawsuit. Her company was suing our company, Philven, and me for several so-called infractions. The premise of the lawsuit was based on the allegation that I willingly and knowingly attempting to solicit clients from her company to mine while I was still employed by her. This allegation couldn't have been farther from the truth.

Shortly after my creditors fucked me over one last time, just before being served with the lawsuit, I began to feel an oncoming collision with a force that I didn't understand and couldn't see. I felt like an evil mass was heading in my direction and it was going to crush my hopes of survival. During the remodel, I built a walk-in closet in the master bedroom that connected to the master bathroom. I installed built-in custom dresser drawers in that closet and, on top of those drawers, I placed all my jewelry including various crosses and rosaries. One day, I stood between the bathroom and the closet entrance and I cried out to God to protect me. I wanted to overcome the evil that I saw approaching from all directions, seeking to destroy me financially and otherwise. Several decades earlier, I had emerged as a gay man from the closet. In my moment of desperation, I reentered that closet from where I had originally emerged seeking God. As I frequently note, He has an amazing sense of humor. After calling on God, I remembered reaching for the little Gideon Bible in that hotel room several years earlier. After embracing that Bible, and sleeping with it in my arms, my overall health improved. It finally dawned on me that it was God that increased my T-cell count to an overwhelmingly high number, where it has remained to this day. It was a miracle. He had made His presence known in Atlanta when I reached for his protection, When I couldn't protect myself, I believe He was there for me in that low-lying place where I had fallen, although I didn't realize that He had done so at that moment.

I believe God is constantly challenging us to refine our character and uses our misfortunes in life to test our commitment to Him. Whether these challenges are self-inflicted, being at the wrong place at the wrong time, or an act of random violence, these hardships will either turn an individual into a heartless soul or they will engender a sense of humility and kindness within that person. I was not humble or compassionate, but the weight upon my shoulders would soon bring me to my knees—and humility would be all that I had left.

Diamonds are formed at very high temperatures and under a tremendous amount of pressure. The incredible amount of heat that I had to endure in that desert city, combined with the enormous financial hardship that was pushing down on me, seemed to be forging me into an extremely durable person that could withstand much and become a tower of strength. I came to see that if money is like air, where the more you have the easier it is to breathe, then God is like water—without it, in the desert, you're just dead. Even though it was becoming hard for me to breathe, I came to have plenty of comfort from God to keep me hydrated.

We often hear that happiness is a choice. I came to understand this theory and was able to accept happiness as part of my life, even when it was extremely difficult. By building a meaningful relationship with God, I was able to find joy when there was none. This realization would coincide when everything in my life seemed as if it was crumbling around me. I came to understand that in the midst of my ongoing struggles, God was willing and capable of offering me comfort and support when I was lonely, afraid, in financial difficulties, and isolated from my family and friends. All the overwhelming and seeming impossible battles that evil thought it could use to destroy me, God would utilize to put an end to the insanity. If I had not cried out to Him to come into my life and protect me, while standing in that closet doorway, I probably wouldn't have made it out of that valley alive.

The state of California began to allow same sex marriages in the month of May in 2008. By November of that same year, California residents voted to ban same sex marriages. Sometime after May and before November, Philven got down on one knee and proposed to me in front of our house, on our pool patio. Careful what you wish for goes the expression, because wishes that seem like they're free are not at all free, they tend to come with a big price—and this was certainly the case with this proposal. I asked Philven if he loved me and he replied that he loved God first and me second. In retrospect, I find his response offensive. How could someone who truly loved God, and claimed to have a relationship with Him, lie and drug their boyfriend to sneak out of the house at night to seek dick? How could he have believed his comment to be sincere? He was a liar and he loved nobody more than he loved himself—not even God. Like many people, he hid behind the concept of God, when in fact he was just selfish and put his own agenda above all others.

I stood in the patio and thought about how I had waited for such a moment all my life. But I was not being swept away by this man who seemed more interested in what he could get from me rather than being interested in just me. I said no. Just like that little girl who dreams of meeting her Prince Charming, I wanted a wedding that I would remember for eternity and we were in no position to afford the wedding of which I dreamed or any other type of wedding. I was also not going to allow the State to dictate when I could or should marry another man. While many gay couples were rushing to get hitched before the November 2008 election that would overturn their right to marry, I was not going to allow Philven to use the upcoming vote to pressure me into marrying him.

I thank God for giving me grace and allowing me to keep the one thing that I still hold very near and dear to my heart—my dream of marrying my Price Charming and living happily ever after. This dream was not stolen from me in that desolate desert valley and I still see it as a possibility, albeit not probable. I may never meet and marry my Prince Charming that was meant to be the father of our children, but if it's meant to be, it will happen and I'll be able to have the fairytale ending that I've always wished.

One of my other favorite movies is *What Dreams May Come*. It's a story about a man and his wife, who had fallen in love, married, and had two children. When they are teenagers, the children are abruptly killed in a random car accident. The couple struggle to cope with their tragedy and, in doing so, they grow apart. Several years later, the husband succumbs to the same fate as their children and he too dies in a car accident. At first, he fails to realize that he has died and, in his confusion, his spirit lingers on earth for a period of time. He is bewildered by what has happened to him and he attempts to connect with his wife who is still alive. Once his spirit finally realizes it's no longer part of the world that he once knew, it leaves it and arrives in heaven. As he enters paradise, he's reunited with his dog who had passed away years earlier. In a place referred to as heaven's dreamland, others teach him that he can shape his surrounding by utilizing his imagination.

Back at home, the wife is overwhelmed with grief from the loss of her children and now her husband. She is an artist and paints the pain of her loss and her love for her family into her paintings. She paints a jacaranda tree into one of her most recent paintings. As she renders the blue tree on her canvas, the tree simultaneously shows up in the husband's surroundings in his dreamland. The wife comes to feel that she can communicate with her dead husband, based on the time that his spirit lingered on earth and spiritually connected with her, which is the reason the painting appears in her husband's dreamland. The love they have for one another is so great that it defies conventional logic.

The wife is eventually overcome by the loss of her family and commits suicide. The husband is very sad that his wife has given up on life, but is somewhat happy that her suffering has come to an end and they can be reunited in heaven's dreamland. But the husband is told that those who commit suicide go to a place called hell. It's not the place of judgment, but one where suicide victims create a nightmarish existence for themselves based on their pain. The wife is unable to remember that she committed suicide and now lives in a version of the home that the family once shared. This home that she has created for herself there is a broken down, lifeless, and dark place inside an upside-down cathedral. She is confused and alone and is visually tortured by her deceitful surroundings that she'll be in for eternity.

The husband's love for his wife is worth more to him than all that heaven has to offer. He believes that he can walk through the gates of hell and enter the nightmare that his wife has created for herself and retrieve the woman that once loved him. It's a beautiful and very colorful story with a dark subplot that captures your imagination and heart while engaging your mind to contemplate a much larger existence of the universe than anyone can prove. The husband is willing to sacrifice his eternal life in heaven rather than leave his wife alone, living her nightmare in hell. This act of selfless love emboldens his wife to see through her pain and, in doing so, she and her husband are spiritually transported and attain a heavenly existence. Once in heaven, they're reunited with their children, in a house that is an exact replica of the home where they all lived together, with their dog, when the family was alive.

Toward the end of the story, once the family is reunited, the husband and wife are told that all people who enter into heaven have the option to spend eternity in paradise or they can choose to be reincarnated and return to the world from where they came. The wife is concerned with how they will find one another, if she and her husband chose to be reincarnated. The husband convinces his wife that they're meant to be together and no matter the circumstances that they encounter along the way, she needs to have faith that they'll find each other. The wife agrees for them to be reborn. At the end of the movie, a little boy meets a little girl and they end up becoming friends. These children represent the husband and his wife and they've been reunited once again, for true love is eternal.

I held an executive design position for many years prior to becoming self-employed and opening ILD. I also have numerous creative projects in my design portfolio that I completed during my professional career. Even though I believe I possess a very creative mind, I still consider myself a realist. I usually approached situations involving money, love, and religion from a very conservative point of view. With this in mind, and as I thought of the movie, I recalled the story about my landlady's poodle and her friend's premonition that it was going to be reincarnated—and her concern that they would not be able to find one another once the dog was reborn.

Philven and I had selected Aston and Bentley as the names of our two miniature schnauzers. Philven yearned to own an Aston Martin and I wanted a Bentley so we thought it appropriate to call the boys by the names of the cars that we so desired, but couldn't afford. Aston was the youngest of the litter and Bentley, as the second youngest, was the older of the two. As the months went by, Bentley began to remind me a great deal of Papi who had died a year earlier. This was even more apparent because Aston didn't remind me of Papi in any way. I began to think that the reincarnation story about my landlady's poodle was really a story meant for me. Had my little Papi been reincarnated? It sounds crazy, but Bentley had so many of the same mannerisms as Papi that he almost seemed to be an exact replica of him. I began to wonder if something spiritual brought us together. I had no intention of getting another dog, miniature schnauzer or otherwise, after Papi had died. Did God reunite me with my little Valentine in that desert to comfort me and know that I was loved and would be protected even though I was going to battle against the Devil? Many times, while I lived in the desert

I wondered if Papi had been reincarnated. It would be just like God to use a puppy to deliver His message of love, companionship, and protection.

A PARABLE | THE COLOR OF MONEY

I've heard people say that God created dogs in the animal kingdom so man would have a best friend. In grade school, I read *Old Yeller*, the one and the only book I've ever read. It's a story about a stray dog that develops a relationship with a boy. The boy encounters the stray when his father is on a cattle drive. While the father is away, the little boy's older brother acts as the man of the house and helps his mother take care of the family farm. Over time, the two brothers become very attached to the dog and eventually it becomes part of their family. I barely remember the details of the book because I read it when I was in fifth grade, but I do recall that toward the end of the book the dog is bitten and becomes infected with rabies while he's defending one of the boys from a pack of wild animals. To protect his younger brother from being attacked by the infected dog that he has come to love, the older brother is forced to do something that no animal lover ever wants to do. It's a very sad story with a very inspiring message about the love between a dog and his family and the bond between two brothers.

Very much like the story of *Old Yeller*, I too felt like a stray dog who was seeking a home where somebody would love me and give me a sense of belonging. I find it interesting that dog reads as God backwards because, just like my dogs who are my best friends, I often feel like God is also my best friend. While living in the desert he gave me something that I sought after my entire life—sincerity and compassion. There's no logical reason that I can provide for why I am alive today, and writing this story, other than for the grace of God. That grace ultimately brought me to a place where I experienced something greater than I can justify with words, although I'm trying to do that by sharing my testimony.

My ongoing coincidences, which I kept seeing, led me to take a closer look at the things taking place around me. Ultimately, my scrutiny uncovered how fate seemed to play such an important role in my life. I saw fate as just another word in the English language to describe inevitable destiny, although I now believe I was mistaken. Once I began to observe my circumstances more closely, I could sense that fate was leading me in a specific direction and it ultimately led me to discover hope. In that desert, when fate brought me to that hope, I experienced a desire to seek and find my purpose when it seemed as if the gloom that was surrounding my life was going to consume me. That purpose led me to realize that I had a destiny I didn't know existed. I then understood that I could attain a better existence than the one I was living. Together, fate and hope gave me the ability to distinguish between my life's purpose and its' destiny, which enlightened me to a point where I could see beyond my crippling conditions. I eventually came to view fate as a spirit and to my amazement it had a feminine aura.

San Francisco has over six thousand homeless people and it's also the second most expensive city to live in the United States. I find it ironic that there's such a great need in such a wealthy area of the country. One night, when I was walking Aston and Bentley underneath the Bay Bridge in San Francisco, I saw a young homeless man in the dog park. He was getting water from a water fountain. The man was carrying a backpack and, because he was in his twenties, he caught my eye. When I see young men and women who are homeless, it makes my heart ache and it saddens me that these kids are living on the street and have to fend for themselves at such a vulnerable time in their lives. While I have compassion for all the homeless, whenever I encounter young people or families with young children that are living on the street, it makes me want to cry. Seeing these people that have to survive without a roof over their head makes me want to do something to make the world a better place for them.

When Aston and Bentley finished their business, I leashed them and we walked to the entrance of the park, which is also the exit. Closing time is at nine in the evening and the gates were being locked. Just beyond the exit of the park, before the sidewalk, there are several benches. I frequently see homeless people use these benches as their resting place for the night, when the sun sets, and on more nights than not. Upon leaving the park, I noticed that the young man with the backpack was also carrying cardboard. He began to lay it on one of the three benches. Under my breath, as I walked by him, I muttered for God to love this boy and look after him. I wanted to do something for this young man, but I was not in a financial position to do much or make a difference in his circumstances.

The following morning, when walking Aston and Bentley, I went to the same dog park. When I got close to the entrance I noticed a man who was sleeping on the sidewalk underneath the bridge. The upper half of his body lay in a cardboard box and the rest of his body was sticking out of that same cardboard box, visible from the waist down. As I approached the sleeping man, I noticed he was the same young man from the night before. A grocery bag sat next to the man's legs that were sticking out of the box. I looked down, as I passed his temporary shelter, and I noticed that someone had placed groceries in the brown paper bag. Someone, unknown to me, had gone to a grocery store a block and a half away from where he was sleeping on the street and bought breakfast, lunch and dinner for him. The grocery store is a small convenience store and much pricier than a large supermarket. There must have been nearly thirty dollars' worth of food in the bag. This unknown someone not only bought the groceries, but he or she had also walked back to the area where this boy was sleeping near the dog park and set the bag of groceries next to his corrugated box.

It's possible that the kind stranger happened to be on their way home from shopping when they came across the young man and pulled items from their own groceries to create an entire day of meals for him. This anonymous person exemplifies the earthly angels that I believe roam among us and protect those in need and I am thankful for these guardian angels performing selfless acts of kindness. I was inspired and humbled. My spirit was moved and I was encouraged to become a more compassionate human being. I can only wish to become one of God's servants and aspire to be like that anonymous angel who goes to the grocery store and shops for a person who's forced to sleep inside a corrugated box on a sidewalk underneath a bridge.

I hope this book helps me to arrive at a place in life where I'm in a position to assist those who are in need of an opportunity, so they can better their circumstances. I understand life is not free, but I believe everyone deserves a chance at making a better life for themselves then the one they're living. It's my dream to be able to establish a bridge that will fill the gap between the haves and the have nots. Through a non-profit organization, I hope to give many of the less fortunate an opportunity and, in many cases, a second chance to be all that they were meant to be. I pray that God will allow me to develop and grow my life's purpose so that no person would be required to sleep underneath a bridge. Bridges are meant to span the gap between two distances and not for people to find refuge under them, once the sun goes down.

Ever since the incident back in Chicago when I encountered an overwhelming sensation that led me to believe I was supposed to be doing something else with my life, I pondered why I had those feelings at a time when I had achieved a level of success that I should have been proud to attain, working for the third largest commercial real estate holder in the United States. My intuition was telling me I should be doing something else with my life. This overpowering, but random emotion, caused me to voice my thoughts out loud even as I was alone in my apartment. I didn't have a clue why I had those feelings or why I felt compelled to vocally express them. My declaration was accompanied by confusion. The question as to why I had these feelings stayed with me for years, but, in time, I completely forgot about the day. Many years later, while living in Palm Springs, I finally understood what it was that I was supposed to be doing with my life. Life never made any real sense to me, nor did it have any purpose, until I added God to my life's equation. Just like the young man in the movie *Slum Dog Millionaire*, who knows all the answers to all the questions because his life experiences mirrored the questions being asked of him on the game show where he's competing, I too began to believe God was using my life experiences to bring me to a place that enlightened me to my purpose.

In Palm Springs, during my lowest moments, several visions were revealed to me that I believe came from a spiritual place. One of these visions consisted of an idea to establish and fund a foundation. Previously, on several occasions, I had thought about forming a charitable organization. Other than having creative ideas about the type of charity I would like to establish, I never thought I would be in a position to take on such an endeavor. One idea consisted of building housing communities in different parts of the world for children without parents. I also thought about gathering unwanted and stray dogs and creating a loving environment for them. I believe every family needs pets to make it a great home and the kids that would live in my housing communities could adopt the stray or unwanted animals. In the vision, I saw myself as the legal guardian of these children and their pets. They would be the family that I always wanted, but was never able to have. The timing of this vision was a strange circumstance. Previously, the idea of setting up a foundation had only been a fleeting idea. I found it strange that God thought it would be advantageous for me to visualize my future, establishing a foundation of this magnitude, in the midst of the aggressive behavior shown me by my creditors, during the global financial crisis. I was fighting desperately to stabilize my finances so my business wouldn't fail and my home wouldn't be foreclosed upon. I was also dealing with my so-called boyfriend who was trying to screw me over. Why would God think I was capable of starting a charity when I was struggling to deal with so much and barely able to provide for my immediate day-to-day needs? But the entire vision for the type of charitable foundation I want to establish wouldn't come into full view until five years after leaving the desert and after meeting Lance.

Around that time, I noticed the writings on a plaque in my possession that I had hung in many homes where I lived over several decades. I had three of these decorative wall plaques created by the artist Sid Dickens. I came across his works two decades earlier when I designed and installed a project in one of the Bigsby&Kruthers stores. I admired his work so much that I bought several plaques for myself, from the many designs in his collection. Two of the plaques had hearts on them and the third resembled a postage stamp with three letters, DLI. I had these plaques for twenty years and, during that time, I never paid attention to the letters. Sometime after I moved into the Whitewater house, I noticed that the letters on the plaque were in the reverse order of the short name of my new company. Even though the letters were the reverse of ILD, it seemed more than a coincidence, which I find to be somewhat overwhelming, even to this day. What were the chances that this plaque that I owned for decades would have the exact same letters as the company that I had no idea I would establish when I bought it? Was it a sign that there was more to my drunken moment in that desert when I thought of a fictitious name for a fictitious company? Was it a marker that foretold ILD two decades before the company was formed?

In my cry for God to protect my little family in the doorway of the closet in the Whitewater home, my life changed forever. I got serious about knowing Him. I needed to understand how God could be a reality in my life rather than just a figurehead that I called upon when I was in trouble. That journey was going to be the most exciting and most overwhelming endeavor that I ever embarked upon. For the next two and a half years, I would intensely seek to know someone that I knew very little about. What I didn't realize at the time of calling out to God for His protection, was that He had already been present from the time I was a little boy and went to church with my parents and grandmother. He had been making His presence known for decades without me ever noticing. What I viewed as unusual occurrences, which I labeled coincidences, were in actuality God reaching out to me. The reason I never saw God's presence up to that moment was because I never took the time to look for Him—until I realized I would never make it out of the desert alive without Him.

Horrific things took place for three years behind that five-foot-high cinderblock fence that surrounded the Whitewater house. This was the place where I fought tirelessly to maintain a livelihood that would support the home that I built for Aston, Bentley, Puckles, myself—and Philven, or so I thought at the time I built it. This was also the place where I encountered wonders at work beyond my imagination. I don't recall the events in the exact order they took place, but I recall the details of each occurrence as they transpired, horrific and amazing at the same time.

I can't recall if God conveyed that He was interested in making a deal with me when I called out to Him in that closet doorway or if He did so shortly afterward. I felt like He was going to honor my request and protect the me and the boys from the evil that I knew was heading in our direction, although I couldn't see it. After screaming for help, I got a distinct feeling that He was, in fact, interested in making a deal. But does God make deals? Many years earlier, after being diagnosed with HIV, I made numerous deals with God for a decade even though I didn't know Him. I asked that He grant me the opportunity to live a few more healthy years and, if my request was granted, I would try to be a better person. When that contract was up, I asked if I could renew our deal for several more years. These deals between us went on for ten years or more. My deals with God seemed to be working and they made sense to me. In time, I stopped renewing my deal with God because He always kept his promise. At some point in Palm Springs, I got the impression He wanted me to do something for Him in return for protecting me and my little family. He wasn't specific about what He wanted and I didn't ask for clarification because it didn't matter to me what He wanted. I knew I needed His protection or I was going to be buried in that desert. Since my time there, I listen to the advice of my inner-voice and let my heart lead me in the direction I was meant to walk. By doing so, I hope to accomplish all that is expected of me.

Before calling upon God, I often let my feelings control how I acted or reacted to a specific situation, especially when it came to fear. Being afraid had become part of my life and who I was. I was afraid of being beat up in the playground at school by the boys who thought I was a sissy. As an adult, I was afraid of what people would think if they knew I was a homo, afraid of people finding out that I was positive, afraid my boyfriend was cheating on me – which they always did – afraid my friends were talking badly about me behind my back, afraid that the people closest to me were lying to me, afraid of becoming ill from a disease related to my HIV status and not being able to work, afraid I would lose my job, afraid I would not be able to pay for my living expenses, afraid I was going to lose my home in the financial crisis, afraid I would become homeless and, ultimately, I was afraid that I would experience a horribly painful death from AIDS. To overcome my fears, I adopted a warrior-like mentality and became a fighter. I became very confrontational, very hostile, and ready for a fight with anyone, over anything, at any time. My financial Armageddon was approaching and it would be a battle like no other. The fight would bring me to my knees, seeking forgiveness and direction, but by the grace of Fate and Hope, I was lifted up to wage the good fight.

After calling on God that day in the closet, I received a second vision. I had begun to question my sanity and whether I was losing my grip on reality. Was I really having visions from heaven or was I hallucinating? Tremendous emotional and financial pressures and its accompanying worries could cause a person to hallucinate. Since I was experiencing visions that foretold a future for myself, as well as others, I knew I was not hallucinating. The timing of these visions may have had everything to do with the fact I was extremely vulnerable, which allowed me to be receptive to them for the first time in my life. In this second vision, I saw three moons in the desert night sky. One of the moons appeared as if it was fading or dying off. It seemed like a vision. After thinking about it deeply, I came to see the vision very much like a riddle, where the three moons represented three worlds.

If God wanted to reach out to me, then why didn't He speak to me in words rather than visions? After pondering this question, I realized that if I had heard a voice speaking out loud to me at the time I was going through my turmoil, it would've put me over the edge. Can you imagine telling a friend that you heard a voice speak out loud to you like Moses and the burning bush? Today, if someone said they heard God's voice coming from a burning bush, I'm sure they would probably be committed or, at the very least, they would be called crazy. I was certainly lost, but I knew I was not crazy. God was communicating with me in a way that I had become accustomed to communicating with others. He was using emoticons and acronyms to get His message heard, hence the visions and the acronyms. The Book of Acts in the Bible (Acts 2:17) states "and in the last days it shall be, God declares, that I will pour out my spirit on all flesh, and your sons and daughters shall prophesy and your young men shall see visions, and your old men shall dream dreams." Once I was able to connect the dots and make a viable reference to the three moons that I believed represented three worlds, it became very important that I ask myself why God wanted me to know this information.

My mind began searching for the reason that God would reveal a riddle-like vision with three moons. I then recalled the World Islands in Dubai. I wondered if God was pissed off that mankind had the audacity to create a man-made world on top of the world that He created. As a designer, I had great admiration for the Crown Prince of Dubai and his vision to conceptualize a project of that magnitude. Was the vision to create the World Islands of Dubai merely a creative idea by the Prince, manifested by his own merits or was it part of a larger plan? Could heaven have inspired the concept for this amazing project? My vision of the three moons came at a time when the American dream was being crushed by the largest financial disaster since the Great Depression and when I was in the midst of trying to weather that financial calamity. I couldn't help wonder if there was a connection between what was going on globally at that time and my vision.

In the movie *2012*, the world is coming to an end and only the rich and the influential were being told of the climate change that would cause the earth to flood for the second time. The governments of the world came together to have China build arks that would save the elite from drowning in the coming flood, while the rest of the population was left to its' own devices. Does art mimic life or does life mimic art? Due to the global climate change, I wondered if the wealthy and influential people of the world were planning to build their modern-day ark in the water off the shores of Dubai.

I believe there's a good chance that God has a plan for this new domain and it doesn't include a safe haven for the few and powerful. The Islands of Dubai that depict the shape of the world that God created seem to be a modern-day wonder, much like the Great Pyramids that were built to connect our world with the world of the afterlife. Could this new man-made domain be used for the betterment of humanity? Could it possibly be the location of the one world government alluded to in the Bible? Perhaps this one world government could be the beginning of man's devotion and commitment to saving God's world from extinction. I see this new domain as being full of humanitarians, from all countries, who work together for the greater good of mankind. Could this new world be the location of heaven on earth? God so loved his creation he created a world for them in which to live, prosper, and procreate. Humanity so loved God that they created a man-made world with the greatest humanitarians from all nations to protect the world He created for them.

18 | A CHEATING HAND

Over my lifetime, I experienced many coincidental situations that led me to think that someone was deliberately staging the events. I began to believe that an unknown someone was screwing with my mind and that's why I kept experiencing situations that left me with a feeling there was more to the circumstances than I knew. My belief that I was being played by an unknown source was the aftermath of the lies that Alex told me over the years of our relationship. Alex's lies, compounded by Philven's deceitful conduct, opened Pandora's Box and released demons of self-doubt that haunted me for many years. The lies that I had to sort through, on a regular basis during my relationships, added confusion to my already complex life. It certainly made more sense that someone was watching me, and screwing with me, rather than believing in an alternative option. I was unable to see how the single coincidences that kept occurring were part of a larger picture. After moving into the Whitewater home, I began to explore a different option to explain the ongoing coincidences than I had previously considered. I was eventually led to embrace an answer that I had not considered before arriving in that desert.

As a middle-aged man, I was lost and roaming aimlessly through life, unaware I strayed from my intended path. I was literally not able to see the forest for the trees. My poor decisions and my not-so-good behavior resulted in a magnitude of situations that kept me in a constant state of damage control, causing me to become a self-absorbed and pissed off individual. In the desert, my suspicions were confirmed that there was a pattern to the coincidences that kept taking place. These events were like breadcrumbs placed in my life's path so I could find my way home, once I realized I was lost. It took me decades to grasp that God had been seeking a relationship with me ever since I had gone to church as a little boy. On the day I finally decided to follow the trail of crumbs that I came to believe were left for me by God, is the day I heard a voice deep within me. That voice led me to explore a world that I knew very little about.

Up to that point, I knew almost nothing about religion or its' respective Gods. I had heard bits and pieces about the story of Jesus in the Holy Bible,

Mohammad in the Holy Quran and Esther in the Holy Torah. In my quest to understand the many religions, I discovered TBN, Daystar, and EWTN, which are faith-based networks on cable television. In my attempt to understand a God that could be a reality in my life, I was enthusiastic about the possibilities of what that relationship could offer. On the other hand, I was confused by which story and which God I should embrace. Watching the religious networks caused more confusion than not and it was unclear which story was the true story and which God was the real God. In the midst of my confusion, however, I began to see more clearly. I was blind and now I can see.

I felt a presence surrounding me as I tried to become more informed on the subject of religion. I find it difficult to explain the existence of this presence without sounding like I should be fitted for a straightjacket. Even though I couldn't see this "thing" that I felt surrounding me, I felt if I closed my eyes I could reach out in any direction and touch whatever it was that surrounded me. The presence of this spirit was that close and very real—even though I couldn't see it with my eyes or touch it with my hands. Many years earlier, when I was partying in San Francisco, I had this same type of feeling although this time there weren't any DJs or singing divas in the equation. Did a spirit follow me all those years without my knowing it? Did it follow me to the desert? Perhaps it wasn't following me at all. It could have been leading me through life the entire time without me realizing it. Did it lead me to that place, for a specific time and for a predestined encounter?

Shortly after I turned to God for his protection, before I had an opportunity to fully comprehend any of the world's religions, I believe God tested my commitment to Him. I had been watching the religious networks for months to understand the different faiths when I began to struggle with my newly found interest in discovering a God that made sense. Even though the words coming out of my mouth were focused on finding God, my inner self struggled with the concept of embracing a God. Was God real or did my mind manifest the belief that He actually existed? I was under a tremendous amount of stress and was hanging onto financial stability by a thread. I wondered if my personal pressures were influencing my subconscious and whether I was capable of convincing myself that I had experienced a vision and believed that vision was from a spiritual place when in fact it was not. As I went through this internal struggle, the feeling of that presence that I felt surrounding me left. Later, I felt that the absence of that presence was a deliberate maneuver by God to seem as if he had abandoned me. I continued to question my developing faith for three more months when a situation occurred that resulted in my having an emotional meltdown that put me over the edge. The pressures of dealing with the ongoing lawsuit from Madame President, combined with my efforts to stay financially above water, finally got the best of me. If there was a God, then where the hell was He and why did He not help me?

One afternoon, I stood in the kitchen and dining area of the Whitewater house and I lost my shit. I felt as if I was falling off a cliff to my death. I had lost all hope of being able to overcome my messed-up existence and felt like my world was coming to an end. I began to rant and rave about how unhappy I was and how pissed off I was at God for not doing anything to help change my circumstances. During my meltdown, the area where I stood in the house became dark. In the mornings, the sun came up on the back side of the house and by the afternoon the sun shone on the front side, which had large sliding glass doors. To keep the house cool in the afternoon, I always pulled shut the drapes on that side of the house. That day, I closed the drapes before noon to keep the sun from causing the temperature to rise. In the afternoon, the central air conditioning system worked the hardest to keep the house cool. The drapes were closed, so it must have been after twelve, but before five o'clock in the afternoon when I lost it. There were several small windows above the sliding glass doors that the drapes didn't cover and some light shone into the house through them. These high windows, though small, kept the main portion of the house well-lit during the day.

As I began to yell about God's lack of support, it suddenly seemed as if the sun had gone away. I walked toward the windows and pulled the drapes open. Upon opening these, I saw that dark clouds had formed in the sky, covering the sun. Before I lost my shit and began to cuss out God, the afternoon had been sunny with nothing but blue skies. As I looked toward the clouds, after opening the drapes in the middle of my tantrum, I saw a bit of light shining through the heavy clouds. The dark clouds seemed to have come out of nowhere and the sunlight was fighting to shine through those clouds. I then noticed an image created by these two elements forming, which resembled a large bird, a white dove to be exact. I immediately walked over to the kitchen counter to grab my phone to take a picture of what I came to see as a sign. I use that picture as the cover of this book.

I had heard the story about how the Holy Spirit appeared to Jesus in the form of a dove when he realized He was the Son of God. Since God knew I was limited in my knowledge about Him, did he use a symbol with which I was familiar? At the exact moment that I questioned my faith, it seemed as if God sent dark clouds to cover the sun's rays to get my attention—and form an image of a dove to reiterate that He was near and aware of my situation. In my eyes, the timing of a dove appearing in the sky, as I questioned my faith and swore at God, can be nothing but a sign. That day was the defining moment when I truly began to believe. After that day, I have never questioned my devotion to God and I have strongly held on to it ever since.

I know God tempted me in that desert to test my faith those three months. He knew I was struggling with my newly found beliefs and He wanted to see how long I would hold onto my faith before I lost it and went back to my old ways. I now know that God does tempt us. He will test our commitment at different times and in various ways so that we understand that our level of dedication to Him should not be dictated by our current situation. As Matthew 3:16 states, "God lead us not into temptation, but deliver us from evil."

I can't begin to understand all the ways in which God interacts with me, although I do think He is amazing and I find Him wildly entertaining. For those who don't believe in a high power…if it weren't for *my* belief in something greater than myself, I would have never been able to muster the energy to fight for a better life—and I wholeheartedly believe this story is proof that God exists. With my faith renewed by what I came to see as God's version of a bat signal in the sky, all hell broke loose and the good fight began. The next several years were the most difficult times I've ever endured. The burdens that evil meant to use to destroy me in that place, God used to rid the demons out of my life once and for all. God began to reveal the prospect of a better life, but for this to become a reality, I needed to learn to have faith in a faithless situation. In the desert, where very little survives unless it can withstand extreme conditions, I too would need to learn to withstand extreme hardships and learn to lean on my faith and not my own understanding, if I was to survive the perils ahead.

Did God send me to the desert to isolate me so temptation had the opportunity to seduce me? While living there, during my effort to build a relationship with Him, I could see comparisons between my life and some of the stories in the Bible. I recalled a story about Jesus going into the desert. While he was in the valley of despair, he became man so he could be tempted. I too was in a similar valley with temptation all around me. I recalled a story about Job, a man who had been blessed by God. An accuser, who was a liar and a thief, told God that the reason Job loved Him so much was due to the blessings that God had bestowed upon him. Since I was young, until I reached the age of forty seven, I too had been relatively lucky in life, on a professional and financial level. In the story of Job, God allowed the accuser to do whatever he liked to Job, except kill him. The accuser began to take away Job's worldly possessions, but despite Job losing his wealth, his faith never faltered and he remained devoted. I felt my life in that dusty dry place mirrored the story of Job. When the accuser began taking my possessions, I grasped onto my faith tighter. I was determined to overcome the hold that temptation had on my life. The harder I held onto my faith, the more the accuser took…until there was nothing left to take. *What does it profit a man to gain the world, but lose his soul?* Just like Job, I held onto my faith and I too would survive my accuser's challenges and fucked up financial games.

In 2009, America had elected its first African-American President, Barack Obama. For the next several years of his presidency, the faltering automobile industry, the bailout of the financial institutions, the introduction of Obama

Care, and the ongoing conflict in the Middle East between Egypt, Israel, Palestine, Iraq, and Iran dominated the airwaves. The national TV networks were also reporting on the natural disasters that seemed to be overwhelming the world. The ongoing doom and gloom in the news added much confusion to my already stressful environment. I felt like my world, and the world as a whole, were on the verge of collapse. I wondered if the Armageddon referenced in the book of Revelations had anything to do with the failing economies and the natural disasters taking place around the globe.

When I arrived in Palm Springs in 2007, California was dealing with an astronomical number of wildfires, which burned nearly a million acres. There were nine thousand separate fires and over three thousand structures burnt. The following year, the state had fewer wildfires, but the fires consumed nearly four hundred thousand more acres of land than the previous year. These 2008 wildfires were the most devastating for the state since the turn of the twenty first century. The next year, in 2009, the Storm Prediction Center counted 1,282 tornados that touched down in America, the seventh most active year since they began keeping records in 1950. All but four of the lower forty-eight states experienced tornados that year.

In 2010, numerous earthquakes shook the world and I felt several small quakes while living in the Whitewater house. One of the quakes caused the pool on my property to splash water out onto the deck. It was unnerving to feel the ground shaking underneath my feet while being able to see how the shaking of the ground caused the water in the pool to splash out. There was an earthquake in Baja California in Mexico that measured 7.2 on the Richter scale. The shaking of the earth was felt in Los Angeles and as far as Las Vegas, Nevada. That same year, Haiti had an earthquake with a magnitude of 7.0, with over fifty aftershocks, that killed hundreds of thousands of people. The extreme nature of the natural disasters around the world together with the financial crisis in America added to my emotional unrest.

On April 13, 2010 while discussing my newly found faith with a longtime friend on the telephone, she stated that she didn't believe in the concept of a God who had a son named Jesus. She told me her faith was more in line with the spiritual beliefs of Buddhism and those of the 14th Dalai Lama, the Tibetan spiritual leader. By coincidence, on February 21 of that year, the Dalai Lama had visited the United States and met President Obama at the White House. His trip was reported by the media so I had a better understanding of who the Dalai Lama was than I did before his visit. The day after having the conversation with my friend, a 7.1 earthquake struck Tibet killing 2,698 people and injuring over 12,000. When I learned about the earthquake in Tibet, one day after debating Christianity versus Buddhism, I freaked out...and became frightened and unnerved. The timing of the earthquake in Tibet – and our debate about the Dali Lama and Jesus and their roles as supreme spiritual leaders – was too coincidental for my comfort.

On April 14, 2010, a volcano erupted in Iceland that closed the airspace over Europe for five days, affecting air travel in twenty countries. A week later, on April 20, an explosion that killed eleven people sank an oil rig in the Gulf of Mexico. Within days after the explosion, underwater cameras revealed a leak in a pipeline that was spilling oil and gas on the ocean floor forty-two miles off the coast of Louisiana. By the time the well was capped, eighty-seven days later, 3.9 million barrels of oil had leaked into the waters of the gulf. The amount of oil that spilled into the ocean and the number of days it took to get the situation under control took way too long, in my eyes, as if the American government didn't take the severity of the leaking pipeline very seriously. Just like the movie *2012*, I wondered if the world that I knew since I was a little boy was coming to an end.

During the years I lived in Palm Springs, there was ongoing debate in the scientific community over the threat of a changing climate. In 2009, the United Nations Climate Change Conference was held in Copenhagen, Denmark from December 7 through the 18. Puckles was very ill that December and I spent a lot of my time on the sofa caring for him while trying to keep him comfortable. Over 190 countries took part in the conference. The representatives for those countries decided to postpone dealing with the most challenging issues that would address climate change to a future date. Lying on the sofa with Puckles, I got the impression that the leaders of the world weren't too concerned about the health and welfare of the environment. Their lack of urgency to such a complicated problem left me with more unanswered questions about the real issues facing the world than the conference seemed to answer. It certainly appeared that the earth was in turmoil and dying on some level. Were the natural disasters taking place around the world simply Mother Nature telling us that the earth was in desperate need of attention? Did my vision warn of the changing conditions of the earth's atmosphere and show what would happen if we didn't take the issue of climate change seriously? I pondered these questions for several more years before I received some clarity on what I believe God wanted me to know when He sent me the vision of the three moons that I saw as the embodiment of three worlds.

The first week that Philven and I started ILD, I purchased an Apple version of QuickBooks so we could manage the financial aspects of our business. While in high school, I had thought about attending college to study finance so I could become a certified public accountant. Even with my interest in accounting, I had no desire to learn the QuickBooks application. My plate was full worrying how I was going to fund a new business. Philven and I agreed that he would handle the books, since he supposedly had a financial degree, while I would be responsible for developing new business to jumpstart the company. The accounting software was imperative to running our business effectively. I charged the five hundred dollars for the software on my credit card. It was an expensive purchase as money was extremely tight. Philven dedicated himself to reading the application manual to effectively use the tool. I was very impressed that he took the time every night before going to bed to thoroughly read the manual. While I on the other hand, was freaking out over what lay before us.

When I was working for Equity, I repaired my damaged relationship with the Italian-based manufacturing company where I worked when I lived in New York. Emily, my former assistant, was in the same position that I had held. The fact that we had remained friends was one of the main reasons why I wanted to repair the estranged relationship, among others. On behalf of Equity, I bought a large fixture program from the Italian organization for several lobby projects that I installed in various buildings. Being a customer and spending a large sum of money with them made it much easier to mend the relationship that I had previously screwed up. Due to my ongoing friendship with Emily, I continued to work with the Italians even after I left Equity. She continued to send me installation projects on which to bid for her clients and, thanks to her, I was able to build a strong business relationship that was mutually beneficial for her company and for Madame President's organization.

One day, a project manager from Emily's company contacted me from their corporate headquarters in Italy to inquire if I would be interested in bidding on the installation services for a national retail rollout in North America. A large international client, who sold sunglasses, awarded the Italians a global fixture contract. The Italians needed to secure a company that could install their client's fixtures around the world. As head of business development, I bid on the project and won the installation for Madame President's company. As the program was being installed, Philven and I met the operations manager for the sunglass company who was visiting the U.S. We were on location overseeing the installation of the program and the operations manager, who was also Italian, was able to experience firsthand how we managed their sunglass fixture setup—and he was very impressed with the attention we paid to the little details when installing the fixtures. After Madame President fired me, the same operations manager reached out to ILD to see if Philven and I were interested in working with their company on upcoming projects. Philven and the operations manager seemed to get along very well and, giving credit where it's due, Philven was instrumental in securing their business for our company. They were both European and this may have played a factor.

ILD was launched in February 2008 and by the end of that year, we had booked over a half a million dollars in business, with two international clients added to our list of other U.S.-based customers. Not bad for two fucked up crack heads that didn't know their ass from a hole in the ground. Despite this success, 2008 was a challenging year, although in September of that same year

I had finally refinanced the house, which brought me much relief, even if it wasn't at the best interest rate.

One morning, in December of that year, I stood in the living room of the completed house and looked through the sliding glass doors at the beautiful landscaping. I quietly thought to myself that it was nothing short of a miracle that I had been able to maneuver through the financial obstacles that faced me that year. I felt like I had accomplished something that seemed impossible when the logistics company fired me in January of that same year. During the most challenging financial time since the Great Depression, I started a new business from scratch, while juggling the finances to complete a two hundred thousand dollar remodel with very little capital. Even though I was one fucked up individual who had no idea how to establish and manage a business, I was able to succeed despite my shortcomings. I still had the pending lawsuit from Madame President hanging over my head and more obstacles to overcome, but I was thankful to have completed the remodel and be able to stand where I stood at that moment to recognize the holiday miracle that was bestowed onto me. By that Christmas, I had completed what I came to Palm Springs to accomplish—to buy and remodel the house on Whitewater Club Drive. I must have had some divine presence guiding me, otherwise there's no way I could have overcome the setbacks I faced. The fact that I could remodel the house while starting a new company without a construction or business loan was proof of this divine intervention and evidence of yet another miracle in my life. Nobody could take that accomplishment or that miracle away from me no matter how hard anyone tried and no matter what would transpire in the coming year. Heaven had made it possible for me to survive another year so I could continue to fight the good fight.

In a tough year, Christmas 2008 would be our first and the best holiday season that we celebrated in the Whitewater house. Aston and Bentley were just over a year old and Puckles was eleven. The week before Christmas, we bought a twelve-foot tree and stayed up all-night decorating it. The holiday celebration took my mind off my financial problems even if for a brief moment. I was thankful, but also hopeful that I could overcome the hardships that lay ahead. A Merry Christmas it was although the New Year wouldn't bring much happiness at all. Bah humbug.

I'm not a person that knows much about sports or the names of their respective teams. Sometime toward the end of 2008, out of the blue, I began to sing *When the Saints Go Marching In* while I was showering and continued to do so for some time. I'm not sure why I decided to start singing this song. Perhaps it had something to do with me trying to keep my spirits up during a difficult time. I never sang in the shower or anyplace else before that moment. Imagine my surprise when I heard in February of 2009 that the New Orleans Saints won the Super Bowl. I was shocked. Several months after I began singing that song, a professional football team – the New Orleans Saints – won the Super Bowl. I had no idea there was even a professional team called by that name until I heard on the news that they won their league championship.

The New Orleans Saints won a franchise record of thirteen games to qualify to play in the Super Bowl. Thirteen is the number of God. During the season, they also lost three games, out of the sixteen games they played, and three is the number of the Holy Trinity. This is a perfect example of what most people would call a coincidence. My singing in the shower, when I had never sung in the shower before, could also be referred to as yet another coincidence. I believe, on the other hand, that these two situations illustrate a pattern that there was more taking place in my life than what I could easily see. I think God was conveying a message, encouraging me, and letting me know that I too was on a winning team…His. Even though it may have looked like I was losing, I was going to be victorious in the end just like the New Orleans Saints. I find it fascinating that God can and will use just about any circumstance to be heard. Was I listening?

From 2007 to 2010, Philven and I had three-ways with random guys. I rationalized that if we had sex with other men together, there would be no need for Philven to cheat and tell me lies to cover it up. Much like Alex, Philven's lies to cover up his unfaithfulness had a more profound effect on me than the actual cheating. His deceitful behavior was part of the reason why I was never comfortable during our sexual escapades. The deception created an underlining layer, which always left me feeling unnerved in that type of sexual environment. I was doing a lot of Tina, which numbed my feelings and kept me from dealing with him and his fucked up lies. To add insult to injury, I had settled in a place where the gay subculture bred unethical behavior in many of the gay men that participate in PNP activities. I was lost in every sense of the word. I was the cracked-out and messed up sacrificial lamb, in the midst of jackals, in a cracked-out den of iniquity.

Even though I was lost and a total mess drowning in stress, while trying to keep myself financially afloat, I tried to maintain a sense of integrity in my personal and professional behavior. I was over the edge in partying and I own up and take responsibility for my inappropriate behavior. I had many aspects of my character that I needed to improve upon, although I was not misrepresenting myself or deceiving anyone to amuse myself or to impress anyone else. Philven, on the other hand, had an agenda of his own and it didn't include the well-being of our family. When we met, I gave him the benefit of the doubt. I didn't judge him for the means by which he chose to support himself or let his escorting influence my decision on the type of person he was before I got to know more about him. Even after everything I had endured at the hands of Alex, I thought Philven could have been a good person. I believed, and I still stand by my belief today, that a person's current circumstance doesn't define them as a human being or determine who they will ultimately become.

I struggled to make sense of the strange events that seemed to haunt me. One day, while Philven and I were working in our office, I heard a faint noise that sounded like a phone ringing, although it was not our home, business, or mobile phones. The sound, however, seemed to be coming from inside the office. I heard the faint ringing noise more than once and I asked Philven if he heard or knew anything about the sound. He replied that he did not. Up to the time I met Philven, I hooked up with other men that I met online via two sites: gay.com and manhunt.com. I had not familiarized myself with other sex sites on the internet and I was not interested in finding more sites, two seemed to be sufficient to get the job done.

Before we arrived in Palm Springs, there were many red flags that were apparent in my relationship with Philven. I was messed up from my time with Alex so I chose to ignore those red flags. I ended up lying to myself as to what was taking place in my relationship. After we arrived in the desert, there were too many red flags to ignore. My mind began to work overtime to process the many unusual situations that didn't add up or make any sense, like the faint ringing of a telephone seemingly coming out of nowhere. When I confronted Philven about a specific situation, like the ringing phone, he always lied to cover-up the situation or he just simply played stupid. I refused to play detective, as I had done in my relationship with Alex. I was not going to spend any more time turning over rocks to see what I could uncover. The only way I knew how to get myself through the fucked-up situation – that I got myself into when I decided to try to build a relationship, a home, a business, and a future with the devil – was to numb myself like I had done during my time with Alex. Our behaviors in life are learned even as adults and I learned to survive Alex by numbing myself with illegal substances. Before hitting myself in the head with one of those rocks that I refused to look under, I instead reached for my good friend Tina. She transformed those large rocks into teeny tiny little pebbles that I could not have cared any less about or what was hiding underneath them.

Several months after I heard the faint noise of a phone ringing while working in the office, I decided to drop my membership with gay.com to save money and came across a gay hookup site called Adam4Adam. I signed up for the free service and created a profile. If another site user liked my profile, they could send me a message. Upon receiving that message, Adam4Adam would send me a notification. If I happened to be logged into the site, Adam4Adam notified me that I had an incoming email—highlighted by the sound of a ringing phone. When I logged into the site, if I had messages sitting in my inbox, I would be notified that I had unread messages, also accompanied by the sound of a ringing phone.

I finally solved the mystery. Once I signed up for Adam4Adam, I informed Philven that I had done so, which is more than I can say for him. Philven had joined Adam4Adam without letting me know and was hooking up with other guys while he was supposed to be working. His workspace faced mine, so I was not able to see what he was working on during the day. If I got up from my desk and walked to face his workstation, he had time to close any internet sites that he may have had open and that he didn't want me to see.

Philven's poor work ethic soon caught up with him and revealed that he was not worthy of owning fifty percent of our company. In March of 2009, the taxes on the business needed to be filed. Philven didn't have the books up to date, so ILD had to file an extension. Since the company was an LLC, a limited liability company, we needed the business taxes to be completed before we could file our personal taxes. I always filed my taxes in April as required by the state and federal governments, but due to Philven not getting his work done, I too had to file for an extension for my personal taxes, which is something that I never had to do prior to going into business with him. I informed Philven that I was not going to continue to look for new business until he got the books up to date. Philven was so far behind on his accounting duties that the client billings for completed projects were not being invoiced in a timely manner. I reluctantly let Philven hire a local bookkeeping company to help him update the company financials and customer billings. I was determined not to get involved in cleaning up his mess. I had done my job by financing the business and establishing a customer base that could support the business and household. Since Philven had made himself a fifty percent partner in the company when it was established, I figured the least that I could expect of him was for him to do his job and to do it well.

I had thought it a good idea to let Philven manage the bookkeeping company, since I was managing our project manager, subcontractors, and customer projects. Once again, I gave him the benefit of the doubt and thought he would step up to the plate and get the financials completed with outside assistance. A few weeks later, I observed Philven and a representative from the bookkeeping company take copies of previously billed client invoices out of the office. I asked what they were doing with the invoices that had been sent to clients for payment and for which we had already received payment in many cases. The bookkeeper responded that Philven's version of QuickBooks was corrupt and it wouldn't populate in the new online version of QuickBooks that the bookkeeping company used. The idiots were recreating the company's financials from copies of previously sent invoices. I freaked. I'm sure an outsider would have thought that Philven and the bookkeeping company were, at the very least, doing something shady. I felt the margin for error was huge. There was also the additional expense from manually entering all the financial data into the online version of QuickBooks. It just so happened that a few weeks earlier, I had the foresight to download a copy of ILD's financials from Philven's desktop version of QuickBooks to my laptop. I was able to give my backup of our records to the bookkeeping company so they could populate the information into the online version. I no longer trusted Philven and I wanted the books to be kept online so I could access the financials at any time.

Between the remodel and the refinancing of the house, combined with trying to establish and jumpstart a new business, eight months passed before I found time to review the books. I assumed Philven was doing his job while I was doing mine, which proved to be a big mistake on my part. There was a lesson to be learned from this ordeal and that was to never let anyone have complete control over my finances. I see now that this very difficult and painful lesson was not without purpose. I believe God planned to leverage this painful, but effective lesson to his advantage. Sometimes the most important lessons we learn in life can and are the most excruciating to experience.

Philven and I worked on Apple laptop computers that I bought for us when we worked with Madame President's company. I purchased the computers with money that I saved prior to meeting Philven and prior to working for the logistics company. After Madame President fired me, Philven and I used the same laptops to run our business. We backed up and stored the company's information on an Apple server that we purchased once we established the company and moved into the Whitewater house. I was a novice when it came to the technical aspects of running our business, although I was learning fast. Unfortunately for ILD, and my peace of mind, I didn't learn what I needed to know fast enough. I felt like the devices that we used were representative of the tree of good and evil in the Garden of Eden. I was using the Apple products for the greater good of running our business, while Philven, like Eve, fell to temptation. He exploited his Apple devices for his own pleasure. He used his computer to look for dick on sites like Adam4Adam when he was supposed to be working. He had an iPhone that I also bought for him and he was using it to contact his tricks when he was out of the office and out of my sight. He ended up using the Apple sever, which we kept in the ILD office, to access and monitor the information on my computer without me knowing it. By monitoring my email, he could ensure that I was not aware of his lies and his cheating. He was also spying on me to see if I was cheating on him or lying about anything, which is hysterical since he was the one that needed monitoring. I've come to understand that a liar and a cheater believes that everyone is a liar and a cheater, hence the reason why he felt it necessary to check up on me.

Several months after hiring the bookkeeping service, and after paying them thousands of dollars to get the financials in order, the books were still not finished. Philven and I fought constantly about his failure to get those fucking books completed so we could file our taxes. At first, I refused to involve myself in this part of the business to straighten out the mess that he created. Since Philven couldn't manage himself, let alone a company hired to help him to update the finances, the relationship with the bookkeepers became estranged and I was eventually forced to fire them. After I let them go, Philven and I were sued over a dispute with the final invoice from the service. I'd never been sued in my entire life and now I had three pending lawsuits, two against me and one against ILD. Fucking Philven was slowly killing me as each day passed. There seemed no end to the madness; it was one fucked up situation after another. I told him on many occasions that his behavior was not only going to cause the business to fail, it was also going to destroy any hope of us continuing our personal relationship. Why the fuck was I in business with this guy, let alone a relationship? I asked myself that question many times. Legally, on the business side, there was little I could do at this point in the game. Philven was a fifty percent owner and he was not going to relinquish that ownership as long as the business was earning income. The only way out of the situation that I got myself into was to try to get Philven to complete the fucking books and do his job. I needed to find a way to hang on as long as I could and hope that God would save me from Philven's fucked up behavior—and my continuous lack of good judgment when it came to choosing a boyfriend who should have been my equal.

When I refinanced my home in early September of 2008, I secured a five hundred thousand dollar loan on an appraised value of six hundred and eighty five thousand dollars for the Whitewater house. If the housing market had not been in a slump, the house probably would've appraised close to eight hundred thousand dollars. When I refinanced it, the financial institutions were only granting FHA loans. Before the global financial disaster of 2007 - 2008, most of the FHA loans that were being processed were for customers who put less than a twenty percent down payment or for individuals who had a poor credit ratings. Since I was refinancing with an FHA loan, I had to pay the monthly mortgage insurance fee, which added one hundred and sixty dollars to the monthly loan payment. In every situation, no matter what I tried, it always turned out to cost me more money than I expected. The fact that I could only borrow between seventy or seventy-five percent of the value of the home left me carrying a considerable amount of credit card debt from the remodel. Being self-employed and having a few large clients that insisted on sixty-day terms for remitting payment, I couldn't always pay myself in a timely manner. On several occasions, my credit card payments were late. Due to the late payments, my creditors fucked me once again. The sharks at the credit card companies used the opportunity to increase my monthly interest rate to a whopping twenty nine percent on all my cards where I had an outstanding balance. It felt like I couldn't catch a break. My life was truly in the shitter. I was in desperate need of an enema to clear out all the shitty people and crappy behavior from my life once and for all. Unbeknownst to me, heaven would dispatch medical assistance. However, it would be two very long years, from April 2009 to April 2011, before an enema could be administered that freed me from the bowels of hell where I had immersed myself. Before I could get any relief, I would endure unbearable circumstances and had to exhaust all options while learning my life lessons in the hopes of surviving my fucked-up existence.

In the movie *Schindler's List,* there's a little boy that survives the Auschwitz concentration camp during World War II by hiding in the excrement below the outhouses where the prisoners go to the bathroom. It's a chilling, but empowering story that shows this lovely little boy that survives against all odds by immersing himself in the feces of the concentration camp. I distinctly remember the scene when the boy, who I thought died earlier in the movie, emerged from the place where he had been concealing himself from the German guards. He had been hiding right underneath the noses of the Nazis, where he knew they would never think of looking for him, in human filth. I too felt like a little boy who was living in the shitter. I had attached myself to a person who was notorious for his vile conduct. Like the little boy in the movie, I too was hiding, although I was hiding from myself and from God.

If we truly must humble ourselves like children to enter into the kingdom of heaven, then I was certainly screwed. My innocence and inner boyish-self had ceased to exist. If my childlike manner had not departed from me, then it was definitely hiding so deeply within me that I thought it was non-existent. The amount of lies that I endured at the hands of Alex, and now Philven, left me feeling used on many levels. Each fucked up lie that I had to sort through slowly killed any boyish traits that once resided within me. Due to my poor choices, I had become a hostile and defensive warrior to survive. God would eventually resurrect the carefree child within me that I thought was once dead. In the years to come, God began to entice the spirit of that innocent little boy who he knew many decades earlier, who called Him BoBo, to come out of hiding. What I believed was gone and never coming back, only God could see was hiding in plain sight. I had covered myself in shame from my bad behavior and poor choices. My inner-child was covered in the vile filth where I had immersed myself. God encouraged me to rise up from that cesspool where I resided. He and I would begin the long drawn out process to clean me up—so when I looked in the mirror I would be proud of who was looking back at me and so would He. Mirror, mirror on the wall who is the man in the mirror?

The company's financials were in a mess. No matter how many times I asked, I couldn't get an accurate report from Philven on the income coming into the business or its' expenses. Although I could never actually prove my theory, I believe Philven was stealing from ILD. This would explain why he never got the books in order. With a messed-up accounting system, it was easy for him to hide his theft. If the books were up to date, it would be very simple to determine if he was stealing money from the company, as I believed he was.

In the midst of the craziness created by trying to get Philven to get the books in order, I had to secure a law firm in California to handle the lawsuits pending against ILD and the both of us. The twin brothers who served as legal counsel for ILD, and who were initially handling the negotiations between Madame President's attorneys and me, were based in Chicago. They believed it would be in our best interest if we secured a law firm on the west coast to handle the litigation on the pending suits. I ended up retaining a firm based in Riverside, California, recommended by them. The California firm requested a fifty thousand dollar retainer from ILD to be deposited into an account that they would draw their fees against. After much negotiation, the firm settled on a thirty thousand dollar retainer. By the grace of God, ILD had the funds in the bank and we issued the check. Could the financial pressures get any worse? Just when I thought I couldn't handle one more person putting their hand in my pocket, it felt like I was buying a new and more expense pair of pants that had more pockets for more people to take more money from me that I didn't have to give.

The new California attorneys indicated that it would cost the company fifty thousand dollars to the point of deposing Madame President. If the case went to trial, it could cost as much as an additional hundred thousand dollars in legal fees. What the fuck? I wasn't living a nightmare existence any longer, I was the main character in a fucking horror film where I was being stalked by a blood thirsty and crazed bitch of a President. As much as Tina worked against me in so many situations, she did allow me to fantasize about becoming a ninja warrior who kicked the financial ass of Madame President and her Lesbian sidekick. I was definitely in hell and needed to find the resources to fight my way out of purgatory. "It usually gets worse before it gets better," goes the common expression—and I would soon experience this firsthand. I needed to learn the skill of knowing when to fight and the wisdom to know when it was time to walk away.

Philven and I were still indulging in messed up, drug-induced sexual activities that seemed to be prevalent in Palm Springs and the surrounding desert cities. For Philven it was more of an indulgence, for it was an environment where he felt like he was a big man. His large dick did get him a lot of attention, even if he acted like an asshole. In my case, I'm not sure why I was partaking in this type of behavior, but for whatever reasons there I was in the midst of cracked-out jackals in a den of sexual insanity. My behavior was not representative of what I wanted people to know about me nor was it the life that I wanted for myself.

Only God could've known I needed to germinate in a dark place before I could shed my shell of despair and begin to discover my life purpose. I now believe He deliberately planted me in that desert like a seed so I could at last be free from my insecurities and feelings of unworthiness. My miserable environment forced me to dig deep within me in the hope of finding the desire that once drove me to see beyond myself and visualize the possibilities of a future. I needed to convince myself that I was somehow going to fix an unfixable situation. Is the desert, where very little survives, unless it can overcome very difficult conditions, the place where God chose for me to spiritually blossom and begin to see hope for a better life? Before I could have any hope of achieving that life and seeing it come to fruition, I would be brought low and be required to humble myself before those who I would've preferred to see buried six feet below the ground.

Madame President fired me in the middle of January 2008 and her company paid for my extended healthcare coverage for six months, after my attorneys got involved. Up to that point, I had been very fortunate when it came to healthcare. Ever since I graduated high school, I was lucky to be employed with companies that offered medical insurance. For the first time since I was diagnosed positive, I was extremely concerned about how I was going to pay for my medications and medical care. Since there were a large number of HIV individuals that lived in the desert cities, there was a nonprofit medical facility that specialized in treating low-income HIV and AIDS patients in Palm Springs. Through this organization, conveniently located less than a mile from the Whitewater house, I eventually enrolled in the Ryan White program. The foundation gave me the opportunity to have medical care and continue taking my HIV medications once Madame President cancelled my health coverage, when I was not in a position to afford a private health insurance policy. Even if I had the funds to cover such a policy, it still would have been impossible for me to secure an insurance provider that would have insured me. If it had not been for the Ryan White foundation, I probably wouldn't be alive today. I believe without a doubt that Ryan White is one of God's archangels in heaven. His foundation has personally impacted and saved many lives, including mine. If it had not been for the devotion of his family to remember and honor him with this legacy, I shudder to think of what would've become of the individuals with HIV or AIDS that couldn't afford or were not able to secure healthcare. What becomes a legend most? An archangel named Ryan White!

Shortly after I was accepted into the Ryan White program, the Affordable Health Care Act was introduced in Congress. It was several more years before the Obama administration convinced Congress to pass the bill that is known today as Obamacare. I always found the timing of the introduction of this act to be an odd coincidence. During the first time in my life that I lost my medical insurance, the U.S. government began to reform the healthcare system. The news networks were constantly reporting on the pros and cons of the Affordable Health Care Act, and Obama was very prominently featured on the news on a regular basis. It seemed that whenever I turned on the television, President Obama was front and center.

I seldom left the Whitewater house between March and May of 2009. I was consumed with managing the company's project manager and its customer's projects and dealing with the pending lawsuits. The television became my connection to the outside world. Since Philven was the COO, he was responsible for taking the payment checks that we received in the mail from our clients to the bank for depositing. Philven also conveniently took on the responsibility of going to the grocery store to shop for our groceries. He regularly used the Jaguar that I bought when we lived in Chicago to run errands. At one point, I thought I had isolated myself behind that five-foot cylinder block fence that surrounded the property—imprisoned by my own accord. I had no interest in leaving the house and so I didn't. My lack of interest in knowing what was transpiring on the other side of that cinderblock fence allowed Philven the chance to schedule his rendezvous with his tricks when taking care of our errands. It was ironic that he was out and about, acting like a big man in a small town and turning tricks in a very expensive car that I purchased for myself. The toughest part for me to swallow about him being the whore of the neighborhood was the fact that he was disrespecting me after I gave him the opportunity to become a fifty percent owner in a business that I built with my connections and the privilege to live in a beautifully remodeled house, which I bought with a down payment from the proceeds from my Chicago condominium. It certainly was a good gig for Philven, although not so much for me.

When Philven went to take care of our errands, and when he was gone for an unusual amount of time, I would challenge him on his whereabouts. By me confronting him, the situation always escalated into a huge confrontation. His arrogance was just another means by which he would try to deflect his cheating behavior. When the hooker went to the grocery store, he was always gone from an hour and a half to several hours even though the grocery store was a five-minute drive from where we lived. On the rare occasion when I did the grocery shopping, I could drive to the store, shop, and drive back to the house in forty-five minutes or less. I was not stupid as to what was taking place when he was out of my sight, but I was not going to babysit him when he left the house to ensure he wasn't cheating. I figured that if he continued to get his rocks off when running errands, his actions would ultimately catch up with him. I eventually found out the crazy hooker had many elaborate means for getting off. Using the bank or grocery store as his excuse to get out of the house and away from me, so he could cheat, was only one of the means that he used.

One evening, when Philven and I were working late in the office, I noticed him get up from his desk and walk through the house. I could see him out of the corner of my eye through the sliding glass door next to my desk. The front entrance into the house also had a glass door. I saw him open the door and walk outside. He walked right passed where I was sitting and toward the carport, which was adjacent to the office. There were no windows on the side of the office that faced the carport so I could not see him from where I was sitting. It was late and pitch-black outside. If you've ever been in the desert at night, then you know what I'm talking about when I say you can't see two feet in front of you without a light of some kind. I opened one of the sliding glass doors in the office and quickly walked around the corner of the house where I thought Philven had gone. I couldn't see him because the lights in the carport were not on. He, on the other hand, must have seen me come around the corner. The illumination from the streetlight in front of the house gave me away. He yelled for me to run back in the house and turn on the lights on that side of the house because there was someone in the yard. Like a stupid asshole, I immediately turned around without thinking he was up to no good and headed back into the house to switch on the carport lights when I heard a loud sound. After I turned on the lights and went back outside, Philven was standing in the carport alone. After inspecting the surrounding area, I noticed that the temporary sprinkler panel that the gardener mounted to a four-foot pole and stuck in the ground had been broken at the base and was now lying on the grass. The sound that I heard earlier when I was heading back into the house to turn on the lights was due to someone running into that sprinkler panel. Whoever was in the carport with Philven took off in a hurry and ran smack into the sprinkler panel that was sticking out of the ground.

I knew exactly what had taken place as soon as I saw the wood pole lying on the grass. Philven must have connected with someone on Adam4Adam when we were working late in the office. The Adam4Adam guy came over to the house. When he arrived, he climbed over the five-foot cinderblock fence in the back. Philven went outside to meet up with Mr. Adam4Adam and was getting a blowjob in the carport. I had to take a minute and laugh to myself. How fucked up was Philven and how fucked up was the gay culture in Palm Springs? What kind of person goes to someone's house when they know that person has a boyfriend and covertly gives a blowjob to the person that they're meeting in a carport in the darkness of night? Welcome to my world. I couldn't escape Philven's despicable behavior no matter how hard I tried. Now it seemed he was able to order blowjobs online and have them delivered to my carport. Whatever next? Like I said, a big dick will get you noticed especially in a small desert town with cracked-out jackals roaming the streets at night, who are willing to jump a five-foot fence to suck off a well-hung hooker at no charge. I had no proof of my suspicions of what had taken place in the carport, but I didn't need proof. It was as black as the dark of night. When I confronted Philven, he of course denied any wrongdoing and began to get hostile to deflect his fucked-up actions onto me for accusing him of inappropriate behavior. The plot thickened.

On my forty-ninth birthday (4+9=**13**), Philven bought four tickets to see Cher in concert in Las Vegas at the Coliseum in Caesar's Palace for Sunday, May 3, 2009, one day before my actual birthday. Since I'm a big fan of Ms. Cher, Philven thought it would be a good idea for us to drive to Las Vegas with Puckles, Aston, and Bentley and stay at Trump's hotel for my birthday weekend. The highlight of the trip would be Cher's concert. We had stayed at Trump's hotel on one of our previous trips to Vegas and enjoyed the accommodations. The hotel also allowed pets, which was perfect since we were bringing the boys with us. Philven invited the realtor that sold me the Whitewater home and her boyfriend to join us for the concert. When Philven originally purchased the concert tickets, it was no sweat off his ass since he paid for the two hundred and fifty dollar a seat tickets with my credit card. As it turned out, my realtor and her boyfriend couldn't attend the concert. Instead, I had two friends, and I use that term loosely, who lived in Texas and would be in Las Vegas the same weekend as Cher's concert. Rather than letting the tickets go to waste, I extended the invitation to this gay couple from Dallas to join us.

I was looking forward to our weekend in Las Vegas and I was especially excited about seeing Cher. As our trip got closer, Philven decided that we shouldn't travel to Vegas. For some unknown and strange reason, he seemed very distant in the days leading up to our trip. I, on the other hand, wasn't letting my birthday gift go to waste. I was not going to let the hooker throw away a thousand dollars of my hard-earned money. I was driving to Vegas to see my lady perform with or without him. Looking back, Philven was probably trying to keep me from going because I had been looking forward to the trip for weeks. His behavior was always very calculated. He may have seemed as if he was acting strange and distant, but that was part of his act. In actuality, he was as methodical in his actions as a mathematician trying to solve a complicated mathematical problem.

In addition to being the company's COO, Philven was also the CFO and handled the finances. When he informed me that he purchased concert tickets, I didn't think to ask if we could afford to go the concert let alone reserve a hotel in Vegas for the weekend. I assumed he knew if we had enough money for such a luxurious birthday celebration, which was another mistake on my part. He probably didn't give a shit either way since the hotel expenses and the tickets were charged to my credit card. He had screwed up his credit before we met and he conveniently didn't have any charge cards to pay for my birthday gift.

Philven was responsible for cutting all the checks for ILD's vendors, payroll, taxes, and other miscellaneous items that required payment from the business. He was also responsible for paying our household utilities in a timely manner from the house account. I took care of making sure the mortgage, Jaguar, and the credit card payments were paid on time. I was constantly fighting with him to get an accurate cash flow report from the business so we could plan our separate payments and operate our business effectively. I'm not entirely sure why Philven never got his act together and got a handle on the financials for ILD. He was obviously capable of doing so, but for whatever reasons he never did. I believe a part of his motive for not having the books current was about control. I think he felt like he had the power, as long as he kept me in the dark. It got so bad that I had a cheat sheet where I manually wrote down the amounts of the checks that I knew were coming into the business from clients and the expenses against that income. My cheat sheet was not an effective means to operate a business, but at least I was trying to keep some type of a record to account for the business' cash flow, which is more than I can say for the high rolling hooker.

Philven was not helpful in getting us ready for our weekend trip to Las Vegas. I handled all the preparations for our travel. When the weekend of our trip arrived, I loaded the luggage in the trunk of the Jaguar and put the boys and their dog beds in the backseat. We were finally on our way, headed to the Mojave Desert to see the Goddess of Pop perform. Philven was extremely quiet the entire trip, which was not a bad thing. Once we arrived at our hotel in sin city, we had about an hour before the concert started. I barely had enough time to get checked into our room, walk the boys, get dressed and travel to Caesar's Palace. Upon arriving at the theater, we met the other gay couple who were joining us for the evening. After a quick cocktail together, we took our seats. Once we were seated in the auditorium, I felt like something was not quite right, although I was not sure why I felt that way. There were various digital pictures of Cher being displayed in numerous areas of the theater from various points in her career. I commented to the other couple that some of the pictures didn't look like Cher. A few minutes after making my comment, Cher entered the auditorium and the concert began.

Once Cher was onstage, I was not able to see her face clearly. It was as if something was keeping me from seeing her up close and personal. I had no problem seeing her silhouette and her costumes, although her face was somewhat distorted. It was as if I was looking through a lens that had a filter over her head causing that part of her body to be out of focus. We were seated on the main floor and close enough to the stage that I should have been able to see her without any issues. Prior to entering the theater, and upon existing the venue, I wasn't experiencing any problems with my vision. Why would her body and costumes and the props onstage be as clear as day, but her face be out of focus? This didn't make any sense to me. While sitting inside the modern-day coliseum contemplating what could be wrong with my vision, I reflected on the time in history when Christian martyrs were killed in the Coliseum in Rome. I now found myself in a modern-day Coliseum, at a place called Caesar's Palace, with my budding faith and the woman that I believed God used to send a message to me at a time in my life when He knew I was not listening for His voice. I wondered if there was something supernatural in the Coliseum that was preventing me from getting a close up look at His messenger, my lady and the world's Goddess of Pop.

I've come to understand that sometimes God will send a vision, but, for whatever reason, I'm not be able to comprehend the meaning of it at the time. It took me almost three years before I understood one of the visions that I encountered in Palm Springs and what it was that He wanted to convey. Perhaps the explanation for the situation involving Cher in Las Vegas is yet to be realized. Possibly, this circumstance was a sign that I needed to begin my walk with God by faith and not by sight. This didn't seem too far fetch of an idea when I considered that He used Cher on other occasions to speak to me. In either case, shortly after leaving the Mojave Desert and returning to Palm Springs, I would be slapped in the face with the reality that I wasn't seeing my circumstances clearly. In building a relationship with the God that I've come to know, I would realize that He very seldom speaks in a point-blank manner when conversing with me. It's as if He wants me to seek out the answer to His riddles. *Seek and you shall find.*

After Cher's concert, I learned that Danny Gans, who was born in Los Angeles and was an entertainer in Las Vegas, suddenly passed away at the age of fifty-two, a few days before I arrived. His first record album contained both Christian and pop genres and was sold in both Christian and mainstream music outlets. Before Danny entered show business, he was a professional baseball player for the White Socks in Chicago. After becoming an entertainer, he spent time working in New York on Broadway. He eventually ended up in Las Vegas as a permanent performer at the Mirage, where the Danny Gans Theater was built. In February 2009, he changed venues and was performing at the Encore when he suddenly died. The news of Danny's unexpected death shocked the entertainment industry.

I'm not sure what Danny's life and death have to do with this story, other than my grandmother, with whom I attended church services, was a big fan of the White Socks. Like Danny, I too was born in Los Angeles county and worked in Chicago and New York. He was a man of faith and I was developing my faith at the time I learned of his passing. Before that night in Las Vegas, I had not heard about Danny or his career. We had a few things in common, but from what I can ascertain, there was nothing out of the ordinary. Although, for whatever reason, I felt like something was drawing me to Danny's life story and his unexpected death.

The following day, Philven and I went to Steve Wynn's new hotel that had opened six months earlier. It was the first opportunity I had to visit this new property since its grand opening. I wasn't a big fan of the Wynn, his other hotel and casino. On the flip side, the Encore was gorgeous on many levels. I absolutely loved the décor and found the venue to be spectacular, definitely a Wynn, Wynn! I walked the entire first floor with Philven and was highly impressed with the visuals and the attention given to the finite details of the design. During our tour of the venue, I came across the theater where Danny had been performing before his untimely death. We ended our tour at one of the entrances into the casino. We were arguing about something, though I don't recall what we were fighting about or who started the argument. The confrontations between us were becoming more frequent and the hostility that we had for one another was escalating. I had finally hit my limit on the amount of shit I was willing to take from him—better late than never.

We sat on a bench outside of the hotel arguing, when I suddenly got up from my seat and said I had some place I had to be. After speaking those words, I began to walk toward our hotel. I had no idea why I said what I said and I wasn't aware of any place where I had to be. Trump's hotel was near where I was standing at the Encore and Philven and I continued to argue, as we walked back to the hotel. Once we arrived at our room, the boys met us at the door. I walked from the entrance of our room to the bathroom. I went in to the bathroom for something, but once I got there I couldn't recall what I needed—so I turned around and walked back into the room. I found Puckles lying on his side next to the bed. He wasn't breathing, which freaked me out. I immediately picked him up, laid him on the bed and began to administer mouth-to-mouth recitation. After breathing several times into his mouth, he began breathing on his own once again. Over the coming months, his health declined. I loved that dog with all my heart and I was nowhere close to mentally accepting his death. I'm not sure what would've become of me, had Puckles unexpectedly died that night in Las Vegas.

If I had not left the Encore hotel when I did, would I have found Puckles dead on the floor when I returned to my room? Did a supernatural presence provoke me to get up from the bench where I was arguing with Philven and prompt me to head back to the hotel? Was Trump's hotel the place where I said I had to be so I could save Puckles' life? While the circumstances that led up to Puckles' collapse were very strange, I'm very thankful for whatever prompted me to hurry back to the room. My presence at the hotel where I was staying was a matter of life or death. My abrupt exit from the Encore possibly also represented a second chance, not only with Puckles, but also for myself. During the drive back to Palm Springs, I contemplated the events that took place over the weekend, which made me realize the importance of being present in the moment. Once I arrived in Palm Springs, the situations surrounding the events that took place in the Mojave Desert on my forty-ninth birthday began to make a little more sense.

Once Philven and I returned to the office, I discovered the company was almost broke. The business didn't have the available funds in its checking account to pay our vendors for invoices that were outstanding or to cover that week's payroll. I was so pissed off at Philven for spending money on the concert tickets and hotel expense for an elaborate birthday celebration when the business was on the verge of financial disaster. I then decided, in early May of 2009, to take over the financials for the company. I discovered that Philven was three months behind in paying the bills for our business cellular phones. He was also three months behind in paying the water, cable, and electrical bill for the house utilities. I don't think our financial situation could've been any bleaker. I knew Philven was behind in getting the financials in order for ILD, but I had no idea the business had such serious cash flow issues. By this point, the company hadn't been operating for more than two years, so trying to secure a short-term business loan from a financial institution was not an option. The economy was still in a serious recession and there were no signs that it was going to improve anytime soon. The value of the house was declining daily and selling the property wasn't an option either. Looking for new employment was not possible since companies were not hiring. Everyone was cutting back on their workforce due to the deepening recession. Just when I thought it couldn't get any worse, it became downright dreadful. I had no other choice but to gamble it all and pray for a mega miracle.

I was able to get the pending lawsuit from the bookkeeping company thrown out of small claims court due to a technicality on how the lawsuit was filed. This was at least one small victory in my favor. I still had the pending lawsuit – against ILD, Philven, and me – from Madame President hanging over my head. In December of 2007, a month before I got fired, I had gone out on a financial limb when I decided to remodel the Whitewater property and believe Madame President thought I wouldn't be in a financial position to fend off a lawsuit on a newly formed business. With the remodel draining my available funds, I believe she thought I would be forced to shut down ILD before it had a chance to become successful. Her miscalculation cost her a tremendous amount of money in legal fees. In the end, Madame President under-estimated my wherewithal and determination. Before it was all over, the lawsuit cost her company nearly one hundred and eighty thousand dollars in legal fees and administrative costs. I had agreed to settle for the nearly forty thousand dollars that she originally offered although she rescinded that offer at the last minute, for reasons that I still do not understand.

I often wonder whether she would be so vengeful if she had to do it all over again. She sent me an email on January 8, 2010 where she wrote "I do know that you never intended any harm and I hate the entire situation and have wanted to write you and have been told by all not to." I'm not sure who she was referencing when she wrote "by all," but I assume she meant her attorneys, the Lesbian vice president and her asshole husband. I believe if Madame President would've taken the opportunity to fly out to Palm Springs, or requested that I fly and meet her somewhere for an in-depth conversation before she made the decision to fire me in January 2008, the two of us could've saved each other a lot of wasted time, energy, and money. I believe our outside influences resulted in a costly mistake for her and me. Besides, for her lawsuit to have validity, wouldn't there have to be intent on my part to harm her company's business?

The problem I have with Madame President's lawsuit is that I believe she ironically did to ILD exactly what she accused us of doing to her company when she fired me. In January of 2009, ILD was asked to submit a bid for a potential large rollout with a national retail client. There were several other companies who were asked to submit bids and Madame President's organization was one of them. This would be the one and only time that her company and ILD bid against each other for the same project. Since I formally held the position as president of business development for her logistics company, I was very familiar with her organization and its pricing structure. Madame President was using her husband's company to secure the labor for her installation projects. I knew for a fact that her husband's organization always bid too high on projects and I was never able to win a project for the logistics company when I used her husband's organization as a subcontractor. Therefore, I was shocked to learn that Madame President's company was the lowest bidder on the submittal—and her company was awarded the project. I often wondered if she accessed my computer or our email account and was able to view our bid prior to submitting her proposal. I was still using the same computer that I had when I worked for her company. I often thought her IT company might have installed a backdoor on my computer for such a moment. She was able to access ILD's emails on a prior occasion and while I'm not sure I can prove my theory of her seeing our bid for this specific project, my gut told me that I was spot on with my assumption.

In the early days of working for Madame President's company, I was very concerned about the security of her company's client information and bids. I worried that if she didn't ensure that the proper security measures were in place to protect sensitive client information, her organization could be vulnerable to a third-party stealing its proprietary data. After speaking with the IT company that Madame President contracted, I discovered that her logistics email accounts were not encrypted so I had the IT service implement the encryption of all company emails. Ever since I started using a personal computer to conduct business development, I had serious concerns about someone stealing my client information and my livelihood by default. My concerns over the possibility of Madame President, or anyone else, being able to pilfer the company's propriety data kept me in a constant state of anxiety. Philven's access of my computer, without my knowledge through the Apple server that we used in the ILD office, exaggerated my feelings that the information was being hacked. I understand my concerns may look like I was being paranoid, but the financial survival of ILD was at stake, due to the pending lawsuit, together with everything that I worked to achieve in my entire lifetime. With my livelihood hanging in the balance, I became extremely suspicious of everything and everyone. I say better to be paranoid and safe than to be carefree and get financially screwed by a vengeful Madame President, a spiteful lesbian vice president, and a lying hooker that also happened to be my partner, my Chief Operating Officer, and my Chief Financial Officer.

19 | A GAME CHANGER

In May of 2009, I needed to secure a short-term loan to keep ILD in business and the Whitewater home from going into foreclosure. I did what any fucked up desperate person would do under the circumstances. I went back to the same gentleman that brokered the refinance on my mortgage and contracted him to find me a short-term loan. Since my credit card companies had reduced my credit lines to almost nothing, I had no choice but to seek unconventional means to survive. The financial institutions were not granting conventional unsecured loans due to the ongoing fallout from the financial collapse. I had to find a private equity firm that would broker a deal. The only type of loan that I was able to secure was a hard money loan, which required me to take out a second mortgage and put the Whitewater home up for collateral on a twenty five thousand dollar loan. I began to seriously ponder whether it was possible to financially recover and be able to save ILD and my house. Had I played my last card or was there a kicker card yet to be revealed that would change the rank of my situation?

I received twenty thousand dollars from the hard money loan. The financial sharks took five thousand dollars in fees to process the loan and placed a lien on my property. I also had to pay a high interest rate on the money for the term of the loan. At the end of the six months, I had to make a balloon payment for the entire amount that I borrowed. It's called a hard money loan because they fuck you up the ass with no lube, which is hard to take, at least for most. In the hood, they call this type of loan what it is – borrowing money from a loan shark at an outrageous interest rate where a gangster will kill you if you don't pay them back. In my case, the gangsters would foreclose on my house. The financial dicks on Wall Street caused the economy to plummet into the shitter and they were still fucking everyone they could by extending these types of loans. Where were the government watchdogs during the aftermath of the financial collapse who could and should have prevented the financial sector from raping the American people? They were too busy bailing out the assholes who got America into the screwed-up situation in the first place. In the meantime, every fucking thief that had a dollar to lend was sticking it to the poor assholes like me that had no other choice but to accept their outrageously high interest rates and enormous fees for processing a loan of this type. I realized then that there was a king that ruled America and his name was almighty cash.

I was not aware that ILD was in such dire financial straits before traveling to Las Vegas for my birthday, although, based on Philven's accounting credentials, it certainly came as no surprise. I was so angry at myself for allowing a lying, cheating asshole of a man to fuck me over once again. My situation made me see the huge difference between the relationship I had with Alex versus the one that I was currently suffering through with Philven. I realized that Alex *was* an honorable man – an oxymoron if I ever heard one – when it came to upholding his financial responsibilities until we could legally and financially separate. I had finally found forgiveness in my heart for Alex and the things that I believe he put me through while we were together. Forgiving him would be the first step that would allow me a second chance at obtaining happiness and my realization about Alex was a turning point in my evolution to become a more forgiving person.

Had it not been for Alex, Philven's manipulative and deceitful behavior would've destroyed me or, at the very least, caused me to become a hateful and vengeful person. The countless lies that I had to sort through with Alex allowed me to see through Philven's cunning and fucked up games. It was extremely difficult to be disrespected by someone with whom I was living, but my time with Alex gave me the wisdom to know that I could overcome a difficult living situation and my new faith gave me the strength to overcome the disrespect I was experiencing in my own home.

Philven thought he could use my past to destroy me or cause me to become like him. Only God could have known that my past was the key to setting me free from the demons that had a hold on me. My financial pressures and deceitful environment ultimately caused me to turn to God for protection. To receive this protection, I needed to learn to forgive myself for the poor choices I made and forgive those who I believed had wronged me. I also needed to learn the art of walking by faith and not by sight. As I thought about this, I recalled not being able to see Cher's face clearly when I saw her onstage in Las Vegas and began to wonder if there *was* a message for me in that event. Prior to arriving in Vegas, I had no idea that ILD was broke, so I was ignorant about its financials. I hadn't focused on the entire business' operation. I was distracted by the pending litigation and my efforts to get Philven to complete the books. Was God utilizing Cher to get me to think about my circumstances in order for me to understand I was not seeing my situation clearly? Since most of these messages were like solving a riddle, I thought it was certainly possible that Cher was being used in this manner—and the issue I had with seeing her face clearly was a possible sign to get me to take a closer look at my immediate surroundings.

In the midst of my financial misery, I turned to the California Department of Industrial Relations for assistance in pressuring Madame President to pay the commissions that I believe were owed me. I began working at the age of sixteen and by the age of forty-nine I had paid employment taxes for thirty-three years. Since I was an upstanding U.S. citizen, with no criminal record, I thought the department would help with my problem. I was informed that this government agency assisted workers in getting their employers to pay their earned wages that were not yet paid after they were terminated. A disputed two hundred thousand dollars in commission was a serious violation, which I believed required an investigation at the very least. I sent several letters to the agency and I visited their offices in Riverside once. At each attempt, I was denied assistance because my dispute with Madame President was in litigation. It seemed as if I couldn't get a fucking break, even if my life depended on getting one. I called my local congress representative to get her office to twist some arms in the hopes of getting the Department of Industrial Relations to help me. The congresswoman's office contacted the department, but their efforts were in vain.

I was forced to take the hard money loan since the government agency wouldn't help pursue my claim. I lent ILD five thousand dollars from the loan and used the remaining fifteen thousand dollars to pay our utilities that were three months in arrears and to get us through our household expenses for a few more months. I didn't take a salary from the business for the next several months to build up equity in the company.

In June 2009, ILD's business was showing signs of slowing. The state of the economy finally caught up with our business and because I was consumed with the pending lawsuit and trying to sort out the company's financials, there was little time left for me to seek new business. It was as if the Titanic was taking on water and I found myself on the main deck throwing chairs overboard in the hopes of keeping the ship from sinking when it was going to sink no matter how hard I tried to keep it afloat. In my attempts to keep the company above water, I forgot to consider whether a life vest was at my disposal. I had gambled it all and failed to think about what would happen to the me and the babies if I couldn't save us from sinking into financial ruin.

My entire life I looked high and low for a man that would love me, not lie to me or cheat on me. I longed to be respected and cherished and I dreamt of building a family, a home, and a life with the type of man who would do so. My relationship with Alex proved to be beneficial in many ways, but unfortunately, he was not able or willing to choose me over temptation. It makes me sad and angry when I reflect on the years when I invested my time and love in men that said they wanted the same things out of a relationship that I did, when in fact they were more interested in themselves and their wants rather than in us. Since the trust between the men that I chose to love always ended in mistrust, how was I to bring myself to a place where I could believe, trust, and ultimately love a man once again? Was I strong enough to take a chance on love again and tough enough to withstand the disappointment if what I so much desired was nothing more than a fairytale? As corny as it may sound, I eventually learned that God is the loving and trustworthy male figure who I had been seeking all my life.

As my situation became more dire, I realized Fate had brought me hope and it was because of that hope that I sought out a relationship with God. Through my faith, I was able to visualize the possibilities of a better life, which allowed me to walk the path of my life by faith and not by sight. I now understand why so many poor people believe in God – He brings hope to hopelessness and I see that through hope we ascertain our faith. I realized that if I was going to survive my situation and emerge victorious, I needed hope, which would strengthen my faith and vice versa. It's then that I learned to live in the moment and do the best I could for that specific day. I had to lean on God to set the stage for a better day than the one that I had previously endured haunted by Philven, Madame President, her Lesbian vice president, my creditors, and the ongoing litigation. I came to understand that God had the ability to forge a way when there seemed to be no way in hell to change an unchangeable situation.

One evening, after working a grueling day at the office, when my financial situation seemed hopeless, I walked to the mailbox at the end of my driveway to retrieve that day's mail. It was dark outside. The only light that illuminated the desert landscape and its surrounding mountains emanated from the streetlights and nearby homes. I arrived at the end of the driveway and opened the mailbox. Suddenly, I glanced over my shoulder and the lights from Bob Hope's residence off in the distance caught my attention. Bob had passed away by then, but Dolores Hope still lived in the house. The home was on top of a mountain and the illumination from the Hope residence shone a spotlight on the concept of seeing hope amid darkness. This metaphor brought a smile to my face. I long believed that Fate is a woman and I see Hope as her sister, so the comparison between her and Dolores seemed appropriate. This situation reminded me of the dove that appeared in the clouds just when I began to doubt my newly found faith. Once again, when hope of surviving my financial situation was diminishing quickly, Fate drew my attention toward a mountain with a symbol of hope. I saw God using the Hope residence as a way to let me know that I should hold on to my faith and not give up. Hope can certainly offer a mountain of possibilities for those who dare to believe in her.

One afternoon when I was getting high, I got into a heated argument with Philven. By this time, our relationship had come to an end and we didn't agree on much. I needed to file the company's taxes for that year and time was running out. September was fast approaching and I did exactly what I said I wasn't going to do. I stepped in to clean up Philven's mess, which really pissed me off. In my attempt to get the books in order, I hired yet another bookkeeping company to assist in bringing the financial reporting up to date. Philven and I were at each other's throats on most days. This afternoon was different. I couldn't have been any angrier with him that day even if I had tried. My heart seemed to be beating out of my chest and it even crossed my mind that my chest pain might be a sign that I was having a heart attack. I kept doing more drugs, which only aggravated the situation, but I didn't care if I dropped dead where I stood. Had I died that day of a drug-induced heart attack, at least my miserable existence would have been over. I cornered Philven in the kitchen, ripping him a new asshole for not doing his job. I was so frustrated with him and had hit a wall in my efforts to get him on board. I took several more hits from the pipe and handed it to Philven. I suppose I subconsciously thought that if I was going to drop dead of a heart attack I might as well take him with me. When I handed the pipe to him, he began to cry. As he did so, the one and only thought that ran through my mind was that he too felt that he was going to drop dead of a heart attack at any moment. But Philven was only concerned about himself so I knew he had to be crying about something that related to him—he was that selfish. I asked him if his heart was beating extremely fast and he nodded in agreement while still crying. I'm not sure what possessed me, but I got in his face and placed one hand over his heart and my other hand over mine. I looked him squarely in the eye and boldly told him that God was going to ensure that neither he nor I was going to die of a heart attack that day. I believed what I said at that moment, but I think I may have been more arrogant than sincere in my declaration.

I had done a considerable amount of partying during my thirties and forties and I was not a novice when it came to ingesting an illegal substance. However, the way my heart was racing and the severity of my chest pain was nothing like I had experienced in all my years of self-medicating. I was also smoking cigarettes every day and had stopped exercising, which didn't help. I was not taking good care of myself, so the possibility that I was having a heart attack was plausible. I became concerned whether I had finally gone too far with the drugs, although I was more crazed than logical at that moment. Five to ten minutes after proclaiming that God was going to ensure we didn't die that afternoon, Philven asked me if my heart was still racing. My heartbeat was now back to normal, even though I was still ranting like a fucking lunatic that just broke out of an insane asylum. I immediately thought that Philven was fucking with me, as he always did, and I thought he slipped me something to calm my heartbeat. It was absolutely crazy. My heart went from beating out of my chest – and hurting as if someone had kicked me in the ribs – to being calm in minutes, after voicing that God would look after us. My chest pain disappeared. Even when God showed up, as I proclaimed he would, my first reaction was to think that Philven had slipped me a drug to calm me down rather than to believe God had done exactly what I said he was going to do. When He arrived on the scene, my knee jerk reaction was to justify the situation in the natural way, rather than believe in the alternative. I experienced grace that afternoon and, on first observation, I failed to identify it as such. Once I took a moment to logically examine the facts, I determined it could've only been an act of divine intervention. I wouldn't call this a miracle, but I believe I experienced a God moment – a moment in my life when He showed up just as I said He would.

Many years earlier, when we were boyfriends, Alex planned a surprise party for my birthday. In the days leading up to my big day, I found out about the upcoming party from Tony, because I believe he was jealous and wanted to spoil the surprise. As my birthday approached, I became increasingly anxious about when Alex would spring the surprise and my friends would jump out of the darkness and yell happy birthday! I kept thinking that everywhere we went during those days would be the place where they would jump out and surprise me. On the day of my birthday, a Saturday, me and Alex, together with our friends went to the club where we first met and where Jeff bartended. As we celebrated, we took ecstasy and other substances. I got the idea in my head that this was the night when Alex was going to surprise me and thought he bought out the club for the night. I was high and not thinking clearly and misread the situation. I stood at the bar talking to Jeff when I determined that Alex had rented the club. Since he had done so, and it was my birthday bash, I felt I could do anything I wanted. I then decided to jump onto the bar and over to the other side with Jeff. As I climbed onto the bar, Jeff looked aghast and said, "Mary, what are you doing?" Two of the doormen immediately came running over as I went over the bar. They were going to throw me out of the club, but Jeff convinced them that everything was all right. I was mortified and disappointed at the same time. It turned out that the surprise party was planned for the next day—Alex had booked an entire restaurant to host a birthday brunch. I was close in my assumption…he did buy out a venue to celebrate my birthday, just not the one I thought.

Ever since that night, I learned an important lesson and made sure I didn't repeat my mistake and over react when I was high. Therefore, my thinking that I was having a heart attack was not the feeling of a delusional individual under the influence of drugs. I assessed the situation logically and determined that the only reason my heart calmed down, after feeling like it would jump out of my chest, was due to some divine intervention, as I believed.

On the other hand, my confusion over my birthday surprise many years earlier became a double-edged sword. Ever since the bar incident, I became very cautious when I was high. I became afraid of misreading a situation and over reacting, which caused me much anguish for many years. This overly cautious behavior allowed people to mentally mess with me and, due to my reluctance to repeat a past mistake, I took way too long to assess situations and act upon them. It didn't take long for Philven to figure out that I was very careful not to react when I was high and when I didn't have all the facts. He knew I would take my time to evaluate a situation properly and he used this cautiousness to his advantage.

By June of 2009, the value on the Whitewater Home had declined significantly and I was upside down on the mortgage—I owed more on the home than it was worth. A year earlier, the house had been appraised at six hundred and eighty five thousand dollars and it was now worth half that and continuing to decline. On several occasions, I tried to get my mortgage company to modify my loan, another complex and time consuming process that was ultimately unsuccessful. I simply didn't have three to five thousand dollars to spend on an attorney to get through the loan modification process. I even tried HARP, a government program that was supposed to assist individuals secure a modification to their mortgage. One of the crazy conditions was that I was not able to speak with a representative from the mortgage company who was handling my case. I needed to fax information to a number that my lender provided. It was very impersonal, which I found to be disappointing because I was trying everything possible to save the most important and expensive asset that I ever owned. I was also emotionally tied to the property since I worked with the architect on the design, selected every element of the house, and I put everything I had worked for my entire life on the line when I bought and remodeled it.

The only people who were receiving loan modifications were individuals who could afford an attorney. Poor suckers like myself who needed to have their mortgages modified due to the drastic drop in their property values, combined with their fiscal hardships, were being fucked over by the financial institutions, which was disheartening since the American people had bailed out so many of the lenders during their financial collapse. The mortgage companies didn't want to modify loans and didn't unless legally forced to do so. Only the King of America could help in securing an attorney to guide one through the complicated process. The individuals that didn't have *almighty cash* on their side were shit out of luck and probably ended up losing their homes, as so many did. Several years after being denied a loan modification, my lender was fined for their actions in foreclosing on properties, along with others, in a class action lawsuit. The case was settled out of court for billions of dollars.

By trying everything in my power, I was able to get most, but not all, of my credit card debt that I incurred from the remodel rolled into the refinanced mortgage. As a result, my monthly loan payment was twice what it was after refinancing the property. I did everything possible to pay my debts and did the right thing by honoring my financial commitments. Unfortunately, my creditors weren't as committed to doing the right thing. Their predatory actions created numerous hardships for me. I believe that most of the unfortunate outcomes from the housing market crash could've been avoided had someone come up with a compassionate solution for all and not just to those who had access to the King of America. I wasn't expecting a free ride, I just needed someone to understand I needed more time so I could honor my debts. My longtime relationships with my creditors didn't seem to matter at all. They tied my hands at every turn and made it impossible for me to have credit available when I needed it the most.

The Book of Revelations in the Bible tells a story about the mark of the beast. *The beast forced all people, great and small, rich and poor, free and slave to receive a mark on their right hands or on the forehead.* Everyone needs to accept his mark to trade and conduct business. This sounded familiar to me, as if the Book of Revelations is referencing today's credit scoring. The mark of the beast is 666 and credit scores are measured by a three-digit number. A credit score of 666 is considered average, though it won't allow you to qualify for the lowest rates available or the best re-payment options. When dealing with me, the only thing the *beastly* financial institutions were concerned about was my credit score that seemed to be tattooed on my forehead. My three-digit mark was all they saw when they looked at my file—and my worth as a person was whatever that three-digit credit score said or didn't say about me. These financial institutions were certainly the beast in my eyes. They cared only about their well-being, which is ironic since they would have been in the same situation as many of their customers if the people's government hadn't bailed their ass out of their own financial mess. What was good for the beast wasn't good for their customers.

The financial collapse that took everyone by surprise, combined with the pending lawsuit by Madame President, her unwillingness to pay my outstanding commissions, and the company's slowing sales created the perfect conditions for the twister that would soon rip everything out from beneath my feet. Had Madame President not sued the company, I would not have needed to write a thirty thousand dollar check for legal fees and I would've had the funds for an attorney to secure a modification that could have prevented the forthcoming disaster.

It seemed no matter how hard I tried, I couldn't get the stars to line up in my favor. On many occasions, I cried…because it seemed the closer I came to knowing and building a relationship with God, the more that seemed to be taken away from me. I recalled the story of Job. Was I strong and resilient enough like Job to hold onto my faith no matter what the cost? If I let go of my faith, would my circumstances change for the better? The story of Job gave me the strength to resist the temptation to dismiss the only thing keeping me from killing myself.

The bookkeeping company I hired to help get the books in order in August of 2009 was a local firm. It was owned by a middle aged white man and he assigned an Asian lady in her thirties to our account. This was my second attempt to help get the books up to date. This time, I oversaw the process. The company's taxes, as well as our personal ones, needed to be filed by the middle of the next month or we had to pay a penalty for filing late. Money was tight and I was once again spending funds that neither the company nor I had to spend. The closer we came to the fifteenth of September, the crazier I became and the more pissed off I was at Philven for not handling the financials appropriately.

I felt sorry for the lady working on our account. Philven was extremely difficult in answering her questions. On a few occasions, when we were at her office, Philven became belligerent. I tried to keep my composure in front of her, but Philven often provoked me to a point where I couldn't contain my frustrations. For some fucked up reason on his part, he was making it as difficult as possible to get the books completed. He wanted to cause as much confusion and difficulty for me as possible. He was clearly hiding something and didn't want the financials to be in order. I wanted to grab him by the throat and bang his head against her desk until the fucker passed out. I was at my wits' end. Had God not entered my life, I would've seriously considered allowing him to have an unfortunate accident—so I could have buried him in the backyard. If Philven was not the devil, then he must have been possessed by a demon or by several demons from the way he was acting. In all my years of managing people, I hadn't come across a more difficult or more determined individual focused on causing as much chaos at all levels. Alex suddenly looked like a saint compared to this demon-possessed asshole.

A power-struggle was taking place. I was determined to overcome Philven's efforts to have ILD default on filing its taxes. He was trying to control me with his passive aggressive behavior that turned violent and abusive. I was messed up and hanging on to my sanity by a thread, but I was attempting to meet my personal commitments and those of the company. I was becoming increasingly terrified that I was going to fail and lose everything. The more scared I became, the angrier and more hostile I acted.

The bookkeeper completed the financials in two weeks. She was my saving grace and a person I will never forget. I remain grateful for her assistance when I needed help so desperately. Once the books were completed, I noticed that Philven had been transferring money between accounts, always for the same amount. A few days later, I hired a certified public accountant to complete the business taxes, as well as our personal tax returns. *A wise old owl once said, the more he saw the less he spoke, the less he spoke the more he heard*—and if you didn't get your fucking taxes filed by the end of your extension date, the IRS would take your nest egg, your house, your business, and whatever else they can get their hands on.

The returns for the LLC were to be filed by September 1, 2009 and our personal returns were to be filed by the 15th of the same month. The LLC returns needed to be filed before our personal returns and Philven hadn't made me aware of this fact. I went to the accountant's office to sign the taxes for ILD that were being electronically submitted, but I was a day late and ILD incurred a penalty for the late submittal. Once again, Philven's lack of commitment cost us additional monies that the company didn't have. I believe Philven deliberately didn't tell me of the earlier filing date because it was his usual passive aggressive way of sticking it to me.

I asked the accountant why he thought Philven would transfer the same amount of money numerous times between various accounts. Philven opened three bank accounts, one for taxes, one for payroll, and a savings account, in addition to the main operating one. The company wasn't conducting enough business to warrant four separate accounts. I knew the answer to my question, but I wanted to get an expert's take on Philven's accounting tactics. The accountant replied that he couldn't say for sure, but if he had to guess, he indicated that it was to make it almost impossible to follow the money from one account to another. He said that someone would conduct this type of financial record keeping if they were stealing funds from the company and wanted to make it difficult to track the transferred money. Once again, I was right with my assessment of Philven's conduct. I was just so over him and his fucked-up behavior. He had very little regard for money and authority, which I found surprising since he never had much of either.

I contacted the IRS to inform them that I thought Philven was stealing from the company. I was told by the IRS representative to report the incident to the local police, but there was nothing they could do for me about my suspicions. Interestingly, when I called the IRS, I discovered that Philven's name didn't appear on any of their records as an officer for ILD. I almost shit my pants when I discovered my name was the only one listed who was responsible for reporting the company's information to the IRS. Since Philven was the Chief Operating and Financial Officer, he should've listed his name as the main contact instead of mine. I wondered if this motherfucker always knew he was going to screw me over and this is why he didn't list himself as an officer. I was so pissed—another example of how deviously calculated he was in his actions. Was this the reason why Philven was being so difficult and fought me so hard when I tried to get ILD's financials completed? The fucker probably thought the IRS would come after me for not filing the company's taxes in a timely manner, and not him. However, I had the IRS add his name as a secondary company contact, together with his COO and CFO titles for the company. Boom!

The perfect storm approached. ILD appeared as if it was going to fail and my fear began to dictate my actions. A terrified person is potentially dangerous—they become unpredictable and may react erratically and aggressively when threatened. This was certainly my case. Each time I seemed to defeat the serpent and cut off its head, it seemed to grow two additional ones. In late September 2009, ILD lost its largest client due to a change in personnel at the clients' organization. The significant revenue reduction from losing our biggest customer caused ILD to cease conducting business. I was terrified from having lost my livelihood and became aggressive with anyone who seemed a threat. The thought of becoming homeless had me in a constant state of trepidation.

Shutting our doors was bittersweet. On one hand, I was freaking out about how I was going to support myself. On the other hand, I was relieved that the constant conflict with Philven to keep the company solvent was over. By closing down the company operations, I no longer had to suffer through days in the office with Tweedledee—and the pending lawsuit against ILD went away. We still had the personal lawsuit from Madame President hanging over our heads, although this too would soon be yesterday's news. Despite the initial breather, Tweedledum and Tweedledee continued to battle against one another in hope of one of them winning the war.

I'd been working night and day to save my tangible assets and in doing so, I was abusing the most important assets that I had. It was not until I was brought low that I realized that my mind, body, spirit, and soul were the most important riches I could ever possess. On many occasions, I placed these in jeopardy due to the drugs I was taking. At one point, I went on a drug-induced bender to numb myself. When I came off my drug binge, I thought I had fried my mind. I was having trouble staying focused and recalling recent events. I thought I had gone too far and had permanently screwed up my memory, which terrified me. A few weeks after this incident, my memory came flowing back and I realized my mind was my super hero. I had acted irresponsibly and placed my body and my mind in great jeopardy, but just when I thought I had gone too far, my super hero returned to save me from myself.

I believe that an individual who has nothing to lose in life is even more dangerous than a person who is afraid. This person understands that by placing themselves in harm's way, there's a risk of a tragic outcome, but their commitment to seek vengeance supersedes any fear they may encounter. As the months went by, the more the accuser took, the less I had to lose and so I began to act more like a warrior who didn't give a rat's ass.

My own accusers – like Job's – had brought me to my knees. When this time came, I found myself isolated, humiliated, ashamed, financially devastated, and used by others. I was soon faced with a choice to follow the evil ways of the world or follow the goodness that I believe God had to offer. The malicious side encompassed anger that was ruled by evil and fueled by fear. This offered me an opportunity to get revenge. The good side consisted of hope that was ruled by faith and fueled by compassion. It offered forgiveness and a plethora of positive possibilities. The angry and fearful person I was before allowing God into my heart would have, without thinking twice, enlisted with the vengeful side. The individual that I was becoming through my relationship with God brought me to a place where compassion, forgiveness, and the possibility of improving my circumstances ruled. This was the side where I chose to enlist. I finally understood that God required me to lay down my sword and that without humility and forgiveness in my spirit, I was going to die miserably. Learning to be humble and to forgive – and the power that comes from these two attributes – came at a huge personal price. However, they became my ticket to salvation and a second chance at having a happy and fulfilling life. It was at that point that I believe God reached down from heaven and calmed my spirit so fear didn't dictate my behavior. In the coming months, I learned to trust God, even when my circumstances were telling me not to. I was concerned about my future, but I was no longer being emotionally strangled by my fear. I became a warrior to survive and, after God touched my spirit, I became part of his military, a solider dedicated to a cause.

It may sound strange, but I believe God allowed the accuser to take ILD from me. I naturally thought God would have protected the company from going under, but that didn't happen. Once I was free from the burden of trying to keep it afloat, I realized I would've died in that office working day and night to keep the business from sinking. I believe God wanted me to stop looking at my immediate circumstances and begin to look toward the horizon to visualize a better future. While I believed this to be true in spirit, my mind was focused on how I was going to financially survive. I was very concerned about what was going to happen to the babies and me if I was not able to obtain a new job in a short time. I was trying very hard not to be afraid and not to lean on my own understanding, but to trust in my faith.

In October 2009, I began to send my résumé to potential employers. Over the months that followed, I sent out hundreds of résumés to potential companies for various positions. The majority of the jobs at these companies were in line with my skills and professional qualifications, although I also expanded my search and sent my résumé to Christian ministries and humanitarian organizations. I was hoping to get a job with an organization that offered me not just a salary, but also provided me with a sense of community. I didn't have an in-depth understanding of religion and I wanted to look for an employer where I could earn an income and comfortably learn more about God, while helping the less fortunate. I dreamed of selling all my possessions and getting on a ship full of missionaries who traveled the world and were focused on helping those with the greatest need. The events in that desert stirred a desire within me to help the less fortunate and demonstrate to them the goodness of God through my actions. The only thing I had to offer was my service and I was willing to sell everything I owned and follow this passion in the hope of finding my purpose. Thinking back, I believe my intentions were in the right place, but I don't think I was emotionally or physically strong enough to take on such an endeavor then. I wonder if God just wanted to know I was willing, even though I wasn't able to take on such a task at that point. Was my desire to help humanity – contrasted with my inadequacy to execute that desire – a major milestone in my walk of faith?

One day, I was watching the Christian networks to learn more about their religion and about their belief in God, when Philven asked me what I would like to do with the rest of my life. If I had a choice, he asked me, would I opt to be the President of the United States or the Pope. Rome was burning all around me and this is what he wanted to know. The question seemed strange, but he always had a hidden motive. By then, my life had deteriorated so much that all I had left of true value, which I could call my own, was my passion to know God. Without hesitation, I picked the position of Pope. I didn't want the distinction or reverence that accompanies the position nor was I capable of holding such a rank, I just wanted to get as close to God as humanly possible. I was feeling alone and isolated in the desert and I felt as if God was the only person that really cared whether I lived or died.

I long believed that someone or something had been watching me for decades, and felt that this unknown presence was the cause of so many coincidences throughout my life. Those situations seemed to be part of a picture that was trying to portray a larger story and the events surrounding these coincidences began to take on a life of their own. When Philven posed his question, a lightbulb went off in my head and I began to see the bigger picture. They were signs that had been laid in my life's path so I could find my way out of the darkness where I lived—and go back to a place where I had once belonged. Being Pope seemed to be the closest I could get to that place. This thinking may seem strange, but I just wanted someone to show me compassion, love, and respect. I wanted to feel the sense of security that knowing God could give me. I had never been able to find a mate that offered me respect and true love, but I then saw that God was the key to achieving this meaningful treasure that I had been seeking my entire life. I eventually came to understand that the love of God is not found in a position, a place, or a thing. While I would love to have the opportunity to meet with the man believed by many to be the closest person to God in this world, I no longer think I need to be a Pope to be near to God or to know Him.

I believe Philven posed the question because he was trying to figure out if I was more interested in obtaining true love or ultimately wanted to hold a position of power. I didn't have the desire to be the individual with the power that comes from holding the highest office in United States, if not the world. Philven was power hungry and he sought influence and authority. Philven didn't want me to find solace or happiness in my spiritual growth so he tried to plant the seed that I should be interested in power and politics rather than in pursuing a relationship with a God that he once believed existed, but in who he no longer believed, as he had lost his way and his faith somewhere along his way.

When Philven was a teenager, he had been very religious and had a best friend who was also very interested in religion. I don't know the specifics, but that young friend eventually committed suicide. I assume that Philven's friend was gay and had issues with accepting his sexuality—and so he took his life. Some gay men may turn to God and the church when they are trying to understand why they're attracted to the same sex, but I believe that in some cases they're hiding from themselves, and the world, in a place where they can feel safe. I expect that many gay men have chosen the church instead of embracing their homosexuality and I understand why someone would turn to God for comfort when the world is judging them. When Philven's friend committed suicide, I believe he drove Philven away from God's arms, rather than moving him closer to them. Philven is a perfect example of how so many people blame God for the tragedies that occur in their life. Evil rules a person's life when the accuser exceeds their faith and their belief that they can overcome and conquer their accuser.

Philven was a master in manipulating a situation to his advantage. When his scheming tactics didn't work, he blamed anyone and everything around him rather than taking responsibility. If I was able to build a solid relationship with God, Philven was concerned he was going to lose the power that he thought he had over me, and he wouldn't be able to manipulate me any longer. I learned from my relationship with Alex that a liar feeds off the power generated by controlling an individual or a situation. Philven wanted to divert my interest from knowing God to politics. If he was successful, he would've have manipulated the situation again to benefit him the most, in the long run. As our conversation turned to politics, Philven mentioned that he would nominate me to receive the Nobel Peace Prize given the opportunity. He often frustrated me with these off-the-wall remarks and he often made comments that had no relevance to anything when conversing with him. I don't understand why Philven voiced this statement. I eventually reached a point where I didn't want to have a conversation with him because of his bizarre remarks. I was trying to find some level of peace in my life and he was causing me much heartache with his bullshit antics. I wanted to find common ground between us so we could reside in the same house without killing one another. Being a peacekeeper was a new approach in my dealing with him.

A few weeks after our conversation, President Obama was awarded the Nobel Peace Prize. Once again, I was unnerved by the coincidence of our random and fucked up conversation that had nothing to do with anything until the President of the United States was presented with the Nobel Peace Prize. I still believed Philven was fucking with me. Was our arbitrary and bizarre conversation the result of a conspiracy to make me a paranoid mess? I naturally thought that someone was trying to push my buttons and drive me over the edge. It made more sense that someone was fucking with my mind rather than believing something unexplainable was trying to get my attention.

My world was failing apart. I had exhausted myself trying to save ILD. I had lost my company and my means of support. I was now broke and broken. I stopped making the house payment in October 2009 because I wasn't earning an income and didn't have much cash on hand. I tried everything I could to uphold my financial commitments, but the harder I tried, the more I lost. I had two life insurance polies that I bought in my late twenties before I was diagnosed with HIV. I surrendered the policies in that desert to get the available cash from both plans. I had these policies for twenty years and was planning to use the money from them if I became ill and unable to work. In my efforts to protect my home from foreclosure, I cashed out these two longstanding polices. It seemed as if I failed on every front in my attempts to keep myself financially solvent. Once again, I was reminded of the story of Job and found strength from his story. I was able to hold on to my faith and decided that I would rather die in that miserable valley than denounce God.

While I have made many references to God, my pursuit to understand how one God – in a world with many religions – could be responsible for creating the universe and every living thing and person in it, was just beginning. Over the many decades of my adulthood, I seemed to be blessed when it came to getting myself out of a tight spot. One way or another, any challenging situation always seemed to work out in my favor. Once I arrived in the desert, for some crazy unknown reason, it seemed that no matter what I tried, my life kept taking a turn for the worse. I was becoming increasingly concerned that I was going to end up homeless or living in my parent's basement. I appreciated that my mother and father had offered to allow me the option to move into their house should the need arise, but I was a full-grown man of forty-nine years and felt I needed to stand on my own two feet. I needed to find a way out of my mess so I could support the babies and myself. On October 31 of that year, the good in my life seemed to merge with the evil. That Halloween, what should have been two opposing forces became cohorts in trying to stamp out any last bit of hope that remained in my life and attempt to entomb me in a miserable existence for eternity.

Papi, who passed away before I moved to Palm Springs, Puckles, who was having major health issues by then, and Aston and Bentley, who were then two years old, had an importance in my life that I have not fully explained. Puckles and Papi stopped me from taking my own life when Alex and I split, because I knew Alex would not take care of them if I were dead. He would have given them away and they would have been forced to live in a new home with people that they didn't know. These two dogs, along with Bentley and Aston, were instrumental in helping me survive. Even though I never found a loving and sincere mate that didn't deceive me or try to control me, I did experience sincere, nurturing and loving bonds with my best friends, Papi, Puckles, Aston, and Bentley.

Puckles wasn't doing well in October 2009 and I didn't expect him to live to see another year. That Halloween I decided to take him to the beach. When I lived in San Francisco, almost a decade earlier, when Puck was young, I would take him and Papi to Ocean beach at the edge of the city, where Puck always seemed to enjoy running on the sandy shore. I decided to make the three-hour drive to Malibu so Puckles could feel the sand underneath his paws, and the sound of the waves hitting the shore, one last time. There were several beaches that were closer, but for some reason I thought I should take the boys to Malibu. This was the last time Puckles was able to enjoy the sandy beaches of California before he passed away.

Once we arrived in Malibu, I suddenly had the idea to stop by Cher's house, which is right off Pacific Coast Highway close to Pepperdine University. I felt like something was drawing me to her home. Upon arriving at the entrance to her property, I pulled into the small portion of the driveway in front of her home. The driveway led to very large wooden gates that keep unwanted visitors from driving onto her property. There was an intercom system at the entrance where a visitor could call the house to announce their arrival. I pulled my Jaguar into her driveway and stopped the car next to the intercom, which was mounted on a pole. There was an envelope at the base of the intercom and it was marked to Cher's attention. My first knee jerk reaction was to take the envelope, but after some consideration, I knew it was the wrong thing to do and I left the envelope alone. Cher had put her Malibu property on the market and I could see that the large packet was from a realtor. The entire event seemed surreal. I was sitting in Cher's driveway when I was once again in great need of guidance. I was lost, broken, fucked up, fucked over, confused, broke, sad, alone, and feeling isolated. Why did I feel the need to drive to Cher's home and pull into her driveway? What was I hoping to find? If Cher had emerged from behind those large wooden gates, I would've shit my pants. She probably would've said to get the fuck out of her driveway, which I would've done immediately. I wondered whether something or someone had a hand in bringing me to her house that day. Trick or treat, I've come to escape my trick and have a retreat.

God had seemed to utilize Cher once before to give me strength and determination to achieve a better life when He knew I wasn't listening for His voice. I began to relive the defining moment in Marin County when I heard a woman's voice in the distance proclaiming that if I believed in myself, there was nothing that I couldn't achieve. I couldn't see past the wooden gates in front of me, but I knew that on the other side of those beautiful doors lived a woman that represented strength and determination. I also couldn't see past my current circumstances or how I was going to survive my messed-up situation. I had to *believe* there was a way, even though I couldn't see one. I cried in my car for a few minutes before I pulled out of her driveway and headed down the hill to one of the many beaches along the shore. I sound as if I was stalking Cher, which was not the case. I believe something sent me to the gates of that Goddess's home to reflect on the words of wisdom that I heard her sing so many years earlier—so that when I returned to the valley, I could overcome whatever awaited me.

I ran on the beach with Puckles and spent time with the babies before we began our long journey back home. The lengthy drive took a toll on Puckles. He was breathing heavily during the entire drive back. His trachea had collapsed on several occasions over the past year, which caused him to pass out from lack of oxygen. The veterinarian had prescribed steroids to keep him strong and breathing properly. I had to keep a very close eye on him when he was outside doing his business. Several times, I found him in the yard, on his side, and he wasn't breathing. Each time, I was able to administer mouth-to-mouth resuscitation and revive him. His veterinarian told me the time would come when he wouldn't regain consciousness. I loved this dog more than I can put into words and now at the time in my life when I was losing everything, I was also losing my best buddy and longtime friend. Like many dogs, Puckles was devoted and loved me and thought the world revolved around me. No one has ever shown me as much affection as Puck, not even Papi, Aston, or Bentley and while I love all my dogs, Puckles stole my heart.

I was emotionally and physically exhausted. I tirelessly sought a solution to my financial problems, but the situation seemed unsolvable. I felt vulnerable. As I was driving back to the desert on the I-10 freeway at 80 miles per hour, it popped into my mind that I could just simply turn the steering wheel sharply. This probably would've caused the car to flip over several times, ending my miserable existence. It seemed like such a simple thing to do. Tempting as this was, I thought of the babies in the car and the innocent people on the highway who might also become casualties from my action and realized this wasn't a viable solution. Once again, my dogs and my conscience saved me from making an irrevocable decision. This was the first time I considered ending my life while living in the desert, although it wouldn't be the last.

I arrived at the Whitewater house early in the evening of that Halloween. As I arrived, I found Philven standing in the kitchen. He was wearing my leather harness, but was otherwise naked. I wondered if he thought that costume was a suitable one. I got the babies out of the car and into the house. I placed Puckles on the sofa and tried to make him as comfortable as possible. Before heading into the kitchen to prepare dinner, I turned on the television to the Trinity Broadcasting Network (TBN), a Christian station. I was still smoking cigarettes, doing drugs, cussing like a pissed off truck driver, and drinking alcohol. I was trying to reduce these vices, but I was nowhere near getting them under control. TBN was broadcasting a program from Hawaii outdoors and I believe it was their first time airing an episode in this format.

Young people were dancing on stage and singing Christian songs. I was desperately trying to learn more about the Christian faith, but I was still relatively green in my pursuit of a sincere relationship with God—and the world of religion made me feel inadequate and ignorant about the formality of worship. I was hoping to obtain a sense of community within the Christian faith by connecting with their belief system through Christian television.

As I watched the program, the narrator said that smokers, drug users, foul-mouthed people, and alcohol drinkers weren't welcomed in the Christian house of God. I felt rejected and hurt. I was trying to become a person who didn't do those things, but I was so far removed from where they were telling me I needed to be—to become part of their family. I cried. I wanted so much to become a part of their social community and be associated with their church. As I sobbed, I realized the irony of the situation. It was Halloween and the man that caused me so much pain was standing in the kitchen, naked in my leather regalia, with his big dick freewheeling about. He looked like he could be the Devil from where I was standing or at the very least a demon-possessed hooker. Trick or treat, smell my feet and give me some crack to eat because according to Christians on television and the naked leather-wearing hooker standing in my kitchen, I was not worthy of anything else.

Philven's behavior, combined with the words from the religious idiots on the television – who were telling me that I was not worthy to become part of their community – seemed to give me the perseverance to fight the evil that wanted to take over my life. Just when I turned to seek some compassion from the Christians on TBN's special presentation that night after returning from Malibu, I was shunned. In that moment of rejection, I realized it was God who brought me to Cher's house earlier that day. He knew the shit was going to hit the fan upon my return to the desert. By visiting the residence of the woman who gave me strength, at times when I had none, God knew she would once again bestow fortitude and determination in me so I could see past the lies I was hearing about not being welcomed in His house by so-called Christians.

The next day, a Sunday, I had tickets to go to Phish, a music festival being held at the Empire Polo Grounds in Indio, California. On Monday, November 2, I had tickets to be part of the audience at TBN's telecast for an episode of *Praise the Lord* being broadcast from Costa Mesa, a two-hour drive from Palm Springs. Between my trip to Malibu on Saturday combined with the activities I had planned for Sunday and Monday, I began to think that I bit off more than I could chew. I was somewhat discombobulated from the events of the previous day, but I pulled myself together to drive from Palm Springs to Indio, a forty-five-minute drive. When I was driving on the 10 freeway toward the music festival, I came across a section of highway where I saw the strangest thing I'd seen in a very long time. There was a large section of trees along both sides of the freeway where the outer bark on these trees appeared like it had been burnt in a fire. Some of the larger trees, which were six to eight feet high, still had their main branches stemming from their trunks, although these branches had no leaves and their trunks were blackened. The dark lifeless stumps, which were once thriving trees, covered a substantial amount of land on each side of the highway. While I initially assumed a fire caused the damage, the pictorial looked too staged to me, like something you would see in a Hollywood horror movie and not like it was caused by a fire at all. The vision of these unnatural, charcoaled, and begrimed trees – absent of any signs of life – with a sandy ground cover and no vegetation in the nearby vicinity, unnerved me. It looked as if I had driven through the gates of hell. I continued my journey to the Phish music festival, but I was rattled by what I had just encountered. I felt like I had crossed a line in the sand and was now in Hades, perhaps a remnant from the previous day's Halloween holiday.

I made my way to the Empire Polo Grounds and proceeded to the parking lot where I parked the Jaguar. There were many people camping on the grounds for the weekend event and I saw strange individuals roaming about, many still in their costumes from the previous day's festivities. Once I was inside the venue, I walked up to a map that depicted the layout of the stages in different areas of the festival. The theaters were identified on the map with scary-sounding names, like dead man's hollow, references that I expect the promoters intended to tie it to Halloween. Based on the chain of events from the previous day…the Christian program airing from Hawaii, Puckles' deteriorating health, and Philven's inappropriate costume and actions, I was feeling emotionally drained. Driving through what seemed to be the gates of hell on the way to the festival, combined with the strange people in costume and the creepy venue references, unsettled me—and they were the last straw. I decided to leave the festival and head back home to hide out in the safety of my house. Standing in Indio at the Empire Polo Grounds, didn't make me feel very comfortable or safe and I didn't want to be in a daunting environment. I wanted to get myself to a safe location so I could rest my overly-active mind. I was in sensory overload and needed to get myself to a place where I could shut down and keep my emotions from running rampant.

If there was a God, or at the very least good in the world, then it only made sense to me that there would be an opposing force to them. It seemed natural to me that the opposing force to God would try to keep me from Him. I was looking high and low for God's presence in my life so I was very sensitive to the things taking place around me. The sight of the begrimed trees only added confusion to my already stressful environment, which was heightened by my sensory overload. I began to wonder if there was a connection between the gates of Cher's home where I stood the previous day, to the charcoaled trees that resembled a Hollywood set depicting the gates of hell. Was something trying to send me a message that there was a deeper meaning to these opposing gates? I thought back on my previous day's journey to Malibu. Could the gates that I stood in front of, and led to the home of Cher, represent all that was good in my world? Did the begrimed trees that resembled the entrance to Hades, represent the evil in my world? If so, were they a sign that good was getting ready to go to battle against the forces of evil? I was concerned that I was able to pass through what resembled the gates of hell twice without any issue, on my way to and from the festival, but I had been stopped in my tracks when I drove into Cher's driveway and faced her security gates. Was I doomed to live my life in the grip of evil?

Seek and you will find;
Keep on knocking and the door will be opened to you.

Once I arrived back in Palm Springs from Indio, I couldn't get the picture of the blackened trees out of my mind. As I recall those days, I see that the events were building upon one another and I'm absolutely certain they were not random occurrences. It was as if the forces of good and evil in my life were beginning to manifest their presence. After I got back in the house, I decided not to go to the taping of *Praise the Lord* in Costa Mesa the next day. Sunday's events exhausted my desire to drive several more hours to attend the Christian program. I was an emotional mess and had very little energy left for such an endeavor.

After settling in at home, I changed into sweatpants and a t-shirt. I got on the sofa with the dogs and turned on the television. I was pleasantly surprised to see that the clarity of the fifty-five-inch plasma screen that hung on the wall of my living room was noticeably better than I remember before leaving for the festival. The colors of the images were heightened. The difference in the quality and intensity of the programing was remarkable and comparable to going from analog to digital high-definition. As I lay on the sofa, I was amazed at the drastic difference in the quality of the visuals. I loved the intense clarity and vibrant colors even as I didn't understand what caused the radical change. I didn't have much disposable income so I spent much of my free time watching TV—so I knew that the picture was much brighter and clearer than it ever was before I left for Indio earlier that day.

I scrolled through the channels until I ended up on TBN. I found Paul Crouch, the network founder, and Paula White hosting a program from TBN's Cost Mesa studio. Paul and Jan, his lovely wife, founded TBN many decades earlier. Paula, a Christian televangelist, was a guest speaker. As I heard her speak, I noted that Paula's sermon that day seemed to apply directly to my situation. A great deal has taken place since I first heard Paula speak that Sunday and I've searched the network's taped broadcasts on their website to watch the episode again, to confirm what I recall hearing, but despite my efforts, I couldn't locate the replay of that episode.

To the best of my recollection, Paula was preaching with much conviction and enthusiasm. Her passionate words prompted me to pay closer attention to what she was saying. In all the times I have seen her before and after this episode, she has never come close to the level of intensity that she exuded that day in November. She spoke about an individual having to cross a line, a point, or a specific place to release something spiritual in their life. She spoke very passionately about being called to a specific place at an exact time and for a distinct purpose. While I cannot recall or do justice to the exact words from her sermon, I do remember several key points from it that made me feel as if she was speaking directly to me. Her words made me think back on my encounter that day with the perfectly assembled charcoaled trees. Did I unknowingly cross over a point or a line in the sand on my way to Indio? As Paula preached, it did seem like I might have released something in my life that was not present prior to traveling through the begrimed gateway on my way to the festival. I pondered her analogy because something seemed different, like the dramatically clearer imagery on the television, as just one aspect. My thought process may sound bizarre, but the events that took place that Halloween and for two days after, finally solidified my belief that something was trying to make a connection of some kind with me. It seemed to me that God may have been utilizing Paula to persuade me to rethink my decision not to travel to Costa Mesa. Could she have been placed in my path to ensure I would keep my appointment? If so, then God was once again utilizing a woman to inspire me to have strength when I was beaten down and had very little desire to look beyond my immediate miserable existence.

I felt like I was being used, like a pawn in a game of good versus evil. In the game in play, I couldn't distinguish the players by status, color, ethnicity, religion or any other distinguishable characteristic. Evil and good were mixed together. Even though there were obvious opponents playing against each other, it was impossible for me to identify who was truly good or truly evil. Both sides had a king, a queen, bishops, many sacrificial pawns, and rooks that represented two kingdoms. Much like a game of chess, each move had to be carefully thought through, otherwise it could be my last move resulting in the demise of my house. A man's house is his castle and an evil queen was trying to take control of mine, while she pilfered the treasury. Should this queen be successful, she would have taken control of my modest desert kingdom and placed me in purgatory.

My feelings of rejection caused by hearing the so-called Christians on the program that aired from Hawaii on that Halloween were not a coincidence. Something evil was trying to keep me from sticking to my plan to be part of TBN's audience that Monday. Halloween that year took place two days before a full moon. After I went to bed that Sunday, after being motivated by Paula to keep my appointment in Costa Mesa the next day, I was awakened in the middle of the night. The moon was so bright and the intensity of the light that shone through the large sliding glass door into my bedroom was so vivid that it awoke me. Before opening my eyes, I initially thought it was Monday morning due to the light emanating from the moon, which was shining directly onto my face. Once I opened my eyes, I saw the moon as large and as bright as I have ever seen it. It hovered outside my bedroom window, just above the five-foot cinderblock fence that surrounded the house. I was annoyed that the moon had awakened me in the middle of the night from a sound sleep. I turned my back to it and to the large window that allowed the moonlight to stream into my bedroom and I quickly fell back to sleep.

The following morning after I awoke, I got out of bed and turned off the alarm to the house. I opened the door that led to the yard so Puckles, Bentley, and Aston could do their morning business. Puckles was not doing very well. He seemed listless and was breathing heavily. After feeding the boys their breakfast, I called the veterinarian to see if I could get Puckles an appointment for later that day. The receptionist informed me the doctor was booked solid, but there was an opening on the following day. I took the available timeslot so the doctor could examine Puckles the next day. I had very little money in my checking account, but since Puckles was looking so ill, I had no choice but to endure the cost of the visit to the vet. Papi had become ill when I had a lot of financial resources available to me and I spent six thousand dollars trying to save his life, to no avail. Now that Puckles was sick, I felt extremely bad for not having the financial resources to help save his life or at least prolong it. I was taking care of the little guy to the best of my financial ability, although I wished I could have done more.

As the day went on, Puckles' condition declined. I had to leave the house in the early afternoon to make the two-hour drive to Costa Mesa. The audience had to arrive at least thirty minutes prior to the start of the show. By this point, I had the impression that God wanted me to keep my appointment at TBN. I'm not sure why I felt this way, I just believed He wanted me there. Sometime in the morning that day, I recalled the story of Abraham and Isaac. God called upon Abraham to offer his son, Isaac as a sacrifice to prove his devotion to Him. I wondered if God was using Puckles to see whether I would choose Puckles over Him. I spoke out loud to God and told Him not to make me choose. If circumstances progressed to where I was forced to choose between staying home to take care of Puck, over being called to TBN, I was going to be a responsible dad and stay home to take care of my little boy. Strange as it may seem, I believed that the situation with Puckles correlated to my level of obedience and loyalty to God. Possibly it was all in my mind and there was nothing more to the circumstances, but this is not what I believed in my heart. Up until then, I had never prayed to God on behalf of another individual or thing. I usually called upon Him when I was in some kind of trouble and needed a way out of a circumstance when I didn't see one. I then laid my hands on Puckles and prayed over him, which seemed strange to me and made me uncomfortable. Religious leaders refer to people like me as a heathen, so prayer made me nervous and made me feel a little silly. Even though I felt silly and uncomfortable, I tried to be sincere in my prayer and asked God to intervene and make Puckles well—so I could keep the assignment that I believe originated from Him. A few hours later, he miraculously and noticeably became better. He was so improved that I no longer felt anxious about leaving him home without my supervision. If his rapid health improvement wasn't a miracle, then it was certainly the indisputable power of prayer, but most possibly both.

The past two days, from Saturday to Monday morning, seemed as if something was bringing me to a certain point or place in my spiritual development. Whether you believe in God or not, certainly you can grasp the concept of good and evil having energy associated with each. When you see an act of amazing kindness that touches your heart, you can't help but feel good. Sometimes an act of kindness will make us want to become a better person and sometimes it will motivate us to do something kind for another individual. There's an action and a reaction, resulting in energy being created and released. On the opposite side of the spectrum, sometimes in an act of hatred, such as a fight breaking out between two or more individuals, a bystander might take it upon him or herself to inject themselves into the fight. That's also an action and a reaction, resulting in energy being created and released. Through the events of the weekend, the situations and circumstances that were taking place were creating energy, some of it good, some not so good, and in a short time an inevitable reaction to these events would need to pass.

Shortly after arriving in Palm Springs, I changed my computer password on a regular basis and used words that related to going home or finding a place of belonging, even though I had a home in Palm Springs. I believed in the back of my mind that I was feeling lost, wondering aimlessly through life. Crazy as it may sound, I thought someone in a cloud was going to intercept my SOS messages – in the form of encrypted passwords – and come to my rescue. I now believe I was subconsciously crying out to God and hoping He would hear my call for help. I was feeling overwhelmed and I was seeking a place of refuge. In my mind, I always thought that if push came to shove and I lost the house, I could always run back to Chicago, a place that was familiar and where I had family and friends that could offer me comfort and a place to lay my head at night.

One day, when ILD was still in operation, a client was executing a project in Los Angeles and requested that I be onsite to oversee the installation of a graphic window display system that a subcontractor was installing. It was already past the time I said I would be on the job site, but it didn't seem to matter to me that I was going to be late. Before getting involved with Philven, I was always on time for my appointments, if not early. Due to all the bullshit associated with our relationship, I had become someone who was constantly late or who wasn't where I said I was going to be.

I sat in my living room in the Whitewater home having a late breakfast before I began the drive to the client's location in Los Angeles. The television was on while I was eating and I was watching a program on one of the Christian networks. I was then trying to get a deeper understanding of the Christian faith by watching those networks as much as possible and I paid close attention to what was being said on any given program that I was watching. At this point, I didn't understand nor did I feel a personal tie or commitment to Israel as many Christians do. While I ate in front of the television, when I was not where I was supposed to be at a time when I said I would be there, Benny Hinn, a Christian televangelist who was televising a program from Israel, made a declaration.

Benny spoke about the time when Jesus would return to this world and stand on the Mount of Olives in Israel. He talked directly to his audience as individuals rather than as a group and addressed them using the word *you*, as if he was addressing one directly. In doing so, his statements became personal ones to each of his viewers. "You'll be here," he said, when the day comes when Jesus returns. I thought that I had no ties to Israel and I certainly wouldn't be *there* as he proclaimed. If I were to be anywhere other than Palm Springs, I would most likely be back at my parent's home in Chicago living in their basement with the babies. "You're always late", he continued to say, "you're never where you say you're going to be, or at the time you say you're going to be there. On the day Jesus returns, you'll not be in Chicago, you'll be here where I'm standing in the State of Israel." I was stunned and amazed at how close his words related to my specific circumstances. I became confused and extremely anxious. I was certain he was speaking directly to me. This was highly unlikely, but I believed he was.

You may think I was paranoid and you may be right because that's what I had become. There were too many of these types of circumstances taking place all around me so I began to think someone was deliberately making these so-called coincidental events happen. I continued to think that someone was watching me and manipulating the events in my life. My thought process made sense and it seemed plausible that someone was trying to control me or at the very least fuck with my head, as so many had done. I had been lied to on so many occasions and manipulated by so many people who were close to me, that it was no big surprise that I thought I was being mentally fucked with once again. I now understand and believe my experiences, such as the one I describe above, was coming from a supernatural place. My world was collapsing, but what I didn't know was that it needed to fall apart so a new world would be created for me.

Philven was supposed to go with me to the TBN studio in Costa Mesa, but at the very last minute, he decided he was not going to make the trip. He was coming down from days of doing drugs and couldn't get his ass out of bed. It was a blessing that he didn't go. He would've made the entire experience a living nightmare. I got dressed and made sure Puckles, Aston, and Bentley were fed and that they went outside to do their business. I knew I was going to arrive back at the house late that evening, so I asked Philven to make sure he let the boys out one more time so they could go to the bathroom before they went to bed. Once I got into the Jaguar, I programed the studio's address into the car's navigation system. I was excited to finally be on my way to be part of the audience for an episode of *Praise the Lord* and see the TBN corporate facility, but I was also anxious over my visit. I didn't know what I was going to encounter once I arrived because the religious world was outside of my wheelhouse. I felt inadequate in every way when I was amongst religious people, so I was quite apprehensive. I was either messed up in the head and there was no real reason for me going to TBN, other than the obvious…to be part of the audience at an episode of *Praise the Lord.* Or my visit was truly an assignment that came from a spiritual place and I had been called there for an unknown reason. I believe my entire life led me to this moment and, in a very short time, I would find out which of the scenarios would play out.

As I tell my narrative, I oftentimes note that a story may sound strange or difficult to believe, but from this point forward I'll refrain from doing so. I ask that you keep an open mind and consider the possibility of my reality. Was I fucking crazy or not? Did I finally fall off the deep end or was I experiencing supernatural encounters? Was it real or was it Memorex? You be the jury and the judge.

As God began revealing Himself to me, I came to understand that He speaks to us as individuals and what makes sense to one may not make sense to another. What makes sense to me and how He interacts with me is more than likely very different than how He will interact with you. My relationship with Him has been designed for me in a way so that I understand and can relate to Him. Traditional religions want to shove us all into the same mold – that their own belief system is the only one – which is contrary to how we've been created and contrary to how I believe He communicates. One size and one story does not fit all!

20 | SECURITY IN THE HOUSE

Whitney Houston, an amazingly talented artist and a devoted woman of God, to whose loving memory I dedicate this chapter, passed away in Beverly Hills, California on February 11, 2012 at the age of forty-eight. There's that number eleven again.

"I look to you, after all my strength is gone - in you I can be strong…"

Whitney Houston

While traveling to the TBN corporate headquarters in Costa Mesa, I flipped the radio back and forth between country and contemporary Christian music stations. My father was born in Nashville, Tennessee and I grew up listening to country songs, developing a fondness for this genre of music when I was a boy. I love me some Jonny Cash, Loretta Lynn, Tammy Wynette, and Dolly Parton. When I was getting close to my destination, *Home* by Blake Shelton, began to play on the radio.

Another summer day has come and gone away
In Paris and Rome
But I want to go home

May be surrounded by a million people I,
Still feel all-alone
I want to go home
Oh, I miss you, you know

And I've been keeping all the letters that I
Wrote to you
Each one a line or two
I'm fine baby, how are you
I would send 'em but I know that it's just not enough
My words were cold and flat and you deserve more than that

Another airplane, another sunny place
I'm lucky I know, but I wanna go home
I've got to go home

Let me go home
I'm just too far from where you are, I want to come home

And I feel just like I'm living someone else's life
It's like I just stepped outside when everything was going right
And I know just why you could not come along with me
This was not your dream
But you always believed in me

Another winter day has come and gone away
In even Paris and Rome
And I wanna go home,
Let me go home

And I'm surrounded by a million people I,
Still feel alone and I want to go home
Oh, I miss you, you know

Let me go home
I've had my run,
Baby I'm done
I'm coming back home
Let me go home
It'll all be all right,
I'll be home tonight
I'm coming back home

The TBN world headquarters are approximately twenty-four miles from Long Beach, where I was born. Once I arrived in Costa Mesa, I found myself close to where I had begun my journey forty-nine years earlier. I longed to be home and at peace, but I had no idea where that place in the world was. I had been looking for a sense of belonging my whole life. I ran from city to city, state to state, coast to coast, and back again. I had exhausted myself by running from one place to another. Ever since God put the concept of three worlds in my heart, and after discovering Dubai, I felt drawn to the Middle East and more specifically to its' World Islands. Possibly God was calling me to this new world, so I began to ponder if Dubai was the place that could offer me the peace and sense of community that I sought. I understand that the Arab nations do not openly accept gay men or HIV positive individuals. I also understand it's against the law to engage in homosexual acts in these countries. Therefore, residing in the World Islands of Dubai seemed like an impossible dream for me based on the laws of that region. But if there's one thing that I've learned about God, is that His instructions may not make sense at the time of receiving them or might seem impossible to achieve. This is where walking by faith and not by sight is the key to realizing the masterful nature of God and how He works. Trust the Lord with all your heart; and don't lean on your own understanding. As I got closer to Costa Mesa, I saw signs on the highway with further directions to Long Beach. I didn't know that my past, present, and future were about to merge in a television studio during a taping of *Praise the Lord* just miles from where I was born.

As I drove, an announcer on the radio talked about a contest and how the winner of that contest would receive a $2,500 diamond engagement ring. Even though I was alone in the car, I voiced out loud that $2,500 wouldn't buy a very good diamond ring and they should, at least, be offering a ring worth $10,000. I was thinking out loud and possibly, in the back of my mind, I was still hopeful that my Prince would propose with a bigger and more expensive diamond. Besides, who doesn't melt over a man who loves you so much that he buys you a beautiful diamond ring to express his undying love or, in this case, wins one on a radio station? The opportunity for me to receive a diamond engagement ring, accompanied by a marriage proposal, may have come and gone, but always being a hopeless romantic…I hope and wish that those who are looking to find their Prince or Princess, and achieving their fairytale wedding, are blessed with finding one another and exchanging beautiful diamond rings as a symbol of their lifelong commitment.

At one point, the navigation system on the Jaguar dropped its satellite connection and I inadvertently got off the highway at the wrong exit. Once the system reconnected, the lovely lady's voice with an English accent noted that the system was recalculating. Shortly afterward, the women's voice directed me to the nearest freeway ramp to re-enter the highway. As I turned the corner to get back on the freeway, I saw a man on the side of the road who was hitchhiking. Since I was somewhat lost, trying to find my way back onto the highway, I only glanced quickly at the man. He looked like he could've been my younger brother. My baby brother lives in Illinois so I knew the hitchhiker was not him. Shortly afterward, I arrived at my destination.

I reached the studio headquarters before they opened the doors to the public so I had to wait in the car for forty-five minutes. I was feeling anxious and afraid that the Christians weren't going to welcome a heathen like me. I spoke to God the entire time that I waited, while I smoked several cigarettes. I told Him how uncomfortable I was and mentioned that the only reason I didn't pull out of the parking lot and head back to the desert was because I believed He had called me to this place, though I still didn't understand why

I felt I had been called there that day.

Cars began to arrive, the drivers exited their automobiles, and they started walking toward the venue entrance. As I was feeling nervous about what I was going to encounter, I too exited my car and began to follow the crowd. A few days earlier, I had watched the TBN program where individuals that smoked, drank alcohol, used drugs, and had a foul mouth, like me, were denounced. These so-called heathens weren't welcome in the Christian community. Since I was still feeling vulnerable and rejected by those statements, I wanted to ensure I was able to get a seat in the back of the auditorium. I wanted to be seated where I could make a quick exit if needed. I wondered why God would require me to come to a place and gather with individuals who weren't accepting of people like me. Was I a sacrificial lamb being led to an emotional slaughter?

I knew I was not strong enough to be humiliated in front of a crowd of that magnitude and mentally survive the experience. I was desperately seeking a place of belonging, where I could immerse myself in a loving environment, so I allowed myself to enter a place where I could be embarrassed, or worse, rejected. I believed this could have been my first step in finding that sense of belonging. I was trying to be strong, but I was close to the edge of no return. Depending on how the events played out, the experience might have sent me deeper into the depths of despair or it could have brought me closer to my goal of finding a sense of community. I was afraid of both options. Hell is where I resided for such a long time that I was concerned I was going to get lost in an abyss of hatred and revenge and never find my way out. I also had reservations about the second option. Would a religious community condemn me for my actions and my sexual preference, based on my behavior and lifestyle? At that point in my spiritual development, God was the only entity that I was willing or able to trust. I still wasn't even sure if the God of the Christian faith was the One that was revealing Himself to me.

I took a seat in the back of the auditorium in the last row, closest to the aisle, on the left side. If I needed to make a quick departure, I would be able to jump out of my seat and head toward the exit within seconds. As the audience began filing into the auditorium, Paul Crouch and his oldest son, Paul Crouch Jr., were on stage, sitting on a sofa. I had previously seen both on TV. I was a nervous wreck. I was so worried that someone was going to embarrass me so I was consumed with anxiety. I had my guard up and was paying close attention to what was taking place. Like so many times when I watched an episode of *Praise the Lord*, TBN always had a guest speaker as they did that night. The guest speaker was a minister of the gospel in the Arab nations, who I believe resided in Dubai. I had no idea an Arab Christian minister was going to be part of the show, although I'd seen him preach on the TBN channel several times. Once he began his sermon, I couldn't stop thinking that his presence was not a coincidence. Could he have been influenced to travel from the Middle East to this studio for this moment? Did he too have an assignment from God? If so, could our assignments be connected? Was his presence a sign for me to pay close attention?

The content of the preacher's sermon was freakishly close to what had taken place in the car when I was traveling to the event. In the physical world, we think in three dimensions…length, width, and height. If you add time to this three-dimensional equation, you have a fourth dimension, which is the one we live. I felt like the events in the car, and the preacher's sermon, were a set of circumstances that originated from a fifth dimension, like *The Heavenlies*, which is believed by many to be the spirit realm on earth.

Earlier, when the song *Home* played on the radio, I thought of the revelation about the three worlds. By that point, I believed the *World Islands of Dubai* were one of the three worlds of which God wanted me to be aware. How could it be a random coincidence that the guest minister on stage was from Dubai? I don't remember all the specifics of his sermon, but at one point he asked the audience if there was anyone who felt like they had an assignment or a calling, or who believed they were anointed—and wanted to come to the stage and put on their garment, cloak, or jacket of praise. I almost shit my pants because I felt like God had called me to that place. I still didn't know why I felt that way, I just did. Not only was a minister asking this strange and unusual question, he came from the place that God had made sure I knew about.

I felt as though I was being set up to look like a fool in front of those Christians who I feared wanted to humiliate me. Many years earlier, when Alex hosted the surprise birthday party for me, I had misinterpreted the day the party was being held, which made me humiliate myself in front of my friends, so I didn't react to the question nor did anyone else in the room. I couldn't help but think that his question was directed specifically to me and that's why no one in the room went to the stage. My mind was racing as to what the fuck was going on. A few minutes later, a speaker announced over the audio system that the elders realized that the person that they were seeking, to come to the stage, was anointed by God, but was not ready to put on their garment or jacket. I became confused as to what the crazy fucking theatrics were all about.

As if this wasn't enough bewilderment for my first time at an event like this, the craziness continued. At the end of the sermon, the minister asked whether anyone wanted to come back to Dubai with him. He said something to the effect that the desert is a lonely and dangerous place, where a family member will drive right past you and not pick you up when you're thirsty and in need of water. By this time, I really thought I was losing my shit. Could I have been hearing him incorrectly? I don't think I did. I then remembered that the navigation system in the Jaguar lost its satellite connection and I inadvertently exited the freeway at the wrong exit, where I thought I saw my brother on the side of the road. I began to wonder if the hitchhiker was an angel and whether the message from the Jaguar's navigation system – that it was recalculating – was a message from that angel that my spiritual navigation had been recalibrated. I hadn't had time to tell anyone about what was happening that day, so I was tripping on how close the minister's comments where to what had just taken place a few hours earlier. His remarks about the desert also unnerved me, as TBN was nowhere near a desert, but I lived in a desert and Dubai, where I wanted to live, was also in a desert.

I wanted to jump out of my seat and run to the stage where he was standing. My heart was telling me to leave all my shit behind and go with this Arab Christian minister to Dubai. Logic, however, was telling me something different, so I kept my ass in my seat. I pondered whether this was my opportunity to reside in *that* place where I so longed to find a sense of community, where I could call home. I've come to know that God's instructions, assignments, revelations, messages, or signs often do not make sense to me when receiving them. In that auditorium, it seemed as if my past was depicting my future. In more cases than not, God had given me the answer to a question before I've posed the question to Him. In this case, He knew I was seeking a place of belonging and I contemplated whether He was telling me that Dubai was that place. I began to think the *World Islands of Dubai* might be *heaven on earth*, at least for me, or they could be the key to help me find my place in the world. Could something have manipulated events to create a means by which the minister was sent from the Middle East to take me to my place of belonging? Was it a test of walking by faith and not by sight? The minister closed his sermon by saying to be sure to stop by Dubai and experience paradise on the way to *The Promised Land*, or heaven on earth. I assumed he was referring to the state of Israel, but that's speculation on my part.

Abraham, the father of many nations and a Jew, had a first-born son named Ishmael. The Prophet Mohammad is a descendant of Ishmael and Mohammad is considered to be the last known messenger and prophet of God according to the Quran. Mohammad died in 632 A.D. If you add the first two numbers of the year he died (6+3=**9**) you get the number nine. If you add all three numbers in the year he died (6+3+2=**11**) you get the number eleven. I found this interesting since the attacks on the twin towers in New York were by radical Islamists, which also coincidently took place on the ninth month of the year and on the eleventh day of that month. These bits of information may seem random at first glance, but if we begin to view these individual strings as being intricately intertwined, we may possibly achieve a higher place of awareness. I believe there's an exceedingly large number of these threads in our past, present, and future. If we begin to acknowledge the importance of these threads, we might see a pattern in the fabric of our existence. I've come to find that the most important messages are usually hidden in plain sight, in the smallest bits of data. By identifying these patterns in our lives, we might possibly discover that the different religions of the world shouldn't divide us, but were meant to form links that would join us.

The conflict that exists between Islam, Christianity, and Judaism is very similar to the disputes that exist between a brother and sister. It's believed by many that we all originate from Adam and Eve and follow some, if not all, of the same prophets of God, although evil has succeeded in dividing the world based on its fears and differences. Fear not, the differences between brother and sister are what makes a family. Siblings have many differences and at times they may even seem like rivals, but they have a common bond that supersedes their differences. Their sense of belonging to a family is always stronger than any differences they may have. I believe the same philosophy should apply between faiths.

Logic didn't seem to dictate the actions of the individuals in the TBN studio; there was *something else* governing the room. Was this *something else* trying to get me to understand that there was a link between the three faiths—Islam, Christianity, and Judaism? Were they symbolic of three siblings who had their own coat of arms, their own stories, to protect them from evil? Were their different shields, their holy books, designed to unite them? My mind was racing with all kinds of elaborate scenarios about what had just transpired in that studio. I was lost in my thoughts, as the minister finished his sermon, when suddenly I heard Paul Crouch let out a boisterous cry, practically yelling, "I want him escorted out of the studio and off the property", he shrieked. While I paraphrase his words, Paul made the demand to his security personnel, as obviously he wasn't happy with the sermon from the visiting minister from the Middle East, who offered free passage to anyone willing to go back with him. I wonder what would have happened if had I gone down to that stage and said, "I will go with you."

It felt so surreal that I wondered if somehow I had passed through a wormhole on my way to the studio and entered another galaxy. I felt like I had stumbled into a twilight zone or someplace like the Bermuda Triangle. Was there more taking place that evening than what met the eye? Whatever the case, I was nervous and fearful that I may have missed my opportunity for tranquility. I understood that it wasn't logical for me to think that I could walk to the stage, leave the studio, and get on a plane to Dubai with this man that I didn't know, but based on what happened in that studio, it seemed like I could've done just that—and been on my way to nirvana.

After the minister left the stage, some of the people in the audience stood up from their seats and began walking toward the exit. My heart skipped a beat. I thought they were going to meet him in the outer corridor of the auditorium and travel with him to Dubai. Reluctantly, I turned to the man next to me and asked him if he knew where everyone was going, but he merely shrugged his shoulders. A young man sat in front of him and turned his head in my direction, when I asked the question. He had a very serious look on his face, which made me more anxious. I was a newborn in that world of religion and new to how these Christians viewed their God. I felt like an abandoned child left in the desert to learn their beliefs without a teacher or any formal education. A few minutes later, the gentleman sitting next to me turned his body in my direction and said, "They're probably going to use the bathroom." That made sense and gave me comfort that I didn't miss my ride to paradise. It sounds funny now, but at the time it was all so serious, at least to me.

When I called TBN to secure the free tickets to be part of the audience, the lady who answered the phone informed me that I had to arrive at least thirty minutes before the show began at 6:00 p.m. She stated that the program would last ninety minutes. If the event started at six, I planned to be out of the studio no later than 8:00 p.m. However, I was in the studio longer than I was told and longer than I expected. Seven years later, my recollection of the event times is fuzzy, but I recall that even if I'm off by an hour, I still should've been back on the road by 9:00 p.m. I'm certain I didn't start my trip back to the desert until around 10:30 p.m., driving one hundred miles, and arriving home after midnight.

If people were running to the bathroom after the minister finished preaching, it gives a good indication of the length of his sermon. By that point, I was overwhelmed with the craziness of it all. When I focused my thoughts again on what was taking place on stage, Paul Crouch was speaking. He appeared to be talking with his son, but may have had another guest on the sofa by then. He was speaking about engagements and I heard him say something about receiving a $10,000 diamond ring. He also made the comment that a dog might be the means by which the $10,000 diamond engagement ring might be delivered to the person getting engaged. Clearly, the dog comment may have been a joke, but I wasn't sure. After that, I didn't hear another word coming from his mouth, or from anyone else on the stage, until the event was over. My mind was baked from all the coincidences that took place that night. How could Paul reference the exact price of an engagement ring that I voiced out loud in the car, on my way to the studio? I was convinced they were fucking with me. This scenario certainly made more sense than believing in a spirit that orchestrated the night's events. To date, I've not told anyone about what took place that November 2 and I still have a difficult time believing what I know transpired on my way to Costa Mesa and in the studio. I know what I saw and what I heard and if someone was not deliberately fucking with my mind, then I can only ascertain that somehow I must have entered the Heavenlies and encountered a spirit or more. Instead of calling it an episode of *Praise the Lord*, perhaps calling it an episode of *Ripley's Believe It or Not* might have been a better description.

When I arrived back home, I discovered that Philven had not let the babies out to go to the bathroom. Once again, he failed to do a simple task that I had asked of him. The boys had pissed on the floor in the guest room and in the office. How fucking difficult could it have been for Philven to get his lazy ass out of the bed and open a door so the boys could do their business? Since there was a five-foot fence around the entire house, Philven didn't even have to watch the boys while they were in the yard, he just had to let them back inside when they were done. He was coming down from his few days of partying and didn't care about anyone or anything, other than laying his lazy ass in bed. I couldn't discipline the puppies for going to the bathroom in the house. It wasn't their fault that they couldn't get outside. I cleaned up their urine and let them out in the yard so they could finish their business before I fed them and we went to bed. I installed tile floors throughout the entire house when I remodeled it, so the cleanup was quick and easy, but I felt sorry that they had to hold it so long, until they couldn't wait any longer, and relieved themselves in the house.

I finally went to bed somewhere around one or one-thirty in the morning. A few hours after I fell asleep, I was suddenly awakened by the moon shining brightly in my face. Before I opened my eyes and realized it was the moon, I thought someone was shining a flashlight in my eyes. The light was that bright. The moon was again hovering outside my bedroom window, just above the fence, like the previous night. This time, instead of being annoyed, I got out of bed to investigate the situation a little closer. I went into the living room and looked up to the sky and saw a vision, which consisted of three moons. This was the second vision I had involving three moons, but this one was different. Two of the three were full moons, like before, but the third was now a crescent moon. They were positioned in the sky diagonally and very close to each other. I wondered if the moon that I saw in my first vision, that appeared to be fading or dying off, had transformed into the crescent moon that I was seeing. Many years later, I came to believe that the dying moon represented the world that I created for myself from my poor choices. I now understand that God was telling me that the world where I resided, for more years than I care to remember, was fading or, for lack of a better description, dying off. The crescent moon represented a new world, where I would find refuge and a place of belonging. I don't believe that it was a coincidence that I went to TBN and thought I experienced an encounter with the Heavenlies and, upon returning to the desert and falling asleep, awoke to a vision in the sky. Based on what I experienced that day, I wholeheartedly believe God was introducing me to a new world. What I didn't know at that time, and wouldn't learn until later, was that the crescent moon is the symbol that sits on top of some, but not all, mosques, much like a cross sits on most, but not all, churches. The star-crescent adornment on the mosques was adopted after the Turks conquered Constantinople, known today as Istanbul – it didn't start as a religious symbol, but as a symbol of state.

I headed to the office, connected to the house, to examine what I was seeing in the sky. As I walked between the living room and the office, I realized that God was reaching out to me. When I entered the office, the three moons were over the highest point in Palm Springs…Mount San Jacinto, which is also referred to as one of the 'Four Saints'. The Four Saints are four mountains in southern California that are named after Catholic Saints: San Jacinto Peak, Mount San Gorgonio, the highest of the San Bernardino Mountains, San Bernardino Peak, and Mount San Antonio, the highest of the San Gabriel Mountains. I reached the furthest point in the office, closest to the mountains and in front of the floor to ceiling glass window, got down on my knees. I looked up at the three moons. Once again, I called out to God. I asked if He was truly reaching out to me and, if so, I asked Him to bestow wisdom and knowledge onto me.

I often think back and wonder why I didn't ask for money. By that time, I had been forced to close my business and had no means of earning an income. I was close to being broke and I still had the pending lawsuit against me. I was worried the bank was going to foreclose on my house in the coming months. With these overwhelming and crippling situations on my plate, I find it strange that I asked for wisdom and knowledge and not for almighty cash. I didn't hear God's voice that night, but right after I posed my request, a heavy layer of fog came over the mountains and into the valley, which prevented me from seeing the mountains and the three moons in the sky. Fog is a rare phenomenon in Palm Springs and its appearance at the exact moment that I called out to God seemed to me a sign that He was there. Shortly afterward, the valley was covered in dense fog and I went back to bed. I was absolutely overwhelmed and exhausted and I fell back to sleep immediately.

The next morning, when I awoke, I wondered if I truly encountered the Heavenlies at TBN the night before and God in the early hours of the morning. At times, when God has shown up in my life, I understand what's taking place at the moment that it's happening, but I usually question it afterward. On other occasions, I question the experience as it happens and usually, after much internal debate, I conclude that I did in fact have a spiritual encounter. On the remaining situations, it has oftentimes taken me days, weeks, months, years and sometimes even decades to realize that a divine presence was reaching out to me. It's only natural to question these supernatural experiences. When the Prophet Mohammad encountered the Archangel Gabriel, he too questioned what he experienced. It was not until he came down from the Jabal an-Nour mountain near Mecca, and after speaking with his wife and her cousin, that he came to fully understand that he encountered Gabriel, God's special messenger – in the cave of Hira.

Shortly after I got up, as I debated with myself about what had taken place the day before, I noticed Puckles was not doing well. I was glad I made an appointment with his veterinarian for that afternoon. His appointment was scheduled for some time around noon that November third. The closer it got to noon, the worse Puckles became. He seemed weak and listless. He was breathing heavily, as if he was having a hard time getting air into his lungs. The sleeping beast also awoke, not by a kiss from a prince, but from the crystals in the devil's pipe.

Philven wanted to go with me to the veterinarian, which was not far from the house. It was hot that day. When we got in the car, I put Puck in the back seat and turned on the air conditioning. Halfway to the vet's office, I asked Philven to ensure that the air conditioning in the rear of the car was working properly. Puck seemed to be struggling harder than ever to breathe and I didn't want him to overheat. My life was falling apart and I was a mess, but I was trying very hard to be a responsible and nurturing father to Puck, Aston, and Bentley. Philven ignored my first request so I asked him again to make sure the air conditioning was working properly where Puckles was sitting. He continued to ignore me. I was so pissed off that I pulled the car over to the side of the road and parked on the shoulder. Once I made sure the air was working in the backseat, I got in Philven's face. He knew I was trying to develop a relationship with God and I believe he deliberately tried to provoke me. I had been manipulated, lied to, cheated on, humiliated and disrespected so much that I could take almost anything that any asshole could dish out, without reacting or letting their fucked-up actions affect me, but I had very little tolerance, if any, for assholes that were dishing their shit onto innocent people or defenseless animals. I had to restrain myself from hitting Philven. He yelled, "hit me, I know you want to." He was right. I did want to hit the fucker in the face, grab him by the neck, and choke some of the life out of him—before opening the door to the Jaguar and throwing him into a desert ravine. I was one angry pissed off fag with a major attitude toward Philven or anyone else who wanted to fuck with me or my little family. However, I was smart enough to know that if I was truly going to advance my relationship with God, I needed to learn to restrain myself from reacting and disappointing Him. Later in life, I learned that when I didn't react emotionally or physically, due to someone's messed up behavior, my self-control came with a sense of power over those who were attempting to screw with me or acting like an ass. Pugs originated in China and the breed was highly valued by the Chinese Emperors, who kept the royal pugs in luxury. They were even guarded by the Emperor's soldiers. I loved Puckles with all my heart and I took great care of him, as if he was royalty. I would've done just about anything for that little dog, even kick Philven's ass to the curb if necessary.

The previous seventy-two hours were jammed packed with unusual circumstance and they seemed to keep coming. Shortly after we arrived at the veterinarian's office, one more bizarre situation happened. After taking Puck into the vet and explaining his symptoms, the doctor decided to take x-rays before confirming his medical condition. Philven and I went outside while we waited for Puck to have his x-rays taken. We stood on the sidewalk, fifteen to twenty feet from the entrance. We were close enough to the building to see the staff at the nurse's desk, although far enough away so they couldn't hear our conversation. I wanted to discuss with Philven why he didn't check the air conditioning after I asked him twice. At that moment, a young Asian man in his early to mid-twenties appeared on the sidewalk, riding his skateboard in our direction. Once he got close to where we were standing, he stopped his board a few feet from Philven. He stood closer to the entrance to the vet's office than us. I could see him from where I was standing, but Philven could not, as he had his back to him. The guy had caught my attention as he was skateboarding in our direction. He never looked at me and seemed to have his attention focused on Philven. I immediately thought he was probably one of Philven's many playmates, which would've explained why he was focusing his attention on Philven. The guy didn't have a pet with him, but after several minutes of standing behind Philven, he went inside the vet's office and sat down in one of the chairs in the waiting room. I was able to observe him sitting in the waiting room through the glass doors. Keeping one eye on the guy and one on Philven, I continued ripping on Philven for being so insensitive toward Puck in the car. I thought Philven wanted to accompany me because he was concerned about Pucks' overall well-being, but his behavior again proved that he didn't care about anyone or anything other than himself. We argued for several more minutes and the guy came out of the vet's office, walking directly toward us. He stopped and stood next to Philven, who didn't say a word, even as the guy stared at him. Philven ignored him, while we keep arguing. After several very long and uncomfortable minutes, the Asian guy dropped his skateboard on the sidewalk and rode off into the desert. I don't believe the guy was one of Philven's tricks, like I initially thought. I chose to believe he was a guardian angel sent on behalf of the emperor's soldiers to protect Puck. At least this version was a positive spin on yet another unexplainable moment, certainly strange, but when I factored in the craziness of the last several days, it seemed small in comparison.

Puck received steroid shots as treatment. I was told again that he had a collapsing trachea and his condition was worsening. The doctor explained that his medical issue would eventually take his life. Five hundred dollars later, I placed Puckles in the car where Philven was waiting for us. I drove home. Puckles' health began to decline significantly over the following several months and I spent a lot of my time caring for him. For the entire month of December, when watching television, I lay on the sofa holding him in my arms while trying to keep him as comfortable as possible. I had hit my limit emotionally and I shutdown, as my little boy's body was shutting down. When I look back on those moments, I'm grateful that I had the opportunity to spend quality time caring for Puck in the last months of his life. Even though my life had fallen apart and I was losing most of what I valued, I would not have traded the time I spent caring for Puck for all the possessions that I lost.

Sometime that autumn, President Obama went to China on a state visit and was photographed on the Great Wall. In December of that same year, the United Nations Climate Change Conference was held in Copenhagen, Denmark from the seventh through the eighteenth. President Obama and the President of the People's Republic of China received major news coverage regarding their involvement, or lack thereof, in the conference. I thought it ironic that Puck's country of origin was consistently in the news when his health took a major decline. I had picked Puck up from the breeder in Rockford, Illinois over a decade earlier and I couldn't help but think that the coincidence of China being in the news was a sign letting me know that the time was fast approaching when Puckles would return to the dynasty from which he came. I was clearly grasping to find comfort in a hopeless situation or, just maybe, the Heavenlies were reaching out to let me know that Puck was in fact returning to his royal ancestors, where the Emperor's soldiers would guard him in his next life, just as the terracotta army of Qin Shi Huang, the first Emperor of China, had done for him in his afterlife.

In late October of 2009, I had been forced to file personal bankruptcy. I sent hundreds of résumés to companies and non-profit organizations for many months, looking for a job, and received no responses. Either nobody was hiring or I was just cursed and unemployable. In either case, the money was almost gone. Since I had no means of earning an income, I had no choice but to file for bankruptcy. In doing so, it got the creditors off my back and the bank couldn't begin the foreclosure process on the house until the bankruptcy was discharged in the courts, which took about three months. I was beat down to my lowest point financially, emotionally, and physically. From that October until Puckles died in early 2010, I resided in an abyss of despair and self-pity.

I had tried everything humanly possible to uphold my financial commitments. It seemed that around every corner there was a creditor, Madame President, Philven, a lawyer, or more out to screw me, making it as difficult as possible to financially recover. In any other situation, I would've been devastated by having to file for bankruptcy, but I didn't have any remorse for filing since the vultures made it impossible for me to find a viable solution to my financial calamity. I placed my house, my life insurance policies, my savings, my company, and my dignity on the table. I gambled everything to keep from losing the one asset that I worked my entire life to achieve...my rare and remodeled mid-century modern home. It was time to throw in the towel and walk away. I had finally been defeated, or so it seemed. I once heard Joel Olsten say, "Bankruptcy is an event, not a person," so I wasn't going to let this *event* define who I was or who I could become.

Every cloud has a silver lining and my bankruptcy was no different. Unbeknownst to me, when filing for personal bankruptcy, any pending litigation against an individual is also discharged along with the debt. Fuck Madame President! I wonder if she ever had any remorse for spending nearly two hundred thousand dollars on legal fees. Interestingly, that was the amount of money that I was willing to forfeit had she followed through and paid me the thirty nine thousand dollars that she agreed to pay, in the early stage of negotiations. She spent all that money to have her lawsuit eventually dismissed. Funny thing, since I had closed ILD International, the lawsuit against the company also went away. I was jumping for joy! Madame President was only left with Philven from her initial suit. He didn't have any assets nor was he working so any further litigation against him was going to lead to a financial dead end. My lawsuit against her and her company remained intact, but I didn't have the funds to pursue litigation. Before her attorneys could get me to stand in front of a judge again, they would have to wait several months until my bankruptcy was discharged, so Madame President was obligated to continue to pay her attorneys.

A few months later, we finally appeared in court. The judge spoke in legal mumbo-jumbo. "I don't understand what you're asking," I replied to a question. "I don't have time to teach you the law," he retorted. I was outraged to be treated as if I was ignorant by a judge whose main responsibility is to help resolve a dispute between two parties—so I proceeded to speak over him. In retaliation, and to exercise his authority as almighty judge, he had me removed from *his* courtroom. A few minutes after I was escorted out of the courtroom by the bailiff, while standing in the outer corridor, Philven approached me and told me that Madame President's attorneys would agree to drop all the charges against him if I agreed to drop my lawsuit against Madame President and her company. For the first time, I had Madame President by her pigtails and all she could do was pursue litigation against Philven because I was free and clear. However, without the funds to hire an attorney to continue the litigation, I had no choice but to agree to drop my lawsuit since the judge didn't have time to explain the law to me or the decency to speak in layman terms…what an asshole! Philven wasn't a U.S. citizen nor was he a legal resident. He had entered the country on an education visa and it had long expired, but the undocumented devil was making deals with Madame President's attorney and the judge on my behalf. It sounded like an illegal agreement to me, but according to the judge, what the fuck did I know. When the document was sent to Philven, from Madame President's attorneys, for dismissal of her lawsuit against him, a line specified that he agreed to release Madame President and her company from any wrongdoing of which he was aware and any wrongdoing that he might learn about in the future. While this may have been standard legal verbiage, I viewed it as Madame President's attempt to exonerate illegal conduct by her or her company that we weren't aware of at that time.

I was just happy and relieved to put an end to a very miserable experience. I was equally as happy that Madame President spent an exorbitant amount of money on litigation. In the end, her arrogance cost her and her company tremendously, although it cost me my business, forced me into bankruptcy, and I lost my house. I learned a very costly lesson...the courts are for rich people who have more money than sense, because unless you have a lot of money to hire attorneys, you're fucked, as I found out. While the experience cost me much, I learned a great deal. Most institutions of higher learning have an expensive price tag associated with them and I believe my experience with the litigation was no different. What I didn't know at that time was that God had a greater plan for my very expensive, but valuable lesson. Even though I never saw a penny of the money that she owed me, God made sure justice was served—and Madame President paid the piper.

Christmas 2009 was a time of refection and humility. I was grateful that Puck was alive and not suffering from his deteriorating health. I was humble and thankful that the babies and I still had a roof over our heads. There wasn't a Christmas tree that year or any presents. I was just grateful that I could afford groceries that holiday season and for having the boys to keep me company. We had a nice dinner to celebrate Jesus' birthday. Philven still lived in the house, but we were no longer boyfriends. We were still sleeping in my five thousand dollar bed and the babies slept between us, becoming a divider to ensure Philven stayed on his side of the bed. It was the first bed that I ever bought, after leaving my parent's house – for myself and by myself – and I had made sure it was special. It came from Ligne Roset, a French furniture company, and it was originally delivered and installed in my condo when I last lived in Chicago. It sat very low to the ground and little Puckles could easily jump on the bed, which was one of the main reasons I picked it. I adored Puck and spending five thousand dollars for a bed that he could easily jump onto seemed reasonable; it was just one of those things you do for the ones you love.

As my world was being shaken, a massive earthquake coincidently struck Haiti on January 12, 2010. It killed hundreds of thousands of people. It was horrific and it made me feel as if the world as I knew it was coming to an end. Shortly after hearing about the devastation, I sat on the sofa with Puck, Aston, and Bentley listening to the news on the situation that was unfolding in Haiti. I glanced out the living room window, on the back of the house, and saw a huge plane coming in my direction. It flew very low to the ground and it looked enormous. I got up from the sofa and walked to the sliding glass doors, on the front side of the house, to get a better view of the plane as it flew over the house and began its descent to land at the nearby Palm Springs airport. For some unknown reason, I glanced back to look at Puck at the exact moment that the plane descended over the runway, when I saw him collapse. As the airplane touched the ground, Puckles returned to his royal ancestors, where the Emperor's soldiers would guard him for eternity. My boy was gone. I was heartbroken and bereft, but also happy that he was no longer suffering. God had given me time to say goodbye to him and to get used to the idea that he would soon be gone. With all the other shit that was on my plate, I'm not sure what would've become of me, had I been forced to deal with his sudden death. My sorrow was boundless, although I found comfort in the love and attention from Aston and Bentley. Suddenly, we were a family of three, with a free loader still living with us in my house.

For one year, my main goal each week was to ensure I had enough groceries in the house to feed us all. Having plenty of food was something I took for granted my entire life, but it became something I thought about every day. Having funds to buy groceries and pay the utilities each month became my full-time job. In the desert, during the very hot summer months, my electric bill was nearly seven hundred dollars. I had ten months left on the Jaguar lease and my payment was nine hundred and fifty dollars a month. I wasn't receiving any call backs from potential employers to whom I had sent my résumé and my financial comeback was looking hopeless. I was still optimistic that I would find a job in Palm Springs or in a nearby town. If I were to find a new job, I would need a car to get to and from work. Within the bankruptcy terms, I could've given the Jaguar back to the dealership before the lease was over, but I wouldn't have been able to lease a less expensive car because my credit was now ruined. I had to make a decision. Try to make the nine hundred and fifty dollar a month lease payment or have no car at all. I owned a car ever since I was sixteen years old and I didn't know how to function without one. By the end of the year, I would be forced to figure it out. There seemed to be no end, I just kept falling further and further into the pit.

At that point, I heard a little voice inside my head telling me I had more than enough to weather the storm. I believe God was using my unfortunate financial situation to test my devotion for the second time. He wanted to know if I would be willing to sell my possessions to survive, without being pissed off. Would I sell what I needed to sell and be glad that I had the stuff to hock, or would I be bitter? I had always been financially blessed and been able to acquire designer clothes, shoes, and accessories, quality furniture, a lot of stylish jewelry, and many fancy home furnishings, which could all be turned into cash if needed. In my quest to survive, I realized I hit a pinnacle in my spiritual development. I believe God wanted to know if I would still follow Him, if I had no choice but to sell my things. I figured that if I sold my possessions, I could always purchase new stuff when the day came when I was financially solvent again. If by some slight chance I couldn't recover financially, then what use did I have for all those things? Strangely, the items that secured me the most cash were jewelry from Chrome Hearts that I owned. I was introduced to Chrome Hearts over a decade earlier by Cher. She wore their pieces throughout her career and through her patronage helped make the two hippies that owned the company, and their brand, superstars in the fashion world. My guardian angel had come through once again without ever knowing it. I sold most of my Chrome Hearts pieces and many other items from the Darrel Loyd collection of stuff on eBay. I shipped things to different states in America, and to far-flung cities in Europe, Asia, Africa, and Australia. Hysterically, my shit is known worldwide. I had Versace silk pillows that I sold to a gentleman in New York. I shipped the pillows to the same building on 10th Avenue where I lived when I resided in Manhattan. What are the chances? Some days, I sobbed as I packed up my things and shipped them all over the world. I cried because I felt like there was no bottom to how far I was going to fall from grace. On the other hand, I was happy that I had stuff to sell and there were individuals who were interested in buying my possessions. Most items would have generated more money had the economy not been in such bad shape, but times were tough for many—and for those who had money to spend they were reaping good bargains.

I was very fortunate to be accepted into SNAP, the government food assistance program. I received two hundred dollars a month to put toward groceries. I was enrolled in the program for a year and during that time I was able to have enough food on the table. I had fallen so far down the rabbit hole that I couldn't see the light of day and thought I would never see it again. It seemed as if Tweedledum and his babies were one step from becoming homeless. At one point in 2010, I was so broke that I didn't have enough money to buy toilet paper. If you don't have toilet paper, paper towels, or paper napkins and you have to take a dump, how do you wipe your ass? You don't! I had to jump in the shower to wash my asshole. I was thankful I still had running water, which can be hard to come by in the desert with or without money. In the midst of it all, I realized God had a wild, but dry sense of humor and there was a thin line between the pain I was enduring and the humor that could be found in my misfortune. Maybe that's why God loves the desert so much, because it's dry like His humor.

After closing my business, becoming penniless, and even after I couldn't afford toilet paper, I continued to pursue a relationship with God. After I filed for bankruptcy, in the midst of selling my possessions and watching everything that I worked for my entire life slip through my fingers, I continued to seek God. I'm sure many people will ask why I continued to pursue Him, when it seemed as if He had let the accuser take everything from me. I had been blessed throughout my life as long as I didn't attempt to build a bond with God. As He began revealing himself to me, after I started to build an alliance with Him, the accuser began taking my possessions. The louder I proclaimed my passion for God in that valley, the more the accuser took, until there wasn't anything left to take. I had been manipulated and lied to so many times, on many occasions, and by many people, not to realize that there was more to what was taking place than me losing my possessions, although I was still not sure what that was exactly. Therefore, I gambled the only thing I had left – my life. I gave it to God. Sadly, when the moment finally arrived and I gave my pathetic life to Him, I gave Him something that seemed to have no value to the world or to me. I now understand this was when God valued me the most. It took me several years after that before I realized that He didn't want it. He had breathed life into me and my life was mine to do with as I pleased. My soul, on the other hand, belonged to Him. He had a vested interest in what I did with my life because my life's path would dictate my soul's destiny. I believe the underdogs of this world will always have God's undying affection and finally saw that God came to seek and save that which was lost and wondering aimlessly through life and now understand that God wanted to test my devotion, so He could help me achieve my life's purpose and, more importantly, so that my soul could achieve its' destiny.

Even though my house was in foreclosure, I was still living in a spectacularly remodeled home. I had amazing healthcare coverage from the Ryan White Foundation, food on the table, and I was still driving the Jaguar. I knew my situation was going to come to an end sooner rather than later, but I realized in the final months before losing my house that I had achieved so much more in my lifetime than most people who work their entire life. I now believe there was more driving the purchase of the Whitewater home than I thought when I closed escrow and also believe the Asian minister from whom I purchased the house was proof of my theory.

If I had been living in an apartment when all hell broke loose, I would've been evicted within three months after I stopped paying the rent. When I ceased making the mortgage payment on the Whitewater house I continued to live in it for eighteen months. By not making the payments, I forfeited my original down payment and the money I invested into the property when I remodeled the house, upgraded the pool, and installed new landscaping. My cash equity, which equated to one hundred thousand dollars, was lost during the foreclosure, so I don't feel too sorry for the mortgage company. I also had an FHA loan, which guaranteed the lender the full value of the outstanding loan amount, should I default. I'm certain this loan guarantee was the main reason I couldn't get the lender to give me a loan modification. Why would they modify my mortgage if they could recover the full amount of the loan by foreclosing on the property? When all was said and done, I believe it was an even trade for both parties. Even though it was a painful time in my life, it was a miracle that I was not homeless, hungry, or without healthcare. On the contrary, I was living in a beautiful house, properly fed, loved by my dogs, medically insured, and driving a luxury automobile. If that's not the love of God, then I don't know what is. The accuser wanted me to be pissed off at God and denounce Him because of my circumstances, but I realized it was God who looked after me when the accuser unleashed wicked forces into my world, resulting in a battle between good and evil and the loss of my possessions.

I still knew very little, if anything, about religion, I was a heathen in every sense of the word. I didn't even know how to pray. When I began watching the Christian and Catholic networks on cable television, I did so to become more informed, while attempting to learn as much as possible, as quickly as possible. On many occasions, I would get high and sit in front of the TV flipping back and forth through channels for days while listening intently to whoever was talking on these so-called religious stations. On more occasions than not, I found myself arguing and yelling at the television, but if it wasn't for these networks, I'm not sure I would've made it out of that time alive. These stations were to me as a life vest is to a man drowning in the ocean, although my ocean was a sea of misfortune.

I was experiencing anxiety and confusion from the unusual events that I believed had spiritual meaning. I was trying to understand what was taking place around me, which I was not spiritually equipped to do. In my pursuit to learn more about religion and in trying to determine whether the visions and spiritual messages I was experiencing were real, I become more confused. The networks I had been watching offered little clarity and I became conflicted by what I was hearing on them because the information wasn't always in line with what I believed was being revealed to me. I felt like a conductor at the helm of an out of control freight train. The locomotive was pulling an endless number of freight cars and each car was caring a different load of baggage. I was overwhelmed and exhausted trying to keep the train from derailing. I was constantly struggling to maintain control so I would eventually reach my unidentified, although predetermined destination. Nobody, not even myself, believed I could make the journey and successfully bring the caboose to the end of the line.

In the three and a half years that Philven and I lived in Palm Springs, he successfully managed to assemble a considerable posse of cracked-out jackals in his den of iniquity. These animals were at Philven's disposal and began circling the Whitewater house after dusk. During the last year of living in Palm Springs, I noticed cars parking in front of my house, or just before they reached the driveway, which was something that hadn't taken place before. The drivers would exit their car and walk on the outside of the cinder block fence that surrounded the property. They always headed toward the back of the house, which butted up against an empty lot. There was also an empty lot on the right side of the house, which was the path they used to get from the street to the rear of the house. I couldn't see where they were going once they walked out of their cars and headed towards the empty lot. It is pitch-black in the desert after the sun goes down and there wasn't a house with outside lights on that side of the property nor on the backside, so it wasn't possible for me to see where they were going or what they were doing.

One morning after waking up, I went to the kitchen to make breakfast for me and the babies. From the kitchen window, I saw a man standing in the empty lot behind the house just beyond the fence. I went outside to find out what he was doing and after speaking with him, I discovered he worked for the city of Palm Springs. He was sent to paint over the word FAGS that someone spray painted in very large letters on the side of my fence that faced the empty lot behind the house, which you could see from the main thoroughfare. The many men who were parking their cars in front of my house were having sex with Philven in the back lot during the night and must have been spotted by our neighbors. Whoever marked the fence must have seen what was taking place between Philven and his cracked-out jackals and this was why they spray painted my fence. I've done a lot of crazy shit in my life, but this behavior was beyond my comprehension and just the tip of the pile of excrement that Philven shat all over our relationship and now over the house.

Philven's behavior became more outlandish. On several mornings after I woke up, I had an overwhelming feeling that he had someone in the house while I was asleep. Logic told my intuition that it must be mistaken. How could he ensure I wouldn't wake up and catch him with someone? In time, I found the simple answer to my question. Unbeknownst to me, on occasion, Philven was still putting sleeping medication in my dinner or drinks to ensure I would sleep through the night even after we split up. I was never able to confirm my suspicion that he was partaking in this fucked up behavior until six months before I moved away from Palm Springs. By medicating me without my knowledge, he was able to move his sexual escapades from the back of the house to the inside. What the fuck was wrong with me that I had suspicions about being drugged and did nothing about them? Had I thrown Philven out of the house, into the street, as I had every right to do – and certainly wanted to do many times – I now believe it would have been the wrong decision.

My past experiences with Alex, the financial pressures I was under, and Philven's deceitful behavior became a lethal combination that drove me to keep self-medicating to subdue my feelings of unworthiness and self-doubt. One of the main reasons why I had developed an abusive drug habit in the first place was to disconnect emotionally, which prevented me from having to confront reality. This behavior started when Alex and I began to have problems—and I continued to self-medicate through my relationship with Philven. I'm an adult and I've learned to take responsibility for my actions and I'm not blaming my drug use on Alex or Philven, although their actions added undue turmoil to an already unhappy and depressed individual.

Evil seemed to want to use the darkness in my life to destroy me, although God used that same darkness to expose my sense of shame, unworthiness, anger, and self-doubt. Through watching the Christian networks, I began to understand that I had to forgive to fully experience the possibilities that God offered. Through God's love, I was finally able to see beyond myself and, by doing so, I was able to understand the power in forgiving those who had wronged me. This allowed a small ray of light to shine in my life. I now understand that without forgiveness in my heart, God wouldn't have been able to fully manifest his presence. Arriving at a place within myself to finally forgive Alex, for what I believe he had put me through, was only possible as a result from my problematic relationship with Philven. God used all the pain that I lived through in that desert to force me to humble myself in front of my problem – and learn to walk around that problem – rather than try to push my way through it as I had done in the past. I also had to learn to converse with my problem, and house and feed it, which brought me to the point where I understood God was in love with my problem…and his name was Philven. This undeniably painful realization brought me to a place within myself where I lost pride of self and gained the power of forgiveness.

Ultimately, my problematic relationships were the solution and the means by which I achieved my freedom from the dark place where I began residing when I was a teenager. Almost a decade after splitting with Alex, I forgave him. I realized God had brought him into my life for a reason. I'm thankful to God for allowing me to see the purpose that Alex had on my life. If it hadn't been for my relationship with him, I wouldn't have survived the time I lived in the same house with Philven. Only the love of God could take the feelings of contempt for Alex that I carried in my heart all those years, and that I felt at that time for Philven, and replace them with joy. I was overjoyed to finally be freed from the darkness where I resided and from my demons who haunted me for decades. Before I could seek a better life, I needed to accept the fact that my freedom was contingent on understanding that God loved the same two people, who caused me so much pain and problems, as much as He loved me.

Before I moved to Palm Springs, when I started to strongly feel that there was something missing from my life, I saw the movie *The Da Vinci Code.* I cried as the movie ending approached. I wanted to be part of something that could offer me a sense of belonging like what was depicted in the movie. At the conclusion of the story, a group of people gather in a place where a woman, who's believed to be a descendent of Jesus, found out she could in fact be from the bloodline of Christ. An older lady in the group introduces herself as the woman's grandmother and declares that the gathered people are her people and they're there to love and protect her. As I saw that scene, at that very moment, I had an overwhelming yearning to have that same sense of community. Ever since, I've longed to be part of a group that would love, honor and protect me. What I didn't know was that I wanted to be part of a community that loved God as much as I did, if not more, and by doing so we would also love, honor and protect each other. I had been searching for this my entire adult life in the form of a man, when I should've been looking to secure this in a heavenly being. Who knew? I certainly didn't.

Four years after seeing the movie, the time came for me to seek out such a community. In 2010, I made my first attempt to go out and find a society with which I could spiritually connect, with acceptance, nobility, and love for God and one another. I had very limited resources. To ensure I found my place of belonging, I was going to do the best I could with the means I had available. I wanted to become familiar with the Christian community in the desert cities and my first attempt to find such a group of people was to seek out a church and attend one of its services in the vicinity. I went to a church in Palm Springs several times before attending its introduction seminar for new congregation members. I was told that this church didn't openly accept those who were gay, which made no sense to me since Palm Springs has such a large gay community. While I enjoyed their worship music, I realized I wanted to be part of a hipper church that had an outstanding worship ministry with a live band, but who were accepting of people like me.

I thought I had found such a ministry in Irvine, California by watching TBN and Daystar. Franklin Jentezen was the pastor of the Free Chapel ministry. The drive to attend a service at Franklin's church was a ninety-five mile trek for me, ninety minutes of travel time each way with no traffic. The Jaguar didn't get the best gas mileage and I was broke, unemployed, and in bankruptcy. However, I made the effort to raise the money to buy gas to drive the two hundred miles in hopes of finding a community that would be accepting of a gay man who just wanted to be loved by God and respected by those who were worshiping in the same room.

The first service I attended at Free Chapel was great though Franklin didn't attend that particular service. It had a worship band that was absolutely fantastic and the energy in the room was over the top. A few weeks later, I made the same drive again to attend another service. This time Mr. Jentezen was heading up the night's services. I had to come up with enough money again to cover the fuel for the round trip, plus the forty dollars I donated to the ministry that night. Once Jentezen came out and began his sermon, he proceeded to trash the Hollywood film industry for their sinful movies, individuals that smoked weed, people who wore skimpy bathing suits in California, and the gay community as a whole. His comments bothered me, but the positive reinforcement that he received for his comments from the congregation disturbed me even more. That church, that pastor, and those people were certainly not representative of a community with which I was hoping to become associated at a place to worship. I was so pissed off that I wanted to say something out loud, although I didn't say a word. I got up from my seat and left the service like a gentleman, which is more than I can say for the manner in which Franklin conducted his sermon. I was devastated. I was spiritually beaten down after hearing him and his congregation. I was also extremely disappointed that I spent a considerable amount of money to get to the Free Chapel to hear such bigotry from a man who I thought would provide a welcoming platform for those like me, who simply wanted to get close to God and worship within a loving community.

I had seen Mr. Jentezen many times on TV and from the way he conducted himself I thought he was a wonderful loving man to all. I never attempted to find another church after he chased me out of his church with his words of condemnation. After much conversation with God in the car on my way back to the desert, I began to think God was trying to tell me to see past the religions of the world and concentrate my efforts on seeing the world He was revealing to me. I was so desperately trying to fit into *their* world and conform to *their* image that they said I had to be to be accepted into *their* church that I began to think I was not worthy of God's love. Each time I tried to be part of the Christian community, I was always left feeling inadequate. I didn't measure up to *their* standards and probably never would. I was also struggling to understand if *their* story of *their* God was the same God that I was encountering.

While I was driving back, during my one-way conversation with God, I realized that the cracked-out jackals in the desert were my people. By all accounts and by definition, I was one of them. I had been doing Tina for more years than I wanted to admit. Even though I believe God considered me a crack head, I wasn't a cracked-out jackal in His eyes. I was one of them, although I was not like them. The main differences that separated this crack head from the cracked-out jackals were the malicious lies, the cheating, stealing, and the disrespectful and cruel behavior in which the jackals partook, at other people's expense for their own personal gain, which I refused to do. I was horrified by the thought that God would group me with the crack heads, although it made me laugh out loud in the car for a moment. Like I've always said, He has a dry sense of humor.

Like Jesus, my so-called people shunned me too. In my case, they turned away from me and embraced the devil residing in my house of iniquity. But like Moses, did God send me to that valley to free the jackals from the grips of evil? If God truly loves me, as I believed He does, then He must also love the entire pack of cracked-out bitches. Possibly He wanted me to write this story so they might know of His love and devotion to them no matter what the world tries to have them believe about themselves. If God loved a cracked-out wretch like me, then I know He also loves the jackals that still reside in that desert. I hope and pray with all my heart to one day mentor as many people as I can, who are called by the same name I once was called, and inspire them to realize their purpose and hopefully help them achieve their destiny. If there's only one reason for me to share this story, it might be to entice the cracked-out pack from their dens of darkness in the hope of them seeing a more promising life than the one in which they're presently living. If God was able to get me to envision a better life for myself, then I know He can and will do it for anyone who will seek Him.

It seemed that organized religion had turned God into a bunch of rules and regulations that left me feeling inadequate in *their* house of worship. They alienated me as I pursued a place within *their* church where I felt accepted. I was left with no choice but to hold *their* abundance of rules and regulations at arm's length. I didn't allow *their* judgment to dampen my joy of building a relationship with God. Without the desire to find a man-made brick and mortar church, I began to look for a heavenly brick and mortar place of worship instead. San Jacinto Peak was visible from my living room. Many times, I found myself staring at the mountain peak while having in-depth conversations with God. I began to think that it was not a random coincidence that I purchased a house with a view of one of the Four Saints from a preacher. If I wasn't able to find God in a church, where else could I find Him, if not in the highest peak of those mountains?

In my pursuit to grasp an understanding of a being that created the world, I began to look at humanity as created by one God. In doing so, I came to view the world as an intricate, but masterful jigsaw puzzle with each of us representing a piece of that puzzle, with each individual representing a smaller puzzle. I was no longer able to divide the world by continent, country, culture, religion, race, gender, or sexual preference—and came to see that the resulting magnificent image depicts a creation that loves each other even if we don't always like one another, in a world without labels, with the exception of one…His.

Upon arriving back home from the Free Chapel, I tried to bargain with the devil and get him to realize I wasn't his enemy. I even went as far as to proclaim to be his friend. The only way I was going to survive my time in the valley was to reach some sense of peace with Philven. I wanted to physically hurt him for all the things he had done to me, but I had realized that God loved Philven too—so reaching out and trying to reason with him to achieve some peace was the only option available to me. God requires you to do things that you thought you might never do under any circumstance and trying to make peace with Philven and being his friend was one of those things and something I thought I would never do.

Joel Osteen rented the Dodgers Stadium in Los Angeles on Saturday, April 24, 2010 for an inspirational service called the Night of Hope. I came to know and was delightfully drawn to Joel through TBN and Daystar. I heard Joel say that one day you'll do something great for God and the people that you once partied with will take notice of your outstanding achievement.

When I heard him make this statement, I felt like he was talking directly to me. At that time, I had no idea what I could possibly do for God that would make a difference in the world, but I still had an overwhelming sensation that Joel's words of encouragement were meant for me. With all the craziness in my life, was it any crazier to think that God could use Joel to send a message that would encourage me to forge ahead? If this story were to be embraced by the public, and were it to sell well, then Joel's statement and my sense that he was speaking to me would have merit. I bought two tickets to attend the inspirational Night of Hope, for fifteen dollars apiece. The outing was going to cost me a considerable amount of money that I didn't have. I was still not working and I needed to buy gas to make the one hundred mile trip in each direction and I also needed to pay for parking at the stadium.

As the twenty-fourth of April approached, the battle raging in my life between good and evil became more intense. After Puckles died, I checked out emotionally and used drugs consistently to subdue my sadness from the loss of my little buddy. Evil will always take advantage of a person's weak moments to gain authority over their life and my situation was no different. Keeping my appointment to attend the Night of Hope came under attack the Friday before the event. I was in the shower when I heard a noise that sounded like tree branches cracking. I immediately knew what was happening, but I didn't want to be right in my assumption. I promptly turned off the shower and grabbed a towel to quickly dry myself. I rushed to the master bedroom to look out the window to see what was causing the crackling noise. The devil was in the backyard, cutting down the beautiful trees that butted up against the fence. The landscaper had planted Angel Trumpet trees after completing the remodel and I absolutely loved those trees. I handpicked them at the nursery and I often looked at them when I sat in the living room, admiring their beauty. They were just small bushes when they were planted almost three years earlier, but they had grown to a considerable height and were quite lovely. They bloomed all year with yellow and orange flowers and they were a perfect choice to conceal the not so pretty cinder block fence, plus they added two of my favorite colors to the landscape.

I was horrified by Philven's actions and perplexed as to why he was cutting down the tress that I so adored. I was a fucked up mess in many ways, but I managed by the grace of God to maintain the house and its grounds for the entire eighteen months that I lived there without making the mortgage payments. I wasn't going to let the property deteriorate, even though I wasn't able to meet my monthly financial obligation. I managed to sell enough of my stuff each month – and my parents were sending me money every month – to help me pay the utilities, supplement my government assisted food program, make my car payment, have the gardener come once a week, and allow the pool boy to maintain the pool twice a week. The gardener and the pool boy cost me one hundred twenty five dollars a month each, which was cheaper than buying the equipment to maintain them myself.

Although the trees would belong to the mortgage company in a short time, I had bought them and I was out of my mind that the devil was cutting down my beloved trees. I ran out to the backyard and confronted him. I asked him what the fuck he was doing. He replied that I needed to get Emily out of the house. Emily, my former assistant, still lived in the Big Apple and I didn't know what the fuck he was talking about since she was on the east coast. Philven often made off the wall comments that made absolutely no sense, so I figured he was out of his mind from being high or he was just acting fucking crazy to inflict additional pain and suffering on me. I screamed at him that Emily was not in the house, but he continued to cut branches off the trees like a cracked-out Edward Scissorhands. He was using a garden clipper to snap the branches from their main trunks. At that moment, all I cared about was getting him to stop what he was doing before there weren't any branches left on the trees. As I drew my hand back to bitch slap Mr. Scissorhands across the face as hard as I could, I suddenly envisioned Edward jamming the garden cutter, which looked like a very large pair of scissors, into my chest after my hand made contact with his face. My vision didn't stop me from bitch slapping him. Edward didn't stab me in the chest nor did he stop cutting off the branches. I went in the house and called the police. I hoped once they arrived they would take Edward Scissorhands off my property before he butchered more of my landscaping.

In the state of California, if you have someone staying with you for thirty days and if they receive mail there, even if they're not on the lease or mortgage, you cannot have them removed from the property without their consent or going through a formal eviction process through the judicial system, which typically takes three to four months. Imagine my amazement when the police showed up and told me that Edward Scissorhands had every right to live in my house as I did. Really? The house was purchased in my name. I secured the mortgage with my credit. I put the down payment on the property. It was my money that remodeled the house and my credit that refinanced it when the construction was completed. Why did Philven have a right to reside in my house when his name was not on the mortgage and more importantly when he was deliberately causing damage to the property? I was informed by the police that not only did he have a right to stay under my roof by California Law, he could also cut down trees on the property that weren't his to cut down.

How about the fact that his visa had expired years earlier and he had stayed in the country illegally? That too didn't matter to the police either because, as they explained to me, that was an immigration issue and not under their jurisdiction. The police went as far as to tell me to leave my house. What the fuck? They said the property wasn't worth jeopardizing my safety and I should consider leaving. Right! I was going to abandon the one asset that I worked my entire adult life to achieve because an undocumented alien had more rights than I did as a natural born citizen of the United States. Girl…even though I was a walking emotional disaster, I knew the statements by the police were about as outrageous as one could imagine.

In a short time, as the police so kindly suggested, I called immigration to have them perform an exorcism on Edward Scissorhands. I hoped to have him expelled from my property. I spoke to a gentleman in Washington D.C. and gave him Philven's name. He looked him up in their system, which I assumed to be some immigration department database, and told me that *they* had been looking for him…aka the hooker, the devil, Tweedledee and most recently Edward Scissorhands. Bingo! The official said he would forward the information to their local immigration office. I waited eagerly for several weeks, but unfortunately nobody from the local immigration office showed up to take Philven back to the United Kingdom.

Our conflicts escalated and I called the police several more times because Philven would get physically belligerent. On one occasion, he threw me up against the sliding glass doors in the living room so hard that I thought I was going to be propelled through the glass. I was trying to be a better person so I refrained from reacting to his physical attacks, although if you hit this bitch one to many times, this bitch is going to hit you back. The police still did nothing to get him out of the house. In their defense, I understand domestic disturbances can be difficult and tricky situation for them to resolve, but it was my fucking house and he was residing in the country illegally. His visa had expired, but nothing seemed to matter. It seemed that Philven had more rights as a British citizen living in the United States illegally than me—a natural born citizen and the single male property owner. I couldn't get a fucking break if my life depended on it, and it almost did.

I called the immigration department in the capital again to see why they never sent anyone to pick up Philven. I was informed that their main office had contacted the local immigration office and it was up to them if they wanted to proceed with deporting him, which they didn't. I was so fucking pissed off at the immigration system, I wanted to jump off a cliff. I just wanted the devil gone because he was causing me so many unnecessary issues on top of all the problems I had on my plate. The immigration official explained that the U.S. had an unspoken agreement with the United Kingdom so they weren't very interested in rounding up and deporting an English citizen. He went on to explain that Philven had rights. I fucking flipped out on the Mr. Immigration. I asked him, "what about my fucking rights, as a natural born citizen, who was being hassled by an illegal resident." He responded that if I was going to talk to him in that manner he was going to hang up. I shouted a few more choice words and I hung up on him. So much for the politicians who rant and rave about how illegal immigrants are ruining America's way of life. I can tell you firsthand, unless the politicians are using the topic of immigration as an emotional ploy with the voters, they don't really give a fuck about illegal immigrants from certain places. At least that's the impression I got from the individual at the immigration agency that I had the pleasure to speak with about Philven.

I was so distressed that I was being ignored that I sent an email to President Obama. I wrote that the White House was going to come under attack. Certainly not a rational move on my part, but a desperate and ballsy one. I wanted someone to show up so I could tell them to get Philven the fuck out. Imagine my surprise when, after sending that email, nobody showed up on my doorstep to inquire why I had sent such an email. I felt insignificant in so many ways. Even Homeland Security didn't think I warranted a visit. As a U.S. citizen, I felt I had the right to live in peace in my own home and start to put my life back together. If the local police, the U.S. Immigration Department, the White House, and Homeland Security couldn't help me, then who was I to turn to? I eventually decided to take guidance from an unlikely federal agency, the U.S. Treasury. The treasury placed their financial well-being in the hands of God and I opted to lean not on my own understanding, but to believe what was noted on all U.S. currency – *in God we trust.* The King of America, *almighty cash*, trusted in the King of Kings and I chose to as well.

On Saturday, I was on the fence about going to Night of Hope. I had been fighting with Philven all morning and was tired from the bullshit of the previous day. I was still devastated that he had hacked the trees in the backyard. I asked God to give me a sign on whether to attend the event that afternoon. Shortly after calling out to Him, yellow and orange hummingbirds began to show up in the backyard. They flew over the fence and arrived a few at a time, perching themselves on the trees that Philven had cut the day before. The number of hummingbirds increased dramatically the closer it got to the time when I had to leave for the event. It was that odd. At one point, the birds were so numerous that it seemed as if someone was on the other side of the fence tossing them onto my side. I took this strange, but heartwarming sign as confirmation that I had to keep my appointment to enjoy an inspirational Night of Hope. I desperately needed to be inspired and I was in dire need of hope, so off I went seeking help.

Yellow is the color of sunshine, hope, and happiness, although it has conflicting associations. On one hand, yellow stands for freshness, happiness, positivity, clarity, energy, optimism, enlightenment, intellect, and loyalty, but it also represents cowardice and deceit. The color certainly represented the contradictions taking place in my life. I believe God was telling me that the color yellow represented my past and the life I was living. The color orange represented the life that he was offering me. It's the color of joy and creativity and it promotes a sense of general wellness and emotional energy that should be shared, like compassion, passion, and warmth. Orange will help a person recover from disappointments, a wounded heart, or a blow to one's pride.

When I arrived at the stadium, I parked the car in the lot and walked to the entrance of the venue. Upon finding my seat and sitting down, I noticed a bird that was smaller than a crow, but larger than a sparrow, fly into the stadium from behind me. It landed directly in front of my view, on a speaker post close to the ball field near the where the stage was set up. I was sensitive to the bird's presence because of what had taken place earlier that day with the hummingbirds. This bird had a large yellow colored underbelly. The bird remained perched on that pole, in my sightline, for the entire duration of the event that lasted several hours. The color yellow in a rose represents friend and I believe God sent this yellow-feathered messenger to convey that He was my friend and I was among friends. I was in a struggle for my life and it was comforting and reassuring to know that my imaginary childhood friend, whom I had left behind many years before, was not only real, but was reaching out to me—wanting me to know He never stopped being my friend.

On my ride back, I reflected on my time spent at Joel's night of hope. I quietly thought about the reasons why I wanted to get to know God on a deeper level. One of my initial attractions was His sense of humor. On more occasions than not, I have found He will use laughter to lighten a difficult situation if I opened my mind to his wittiness. He moved from having the architect *verbally* plant a seed in my mind about a new world being built in the Middle East, to having a friend *email* me information about the World Cruise ship under construction, to *texting* emoticons of three moons that represented three worlds, to *tweeting* via yellow and orange birds. God may be the same as he was yesterday, today and tomorrow, but in today's culture I find Him as savvy and as current as a teenager with a smart phone.

I also thought about how I was going to financially support myself. I had been sending my résumé when I applied for jobs posted online on various job boards, but the companies were not responding. 2010 was the year I hit my lowest point. After Puck passed away, I checked out for several months, continuing to take a considerable amount of drugs to numb my concerns, my worries, my feelings of rejection from potential employers, my financial problems, and my broken heart caused by Puck's death. I stopped taking care of myself emotionally and physically. I became inconsistent when taking my medical regiment to treat my HIV. I would go weeks, and sometimes months, without taking my meds. When taking into consideration the tremendous pressure I was under for such a long period, combined with my irresponsible behavior of not taking my medications prescribe by my doctor, on top of my illegal drug use, it's a miracle that I managed to stay physically healthy.

From the moment I had driven into Palm Springs in 2007, I had fought a daily battle and Philven was the common denominator to my many problems. In my desperation to free myself from all that tormented me in that desert, I had tried to take my own life that would end my battle. But in the midst of the tempest raging around me between good and evil, God had a plan and it didn't include allowing the accuser to reap my life by a self-induced drug overdose. The accuser would not become the victor. God would ultimately use my poor choices and Philven's deceitful behavior to finally free me from the demons that haunted me. I then realized that there was a reason for what was taking place around me and these reasons led me to understand that life wasn't a random shuffle of the cards, it had purpose and I needed to find and acknowledge mine.

I believe our purpose in life is very much like that brass ring that you try to grab when riding a carousel. The point of seizing the brass ring is to win a free ride, but it also brings a sense of joy, determination, and achievement to the rider. I had fallen off the carousel of life decades earlier while trying to reach for a man that wanted the same things out of life as I did and by doing so I ended up in a pit rather than with a ring around my finger. With each choice, I descend further into that pit until one day I hit rock bottom. At times, I wondered if my life's path was pre-destined or just a bunch of bad choices that brought me low looking for God's grace. Was the fate of my journey always meant to bring me to my lowest point and enlighten me to the fact that I had a purpose? Or did God utilize all my wrong choices and bad conduct to reveal that fact? I'm not entirely sure which of these scenarios applies, but it doesn't seem to make a difference anymore. The moral of this story is that it doesn't matter how and why I hit rock bottom because if I hadn't, I wouldn't have discovered who I was and the person that I wanted to become. When I hit bottom, while covered in shame, I was finally able to see, for the first time, that ring that I so longed to achieve. My brass ring was lying on the floor of that pit covered in filth.

When I couldn't take any more, I began to understand that God was going to utilize the horrific things in my life for my greater good, if I allowed Him. But God's ways are not our ways...and with each choice I made, God turned that bad choice into a stepping-stone that He used to construct a staircase—so when I was ready, I could climb my way out from the place where I had fallen and escape the filth where I resided. I needed to look beyond my immediate circumstances to the future that I wanted. It was at my lowest point that I discovered who I was and the person that I wanted to be and for the first time in my life these two individuals were in union. Even though I had tripped an infinite number of times in my attempt to reach a point where I could achieve my American dream, I was determined to hold onto the hope of someday finding a sense of community and a family that loved me as much as I loved them.

After hearing Joel's words of encouragement, I was in a much better place mentally then I was before I left for the event. Once I arrived back home, I began to argue with Philven about his fucked up actions that led to him hacking the trees. I was still upset, but I was now inspired that things were going to get better, so I went easy on him. I realized that the trees would grow new branches with time. I told Philven while he lay in bed that I believed humanity – in my mind referring to him and me – would eventually realize their life's purpose and stop their bullshit antics towards one another. I purposely didn't specifically refer to us to avoid a physical confrontation, although I was hoping to get my point across. I told him that I believed this would happen before "they" destroyed one another. This epiphany of "theirs" would come to fruition by the skin of their teeth. Later, I learned that the expression *by the skin of my teeth* is in the King James version of the Bible, in Job 19:20. Shortly after our conversation, I went to bed. The next morning when I awoke, I was missing a tooth, a seven hundred dollar cap, and it was nowhere to be found. Whoever said God doesn't have a sense of humor, clearly has never had Him take one of their teeth in the middle of the night. After I fell asleep, he sent the tooth fairy to my house to make his point, although His point cost me quite a bit.

God knew I wanted to live in a world based on truth more than I wanted life itself. I believe He also wanted me to live in a world built on facts and this was especially true when it came to learning about Him. He knew I had been lied to on so many occasions, by so many people, and for so many screwed up agendas that I acquired the ability to determine if someone was telling me the truth or a fictional tale. In my pursuit to learn more about God, I needed to sift through a multitude of sermons from preachers, so-called prophets, ministers, and priest. With my history of scrutinizing information given to me by people who preferred to deceive me, combined with the spiritual encounters I had experienced, I believe God saw me as a perfect candidate to determine which stories about Him made sense and which did not. He cleared my schedule for months and sat me in front of the television like a puppet, watching and listening to the religious networks. I was a real live Pinocchio and without their knowledge they were preaching to the puppet of the master puppeteer. Unlike the story of Pinocchio, who was a marionette created by his master not to tell a lie, or his nose would grow longer, my master created an opportunity for me to use the skills I honed over decades that gave me the ability to spot a bullshit story when I heard it. I was committed to identifying whether an account of God seemed to be truthful or if it sounded like it was fabricated. If God was tugging on my strings to do this for Him then whose strings did I need to pull to find my own magical being, my Blue Fairy? Could the Blue Fairy help me determine which stories about God were true and which were not? If the Tooth Fairy was in fact the one who stole my tooth in the middle of the night, then the Blue Fairy must be real too.

Come away O human child!
To the waters of the wild
With a fairy hand in hand
For the world's more full of weeping than you can understand.
The Stolen Child

W. B. Yeats

The many individuals who told me endless lies for years stole my innocence. If the Blue Fairy in the tale of Pinocchio had the power to make him into a real boy with real childhood experiences, then could she help restore my lighthearted nature while helping me determine what was true and what was not? In the movie *A.I.*, an animated computer program, called Dr. Know, told David that he must seek the Blue Fairy for him to become a real boy. Dr. Know also told David where to find her, in a restricted area. Was the worldwide web my Dr. Know? Could the internet help me obtain information from a restricted area? If so, would I be able to determine if the Blue Fairy was a person, place, or a thing—at the end of the world, in a lost city, at the edge of a sea where lions weep?

The unrest in the Middle East escalated in 2010 and peace talks between Palestine and Israel broke down. The United States was involved in the negotiations and the news networks and religious stations were reporting how the U.S. government should unite and stand strong with Israel. The timing of this political unrest and the volume of news coverage it received was an important element in my spiritual development. Up to then, I hadn't traveled to the Middle East for any reason and I didn't have a comprehensive understanding of the political and religious issues in that part of the world.

During my last year in Palm Springs, I became obsessed with the three moons, especially with the crescent moon that I saw together with the two full moons. I wondered if God sometimes keeps us in the dark until He wants us to be enlightened. When the crescent moon was visible at nighttime, I was always drawn to a bright star in its vicinity. To me, they looked like they were hanging out together in the sky, like a couple. What I did not know was that it wasn't a star at all that was shining so brightly, it was the planet Venus. For some unknown reason, I began to associate the crescent moon and the one bright planetary star with the country flag of China. I wasn't good at geography and almost flunked that course in high school, so I expect this shortcoming followed me to the desert. To my amazement, I later discovered that a crescent moon and a star were not symbols depicted on the Chinese flag, they were the symbols on the Turkish flag.

When I saw the image of the crescent moon and Venus, which looked like a bright star, they stirred a desire within me to visit the Middle East, especially Dubai. Since I was flat broke and concerned that I might soon be homeless, the desire to travel overseas made absolutely no sense. What I didn't know was that once my time in the valley came to an end, I would travel to Istanbul, Turkey—one year after my exodus from the desert. Turkey straddles Europe and Asia. I saw this as the reason why the crescent moon and Venus drove a desire within me to travel to that region and why I associated the two symbols with Asia. The fact that Istanbul had a footprint in two continents was the common denominator in making some sense out of my thoughts and feelings about the Middle East and Asia. Istanbul was once known as Byzantium and later Constantinople. It was a city where Venus, the Roman goddess of love, was once worshipped before Christianity became the dominant religion of the Roman Empire. Constantinople was eventually conquered by the Ottomans and became the capital of their empire, when the star-crescent adornment on the mosques was adopted – it didn't start as a religious symbol, but as a symbol of state. While all this may seem random, I saw a connection in what I believe was an intricate plan to connect my faith to Europe, the Middle East, and Asia.

When I checked out from my miserable life, doing too many drugs, I often laid my weary bones on the sofa watching religious and news networks. Israel and the Middle East were constantly being discussed from the unrest in the region. One day, while watching a program, I heard a plane ramping up its engines in the distance. I got up from the sofa to look out the window to see what type of plane was taking flight from the airport. At that moment, I saw a blue and white-feathered bird perched on top of the cinderblock fence in my front yard. Seconds after spotting my feathered friend, who was in my same direct sightline as the plane taking flight, I noticed that the colors on the plane were the exact same as the bird on the fence. The blue and white feathers of the bird, combined with the same two colors of the plane, made me think of Israel. I went back to lie on the sofa to watch the television and didn't give any more thought to what had just taken place. A few minutes later, I heard another plane ramping its engines to begin its takeoff. I got up again and walked to the window. This time, a bird with black, red, yellow, green, and white feathers perched on the fence. Imagine my astonishment when I saw the second plane take flight with Arabic writing on its side, with the same colors as the second bird. Now, as I recall the second bird and plane, I am not entirely certain that their colors were as I remember them, but at the time they were identical. There is a private airfield next to the Palm Springs airport so it could've been a large and extravagant privately-owned plane that I saw takeoff. Regardless, I went back to lie down on the sofa and watching television.

The coincidences baffled me. I began to ponder if the birds on my fence, with the same colors as the planes that took flight, were a sign. Was Israel supposed to unite with the Arab countries and not just with America? I had seldom seen these beautifully colored birds on my property. At the exact time that these two birds perched on my fence, with the same coloring as two planes taking flight one after another, the news programs were reporting on the conflict in the Middle East. The colors of the first plane and bird reminded me of Israel. The Arabic writing on the second plane, combined with its colors and those of the second bird reminded of the Arab nations. Until that incident, I was in agreement with the popular consensuses that Israel should stand united with America and vice versa, but upon receiving the unison vision of the birds and planes I adjusted my thinking, as it felt like a sign for me to see a different point of view. It seemed that something used the birds and the planes as metaphors to get me to understand that perhaps Israel and its Arab neighbors should unite and that America isn't necessarily the answer to unification and peace in the area. Obviously, if there's going to be a peaceful resolution in that part of the world, Israel and the Arab nations need to come together.

During my last year in the desert, I spoke to God nearly every day. When I experienced what I believe were many signs and wonders, I never encountered a manifestation of an actual spirit in human form who claimed to be God or the son of God and I find it difficult to believe a person when they say Jesus appeared to them. I do understand that God speaks to each individual in a manner specifically designed for that individual and, possibly, I'm still in my initial stage of getting to know God and the different ways in which He communicates with me—whether via email, text, tweets, or otherwise.

I believe that the church has tried to bring people to know God through fear. Fear can persuade people to say many things, but it can't get them to build a true relationship with God. Faith without works is dead in my eyes! Putting your faith in God and building a meaningful relationship is a lot work, which I've learned firsthand. The more work I put into building my relationship, the better it is and the more satisfying the experience. The church and many priests and ministers have said that people like me were not accepted in the eyes of God. Had I listened to them, I would've never tried for a better life. It was God who showed me that these so-called religious people didn't represent His true feelings towards people like me. He loved me when I felt like no one else did. Even when I didn't love myself, He made sure I knew He did.

I don't view the phrase *God created us in His image* as a literal one. I believe God created us to be creators and created us in His figurative image. Whether a person is an architect who designs high-rise buildings, a carpenter that builds residential homes, a machinist that works in a factory making automobiles parts, a chef that cooks at a five-star restaurant, a busboy who creates a pleasant dining experience, a code developer for a software company, or a stay-at-home mother or father who create a loving environment to raise their children, we all are creators in our own right. I believe this is why I relate to so many movies, entertainers, and songwriters shared in this story. Through the creation of these stories and songs, I've been able to see and hear God more clearly.

I've come to understand that there are many religious leaders that have an enormous amount of personal wealth. Even though I'm a strong believer that God wants His creation to live a good life, I also believe that if you walk, preach, and live by the Bible, you can't have an enormous amount of personal wealth and truly be a legitimate spokesperson for God when so many of His creation are suffering. I think Joel Osteen is an amazing man so I'll use his situation as an example. Oprah Winfrey once aired a special on Joel's life, which included his ministry. During the program, it was revealed that Joel had a personal worth of forty million dollars. Joel defended his portfolio by saying that he earned that money from books that he wrote and none of his wealth was from his church where he serves as its pastor.

I wonder what God will ask Joel on judgment day? I expect Joel would say something to the effect of "look at all the good that I've done in your name." God might then say, "How could you let my people suffer when you had so much wealth that you acquired in my name?" In Joel's defense, I think it's fair to break down the numbers. If he had a five-million dollar house, including its furnishings – a fantastic house for Houston where Joel's ministry is based – five million dollars allocated for each of his two children, and if he had another five million dollars in cash in the bank, it would amount to twenty million dollars, an extremely generous to allocate to his portfolio in my opinion and would provide a fantastic lifestyle for anyone. Twenty million dollars is certainly more assets than most people in America will ever acquire. Yes, Joel will continue to have living expenses, but he'll also continue to make more money.

I love Joel even though he doesn't accept my lifestyle and believes that God will condemn me to hell on judgment day for being a fag. If I'm right in my assumption about God questioning Joel's personal wealth, then I expect that according to the numbers above and according to Joel, we'll see each other in hell.

I don't mean to be disrespectful to Joel in anyway, that's not my intent. I love Joel and truly believe he was one of the people God empowered to comfort me while I was imprisoned. I've not met him nor do I know anything about his life. I've made a generalization based on what I heard in Oprah's show. If the numbers are correct, then his extraordinary wealth is a perfect example of why so many people are turned off by religious leaders. He is only one example of the outrageous and scandalous amount of wealth many religious leaders and the church have in their possession while so many continue to suffer. I wholeheartedly believe the church has the resources and the power to change the world for the better, if they only got themselves out of the way and make room for God. I may piss off a whole lot of rich leaders in the church with these comments and to them I say…good!

I expect the church to be familiar with the expression *from the ashes we shall raise.* The catastrophic earthquake of 2010 that devastated Haiti, was a perfect opportunity for the church to go into that country and assist the citizens and its government in rebuilding the nation. I watched the Haiti situation unfold and was horrified by the level of suffering the people had to endure—and continue to endure. Some churches in America showed up in Haiti shortly after the earthquake and offered assistance to relieve a portion of their immediate needs, building houses for some of the people who lost their homes. This is certainly tremendous and more than I've done for anyone so far in my life. I'm not judging the church, but I question why it didn't do what I believe it was established to do. How better to tell the citizens of Haiti and the people around the world that God loves them, if not by helping them rebuild and help them become a self-sustaining and prosperous nation. A project of this magnitude, headed by the church, would be a spectacular outpouring of God's love and the power of a unified church.

There're over three hundred thousand Protestant and other Christian churches in America, plus twenty-four thousand Catholic and Orthodox churches, over three hundred and twenty-five thousand churches in total. Why was this establishment unable to ensure that Haiti wasn't forgotten after the initial devastation of the earthquake became yesterday's news? I believe the reason the church was unable to handle a project of that scale is because each church and each pastor is operating their church under their own agenda. Many religious leaders want to be a star rather than allowing God to be the superstar. In my eyes, other than the Catholic church, there seems to be very little hierarchy in the religious denominations, so individual churches are incapable of unifying. Again, in my opinion, the unification of the church is where the real power lies. Its seems impossible to get the egos of the individual preachers, ministers and pastors out of the way, so the church is unable to do what it was established to do—take care of those who can't take care of themselves and spread the word and love of God through their actions. Faith without works is dead!

If the church would fund a project to supply the manpower and the resources to rebuild Haiti and would be willing to appoint me to be their project lead, I would spend the rest of my life, or until the project is completed, working with the people and government of Haiti to rebuild their country and its economy so they could become a self-sustaining nation. If the government of Haiti agreed to accept the support of the church for its' restructuring, Haiti would have the opportunity to be a crown jewel, illustrative of what the church in America and around the world are capable of achieving in the name of God. If church leaders were interested in my offer to be their project lead for this endeavor, I would forward them my résumé immediately.

When I was financially broke, I heard prosperity preachers say to give money to their organization. They quoted examples from the Bible and told good fortune stories to entice people to donate money. As I was trying to learn more about and become closer to God, I kept being bombarded by their prosperity sermons. I was told that if I gave money to their organization, the windows of heaven would open and blessings would pour out onto me. I had very little money, but how was I to be blessed and get closer to God if I didn't give money to their organizations as they proclaimed I should? I heard on many occasions, by many so-called preachers, the story about a woman who only had enough food for her and her son when a prophet showed up and told her to bring their food to him. The prosperity preachers went on to say how God so blessed the woman for giving the food to the prophet. This story may be true, although I'm absolutely sure that if a woman only had enough food to feed herself and her son, God wouldn't require or expect the woman to give their food to a prophet. No man of God, or woman, should ever take food from a starving person and their child unless that person is willing to share by their own free will. End of story, prosperity preachers! I'm sure the tale of this woman who had so little, is not meant to be used as a story to entice people to give money, or in her case food – that they don't have the luxury to give – to reap the rewards of heaven. Outside of the religious sector, this kind of situation is called a con, perpetrated by a con artist and punishable by imprisonment.

I was a newbie to the concept that the prosperity preachers were declaring. I didn't believe what they were saying was true. The God that revealed himself to me was not about money. My God was about loving relationships. I understand that it takes money to run a ministry and I believe He does too, but not at the cost of people putting their well-being in jeopardy because some so-called man of God has convinced them that if they give what little they may have, God will grant them blessings. What I've learned about God in the short time that I've known Him is that He does what He wants when He wants to do it, at least in my case. He may bless an individual who donates money to a religious organization, but I believe it's about the act of giving and not because you'll receive a blessing in return. I believe without a shadow of a doubt that God wants us to live a quality life, which does take money, but I also believe He wants to ensure we love Him more than we love our money and our possessions. *It's easier to get a camel to go through the eye of a needle than for a rich man to enter into the Kingdom of God.* According to this biblical declaration, the enormously rich religious leaders may encounter an issue when they attempt to enter into the kingdom of heaven.

There's a story in the Bible were Jesus and his disciples travel to Jerusalem for Passover. Jesus expels the merchants and money changers from the Temple, while accusing them of turning the Temple into a den of thieves through their commercial activities. I believe if Jesus were to return today, he would feel the same today as he did that day before Passover centuries ago. To prove or disprove the prosperity preacher's claims, I decided to put my money where their mouth was. I came to feel that unless I gave money to one of these prosperity preachers, how else was I going to be able to say with a clear conscience that they were con artists? I had four thousand dollars in my bank account, so I donated twenty-five percent of that money to one of the Christian networks. I was familiar with TBN and Daystar, but on the evening when I was compelled to test the claims of the prosperity preachers, I came across a new station called INSP. When I finally decided to call the bluff of the prosperity preachers, INSP was broadcasting an episode to raise money for their network from Israel. I called in my donation and several weeks, or perhaps a month afterward, I received an unexpected check in the mail for three thousand dollars. When I opened the envelope that contained the three thousand dollar check, I laughed out loud in my office. I was thrilled to receive the money and was certainly able to find a good use for the additional cash. What were the chances of receiving money in the mail that I should've never received, after calling in my donation? I was dumbfounded to discover that the prosperity preacher's sermons may have merit.

I had donated one thousand dollars and three thousand dollars was returned to me, resulting in a two thousand dollar gain. I believe I received a divine return on my investment, as claimed by the preachers, due to the fact I received three times my donation, a number represented by the Holy Trinity. The additional two thousand dollars was helpful, but a far cry from being enough money to change my financial situation. If an individual uses the standard of three hundred percent return on their donation then, according to this equation, a person would need to donate a whole lot of money to receive a substantial profit. I believe God rewards those who give with a loving heart and who give expecting nothing in return, as I had done. I also believe God will hold us responsible for ensuring the money we donate to an organization is being used in a manner that will benefit those with the greatest need. When I sent the funds to INSP, I was not expecting to receive anything for my donation other than the gratification that comes from giving. If you give because you expect to double or triple your money, I believe you're setting yourself up for a disappointment. Many of the prosperity preachers have turned God into a money-making concept, when I know He's really all about relationships and we're the commodities that He's looking to acquire, not cash. I also donated money to Daystar and TBN, but after sending in my modest pledges to them, not nearly as much money as I donated to INSP, I didn't receive any unexpected cash in the mail. While incarcerated in the valley, I gave more money to religious organizations than I had ever done in any other time of my life, for the same time period. Did I buy my freedom or did I invest in my future?

I love *Judge Judy*, the TV show. She's constantly sifting through people's bullshit stories to get to the truth. Based on the number of years she has listened to liars tell their tales, she can determine from the details of their story, if something makes sense or if it doesn't. She's the highest paid person on television so it seems that according to her salary, the effort to establish the truth is certainly worth much. In my effort to build a relationship with God, He knew I wanted the truth and used my skills to spot a liar to His advantage. I hate when people use me for their own agenda, but when God takes advantage of my skills it makes me happy. This is a perfect example of how God can take a person's pain and use it for the greater good. He knew I would dissect the information that I heard from the religious networks before I accepted their word as truth. He also knew I would compare their stories against the relationship that He was developing with me. I wouldn't accept a story about Him from a preacher, minister, pastor, or priest if it didn't resonate as being in line with the God that I was getting to know.

I naturally consider myself a creative person. As I built a closer relationship with God, I had daily conversations with Him, with me doing most of the talking. I wanted to do something great for the world in His name. I was stuck in a situation where it didn't look like I was going to be able to take care of myself, let alone do something great for mankind. My ambitions seemed more like a fantasy than a reality. I didn't have any disposable income, so my imagination and conversations with God got me through that lonely and difficult time. Part of the reason I survived the days, months, and years in Palm Springs was because of our talks. Since most of my professional background was in retail, I thought about building a house for God, though not a literal house like a church. I wanted to establish a figurative or a virtual house, much like the ones that represent a clothing or fashion line. This metaphorical house would be the umbrella for the many elements that would be tied to the brand. Since I had ILD, a company with a three-letter acronym, one rainy day, I decided to come up with a different three-letter acronym to identify the brand that I could establish. I came up with LVG, an acronym that stood for Love, Valor and Goodness. I originally came up with the word Godliness, rather than Goodness, but I decided to go with Goodness because it sounded less religious.

I stood outside the house, speaking with God about my idea and noted that the acronym I came up with included the same two letters used by the Louis Vuitton brand, LV. Shortly after my conversation, I had a feeling that God was claiming the twenty-something generation, referred to as generation Y, or millennials, as His own. I can't claim to understand what He places in my heart at different times, but I've learned to ponder the idea until He decides to fully allow me to see what He envisions. I assumed that He meant the millennials were going to be the generation that He would empower in some way, at some time in the future, to do something that He wanted. Maybe that's why He began tweeting…He wanted me to know He was more like a millennial. Around that time, I also got the impression that He didn't want me to put anything in my name, which didn't make sense to me. But I've also come to view His messages like riddles and I've learned to place them in my memory bank and wait until the exact time when He decides to reveal their meaning. One year after I exited the desert, two years after my conversations about building a brand, I moved to Los Angeles where I met Lance.

I forgot all about the conversation where I came up with the acronym of LVG, until Lance passed away almost one year after meeting him and three years after conceiving the idea. Shortly after Lance died, I recalled the conversation with God and was flabbergasted that the letters that I came up with to identify His brand two years before meeting Lance, tied back to Lance's initials, who was also a millennial. It's impossible in my eyes for this situation to be anything but representation of a larger plan, of which I was unaware when I came up with the concept to build a brand and use the letters LVG to identify it. My idea was not the crazy rant of a desperate man talking out loud to himself because he was lonely in the desert. I now believe my one-sided conversation was not one sided at all. I naturally assumed that the concept to build a brand around God in the form of a figurative house by using the letters LVG was all my idea, but I now wonder if that's not the case and it was all His idea after all. The original twelve tribes of Israel were referred to as a house, such as the *House of Saul.* I didn't learn that the original tribes were referenced as different houses until five years after having the idea to call the brand, the *House of* ***LVG***. Certainly it's impossible for this to be a coincidence, and in my mind I can only view it as a revelation.

I returned the Jaguar to the dealership a few months before the lease expired because I was no longer able to come up with the money to make the three remaining lease payments. This would be the first time since I was sixteen years old that I didn't have a car of my own, apart from the time I lived in New York City. Curiously, the Whitewater property was built on the second lot in from a major street where there was a bus stop on the corner. I don't think I ever noticed the bus stop until my car was gone and I needed to use public transportation. Yet, two years after I bought the house, when I wouldn't have considered the concept of using public transportation, I discovered that the nearest bus stop was less than a few hundred feet from the house. I love God, who planned for the future when I didn't.

I still didn't know who Jesus, whom the Christians spoke of as being God, was. Jesus was not the God that was revealing himself to me. I understood who Jesus was supposed to be, but I couldn't understand why the Christians always put Jesus before God, or so it seemed to me. When different people abused me and after they were finished with me, they pushed me aside and I became yesterday's news, so I was very sensitive about people giving Jesus more attention than God because I knew how it felt to be pushed aside. It pissed me off that the Christians were consistently giving more admiration to Jesus than to God.

During the last year Philven and I lived together, when I couldn't bear any more pressure, he began to lash out more than he had done in the past. I seriously began to believe he was indeed the devil, or that an evil demon possessed him. One day, he was off and running with his crazy antics, and I became concerned that he was going to physically hurt me or mentally destroy me. I heard preachers on the TV tell a story about how their Jesus could vanish demonic spirits. They said Jesus had dominion over demons and if a person prayed to God, asking Him to vanish the demons in the name of Jesus Christ the evil spirits must leave. Since I was concerned that I might be living with the devil, or at a minimum a demon possessed crack head, I thought I should bless the house and pray for the demonic spirit to flee in the name of Jesus Christ. I used the garden hose to spray water on the roof of the house, while holding my thumb over the open end of the hose, as I walked from one end of the house to the other, while praying for the demons to flee in the name of Jesus Christ. I felt very stupid at first, but I was desperate and concerned, so I thought it couldn't hurt to put the claims of the preachers' Jesus to the test even though it made me feel ridiculous.

The house was a large u-shaped home with the business office on the right side, the main house making up the bottom portion of the u and the casita making up the left side, directly across from the office. When I started praying to God to vanish the demonic spirits, I spayed a fine mist of water over the roof of the house where I was praying. I began my demonic cleansing over the office and worked my way to the opposite end of the house. As I was saying my prayers and spraying the roof with water, to my amazement and confusion, I noticed two yellow suns above the roof over the office. One sun was directly over my desk and the other was directly over Philven's desk, with ten feet between them. You might think I was seeing things, but that was not the case. At some point in your life, when washing a car or watering the grass, you may have had a garden hose in your hand and while spraying water in the air, the fine mist might have revealed a rainbow. When you turned off the water, or stopped spraying that area, you could no longer see the rainbow. My situation was the same, when seeing the vision of the two yellow suns. I thought I was seeing things that weren't there, so I stopped misting water over the roof of the office—and the yellow suns went away. I began to spray water over the roof again, and the two yellow suns reappeared. Each time I turned off the water, the suns disappeared and each time I began to mist water over the roof again, the two suns reappeared. The vision freaked me out! I wondered if God was texting a message, using emoticons, and if so, what was he trying to convey?

Even though I was unnerved by what I just experienced, I kept to my quest. I continued to pray to bless the house while misting the roof, in my attempt to vanish any possible demonic spirits in the name of Jesus. I didn't encounter any more emoticons when I reached the guest bedroom, which had become my bedroom. Even though it was my house, I moved to the guest bedroom and was now sleeping on the sofa in that room as I had moved out of the master bedroom a few months earlier. I no longer wanted to be anywhere near Philven, so I had given him the master suite. It gave Philven a sense of being a big man because he ended up with the larger bedroom and he was sleeping on my five-thousand dollar bed, while Aston, Bentley and I were sleeping on the sofa in the guest room. Never let it be said that I didn't try to achieve some level of peace in an environment that offered me very little.

Once I finished praying over the guest bedroom, I began to spray water on the roof above the living and dining room. Once again, while praying, what appeared to be two emoticons appeared, although this time they were two rainbows void of color. The rainbows were white, ten feet apart. I was freaking out big time. What did two suns and two white rainbows represent? As I pondered the question, two birds flew between the two white rainbows. The bird's feathers looked as if they were the same colors that one sees in a rainbow, although they flew so fast that I'm not certain if their feathers represented all the colors in a rainbow. Thinking back, I believe the birds looked much like the bright colors one sees on a Toucan. It was as if God threw the colors of the rainbow on both of these birds and then tossed them out of heaven's window at the exact moment when the colorless rainbows appeared. Even if I could make these stories up, I'm not sure I could imagine tales of this magnitude.

The master bedroom where Philven slept was adjacent to the living room. As I made my way over to that area of the house, and continued to pray while misting the roof, I encountered no emoticons. I found it strange that in the areas of the house where Philven and I didn't cohabitate, like the bedrooms and bathrooms, no emoticons appeared. In the areas of the house where we did cohabite, such as the office, the living and dining rooms, adjacent to the kitchen, emoticons *were* present. Were they signs from heaven? If so, what did they mean? I was out of my mind as to what was going on and what these signs meant. At that time, the best scenario that I could come up with was that the suns represented one of my two brothers and me. Of all the things that appeared to me in my visions…the two suns, the colorless rainbows, and the two birds with the colors of a rainbow were the most gratifying I encountered, even though I had no idea what they meant. God's is certainly entertaining; I was not only amused, I was left wanting to see more, experience more, and to know more. Looking back, I can find humor and happiness in the most difficult time of my life because of Him. I sometimes miss those days. Only God could take the shittiest time of my life and turn it into something that I can reflect upon fondly—one of the main reasons, I'm certain, why He's often referred to as The Almighty.

Almost three years after I experienced these visions, and a few months after Lance's passing, the meaning of these signs came to me out of nowhere. To this day, I'm not sure if the timing of my sudden realization as to the significance of the emoticons had anything to do with Lance's passing, but I often wonder if it did. I now understand that the two suns were God telling me that Philven and I belonged to Him, like two sons, and He was with us. In God's eyes, we were truly Tweedledee and Tweedledum, much like brothers, and certainly the same in His eyes. I had realized that God loved Philven, but I was still shocked to learn He considered us to be equal. Possibly, I wasn't able to understand the vision earlier because I wasn't ready to accept that God viewed Philven as my equal. I came to see that the white rainbows, void of color, represented the life that Philven and I were living—a life without purpose. The rainbow hued birds represented the lives God wanted us to live. He wanted us to spread our wings, broaden our horizons, seek new adventures, and pursue our life's purpose.

To avoid dealing with my issues, I ran from one place to another my entire adult life. Once I encountered God in that desert, I made the Whitewater house my foxhole and I dug in for the long haul. I refused to run from my problems any longer. I was waiting on Him for direction. *Isaiah 40:30-33. Even youths shall faint and be weary, and young men shall fall exhausted; but they who wait for the Lord shall renew their strength; they shall mount up with wings like eagles; they shall run and not be weary; they shall walk and not faint.* One year after receiving the vision of the suns and white rainbows, I abandoned my foxhole in the hopes of spreading my wings, broadening my horizons, seeking new adventures and ultimately pursuing my life's purpose.

A creative person who stops dreaming is like a fish out of water, eventually they both will suffocate. The entire time I lived in the desert I only dreamt three times. The first time, I dreamt Philven was moving back to Chicago. The second dream I had involved Dubai...the city-state was adding English text to all their Arabic signs because I couldn't read Arabic and I was moving to *The World Islands*. This dream could be due to my obsession with living in the United Arab Emirates. I understand the Arab nations don't allow openly gay foreigners, or those with HIV, to reside in their countries, although it doesn't stop me from hoping that one day they will.

My third and last dream in that desert was about Rick. I hadn't spoken to him in nearly five years, but I dreamt that he and I were having a conversation. During our talk, Rick cussed a great deal and seemed particularly stressed. Prior to our falling-out, I was the one that was always stressed and had a very sharp tongue. In my dream, I had become more like Rick, calm and a genuinely happy person. Our dispositions had flipped; he was more like me and I was more like him. I told Rick that God was real and I laughed as I told him. I believe my laughter symbolized that I was in a very happy place, contrary to my actual deposition at the time. Rick swore like a truck driver and he was frazzled about something the entire time I spoke to him about my beliefs. As I laughed, I kept repeating to Rick, over and over again, that God is real.

Philven deliberately did shit to piss me off and we were constantly butting heads. It was a struggle each day, for almost eighteen months, to ensure we had enough food on the table and that I had enough money to pay the utilities at the end of each month. Out of necessity, I became thrifty. I had been extremely fortunate up to that point and never struggled to meet my living expenses. Thriftiness was a new characteristic that I had to learn to survive. Philven, who claimed he always struggled to have enough money to get by in life, certainly didn't act like it when we were together. He conducted himself as if he had been a spoiled rich brat his entire life. When I was forced to close down ILD, I began to do everything I could to reduce the household expenses. I started washing the dishes by hand. I would put them in the dishwasher to dry. When I was not around, Philven would turn on the dishwasher, with the clean dishes in it, every chance he got. He ran every extra cycle that he could to use up as much electricity as possible, resulting in a higher utility bill that I had to pay. I would get so angry at his fucked-up passive-aggressive behavior. I often wondered that if I was an escort with very little money, as he was when I met him, and I met a man that was willing to love me, build a home, and let me live with him in that newly remodeled home, make me a fifty percent owner in a company, let me drive his brand new car, give me credit cards, buy me clothes, a computer, and a cell phone, feed me, and if he made every attempt to make me an equal in his life, would I disrespect him, as he was disrespecting me? My answer was always the same, no…I would not! I'm a lot of things and many of them are not so great, but I didn't deserve to be treated so disrespectfully by Philven. The part that was the most difficult for me to choke down was that I eventually had to accept that Philven was my equal in God's eyes. If that analogy didn't eventually sober me up, nothing ever would!

During a heated argument, I told Philven that if I had the power, I would lock his ass up, preferably in the international space station because I wanted him as far away from me as possible. Since everything that came out of his mouth was a lie, I told him I would make him write his life story. The only way to be released from prison was for him to write the truth about his life. I wanted to physically hurt him for all the things he had done to hurt me, but I was smart enough to know that God wouldn't be happy with me if I acted on those feelings. I knew it was acceptable to God to have ill feelings towards Philven because of the pain that he inflicted on me, but I also knew without a doubt that God was going to hold me accountable for how I treated him and the things that I acted upon when it came to interacting with him. Six months after making the comment about wanting to lock him up and have him write his life story, I began writing this story. A year and a half after I began writing, Philven was arrested and locked up in a prison cell for several months. When I heard this, I thought that the moral of that story is to be extremely careful what you wish onto your enemies because God just might make you live out the ill words that you wish upon someone else.

When Philven and I engaged in three-ways there was always an underlining agenda taking place, which never allowed me to relax. When I reflect back on those encounters, I can clearly see the reason why I was never able to get comfortable. More times than not, I had been lured into a den of liars and thieves. When Philven hooked up our party play dates, he did so with guys with whom he had already fucked before he and I played with them. It defeated the purpose to ingest recreational drugs to escape from my problems and to enhance a sexual experience when Philven and his jackals were playing games. I'm sure many individuals who knew me when I was going through my breakup with Alex would say I seemed unstable on many occasions. In retrospect, my behavior back then seemed like child's play compared to how unstable Philven tried to make me. The situation was beyond unstable, it was insanity at its worst.

My fears and the shame I carried from using drugs imprisoned me. Philven knew I was terribly afraid that ILD clients would discover my recreational drug use. I was concerned and extremely paranoid that someone was going to videotape me doing drugs while having sex and that video would end up on the internet. This was my single biggest worry when partying with others outside of the house. Philven knew I was terrified of being found out and he played on my fear for his amusement. He consistently tried to fuck with my mental state when we hooked up with other guys. One day, when we were partying with a younger man, he and Philven moved away from the computer screen, where porn was playing, when I took a hit of Tina. They were trying to get me to believe I was being filmed via the built-in camera in the computer. They made it look like they were moving away from the camera to make me think the computer was recording my actions. I don't think I was being filmed on that particular occasion, but Philven and his jackal were playing psychological games and attempting to get me to believe that I was being filmed so they could cause me undue stress. Unfortunately, I believe there were probably several instances when I was videotaped without my knowledge or consent while having sex and doing drugs. Sex and drugs are supposed to be fun, but they ended up being my biggest nightmare. I don't think there's anything wrong in having a sex tape of yourself it that's what you want, although in my case, I never authorized anyone to film me while having sex and doing drugs or having sex with or without drugs. The only reason I agreed to do three-ways with Philven, was to keep him from cheating on me, as Alex had done and keep him from telling me lies to cover up the affairs. *Damned if you do and damned if you don't*, certainly applied to my situation.

By sharing this story, I've been able to release myself from the place where I locked up my feelings, hid my fears, and concealed my shame. The truth has set me free or at least the truth has allowed me to be free.

Philven was the leader of the pack. One day, we invited a guy to our house for sex. Once he arrived, he commented on a picture that I had hanging in the kitchen of the *Cloud Gate* sculpture, the silver "bean" in Chicago's Millennium Park. He told me that the sculpture was going to tour the country. When someone comes to my house for sex that I've never met, I'm certainly going to be polite and try to make that person feel as comfortable as possible. Since the sculpture is enormously large and an extremely heavy piece of art designed specifically for Millennium Park, I knew it was not leaving the spot where it had been installed. The trick was a lying piece of shit, but I politely told him I didn't believe his story to be true. Philven told many people in the desert that I was stupid and I would believe just about any outlandish story that I was told and this guy was clearly being an asshole, disrespecting me in my house by telling me this outlandish tale. I guessed he wanted to see whether I was naïve enough to believe what he said so he could amuse himself by my stupidity. I had become the joke of the desert, the stupid faggot that would believe whatever anyone told me, no matter how outlandish a story. I thought I was getting high and engaging in a three-way with two other men who were looking to fuck. Instead, I found myself playing with a bunch of immature boys that acted like little sissies and who were more interested in playing pussy games than on having mind-blowing sex. Fucking crack heads – crack is indeed whack!

When Philven and I moved to the desert, we lived in the temporary house while the house remodel was underway. I had so many elements on my plate that I didn't pay attention to every detail in my personal life. While I was focused on saving my livelihood and building a wonderful home, Philven was taking personal items of mine out of the house and giving them to God only knows who. When we finally moved into the Whitewater house and unpacked the household items that had been in storage for six months, I noticed several things were missing. I had several expensive bottles of men's cologne that somehow got "lost" during the cross-country move. Coincidentally, one evening, during a party-and-play date at a trick's house that Philven had arranged, the exact same designer colognes that were lost in the move were in his bathroom. Awfully coincidental.

Several months afterward, some of my expensive lead crystal glassware turned up missing. After initially unpacking the kitchen items and placing them in the cabinets, I ended up with two complete shelves of Ralph Lauren lead crystal glassware. One shelf held twenty-four rock glasses and another shelf held twenty-four tumblers. A few months later, I discovered that the two shelves of glassware had somehow manifested into just one shelf. The mother-fucker took half the inventory of the Ralph Lauren glassware and gave it to someone. My personal household items were being dispensed to Philven's jackals all over the desert cities without my knowledge. Philven, of course, insisted that there had only been one shelf full of Ralph Lauren glassware after the kitchen items were unpacked and put away. There were several other situations where my personal shit came up missing during the time we lived together. I believe Philven was stockpiling goods from my house, at someone else's place, because he had planned on leaving me so he was stealing so he could furnish his new digs. When I tell you that the desert is full of cracked-out liars and thieves, I'm not kidding…my missing lead crystal glassware is proof enough for me. Does it get any more fucked up than your boyfriend stealing your stuff right from underneath your nose and keeping it at someone's place while lying about what he had done to your face?

I often wondered what was so wrong with me that I always invested in the wrong people. I sought professional help to understand why I was always attaching myself to people who wanted to use me for their personal gain. I spent thousands of dollars with psychiatrists in several cities to eventually conclude that I was just fucked in the head, or so I had thought. It was not until I built a relationship with God that I realized I was more like Him than I ever thought possible. I was drawn to the lost souls of the world. This analogy would certainly explain my behavior of repeatedly investing in the wrong type of person. I understood at last that my biggest fault was a trait that I needed to embrace. My inability to correctly judge someone's character would eventually lead me to see my life's purpose and ultimately it may assist me in achieving my life's destiny.

It's Not Right But It's Okay

Friday night you and your boys went out to eat
Then they hung out
But you came home around three
If six of y'all went out
Then four of you were really cheap
'Cause only two of you had dinner
I found your credit card receipt

It's not right
But it's okay
I'm gonna make it anyway
Pack your bags up and leave
Don't you dare come running back to me
It's not right
But it's okay

I'm gonna make it anyway
Close the door behind you
Leave your key
I'd rather be alone
Than unhappy

I'll pack your bags
So you can leave town for a week
The phone rings
And then you look at me
You said it was one of your friends
Down on 54th Street
So why did 2-1-3
Show up on your caller ID?

I've been through all of this before
So how could you think
That I would stand around
And take some more
Things are gonna change
That's why you have to leave
So don't turn around to see my face
There's no more tears left here
For you to see

Was it really worth you going out like that
See I'm moving on
And I refuse to turn back
See all of this time
I thought I had somebody down for me
It turns out
You were making a fool of me

It's not right
But it's okay
I'm gonna make it anyway
Pack your bags up and leave
Don't you dare come running back to me
It's not right
But it's okay
I'm gonna make it anyway
Close the door behind you
Leave your key

I'd rather be alone
Than unhappy

It's not right
But it's okay
I'm gonna make it anyway
Pack your bags up and leave
Don't you dare come running back to me
It's not right
But it's okay
I'm gonna make it anyway
Close the door behind you
Leave your key
I'd rather be alone
Than unhappy

It's not right
But it's okay
I'm gonna make it anyway
Pack your bags up and leave
Don't you dare come running back to me
It's not right
But it's okay
I'm gonna make it anyway
Close the door behind you
Leave your key
I'd rather be alone
Than unhappy

It's not right
But it's okay
I'm gonna make it anyway
Pack your bags up and leave
Don't you dare come running back to me
It's not right
But it's okay
I'm gonna make it anyway
Close the door behind you
Leave your key
I'd rather be alone
Than unhappy

It's not right

But it's okay
I'm gonna make it anyway
Pack your bags up and leave
Don't you dare come running back to me
It's not right
But it's okay
I'm gonna make it anyway
Close the door behind you
Leave your key
I'd rather be alone
Than unhappy

Whitney Houston

In 2010, a sketchy and random thought popped into my mind. Almost a year later, I finally understood what transpired. I had experienced a premonition. A year before Whitney Houston died, I had an overwhelming sensation that she was dead. I searched the internet to see if there was any information about her death and, as I searched, I came across a video of her singing her new hit song, *I Look to You.* As I saw her video, it seemed to me as if she was signing from heaven's throne. Strangely, the following year, Ms. Whitney Houston would in fact pass away. I'm not sure if God was using this particular premonition to get my attention, or not, but the incident left me wondering if there were more of these forewarnings in my future.

Much like the situation with Whitney, I had random thoughts pop into my head about religion, politics, and foreign affairs—and have no idea where they originated, as I was not very knowledgeable on these topics when I lived in the desert. I'm not sure if these thoughts were spiritually inspired or if they were drug induced. Regardless, these eleven notions have stuck with me ever since I left the desert many years ago. You can judge whether you think there's any truth in these statements or if you simply believe that *crack is whack*, as Whitney once did when she made the comment.

1. Why does the world adorn the dead and walk over the living? Why doesn't the church ordain living Saints and honor great men and women of God that have accomplished much for humanity while these individuals are still alive?

2. One day Africa will be the richest continent in the world.

3. Turkey will allow Asia safe passage through their country in order for Asia to bring peace to the Middle East.

4. Twenty four Arab countries will enter into a peace agreement with one another and Israel. These twenty-four nations will remain separate countries. The nations that unite under the new peace agreement with

Israel will be known as the Israeli Union of Territories.

5. Tel Aviv will remain the official capital of the Israeli Union of Territories and the rest of what is known today as Israel will become Palestine.
6. The New Jerusalem referenced in the Bible will be in Egypt – the place where Joseph originally led the Israelites.
7. The Holy Royal Family will one day reside in Saudi Arabia.
8. The Arab countries will embrace women and will consider them as equal to men.
9. The Arab countries will embrace gay people within their nations and consider them as equals.
10. One day, I will reside in Dubai in the World Islands.
11. One day, the Saudi Arabian government will invite me to their country and allow me to visit Mecca and more specifically the Holy Kaaba.

21 | THE ACE OF SPADES

If today is your past come tomorrow, then make your past your future of today.

I began to lay out this chapter before I wrote, or even drafted, chapters 15 through 20. Come tomorrow, what I write in this chapter today will encompass my past. Once I finish writing the previous five chapters and come back to complete this one, chapter 21 will embody my past, my present, and my future. This helps me understand when I've heard some ministers say that "God knows the beginning from the end and the end from the beginning." I feel as if God has had a hand in guiding this book from the beginning to the end or, in this case, from the end to the beginning. Corinthians 5:17 states, *the old things have passed away; behold all things have become new.* I truly feel that after writing my testimony, the former things in my life have passed away and all things have become new. I now see the world differently. I've learned that the key to overcoming adversity is to find hope through faith and believing that all things are possible.

I dedicate this chapter to Cher – the goddess of pop, for she is my idol. If it had not been for her, I believe my love story, which you might think is more a horror story, wouldn't have been written. I've come to think of Cher as the person God placed in my life so I could hear His voice at a time when I was not listening for it. In Exodus 20:4, it is written that *you shall not make for yourself an idol of any kind.* Cher is not my idol before God; I believe she is the means by which God chose to bring me closer to Him. A star, a favorite, and a hero are three synonyms for the word idol that I *Believe* best represent my feelings for Cher. She is the star God chose for me to gaze upon so I could hear Him more clearly. She will forever be my favorite hero for bringing me to a place where I could experience the love of God.

Feeling broken
Barely holding on
But there's just something so strong
Somewhere inside me
And I am down but I'll get up again

Don't count me out just yet

I've been brought down to my knees
And I've been pushed way past the point of breaking
But I can take it
I'll be back
Back on my feet
This is far from over
You haven't seen the last of me
You haven't seen the last of me

They can say that
I won't stay around
But I'm gonna stand my ground
You're not gonna stop me
You don't know me
You don't know who I am
Don't count me out so fast

I've been brought down to my knees
And I've been pushed way past the point of breaking
But I can take it
I'll be back
Back on my feet
This is far from over
You haven't seen the last of me

There will be no fade out
This is not the end
I'm down now
But I'll be standing tall again
Times are hard but
I was built tough
I'm gonna show you all what I'm made of

I've been brought down to my knees
And I've been pushed way past the point of breaking
But I can take it
I'll be back
Back on my feet
This is far from over
I am far from over
You haven't seen the last of me

No no
I'm not going nowhere
I'm staying right here
Oh no
You won't see me begging
I'm not taking my bow
Can't stop me
It's not the end
You haven't seen the last of me
Oh no
You haven't seen the last of me
You haven't seen the last of me

Cher

Around June 2010, I decided to come out of my drug-induced coma and re-enter the working world. Since I couldn't find anyone who was interested in hiring me, or even in interviewing me, I decided to partner with a previous ILD vendor. This former vendor had the field personnel to handle any installation projects that I could bring to the table, so we formed a partnership. I would sell installation services and his organization would supply the staff to implement them. We agreed to split the profits we earned fifty-fifty. His company would also handle all the billing and receivables for our projects. Since I had nothing but headaches with Philven, I welcomed the idea of having the company of my new business partner handle the financials. The economy was still very soft and finding new and former clients who had projects and needed installation services was going to be an uphill battle. I didn't have many other options to earn an income, so I had to at least try to make this new business endeavor a successful one.

For at least a decade, I had a desire within me to write stories for a series of children's books. One day, in September 2010, I heard on the news that President Obama wrote two children's books and had them published while in office. At every turn, it seemed that the President was on the television at an event that was somehow related to what was taking place in my life. I was possibly just being overly sensitive because I had emailed the White House in my desperate attempt to remove the illegal resident from my home. Since I never heard from anyone, I was holding onto some ill feelings. I felt like Obama was needling me and the situation was starting to piss me off in a big way. A few months later, Philven asked me if I ever had sex with an Indian man. His question came out of left field, but Philven often said things that made no sense. When I lived in New York, I had slept with a man of Indian descent, my first and only encounter. A few days after Philven posed his nonsensical question, guess who appeared on the news talking about deepening the economic relationship between India and the United States? President Obama indeed.

In November of that year, Obama traveled to India to meet with their Prime Minister. On its own, this seemed to be a simple coincidence, but when you consider all the times that the President seemed to appear on the news, seemingly out of nowhere, at the exact time I had something going on in my life that related to whatever he was doing, I began to think that the President and Philven were screwing with me. I know I sound paranoid and you're correct. Too many coincidental events that involve the same person will place an overly sensitive individual on heightened alert after they have been mentally fucked with on many occasions. I don't understand what it was with President Obama and me. We both began our careers in Chicago, wrote our biographies, and seem to share a passion to write children's books, but nothing more. I wonder if God was trying to convey a message that involved the highest office in the United States. Maybe the connection was simply that the President represented America—built on the premise that *in God we trust.* Possibly God wanted me to trust in Him. *Trust the Lord with all your heart and lean not on your own understanding.*

While I don't believe in coincidences, an interesting event happened to me on April 20, 2016 involving President Obama. After writing the above paragraph, I heard on the radio – and later on the television – that Mr. Obama had landed in Saudi Arabia, the fourth time he visited the kingdom during his two terms in office. His arrival in Saudi Arabia seemed interesting, as I had just finished chapter 20, where I wrote about the Middle East and specifically Saudi Arabia. These situations give me hope that God has a plan for the world and it's more elaborate and fantastic than anyone can see. I certainly do not claim to understand that I know how God operates, but I believe with all my heart that He's on the move and has a master plan for us all.

Cher's movie Burlesque was released on November 24, 2010. I didn't see the movie during its theatrical release, but I did see it on cable television later. In the movie, Cher sings, "You've not seen the last of me." Once again, her timing was spot on.

I've been brought down to my knees
And I've been pushed way past the point of breaking
But I can take it
I'll be back
Back on my feet
This is far from over
You haven't seen the last of me
You haven't seen the last of me

Oh, my God! If this woman is not my guarding angel than she must have been handpicked by God to be His messenger and deliver words of encouragement so I would be inspired to get off my knees, brush myself off, and push onward. I love this woman for all that she represents to me – strength, determination, intelligence, beauty, entertainment, creativity, sophistication, love, kindness, devotion, and most of all – a beautiful spirit. It's important to me that she know I believe God loves her beyond any level that any one person can comprehend. I'm certain, without a doubt, that all the angels in heaven smile when they hear God mention the name of this goddess.

I was first introduced to Cher when I was a little boy and watched the Sonny and Cher variety show with my father. When I was in my thirties, I had a tall and very lanky friend who was the visual merchandising director for Merry Go Round, a specialty retail chain that once had over five hundred stores. I was a guest at his house in Baltimore, Maryland for a weekend and I discovered that he idolized Cher. I sat at his dining room table having breakfast with him one morning when I noticed a framed poster of Cher hanging on his wall. This became my second introduction to her. I commented on the poster and my friend went on and on and talked about how much he loved her. I thought to myself, "Oh Mary, please, you need to get a grip on yourself." Little did I know that this woman, who I saw for the first time as a boy, would be the means by which God would save me from a lifetime of poor choices. After that morning in Baltimore, when I had breakfast with one of her mega fans in front of that poster, I would not think of her again until several decades later when she and her music entered my life.

I experienced my third encounter with Cher when I was living in San Rafael and I walked into the house to confront Alex about his sexual indiscretions that I discovered earlier that morning. Cher was being interviewed on some show as she was promoting *Believe*, her new album that she had just released. I don't recall the exact conversation she was having, but, when she caught my attention, I am one hundred percent certain that I heard, "If you believe in yourself, there's nothing you cannot achieve." As a child, I recalled that my father once stated, during an episode of Sonny and Cher, that "she'll be a big star one-day." My father's comment when I was a child, combined with Cher's iconic status that she achieved many years later, gave credence to her words of wisdom that I heard emanating from the large screen television in the den. As my senses perceived the insightfulness of her wisdom, I mustered the strength to demand a better life for myself than the one I had endured at the hands of an unfaithful boyfriend for the past three and a half years. *Believe* me when I tell you, God knew I was not listening for his voice, but He knew that by utilizing Cher's words at that precise moment,

I would realize I could have a better life. Is there life after love? I was not sure I could go on living if my relationship with Alex came to an end, but Cher's words combined with her number one hit song *Believe*, gave me the strength to initiate a chain of events that gave me hope of achieving a better life. If I believed in myself, as Cher said I should, then there was nothing that I could not achieve or overcome. The life that I hoped for myself did not include a liar and a cheater, who was my life partner, so I ended that relationship.

My fourth and fifth encounters with Cher were through her *Do You Believe* tour, when I saw her perform this concert twice while living in San Francisco. The sixth time, I went to her *Living Proof: Farewell Tour* at Madison Square Garden when I lived in New York. I encountered her a seventh time at her *Cher at the Coliseum* concert in Las Vegas when living in Palm Springs. It pains me to admit that each and every time I saw her perform in concert, up to this point, I was high. I had become a functioning drug addict.

When I was at my lowest point, brought down to my knees, she once again showed up in my life for the eighth time. She released another song and starred in a new film, *Burlesque*, that related to my situation. In this movie, which captured my attention, Cher's character was going through difficult financial times, just as I was. In the film, when things were dire and the bank was about to foreclose on her property, an earthy angel appeared offering an unforeseen solution. The final outcome to my situation was very different from what was portrayed in the movie. Cher's character was able to save her business from foreclosure whereas I had lost my business and my home. But I lost more than just a house. I also forfeited all the equity I had in the world. After buying the house in Palm Springs, I had invested every last dollar in the remodel. When I bought the property, I planned to live in it for at least five years. I planned on taking whatever equity I would have made when selling the house to relocate to the City of Angels. I was fifty years old and I'd been dealt a different hand. My midlife crisis had arrived right on schedule. At that time, I heard Paul Crouch from TBN say, "God never arrives on the scene early and God never arrives on the scene late, although he always arrives exactly on time." In the midst of my midlife crisis, God arrived exactly on time – not a moment too soon and not a moment to late – delivering an important message through His best messenger, Cher. You've not seen the last of me.

Before leaving Palm Springs and moving to Los Angeles, I made one more trip to Cher's house in Malibu. I arrived in her driveway and the large wooden gates opened. A few feet beyond those gates, stood a woman holding a tennis racket. She waved me onto Cher's property. I was freaked out that the doors had opened on my arrival and even more so to be welcomed to her home by the lady standing just beyond the gates. I was so nervous, I put the car in reverse, drove out of the driveway, and headed down the hill as fast as

I could. Was this a sign that I was finally free from the grips of evil?

Seek and you will find;
keep on knocking and the door will be opened to you.

One week before Thanksgiving 2010, a yellow hummingbird perched a few feet from the kitchen window on a branch of one of the beautiful orange trumpet trees that I planted in the backyard. The little hummingbird returned to the exact same branch just outside my kitchen window each morning. The bird's visits were so regular that when I woke up in the morning, before pulling the shade open, I would ask out loud, "are you there?" and each time the little bird was on the same branch where it always perched. One day, I opened the shade and the little bird wasn't on its branch. I called out to the bird and sure enough it came out of nowhere and alit on the same branch where it always perched. This went on for three days in a row. Each time I called out to the little bird, when it was not on its branch, it seemed to fly in out of nowhere, landing on the same branch that it always occupied. In my mind, God had to be behind this strange and unusual phenomenon. How could I open the shade, not see the bird, call out to it, and have it come flying out of nowhere and land on the same branch where it always perched? It seemed impossible and it freaked me out. The little hummingbird returned every day to the same branch at the same time, and hung out for hours. This went on for a little longer than a month. The hummingbird perched on the same branch so often that I bought it a little birdhouse and hung it next to the branch where it perched, but the bird never occupied the house that I so lovingly purchased for it. I learned that hummingbirds usually travel in pairs, but my hummingbird flew solo, which was strange. The week between Christmas and the New Year was a stormy week in Palm Springs. I saw the little bird on December 30 of that year for the last time. It never returned, which made me sad. The following spring, when I left the desert on April 15, 2011, I took the little house that I bought for my feathered friend, which I still have in my possession. I hope someday to purchase a new house and hang that little birdhouse in a tree on my new property and maybe, just maybe, my little feathery friend will return home.

That New Year's Eve of 2010, birds and fish began showing up dead in different parts of the world. A bizarre sequence of events resulted in the massive deaths of these animals. It was reported that night that nearly 3,000 birds fell from the sky in Arkansas and, 100 miles from where the birds fell from the sky, 10,000 fish washed up on the shores of a river in the same state. On the same day, 500 of the same bird species were reported to fall from the sky in Louisiana and two million fish washed up dead in Chesapeake Bay. If this wasn't enough, 100 tons of fish washed ashore in Brazil and several thousand doves fell dead from the sky in Italy. As if these odd events weren't enough for one day, several more situations of unexplained animal deaths were reported taking place between New Year's Eve in 2010 and March 9, 2011. Twenty states in America and 39 other countries reported at least one incident, if not several, where large number of unexplained animal deaths took place. I wondered if this was another sign. If nothing else, it was definitely bizarre and seemed beyond coincidental that my little hummingbird left the day before New Year's Eve.

In January 2011, I began writing my testimony. By this time, I was self-employed for the second time and had been developing business opportunities with my new partner for six months. I was finally earning an income and had some cash on hand. Not a lot at first, but I was building momentum. I was chasing a large project with a former client and was hopeful that I would be awarded the project. Every evening, when I went to bed, I spoke to God about the possibility of Him helping me, so I could secure the business. I needed this deal and I needed it in a big way. It would make the difference in me getting back on my feet financially sooner rather than later—or not at all. I was fifty thousand dollars behind in my mortgage payments and the house was worth less than half of what I owed on the mortgage. There was no way I was going to get my hands on fifty thousand dollars to become current on the mortgage before the bank repossessed the house in the next four to five months.

I also spoke to God about getting ten thousand dollars saved by my birthday, in the month of May. I decided that if I were able to get that amount of money put away before my birthday, I would vacate the Whitewater house and rent an apartment in downtown Los Angeles. In my former years, when I was financially solvent, a hundred thousand dollars would have been equivalent to what ten thousand dollars now represented, which exemplifies how difficult my situation had become and how monumental ten grand was for me to obtain. Low and behold, by March 2011, I had ten thousand dollars in my savings account, more money than I had in my possession in almost two years. *Ask and you shall receive.*

One hot sunny afternoon, I was shirtless outside, washing off the pool deck with a water hose, when I caught a quick glance of a man's reflection in one of the tinted sliding glass doors on the front of the house. I thought to myself, "who's that fat fucker in my yard?" Sadly, it was me. I had gained forty pounds in four years. I had quit going to the gym from all the pressures in my life during my time in purgatory. I had worked out for twenty years to ensure I kept my body in good shape and, in less than four years, I lost the body I worked so hard to attain in those years. But even though I lost so much financially and physically, and endured much mental duress in that desert, I gained something greater than all that I had lost and all the pain I endured—my encounters with God.

In March, I rented a car and drove to Los Angeles. I leased a seven hundred and fifty square foot loft apartment in downtown Los Angeles for Aston, Bentley and me. Ever since I could remember, I wanted to live in LA and now that dream had become a reality. Even though my circumstance were not ideal when I arrived in the City of Angels, I was still very excited to be moving there. My fifty-first birthday had not yet arrived, but it was fast approaching. I wanted a fresh start. Los Angeles represented the beginning of a new life. I was eager to start the second half of my life in the same place where I began my first half. In a strange way, it seemed as if I was returning home.

I had to downsize. The apartment I rented was half the square footage of the Whitewater house so I needed to decide what I was taking with me, what I wanted to sell, and what I was willing to leave behind for Philven, if anything. I signed the lease on unit 9**13** (9+1+3=**13**), at 650 (6+5+**11**) South Spring Street, which began on April **13**, 20**11**, although I would not move into the unit until Friday, April 15. I was excited to finally be free from Philven's grasp. In the midst of my newly found freedom, I became concerned I would not be able to secure enough business consistently and get paid from those clients on time so I could meet my living costs. My rent was one thousand four hundred and fifty dollars a month, which wasn't much compared to the Whitewater mortgage of over four thousand dollars, although I hadn't been earning a regular income in over a year and hadn't made a house payment during that time. Out of the ten thousand dollars I saved, nearly three thousand went to my first month's rent and security deposit. I allocated one thousand dollars to pay for my move, which left me with six thousand dollars. I placed this money in my savings account to cover three months of rent and living expenditures, so I had room to seek and secure new business. Now that I had an exit plan and felt like God was telling me it was time for me to move on, I needed to get organized, pack my things, and sell some furniture and large appliances that I knew I wasn't taking with me or willing to leave behind.

I couldn't believe I was finally able to take the initial steps that would hopefully lead me to recover from my financial disaster. I thought many times that I was never going to be able to escape from the life I had been living—full of disappointments, abuse, and deceit. In the midst of my misery, I had asked God for divine intervention and to send someone to rescue me. I just wanted somebody to come and put their arms around me and tell me it was all going to be OK…and then take me way from that place where I had fallen so far down the rabbit hole that I couldn't see the light of day. I didn't think I had the energy to clean up my mess nor did I want to. I found out the hard way that God wasn't going to answer my sincere request with a miracle just because I didn't want to do something I found difficult. To my disappointment, an angel wasn't dispatched from heaven to take care of my mess. I was held responsible again for cleaning up the crap I created. He did grant me a significant miracle while I lived in the desert—surviving twenty years of bad behavior and poor choices. But *God helps those who help themselves.* I realized the painful truth in this statement. He required me to do my best each day. As long as my heart was in the right place and I truly tried to do the right thing, he would help me with the rest, hence the saying, I suppose.

At that point, God introduced me to my teacher. My new spiritual professor wasn't a priest or some other religious individual, it was Jesus. One day, I was on the phone standing in the kitchen of the Whitewater house talking to a friend about leaving some of my furniture behind for Philven. He was upset with me because he knew the abundance of pain Philven had caused me. I got a bit angry at his abrupt outburst and I told him that maybe my good fortune of being able to depart from what had become my purgatory was a test. He laughed nervously, but sounded concerned and annoyed at the same time. He asked me what I meant by a test. I explained that I believed God was perhaps testing me to see how I treated Philven when I physically separated from him. I knew God loved Philven, but at that point I had not put the puzzle together about the vision of the two suns that I saw over my office months earlier. I had not told my friend about my vision, as I was sure he would have thought I had lost my marbles. I told him firmly that maybe my situation was not all about me; possibly there was a larger picture that I needed to take into consideration. He backed away from our discussion as he sensed I was becoming angry. I can't explain why I felt I needed to treat Philven with compassion – even as I was leaving him – especially after all the shit he had put me through, but a little voice from within was telling me to be careful and not to hold on to a grudge or take that opportunity to get even with him. I had the conversation in early March and by Monday, April 18, I came to understand why I had those feelings and why I needed to show Philven kindness on my way out of that scorching city. Showing kindness to Philven didn't mean that he deserved my kindness. On the contrary, he deserved little sympathy in my eyes. Any compassion I expressed for him came from seeing him through the eyes of God. It was God who wanted me to be kind to him and I was smart enough to listen to what my inner voice was telling me. I shudder to think what would have become of me had I ignored the advice of that voice.

It was six weeks between signing my new apartment lease and taking occupancy of the loft. In the weeks leading up to my departure, I went through all my things. I gave Philven many of my clothes, half of my kitchen items, a $2,000 sofa, a $3,000 wool rug, two $750 yellow suede side chairs, several side tables, a coffee table, an $800 floor lamp, a $750 desk, a $1,500 white leather desk chair, a server, and a $2,200 laptop. These things weren't brand new, but they were in like new condition. Philven paid for none of the items…I bought them before I met him or purchased them on my credit cards when we were together. As if my generosity wasn't enough, my new teacher told me to give Philven the most expensive asset I owned at that time…the five thousand dollar bed I bought when I lived in Chicago, prior to meeting him. I had placed that bed on Craigslist before I was instructed to give it away. A woman in Palm Springs had answered my ad. She was willing to pay somewhere in the neighborhood of $2,100 for the bedroom set. I could have used the extra money, but Jesus told me to give it to Philven and I obeyed. I told a few people that I was leaving furniture for Philven and they said I was absolutely nuts, but I had listened to what that inner voice was telling me. I had begun to trust God with all my heart and did not lean on my own understanding. A true relationship with Him is not for the faint-hearted. He'll make you do stuff you never thought you would do in a million years, like treat Philven with kindness and generosity by giving him two rooms of furniture and much else.

I sold all the outdoor furniture and potted plants from the exterior of the property before I moved out. I also sold a top of the line washer and dryer and split the $2,000 from the sale of these items with Philven. I didn't have to give him any of the money from the sale of these things, but I tried to do the best I could for him on my way out without jeopardizing my own financial well-being. I had supported him for eighteen months after I closed the company. I paid for all the food, personal items, haircuts, utilities, gardener, and pool boy when neither of us worked. I sold much of my personal stuff to make this happen and my parents had also sent me money regularly. A few days before I left, I gave Philven the $1,000 in cash and paid the utilities in full up to the day I exited from the house. The day before I moved out, I went to the store and bought him groceries for one week and left them in the refrigerator. I also bought him a pay-as-you-go cellular phone and placed several hours of talk time on it.

Earlier in the week of my departure, Philven had been on a drug induced sex binge and he was coming down. He only came out of the bedroom to get food at night. On the day I left, he never came out of his room, not even to say goodbye to little Aston and Bentley. I was glad I didn't have to deal with the emotion of having to say goodbye, but it broke my heart that he seemed to care nothing about Aston and Bentley who had considered him one of their daddies for the last three and a half years. The hooker was as cold as ice! The movers loaded the truck and shortly they were on their way to 650 South Spring Street. I rented a SUV for a few days. I loaded the babies in the car and we too were on our way to meet the movers at our new home. At last, I had done exactly what the Palm Springs police told me to do almost a year earlier—I vacated my house. The police were right; living in an unhealthy and unsafe environment was not worth jeopardizing my well-being for any material possessions. I'm a slow learner, but I eventually learn my lessons.

By the time the babies and I reached the main street heading out of Palm Springs, Philven called from the mobile phone I bought for him and said,

"Well done!" I thought to myself, "Yes, you're right, well done indeed." No thanks to him, I had been able to secure work, save ten thousand dollars while supporting the household in the best way I could, sold what personal items I needed to sell, found an apartment for me and the babies, got myself organized and packed and hired movers, while the entire time Philven was running the streets doing drugs and having sex at all hours of the day. I'm not judging him for what he did, but I did all I could for him on my own and supported him the entire time that he was fucking around with other men and lying about what he was doing. The night before I moved out, I cleaned the entire house and rearranged the furniture that I left for him so the house looked nice for him when he finally emerged from his room. I may sound pathetic for doing so much for someone who seemed to care little for me, but I knew that in God's eyes, I was supposed to do the right thing by Philven and there was a larger purpose in my doing so.

I also notified the mortgage company that I was vacating the house and I took pictures of the property and grounds to prove that the interior and exterior of the house were in excellent condition. I asked them to let me know where I was supposed to send the keys, which they never did. I kept the landscaping, the pool, the interior, and the exterior of the house in *like new* condition until the day I left it. I tried to do the right thing even when I was in the process of being evicted, which was the major difference between me and Philven. At least I tried to do the right thing, even if I didn't always manage to do so.

I arrived in Los Angeles on Friday, April 15 and took the weekend to get settled. On Monday, April 18, **three** days after departing the desert, I received an email from my client about a large project to install graphics at fifteen hundred locations. I had been pursuing the project for the last six months. She informed me that my business partner and I were awarded seven hundred and fifty of the fifteen hundred locations. This was the crème de la crème after my release from my hellish existence. Was I awarded the project because I went above and beyond to do the right thing for Philven in the eyes of God? I believe, without a doubt, that the answer is absolutely yes! It was nothing short of divine restitution for listening to the voice of my teacher.

Once the project commenced, it took a little over two months to complete it and several weeks to get the first invoice processed. The first payment arrived just as my savings were depleted of the six thousand dollars that I had put away and when I had no money to buy groceries for that week. The notification that I was awarded the project, and the timing of the arrival of the first check was no coincidence. It would be impossible for these two situations to be random, since the timing of the events were so critical to my well-being. I believe with all my heart – and know without any reservation – that my good fortune was directly related to that voice that was telling me what to do, and that I obeyed, even though it didn't make any sense to be kind to someone who had been so unkind to me. Romans chapter 12:20 through 12:21 states, *Therefore if thine enemy hunger, feed him, if he thirst, give him drink. Be not overcome with evil, but overcome evil with good.*

If Jesus was a carpenter who is a fisher of men, then God must be an architect who is a hunter of souls. If this is true, then I believe God is very much like a hunting doG. He's searching for the ones who are wondering aimlessly in the wilderness and who have been injured in some way. Once these individuals are located, I believe He points them out to Jesus, whose responsibility it is to gather the lost and the sorrowful. It's what happened to me. God found me when I was shattered and brokenhearted and showed me what real love and compassion felt like. I had been involved with men over several decades who said they loved me, but they used the word love to get what they wanted from me. I began to believe love was a weapon, a sword that people used against one another for their own gain. Although, through my relationship with God, I eventually understood that love was like a shield, to safeguard what was important. More importantly, His love was like a coat of arms that offered protection and comfort when their seemed to be none. Once I comprehended the limitless dimensions of God's love, He sent Jesus to teach me the importance of forgiveness and the art of being kind to others, especially to those individuals that didn't deserve forgiveness or kindness. I don't believe that a person who has been deeply hurt can show kindness and forgiveness to another individual until they grasp the depth of love that God has for them, but to bestow these two attributes onto others through the eyes of God comes with many rewards. The story of Jesus' life and death is proof of what kindness and forgiveness will get you when you have been introduced to God's love and see others as He does. His boundless love and unwavering compassion is something that can only be ascertained after you have sought after Him in the same manner in which He has hunted for you—tirelessly.

A few weeks after moving to Los Angeles, I went back to check on Philven. I wanted to make sure he was doing all right on his own. I don't know why I felt like I was responsible for him, but I worried about his well-being. I also wanted to ensure that Philven was looking after the property. After I arrived at what was still my house, we spoke. During our conversation, he told me that *they*, who I assumed to be the jackals in his den of iniquity, had told him that *he* ran me off. He seemed bewildered by their comment and I was amazed that Philven hadn't realized the obvious, but it also surprised me that his pack of cracked-out jackals was coherent enough to determine what should have been so apparent to him. To this day, this was the last time I traveled to Palm Springs and to the house. Before heading back to Los Angeles, I went to the store and bought him groceries. I never saw Philven after that day.

Philven and the mortgage company allowed most – if not all – of the landscaping, which cost me over five thousand dollars, to die. Around August or September of 2011, the city of Palm Springs sent me a letter to clean up the dead landscaping around the house or they were going to fine me and then charge me for clearing the dead shrubbery. The mortgage company had foreclosed and taken possession of the house by then so it was no longer my problem. As I wrote these words, the Whitewater property was on the market for $519,000. The owners bought the house in February 2012, six months after the bank foreclosed on it, for a mere $190,050. I had purchased it for $370,000 and invested $200,000 on the remodel. The mortgage company recouped all their money because I had an FHA loan, which guaranteed the loan when I defaulted. The new owners ended up with a fantastic deal because of my misfortune. In October 10, 2016, the Whitewater house sold for $487,000 – a profit of $296,950 dollars. One man's misfortune is another man's fortune.

I was concerned and worried about Philven for a long time after I moved to Los Angeles. In the first few months after I left Palm Springs, he called on several occasions looking for money, but I wasn't in a financial position to do any more for him than I had already done. I did include him in my nightly prayers and asked God to look after him and keep him safe. I prayed for his well-being and safety every night for the entire first year that I lived in downtown LA.

During my first week in the city, I had a project that was being installed at the Beverly Center, a shopping mall in Beverly Hills. I needed to be onsite to handle a few issues. I didn't have a car so I took the bus, which took an hour to travel from downtown to the mall. I was unfamiliar with the public transportation system in LA and I got off the bus too soon, at the wrong stop. I walked a few miles before arriving at my destination. As I walked, I had a conversation with God about all the times I had previously traveled to Los Angeles. I told Him that I wasn't happy that I was forty pounds overweight and living in the city without my own transportation. Previously, when visiting Los Angeles, I had been in great shape, had considerable disposable income, and drove expensive cars. As I continued to make my way to the Beverly Center, I heard that inner voice again. The voice told me, in so many words, to quit whining and get my ass back to the gym if I wanted to get back in shape. I didn't get any instructions on transportation, however. I guess He thought walking would help me lose some of those forty pounds that I was complaining about. God is funny, but I wasn't featuring His humor at that moment.

A few months after that conversation, I did as instructed. I had arrived in Los Angeles in April and by October of that year I joined Gold's gym. Thirteen months later, I met Lance and we became workout partners on November 13, 2012, usually meeting up at three o'clock in the afternoon. It wasn't until I wrote these words that I saw the connection between the time we would meet at the gym to the number three, representative of the Holy

Trinity. After all that has taken place throughout my life, I've come to look for signs in everything that I do and in everything that happens. In relation to my friend Lance, there are an overwhelming number of signs that link us to one another that I feel are indisputable. I believe God brought Lance into my life and see these indicators as proof that He brought us together for a greater reason than just working out.

I had been awarded the large project three days after arriving in Los Angeles and my good fortune continued to grow that year. By the end of 2011, I was doing fairly well financially, especially when compared to my income from the previous two years. In the fall of 2011, I established a new company, ILDworld. In doing so, I recalled a sensation I experienced while living in the desert. While I was in the valley, I heard God tell me not to put anything in my name. I had no idea what He was referencing. As I established a new business, I thought He may have been referring to the new company I was forming. Therefore, I established the new business as a "C" corporation. In doing so, the company was its own singular entity. There were several other reasons that drove my decision, but one of the main factors why I established a corporation, rather than a DBA or an LLC, was because I had the impression that it was what God wanted me to do.

I was happy to be earning an income again. When I went to the store to buy groceries, I didn't have to worry whether I had enough cash to buy ample food for the week. Even though I was working, I kept a close eye on my expenditures and tried to stretch my cash as far as it would go. For the first time in my life, I realized how fortunate I was to have a refrigerator full of food. I didn't appreciate the luxury and privilege of not worrying whether I had enough money to buy groceries for the week until I became bankrupt and penniless. I ended 2011 with more money in the bank than I had in years. I was grateful for what I accomplished that year and for all of God's help in achieving those accomplishments.

A few weeks after I arrived in Los Angeles, I went to see a psychic. I asked many questions about Philven and she advised that I stay away from him. I didn't need a physic to enlighten me to that answer. She touched upon an interesting subject without me soliciting the information from her. She told me I would start traveling once again. She continued to tell me that I traveled a great deal in the past and that I was wondering if my traveling days were over. She was correct; I had thought that my vacations had come to an end since I didn't have the income that would provide me with the luxury to travel. She added that not only would I travel for business and pleasure within the United States, but that I would also travel extensively overseas. The U.S. travel made sense to me, but the part about traveling overseas seemed far-fetched from where I was standing.

I recalled the dream I had about Rick and I decided to reach out to my old friend. A month after I arrived in LA, I sent him an email. He had the same email address ever since I knew him and I assumed he was still using it. My one single communication to his inbox changed my life. I now understand and believe that God separated us for a reason. Rick grew his career and I needed to conquer my demons. My walk in the desert was an uncharted path that I had to travel alone, without my best friend at my side. If Rick and I had remained in contact, there was a good chance that I may have taken him down with me. He would've helped me through my financial difficulties and by doing so he could've jeopardized his own economic well-being in an effort to assist me in throwing deck chairs off the Titanic when it was going to sink no matter what I did or how hard I tried to save it.

As I rebooted my life, I began to rid Tina from my house. I've heard many people say that a person can't overcome an addiction without professional help, but I don't believe that is always the case. If one addiction wasn't enough to conquer, I also decided to quit smoking cigarettes. I had been smoking between one to two packs a week for the past ten years and cigarettes were entrenched in my daily routine. Once I decided to quit, it took me several months to completely shake the habit, but I eventually overcame my nicotine addiction. I did it cold turkey, without using nicotine gum or patches. I was on the right track. According to those Christians I saw on the television back in Palm Springs that Halloween night of 2009, I was one step closer to becoming one of them…not!

Overcoming Tina, however, and kicking her out of my house and eventually out of my life was going to prove to be more complicated. I realized that if I made contact with a drug dealer and had a reliable connection, I would probably reach out to that person in a weak moment. I knew myself and if I purchased the drug and kept it in my possession, I would do it until it was gone. Unfortunately, during the twenty-seven months I lived in Los Angeles, I bought Tina on several occasions in the first year. Addictions are not something you can overcome easily or quickly. Like most things in life, it's a process and that process varies from one person to another. What works for one, does not work for another. You don't have to be a scholar to know that if you've had issues with an illegal substance, it's probably not a good idea to have it readily available. The first step in my recovery was to admit to myself that I had a substance issue. My second step was not to make a connection with a drug dealer so it wasn't easy for me to attain it. My third step was to keep myself from bringing Tina into my apartment because once she was inside I would use it until there was nothing left. When she was in the same room as me, she was in control. I needed to outsmart the bitch. It wasn't a problem for me to stay away from finding a drug dealer or stop myself from bringing Tina into my apartment—that was the easy part. Without me ever realizing it, Tina developed a new and more complicated problem for me to overcome. The fucking bitch is relentless.

It had been more than four years since I had sex without Tina in the room.

She rewired my sexual desire—when I thought about having sex, I thought about her. I've learned that until an individual has personally gone through a specific situation, they have no idea what it's like. I believe this is why Jesus said, "Judge not or though shall be judged." So many people look down at other people for the bad choices they've made, their problems, or for their race, sexual preference, addictions and much else. Until a man or woman has walked in another person's shoes, they have absolutely no idea what they're talking about when they comment on another person's situation or circumstances. If I hadn't experienced so many hardships first hand, I would've had little reference on those situations, such as having Tina rewire me to include her when having sex. Having her control my sexual urges was fucked up. Sadly, it's why many gay men have a hard time cutting Tina out of their lives once they've decided to kick the bitch out of their bed and to the curb. My situation was no different. Rome was not built in a day nor was breaking my co-dependence on Tina. When Rome burnt, the city burned a hell of a lot faster than it was built and so would my dysfunctional association with the bitch.

I hope to put what happened to me, self-inflicted or otherwise, to good use one day. I would like to eventually mentor young gay men who find it difficult to break away from the drug culture and who are unable to muster the courage to envision a better life. In many cases, addictive behavior can be attributed to an abusive relationship or from simply making poor choices. I've been through enough messed up circumstances that I can offer guidance and hope to achieve a better life for those people who are self-medicating to make it through their own lives. Possibly my story will encourage an individual, if not many, to face their own demons. I know I can't save the world, but I believe God expects me to try and He'll do the rest. I'm going to do all that I can to arrive at a place where I'm in a position to be the change that I want to see in the world. I heard a Christian song once that sums up my feelings and the lyrics go something like this… "I saw all the injustices in the world and I shook my fist at heaven and asked God why he doesn't do something and he replied, I did, I created you." Christians say that if we accept Jesus as our savior, God will not judge us for the awful things that we have done. I think they've left out a critical piece of information—for while I generally agree, I also believe God will judge us for what we didn't do. He won't judge us for picking up the sword against our neighbor, but He will judge us for not putting it down.

I suffered from intimacy issues my entire life. The household where I grew up wasn't a place where we openly expressed our affection. I can't remember ever hugging my parents or kissing them as a child. The thought of them hugging or kissing me and vice versa actually makes me uncomfortable—probably from the lack of childhood affection demonstrated by my family. I don't think my parents did anything wrong in raising me, but I believe many of our adult behaviors are learned when we're young. As a teenager, I was uncomfortable with affection. The fact that I had to deal with my sexuality when it was not entirely acceptable to be openly gay added to my intimacy issues. As a young adult, I usually got intoxicated before picking up a man and having sex. The alcohol allowed me to be less inhibited and I was able to relax and become more aggressive in bed. Without making a conscious effort, I replaced alcohol with recreational drugs to lower those inhibitions. When I was diagnosed positive, this created even deeper intimacy problems for me. I felt I was not worthy of a loving relationship. The fact that several of my boyfriends cheated on me, while professing their love for me, affected the way in which I physically interacted when having sex. I believe that if a person meets the *right* individual who treats them lovingly and respectfully in their committed relationship, it can solve any intimacy problems. I understand that another individual can't make another person whole, but the right person can be the missing link in someone's life to help them be intimately comfortable. I've longed to attain the type of connection where each person in the relationship complements the other. Possibly the solution to true intimacy is like a fairytale ending. Unlike most fairytales, it's not about finding one's Prince Charming. I've personally fallen too many times for the charms of the prince of darkness. The key element in a happy ending is meeting one's knight in shining armor, with a coat of arms, who offers love and protection.

I heard Cher's son, Elijah Blue, give an interview on the television one afternoon where he made several comments that caught my attention. When he was asked about his former drug addiction, he stated something to the effect that doing drugs when he did saved his life. He added that this comment would only make sense to a former drug addict and that the key was to quit doing drugs before they killed you. What the fuck was he talking about? While that statement might make no sense whatsoever to most individuals, his words resonated with me. I believe Elijah was referring to the reason why he and so many other people begin using a substance to alter their perception of reality or numb themselves, as I had done. I understood Elijah's statement to mean that if it hadn't been for the drugs, he would have probably killed himself or his life would have ended tragically. The drugs numbed him long enough until he was able to find a way out of the darkness consuming him. I cannot speak for Elijah, but this is what drugs did for me when I was doing them. I now realize that there are more effective and less destructive means to deal with my depression and my feelings of hopelessness, but at the time I thought recreational drugs were my only option.

Elijah's television interview revealed a fact of which I was not aware—his estranged relationship with his mother. During his adolescent years, he felt Cher chose her career and fans over him and this possibly resulted in him feeling neglected or emotionally abandoned when he was a child, causing their estrangement. I cannot begin to speak for them or their relationship, but I can explain the impact that Elijah's mother and her career have had on me. Cher's absence in the early years of his life literally saved mine. I sincerely believe that Cher and her career were a means to reach me. After I began a relationship with God, and for many years afterward, He continued to speak to my heart through Elijah's mother. During the many years when I used drugs, Cher always seemed to be there offering words of wisdom and comfort. If she had chosen a different path, my life probably would have ended up differently too. Without her influence, my story may not have come to fruition. If my book is published and this story helps or influences even one individual in a positive way, then I'll be certain that it was God who utilized Cher as a means to help me. I hope Elijah finds comfort in knowing that his mother didn't choose her career over a relationship with him, but that just possibly God had a larger plan. I *Believe*, much like the name of Cher's album, that God brought us *Closer to the Truth*, and that Cher brought us closer to one another. I'm grateful to Elijah for sharing his story and, more importantly, his mother with me.

Once I sent the email to Rick, he welcomed me back into his life. Over the months after reaching out to him, we rekindled our longtime friendship. After a short time, the disagreement that separated us for years became irrelevant. In September of 2011, Rick planned to attend the baptism of the daughter of one of his dearest friends, which was being held in the family vineyard in Greece, not far from Athens. He invited me to join him on the trip and we decided to add Istanbul and London to the itinerary.

We arrived in Istanbul on Monday, September 12. Upon reaching our hotel, when I exited the taxi, a flag flapping in the wind on the flagpole in front of the hotel caught my attention. It looked to me like the flag of China, but it was actually the national flag of Turkey—with its crescent moon and one single star. I was speechless. Did I confuse the Turkish national flag with that of China because I was simply being ignorant or was there more to my ignorance than what met the eye? Turkey's location, straddling Europe and Asia, could be why I had China on my mind and why I confused their flags. In Palm Springs, I had been inexplicably drawn to the Middle East and wanted to travel to the region when I was bankrupt without the financial means to do so, and my yearning had become a reality. In my eyes, it was impossible for my unexpected travel to Turkey to be a coincidence. Discovering that the Turkish flag had the same two elements – a crescent moon and one star – that I gazed upon in the desert sky when I felt like something was pulling me to the Middle East seemed like fate. There I stood, in that exotic city, staring up at a flag that depicted those exact two symbols. Through the rekindling of my friendship with Rick, God had seemed to orchestrate what I saw as impossible when I was penniless and thought I would never make it out of the desert alive.

Istanbul was once the capital of the Byzantine Empire, the continuation of the Roman Empire, and it had been called Constantinople. This was where Venus, the Roman goddess of love, was worshipped before Christianity became the dominant religion of the Empire. The city was named after Constantine the Great, or Saint Constantine, who was a Roman Emperor. Some scholars suggest that Constantine used his faith to his political advantage. In any case, Constantine stopped the persecution of the Christians and legalized Christianity, making it the state religion. Eastern Orthodox Christians, Byzantine Catholics, and Anglicans venerate him as a Saint. In time, Constantinople was conquered by the Muslims and became the capital of the Ottoman Empire, when the star-crescent adornment on mosques was adopted, as a state symbol not of religion. The fact that Paganism, Christianity, and Islam were so deeply rooted in this city that I happened to visit out of the blue, left me in a state of wonderment.

We visited the Blue Mosque and Hagia Sophia. The basilica of Hagia Sophia was built in the sixth century, as a cathedral of the Greek Orthodox faith and it remained so until 1453, except for a brief period when it was converted to a Roman Catholic cathedral under the short-lived Latin Empire in the thirteenth century. In 1453, it was converted into a mosque and in 1931 it was secularized and became a museum. This impressive building represents both Christian and Islamic faiths under one roof. As I looked up and marveled under its massive dome, I thought it proof that God wanted me to know that Islam and Christianity where intertwined.

Our trip to Istanbul was riddled with puzzling events. Coincidently, we visited Hagia Sophia and the Blue Mosque on September **13**, 20**11.** Could the mythical Blue Fairy be an actual person, place, and thing? If so, then could Elijah Blue be a symbol for Elijah the Prophet and could the Blue Mosque be the symbol of faith – *the substance of things hoped for and the evidence of things not seen?* If so, then how was I to identify the third symbol that represented the place where one would find the Blue Fairy? Was it as simple as finding a restricted area at the end of the world in a lost city that is located in the sea where the lions weep? Was the "the end of the world in a lost city" a reference to a lost city from the ancient world? Is the Winged Lion Temple in the Lost City of Petra the place of the Blue Fairy? Kadesh, referenced in the Holy Quran is in Petra, and is believed by many to be where Moses struck a rock with his staff and produced twelve springs of water for the Israelites. Could this biblical phenomenon be a metaphor for the phrase "in the sea where the lions weep?" Or is the restricted area at the end of the world in a lost city where lions weep simply Mecca? Wherever it might be, it seems likely to be somewhere in the Middle East.

On September 16, 20**11**, Rick and I visited Topkapi Palace. While touring the palace, we saw a footprint of Mohammad and the staff of Moses. I was amazed and overwhelmed to see these two religious relics next to one another, in a glass showcase. Stumbling upon these artifacts from antiquity felt like more than causal coincidence. Rick was normally very well informed on the historical highlights to see whenever we visit a new city in a country that we have not visited, but I was amazed that he was not aware that these two items were on display. Had it not been for his invitation to join him on holiday, I would not have gone to Turkey then or now, if ever. I felt like a divine force helped orchestrate my visit to this city and the sights that Rick chose for us to see.

There seemed to be more to visiting Istanbul than just tourism. Traveling to this modern and vibrant city, with such old-world history and a deep and complex religious foundation, did not seem accidental. I found myself standing on the ground where Christianity was legalized and embraced by an Emperor—and was amazed by its many other wonders. Several years after visiting the country, I learned that over sixty percent of the places mentioned in the Bible are in Turkey, which is often called the other Holy Land as it has more biblical sites than any other country. I learned that Saint Nicholas was a bishop who lived in the fourth century in a place called Myra in Asia Minor, now Turkey. A famous story about Saint Nicholas explains how the custom of hanging up stockings to get presents originated. A poor man had three daughters. He was so impoverished that he didn't have the money for dowries for his daughters, so they were unable to marry. One night, Nicholas secretly dropped a bag of gold down a chimney into the house of the poor man and it fell into a stocking that had been hung by the fire to dry. The older daughter could now get married. Nicholas repeated the deed for the second and third daughters so they too could marry. The bishop was eventually proclaimed a saint and is not only the patron saint of children, but also of sailors.

On September 12, the day of our arrival in Istanbul, a full moon glowed in the night sky. Was it symbolic of a blue moon, traditionally an extra full moon in a year that normally sees twelve full moons? Was something trying to convey to me again that Islam, Christianity, and Judaism were all linked together? Did I randomly stumble into this country with such a rich religious legacy or did something deliberately lead me to the land of the Blue Fairy without me realizing it? Judaism, Christianity, and Islam are the sequence in which each religion came into existence. Aramaic, the language spoken when Jesus lived, is read from right to left. If you take the first letter from each faith and read it from right to left you end up with ICJ – I see Jesus. In reverse, the way in which we read today in the west, it reads JCI – Jesus sees I. Are these signs and wonders or are they just simply random minutiae without any significance whatsoever?

The signs seemed to keep fitting together like a puzzle. With each piece of the puzzle, a clearer and more detailed picture of the master puzzle seemed to be revealed. It's either signs and wonders from God or my extremely imaginative mind can construe a story from random bits of information. Do I have the creative ability to take unrelated coincidences and weave them in an intricate manner to tell a story that always ends with the same common denominator? Possibly, but based on what I've experienced there was more taking place around me than me losing touch with reality and having paranoid delusions of grandeur.

Gene from Bigsby is one of the most creative individuals I've met during my professional career and one of the most committed. However, Gene did have a big flaw—he couldn't stop himself from rethinking his concepts and continued to refine his ideas up to the point when they were implemented. This perfectionist behavior caused construction delays and cost overruns. The idea, in its perfect form, ended up becoming the driving force rather than the rationale for the idea in the first place, to make money. I had heard that Gene had a nervous breakdown before I came to work for his company and that while he was in the hospital he kept telling himself that he was not crazy. After he left the hospital, he opened a new retail store concept selling men's neckties and accessories called Knot Crazy. This concept evolved from one retail store in Chicago to become the Knot Shops, the national chain and separate division of Bigsby&Kruthers. His constant tinkering to refine the concept to perfection caused the company to spend more money on the design of the stores than it earned in profits, which resulted in the demise of the Bigsby empire. As I wrote my story, I realized how much the Mad Scientist and I were alike and that we had more in common than I realized when I worked for him. I too told myself that I was not crazy when I was with Alex and then with Philven. Those two bitches were doing exactly what I feared they were doing—cheating and lying at length to cover up their infidelities, which made me think I was crazy. Even now, I feel the urge to remind myself that I'm not crazy. In some strange way, Gene and I are like two peas in a pod. Who knew? Certainly not me.

Like David from the movie *A.I.*, I too was in pursuit of a mythical being. In our quest to find something greater than ourselves we found a divine presence that offered us the means by which we could love again and allow ourselves to be loved in return. During the most difficult and stressful period of my life, I was forced to look beyond myself for an answer to what seemed an unsolvable problem. In my pursuit to break free from the depths of my hell, I looked beyond me and God began to reveal Himself. He offered hope and captured my curiosity. In my case, curiosity didn't kill the cat, it allowed the doG to chase away my insecurities and self-doubt. I was renewed and regained an inquisitiveness that was almost childlike. I wanted to learn all that He wanted me to know and my relationship with God became like a scavenger hunt. *Seek and you shall find! Truly I say to you, unless you are converted and become like children, you will not enter the kingdom of heaven. Whoever then humbles himself as this child, he is the greatest in the kingdom of heaven.*

Overall 2011 was a good year for me financially and spiritually. My new business was doing well and I continued to seek a deeper understanding of God. I went back to working out, which I had neglected for years. I was moving in the right direction to reclaim what the accuser had taken from me when I lived in the desert.

In 2012, I continued to obtain more clients. It was not easy and landing a large project or major rollout as I had done in the previous year was challenging, but in the third quarter of 2012, I secured a national contract with a store fixture manufacturer in the Midwest to install their fixtures and millwork for an international retail client of theirs. The contract came from the would-be priest, my former boss in New York, who was heading the organization. His new company was based in Michigan and he was its president and co-owner. It awarded me six large retail locations. The contract entailed the installation of fixtures across the entire seventeen thousand square feet of each of the retail spaces by early December of that same year. This job would generate a sizeable profit for my partner and me. The would-be father was my saving grace that year. I intensified my workout regimen. In November, I met Lance. It looked as if I was on my way to recover finically, physically, and mentally from my ordeal. During Christmas, Rick and I traveled to Madrid and Barcelona where we visited the Sagrada Familia, the highlight of my Christmas that year.

Since my main focus was to build a new business from scratch once I arrived in Los Angeles, I spent a large portion of my time seeking and developing new business. I felt like God was pulling on me to spend more time writing, but I ignored those feelings. I rationalized my lack of commitment by telling myself that I'm sure He understood that I had to earn a living and that my time was limited. I began to write my story in January of 2011, when I still lived in Palm Springs, and by the end of 2012 I was still working on the introduction. I was having difficulty in collecting my thoughts in a cohesive way that would make sense to others and I spent much time and energy on the introduction to set the correct stage for the overall story. As I wrote sporadically over the coming months, I realized I was trying to cram the highlights of the entire book into the introduction.

One Friday afternoon, in March of 2013, I suggested to Lance that we workout at the Gold's Gym in Hollywood. The Gold's in downtown LA had a very straight clientele and the Gold's in Hollywood got the gay crowd from West Hollywood. I worked out at that gym several times when I previously traveled to Los Angeles and knew that the clientele at the Hollywood gym was very different than the downtown gym. I was curious to see how Lance would interact in an environment where the patrons were openly gay. It was a Friday, a day when we always went drinking after the gym, so I thought Hollywood would be a good place for Lance and me to have a few drinks as a reward for working out that week. On the train to Hollywood, I told Lance that my business partner owed me fifty thousand dollars and I was having a difficult time getting him to cut me a check for my share of the profits we earned. The look on Lance's face when I told him the story was unforgettable. I was a whole lot angry and upset when telling Lance my woes because fifty thousand dollars was a great deal of money to me. Besides, it was the beginning of the same old shit that I went through with Philven, when I was not able to get updated reports on the profits that the business earned. It seemed that I couldn't escape from the people that wanted to keep me in the dark, feed me bullshit, and take my hard-earned money. I was terrified that I would end up back in the same situation—penniless. I worked so hard for the previous two years to get myself out of my financial difficulties and it seemed that, if I wasn't careful, there would be a good possibility that I would end up having money problems once again. By the look on Lance's face you would have thought that my partner tried to steal his fifty thousand dollars. Lance was visibly upset and showed genuine concern for my ordeal. From Lance's painful facial expressions and his overwhelming concern for my situation, I acted like it was all going to be OK when in fact I knew it was not. I made a joke about the situation and changed the subject. At that moment, while we were in the subway, I realized what a kind hearted and genuinely caring person Lance truly was. I was fortunate to have him as my friend.

Once we arrived at the gym, Lance and I dumped our backpacks in a locker and hit the free weights. It wasn't long before Lance caught on that the guys were checking him out. Being the gentleman that he was, Lance never let on that he knew he was being admired from a far until we finished our workout and left the building. While having a few drinks at a nearby bar, Lance told me he caught the reflection of two guys kissing in the mirror when we were in the free weight room. He didn't react in the gym to the guys kissing, although he was laughing as he told me the story. He said he didn't expect to see guys kissing in the gym and they caught him off guard. He also told me he saw some guys checking us out while we were exercising on the same machine. His story brought a smile to my face. The guys at the gym were probably wondering what such a hot young stud was doing with an older man. I was flattered at the thought of the West Hollywood gays thinking I was his boyfriend—it certainly made my afternoon.

Rick's friendship was essential in maintaining my sanity when I was trying to get the money owed to me. After many painful and unpleasant email exchanges with my fucked-up business partner, I ended up getting all my money, except for about thirteen thousand dollars, but by this time, my professional and personal relationship with my partner had soured. I learned in Palm Springs that I had no control over what other people did or how they treated me, although I did have the power to keep them from mistreating me.

Another failed relationship. No matter how hard I tried, I could not seem to break the cycle of getting involved with people who wanted to take something from me and then throw me away. Our entire client base was comprised of companies that I brought to the business. My partner brought none. As our relationship came to an end, I refused to fight him for the customers. I walked away from the partnership and let him have the clients that I sought, secured, and nurtured into a successful business for both companies. Even after I was the bigger person and didn't fight him for the clients, he still kept my thirteen grand. My relationship with God allowed me to have the strength not to go postal over the ordeal and try to get revenge. I was angry to be cheated out of money by someone who I had known for over a decade. To add insult to injury, I had hired my partner's company to install my projects at several companies where I had worked in the past. I gave him a lot of business during my career and I still got fucked out of thirteen grand in the end. Did thirteen signify that there was more to this ordeal than what met the eye? Only time would reveal the answer.

Several of my former business partner's previous clients noted via derogatory comments on the internet that his company had screwed them out of money prior to us joining forces. When I partnered with his company, I was aware of his shady past, although at that time I didn't have many options, so I hoped for the best. It should have been no big surprise that he ended up screwing me too. He was filthy rich by most people's standards and I learned just how he got so rich—by cheating people out of their hard-earned money. Today, I believe God hooked me up with this shady character because our business relationship was always intended to be a temporary one. I believe God had a larger plan and it didn't entail me working with a thief for the long haul. But for the plan to come to fruition, I had to follow the wisdom of my spiritual teacher. I had to forgive those who I thought had taken advantage of me no matter how many times it happened. I was to remind myself I was not defined by an unfortunate circumstance and needed to look beyond my current situation. Instead, I would be defined by the *Love* that I bestowed onto others, even if they didn't deserve my love, the *Valor* to stay hopeful amidst hopelessness, and the ability to see *Goodness* in a world when oftentimes there seemed to be very little of it—*LVG.*

Rick was still living in Chicago, in the same condominium that he bought when I convinced him to move back there almost eight years earlier. During the four years that we were estranged, Rick had flourished professionally. I once heard T.D. Jakes, the minister, make a statement during one of his sermons on TBN. He said not to get jealous of a friend's success when you're down and out. If God had allowed your friend and you to go through difficult financial times at the same time as one another, then you wouldn't have the good fortune of having your friend help you through your hardship. This was certainly the case between Rick and me. He advanced considerably in his career between the time we stopped speaking and the time we reconnected and he has continued to thrive professionally. If it hadn't been for his kindness and generosity, this book would not have ever come to fruition. He is definitely my BFF, my best friend that I hang out with all the time.

Through my story, I hope you can see the importance of helping people when you can do so. Throughout my life, when I was in a position to help, I tried to lend a hand to individuals to advance their careers and assist them in achieving a better life for themselves. Some of these people are still in my life today while others are not. The key to helping people is not to expect anything in return and to not get bitter if those who you've helped turn out to be less than appreciative. Had I not hired Rick to work with the creative team at Bigsby, and later convinced Alex to hire him, I would have been up shit's creek without a paddle. By helping Rick early in his career, and as a result of the friendship we developed over the years, he became my saving grace. To be clear, I did nothing for Rick but present him with an opportunity. What he did with that opportunity was orchestrated by his own efforts and he owns his success. As his friend, I am proud of all that he has accomplished. Interestingly, in the time that Rick and I were not speaking to one another, his career path changed direction and he entered the field of corporate communications, which set the stage for him to be the editor of this book. What are the chances that Tweedledum would write his life story and his BFF would become a writer and ultimately my editor? It's impossible for all this to be just random occurrences that just so happen to work out in my favor.

I'm grateful for the day when Rick came into my life and helped me become a better person. We remain loyal to each other and he and I are two of the original three musketeers. At the conclusion of the movie *Slum Dog Millionaire*, the last question on the game show, worth a multi-million dollar jackpot, is "what's the name of the third musketeer?" Even though Rick never met Lance, he heard many stories about him. Rick was happy to learn that Lance and I had not only become workout partners, but also managed to develop a friendship. He knew I needed a positive influence in my life while living in Los Angeles, especially after the shit that happened in the desert. He was also happy to know that through my friendship with Lance, I found the encouragement that I so desperately needed at that time. Since this story is about **L**ove, **V**alor and **G**oodness, the answer to the multi-million dollar jackpot question, as it relates to my inner circle, is that the third musketeer is my friend **L**ance **van****G**ils**!**

Did God have a hand in bringing Lance and me together? I now believe the answer to this question to be yes, He certainly did. I believe the last-minute change to Lance's friend schedule at his job, which resulted in Richard not being able to work out with Lance, as they originally planned, was orchestrated by a divine presence. The sudden change to Richard's work day allowed me to befriend Lance and become his gym partner and eventually one of his close friends.

When hanging out with Lance after the gym, on the night of his murder, his wallet fell out of his backpack. It hit the ground at a place close to my apartment where we had our last drink together. He did not realize that his wallet had fallen on the floor, so I bent down, picked it up, and handed it back to him. Later, I asked his mother if I could have that same wallet after she retrieved his belongings from the coroner's office. I felt it was no coincidence that we both simultaneously touched that specific item on the night of his death. In some strange way, I feel that his wallet binds us together. In Greek mythology, the word *kibisis* is defined as the sack carried by the god Hermes, typically translated as *wallet*. Hermes is described as moving freely between the worlds of the mortal and divine. He is also portrayed as an emissary and messenger of the gods, an intermediary between the two worlds. Today, I carry Lance's wallet in my pant pocket wherever I go. I like to believe that the incident involving his *kibisis* was deliberately orchestrated and is a marker left by a divine presence to let me know that Lance moves freely between two worlds and he's my intercessor in heaven.

After my business partner and I went our separate ways, I was again terrified that I would end up in the same situation as before—when I didn't have enough money to buy groceries and pay my rent. I had to hang on to my faith and believe that it was somehow all going to work out as long as I didn't try to get even with the bastard. Once I broke away from the thief who stole my money, I informed my clients that I was no longer working with him and thanked them for their patronage. However, splitting from him when I did worked out in my favor. The same guy who hired me to work for his company in New York – when I originally moved from Chicago to San Francisco – had contracted me to handle a few projects for his clients while the pickpocket and I were still working together. This former boss from New York expressed his satisfaction in the way I managed his client's projects and he wanted to know if I had any interest in working for his new company. When the rug was pulled out from underneath my feet again, and the door was slammed shut in my face, God made sure there was a welcome mat in front of the next door that He opened for me.

In the spring of that year, Rick decided to sell his apartment and he bought a two-bedroom unit in downtown Chicago. Knowing the situation in which I found myself, he invited me to come live with him. His invitation was my ticket out of a bad situation and allowed me to walk away from the thirteen thousand dollar loss without having to worry whether I would soon find myself in a financially compromised situation again. Because we rekindled our friendship, I was able to split from my business partner. Had we not reconnected, I would have fucked myself big time, without ever knowing it, because then I wouldn't have had the option to split from the thief when I did. Without Rick's unwavering friendship, I shudder to think what would have become of me. Without a doubt, I believe that God had a definitive plan for our friendship since we met over two decades earlier. I also believe that the last dream that I dreamt before my exodus from the desert was not a random one. Rick is aware of that dream, where I tell him that God is real. To this day, Rick believes in God differently than I do and I believe that the full meaning of my dream is yet to be realized by both of us. What I know for certain is that, in forgiving Rick, God hid my redemption, deliverance, rescue, recovery, and future, for whatever I thought he may or may not have done many years earlier—and he became the means of my salvation.

Moving back to Chicago and living with Rick would lower my living expenses drastically. However, my relocation cost me over five thousand dollars. It seemed that I was constantly rearranging my life and spending money that I couldn't afford to spend because some asshole was stealing my money and using me for their own gain without regard for my well-being. While I made the decision, the move back to the Midwest wasn't ideal because of the cold winters that I disliked so much. Little did I know that the winter of 2013 - 2014 would be one of the coldest in many years.

In late March or early April, I informed Lance that I was moving back to Chicago because I needed to lower my cost of living. I had lived in Los Angeles for twenty-seven months and the one person that I was going to miss the most when I moved away was Lance. I was sad that our weekday workouts at three o'clock, which had become part of my daily routine, were coming to an end. I was also going to miss spending time with Lance after the gym and hearing his stories during our happy hour excursions. Lance told me that one of things that he liked the most about our friendship was that I listened to him. I genuinely enjoyed his company and was thrilled to hear he enjoyed our time together as much as I did. I learned, at that moment, that young adults just want older adults to take them seriously. Before I entered the desert and experienced my financial meltdown, my friends, colleagues and business associates always took me seriously and came seeking my advice. Once my life fell apart, those same people that frequently turned to me for advice or guidance, stopped seeking my wisdom. For whatever reason, they stopped coming around and it made me feel like I had nothing of value to contribute to anyone any longer. Lance's friendship made me feel like I had value once again. He cared about what I had to say and he took the years of wisdom that I could offer him to heart. Through my friendship with him, I learned there's no difference between a twenty-one-year-old and a fifty-one-year-old man besides their obvious age difference—they both want to be taken seriously and feel like they have something of value to contribute, whether to a friend, a family member, a work associate, or to the world at large.

After the gym on Wednesday, July 3, Lance I went out for drinks. Since the following day was the Fourth of July holiday – and Lance was off from work on Thursday and Friday – we decided to move our Friday drinking outing to Wednesday. During drinks, Lance told me that his sister had gone into labor that day with her second daughter. He was very excited about becoming an uncle for the second time. We had several drinks and got a bit loopy before heading to our homes. A few days later, I learned that on Lance's way to the station to catch his train to go to his apartment, he decided that he would walk to the hospital where his sister was having her baby. Upon his arrival, he met up with his mother. After his death, when I spoke with his mother for the first time, she informed me that Lance told her about our friendship the night he went to the hospital to see his sister. Based on what he was telling her about our relationship, she got the impression I was mentoring him and I was flattered to hear that she thought I was a positive influence on her son.

That evening, when Lance's second niece was born, I had a dream. I dreamt that his new niece would grow up to be a great leader. At some point in her career, she would land a position where she would impact many people's lives in a positive way while creating financial independence for many. In my dream, her name was Purity. Seven days after my dream, on the night of the fourth of July, and seven days after Lance's niece had been in this world, Lance left it (4+7=**11**). His niece wasn't named Purity as I dreamt. She was given the name Milani. According to an encyclopedia of names, Milani stands for *union*, *people*, *favor*, and *grace*. After Lance's death, I wondered if there was more to my dream than I originally thought. Could God have chosen Lance and me to be the conduit to establish the *House of* ***LVG***? Is God's *grace* on Milani and if so, is she the person He will use to bring many *people* in *union* with His *favor*? I wonder if she's the main character of this story. It would be just like God to take one paragraph from this entire book and have it contain the most important message—about a little baby girl and her purpose. If I'm able to establish and fund a non-profit called the *House of* ***LVG***, I believe she just might be the one God has chosen to become my successor and the trustee of the foundation after my death. If this is true, then I also believe she might positively impact a greater number of lives than I could ever have thought. I do know that God has a larger plan and just maybe, I've seen a glimpse of what that plan entails.

Lance worked with a young lady who joined our gym and who I got to know. One afternoon, while working out, she kept interrupting my gym regimen. She was trying to share a personal story with me, but what she was telling me didn't make much sense. I expressed my frustrations with her to Lance. Being the gentleman that he was, he immediately came to her rescue and asked me to be more patient when dealing with her. On my walk home that evening, I realized that even though Lance was thirty years my junior, I was inspired by his kindness and gentle nature toward others. I wanted to become more like him. After he died, I reflected back on the conversation I had with his mother when she told me how she got the impression from Lance that I was mentoring him. I wondered whether I was mentoring Lance or was he mentoring me. At the gym, I only saw the serious side of him, but on occasion I would get a glimpse of his silly side after he had a few drinks during our happy hour outings. His sister later told me that he was a jokester when he was around his close friends and family. She also told me that he enjoyed making people laugh and seeing them smile. He was a beautiful person who was extremely pleasant on the eyes, but more importantly he was extraordinarily beautiful on the inside.

Before I left Los Angeles, I wanted to get Lance a surprise gift to express my gratitude for his friendship. My first thought was to buy him a miniature refrigerator for his bedroom, but I found out that he already had one. My second idea was to buy him a microwave, but shortly after I had this idea, he told me he recently purchased one. I was out of ideas until one day, at the gym, he gave me the perfect idea. Lance told me he wanted to buy a good suit once he saved enough money to afford one. He was young and he hadn't acquired certain personal possessions that an individual usually accumulates as they get older, like fine clothing. I, on the other hand, had acquired many designer suits that I had hanging in my closet, which I never wore because I worked from home. I decided to give him one of my suits that I bought on a trip to Italy. I offered him a beautiful light brown Pal Zileri two-piece suit, a dress shirt, and tie. The great thing about investing in quality clothes is that they are usually timeless and remain in style for many years, if not decades. I also decided to give him other items that I bought before I gained weight. I had lost many of the pounds that I gained while I lived in Palm Springs, but I was still not at my ideal weight. There were certain clothes that I loved, but knew I was never going to be able to fit into again so I decided to give Lance more items from my closet than just the one designer suit that he was hoping to buy for himself someday. I gave him a black leather blazer from Barney's in New York, several Emporio Armani sweaters that I purchased when I lived in San Francisco, a Dolce Gabbana reversible sweater-jacket, and several jeans by different designers. He was now well outfitted with enough designer digs to get the attention of the ladies, even though he didn't need any help in getting women to notice him. Sadly, Lance never got the opportunity to wear his suit before he died. His mother cremated Lance in the suit, dress shirt, and tie that I gave him. I wondered whether there was more to Lance telling me he wanted a good suit and me giving him one. It saddened me that Lance never got the chance to enjoy his designer clothes, but I was honored to have him wear a suit that once belonged to me when he was cremated and see this inconsequential suit as one of the many elements that bond us to each other.

I enjoyed hanging out with Lance and immensely appreciated the friendship that we were able to develop over the eight months we knew each other. I was captivated by his beauty and genuine caring personality and I could see that he appreciated and cared for me too. Ours was definitely a bromance, although I was very careful not to let myself get overly emotionally involved. I could have fallen in love with him, but the only one that was going to get hurt in that scenario was me. I never accepted the fact that I loved him until he was gone. I can now admit to myself that I did in fact love Lance and I'm in love with him for any of the traits that he demonstrated—for the kind man he was, his devotion and commitment to becoming a U.S. Marine, for being a dedicated and caring brother to his sister, the amazing companion he was to his friends, and the loving son he was to his parents. He was very proud of his family and friends and often spoke highly of them, which is evidence of him loving those who were close to him. Most significantly, my bromance with Lance ignited a passion within me to follow my dream of establishing a charitable foundation. I envision Lance living forever in the hearts of the people's lives that are impacted and changed for the better through the *House of* ***LVG***.

On Thursday, July 11, the day Lance died, we worked out together at our usual time. Lance's female friend from work was also working out that day. The three of us hung out and chatted between sets. She knew it was the last time I was going to be at the gym before the movers came to pick up my things the following day. Toward the end of our workout, she asked me for my cellular number so we could stay in touch. Had she not asked for my number at the last minute, I'm not sure when I would've discovered that Lance had passed away. None of his family or other friends had my contact information.

The following afternoon, I received a call from her wanting to know whether I knew of his whereabouts because he hadn't shown up for work. He appeared to be missing. I had no idea where Lance was, but I immediately called him and left a voicemail on his phone, asking him where he was. The next day, on Saturday, July 13, I received a second call from his work friend informing me that he was gone. I was confused by the term "gone". I asked her, "Where did he go?" She replied that he had been murdered. I heard what she said although I couldn't unite or comprehend the words Lance and murdered in the same sentence. His unexpected and tragic death hit me like a ton of bricks and it certainly tested my faith.

After his death, I talked to him every night before I went to sleep and apologized for not being with him on that bridge where he met his assailant. My one-way conversations with him went on for a full month before I traveled from Chicago to Long Beach for his memorial service. After Lance's eulogy, a young girl, a relative of Lance, went up to his mother and asked who Darrel was and where she could find him. Lance's mother didn't see me inside the building where the service was held so she told the young lady that

I must be in one of the hallways in the outer corridor. I was standing with Lance's friend from work, the same lady I knew from the gym, when Lance's relative approached me and asked whether my name was Darrel. I told her that yes, it was. She then informed me that she had a supernatural gift and wanted to know whether I believed in such things. I told her that I did. She then told me that Lance wanted her to relay a message. He wanted me to know that there was nothing I could've done that would have changed the outcome of what happened on that bridge, which resulted in his death so I needed to stop feeling guilty. I began to cry. There was no way she could've known about the conversations I was having with Lance because I hadn't mentioned them to anyone, not even Rick. Lance's message brought me much comfort and was one of many unusual and unexplainable situations surrounding his death. I believe these strange occurrences were taking place so I would know that there was more to his death than a random act of violence and I was to refrain from becoming bitter or from wanting to seek revenge for his death.

Later, Lance's mother told me that a psychic conveyed to her that her son's assailant would be identified, but not for many years, which I believe to be true. For some strange reason, I believe that when Lance's perpetrator is finally known, God will want us to meet. In my mind, I see Lance's assailant expressing deep remorse for what took place on that bridge and while expressing heartfelt remorse, the attacker emotionally breaks down, we embrace and I too begin to cry. I forgive whoever caused Lance's death, because I know I can't carry the alternative with me and expect there to be room for God in my life. I question why I see myself embracing the person who is responsible for taking my good friend away from his family and friends and the only answer that makes sense to me is that I believe God wants me to openly express my compassion for the person who has taken someone from me that I would've given up my life to protect. I've come to know that God offers hope and through hope anything is possible, even forgiving an unforgivable act. Perhaps this book will become well known and through this story the person that is responsible for Lance's death will find the valor within to come forward. As a rule, forgiveness and remorse are usually articulated through words, but true forgiveness and deep remorse can only be defined through actions. I believe Lance's legacy embodies the *Love* that's bestowed to another through heartfelt forgiveness, even if that individual doesn't deserve to be forgiven, the *Valor* that it takes to express one's deepest remorse when seeking someone's forgiveness, even when you know you don't deserve to be forgiven, and the *Goodness* that's created when these two opposing forces embrace one another – *LVG.*

There's a building on the corner of Main and 2nd Streets in downtown Los Angeles that was once the city's first Catholic Cathedral, dedicated to Saint Vibiana. She was a third-century virgin martyr of the Roman Catholic Church and she is the patroness of the Archdiocese of Los Angeles. Her remains were rediscovered on December 9, 1853 in ancient catacombs near the Appian Way close to Rome. A marble tablet, inscribed with the words *to the soul of the innocent and pure Vibiana* adorned her tomb. Her cathedral is one of the few remaining nineteenth century landmarks in LA. It was finished in 1876 and designated a cultural monument in 1963. Following the 1994 Northridge earthquake, the Archdiocese determined that the building sustained irreparable damage and the church was decommissioned. A new cathedral, Our Lady of the Angels, was built a few blocks away. Since 2002, Saint Vibiana's relics have been housed in the mausoleum of the Cathedral of Our Lady of the Angels. In 1999, the former cathedral was acquired by a team of developers whose vision was to transform the dilapidated structure into a state of the art venue for the performing arts and special events, with a beautiful courtyard garden. Shortly after the acquisition, a team of architects and structural engineers began the seismic retrofit and renovation. Painstaking efforts went into the restoration of its century old historic details.

I came across this building shortly after moving to LA in 20**11**, over a year before meeting Lance. For an unknown reason, I found myself immediately drawn to the building when I stumbled upon it. On many days, when walking Aston and Bentley, I took them to play in the park on the opposite side of the street and kitty-corner from the former cathedral. After the boys were done playing in the park, on our way back to the apartment, I would stand across the street from what was once a church and just stare at the building. I always thought there was something special about the structure and felt like one day I might own that building. After meeting Lance and realizing what transpired on the evening of his passing, I wondered if there was more to my affection for this LA landmark.

The last day I saw Lance, that Wednesday, July **11**, 20**13**, we hugged each other twice after having drinks, said goodbye, and parted on Spring Street between 5th and 6th Street (5+6=**11**). On his way home, he walked to Main Street and stopped at the Five Star Bar, between 3rd and 2nd, on the opposite side of the street from St. Vibiana. At the bar, Lance used his bankcard at the ATM inside before heading home. After leaving the Five Star Bar, on his way to his apartment, he continued walking north on Main Street until he came to 2nd Street, where he made a right turn. This was his usual route when walking home from my place. On Main Street, he walked directly in front of the entrance to the former cathedral. As he continued to make his way home, he walked past the outdoor gardens of the building when he turned the corner to head east on 2nd Street. Somewhere on the 1st Street Bridge, which leads into East Los Angeles, he was murdered. Later, I realized why we hugged each other twice before we parted from one another on the evening of his death, rather than shaking each other's hand as we had always done every other evening when parting ways—one hug was for this life and the other hug was for the next.

I now believe that the reason I was drawn to the old cathedral, and felt like I would own it one day, is because it was always meant to be the home offices for ***The House of Love, Valor and Goodness.*** After Lance's untimely death, I've come to believe that I'm not to be the owner of the former church on the corner of Main and 2nd Street as I originally had thought. I now believe I'm to be the trustee of the foundation that will hopefully own this property one day in the future. In some bizarre way, I feel I'm destined to establish the offices for the non-profit on this parcel of land. I understand establishing the offices for the foundation in this former church seems impossible from where I'm standing at the present, but I've come to know that I'm to trust the Lord with all my heart and not to lean on my own understanding. This structure is a perfect place to house the offices of the foundation. The building has the capacity to accommodate its' administrative offices and the main hall can be used for large fundraising events and could be rented for weddings and other events to generate income for the organization. I'm either as crazy as a loony tune cartoon character on crack or there's a larger plan in play. Lance was born in Los Angeles and died in the city of Angels. Therefore, I can't think of a more perfect place to establish this foundation than in a building that once held a formal house of worship, in a parcel of land that Lance passed by – and more than likely stepped upon – during his route home on the evening of his tragic death. Possibly a greater force had already chosen this specific location for the foundation before I became enchanted with the building and before I even met Lance. I wholeheartedly believe that God does work in mysterious ways and He will use all things for the greater good if we allow him. If this former cathedral becomes the center for the *House of* ***LVG*** then it will be indisputable proof that God took my mess and used it to create a legacy for Lance—and a better life for many.

When I moved with Alex from Chicago to San Francisco many years earlier, I secured the position with the New York firm to be their account executive in the west coast and received that job offer before the movers physically transported our things to the bay area. Fifteen years later, as I was moving back to the Windy City from California, the same boss that offered me the job when I moved to San Francisco from Chicago once again offered me a job at the exact time that I was going back to the Midwest, before my household items were transported. It seemed as if my career path was retracing its steps. I thought it unusual and possibly a sign of some kind. Did this mean my career path had completed a 360 degree turn or was it merely 180 degrees? If it had gone full circle, did it mean my new job was going to bring an end to my cycle of disappointing business relationships? If it was a 180, did it mean there were more disappointments yet to come?

I settled back into life in Chicago. Shortly after moving there, I found out that Cher was passing through town during her *Dressed to Kill (D2K)* tour. I had planned to finish writing this book before I saw Cher again, but that did not happen. On June 9, 2014, I saw her at the Allstate Arena in Rosemont, Illinois. Three years after seeing her at that concert, I found myself still writing. In the end, it took me nearly seven years to finish my tale.

Those who have had the pleasure to see Cher, in the cities where her *D2K* concert was held, are aware that she sings *I Hope You Find It,* from her *Closer to the Truth* album, as her last number. When she stepped on stage for her last song of the night, she walked over to an open structure on stage. She wore an elaborate costume and her headgear resembled a halo. The open cage to which she was strapped gave the visual illusion of a playing card from a deck of cards, and she resembled the ace of spades. Once she was safely strapped into the cage, it lifted off the stage and elevated her over the audience taking her on a journey above the crowd through the auditorium. She seemed to me like a flying *ace of spades*. A Chicago Tribune writer later wrote that "it was as if the Virgin Mary levitated herself over the audience visiting her people." She was truly a vision, very much like the Virgin Mary, a woman who represented perseverance, beauty, strength, love, hope, dedication, motherhood, and – most of all – salvation. Just like a heavenly vision, Cher was there one moment and gone the next. I refer to Cher's *D2K* concert as her ace performance—first-rate, excellent, brilliant, and great, nothing less than top-notch. When I got home that evening I googled "ace of spades" and learned that the ace of spades is the highest-ranking card in the deck and it's only fitting that this chapter be dedicated to *The Goddess of Pop* since twenty-one is the winning hand in blackjack.

As I reflect on that concert that night, I came to see that the evening was full of **love**—for a woman that I saw with my father when I was as a little boy and who empowered me as an adult to get myself out of a bad relationship when I could see no hope of a better life. The same woman helped me to find the **valor** to seek out my purpose in life while inspiring me to envision my destiny. God utilized Cher and her talent to assist Him so I may see the **goodness** that the world had to offer. With Cher hovering just several feet above my head, she did in fact resemble the Virgin Mary or at least a loving angel sent from heaven. As she hovered above the crowd, she gave her audience exactly what we all wanted from her, a closer look at an amazing entertainer and a woman who was nothing less than an icon. It was the most incredible and extravagant ending of the many encounters that I experienced with Cher. That evening would leave an everlasting impression upon me. Unlike all her other concerts that I attended, I was sober. Had Tina finally played her last card, ending a long and drawn out game of self-medication?

Cher played her hand well that night. She packed the house and one might say she was holding a full house. Earlier that evening, Cher proclaimed that this would be her final concert series of her career. Was that night the last time I would physically be in the same room with her? Did my lady who brought me so much comfort sing her last song onstage? Did we dance our last dance together?

Rick attended the concert with me. When we arrived, we made our way to our seats, on the main floor of the stadium. My seat was in row twenty-three, in seat number six (2+3+6=**11**), and Rick sat next to me in seat number five. We found an oversized postcard on our chairs with a beautiful picture of Cher on one side and a note from her on the other. On it, Cher wrote that "There are hungry children living in our neighborhoods and communities across the U.S. who need our help – and I hope you will join me in this great campaign to make their lives better and healthier." She went on to say, "This initiative to help poor children touches my soul." She finished her plea by stating that she had been a poor child growing up and that together we could make an enormous difference. She thanked everyone from the bottom of her heart and wrote that she would match all donations. There was a phone number listed on the card where one could text the word "food." By sending a text, you would make a ten-dollar donation. I say Cher and Cher alike, so I texted the word food to the number on the postcard. I then learned that the donations were given to the "Chef's for Humanity" and "Wholesome Wave" organizations. I was once again amazed and delighted by Cher. She and I shared a mutual passion…we both want to assist those who would go to bed hungry that night, or any other night, from ever having to go to bed hungry again.

Someday, I hope to meet Cher, befriend her, and possibly partner with her on a program to feed the hungry. I understand my desire to meet and establish a relationship with her is probably nothing more than a fan's pipe dream. If this book has a purpose and a destiny then possibly its purpose is to engage someone, and hopefully many, to seek out their own purpose in life—and its destiny is to build friendships and alliances for the betterment of humanity in the form of the *House of* ***LVG***. I also fantasize that the book brings Cher and I together in the same room so I can personally thank the woman that God used to get His voice heard when I was not listing.

I Hope You Find It

These clouds aren't going nowhere, darling
Rain keeps coming down
I just thought I'd try to call you
For you got too far outta town
And I hope that you get this message that I'm leaving for you
'Cause I'd hate that you left without hearing the words that I needed you to

And I hope you find it
What you're looking for
I hope it's everything you dreamed your life could be
And so much more

And I hope you're happy, wherever you are
I wanted you to know that
And nothing's gonna change that
I hope you find it

Am I supposed to hang around and wait forever?
Last words that I said
But that was nothing but a broken heart talking, darling
You know it wasn't what I meant
Call me up, let me know that you got this message that I'm leaving for you
'Cause I'd hate that you left without hearing the words that I needed you to

And I hope you find it
What you're looking for
I hope it's everything you dreamed your life could be
And so much more

And I hope you're happy, wherever you are
I wanted you to know that
And nothing's gonna change that
I hope you find it

Whatever it is out there that you were missing here

Well, I hope you find it
What you're looking for
I hope it's everything you dreamed your life could be
And so much more

And I hope you're happy wherever you are
I wanted you to know that
And nothing's gonna change that
I hope you find it
I hope you find it
Oh, oh

Cher

I can't say it any better. God's promise of a purpose for our existence is much like that perfect Christmas present sitting so beautifully under the holiday tree. It's impeccably wrapped and waiting for its recipient. *I hope to find mine and I hope you find yours* – destiny awaits us.

THE BEGINNING | THIS IS IT

With every ending, there's a new beginning. This is the end of what was—and the beginning of what's yet to come. I dedicate the end and the beginning of this book to Michael Jackson, who famously uttered, "this is it?" just days before his tragic death. Michael won countless awards for his humanitarian efforts and, in some ways, his life exemplified what this book is all about, **L**ove for our fellowman, the **V**alor to overcome adversities, and the **G**oodness that can be found in the world, when at times there can seem to be so little.

Like many people, I believed that Michael was guilty of the child abuse charges that were brought against him, although never proven. After I got to know God on a more personal level, I realized I was mistaken. I now believe Michael was innocent of the allegations brought against him. My relationship with God allowed my heart to be cleared of judgment and my mind to be freed from hatred. For the first time, I could see Michael as a little boy who had been used by so many for financial gain. I believe the actions of these people birthed a deep level of sadness within Michael that created disorder.

I heard a story about Michael from a business associate who worked for a mannequin company in New York. One day, he got a call from one of Michael Jackson's people wanting to know whether his company sold children mannequins. My associate responded that they did sell children mannequins and offered them in a variety of ages. The caller then indicated that Michael would stop by the following day to look at the mannequins in his showroom. The next day, a group of men came to the showroom and scoured every room to make sure they were empty of other people before Michael entered the building and sales floor through the freight elevator. Michael quickly walked around the showroom and pointed at various mannequins. Then, just as quickly, he exited the building. One of his people approached my associate and asked him if he could sell the mannequins with the clothes with which they were dressed. He also wanted to know whether my associate could deliver them to Michael's hotel room in Manhattan and place the mannequins throughout his suite. Sounds fucking weird—until you realize that Michael related to children because kids wanted nothing of monetary value from him. They just wanted Michael to be their friend.

Mental and physical abuse affects everyone differently. It can make an abused person do things that look fucking crazy to the outside world…like having child mannequins delivered to your hotel room. I know this to be true because I was abused on many levels for many years. Being used by people caused me to do things that made me appear to be fucked up in the head to many people who often said I was paranoid. In actuality, much of my crazy and messed up behavior was fueled by those that used me for their own gain without regard for my well-being.

On July 14, 2013, Aston, Bentley and I landed in Chicago and moved into Rick's new apartment, located two blocks from the iconic Willis Tower, which was formerly Sears Tower, in the financial district. What I thought was going to be the beginning of a new chapter in my life, turned out to be the end to an old one.

A month after I arrived in Chicago, I began to work for my former boss, who was now my business partner, and his New York based company. Since I worked for him previously, I didn't want to put myself back into the same position with him again. Therefore, I added his company products to the array of services that ILDworld offered, and worked for him as an independent contractor, whereby ILDworld would sell his company's goods and it would receive a 10% commission on every sale. I guaranteed him a minimum of twenty hours a week, even though I ended up working close to forty, and he guaranteed me a five hundred dollar a week draw against future commissions. I had a global territory, with only two retailers off limits, as those two companies were already his clients.

In December of 2013, I traveled to New York for a store fixture tradeshow in which my new business partner's company was participating. Rick traveled with me and we stayed at the W Hotel in the financial district, directly across the street from ground zero. When we checked into the hotel, we were given room number 902 (9+0+2=**11**). The same day we arrived, we went to see the memorial built to commemorate the individuals who perished on 9/11. Once we arrived in the park, my breath was taken away by the magnitude and the splendor of the memorial. It includes two square in-ground waterfalls that outline the footprints of what were once the two World Trade Towers. I randomly walked up to the edge of one of the waterfalls and noticed that the names of the people who perished during the collapse of the towers were listed in the stone balustrade that surrounds the waterfalls. There was an engine number listed under one name, which I believed to be the name of a fireman who was lost during the collapse of the towers. The engine number was 238, which adds up to the number thirteen (2+3+8=**13**). The memorial is enormous, with thousands of names, so the chances of me walking up to that exact name, with an engine number that added up thirteen, seemed impossible unless an unknown spirit was directing me to that specific spot. I'm not sure what this spirit was trying to convey to me, but I believe with all my heart that it was no coincidence that the two numbers that are so significant in my life were so prevalent on that day we arrived in New York.

If and when this book is successful, I hope to transform ILDworld into an **I**nspirational, **L**iterary, and **D**evotional organization. What I love about God is that through knowing Him all things are possible. Having a relationship with Him is very much like playing the lottery. Half the fun in playing is imagining what you would do with all that money if you won. Half the fun in having a relationship with God is imagining all the things that are possible. Perhaps the prominence of the number eleven and thirteen on the day I visited the 9/11 memorial is a sign that someday in the future ILDworld will occupy offices in Freedom Tower. Like the lottery that offers hope of winning more money than one can imagine, God offers hope that the impossible is possible, such as a small company like ILDworld leasing office space in one of the most expensive buildings in New York.

Between January and October of 2014, my company sold almost seven hundred and fifty thousand dollars for my new business partner's organization. In that time, I was able to secure nearly forty client meetings in the U.S. to promote his products. ILD incurred the travel costs for me to meet with these clients and based on those meetings, I ascertained the client's future interest in the products I represented. From those interests, I was forecasted to sell five million dollars of store merchandising fixtures in 2015, which would have generated five hundred thousand dollars in revenue for ILDworld.

Throughout my career, I built something out of nothing at the various companies where I worked. These so-called professional accomplishments of mine were much like building a pyramid. Like the great pyramids of Egypt someone was always trying to loot the pyramids I painstakingly built. Madame President withholding my commissions upon my exit from her company, Philven stealing from our business, and my former business partner stealing my thirteen thousand dollars caused me to become disenchanted, to say the least. Each of these relationships – into which I poured my blood, sweat, and tears to make them financially successful – always came to an end. Every time I found a new business opportunity and began the tedious and tiresome process of building my next pyramid…it was looted. It felt like each time I created something out of nothing, that when that something began to show signs of turning a profit, someone would try to cheat me out of the success I built. I was exhausted and with my latest business endeavor, I thought I finally found a partner with whom I could build my latest and greatest pyramid, where I could store my riches for eternity or until I retired, whichever came first.

Before I left Los Angeles, when I was still working out with Lance, he told me that he once found a little bird on the ground, in the walkway behind where he lived. He realized it had fallen out of its nest, at the roofline of the garage behind his apartment. He secured a ladder to reach the nest so he could place the little bird back in its home. When Lance told me this story, he mimicked the little bird's walk back to its nest after he placed it back on the roof. His acting skills brought a smile to my face. His interpretation of the bird's walk was adorable and amusing. What made me smile further, and what seemed to be even funnier, is that Lance didn't realize he was imitating the little bird's walk as he told the story. I only saw the serious side of Lance at the gym, so his walking bird imitation was a big departure from his usual demeanor.

While living back in Chicago, I went to see a well-known and reputable psychic to ask her questions about Lance and learn more about the future relationship with my new business partner. When I arrived at her place, we went to the second floor of her condominium, where she had a sitting room. She sat in a chair in front of a large window and I sat on a small sofa on the opposite side. From where I sat, I could see her terrace through the window. It was still winter and snow had accumulated on her patio, which was barren of any plant life. I noticed a small bird carved out of wood that was mounted on a stick and stuck in a pot of dirt that must have held some foliage before winter arrived. As she began to speak, I wondered if this woman was truly legitimate or a hoax. I began to concentrate on the little wooden bird hovering over her shoulder. It reminded me of the encounters I had with my feathered friends while I was living in the desert and the story Lance told me about the little bird falling out of its nest. As I contemplated whether the wooden bird was a sign that the woman was legitimate, my mind began to wonder. I then heard her say that Lance was with us and he had a toucan with him. She told me that Lance spoke to the toucan and the toucan repeated whatever Lance told it. She began to laugh and said, "Oh, I get it now." She then told me that Lance told her, "Two can do it better than one." She got my attention, mainly because I had focused on the bird outside and because the first thing out of her mouth was about Lance having a pet bird in the spirit realm. Later, when I mentioned to Lance's sister and his mother about my visit to the psychic, they immediately told me that Lance would often say to them, "Two can do it better than one." The psychic and I spoke at length and she also told me that Lance and I were more than likely brothers in another life and this was possibly why when Lance and I were out together and people met us for the first time, they would ask whether I was Lance's father, or if we were brothers. I was comforted by the visit and was absolutely amazed to be in the same room with someone who connected with Lance's spirit. I recalled my time in Palm Springs and remembered how strange it was that I had seen what I believed to be two toucans in the sky when I saw the vision of the two yellow suns and the two white rainbows. Was that somehow connected to this encounter with Lance?

The Chicago winter of 2013 - 2014 was relentlessly horrendous and that's putting it mildly. It had the most days at zero temperature or below than any other winter in recorded history. The winter began on Saturday, December 21, 2013—lasting for only **eleven** days of what was left of that year. If you add the two years from that winter (2+0+1+3 plus 2+0+1+4=**13**), it appears like a distinct pattern, much like a footprint. It was like seeing a shoe impression in the snow and knowing that someone had walked in my same path even if I didn't know who that was. I now think the numbers thirteen and eleven are a sign from God letting me know that no matter what brought me back to Chicago during one of its coldest winters, He was at the helm navigating my journey—even as I was freezing and not certain where I was headed. Mercifully, in the spring of 2014, Rick received an offer from his company to relocate back to the bay area where the company's corporate headquarters were based. Still reeling from the harsh winter, I was thrilled that Rick had received an offer to move back to San Francisco. He accepted the transfer and placed his condo in Chicago on the market. By October of that year, Rick and I were back in San Francisco where we had many fond memories of the city from the first time we lived there.

Now that I was living back on the West coast, when ILDworld was forecasted to sell five million dollars in 2015 within the territory that I had built over the year, my business partner suddenly made the decision to pull the East coast and Midwest territories from my sales jurisdiction. I was left with the West coast territory, which reduced my projected 2015 earnings from five hundred thousand dollars to one hundred and fifty thousand dollars. Once again, the pyramid that I painstakingly built over the last year was looted. I was disappointed and pissed off! What *was* wrong with me that I kept getting myself involved with people that didn't keep their word and kept using me? I realized my career had taken a 180 degree turn when I moved from Los Angeles back to Chicago. Now that I was living in San Francisco for the second time, my career had completed a full 360-degree circle. Soon after, my business partner and I ended up going our separate ways, just as we had done over a decade earlier. History had repeated itself. We parted ways because he reduced my territory and took money out of my pocket that was not his to take. Why would God allow me to be taken advantage of time after time? I thought I was His boy and He was going to look after me and ensure that people didn't continue to exploit my talents without taking my welfare into consideration.

My business partner with whom I split lived in a state that bordered New York. The street that he lived on was called Church Road. I thought this was a sign that I was finally involved in a business relationship with someone that I could build a partnership with that would develop into a prosperous venture for both parties. I was sure that his living on Church Road was a sign that my newest pyramid was going to be protected by angels, but I don't always interpret what I believe to be signs correctly at first. I've also learned that God will, more often than not, send me the answer to a question before I ask the question. Possibly, I was *supposed* to believe my newly formed partnership was going to be fruitful so I would put forth the effort to make it successful. In either case, I now believe God was telling me that it was the last time the looters would be allowed to pilfer from me.

I had been robbed of my confidence when I lived in Palm Springs and once I moved to Los Angeles I questioned whether I had the strength and skills to be successful again. I now understand that God gave me two opportunities to build a business from the bottom up after leaving the desert to restore my self-confidence. In both situations, I accomplished a great deal with little resources available to me. I believe God wanted me to understand that I was still capable of building something from nothing. In doing so, I became self-assured again and could take on the monumental task of building another pyramid, although this one would be built for Him. Like the pyramids of the ancient world, my latest and greatest monument would take decades to unfold. In my eyes, writing my testimony is a paramount achievement and a dream come to life. I started writing in 20**11** and I finished the first draft of the manuscript in 2016 (2+0+1+1+2+0+1+6=**13**).

On May 4, 2016, I turned fifty-six years old (5+6=**11**). Are the numbers thirteen and eleven a sign that this book is ***the beginning*** of my greatest pyramid yet? I hope and pray with all my heart ***this is it***, the one that I've always dreamed of building.

When You Wish Upon A Star...

When you wish upon a star
Makes no difference who you are
Anything your heart desires
Will come to you.

If your heart is in your dream
No request is too extreme
When you wish upon a star
As dreamers do.

Fate is kind
She brings to those who love
The sweet fulfillment of
Their secret longing

Like a bolt out of the blue

Fate steps in and sees you through
When you wish upon a star
Your dreams come true

When a star is born
They possess a gift or two.
One of them is this
They have the power to make a wish come true.

When you wish upon a star
Makes no difference who you are
Anything your heart desires
Will come to you,

If your heart is in your dream
No request is too extreme
When you wish upon a star
As dreamers do.

Fate is kind
She brings to those who love
The sweet fulfillment of
Their secret longing.

Like a bolt out of the blue
Fate steps in and sees you through
When you wish upon a star
Your dreams come true.

Leigh Harline *and* ***Ned Washington,***
for Walt Disney's 1940 adaptation of Pinocchio

After I split from my business partner in October 2014 – another failed business venture – I decided I would devote a full year to finish this story. Unbeknownst to me, a year was not going to be enough time. I would need three years of my undivided attention to complete the book. I felt like God was rearranging my circumstances so I would take the time to finish writing my testimony. Possibly, he was getting impatient and cleared my schedule. I feared that I would fail as a writer and end up with yet another failure. One day, I asked God for a sign that I wasn't going to fail in my quest to write a story that would capture the hearts and minds of its readers. That same day, I walked Aston and Bentley on the Embarcadero, which borders the San Francisco bay. As I walked the dogs on the promenade, I looked over my left shoulder at a concrete bench positioned between where I stood and the road that runs the length of the waterfront. I saw the words *fear no failure* spray-painted on the bench. What were the chances that I would see these words on the same day that I asked for a sign that I wasn't going to fail in my effort to write a compelling story? One week after I saw what I've believed to be a sign, I went back to the same spot. By that time, the city had the graffiti removed by painting over the words. I could still barely make out the outline of the phrase *fear no failure* if I looked for it carefully. Had I asked for my sign at a different time, I would not have seen the *fear no failure* graffiti, as it would have been painted over. It's impossible for this to be a coincidence. I knew without a doubt that this was the sign that I asked God to send me—and the sign that I so desperately needed to receive. It was the encouragement I required to keep moving forward when I was not sure I was moving in the right direction.

It's hard for me to remember the person I was before I encountered God in the desert. Before entering that valley, I had little knowledge of religion and religion still makes me uncomfortable to this day. When I tried to become part of the Christian community, I was always left with the impression that I was unworthy of God's love. I had been met with opposition when I tried to find a place of belonging in two Christian churches, but through Christian television, I familiarized myself with various religious leaders and their viewpoints. Since that time, God has revealed much to me and I've become a better person from what I've learned. I love God with all my heart, but – and this is a big 'but' – I'm not that Bible pushing religious naysayer who believes I'm covered in sin and destined to end up in hell if I don't believe as others do…whatever that might be. On Halloween of 2009, I heard the Christians on TBN say that people who smoke cigarettes, cuss, and drink were unworthy to be Christian. Since I was doing all those things and much more at that time, I was not fit to be part of their community according to them. I didn't measure up to their standards. If I had listened to those so-called Christians leaders who were telling me that I was unworthy, I would've never made it out of the desert alive. I probably would've killed myself or, worse, became a judgmental and vengeful person for what people had done to me. Certainly not all Christians or their organizations are judgmental of others or bad people and there are countless religious organizations that implement many great projects for the betterment of humanity in the name of God. Unfortunately, many religious people that I encountered when I was hoping to be accepted in a community that loved God as much as I did, shunned me. I'm a Taurus and very stubborn and, due to my stubbornness, I refused to be told by anyone other than God that He didn't love me. From experience, I knew what a lie looked like, smelled like, and sounded like and I felt like many religious leaders and their organizations were misleading me in my spiritual development. I could tell I was being misguided by their views. I knew I was worthy of God's love because He had been revealing Himself to me in that dry and hot valley.

The world has divided itself into so many categories and sub-categories that everyone and everything has a label. It seems that religion has divided itself even further and has added even more labels to a world that already has too many. I've learned over many years that God doesn't divide, he adds—all for one and one for all. I don't really know much about religions, but I do know what God has shown me and it doesn't line up with what I heard from many. Religion consists of believing a story about God that someone else has experienced, but being spiritually religious is experiencing God for yourself and having a story of your own in the form of a testimony to share with others. When it was all said and done, I got the impression God wanted me to build my own world since religion wouldn't allow me to be part of theirs. Possibly the new world that God wants me to build is as simple as taking ILDworld and converting it to an **I**nspirational, **L**iterary, and **D**evotional organization.

Who's the face of Facebook? I have this idea to get people to write stories, whether fiction or non-fiction, and submit them to Facebook. Every year, Facebook would choose a story, or one from each category, and post that story as the face of Facebook for one year. It would be a fantastic way to engage people, especially young adults, to become interested in writing, while engaging their creativity. Maybe I have it all wrong and my idea was meant for the new version of ILDworld, its **I**nspirational, **L**iterary and **D**evotional phase. In either case, if Facebook is not interested in exploring my concept, then I hope someday I'll get the opportunity to implement my idea in the new chapter of ILD.

I believe there are two types of people on this planet, those who love and those who accuse. The lover seeks forgiveness and the accuser seeks vengeance. I've learned the hard way that God loves the accuser as much as He loves the lover. While I don't believe God divides, I believe the day will come when He will begin to separate the lovers from the accusers. Until then, I'll leave religion in God's hands and I will continue to work toward refining the person that I want to become so some day when I walk past a mirror and catch a glimpse of the man in the mirror, I will see the reflection of my spiritual teacher in that mirror. For I believe Jesus is the ultimate reflection of God's love.

Can one bad apple spoil the bunch? Jesus had twelve disciples that professed their everlasting devotion to Him. When Judas betrayed Jesus, it caused the other disciples to abandon Jesus in his time of need. One bad apple can and has spoiled the bunch. I once heard someone say that it was Judas' destiny to betray Jesus, which was what God created Judas to do. How ridiculous does that sound? If it was Judas' destiny to betray Jesus, then why would any of us ever try to crawl, kick, or climb our way out of a bad environment, if God creates destinies, as the one that *they* said He created for Judas? Judas had a choice and he chose to betray Jesus. Later, he realized he made a bad choice and regretted his decision—so it's impossible for God to have created him to betray Jesus, or Judas wouldn't have regretted what he had done.

Constantine played an instrumental role in deciding which books would go in the Bible. Obviously, there were books he favored and those that he did not. He embraced the church as another means to help him and his government control the people. The Gospel of John was written by one of Jesus's closest disciples. Many of the other books in the Bible were reports of another person's words by someone other than the person who heard them. In a court of law, this is *hearsay* and not allowed to be taken as testimony. If some of the testimonies in the Bible are truly based on hearsay, then I do not believe that every last word in the Bible is an accurate account. I'm certain to piss off a whole lot of people, but before anyone gets their panties in a bunch, understand that I'm not challenging anyone's faith or beliefs, but in return I ask you to respect the fact that I too have the right to believe what I know to be true.

In the Book of Revelations, it's written that one-third of the world's population will perish in the end of days. I believe this statement has merit, but I also believe it's a warning. I'm sure the number of referenced people is not an absolute. More people could perish, or less, but I believe it's God wish that none perish. It can only be God's wish and not His will because He gave free will to humanity—so the decision lies in the hands of human kind. Unless you believe, as I have come to believe, that we need to give our will back to God and ask, as Jesus did in the Garden of Gethsemane when he said, "Thy will be done, not mine." Again, if humanity can't change its circumstances, then why would any of us ever try to become better human beings and help those in need if we believe one-third of the population is predestined to perish? With this mentality, it leaves a person to adopt the philosophy of everyone for themselves and fuck the rest. In the Bible, it's written that "If my people who are called by my name, shall humble themselves and pray and seek my face, and turn from their wicked ways, I shall hear from heaven, and forgive their sin and heal their land." This sounds like the answer to the conundrum of how to change the outcome to the end times referenced in the Book of Revelations.

At all times, I wanted the truth and, in many circumstances, I wanted the truth more than anything in life, especially when it came to knowing the truth about God. The stories I heard about Him didn't always make sense or after hearing them I ended up with more questions than the stories left me with answers. I believe most if not all stories about God contain some degree of truth. Some stories, such as mine, can be an interpretation of how a person sees God and how God has revealed Himself to them. Other stories can be an abstract tale of how a person views God. As it pertains to the three holy books – the Quran, Torah and the Bible – I believe these three stories are too close in nature to not be linked to one another and be the means by which God meant to unite us rather than divide us. I knew there could only be one God for all of creation, but according to the various religions each of them has their own version of God. Rather than trying to find the answer from a religious leader or in a religious book, I looked to God to guide me to the truth. This book is what I believe to be my truth—after I painstakingly searched for a story that properly represented the loving God that came into my life.

Since God is a story and, more specifically, a love story, I'm going to be your shaman DJ and spin the love story that I've come to believe. In the beginning, God created Adam and Eve. He told them not to eat from the tree of good and evil. The church claims Satan deceived Eve in the garden and she defied God's will. Why would Satan have the power to be in the Garden of Eden? I think the church places way too much emphasis on evil, which diminishes God's authority. I believe it was God in the form of a serpent that tempted Eve. He told Adam and Eve not to do something and He tempted them to see if they would honor His command or if they would fall to temptation. The proof is in the Lord's Prayer, *God lead us not in temptation but deliver us from evil.* In my eyes, the serpent in the Garden of Eden represents temptation and not evil. The Bible states, *death and life is in the power of the tongue.*

The devil that the Bible references as being the root of all evil is nothing more than people who haven't accepted God into their hearts and minds. The Book of Revelations speaks of the Anti-Christ and Satan. I believe the devils of the world will one day hold an election to elect one of them to lead many devils and that leader will call himself Satan. Again, Satan is nothing more than a man who has not submitted to the will of God and who becomes the leader of the many devils. The Anti-Christ is more than likely a religious leader, or an organization, that defies the will of God and joins forces with Satan and his evil followers. Lucifer is an angel that was cast out of heaven and whom the church, the many devils, and Satan blame for all the bad behavior. The only real fear that exists on this planet is pissing off God and receiving His wrath as judgment, which I'm sure is much worse than whatever any devil, Satan, Anti-Christ, or fallen angel could release into this world. *The Lord is on my side, I fear not.*

There are many great religious leaders throughout time who loved God, but who disappointed Him. After the flood, God commanded Noah's family to disperse and go out and procreate to replenish the world. Noah's family was afraid to leave one another and didn't do as God commanded. Abraham and Sara were told by God they would bear a son, although Sara doubted God and convinced Abraham to mate with her handmaiden. Saul deliberately went against the instructions of Samuel the prophet, who spoke the prophetic words of God. King David fell in love with his best friend's wife and David sent that same friend into battle so he would be killed. David then married the wife of his best friend. It was not until the birth of Jesus that God created a man that loved God more than that man loved himself. I believe it was Jesus' unwavering commitment to God and humanity that changed God's spirit from a judgmental one to a loving one. I've come to understand that God's wrath is much like a loaded gun and the trigger on that gun could be pulled at any time, but due to the love that God has for Jesus and Jesus has for God, Jesus has become the safety in that gun and the one who keeps God from releasing His wrath onto humanity.

On several occasions, I've heard Christians say they don't belong to this world, which begs the question, if they don't belong to this world then where in the hell do they think they belong? I believe this world is and always will be God's first love. From the beginning of time, His intention was to live among His creation. It seems to me that God has put forth painstaking effort to reconcile the master plan that Adam and Eve derailed in the Garden of Eden and I believe the facts speak for themselves…it is all about this world. Personally, I'm in no hurry to abandon what I believe is and will always be God's main priority, and one that has His deepest affection. Possibly those Christians are pining for their gold mansion in the sky and that's why they don't think this world is their home.

I believe without a doubt that Jesus was the *man in the mirror*. He was the perfect representation of what humanity was always meant to become before Adam and Eve fell to temptation. I strongly believe God didn't send Jesus to this world to be crucified. The God that I've come to know and love is not a God that sends a man to his death by a brutal beating before he's crucified on a wooden cross. The manner in which Jesus met his death can be nothing short of the devil's doing. I wouldn't follow a God that sends a man, let alone one who is believed by so many to be the son of God, to his death in the horrific way in which Jesus died. A God that would redeem humanity through the torture, suffering, and shedding of blood is not a God I would follow and I know it's not the God that I've come to know and love. It's just like humanity to blame God for Jesus's death when in fact God had nothing to do with orchestrating his demise. Jesus didn't die **for** our sinful nature. Jesus died **because** of our sinful nature. It's interesting how one word can change an entire belief system. The horrors of humanity brutally beat Jesus and then placed him on a wooded cross to die of a painful and horrific death, not God.

While living in San Francisco, I learned about Reverend Moon. He believes Jesus was not sent to this world by God to be sacrificed for our sins, but was sent to educate and reconcile humanity back to God, which is something with which I wholeheartedly agree. As I got closer to finishing my story, I began to understand that Jesus's destiny wasn't to die on a wooden cross—it was to live among humanity to educate them on the magnitude of God's love. Jesus was the reflection of humanity – in its most perfect form – that God created us to become…His sons and daughters.

I was becoming increasingly concerned that people would think I was crazy when I told them of my beliefs, as they related to Jesus. As I had these feelings, I stumbled across information about Reverend Moon. One afternoon, as I walked Aston and Bentley on the same promenade where I had seen the words *fear no failure* almost a year earlier, I saw a two-sided board sign detailing Reverend Moon's beliefs. It's seemed unlikely that my discovery of Reverend Moon and his teachings, a decade after I began building a relationship with God, was a coincidence. Discovering there was an entire religious movement called the *Moonies* who believed that Jesus was always meant to be humanity's teacher and a reconciler, rather than its sacrificial lamb, was nothing short of a revelation in my eyes. The timing of my discovery was too perfect to be anything less than a divine unveiling. I came across Reverend Moon and his beliefs at the same time as I reached the last chapter of this book. Up to that point, I was concerned that people who read my testimony would think I was crazy. I always loved the song *You are not alone* by Michael Jackson and suddenly I understood why…because I'm not alone in what I believe to be true about Jesus. Could my vision of the three moons be a sign that Reverend Moon's world is *Closer to the Truth*, as to what I was to *Believe* about Jesus? *My people perish for lack of knowledge.*

Through knowing God, I've learned I can be empowered to demonstrate self-control over the things in my life that once dictated my actions. Wisdom through building a relationship with Him is the answer to achieving self-discipline and not religion dictating what a person should and should not do. I've discovered God is not seeking control of my life and I believe He's not seeking control of anyone's life. I've also discovered He's not seeking vengeance for my sinful nature and also believe He's not seeking vengeance for anyone's sins. What I do know is that God is seeking love and inclusion. Since humanity shunned Jesus when He was alive, God made sure that humankind would accept Jesus as their Lord and Savior in this world to make it to the next world. I believe Jesus represents the highest achievement that humanity can realize on earth and in heaven. In other words, if a person fulfills their purpose and destiny, I believe God is capable and willing to create a planet where that individual can be the God of his or her own world, as He did for Jesus. Shortly after having this revelation, I heard that a representative at the NASA Science Mission Directorate in Washington said that they had discovered seven earth-like planets that they believed could sustain life. These seven planets are in what has been nicknamed as our sister star system called TRAPPIST-1, 40 light years from earth. I believe this discovery by NASA gives proof to my above theory. The potential opportunity to have a world created in my image that I would love, nurture, and protect is certainly a heavenly reward that gets my attention and more importantly my unwavering devotion to God and His plan for my purpose and ultimately my destiny, the same world that I would like to see created on earth for everyone—a world where people don't lie, where truth is the foundation of society, and where love for our fellow man ruled our existence. Whatever you believe or do not believe about the love story of God, I hope you come to your own conclusion about Him through your life experiences and you don't blindly follow what someone tells you or what you read in a book. Possibly you'll find your voice and you too may someday declare to the world your spiritual testimony in the form of a love story.

The first fifty years of my life were all about serving my needs and my wants. At the onset of my fifty-first birthday, I was enlightened to what I wanted to do with my next fifty. I hope, wish, pray and – by the grace of God – plan to do everything I can to spend the rest of my life bringing hope to as many people who are living a life of hopelessness. I believe that through hope, opportunities are birthed. Without opportunities, there can be no hope and without hope there's nothing but despair. When my own hope was lost in the desert, God revealed Himself, which allowed me to envision a better life. I've recently heard that there are somewhere in the neighborhood of one hundred forty three million to two hundred thirteen million orphans in the world. I was shocked and appalled at the number of children on this planet who don't have a mother or a father to care for them. I know it's impossible to think I could impact all the lives of all the orphans on this planet, but I believe God expects me to at least try and He'll do the rest. I truly believe His plan is already in play, I just need to ensure I do my best – whatever that might be. If I could choose my destiny, I would take on the monumental task of eradicating the word *orphan* from every language on this planet.

All my life, I always wanted a family of my own, but for many reasons, I wasn't able to have one. Possibly, God has another plan and it doesn't include me being what the world deems as a conventional father. Through the *House of* ***LVG***, I hope to partner with many organizations, churches, synagogues, mosques, businesses, individuals, and even countries, to show God's parentless children as much of His **L**ove, **V**alo**r** and **G**oodness as I can possibly spread across this world in the time I have remaining. From what I've learned about God, it would be just like Him to take a broken down gay man that always dreamed of having a family of his own and trust him to be a *trustee* for His parentless children. Only He would pick the most unlikely person to do the most unlikely assignment. By doing so, the world would know without a doubt that the concept for the *House of* ***LVG*** could have only been orchestrated by God. If I'm correct, then I will not only fulfill my purpose, I believe I will have the opportunity to fulfill my destiny.

When I was still a baby, my parents moved from California to Chicago. They loaded their personal items into a trailer, something like an airstream, which they towed with the car that they drove to the Midwest. My mother and father took turns driving without ever stopping to rest. At one point, my dad and older brother were sleeping in the trailer while my mother drove. Car seats were not used then and I was nestled in the front passenger seat next to my mother. Does that make me a mommy's boy? Somewhere during the trip, my mother fell asleep behind the wheel just before driving onto a bridge, or just as she exited the bridge, where there was a river that flowed underneath. After my mother nodded off, the car and trailer veered from the road and went down an embankment toward the river. I was too little to remember the ordeal, but I was told that I ended up on the floorboard of the car by the time it came to a stop. I cried. Does that make me a crybaby? Miraculously, the car and trailer stopped just before they hit the river. It was nothing short of God's grace that saved my family and me from harm that evening. Possibly, God had a plan for the Loyd family and it didn't include us drowning in a river. Maybe, like baby Mosses, I too was saved from the river because God had something I was supposed to do for Him later. Did He choose me to be His *trustee* when I was but a child to lead an exodus of parentless children from orphanages or from the streets of the world to a house they would be happy to call home, where they would be loved? Would I in fact be able to deliver on this house's mission... *all for **L**ove and with **V**alor, in which one stands for the **G**oodness of the indivisible **H**ouse in a world united, to God's allegiance I pledge, the House of **LVG**?*

After I moved to San Francisco, I had a casual conversation with a man I met at a social event. I told him about my idea to establish a nonprofit organization to assist less fortunate children. After I told him about it, he said that I would do it to make a name for myself. At that moment, I reflected on my feelings in Palm Springs when I heard my inner voice tell me not to put anything in my name. I finally understood what I believe God was trying to convey. He didn't want me to be accused of establishing the *House of **LVG*** to glorify my name, as the gentleman had accused me of wanting to do. I now truly believe the name of the charity was God's idea, even though I thought I was the clever one that came up with the concept. He didn't want my ego to get in the way of His plan. He wanted to ensure that I and everyone else knew that the *House of **LVG*** was about His parentless children. I think many of the religious leaders today let their egos get in the way of their mission and end up making it all about what they accomplish, rather than what God has done. If I do as I believe God has instructed me to do, then there will be a good chance that I'll have the opportunity to fulfill my heart's desire and build a legacy for Lance, become the father that I always dreamed of being, while showing many parentless children God's devotion and love for them. The world may have forgotten about these kids, but I whole heartedly believe He has not.

When I lived in San Francisco for the first time, before I moved to New

York, I traveled to Berlin for Christmas one year. I went with Rick and another friend of ours who was also living in San Francisco at the time of our trip. While in Berlin, we had our holiday dinner at the Adlon hotel, where Michael Jackson famously dangled his newborn son, Prince Michael II, out of his room's window so the photographers outside of the hotel could take a picture of him. A few days after Christmas, we were walking around the city and ended up at the same hotel. In front of the Adlon, we encountered an outdoor bar sculpted out of ice. The bartenders at this ice bar were serving champagne and we had several glasses to celebrate the upcoming New Year. We learned that on December 30 through New Year's Day, a huge outdoor celebration was taking place between the nearby Brandenburg Gate and the Victory Column on its opposite side, and the bar had been installed for the upcoming festival. The program included live music performers, light and laser shows, DJ sets, and food stands from all over the world. The ice bar was one of the coolest vendor set ups that I saw while walking the grounds of the festival. We left Berlin before the festival officially opened, but at least we were able to walk the venue and have a few glasses of champagne to celebrate the approaching New Year before we traveled back home.

The same psychic that told me about Lance and his pet toucan also told me something interesting about this book. When I told her I was hoping *The doG House of Cards* would be published nationally and internationally, I asked her whether the book would be well received in different parts of the world. She said it would not be popular in the entire world, but it would be in many countries. She said it would have a sizable audience in several large nations and specifically stated that it would have a German following. I found her comment interesting because I had a feeling, when I was living in Palm Springs, that one day I would *unleash* an international launch introducing the story of the God that revealed Himself to me. At the time, I had not started writing this story so my feelings were premature and didn't make much sense to me. I envisioned the international launch taking place in Berlin around Christmas. As I've said before…I often receive unsolicited answers to a question via a sign before the question is ever asked. It's like someone hands me an envelope, which contains the answer to a question, but the question that is supposed to be in the envelope with the answer arrives later. In this case, fast-forward seven years and the question finally arrived.

I now think something greater than me might have chosen Berlin at Christmas as the location and time for the international launch of *The doG House of Cards*—before the idea of this book was ever conceived. It seems far-fetched, even for me, but when I take into consideration the fact that three of my dogs – Papi, Aston and Bentley – are miniature Schnauzers, which is a German breed, I can see a connection, however tenuous. Upon further consideration, I realized the number three is the number of the Holy Trinity. During the time that I had these feelings I heard my inner voice speak to me again. One day, I happened to see the DJ Zedd on television. Prior to that day, I had never heard of this entertainer, but I heard my inner voice tell me that this particular DJ was to be the opening DJ for the launch of *The doG House of Cards* in Germany. I decided to look into Zedd the DJ. He is a record producer, DJ, musician and multi-instrumentalist who won the award in the best dance-recording category for his song *Clarity* at the 56th Grammy Awards (5+6=**11**). I found out that he was born in Saratov, Russia and when he was four years of age his family moved to Kaiserslautern, Germany where he was raised. He was also born on the nine month on the second day (9+2=**11**). To my amazement, there suddenly seemed to be merit to what the psychic said about this book having a German following and my feelings about Berlin when I was living in the desert and that inner voice spoke to me about Zedd.

I can't think of a more fitting place to bust down the barriers of preconceived religious ideology that has divided people than in a city where its people were once divided by a wall. I absolutely understand there's a good possibility that this book will not be well-received and I won't have the opportunity to introduce my story anywhere. On the other hand, I dream that this book could end up on the New York Times best seller list and become an international best seller too. I entrust God with this book's destiny and with my future because I trust Him more than I trust myself. What I love about having faith in something greater than myself is the hope that comes with that faith and knowing that anything is possible. If believing is seeing and seeing is believing then based on what I've seen I've come to believe that I'm an *omnist*, one that believes in all religions. Many omnists believe that all religions contain truths, but no one religion offers all that is truth. I've found that the truth over time has a habit of revealing itself and so does God. Keep calm, I trust He will ensure it all works out in the end and if it doesn't then that means it's not **The End**, it's just **The Beginning.**

P.S. When I was a child, I played a game with my brothers called *king of the mountain.* The goal of the game was to occupy the highest point on a raised platform or hill, while resisting attempts by my brothers to knock me off. If they were successful in taking my position they would conquer the mountain and become the new reigning king. Ever since I was that little boy who fought so desperately to protect his place on that hill, I can recall wanting to find a place where I felt like I fit in. For the next three decades, my spirit tirelessly sought to find a place where it could feel at home. This is why my inner-self yearned to find a sense of community and the reason why I climbed so many mountains to ultimately find myself in the lowest valleys. I now realize that, as early as a pre-adolescent, my spirit longed for a connection with a high power. My soul required a relationship with God for my mind, body, and spirit to be in union. It was this union that gave me peace and allowed me to visualize my life's purpose.

Cher said it best when she sang, "Take me home." I have come to *Believe* that home represents love and I now understand *love is where the doG lives.* I'm certain a person can live a fulfilling life, but without experiencing the love of God they may never achieve a sense of tranquility. Perhaps I'm being selfish in my thinking and I have it all wrong. Maybe it's God who yearns to be reunited with creation in the place where it first existed and instead of me wanting to go home, it's He who aches for us to bring Him back home. I no longer seek a place of belonging because I have been enlightened to my place in life and identify that place as being the *House of* ***LVG***. This home embodies **L**ove, **V**alor and **G**oodness for all who reside inside the house, as well those who live outside of it. Through sharing my testimony, I hope the King of Kings and His mountainous kingdom shine a little brighter on earth and in heaven.

ABOUT THE AUTHOR

I, Darrel F. Loyd, am a first-time author.

Born in 1960, in the county of Los Angeles, California, my parents moved my older brother and me to Chicago, Illinois when I was still a baby. The Midwest region of the U.S. is where I grew up to become a shy gay man and where I would spend the next four decades before moving back to California. I worked as a part-time stock boy on a retailer's loading dock for several years while attending high school. I graduated at the age of seventeen, six months earlier than most of my classmates. Four months before my eighteenth birthday, on the day of graduation, I was promoted to shipping and receiving manager. In my new managerial role, my life soon became all about the working world and the things I could afford to buy.

Over the next thirty years, I would devote my time and energies to advance my professional career. During this time, I entered the visual merchandising field where I worked for several large retail companies, most notably at Bloomingdales. When my career ended at Bloomies as director of visual merchandising, I utilized my experience to secure another visual merchandising director position at Bigsby&Kruthers, a high-end men's and women's clothing chain in Chicago. During the six years I was employed at Bigsby, the company grew exponentially and I was promoted to vice president of store development and visual merchandising for their three retail divisions consisting of fifty-three stores and a retail shop in the Michael Jordan restaurant. My department was recognized by the retail industry for our projects and my work was published in many trade magazines. My team also won numerous design awards for our creative store and shop concepts. I went on to become vice president of operations for a lighting distributor in Chicago, creative director for a store fixture manufacturer in New York City, president of business development for a logistics company in Arizona, and eventually established my own company in California, where I reside today.

While I realized that I was gay early on in my teenage years, it was something that I hid from most everyone until I was twenty-five years old. Around that time, the AIDS epidemic ravaged the gay community and I was diagnosed as being HIV positive, which made me withdraw from those who would have judged me for my medical condition. This caused me to revel in hedonism and reckless behavior, self-medicating to subdue my fears of dying a painful and horrible death. During my years of recreational drug use and eventual isolation, I lost my way. My dream of finding a loving man and eventually having a family of my own became a living nightmare, until one day when I had an epiphany—I came to realize that my life without "something" to give me hope, understanding, and love, was a life that made very little sense. At last, I was finally able to embrace the world and all its possibilities.

The doG House of Cards is the story of my life and my spiritual journey of self-discovery.

www.ildworld.com

www.ingramcontent.com/pod-product-compliance
Lightning Source LLC
Chambersburg PA
CBHW051848090426
42811CB00034B/2257/J

9780692989616